W9-CTM-449

099

DATE DUE

WITHDRAWN

A COMPREHENSIVE HISTORY OF WESTERN ETHICS

WHAT DO WE BELIEVE?

A
COMPREHENSIVE
HISTORY OF
WESTERN ETHICS

WHAT DO WE BELIEVE?

WARREN ASHBY

EDITED WITH A FOREWORD BY
W. ALLEN ASHBY

 **Prometheus Books**

59 John Glenn Drive
Amherst, NewYork 14228-2197

Published 1997 by Prometheus Books

A Comprehensive History of Western Ethics: What Do We Believe? Copyright © 1997 by
W. Allen Ashby. All rights reserved. No part of this publication may be reproduced, stored
in a retrieval system, or transmitted in any form or by any means, electronic, mechanical,
photocopying, recording, or otherwise, without prior written permission of the publisher,
except in the case of brief quotations embodied in critical articles and reviews. Inquiries
should be addressed to Prometheus Books, 59 John Glenn Drive, Amherst, New York
14228–2197, 716–691–0133. FAX: 716–691–0137.

01 00 99 98 97   5 4 3 2 1

Library of Congress Cataloging-in-Publication Data

Ashby, Warren, 1820–
    A comprehensive history of Western ethics : what do we believe? / Warren Ashby ;
edited with a foreword by W. Allen Ashby.
        p.   cm.
    Includes bibliographical references and index.
    ISBN 1–57392–152–1 (cloth : alk. paper)
    1. Ethics—History. I. Ashby, W. Allen. II. Title.
BJ71.A84   1997
170′.9—dc21   97–8613
                                                                                CIP

Printed in the United States of America on acid-free paper

For Helen Bewley Ashby

sine qua non

CONTENTS

CHAPTER 3: THE ETHICS OF MARCUS AURELIUS   141

CHAPTER 4: AUGUSTINE: THE FAILURE OF THE CLASSICAL IDEAL   165

CHAPTER 5: THE ETHICS OF MEDIEVAL CHRISTENDOM   191

CHAPTER 6: THE ETHICS OF THE RENAISSANCE AND REFORMATION   249

CHAPTER 7: THE ETHICS OF THE RELIGIOUS AND SCIENTIFIC REVOLUTIONS: THE SEVENTEENTH CENTURY — 307

CHAPTER 8: THE ETHICS OF THE ENLIGHTENMENT — 375

FOREWORD

"We are children of the Greeks," my father begins in chapter 1, "and we are also," he adds in chapter 2, "the children of Israel." Those of us who have made our homes in the Western world are the inheritors of these two illustrious traditions; but more than just being the children of these parents, we are also parents ourselves, passing on to the next generation the accumulated values and beliefs that have supported us, the beliefs we have embodied in our lives. Thus we are part of a process of over two millennia, a process we are often unconscious of, living as we do so deeply immersed in a brief generational span of its life.

This book is the work of a lifetime, and not even the lifetime of one man only, though certainly it is that. My father began writing it in the early 1950s, and had completed an early draft when he was given a Ford Foundation Fellowship in 1952–53, which allowed him to conduct research at the Princeton University Library, while my brother, sister, mother, and I lived in Havertown, Pennsylvania. But more than this I think, as you can see from the final chapter, the book really began for my father in the living relationships of his own family and their living relationships to a particular perception of American history as seen by a boy growing up on the banks of the James River in Newport News, Virginia. For it is a central thesis of the book that we are individuals who live in community, being ourselves shaped by these communities as we try to give shape to them in turn.

At his death in October 1985, my father left behind a completed manuscript. By then it had been through numerous drafts. Authors had been added, authors deleted. A whole new section on Romanticism had been included. There were still changes my father wished to make, and in fact he left behind a detailed account of the number of pages he wanted to delete from each chapter, as well as, in a few cases, the number of pages he wished to add. After his death my mother asked me if I would undertake the responsibility of preparing the manuscript for publication, and off and on for more than a decade I have labored over this task, with some joy and a great deal of trepidation.

I have felt the most confident in deleting passages. More than twenty-five years as an English teacher at Union County College in New Jersey had, I thought, at least prepared me for that task. I felt less confident about expanding various sections, for although in a sense my undergraduate and graduate educational background in philosophy and in religious studies was similar to my father's, still I am not my father, and so, with two exceptions, I did not attempt to make the few additions he had wanted to make. First, I did attempt to add concluding sections to approximately half the chapters. My father had completed summation sections for the other half and had left extensive notes, including prioritizing the points he wished to make, for most of the others. And so I undertook the task of trying to finish those summation sections in order to give the book a symmetry and continuity that I know was his intent.

Second, I have added the concluding chapter "Retrospect and Prospect: A Personal View." This was the chapter that my father had always wanted to write, and in some ways he had lived his whole life in order to be able to write it. It was a long-standing family joke between us: I would tease him by asking him if he ever thought he would get to the twentieth century before we entered the twenty-first. And he would remind me of T. S. Eliot's "a lifetime burning in every moment." In the case of this chapter, there were no notes, but there were numerous unpublished articles, scraps and fragments of thoughts and ideas, journal entries, and letters. I collected these and then I tried to put them together into a coherent whole. Where this chapter fails, the faults are clearly mine. Where it succeeds, as I believe it does, the success is clearly my father's. In reading it the reader will certainly notice a more personal and intimate tone. That tone is my intention; I do not know if it would have been my father's intention. But the words are wholly his. Except for phrasings to connect sections, the words and the ideas in that chapter belong to him.

It was my decision to include this chapter and in this form, because although my father was a private man, the history of ethics for him was not a private nor solely an academic endeavor, but was meant to connect us to the deepest and most fundamental sources of our lives. It was meant to connect us to our own communities, and especially to our own families, those we are born into, those we create, those families of religion and nation, state and village that continue to give shape to our lives as we continue to try to shape their control over us. For more than anything, ethics for my father was a con-

versation, a dialogue, not only within each of us between the Greek philosophers and the prophets of Israel, but between each of us individually and the
people we love, as well as those we do not love.

As a teacher my father always sought out those places of personal conversation and attempted to enter them with others. His classes were meant to
be seminars, conducted around a table, and not lectures delivered from behind
a podium. So, I know that for him this book was not meant to be a lecture, but
a dialogue with you, the reader, and so, as my own personal choice, I wanted
to put his voice in the book as a living presence, so that you could feel engaged by a living man. It was the way my father engaged us in the family; his
colleagues at work; his life in the community; and, most importantly for him,
his life in the university classroom which was, for him, always meant to be an
abiding and enduring conversation, continuing long after the semester ends. It
is my hope, as his son, as I know it is my mother's, brother's, and sister's, that
by reading this book, you, too, will feel a part of that conversation not only
with him, but through his words, with the remarkable history of ethics in the
Western world, and of the courage of the individuals who have lived in community and given their lives to this conversation, as my father also gave much
of his life to the creation of the text you hold in your hands.

❈ ❈ ❈

It is difficult for me to know specifically whom my father would have chosen
to recognize in his acknowledgments, and if I omit individuals, it is because
of my ignorance. It is my hope, however, that, as my father wrote in his final
journal entry, "you know who you are," and "you really feel my love so
deeply it abides in you. For that would be the return of your gift."

Certainly I believe he would have begun with his own family, his parents
and grandparents, and his five brothers and sisters. For it is certainly true that
the concerns that you as a reader will find in this book began in that family
and in that community. Next I think he would have thanked his teachers,
from elementary school through his undergraduate work at Maryville, and
his divinity and graduate school work at Yale University. In this respect I
know that he would have singled out a number of individuals whose names
I would not know; but from our own conversations I know he would at least
have included Horace Orr and Edwin R. Hunter from Maryville, and H.
Richard Niebuhr from Yale.

Judging from his acknowledgements in his earlier published biography,
Frank Porter Graham: A Southern Liberal, I know that my father then would
have thanked a number of specific authors and even mentioned some individual works. While many of these thinkers will be found in these pages,
many more will not. What is true of all of them, however, would be his deep

appreciation for their commitment and their influence on his life, for books were friends for my father, and ideas were alive with a palpable presence. Then I think he would have thanked his own colleagues and friends, first at the University of North Carolina at Chapel Hill where he taught briefly from 1946–49, and then those colleagues at the University of North Carolina at Greensboro (UNCG), where he taught from 1949–83; in particular, Anne Queene, Charlie Jones, Henry Ruark, Mereb Mossman, Marc Friedlaender, Gregory Ivy, Edward Lowenstein, Franklin Parker, Gene Pfaff, and most especially Bill and Frances Mueller, whose generosity after my father's death in establishing two scholarships in his name was matched through the years with a close and gracious friendship.

More recent colleagues and friends would have included Robert Calhoon (with a special appreciation), Jim Clotfelter, Bob Miller, Dick Whitlock, Charles Tisdale, Henry Frye, Devendra and Louise Chawla, Alice Irby, Betty Carpenter, Henry Levinson, Mary Hill, Mary Jellicorse, Carolyn Cooper, McNeill and Louise Smith, and again especially Fran and Murray Arndt. Next would have come the students in his classes over the years, especially those on ethics, where my father explored these ideas in living conversations. Some I know he would have mentioned by name, and he would have especially thanked the students in the Residential College, an institution at UNCG that he was instrumental in creating and where he served as director from 1970–76.

Thanks would have gone to many of the staff at the UNCG library, the Ford Foundation for its direct and substantial support during the writing of the first draft of this book, and to the American Friends Service Committee for the two years he and the rest of my family spent working in India in 1964–66. Finally my father would have thanked my brother, Paul, my sister, Ann, and our children, and especially his lifelong and dearest friend, my mother, Helen Bewley Ashby.

In preparing this manuscript for publication, I would be remiss if I did not thank my father's sister Margaret Williams for working closely with my father and diligently transcribing onto a computer the original manuscript in both its typed and handwritten form long before it was given to me. And then my sister for arranging and maintaining my father's vast files, both the unpublished articles and those that were the source of this text. And my brother, who for years continued alone to send out letters on behalf of the family, and to enhance the book's visual appearance on the computer, and who has created a special Web page (www.ashbydialogues.org) to promote the book, to act as a bibliographic resource, and to provide a place to continue discussions of ethics and ethical issues. I also want to thank Robert Calhoon for his continued support and faith in the manuscript, for his ideas and warmth and encouragement, and also the students who checked the references for each chapter: Roger Brown, Patricia Callahan, Edward Roush, and Sam Hieb, and a longtime family and personal friend, Joanne Daniels, for her consistent and specific support. Union County College has been generous in its resources and it, too, deserves my appreciation. Thanks to Steven Mitchell at Prometheus Books, whose unwavering and persistent encouragement has finally been singularly instrumental in bringing this book to completion. And, as my father's son, last and certainly not least, I need to thank the lifelong support of my mother and her belief that I could do what I was never sure could be done, and what I am not sure that I have done well, namely, to deliver into your hands my father's words without damaging them.

From all of us, we welcome you into what we feel is this remarkable conversation about the Western community. We hope you will find in these words a clearer sense of what it means for you to be an individual, living and loving in community, and experience what my father wished for all of us, "a satisfying happiness."

Dr. W. Allen Ashby
Plainfield, N.J.

PREFACE

It is an important fact that there is no adequate history of Western ethics. There are many satisfactory histories of philosophy and of theology, even of political thought, of economics and of aesthetics, but none of ethics. *A Comprehensive History of Western Ethics: What Do We Believe?* is an attempt to address this omission by providing an adequate and inclusive history of Western ethics from antiquity to the twentieth century.

In writing the book I have consciously had two types of readers in mind. The first are university students interested in history and ethics. In this respect the book has been designed to serve as a primary or secondary text in courses in philosophical, business, or medical ethics as well as in courses in history, philosophy, religious studies, literature, and related subjects. But the second and perhaps more important group that I wish to appeal to is more difficult to describe. It consists of those persons who, interested in and perplexed about moral values in contemporary life, are looking for clearer personal and social bearings about what it means to be a person in today's society. These are persons interested in extending human right and human rights, in finding appropriate ways to think of moral experience, and in discovering an ethical perspective appropriate for life. While this book cannot directly satisfy these interests, it can provide what is requisite to their satisfaction: a sense of the Western ethical past that has led to the present.

However, more specifically and regardless of the particular interest that brought the reader to this book, this text should enable its various readers to participate, to reflect, to suffer, and to enjoy, for these, rooted in moral principles of Western ethics, are the deeper purposes of the book.

(1) "To participate" does not mean only to participate in the recreation of

17

the book, such as accompanies any serious reading. It means, more particularly, to participate in the life the book attempts to reveal. This is to participate in our past by participating in the societies and lives that have shaped much of our moral experience.

(2) "To reflect" is, first, to reflect upon what ethical thinkers of the past have said and why, given their societies, their lives, and their basic beliefs, they thought as they did. But the book will be unsuccessful unless at certain points it enables the reader to reflect upon the reader's life, and upon that life's personal and social pasts as well as upon its present values and future prospects.

(3) "To suffer" in the contemporary world does not require a history of ethics but, strangely, such a history can and should make suffering more accessible. To experience life today and to question what has happened to the Western ethic in the present world are causes enough for suffering. But nevertheless, paradoxically a subsidiary purpose of the book is to intensify pain. By this is meant both the intellectual pain of difficult thought and also the more intense pain of sharing imaginatively the lives of many who had to undergo suffering to create their ethics. To intensify the pain also means to keep alive those feelings that accompany the remembrance and recognition of the ethical tensions of what we have been, what we became, and what we now are.

(4) "To enjoy" is by far the most important purpose of the writing. This not only implies what any author wants, that the reader will enjoy the reading. It is also meant to point to the fact that to reflect seriously and to participate fully provide some of the greatest joys human beings can know. To participate in the lives of cultures and persons of our past and to reflect upon ideas from our past and our own incomplete ideas: these make for genuine joy. For the participation provides a sense of shared life, of having a history and community; and the reflections, if sufficiently serious, emerge into some degree of clarity of thought and life. Both, together, provide an aesthetic sense of coherence, not of the book but of actual life imagined and known.

To participate, to reflect, to suffer, to enjoy have been a part, an important part, of what the Western ethic has informed us it means to be and become a human individual in a human and humane society. So a primary purpose of the book is to enable persons not only to look at a history of Western ethics but to experience the ethic.

These purposes have had influences upon the style of writing. My attempt has been to keep the writing "open," not to force or be dogmatic about positions, but to leave space for the reader to think, to agree or disagree, to discover and correct ideas which I have missed. The writing has been based upon an appreciation of all the societies, all the persons portrayed in the book, not least when I have disagreed with them. It is, therefore, a critical inquiring appreciation. This, after all, is our history; these persons constitute our family. The introduction to each section, then, begins with "we," trying to make some connections between that ethical community and our lives. After each introduction there is the change from the personal "we" to an impersonal perspective more suitable to an objective understanding that must precede any subjective appropriation. It is that subjective appropriation which is the basic purpose of this history of ethics.

This book is also guided in both its structure and content by other specific principles. In addition there are principles related to the motive of writing that are reflected in the purposes and style of the book.

In terms of the principles relating to the content and structure, it is important in the first place to know that an understanding of Western ethics requires an understanding of the inclusive intellectual moral history. This principle implies that a history of ethics should interpret both the philosophical and the religious expressions of moral thought. The Greek philosophers and the Hebrew prophets provide the bases for all later Western ethics, and so both must be included. Similarly, throughout history the dominant and creative modes of moral expression at any given time, whether religious or secular, philosophical or theological, must be dealt with if the history is to be understood.

In the second place, there are a limited number of ethical communities that provide basic assumptions for all thinkers within those communities. An ethical community is established by persons who live in a specific time and place, and who, from this fact, are led to share basic assumptions. These assumed beliefs set the problems and provide the direction for all of the ethical creations within that context. An ethical community is not a matter of sociology but of ethos, though the ethos is necessarily related to a society. Moralists who share an ethos and who often, in later historical interpretation, are viewed as opponents usually have more similarities than differences. It is these similarities that make possible the disagreements, and for an adequate understanding of the contributions of the individuals and communities it is the similarities as well as the unique ethical developments of representative persons that require clarification.

In the third place it is important to recognize that two indispensable sources for the creation of any ethic are the social context and the personal life of the individual moralist. The creative mind at work, drawing upon its own life-experiences, is the most essential and immediate source of any ethic, but that creative mind is partially shaped by many social influences. Therefore, any ethic can be understood more completely by an awareness of the social context that was critical in its formulation. Indeed, it is essential to see an ethic in its society and not from the perspective of another society. Anyone who would satisfactorily comprehend an ethic must place his or her imagination in the society within which the moralist wrote, making a strenuous effort to avoid the provincialism of one's own time and place. Essential insights into the social structure, economic and political events, cultural milieu, and geographical environment of the author will illuminate the ethic.

Along with this is the realization that the personal, often hidden, life of the originator has an even greater influence on the creation of an ethic. Every ethic that has added substantially to human experience has been the consequence of individuals struggling with inescapable problems, usually of a personal nature. One of the most obvious facts about the history of Western ethics has been the recurring relation between personal suffering and the development of an ethic. So while an awareness of significant events in a thinker's life does not explain the ethic any more than does the recognition of the social context, nevertheless an imaginative grasp of important inner experiences of the writer can often help to bring the ethics to life.

This book has taken its shape as a result of these principles. First, the most important types of content are the identification and interpretation of ethical communities and of individual ethics. There are only a limited number of significant ethical communities in Western history, and the essential task in understanding ethics is to identify those communities through which something important, new, and lasting occurred in moral experience and thought.

Next, the selection of individuals whose views deserve reporting is critical. While, in this volume, most of the writers would appear on any list of major moral thinkers, there are others, obscured in history, who deserve recognition. There is inevitably some arbitrariness in the choice of the latter, and certainly I am conscious of others who could appropriately be included. However, the primary criterion for selection has been to identify individuals who have made significant and new contributions to ethics. The choices have been persons who are recognizably philosophical and/or religious; and since both traditions have been influential, the attempt has been made to give a balanced view of their contributions, emphasizing the mode of experience dominant in a given community, whether philosophical or religious or both.

The structure of each major section has been to interpret the ethical communities in terms of the social context and the assumptions developed in the community, to provide biographical insights of individuals, to interpret in detail the ethics of individual moralists, and finally to provide a summary of the ethics of the community. Consequently, the contents of each of the ten chapters in the book have been organized as follows:

(1) There is a description of the society in which the ethical community was initially shaped. This is to describe social structures and events as well as geographical factors that were influential in ethical developments. In the space available, it is only possible to make hints and suggestions of such elements, but these should be sufficient to enable the reader to make connections between the contextual elements and the assumptions, the biographies, and the ethics.

(2) There is the statement of the presuppositions of the ethics of any individual within that community. These presuppositions constitute the essential meaning of "ethical community," for the concept of such a community is not sociological or historical but cultural and spiritual. The presuppositions are those beliefs, usually intensely held, that provide bases for the individual's existential and intellectual explorations, making possible the kinds of moral problems and the available answers to be found.

(3) When the individual whose ethics are to be interpreted is first introduced, there is the presentation of brief biographical data relevant for the ethic. Here the interest is not in external facts except when those facts were internalized by the person. There is, rather, the identification from diverse sources of events in the inner life of the person that would subsequently have a direct bearing upon the ethic.

(4) The ethics of individuals constitutes the major subject matter of the book. All preliminary considerations of ethical community, assumptions and biography, all subsequent considerations of a community's answer to basic moral questions are secondary to the moral thought of individuals. For, finally, if the history of Western ethics is to be understood, it must be through those creative individuals who have given shape to Western moral experience and reflections.

Consequently, the purpose here is to report what the moralist actually said or was trying to say. The latter would often enough have been clear at the time in its context, but may no longer be obvious. Therefore, I will sometimes go beyond a mere reporting, as complex as that frequently is, to state candidly what I, as an interested reader who respects every ethical thinker included, understand their meanings to be, but even in these cases, there is no attempt to criticize or to correct their views.

(5) After presenting the views of individuals, I summarize the moral position of the ethical community concerning the human individual and society. The dominant and recurring problems are the nature of the human individual and human society, the definitions of "good" or "right," and how the good or right is achieved in a specific situation. In addition, there is mention of unique problems considered by the community. Finally, for each section there is a description of the permanent ethical value contributed by that community.

Here are a few additional principles that reflect the values of the author that have motivated my writing and have established the purposes of the book.

1. There is a Western ethic that has developed in and through Western history.

This principle implies no judgment of the many forms of non-Western ethics. It is simply to assert that out of varying shared experiences in Western history recognizable ways of looking at life have emerged both in terms of types of perspectives and types of moral values. The perspectives refer to the kinds of questions that are asked in and of moral experience; the moral values refer to the answers that have been given to these questions.

2. The discoveries made by individuals in Western ethics have been the discoveries of truth.

This is to claim that there are truths about the moral life and that, therefore, a history of ethics is as much the development of the history of truth as is the history of science. It is futile to make comparisons about the relative values of the different kinds of truth. But it is also clear that our future as individuals and societies depends upon our success or failure in comprehending and using the ethical truths, or insights, our history offers us.

3. The self has a history that is important to grasp.

One of the essential tasks for every human individual, including the readers of this book, is the understanding of the self's past, and this understanding is essential to accomplish that more important task of giving shape in the present to the self's future. "The self's past" refers, first of all, to one's personal and unique history. It also refers to one's societal history. Neither remembrance nor reconstruction can be perfect, neither is ever finished. However, it is important that throughout life the individual recover significant elements from the individual and social past, discovering in and creating with those elements an understandable order.

A major theme emphasized throughout Western ethical theory has been that the self accept responsibility for its own life. This theme has often been accompanied by a recognition of those forces, often overwhelming, over which the individual has little or no control, no matter whether those forces are outside or within the self. To have a cause or reasons for living, to be responsible or have goals for one's life, and therefore to give form and content to life is essentially what it means to be human.

4. The primary theme of Western ethics has been what it means to be and to become a human individual in a human community.

This theme has been so often disguised and so variously developed that it is often difficult to disentangle the details in order to recognize the fundamental issues at stake in all Western ethics. But again and again, sometimes in the most unexpected places and ways, the questions emerge: "What does it mean to be a human individual?" "What does it mean to have a human society that is, by this very fact, a humane society?"

The philosophical distinction between human right and human rights cannot adequately capture the complexities of this theme. But it can point us in the direction of the four most important perspectives from which Western ethics have viewed the theme. "Human right" suggests the obligations or duties, the motives or responsibilities that human life implies. This is to ask what is right or fitting, what an individual *owes* to various other realities, especially other persons, and to the self. "Human rights" suggests what an individual can legitimately *claim* in terms of what is necessary or good for life. This is to think of goals or consequences. In technical terms the first has been an ethic of the moral agent, the second of the moral recipient, and throughout the past these two primary types of ethics have been entertained in complex patterns.

These two major types of ethics, in diverse forms, have been extraordinarily successful in providing moral guidance in various historical situations. But because of the failure, perhaps inevitable, to reach a widely acceptable ethical theory incorporating both types, two additional perspectives developed. One has been the attempt to understand how human beings make moral judgments and how such judgments can be validated. If the first position is that of the moral agent, the second of the moral recipient, this is that of the moral judge; though, of course, each of these types normally incorporates elements from the others. A final viewpoint, arising from doubts about the possibilities of theoretical ethical formulations, turns away from these dominant positions even while accepting something from each. Its doubt has to do with the adequacy of a conceptual and abstract approach to ethics, and its attempt is to establish a human stance from which the moral life in its actual forms can freely develop. All four perspectives are clearly diverse attempts to discover what it means to be and to become a human individual in a human society.

The title of the final section of the book is "The Last Western Century." In this chapter I am attempting to capture something of the twentieth century's amazing complexity of actions and ideas which almost defy ethical mapping. The mapping of the ethics of the last half of the nineteenth century is difficult enough, but for the twentieth it is a near-impossible task. In the late twentieth century we receive a continuous flow from our nineteenth-century delta. We are the inheritors of the last Western century and we must live with, accepting or transforming, the institutions and ideas we have received. The late-nineteenth-century map reveals that those institutions and ideas of the past century both continue and contradict previous structure and thought. On the one hand, there was a developing continuation of the Enlightenment and Romanticism with all that had gone before, both religious and secular, but there was also a fundamental rejection of essential earlier ideas and institutions. It was this rejection, coupled with worldwide technological developments, that made the period before the First World War the last Western century. The ideologies of the future cannot be exclusively Western; future history cannot be Western history.

With this perspective in mind, it is now possible to attempt to write an inclusive history of Western ethics. *A Comprehensive History of Western Ethics: What Do We Believe?* can be seen, therefore, as the first attempt to undertake this task and to engage the reader both personally and intellectually in that quest.

1

GREEK ETHICS

We are children of the Greeks. The character of our Greek ancestry is re-flected in our daily lives, in our manner of speaking and the things we speak about, our interest in politics and the ideals we have for our political community, our sensitivity to beauty and to art, our courts of justice and our caste and class divisions, our philosophy and our science. One of the greatest influences of the Greeks upon our lives has been the influence of ethics. The ideals that we profess in a democratic society and the ways we think about those ideals are to no small extent the influence of the Greek character upon our own. Probably no single society has been more influential in shaping our ethic than that of Greece in the fifth and fourth centuries before Christ.

Even the language of our moral reflection bears the imprint of Greece. The word "ethics" has its root in a Greek term meaning "custom, usage." "Philosophy," both the word which originally meant "love of wisdom" and the reality out of which the word came, were Greek inventions of the fifth century. "Ideals" and "politics" are, the Greeks assumed, a part of ethics; and both words are Greek. Greek ethical words and ideas (itself a Greek word) were the creative work of specific individuals who lived in a particular com-munity under a definite set of circumstances. To begin to know the thoughts of these individuals and the life of this community is to begin to know our own heritage.

THE SOCIAL SOURCES OF THE ETHIC

At the beginning of the sixth century B.C.E Athens was in as weak and impoverished a plight as any of the city-states between the Aegean and Adriatic.
Tenant farmers who could never rise above their indebtedness to a hereditary
land-owning aristocracy comprised the bulk of the population. The land the
farmers ploughed showed pockmarks of erosion, symptoms of economic
sickness. Debts were passed from generation to generation; so a man's sons
began life with the same bondage and hopelessness with which the father
died. Overpopulation threatened the entire community, and neither war nor
colonization, both of which were tried, was able to meet that threat. Currency
was cumbersome and difficult for the simple folk to understand. Commerce
between Athens and other city-states was sparse, and crafts in Athens had not
been widely developed.

In the face of these ills Solon (ca. 630–ca. 560 B.C.E.), poet and chief officer of the state, in 594, began improving the lot of the tenant farmers.
Through a series of measures, all based upon recognition of the worth of the
individual and the community, Solon created a freedom and hope for the dispossessed. It became illegal to sell one's family into slavery, and all debts on
the land were canceled. The system of currency was simplified. The production of olive oil, the crop for which the soil was most suited, was encouraged.
And, since man cannot live by olive oil alone, this further stimulated commerce. When Athens became a center of trade, "industries" became essential.
Thus, on the basis of moral insight into the needs of human beings coupled
with practical wisdom, Solon introduced an era of Athenian history in which
there developed for many a freedom from fear and want. The flowering of that
freedom came a full century later with the fifth-century poets, statesmen,
artists, philosophers, and the entire Athenian community that encouraged the
work of its leaders. In ethical practice, moral valuations expressed by Solon's
reforms were fulfilled with the political life of the Athenian community prior
to the outbreak of the Peloponnesian War in 431; in ethical theory, the ideals
were realized in Socrates (469–399), Plato (427–347), and Aristotle (384–322).

The passage of Athenian history from Solon to Socrates was neither
smooth nor easy. Solon, with his valuations of human worth, had met a group
of threats that challenged the existence of Athens. But his solution, coupled
with geographic, economic, social, and political factors, created further inescapable problems. The first problem was, "How shall we Athenians live
with our Greek neighbors and create a just order and peaceful relations
among societies that have been in continual conflict?" And the second question, no less difficult than the first, was, "How shall we Athenians live with
one another? On what basis shall we establish our community life?"

The geography of Greece itself posed these problems. Town was cut off from town by rugged mountain terrain, by rivers, and, since much of the Greek world consisted of islands in the Aegean, by the wider sea. The cities developed independent traditions. With the double disasters of increasing population and decreasing food supply the raids and wars between city-states became inevitable. Then in the early years of the fifth century the rival city-states were united in opposing the Persian invasion. Taking advantage of the feuds between the city-states, the Persians had tried to destroy each community separately, placing the entire Greek world under Persian hegemony. In 490, King Darius, after several unsuccessful attempts to destroy Athens, organized an invading force of six hundred ships. One by one the islands of the Aegean were conquered until Athens was next in the Western advance. There seemed no hope that a small isolated city could survive the onslaught of the disciplined and powerful army. Yet the Persian professional infantry was defeated for the first time in the West at Marathon, and it was defeated by a civilian Athenian army.

Ten years later Xerxes made careful plans for another Persian campaign against the Greeks, and this time the Greek communities organized together under the leadership of Sparta and Athens to meet the invaders. In 480 Thermopylae, a narrow, strategic communications base, was taken at great cost to the Persians. Athens was invaded and destroyed. But off Salamis, an island southeast of the mainland, the Greek fleet, manned mainly by Athenians, defeated the Persian navy. And the next winter decisive land and sea battles were fought on the same day with Greek victories in the West at Plataea and Mycale. The threat of Persia had been repulsed by the cooperation of the city-states.

If cooperation was successful in war it might be similarly successful in peace. In 478 there was formed the Confederacy of Delos, an organization of independent city-states that united to prevent war. For almost fifty years (480–431) the aim of the confederacy was realized. In this period there was the development of international trade. In Athens, there was the flourishing of culture.

Commerce called for new classes of citizens, for city merchants and artisans and sailors. Immigrants flowed into Athens, and conflicts between the newer classes and the older citizens naturally occurred. A new aristocracy based on slavery appeared. The Greek slaves were treated as "fellow-workers," but the slaves were slaves nonetheless. The size of Athens (with a population of perhaps 350,000, with 40,000 adult males during Socrates' life) meant that a maximum of face-to-face relations existed in which the relation of master to slave, or ship-owner to artisan was on a personal basis. The types of work, for example, sailing a ship, with its the mutual dependency upon winds and the skills of the seamen, were those in which the co-laborers shared common dangers and common hopes. These characteristics were important for the Greek ethos.

The presence of diverse social classes raised the crucial problem of how different persons and groups could live together in harmony in the city-state. Fifth-century Athenians solved this problem creatively, and for a time it seemed to the Athenian that he with his fellows had achieved the rule of life by which men live together harmoniously in a community. Economically there was a division of labor that required cooperation as well as friendly competition between members "of the same family." Within the community there was mutual respect for one another, a regard for individuals that was furthered by the possession of a common tradition and the gentleness of the civic religion. Politically there was a sharing in the creation of the laws and a life according to the laws. All free citizens received the benefits which the Athenian society had to offer in art, in education, and in amusements.

In 429, Pericles (ca. 495–429), the great democratic leader, reminded his fellow-citizens of their heritage and pleaded with them to dedicate themselves to the same ideals in the difficult days. He expressed the spirit of the Athenian life at its best.

The first battles of the Peloponnesian War had been fought. Athenian youth had been killed. The bodies of the dead were returned to their home-city; and then, in accordance with custom, there was a public funeral. The crowd, an entire city, assembled. For the most part there was an awesome silence as the people came together. After the coffins were lowered into the earth Pericles stepped from beside the graves to a high platform and spoke to the hushed assembly, clearly elucidating the basic principles which had contributed to Athens' greatness:

> I shall begin by speaking about our ancestors, since it is only right and proper on such an occasion to pay them the honor of recalling what they did. In this land of ours there have always been the same people living from generation to generation up till now, and they, by their courage and their virtues, have handed it on to us, a free country. They certainly deserve our praise. . . .
>
> What I want to do is . . . to discuss the spirit in which we faced our trials and also our constitution and the way of life which has made us great. After that I shall speak in praise of the dead . . . .
>
> Let me say that our system of government does not copy the institutions of our neighbors. It is more the case of our being a model to others, than of our imitating anyone else. Our constitution is called a democracy because power is in the hands not of a minority but of the whole people. When it is a question of settling private disputes, everyone is equal before the law; when it is a question of putting one person before another in positions of public responsibility, what counts is not membership of a particular class, but the actual ability which the man possesses. No one, so long as he has it in him to be of service to the state, is kept in political obscurity be-

cause of poverty. And, just as our political life is free and open, so is our day-to-day life in our relations with each other. We do not get into a state with our next-door neighbor if he enjoys himself in his own way, nor do we give him the kind of black looks which, though they do no real harm, still do hurt people's feelings. We are free and tolerant in our private lives; but in public affairs we keep to the law. This is because it commands our deep respect.

We give our obedience to those whom we put in positions of authority, and we obey the laws themselves, especially those which are for the protection of the oppressed, and those unwritten laws which it is an acknowledged shame to break. And here is another point. When our work is over, we are in a position to enjoy all kinds of recreation for our spirits. There are various kinds of contests and sacrifices regularly throughout the year; in our own homes we find a beauty and a good taste which delight us every day and which drive away our cares. Then the greatness of our city brings it about that all the good things from all over the world flow in to us, so that to us it seems just as natural to enjoy foreign goods as our own local products.

Then there is a great difference between us and our opponents, in our attitude towards military security. Here are some examples: Our city is open to the world, and we have no periodical deportations in order to prevent people observing or finding out secrets which might be of military advantage to the enemy. This is because we rely, not on secret weapons, but on our own real courage and loyalty. There is a difference, too, in our educational systems. The Spartans, from their earliest boyhood, are submitted to the most laborious training in courage; we pass our lives without all these restrictions, and yet are just as ready to face the same dangers as they are. . . .

Our love of what is beautiful does not lead to extravagance; our love of the things of the mind does not make us soft. We regard wealth as something to be properly used, rather than as something to boast about. As for poverty, no one need be ashamed to admit it: the real shame is in not taking practical measures to escape from it. Here each individual is interested not only in his own affairs but in the affairs of the state as well: even those who are mostly occupied with their own business are extremely well-informed on general politics—this is a peculiarity of ours: we do not say that a man who takes no interest in politics is a man who minds his own business; we say that he has no business here at all. We Athenians, in our own persons, take our decisions on policy or submit them to proper discussions: for we do not think that there is an incompatibility between words and deeds; the worst thing is to rush into action before the consequences have been properly debated. And this is a another point where we differ from other people. We are capable at the same time of taking risks and of estimating them beforehand. Others are brave out of ignorance; and, when they stop to think, they begin to fear. But the man who can most truly be accounted brave is he who best knows the meaning of what is sweet in life and of what is terrible, and then goes out undeterred to meet what is to come.

Again, in questions of general good feeling there is a great contrast between us and most other people. We make friends by doing good to others, not by receiving good from them. . . . We are unique in this. When we do kindnesses to others, we do not do them out of any calculations of profit or loss: we do them without afterthought, relying on our free liberality. Taking everything together then, I declare that our city is an education to Greece, and I declare that in my opinion each single one of our citizens, in all the manifold aspects of life, is able to show himself the rightful lord and owner of his own person, and do this, moreover, with exceptional grace and exceptional versatility. . . .

This, then, is the kind of city for which these men, who could not bear the thought of losing her, nobly fought and nobly died. . . . And it was for this reason that I have spoken at such length about our city, because I wanted to make it clear that for us there is more at stake than there is for others who lack our advantages; also I wanted my words of praise for the dead to be set in the bright light of evidence. And now the most important of these words has been spoken. I have sung the praises of our city; but it was the courage and gallantry of these men, and of people like them, which made her splendid. Nor would you find it true in the case of many of the Greeks, as it is true of them, that no words can do more than justice to their deeds. . . .

They chose to check the enemy's pride, . . . and when the reality of the battle was before their faces, they put their trust in their own selves. In the fighting, they thought it more honorable to stand their ground and suffer death than to give in and save their lives. . . . So and such they were, these men—worthy of their city. . . .

For the time being our offerings to the dead have been made, and for the future their children will be supported at the public expense by the city, until they come of age. This is the crown and prize which she offers, both to the dead and to their children, for the ordeals which they have faced. Where the rewards of valour are the greatest, there you will find also the best and bravest spirits among the people. And now, when you have mourned for your dear ones, you must depart.[1]

Here is the expression of Athenian ideals at their best. It is a statement of the ethos which formed the basis for the ethic of the greatest Greek philosophers. In it the Athenian recognized himself, his neighbors, and his city. A year before Pericles' speech, just prior to the outbreak of the Peloponnesian War, Athenians assumed that their city had finally solved the dual problems of how to live with internal and external neighbors. This assumption proved to be false.

The difficulty was the Confederacy of Delos had created a new problem, namely: How can central control be balanced with local city-autonomy, i.e., how can a federation of states be reconciled with the sovereignty of each state? There was also the question as to how the league would be effectively and cooperatively controlled. For example, since individual state autonomy was not to be tampered with, there was no effective "international" organization. Then, when the control of the league passed into the hands of the most powerful state, Athens, a failure within Athens, coupled with the jealous ambition of other Greek communities, caused the breakdown of the confederacy. To the citizens of other cities—the Spartans, the Corinthians, and the Macedonians—the Athenian control became increasingly oppressive. In 431 open war broke out between the Greek communities. The start of that war was the first visible sign of the breakdown of Hellenic civilization. It was a tragic breakdown, for when Athens with her neighboring city-states had almost achieved a solution to the basic problem of political relations, there was a failure of spiritual relations. It was a failure that, paradoxically, produced a disordered world and simultaneously a serious moral inquiry.

Similarly, when it appeared on the surface that the internal life of Athens was organized in a harmonious manner, there occurred the failure of ethos that disrupted the common life. Individuals became more conscious of their status; class lines became more sharply drawn. Mutual respect gradually disintegrated, and the ideal of life under law was dissipated through political revolutions. Athens had failed to find an answer to the vexing problem, "How shall different individuals and diverse groups live together in one community?"

Two events that occurred, the first in 416, the second in 404, reflect the disintegration of the inner core of Athenian ideals. At the time neither seemed decisive to the Athenians, but to a later age both reflect a transformation of the Athenian moral ideal.

Shortly after the beginning of the war, the Athenian citizens became discontent with the burden of military operations and taxes. Cleon, the recognized political leader described by Thucydides as "the most violent man in the city,"[2] proposed a policy by which the subject states of Athens would pay the cost of the war. So, in the fall of 421 Athens doubled the rates of tribute required of its subjects despite the fact that this involved an open breach of a treaty made two generations previously. More surprising than the breach of a treaty was the fact that without advance warning and for the first time, the tiny island of Melos in the Aegean, ninety miles from the mainland, was required to pay tribute to Athens. Melos had preserved its neutrality through all the Grecian conflicts. It had neither asked for protection from Athens, nor had it received any aid. It had a history of more than seven hundred years of independent life. These traditions were suddenly shattered by an aggressive Athens which demanded, by reason of superior strength alone, that the weak Melians help support the wars for the strong Athenians. The Melians refused, and in 416 Athens made military preparations, and envoys, accompanied by an army, were sent to negotiate with the people of Melos. Thucydides gave an account of the conference in which he emphasized the brutal frankness of the Athenian leaders in appealing only to their superior strength and in rejecting as foolhardy any notions of religion, or justice, or pity.

The Athenian envoys suggested that the points of difference be taken up quietly and individually, to which the Melians replied,

> "We have no objection to your reasonable suggestion that we should put our respective point of view quietly to each other, but the military preparations which you have already made seem inconsistent with it. We see that you have come yourselves to be the judges of the debate, and that its natural conclusion for us will be slavery if you convince us, and war if we get the better of the argument and therefore refuse to submit."
>
> ... "We will not make a long and unconvincing speech, full of fine phrases, to prove that our victory over Persia justifies our empire," continued the Athenians with an open moral cynicism, "nor to prove that we are attacking you because you have wronged us. You know and we know, as practical men, that the question of justice arises only between equal parties in strength, and that the strong do what they can and the weak submit. . . . We believe that Heaven, as we know that men, by a natural law, always rule where they are stronger. We did not make that law, nor were we the first to act on it: We found it existing, and it will exist forever, after we are gone. . . .
>
> "You will show a great want of judgment if you do not come to a more reasonable decision after we have withdrawn. Surely you will not fall back on the idea of honor, which has been the ruin of so many when danger and disgrace were staring them in the face. The greatest of cities makes you a fair offer, to keep your own land and become her tributary ally: there is no dishonor in that. The choice between war and safety is given to you: do not take the worse alternative. The most successful people are those who stand up to their equals, behave properly to their superiors, and treat their inferiors fairly. Think it over after we withdraw, and reflect once and again that you have only one country, and that its prosperity or ruin depends on one decision."

The Melians held a closed conference and arrived at the decision which they reported:

> "Our resolution, Athenians, is unaltered. We will not in a moment deprive of freedom a city that has existed for seven hundred years; we put our trust in the fortune by which the gods have preserved it until now, and in the help of men; and so we will try and save ourselves."

The conference was ended by the coldly calculating remarks of the Athenians:

"To judge from your decision, you are unique in regarding the future as more certain than the present and allowing your wishes to convert the unseen into reality; and as you have staked most on, and trusted most in, the Lacedemonians, your fortune, and your hopes, so you will be most completely deceived."

The conclusion of the entire matter was stated simply by Thucydides:

Reinforcements were sent from Athens, and the siege was now pressed vigorously; there was some treachery in the town, and the Melians surrendered at discretion to the Athenians, who put to death all the grown men whom they took and sold the women and children for slaves; subsequently they sent out five hundred settlers and colonized the island.[3]

If the previously maintained moral ideal of just treatment for allies was not maintained in international relations, neither in internal affairs were the old traditions defended. Athens, Pericles had reminded his fellow-citizens, was a democracy ruled by law. But in the last decade of the fifth century there were a series of political revolts, based primarily upon class and economic divisions, that destroyed the inner sense of unity of the Athenian people.

A number of factors contributed to the unique upheavals. An unsuccessful, senseless, and interminable war produced a divisiveness and querulousness among the people. A new set of leaders, the demagogues, arose, and it was the frantic, selfish policy of these men, critics and not formulators of policy, members of the new proletariat and not the established country families, that accounted for much of the turmoil. A vigorous anti-traditionalism, along with an irreverence for the old values, became rampant. On a single night in 415 there was a total desecration of religious statues throughout the city. Secret political clubs were organized; class divisions were sharpened. In 411 there was a union of the upper-class clubs, and in the ensuing revolution the democracy was overthrown. The following year the democratic leaders were returned to power, and now the democrats formed secret associations in which the members pledged to treat the opponents of democracy as foreign enemies. The politicians resorted to judicial murder, to blackmail and bribery. Any persons who were charged with having supported the revolution of 411 were executed or deprived of all civil rights.

In 406 the Athenians won a sea-battle at Arginusae, and for a time victory united the warring factions. But the internal conflict had gone too far to be appeased. The victorious generals were brought to trial on the charge that they refused to rescue the Athenian wounded and allowed the remnants of the enemy to escape. Two of the generals went into voluntary exile and the remaining eight were put to death following a vitriolic public trial. In 404 thirty aristocratic leaders overthrew the waning and degenerate democratic government. Relatives of Plato were among the thirty, and Socrates was invited to participate in the new government. Some reforms were introduced, but the nerves of the thirty were too frayed for the reforms to be moderate. The teaching of oratory was forbidden in the attempt to quiet the criticisms of Socrates and the sophists. The former democratic leaders were put to death, and no opposition to the government was tolerated. In February of 404 the "thirty" were overthrown by returning exiles, the new leaders promising not to avenge the treatment former democratic leaders had received. For three years, purely because of political expediency, the promise was kept. Then, in 400, the thirty were drawn into a trap, and, without exception, they were either executed or driven into permanent exile.

Such was the internal life of Athens in the last days of the fifth century. After having approached a solution to the problem of community life a degeneracy in the ethos of Athens brought—though it was not generally recognized at the time—catastrophic failure. Yet not only failure. For this was the community in which Socrates lived. This was the city that had its lasting impact upon the young Plato, and this was the community out of which there came an ethical ideal that has shaped life in the Western world. Events in the community drove some men away from involvement in political life into the shelter of a philosophic retreat, but what they did in that retreat has been "woven into the stuff of other men's lives."

THE PRESUPPOSITIONS OF THE ETHIC

There is a primary significant fact to note about all Greek ethics: that in terms of their ethical perspectives, all the major Greek writers are in basic agreement. That is to say, appearances to the contrary, Aristotle's *Nicomachean Ethics* is in more agreement than disagreement with Plato's *Republic*. And despite profound differences in vocabulary, the moral thought of Socrates, Epicurus, and the early Stoics are more like than unlike Plato and Aristotle. Of course, in recognizing basic similarities, differences must be neither ignored nor minimized, but the more frequent error to which interpretations of Greek thought succumb is to emphasize the differences among the various Greek philosophers, leaving the erroneous implication that in matters of real importance they were poles apart.

There were four groups of ideas, taken over from the Greek ethos, that formed the basis of all philosophical ethics. These ideas were more than rational definitions which the mind accepted. They were a part of the personality, and as such had a far richer, and vaguer, content of meaning than could possibly be expressed in a definition. They were the presuppositions of the Greek ethical theory, the windows through which the Greek looked at moral issues. As presuppositions or windows they could not be dispassionately observed by the person who lived within them, nor can we, from our more dispassionate and objective position, completely sense the fullness of their meaning. Still they were the foundation of the Greek ethos.

These four groups of ideas that were the basis of Greek ethical thought were the convictions that: (1) The being of man exhibits a purpose, or a definite structure; (2) The good life is the harmonization, or ordering, of human functions; (3) Rationality is the distinctive, and primary, aspect of man's life; and (4) The human individual is interdependent with the human community.

1. The being of man exhibits a purpose, or definite structure

The Greeks looked at their world through the concept of causation. This, indeed, was one of their greatest contributions to philosophy and science. They recognized, too, that there were various types of "causes," and one of the most important was what Aristotle called "final." The word alone is Aristotle's, although the concept existed long before him in the common Greek consciousness. For Aristotle a final cause of any thing or event is the purpose, or end, for which that thing or event exists. Thus the final cause of an axe is to cut; the final cause of a musical instrument is to produce music. To the Greek mind it was absurd to suppose that while an axe or a lyre had a final cause, man, alone of all objects, had no purpose or structure. To have a purpose, to this way of feeling, is to have a structure. An axe, whose purpose is to cut, will not be made of feathers or water but of a hard metal. Similarly, the purpose of man involves a definite structure. Thus when Aristotle began his lecture on ethics with the statement: "Every art and every science, every action and every moral choice aims at some end,"[4] he was saying what everyone assumed.

It is because all of the important Greek ethicists accepted this view as basic to their theories that all of the Greek moral systems have been interpreted as "teleological," arising out of the Greek work *telos,* which means "end." Therefore, since man has an "end" or "goal," the good life will be conceived in terms of "purposive living," of the realization of goals.

2. The good life is the harmonization, or ordering, of human functions

The notion of harmony is a crucial one. Plato makes use of the analogy of the art of living and the art of tuning an instrument: when the musician has the proper relation existing between the various tones he does not ask for anything further but knows he has achieved perfection. Aristotle incorporates the idea in his conception of the "golden mean," and it can also be seen in the Greek notion of "a sound mind in a sound body."

3. Rationality is the distinctive and primary aspect of human life

To the question "What is man?" the Greek catechism contained a clear answer: "Man is a rational animal whose chief end is to think." And a typical Greek way of thinking was, "Man is superior to all other animals; man is different from other animals in possessing reason; therefore, reason is the cause of man's superiority to other animals." The use of reason, then, for all of the Greeks was essential to the good life, and it was reason that informed man what was to be sought, how the end should be achieved, and then assisted in the control of his life that the goal might be reached.

4. The human individual is interdependent with his community

It was inconceivable for the Athenians to think of the life of the individual apart from the life of his community, and so it followed that the good life could not be completely achieved apart from a community relationship. Politics and ethics were indissolubly united. The Epicureans, who advocated withdrawal from the civic life, and the Stoics, with a theory of universalism, might, at first, seem to disagree with this principle; but it was with the particular application of the principle, and not with the view itself, that their theories were in disagreement. It follows from this premise that there can be no separation between ethics and politics, no disjunction between individual and social morality.

These four groups of ideas were not theses that the Greek philosophers dispassionately and rationally examined, and then, after careful analysis, accepted as true. They were, rather, the materials with which they began their moral reflection. And these notions were so obvious, so compelling in their truth, that the greatest of the Greeks were as incapable of questioning their adequacy as the Hebrews were of questioning the existence of Yahweh, as the men of the eighteenth century were of questioning the truth of progress, or as many today are of questioning the adequacy of the scientific method.

THE SOPHISTS

Philosophy began about 600 B.C.E, 150 years before the birth of Socrates. It was, at first, highly speculative, but its importance lay in that it was an attempt to speculate, for the first time, in an objective, rational way about nature. Advances were made in mathematics, music, medicine, and in many areas of the sciences. But the advances were only tentative, and because progress toward truth was so slow and so contradictory, impatient men became skeptical and insisted that there was no scientific "truth."

These men were called "sophists," or "wise ones," and their teaching reached its peak popularity about the time of the birth of Socrates, in the mid-fifth century. They were not native Athenians, but men of the world, cosmopolites, from large cities of the Mediterranean. Athens, by contrast, was a relatively small town. The sophists daily attacked the small customs, the small thought of Athens.

Protagoras of Abdera was one of the first sophists. Two statements that he made are important: The first is from his treatise *On the Gods*: I will not speak of them, he said in effect, because of "the obscurity of the subject and the shortness of human life."[5] Protagoras was a religious skeptic, and he thereby called into question all that conservative Athenians held sacred. The second statement is more significant: "Of all things the measure is Man, of the things that are, that they are, and of the things that are not, that they are not."[6] Thus for Protagoras moral truth was subjective and relative. What seems true or false to any man *is* true or false. The ethical consequence of this position was that there was no higher authority than the individual. The Greek virtues of temperance, courage, wisdom, and justice became mere words, having no "true" meaning apart from the meaning of the particular speaker.

But the sophists not only questioned philosophical truth, they questioned the social customs of men. They came to Athens as great world travelers, as reporters who gave eyewitness accounts of how men elsewhere lived differently. So they taught the youth of Athens to question the ways and wisdom of their parents. And all of this was disastrous, not only for the parents of the teenagers of Athens and for science, but for ethics as well. For the teachings of the sophists denied the objective validity of any ethical truth, and yet out of this denial came a source of new life.

That new life was Socrates.

SOCRATES (469–399 B.C.E.)

The father of Socrates was a stonecutter, a man of repute in his community; his mother was a midwife. Socrates often referred to himself as having fallen heir to his mother's profession because he was always assisting at the birth of embryonic ideas. Aristophanes joked about Socrates' role as a philosophical midwife when he banteringly referred to the "miscarriage of an idea."

Socrates was strictly the product of the city. He loved its crowded streets, and he was never absent from it except during his service in the army. In one of the Platonic dialogues Socrates is pictured on an infrequent walk in the country; but while appreciative of the beauties of nature, he is more appreciative of human nature: "You must forgive me, dear friend," he says, "I'm a lover of learning, and trees and open country won't teach me anything, whereas men in the town do."[7]

It was partly because Socrates was so gregarious that he was confused with the sophists. But it was his aim to refute what he saw as skepticism and relativism. He attempted to refute them on their own terms, with their logic and love of human discourse.

1. The Socratic Method

The method which Socrates used was rationalized and complicated by Plato and Aristotle to meet their needs as philosophers. But with Socrates the method was simple, and it included two aspects: a confession of ignorance, and an argument, with questions and answers, in the attempt to arrive at truth.

Socrates described the meaning of his confession of ignorance with a whimsical touch. One of his friends upon visiting the oracle at Delphi asked who was the wisest of men and received the answer from the god that, of all humankind, Socrates was the wisest. Socrates knew that he did not possess what was commonly called human wisdom, so he was perplexed by this answer. He decided to refute the god, and this, he thought, could best be accomplished by finding a man wiser than himself. So he began his search, first visiting a leading politician who had a reputation for wisdom; but as a result of Socrates' conversation with him that reputation seemed unwarranted. "So I left him, saying to myself, as I went away: Well, although I do not suppose that either of us knows anything really beautiful and good, I am better off then he is,—for he knows nothing, and thinks that he knows; I neither know nor think that I know."[8]

The attempt to find a wiser man than himself was futile. Socrates discovered that the men most in repute were often the most ignorant. Even the artisans who knew something, who knew how to make shoes, and build ships, and construct houses were ignorant and not aware of it, for they discussed with authority all the affairs of the state, religion, and philosophy. Socrates concluded his search with these words:

> The truth is . . . that God only is wise; and by his answer he intends to show that the wisdom of men is worth little or nothing; he is not speaking of Socrates, he is only using my name by way of illustration, as if he said, He, O men, is the wisest, who, like Socrates knows that his wisdom is in truth worth nothing.[9]

Socrates' confession of ignorance had a double meaning.

(i) Socrates intended to say that he was not in the possession of truth which he could give to any man. He had no system of philosophy to pass out for a fee, and he insisted that any man who thought he had such a system to sell was mistaken. And the reason that he did not have such a system, he thought, was simple: there was no such system. For truth must be discovered within a man and tested there. It was no use to tell a man what he was to find, for each person must understand with his own mind what to accept and reject.

(ii) But if it was of no use to tell a man what he must find, it was still essential to tell a man *that* he must find, and this was the second meaning of the confession of ignorance. Because Socrates was aware of his ignorance, he had a yearning to become wise. Because he was not in possession of truth, there was an inner drive to discover what was true. He attempted to convince men of their ignorance with his belief that once aware of their limited knowledge they, too, would be driven by the desire for truth.

At this point in the attempt to arrive at a definition there entered the second element in the method of Socrates, the discussion.

This part of the method, too, was simple. In a casual conversation some term arose about which there was a difference of opinion. The term was always moral, such as "piety," "temperance," "courage," or "justice." Socrates suggested that the meaning of the term must be found, and asked someone to define what he meant. Usually the first attempt at a definition was crude, nothing more than an illustration of the term in question. But by more questions and with the use of concrete illustrations taken from everyday life, from cobblers and cooks, from merchants and doctors, Socrates indicated the inadequacy of definitions carelessly used.

Socrates and his friends never arrived at a definition that was entirely satisfactory. But in the attempt there was a double value:

(i) The speakers examined their own ideas. They questioned untested dogmas and vague beliefs. In this examination they would, if honest, discard anything in their thought that had no adequate foundation. They thus discovered their own mental lethargy, that they have been living all along in ignorance, with false or incomplete beliefs.

(ii) The speakers would not just be content to discard unsatisfactory ideas. They would replace inadequate beliefs with new thought. They came to understand what it means to search for truth, and, though they never arrived at the final truth, they would find a kind of truth, by which they could live.

Socrates wanted to discover a definition because of a simple conviction. It was the conviction that in ethical terms about which there is disagreement, in such terms as "piety," "temperance," "courage," or "justice," there is valid meaning. These are not words which men have invented to hide behind; rather, behind the terms there is a valid human experience that men have, even though they cannot put that experience into clear speech. This conviction was the beginning of both the method and the ethic of Socrates.

2. The Socratic Ethic

Socrates the man, his method, and his ethic are not to be divided arbitrarily. The three form a whole: the life of Socrates was a commentary, and an almost perfect commentary, on his ethic, and the method and ethic arose from his life. The ethic was never developed into a consistent system, yet his essential moral theory, resting upon the Greek ethical presuppositions, was clear: (a) virtue has an objective existence; (b) virtue is knowledge; and (c) virtue is knowledge of the good.

(a) Virtue has an objective existence.

The sophists, of course, disagreed with this theory. For the sophists, man was the measure of all things, and virtue was whatever the individual wished to make it. Socrates, however, insisted that virtue has meaning, and that the meaning is objective. Morality is something to be discovered, not something to be invented. If this is true, the important task for the philosopher and education is clear: it is to discover the "essence," the "form" of the particular virtues.

(b) Virtue is knowledge.

To speak of "virtue as knowledge" meant that without knowledge there is no virtue and that apart from knowledge the good life is incapable of realization. This was a cherished belief of Socrates; but it was not merely a scientific or a dry intellectualist belief, for there was emotion in Socrates' intellect and a mystical streak in his nature. Out of this combination of emotion and intellect, mysticism and logic, Socrates meant two things in claiming that "virtue is knowledge":

(i) He was talking about a certain kind of knowledge. That knowledge was not the science or theory of a physicist or metaphysician nor the knowledge possessed by the artisan at his work. The virtue that is knowledge is more basic: it must be identified with whatever it is that makes human life human. This was the *sine qua non*.

(ii) The second meaning of this doctrine is that it was a knowledge possessed by the whole man: the reasons of the heart combined with the reasons of the head. When Socrates referred to a man as knowing a thing, he intended to say that the man possessed that knowledge and was possessed by it. In this respect he regarded his own mystical experiences, which for him were times when he gained knowledge, as perfectly normal. They were normal not in the sense that all men had them, but that they were a valid way of arriving at moral truth.

(c) Virtue is the knowledge of good.

Moral good has reference to man, and so this knowledge that is virtue is first of all a knowledge of what is good for man. The "know thyself" of the Delphic oracle is the first kind of wisdom for a man who would lead a life of virtue. This is the reason that Socrates prodded men into questioning their own most cherished beliefs, the reason that he spurred them to make an analysis of their own crude way of living. "The unexamined life," he said, "is not worth living."[10] So, as virtue depends on knowledge, it is first of all, self-knowledge, a knowledge of what is good for humankind.

But good, Socrates believed, is also related to what is beyond man, to what is most real in the universe. So man becomes, in truth, virtuous when he apprehends with his total life, when he understands the perfection of all the virtues. It is this knowledge that the soul of man always strives to attain. It is this knowledge, joined to the knowledge of the self, that alone is virtue; it is this alone that is worth anything.

3. The Paradoxes of Socratic Ethics

With this understanding that for Socrates virtue is knowledge of the good, five unexpected theses in the ethic of Socrates appear:

(a) Virtue is not teachable.

This is a strange thesis in light of the fact that virtue is knowledge. But Socrates based this opinion upon empirical fact: he noted that there were no teachers of virtue. His insistence that virtue was not teachable was a double-edged sword. One side cut against the sophists: "If you claim to teach virtue," Socrates asked them, "what is the virtue that you teach?" And to that question no satisfactory answer could be given. The other side of the sword cut into the life of one seeking virtue: morality is to be found in self-examination, and in the personal apprehension of good; it cannot be brought about by the instruction of any teacher, though a teacher may aid, indeed, may be essential to, securing this knowledge.

(b) Virtue is useful.

Again and again Socrates returned to this test: it is not virtue unless it is useful for man. It is not useful as a means to an end, but always as an end in itself. Pleasure, money, and possessions are all secondary goods. Virtue is useful for the essential nature of man.

(c) "No man does evil voluntarily."

For Socrates, to know what is good and to choose what is evil was an absurdity. No man could willingly ever choose evil. Men choose evil *in spite of the fact* that it is evil, never voluntarily *because* it is. For when they choose evil they must believe that some good will result. Evil is only the necessary result of ignorance. It arises because a man, at a particular time, does not know with his entire being what is right.

There are three things that should be noted in connection with this doctrine:

(i) Socrates is not destroying freedom of will. His belief that a man cannot will to do evil has nothing to do with the freedom of the springs of human activity.

(ii) Since evil is the result of human ignorance, it is merely negative. There is nothing in Socrates, and indeed in all the Greeks, that can correspond to the Christian doctrine of human sin which we shall meet later, especially in Paul and Augustine. Socrates' view of human nature is wholesome: man is basically good and was made for goodness. There is no concept of original sin, of a dynamic, demonic element within man.

(iii) But if evil is negative and not positive, then it cannot be said that Socrates has solved the moral aspect of what has been called "the problem of evil." In this area he has not faced the essential question of his own philosophy, namely: "If evil is never committed through choice but is only the result of ignorance, and if man *is able* to arrive at knowledge, then why has he *chosen* ignorance? Why is man ignorant?"

(d) It is better to suffer evil than to commit evil.

Socrates was well aware that this was not a usual opinion, but he was convinced of its truth. When evil is done *to* a man he is, at the very most, deprived of external goods that have, at best, only a secondary value. He may lose his possessions, his power, his prestige, even life itself. None of these is the ultimate human good. But when a man *commits* evil he deprives himself of what is of supreme value. He destroys that which gives meaning to his life, he bores into the core of his being, and his life becomes a hollow shell. Furthermore, secondary goods may be replaced, but when a man commits evil something is irretrievably lost and can never be replaced.

(e) The unity of virtue

The final doctrine in the Socratic ethic asserts that in the final analysis all the virtues are one. In saying this Socrates was pointing toward several facts:

There is a unity of all the virtues because each is related to the same root, to knowledge. In the knowledge of the good, then, all virtues are bound together and become a unity. It is therefore impossible for a man to have knowledge of one virtue without having knowledge of the whole, of all virtues that make human life human.

4. The Trial and Death of Socrates

Socrates was not a system-builder. He did not present in outline form his philosophical conclusions. His ethical theories can be discovered through a sympathetic observation of what he said and did, but his moral convictions have a vitality that breaks through any formal presentation. If Socrates was not a systematic philosopher neither was he brought to trial because of his ethical theory. He recognized that his theory implied certain practical consequences, and it was those consequences, as they appeared in his life, which caused him trouble.

When Socrates was seventy years of age, a formal charge was made against him: "It says that Socrates is a doer of evil, who corrupts the youth; and who does not believe in the gods of the state, but has other new divinities of his own."[11] Conviction brought a penalty of death.

The charge was brought by Meletus at the instigation of Anytus, a political leader of sincerity and integrity. In a sense Socrates was guilty of both charges: he was not orthodox in his beliefs, though he was deeply religious, but he did encourage youth to question traditional beliefs and to become dissatisfied with conventional answers. Honest Anytus, aware of the dangers to a stable order that existed in those times, was firmly convinced that the legal guilt was sufficient reason for removing the troublemaker from the public arena, though it is doubtful that Anytus desired the death penalty.

The trial was brought to a court of 501 Athenian citizens. Plato, who was twenty-eight at the time, gave an eyewitness account in the *Apology*. In the trial all of the blunt and offensive manners of Socrates were manifest. Unlike the ordinary defendant he did not defer to the jury but was indifferent to them, and to his fate as well. His account of his own mission, while accurate, was not couched in the tactful language which would remind the Athenian jurors of their intelligence and justice, but almost everything he said brought to their minds the disorder in the political life; the mismanagement of the democracy; the possibility of their lack of knowledge; and, finally, what was unbearable, the suggestion that they were not morally good.

> If you [should] say to me, Socrates, this time we will not mind Anytus, and you shall be let off, but upon one condition, that you are not to inquire and speculate in this way any more; if this was the condition on which you

would let me go, I should reply: Men of Athens, I honor and love you; but I shall obey God rather than you, and while I have life and strength I shall never cease from the practice and teaching of philosophy, exhorting anyone whom I meet, and saying to him after my manner: You, my friend,—a citizen of the great and mighty and wise city of Athens,—are you not ashamed of heaping up the greatest amount of money and honor and reputation, and caring so little about wisdom and truth and the greatest improvement of the soul, which you never regard or heed at all? And if the person with whom I am arguing says, Yes, but I do care; then I do not leave him or let him go at once; but I proceed to interrogate and examine and cross-examine him, and if I think he has no virtue in him, but only says that he has, I reproach him for undervaluing the greater and overvaluing the less. And I shall repeat the same words to everyone whom I meet, young and old, citizen and alien, but especially to the citizens, inasmuch as they are my brethren. For know that this is the command of God; and I believe that no greater good has happened in the state than my service to the God.[12]

The verdict was guilty, 281 to 220. Then, in accordance with custom, Socrates was given the opportunity to state what he considered a fair penalty instead of the requested punishment of death. Socrates suggested that because of his service to the city he should be maintained at the public expense with all others who have brought honor or rendered distinguished service to the state. The vote was then taken on the death penalty, and this time Socrates lost by a far larger majority.

Once more, according to Plato, he was given the opportunity to speak. This last reported address to the jury was a Platonic literary addition, but even so it expressed the Socratic spirit:

[My] judges, be of good cheer about death, and know of a certainty, that no evil can happen to a good man, either in life or after death. . . .

Still I have a favor to ask. . . . When my sons are grown up, I would ask you, O my friends, to punish them; and I would have you trouble them, as I have troubled you, if they seem to care about riches, or anything, more than about virtue; or if they pretend to be something when they are really nothing,—then reprove them, as I have reproved you, for not caring about that for which they ought to care, and thinking that they are something when they are really nothing. And if you do this, both I and my sons will have received justice at your hands.

The hour of departure has arrived, and we go our ways—I to die, and you to live. Which is better God only knows.[13]

Socrates was taken to prison to await his execution. One of his friends, Crito, made plans for an escape from prison into self-imposed exile. He presented imposing arguments why Socrates should escape. Socrates listened, but he refused the temptation, primarily on the grounds that his punishment was being imposed through proper legal action and that by living in Athens he had made a covenant with the state which it would be immoral to break. His refusal was concluded in simple words that it was better to "depart in innocence, a sufferer and not a doer of evil; a victim not of the laws but of men."[14]

On the final day of his life Socrates talked with a group of friends about his beliefs in immortality. Plato, ill at the time, was not present, but was told what happened. At the end of the discussion Socrates made a few requests, visited with his wife, three sons, and other members of his family, and then he announced he was ready for the poison. The jailer handed the cup to Socrates who, said Phaedo, describing the scene,

> in the easiest and gentlest manner, without the least fear or change of colour or feature, looking at the man with all his eyes, . . . as his manner was, took the cup and said: What do you say about making a libation out of this cup to any god? May I, or not? The man answered: We only prepare, Socrates, just so much as we deem enough. I understand, he said; but I may and must ask the gods to prosper my journey from this to the other world—even so—and so be it according to my prayer. Then raising the cup to his lips, quite readily and cheerfully he drank of the poison.[15]

The sight of Socrates drinking the poison was too great a strain upon his friends and several of the men who prided themselves upon their self-control began to weep. And when one of the group sobbed aloud everyone present broke down. "I covered my face and wept," said one of them, "Not for him, but at the thought of my own calamity in having to part from such a friend."[16] Socrates restrained them with the reminder that he had sent the women away that he might go to his death in silence. When the room became quiet, Socrates walked about that the poison might be distributed through his body. The jailer watched his feet and hands closely and then pressed firmly upon Socrates' foot. There was no feeling. He lay on the couch and covered his face. His leg became numb. The lower part of his body began to get cold, the poison working steadily toward the heart. Uncovering his face, he spoke his last words, "Crito, I owe a cock to Asclepius; will you remember to pay the debt?"[17] He lay down once more, covered himself again, and a moment later was dead.

The debt to Asclepius was a debt to the Greek god of health and healing. For Socrates it was a debt incurred in his last moments as he passed easily from the fitful fever of life into the serenity of death.

PLATO (CA. 427–347 B.C.E.)

When, in 399, the Athenian court sentenced Socrates to death it was, unknowingly, also passing a sentence to life upon a younger man who was present at the trial. Plato was deeply affected by the injustice of the charges brought against his friend, and more affected by the unexpected penalty. Some years later when he wrote an account of the death of Socrates Plato put into the mouth of Phaedo his own anguish and adoration:

> Such was the end . . . of our friend; concerning whom I may truly say, that of all the men of this time whom I have known, he was the wisest and justest and best.[18]

Plato had been born into a distinguished family and it was expected, by himself most of all, that when he came of age he would enter public life. But the life and teaching of Socrates, culminating in his fate, confronted Plato with the question whether it was possible to enter politics. Faced with the problem of what he should do with his life, he, with some friends, went into exile from Athens in order to come to terms with what had happened.

A half century later Plato wrote a letter which gives an account of his feelings as he remembered them. He reported his youthful hopes for a revolution in Athens, a revolution in which he participated because his relatives had key roles. Soon he withdrew in disgust, for they made the previous government "seem like an age of gold." Years later his chief complaint was that they had tried to implicate Socrates in their "wicked deeds." There was another revolution; "Once more," Plato remembered, "I was moved by the desire to take part in politics and in public life." At first the new leaders showed moderation; then they brought Socrates to trial.

> Now as I considered these matters, as well as the sort of men who were active in politics, and the laws and the customs, the more I examined them and the more I advanced in years, the harder it appeared to me to administer the government correctly. For one thing, nothing could be done without friends and loyal companions, and such men were not easy to find ready at hand, since our city was no longer administered according to the standards and practices of our fathers. Neither could such men be created afresh with any facility. Furthermore the written law and the customs were being corrupted at an astounding rate. The result was that I, who had at first been full of eagerness for a public career, as I gazed upon the whirlpool of public life and saw the incessant movement of shifting currents, at last felt dizzy, and, while I did not cease to consider means of improving this particular situation and indeed of reforming the whole constitution, yet, in regard to action, I kept waiting for favorable moments. . . .[19]

The "favorable moments" never came in Athens. Plato was torn between two conflicting forces: that of his political ambition with friends pleading for him to enter politics, and that of Socrates' personality and moral discoveries. Before choosing to enter politics he had to think out the implications of Socrates' moral convictions, which meant he had to remember and clarify those convictions. After Socrates' death, Plato went into self-imposed exile, traveling widely and staying at Megara with other Socratics. It was during this period that he hit upon the happy scheme of writing dialogues in which he would present Socrates as the principal speaker showing how absurd the charges brought against him had been. These early dialogues were relatively calm. They were purely Socratic, and in them Plato did not interweave his own personal problems. But as he remembered Socrates, there gradually emerged his primary problem, "what is just for communities and for individuals."[20]

The more complex dialogues which Plato began to write in his late thirties continued to be about Socrates. But in them Plato gradually found his own voice and ideas, and frequently, through the words of Socrates, he expressed his personal moral dilemmas. This presence of himself, even when half-concealed, accounts for the passion and love in the writings. It also provides clues to the sources and nature of his ethic.

Plato's personal searchings of heart broke through the serenity of the dialogues with the *Gorgias*, written just prior to his first visit to Sicily when he was forty. With impassioned writing he gave the answer to those who pleaded with him to enter politics. The intense, malicious tone of much of the conversation made clear that there was much more taking place than an impersonal philosophical discussion.

When Socrates, as the major character, stated his ethical convictions that it is better to suffer wrong than to commit a wrong, better to be punished for a wrong committed than to escape punishment, Callicles, a sophist, broke into the argument. The true object of the work now became clear: it was to place in conflict a life that extols political power against a life of philosophical devotion to moral searching. Callicles was not a literary gentleman discussing a theory of life for the sake of winning an argument. He was convinced he had had a true vision of Nature in which only the fit survive and the rest are crushed, and by this ethic of power he justified human society. The mere possession of power gives the possessor the right to use it as he sees fit, regardless of conventional morality. Socrates was absurd, then, when he said that it is better to suffer evil than to commit it, and Callicles pleaded with Socrates to forsake philosophy:

> This is the truth then, and you will realize it if you will now abandon philosophy and rise to greater things. For philosophy, you know, Socrates, is a pretty thing if you engage in it moderately in your youth; but if you continue in it longer than you should it is the ruin of any man. . . . When I see

a youth engaged in it, I admire it and it seems to me natural and I consider such a man ingenuous, . . . but when I see an older man still studying philosophy and not deserting it, that man, Socrates, is actually asking for a whipping. For as I said just now, such a man, even if exceptionally gifted, is doomed to prove less than a man, shunning the city center and market place, in which the poet said that men win distinction, and living the rest of his life sunk in a corner and whispering with three or four boys, and incapable of any utterance·that is free and lofty and brilliant.[21]

This choice between the life of philosophy and politics could not have been presented to Socrates at the time of the conversation.[22] He was then too much engaged in his mission. Indeed, there is no evidence that Socrates was ever tempted to enter politics. But it was Plato's problem, a problem that he could not resolve until he was forty years old. Callicles, with his practical, commonsense view, was Plato's alter-ego. And the only way Plato could work out this problem was to discover what he believed about human life and what he had found in Socrates. This moral journey, along with his dual concern for what constitutes the best life for the individual and society, was revealed primarily in the *Gorgias, Symposium*, and the *Republic*.[23]

In the *Gorgias* Callicles attempted to establish his ethic by appealing to the majestic ethic of nature where the stronger animal always devours the weaker. The thesis of Callicles is simple: one ought to have violent desires, and one should gratify all those desires. He was an unequivocal hedonist. The good is the same as pleasure; evil is identical with pain.

There are two reasons Socrates considered this thesis absurd. (1) Good and bad are opposites, and cannot both be possessed at the same time, but pleasure and pain are not opposites since they can exist simultaneously. (2) In Callicles' view the good men are those who are wise and courageous, the bad those who are ignorant and fearful. But foolish men and cowards seem to feel as much pleasure and pain as the intelligent and bold; so the foolish man is as good as the wise, the coward as good as the brave.

Callicles finally agreed with Socrates that pleasure in itself is not the good. He made his last stand: there are good and bad pleasures. The important thing is to make the right choice of pleasure, and this means there must be a competent judge. The only competent judge is the man of action, the politician. Here is the final problem raised by the dialogue, and from this point the words rush headlong, and Plato's dual concern for the good of the society and of the individual as well as his reaching for the right relation between thought and action, between philosophy and politics, became clear.

Just as the physician has an ideal of health for his patient, the statesman should have an ideal of health, of order and justice, for the state and for its citizens. The object of the statesman is to produce a "national character"; and if that national character becomes distorted, if the ambitions of the citizens and nation are unhealthy and evil, then the true statesman will attempt to change that character. He will try to redeem the national soul by chastisement. (Greek medicine, tragedy, and political ideas are clearly present in these views.)

Callicles was so disgusted with the turn in the argument toward the original paradox of Socrates, that it is better to be punished than to go unpunished, that he refused to argue further, so Socrates drew his own conclusions. They were Plato's conclusions, which are not developed in the dialogue but form a lure for his later thinking. Good is not the same thing as pleasure; the good depends upon order and rightness. The good soul is the disciplined; the evil is unchastized, undisciplined. The former acts appropriately to any situation, and so is happy. The undisciplined soul is not able to meet all the situations of life adequately, and so it is not merely bad but is also unhappy, especially if it is not held in check by punishment. These principles should guide the state as well as the individual. The life of the superstate and that of the superman are the lives of bandits, and these lives are both evil and miserable. To do wrong, then, is the worst evil that can happen to a person. It is much worse than to suffer evil.

Since this is true for the state as well as the individual, the chief task of the statesman is to produce "national character." It is useless to increase the wealth and power of a nation unless the citizens have the character to use that wealth and power legitimately. The work of the statesman, then, depends upon a knowledge of moral values. And how do the statesmen of Athens stand up under this test? One and all they have failed: they have filled the city "with harbors and dockyards and walls and tribute and such stuff, without justice and temperance."[24]

What did Callicles mean then when he asked Socrates (or Plato) to enter public life? Did he want Socrates to forsake his moral convictions for the expediency of the practical politician? As a matter of fact, Socrates continued, he is the only statesman in Athens, for he is the only Athenian who does not aim at giving pleasure but in developing the character of those with whom he speaks. True, he may be hauled into court as a "corrupter of youth"; and if so, his condemnation is certain. However, it is not evil to die, but only to die at the end of an evil life.

The importance of the dialogue for the life of Plato is that it marked the definite step in his turning away from politics and toward philosophy. Yet it was not the completion of this process. That came only several years later with the establishment of the Academy and the writing of the *Republic*.

Years afterward, Plato recalled his attitude toward existing societies at the time he wrote *Gorgias*, and the momentous discovery he made:

> I . . . finally saw clearly in regard to all states now existing that without ex-
> ception their system of government is bad. Their constitutions are almost
> beyond redemption except through some miraculous plan accompanied by
> good luck. Hence I was forced to say in praise of the correct philosophy that
> it affords a vantage point from which we can discern in all cases what is just
> for communities and for individuals, and that accordingly the human race
> will not see better days until either the stock of those who rightly and gen-
> uinely follow philosophy acquire political authority, or else the class who
> have political control be led by some dispensation of providence to become
> real philosophers.
>
> This conviction I held when I reached Italy and Sicily on my first
> visit.[25]

Plato had refused to enter politics in Athens, but in his first visit to Sicily
there arose the possibility of contributing to political life. While the ruler,
Dionysius I, was a corrupt tyrant, he had a younger brother-in-law, Dion,
with whom Plato became friends. When Plato was invited to teach Dion, he
saw the possibility of uniting philosophy and political power. Dion was an intelligent pupil. He absorbed what Plato had to teach and resolved to live a different life from that of the luxurious court of Dionysius, "an existence that
consists in filling oneself up twice a day, never sleeping alone at night, and
indulging in all the practices attendant on that way of living."[26] Plato's first
visit to Syracuse, however, was ill-fated: with his talk of human excellence
and of virtue in the state he made himself obnoxious to the favorites of the
court and had to flee the country. Again he knew political failure. After returning to Athens, Plato started a school which he named after the land on
which it was built, the Hecademus grove.[27]

That was in 386, when Plato was forty-two years of age. It was a decisive
moment for him. He decided to spend his life "sunk in a corner and whispering with three or four boys."[28] But there may have been another desire in
the founding of the Academy. This was to establish a community where
friends could meet, assisting each other in the most important matters of life.
Socrates' teaching had occurred among friends who were essential for its existence, and Plato was also convinced that a good society could not be created
without friends and loyal companions. Through his experience Plato knew
that friendship and its primary characteristic, love, were indispensable for
moral thought and life. But there were no readily available theories of love or
friendship that explained this; so in order to complete his essential ethical task
of finding the best life for himself and society, Plato had to discover the
meaning of friendship and love. What place do these have in human life and
learning? An early and delightful dialogue, *Lysis*, is about friendship; but after
examining various meanings it concludes with the typical confession of ignorance when Socrates says to the two youths with whom he has been talking,

"We suppose we're one another's friends—for I also put myself among you—but what he who is a friend is we have not been able to discover."[29]

In *Lysis* Plato was reaching toward the view that love implies needs and wants and that real friendship, which can only be of the good for the good, must be based upon love for an ultimate, "the first beloved." These insights are developed in that matchless dialogue, the *Symposium*; and the insights had a significant bearing upon the way his ethic unfolds. The *Symposium* is unique in Plato's writing.[30] It is not a dialogue, except for one brief section, but rather a series of speeches on the subject of love. The various views expressed are not contradictory but build upon each other, culminating in Socrates' speech which moves the subject matter to a new depth. "Love," he surprisingly says, "is the one thing in the world I understand."[31] Indeed, the *Symposium* not only states Plato's views of love, connecting it with education and ethics, but it is an expression of love in the relations of the friends present and in the typical Athenian importance of conviviality for enlightened conversation. Love is further artfully expressed in the longing of the speakers and in the deft manner the different ideas of love complement, harmonize with, and seduce each other.

Phaedrus, who had proposed the subject of Eros for the friends' entertainment, makes the first speech, in which he extols love as essential for a full human life. "For neither family, nor privilege, nor wealth, nor anything but Love can light that beacon which a man must steer by when he sets out to live the better life."[32] Without Eros communities or individuals cannot achieve anything great or noble. It is love that leads both a man and a woman to sacrifice their lives for another. Eros is "the great giver of all goodness and happiness to men."[33]

The second speaker, Pausanias, feels that Phaedrus has been too general in his eulogy of Eros. He distinguishes between two types of love, the "heavenly" and the "earthly" Aphrodite which, as with all moral actions, are distinguished by the purpose of love. The former has as its goal intellect and virtue of a boy who is loved; the latter, loving at random, is governed by "the passions of the vulgar":

> their desires are of the body rather than the soul; and finally they make a point of courting the shallowest people they can find, looking forward to the mere act of fruition and careless whether it be a worthy or unworthy consummation.[34]

Different societies, Pausanias argues, have different attitudes toward love, but the best attitude is that of Athens, which combines the affirmation of the love of boys with "the pursuit of wisdom and virtue."[35] The heavenly Aphrodite is precious to communities and individuals, for she leads "to a submission which is made for the sake of virtue" and "constrains both lover and beloved to pay the most earnest heed to their moral welfare."[36]

Aristophanes, the comic poet, was to have been the next speaker, but since he had the hiccups his place was taken by the physician Eryximachus, who presents a medical perspective revealing how significant medicine was for the development of Plato's ethic. Love extends beyond humans to all of nature; and among humans it is closely aligned with music. For medicine (like morality) is under the direction of the god of love: it is a seeking of harmony, and concord is a kind of sympathy of one being, one act for another.[37] Eros is found in a "rhythmic and harmonic union" and it is important to distinguish the muse of heaven, which is a temperate and balanced order, from the "muse of many songs"[38] characterized by excess. Even the end of religion, "communion between god and man—is either the preservation or the repair of Love."[39] The harmonious Eros, that medicine and proper music reveals, "tends toward the good. It is he that bestows our every joy upon us, and it is through him that we are capable of the pleasures of society and friendship with the gods our masters."[40]

Aristophanes, having recovered from his hiccups, presents a humorous picture of the origin of Eros, but it is humor with profound meanings. Originally, human beings were one of three sexes: man, woman, and man-woman. Each being was round with four arms, four legs, two faces, two genitals, and each walked erect but when running turned cartwheels. Such beings became a threat to the gods, so Zeus divided them. When that happened "it left each half with a desperate yearning for the other, and they ran together and flung their arms around each other's necks, and asked for nothing better than to be rolled into one."[41] Love is thus a yearning for what one essentially is and was meant to be, a seeking for wholeness, and, if it is not sought with reverence and piety, human beings will be split asunder again.

Agathon, poet and philosopher, is the last speaker who prepares the way for Socrates' view of love. He praises Eros for what it is and what it gives. Love is the loveliest and best, and also the youngest, of the gods. He "lives and moves in the softest thing in the whole of nature,"[42] in the hearts of men. He is tender and supple, never injures nor is injured by god or man; and he does not work by violence, by force, by compulsion. Love is temperate and valorous. Love is a divine poet, "the creative power by which all living things are begotten and brought forth," and all arts and crafts, too; so "we are every one of us a poet when we are in love."[43]

Eros gives peace and rest.

And it is he that banishes estrangement and ushers friendship in; it is he that unites us in such friendly gatherings as this—presiding at the table, at the dance, and at the altar, cultivating courtesy and weeding out brutality, lavish of kindliness and sparing of malevolence, affable and gracious, the wonder of the wise, the admiration of the gods, the despair of him that lacks, and the happiness of him that has.[44]

These speeches were a prelude to Socrates, introducing themes that he would now develop and enrich. It is not that the earlier views were false but that they were too abstract, too elementary. They failed to reach deeper human meanings in their affirmations of love. Here, as elsewhere in his ethics, Plato kept close to actual human experience, eliciting the meanings and possibilities of ordinary moral actions, and having Socrates develop their possibilities by transforming their abstract assertions into specific human experiences.

First Socrates engages in a dialogue with Agathon, correcting a minor point in his speech but turning the correction into a significant idea. Then he reports a conversation he had with the goddess Diotima, so his truth about love ("the one thing in the world I understand") is the goddess's truth or, more accurately, Plato's truth.

Agathon had asserted that love is beautiful, lacking in nothing. But, Socrates argues, love cannot itself be beautiful since it wants, and therefore lacks, the beautiful. When Agathon confesses, "I begin to be afraid I didn't know what I was talking about,"[45] Socrates, quoting Diotima, reveals the deeper meanings of love.

First is the fact that love is the child of Plenty and Need. The emphasis upon Need points to the goal-oriented character of Plato's ethic: it is a matter of wanting, of aspiring, of self-fulfillment. The aspect of Plenty ("the son of Craft"[46]) emphasizes the centrality of reason in reaching ethical goals. Love is "at once desirous and full of wisdom, a lifelong seeker after truth, an adept in sorcery, enchantment, and seduction."[47]

Eros is the love of wisdom,

> For wisdom is concerned with the loveliest of things, and Love is the love of what is lovely. And so it follows that love is a lover of wisdom, and being such he is placed between wisdom and ignorance.[48]

This love enables one to make the beautiful and the good one's own, and, in gaining what is good for the self, one gains happiness.

Aristophanes had suggested that lovers are people looking for their other halves, but Socrates also corrects this view. "Love never longs for either the half or the whole of anything except good."[49] The fact that everyone wants the good to be his own forever accounts for conception, both physical and spiritual. "The mortal does all it can to put on immortality,"[50] that is, to have the good forever. This longing for an eternal good explains the love of fame and so accounts both for the creation of a family and "the things of the spirit." These latter are "Wisdom and all her sister virtues; it is the office of every poet to beget them, and of every artist whom we may call creative."[51] But love accounts, too, for the creation of laws and institutions. It is also both the beginning and the end of education, which begins with love and ends with the fruits of love. When one is attracted to a beautiful body and an agreeable soul, "it is easy to discuss what human goodness is and how the virtuous should live—in short to undertake the other's education."[52] In all of this there is no contradiction between the love of the other and of the self, between wanting the good of the other and of the self. Plato, having begun his view of love with a self-love and a wanting for the self, has been led through the love of wisdom, which is also a love of the beautiful and the good, to a creativity that leads to a friendship which, with love for the other, wants the good of the other and willingly nurtures the good that the other and the self have brought into being.

Now Plato moves from these "elementary mysteries of love" to "the final revelation"[53] of how one loves and the culmination of loving. There are four stages in learning to love, culminating in a vision beyond knowledge. First, one is taught to begin with the love for the beauty of an individual body, a love that leads to "noble discourse" which leads to the discovery that the beauty of one body is related to that of another; so "he must set himself to be the lover of every lovely body." Then one must grasp that bodily beauty cannot compare with "the beauties of soul" even when it is in an unlovely body; and this leads to the "longing for such discourse as tends toward the building of a noble nature." In this state the true lover is led "to contemplate the beauty of laws and institutions." In the third state his attention is diverted to the sciences, seeing the beauty of every kind of knowledge. From the sciences looking toward "the open sea of beauty" he will find the origin of "the most fruitful discourse and the loftiest thought, and reap a golden harvest of philosophy." That will provide a "single form of knowledge," leading into the final stage. As Diotima has explained to Socrates:

> Whoever has been initiated so far in the mysteries of Love and has viewed all these aspects of the beautiful in due succession, is at last drawing near the final revelation. And now, Socrates, there bursts upon him that wondrous vision which is the very soul of beauty he has toiled so long for. It is an everlasting loveliness which neither comes nor goes, which neither flowers nor fades, for such beauty is the same on every hand, the same then as now, here as there, this way as that way, the same to every worshiper as it is to every other. And if, my dear Socrates, . . . man's life is ever worth the living, it is when he has attained this vision of the very soul of beauty.[54]

Thus, Eros, that love and longing for beauty, becomes the driving force of Plato's ethic. And the vision of a reality that makes possible "attending to all that is, in the fullest sense, a man's proper concern,"[55] becomes the goal of that ethic. Plato still has to discover the meaning of both the driving force and the goal, and this will become the task of the *Republic*. But the *Symposium* makes clear that ethics is essentially a matter of the inner life reflected in external behavior, related to an understanding of what is true.

However, the *Symposium* does not conclude with the exalted vision of beauty. There is, rather, a comic scene in which the young Alcibiades (later to become a tragically flawed statesman and man) breaks drunkenly into the party. He has not heard the speeches on love, but, when invited to participate in the competition, he gives a eulogy of Socrates which, through Alcibiades' wistful, comic descriptions, reveals that Socrates is the embodiment of Eros in its finest, fullest sense. It is the fulfillment of the Socratic prayer in the *Phaedrus*, the only prayer in Platonic writing:

Dear Pan, and all ye other gods that dwell in this place, grant that I may become fair within, and that such outward things as I have may not war against the spirit within me. May I count him rich who is wise, and as for gold, may I possess so much of it as only a temperate man might bear and carry with him.[56]

Socrates, clearly, is the model for Plato's ethic.

After Alcibiades, in his humorous way, describes the beauty and strength of Socrates' character, the speeches end when a whole crowd of revelers breaks into the party. Drinking continues, and at daybreak all have gone home or are asleep except for three who continue to drink and talk: the tragic poet, the comic poet, and the philosopher. "Socrates was forcing them to admit that the same man might be capable of writing both comedy and tragedy. . . ."[57] They were scarcely able to follow the argument. First Aristophanes, then Agathon, went to sleep; "whereupon Socrates tucked them up comfortably and went away"[58] spending the day as usual. It was a victory for the philosopher who unites the comic and the tragic in his life, for the *Symposium* as writing is both comedy and tragedy. In it Plato has revealed, through the life of Socrates, the exalted vision of beauty wherein it is possible to live a good life.

These understandings prepared the way for Plato's next creative discoveries in ethics. The *Republic* is, in itself, one of the most reasoned and certainly the most readable expressions of the Greek ethic, but it is also an incomparable work of art which, with the possible exception of some few books of the Bible, has exerted more influence upon Western ideas and ideals than any other single piece of writing. No other work of Plato interweaves his varied ideas—ethics, politics, metaphysics, religion, knowledge, and education—with such a harmonious dramatic intensity. Part of the reason for its emotional urgency is that is was written at the time Plato had finally resolved the difficult problem of what to do with his life; so it was an *apologia pro vita sua*.

Book 1 is a perfect example of the Socratic method, and it could stand alone as one of the earlier, minor, Socratic dialogues. But Plato has artistically made it more than this by creating it as a prelude which presents the theme and snatches of motifs that are to be developed. The central question is "justice": what is the nature and effect of justice in the life of the individual and society? Plato was convinced that if he could answer this question he would complete his essential task of discovering the best kind of life for a human being and a human community.

After some preliminary, unsatisfactory answers to the question "What is justice?" a sophist, Thrasymachus, suggests the same answer that had been given by Callicles in the *Gorgias*, that "justice is nothing other but the advantage of the stronger."[59] The first arguments focus upon the question whether the function of a ruler is to serve his own interests or the interests of his people, and since they can reach no agreement, the disputants blurt out their most cherished views.

Thrasymachus: "Injustice on a sufficiently large scale is a stronger, freer, and more masterful thing than justice."[60]

Socrates: "I will make no secret of my own conviction, which is that injustice is not more profitable than justice, even when left free to work its will unchecked. No; let your unjust man have full power to do wrong, whether by successful violence or by escaping detection; all the same he will not convince me that he will gain more than he would by being just."[61]

Socrates elicits from Thrasymachus his views that the unjust (or knowingly immoral person) (1) has more intelligence and character than the just, (2) is stronger and more effective in action, and (3) has a happier and better life. He attacks these views in arguments that anger and confuse Thrasymachus. But the arguments confuse Socrates as well, and he concludes by admitting he has not solved any of the problems satisfactorily:

> So now the whole conversation has left me completely in the dark; for so
> long as I do not know what justice is, I am hardly likely to know whether
> or not it is a virtue, or whether it makes a man happy or unhappy.[62]

If, then, at the end of book 1 a reader is left with a sense of the importance of the question but confused with the inadequate answers, it is precisely what Plato intended.

Dissatisfied with the conversation, Socrates thought the argument was over, but two younger men, Glaucon and Adeimantus (in real life Plato's older brothers), who do not believe Thrasymachus's thesis, yet are perplexed because they do not know how to answer it, restate his argument. It is Plato's way of saying, "You sophists present a serious problem. Let me create your best argument, and then let us examine that." It is the insignia of the genuine philosophic temper to understand and take seriously the strongest, and not the weakest, argument of an opponent.

Glaucon presents a "social contract" theory of ethics: right and wrong are determined by laws, and laws arise because men make a compact to respect socially established "rights" of each other. Selfishness, not love, creates the compact, for each desires to gain by any method and to avoid having wrong done to him. Human beings, therefore, are moral with reluctance, and the life of injustice, when one can get away with it, is really the better life. In support of this view Glaucon presents Socrates with dramatic challenges he must meet.

The first challenge comes in the story of a shepherd who steals a magic ring which, turned on the finger, makes him invisible. By it, through "immoral" actions he gains a kingdom.

> Now suppose there were two such magic rings, and one were given to the just man, the other to the unjust. No one, it is commonly believed, would have such iron strength of mind as to stand fast in doing right or keep his hands off other men's goods, when he could go to the marketplace and fearlessly help himself to anything he wanted, enter houses and sleep with any woman he chose, set prisoners free and kill men at his pleasure, and in a word go about among men with the powers of a god. He would behave no better than the other; both would take the same course. Surely this would be strong proof that men do right only under compulsion; no individual thinks of it as good for him personally, since he does wrong whenever he finds he has the power.[63]

The second challenge is to compare the "perfect type" of the unjust and just individual. The former, a consummate artist, must know exactly how far to go with his injustice, so that he has the reputation of being a just man while getting all the rewards of his actions. The just man, in his simplicity, cannot receive honors and rewards and, indeed, must have a reputation for evil. Otherwise it cannot be known whether it is the rewards and reputation that make his life better or whether it is for the sake of these that he is moral.

When Glaucon has completed his brief, Adeimantus takes up the theme with what he considers more convincing points for the "social contract." When one listens carefully to the arguments in support of justice, it is clear that it is not justice that is considered good but the supposed rewards of justice. "Honesty is the best policy" not because it is good in itself but because it brings the best results. Children are taught to be good by their parents with promises of rewards, and the rewards do not require a moral life but the reputation for morality. Moreover, the poets teach that justice is difficult to achieve but a life of vice is pleasant and easy. And what the poets say about the gods and justice is most surprising of all: it is that "heaven itself often allots misfortunes and a hard life to the good man, and gives prosperity to the wicked."[64] Moreover, even the gods can be bribed: through proper sacrifices the evil person can atone for evil.

It is at this point that Plato reaches the ultimate development of his view of the sophist ethic: ethics and religion are not united except in the mind of simple folk. Adeimantus waves aside religion:

> Suppose there are no gods, or that they do not concern themselves with the doings of men . . . or if the gods do exist and care for mankind all we know about them comes from the poets who assure us that they can be won over by "sacrifice and humble prayers"![65]

The sum of the arguments of Glaucon and Adeimantus is that if the just life is really better than the unjust, it must be because of what justice is and what it does to an individual. So this is the final challenge they present to Socrates:

> You have agreed that justice belongs to that highest class of good things which are worth having not only for their consequences, but much more for their own sakes—things like sight and hearing, knowledge and health, whose value is genuine and intrinsic, not dependent on opinion. So I want you in commending justice, to consider only how justice in itself, benefits a man who has it in him, and how injustice harms him, leaving rewards and reputation out of account. . . . You must not be content merely to prove that justice is superior to injustice, but explain how one is good, the other evil, in virtue of the intrinsic effect each has on its possessor, whether gods or men see it or not.[66]

In response to this challenge which confronted him personally, Plato begins with Socrates' conviction that important human realities have single, true definitions. Justice in the community, therefore, is essentially the same idea as justice in the individual; and it is assumed, further, that its meaning in the community can be more readily found.

Plato, too, starts with a social-contract theory of ethics; but he asserts the community is a contract based upon a given structure of human needs, not merely individual desires. His initial point is to deny the egoistic interpretation of "social contract." Society is not unnatural, the product of selfish human contrivances. The origin of society is that human individuals have many needs and no one individual is self-sufficing. There are, first of all, the economic needs, then the need for security, protection against aggression from without and violence from within.

Through an extended discussion Socrates arrives at a conception of an "ideal community":[67]

Classes	Function	Characteristic Virtue	Characterized by
1. Tradesmen or Craftsmen	Productive (economic)	Temperance	Ownership of property, families
2. Auxiliaries	Public servants: Military, police, executive, but not policy makers	Courage	Communal life
3. Guardians or Rulers	Legislative and judicial	Wisdom	Communal life

This outline of the state requires clarification.

(a) First in importance is the goal of the state:

> Our aim in founding the commonwealth is not to make any one class specially happy, but to secure the greatest possible happiness for the community as a whole. . . . As the community grows into a well-ordered whole, the several classes may be allowed such measure of happiness as their nature will compass.[68]

(b) There is no attempt to propose that the state should exist along static class lines. The classes represent different functions as these are determined by differences of individual ability. When an individual finds his proper work he must remain in it, but the classes themselves are not hereditary.

(c) All in the state will receive the same opportunities for education, girls and boys, men and women alike. (There is no notion that education stops with the end of formal schooling.) Each person will be placed in his proper work as this is determined by competitive "civil service" examination. The education and examination alike are in literature and music, physical skills, leadership ability, morality (courage and self-control), mathematics (including astronomy and harmony), and culminating in "dialectic," which is Plato's conception of philosophy as the art of asking and answering questions.

It is essential to recognize that Plato had given up the hope of transforming society, so his Republic is not a political model for social reform. It is, rather, a moral model, the attempt to define what is good for communities and for individuals, and, in particular, to discover those ideas in which the individual must find his life if he is to become fully human. This society which Plato creates in imagination does not exist on earth and may never exist, yet it is man's true home, "a pattern set up in the heavens for one who desires to see it and, seeing it, to found one in himself. But whether it exists anywhere or ever will exist is no matter; for this is the only commonwealth in whose politics he can ever take part."[69]

Justice has not yet been identified within the community but with an important supplementary assumption its meaning will become clear. This is Plato's assumption that the four virtues—temperance, courage, wisdom, and justice—constitute an essential framework of ethics.

(a) Temperance is "the agreement between the naturally superior and inferior elements on the question of which of the two should govern."[70] (b) Courage in the state is the social power of constantly preserving "the right conviction about things which ought, or ought not, to be feared."[71] (c) Wisdom in the state is that knowledge which makes possible wise public policy. It is the knowledge that determines "the best possible conduct of the state as a whole in its internal and external relations."[72] (d) Finally, justice is the active, proper ordering of the whole "which makes it possible for wisdom, courage, and temperance to take their place in the commonwealth." It is thus the proper performance of citizen functions as these are determined by nature, ability, and status: "when each order—tradesman, auxiliary, guardian—keeps to its own proper business in the commonwealth and does its own work, that is justice and what makes a just society."[73]

It must be remembered that Plato's aim of finding "what is just for communities and individuals" had begun with his questioning about what to do with his life, and that the *Republic* had begun with his concern to define the best life for the individual.[74] Individual good is its main theme throughout. How, then, does the picture of what would be good for the community clarify what an individual should become? The answer is given on the basis of the assumed parallel between the person and society, with the assertion that the characteristics that appear in the state must come from the individuals who compose the state.

There are, in each individual, desires of the senses, reason, and a "spirited" element. The first is the bare craving for the satisfaction of physical appetites; the second is the rational determination of choices; the third is the feeling of a "sense of honor" present, for example, in justified indignation, determination, and loyalty. (a) Temperance exists when there is the subordination of the spirited and appetitive elements to the rational. (b) Courage is the virtue of the spirited part which enables the individual to be loyal in any situation to the determination of reason. (c) Wisdom in the individual is the virtue of possessing "knowledge of what is good for each of the three elements and for all of them in common."[75] (d) Finally, justice in the individual, as in the state, is the name for the condition that exists when each part of the self fulfills its proper function. It is a matter of the inner self and the fulfillment of the one Platonic prayer, "grant that I may become fair within," enabling an individual to "set all in order, and become a friend to himself."[76]

In reality justice . . . is not a matter of external behavior, but of the inward self and of attending to all that is, in the fullest sense, a man's proper concern. The just man does not allow the several elements in his soul to usurp one another's functions; he is indeed one who sets his house in order, by self-mastery and discipline coming to be at peace with himself, and bringing into tune those three parts, like the terms in the proportion of a musical scale. Only when he has linked these parts together in well-tempered harmony and has made himself one man instead of many, will he be ready to go about whatever he may have to do, whether it be making money and satisfying bodily wants, or business transactions, or the affairs of state. In all these fields when he speaks of just and honorable conduct, he will mean the behavior that helps to produce and preserve this habit of mind. . . . Justice is produced in the soul, like health in the body, by establishing the elements concerned in their natural relation of control and subordination, whereas injustice is like disease and means that this natural order is inverted.[77]

In this passage describing what is good for the individual Plato compresses much of his ethic. The good life is a matter of internal, not external, action and achievement. Just actions in society are just because they either reflect or produce and preserve a condition of the inward self. Central to this morality is human freedom: it is the individual's choice and mastery of life. The moral accomplishment is related to music and medicine as both are of crucial importance in Plato's theory of education. Virtue, then, "would be a kind of health and beauty and good condition of the soul, and vice would be disease, ugliness, and weakness."[78] Such morality makes human life possible since life can exist only because of a principle of order.

Now it is possible to examine the initial question: is it better to be unjust if you can escape the social consequences of your behavior or to be just whether or not anyone knows what kind of person you are? Since justice is the health and beauty of the inward self, the brothers of Plato think the question ridiculous.

People think that all the luxury and wealth and power in the world cannot make life worth living when the bodily constitution is going to rack and ruin; and are we to believe that, when the very principle by which we live is deranged and corrupted, life will be worth living as long as man can do as he will, and wills to do anything rather than to free himself from vice and wrongdoing and to win justice and virtue?[79]

With this conclusion Plato has answered the problem of what is the best life, both for individuals and communities. If the questions facing Plato had been solely theoretical, these conclusions would have satisfied him; but he was dealing with burning personal issues. Under the influence of his Socratic ideals he had made the decision not to enter politics. Now he had to justify that decision, explaining it to himself. This required a more detailed definition of the good for communities and individuals. This necessity led him to a consideration of (1) how justice could be achieved in society; (2) what would be the basic qualities of the best citizens (or rulers), and why these are not always developed; and (3) what an individual must be, do, and know to become fully human. These considerations, in the context of the social realities, caused Plato also to examine the degrees of the failures of societies and individuals, and to compare in detail just and unjust lives. Throughout this inquiry his thought interacts between the individual and society, and while his primary concern was the individual, and although he had no hope that society could become just, he could not give up thinking about the good for communities.

It is significant that before moving to these questions Plato considered the place of women in his state and ethic. He was reluctant to introduce the issue, because on this question he, as a "doubting inquirer," was afraid of his influence in challenging accepted social views. The inequality of women in law and custom was deeply ingrained in Greek culture, and so Plato's intrusive radical questioning of the role of women in the structure of his moral thought must have been based upon intensely held ethical beliefs.

Women are to have equal opportunities in society because the needs of the state demand equal responsibilities. There is the further fact that there are no significant differences between the sexes relevant to the purposes of developing a good society and good individuals. The male rulers are to have "wives and children in common"[80] for two reasons. First, socially planned sexual life for the rulers will have beneficial eugenic effects both in the control of population and in the guarantee of the best possible human stock. Second, the communes will prevent the selfishness associated with private property and families, thus enabling the rulers to serve the social good. So communal life will lead to unity in the state.

1. The only means by which a just society can be established

Plato has described a just society as one which is properly ordered, one in which the different parts function according to their purposes. The function of the ruler is to rule, and given the fact that wisdom is the essential virtue of the ruler, this provides a clue to the only way a good society can be created:

> Unless either philosophers become kings in their countries or those who are now called kings and rulers come to be sufficiently inspired with a genuine desire for wisdom; unless, that is to say, political power and philosophy meet together, while the many natures who now go their several ways in the one or other direction are forcibly debarred from doing so, there can be no

rest from troubles for states, nor yet, as I believe, for all mankind; . . . there is no other way of happiness either for the state or for the individual.[81]

Because the desire for wisdom and political power are contradictory and cannot naturally combine in the same person, the philosopher must be compelled to serve society, for "access to power must be confined to men who are not in love with it."[82] Only by such compulsion of the best can a just society come into existence.

2. The qualities of the best citizens, or philosophers, and why they are not developed

Most human beings are uncertain about what is "beautiful or honorable or just" because they do not think through to the realities of human life. "The name of the philosopher will be reserved for those whose affections are set, in every case, on the reality."[83] He is one "habituated to thoughts of grandeur and the contemplation of all time and all existence"[84] who develops a clear pattern in his mind of the good individual.

What is that pattern of human life at its best? There are traits of an inborn disposition beginning with "a constant passion for any knowledge" that reveals reality or permanent principles, and a longing, related to eros, to possess the whole of that reality. Another characteristic is the love of truth and hatred of falsehood. The love of wisdom and truthfulness make impossible the love of money or the physical pleasures which money can buy. In such a person there will not be the least touch of meanness or fear of death. He will be gentle, fair-minded, and friendly. Quick to learn and able to remember, he will have a "mind endowed with measure and grace, which will be instinctively drawn to see every reality in its true light." These qualities which Plato repeats in an imperfect summary ("quick to learn and to remember, magnanimous and gracious, the friend and kinsman of truth, justice, courage, temperance")[85] must be matured through education. But, unfortunately, of those who continue their education, "the majority become cranks, not to say rascals" while "the finest spirits among them are still rendered useless to society."[86]

Why is this? Why is it that most human beings are corrupted, and that those who escape corruption become socially useless? First and strangest is the fact that "every one of those qualities which we approved—courage, temperance, and all the rest—tends to ruin its possessor and to wrest his mind away from philosophy."[87] In addition, so-called good things like beauty, wealth, strength, and good family connections also corrupt and divert. This happens because "evil is a worse enemy to the good than to the indifferent," so "the best endowed souls become worse than the others under a bad education."[88]

But formal education, when bad, is not as corrupting as social influence.

"Is not the public itself the greatest of all sophists, training up young and old, men and women alike, into the most accomplished specimens of the character it desires to produce?"[89] Social pressures produce a low conformity in moral standards and behavior.

Not only society but specific persons corrupt a talented youth: "His kinsmen and fellow citizens then, will desire . . . to make use of him when he is older for their affairs."[90] They will flatter and regard him, so he will have unbounded hopes, thinking himself capable of managing the affairs of Greeks and barbarians.

> And if to a man in this state of mind someone gently comes and tells him what is the truth, that he has no sense and sorely needs it, and that the only way to get it is to work like a slave to win it, do you think it will be easy for him to lend an ear to the quiet voice in the midst of and in spite of all these evil surroundings?

When "one such youth apprehends something and is moved and drawn towards philosophy," how will his kinsmen and friends react when they see "they are losing his service and fellowship"?

> Is there any deed they won't do or any word they won't say, concerning him, so that he won't be persuaded, and concerning the man who is doing the persuading, so that he won't be able to persuade; and won't they organize private plots and public trials?[91]

How can a gifted individual with all these corrupting influences—a bad education, social pressure, manipulation by friends and relatives—become a lover of wisdom? The answer is that many of the most talented cannot, and so a lover of wisdom, if he would keep his integrity amidst brutal social realities, "keeps quiet and goes his own way."[92] Here Plato's ambivalence toward social reform becomes evident. "So the philosopher, in constant companionship with the divine order of the world, will reproduce that order in his soul and, so far as a man may, become godlike."[93] What is the final pattern of that divine order for the soul, and how is it achieved? Plato's ethic culminates in the answers to these questions.

3. What an individual must be, do, and know to become fully human

In the *Symposium* Plato had shown how man at his best must be eros, aspiring for the highest. He must pass through stages to achieve the goal, and he must understand both the stages and the vision of beauty. These interactions of being, doing, and knowing are all paralleled in the ethic of the *Republic* when Plato interprets "the divine order" and how it is achieved in human life. In the *Symposium* the divine order revealed by the priestess Diotima is the order of "the beautiful itself." "And if . . . man's life is ever worth the living, it is when he has attained this vision of the very soul of beauty."[94] The divine order revealed by the philosopher is "the essential nature of the Good, from which everything that is good and right derives its value for us."[95]

Thus there is a "natural tropism of the soul."[96] It is the Good which is "a thing, then, that every soul pursues as the end of all her actions, dimly divining its existence."[97] But paradoxically this Good cannot be defined literally, and so as Plato makes several attempts to state his understanding or, more accurately, what he is trying to understand, he speaks in metaphors: (a) with an analogy; (b) with stages of knowledge; and (c) with an allegory. Each reveals his theory of education, or *paideia*,[98] which is his essential ethic.

(a) Analogy of the sun as the Good

The sun as the source of light makes vision possible, though the sun is neither light nor vision but beyond both. The sun also is the origin of things, it "brings them into existence and gives them growth and nourishment." As the sun is to visibility and vision and existing things, so is the good to intelligibility, knowledge, and essential being. The Good is the source, or basis, of knowledge making reality intelligible; and it is the source of knowing, giving the power to know. But it is also the creative and sustaining source of the objects of knowledge and (Plato implies but does not state) of the knowers. Yet the Good "is not the same thing as being, but even beyond being, surpassing it in dignity and power."[99] A person's life becomes morally good to the extent that it has an order and harmony which is a comprehensive, creative, and sustaining purpose.

Yet, the Good has not been adequately interpreted, and when Glaucon pleads with Socrates not to leave anything out, Socrates replies, "I am afraid much must be left unspoken. However, I will not, if I can help it, leave anything out that can be said on this occasion."[100]

(b) Stages of knowledge in the ascent to the Good

There are clear parallels between the four stages of love in the ascent to beauty in the *Symposium* and the four stages of knowledge (also based upon love) in the ascent to the Good in the *Republic*. (Indeed, Glaucon speaks of the Good as "an inconceivable beauty" or "an overwhelming beauty.")[101] First, there is an interest in shadows or reflections of actual things which implies the ability of imagining. Second, there is a focus upon "the animals around us, and everything that grows, and the whole class of artifacts,"[102] for which the corresponding intellectual activity is belief. In the third stage, the subject is mathematics, which proceeds deductively, and corresponds to the mental activity of thinking. The fourth stage begins with hypotheses and proceeds inductively (or adductively) by dialectic. The desire is to arrive at real knowledge, whatever the subject matter, through an understanding of the "Forms," laws, or principles. The mental activity here is a form of "rational intuition"[103] or insight.

Still, the soul is "unable to get a sufficient grasp of just what [the Good] is" because the Good reigns over the intelligible world yet surpasses it "in dignity and power."[104] So, since it is impossible to define the Good in philosophical language, Plato, as he often did, resorts to an image which elicits reverberations of both thought and feeling.

(c) The allegory of the cave

This simple story has become one of the most famous metaphors in religious and philosophical thought (*Republic* 514–527a). In an underground cavern prisoners are chained, able to see only what is in front of them. Behind the prisoners is a fire, in front of the fire a parapet with hidden men carrying models of objects which cast shadows on the wall; and from the voices of the men there are echoes from the wall. The prisoners could only think that the shadows and the echoes were the reality. But, if one prisoner were released and forced up "the steep and rugged ascent" he would, after much pain, come out of the cave. At first blinded by what he saw, he would have to grow accustomed to the sunlight, and ultimately he would make the connection that the sun is the source and revealer not only of what is in the actual world but of all the illusions in the cave as well. Though feeling sorry for his fellow prisoners, if he went back to help them, he would once more be blinded, this time as he attempted to adjust to the dark; moreover, his former fellow prisoners would laugh at his confusion and say it was not worthwhile "even to attempt the ascent. If they could lay hands on the man who was trying to set them free and lead them up, they would kill him."[105]

Plato is insistent upon making his meaning clear. As he tells the story he interrupts to point out that the prisoners are "like us." Immediately after concluding the story he asserts, "Every feature in this parable . . . is meant to fit our earlier analysis"[106] of the image of the sun and stages of knowledge. Then, to make certain his meaning is understood, Plato interprets the story, although there is even more ethical meaning in the story than in his interpretation.

If one is to know and achieve what is good in his own life or in society, one must make the upward ascent of knowledge in which "the last thing to be seen and hardly seen is the idea of the good . . . that is indeed the cause of all that is right and beautiful."[107] This being so, anyone who has once had the vision will not want to busy himself with the affairs of society but will have the yearning to live totally in the upper world. When someone who has seen the origin and meaning of justice enters the life of the state, he is likely to appear awkward and confused.

The ultimate ethical meaning of the story is that every person has the power within himself to make the ascent. Indeed, the ascent—the disciplined life toward knowledge and achievement of the Good—must be made by the individual since no one else can do it for him.

> If this is true, then, we must conclude that education is not what it is said to be by some, who profess to put knowledge into a soul which does not possess it, as if they could put sight into blind eyes. On the contrary, our own account signifies that the soul of every man does possess the power of learning the truth and the organ to see it with; and that, just as one might have to turn the whole body round in order that the eye should see light instead of darkness, so the entire soul must be turned away from this changing world, until its eye can bear to contemplate reality and that supreme splendor which we have called the Good.[108]

The good life for individuals and for communities can be realized only by the turning of "the entire soul" away from the ordinary social and natural world toward the objectively true and lasting. And the noblest natures must be compelled both to climb the ascent to the Good and to return to improve society.

When Plato completed his pattern of the ideal life his mind turned to the social realities of states and the kinds of individuals who corresponded to them (no doubt to individuals he knew as well). First, there is the timocratic state like Sparta, dominated by ambition and the desire to excel, military and warlike, fearful of admitting intellectuals to office, caring nothing for culture but, with a love of honor, cultivating the body. The corresponding individual, dominated by the spirited element, is motivated by ambition and becomes arrogant.

The oligarchic state is "one which is also based on property qualification where the rich are in power and the poor cannot hold office."[109] Because it is divided into rich and poor, the state lacks unity, with the consequent inability to defend itself effectively. The oligarchic individual is one dominated by the money-loving spirit. All he does is for the sake of money, and both reason and ambition are slaves to its service.

In the democratic society (perhaps more accurately characterized as "an agreeable form of anarchy") all segments of society rule; "anyone is allowed to do what he likes"[110] and does not submit to authority if he prefers not to. For such an individual, freedom and equality apply to the major elements of the self—sense desires, reason, and the spirited quality—and indeed to all the appetites. Each erupts and for a time controls life as happenstance allows.

Such disordered freedom and equality is intolerable whether for a state or an individual. The society will be divided into classes; the people will put forth a single ruler who, given complete power, will become a despot.

> The people's champion, finding himself in full control of the mob, may not scruple to shed a brother's blood; dragging him before a tribunal with the usual unjust charges, he may foully murder him, blotting out a man's life and tasting kindred blood with unhallowed tongue and lips; he may send men to death or exile with hinted promises of debts to be cancelled and estates to be redistributed.[111]

An individual with similar characteristics develops a master passion that rules his life, while the passion is itself unruled.

Earlier the discussants had agreed, given the definition of justice, that it was ridiculous to ask whether "to do right and live honorably and be just"[112] is more profitable than a life of injustice. Now that he has the complete picture of what it means to be fully human ("all that is, in the fullest sense, a man's proper concern"),[113] and the various degrees in which states are inhumane and individuals inhuman, Plato is driven to make comparisons.

First, the unjust man has no freedom and is insecure. The "best and most reasonable parts" of the self, which make freedom possible, are enslaved while the "worst and most frenzied"[114] master his life. Accompanying the servitude is an insecurity that comes from not knowing when a passion might disrupt and destroy his life. Consequently such an individual is "haunted throughout life by terrors and convulsed with anguish."[115] Second, to know the best life we must turn to the best judge. This is the person who has experienced the unique pleasures of all parts of experience, and that is the just man (or lover of wisdom) who can understand the whole range of life, an understanding impossible for the unreflective. Third, there is a distinction between pure and impure pleasures, the latter being dependent upon or mixed with pain. Once more it is the just man whose life is guided by reason and wisdom who experiences pleasures fully.

Finally, all the meanings of Plato's ethic are united in his unforgettable image of man as a composite beast, and in a concluding myth.[116] Three elements constitute the composite beast: inwardly the multifarious beast, like the Chimaera or Scylla or Cerberus, has many heads, tame and wild, which it can reproduce at will; the form of a lion; and the form of a man. Outwardly, the beast is shaped in the likeness of one of the three, a man. What, then, does it mean to say that wrongdoing pays and that righteousness is futile?

> This simply means . . . that it pays to feed up and strengthen the composite beast and all that belong to the lion, and to starve the man till he is so en-

feebled that the other two can drag him whither they will, and he cannot bring them to live together in peace, but must leave them to bite and struggle and devour one another. On the other hand, to declare that justice pays is to assert that all our words and actions should tend towards giving the man within us complete mastery over the whole human creature, and letting him take the many-headed beast under his care and tame its wildness. . . .[117]

This is the man who, doing everything that will make him a better man and avoiding all that would destroy his inner order, seeks to see a pattern for his life and "to found [upon it] a commonwealth in himself."[118]

This commonwealth is the moral meaning of the myth of Er with which the *Republic* concludes, and Plato makes clear the meaning of the myth first by quoting "Lachesis, the maiden daughter of Necessity," who says to those who appear before her, "You shall choose your own destiny."[119] Then, Plato asserts,

Here . . . a man's whole fortunes are at stake. On this account each of us should lay aside all other learning, to study only how he may discover one who can give him the knowledge enabling him to distinguish the good life from the evil, and always and everywhere to choose the best within his reach. . . . This is the supreme choice for man.[120]

ARISTOTLE (384–322 B.C.E.)

The Academy of Plato was two years old when Aristotle was born in 384 in Stagira, a predominantly Greek town in Macedonia. By the time he was eighteen, the Academy had developed into the greatest educational center in Greece, so it was natural that as a young man desiring the best training, Aristotle should go to Athens to study. When Aristotle arrived at the Academy, Plato, sixty years of age, was on leave of absence as political adviser to a foreign government. Following Plato's return the next year and until his death in 347, Aristotle was, for nineteen years, first his student and then an associate. It would be strange, indeed, if with this close relation Aristotle had not become a disciple of his teacher. After Plato's death, Aristotle was away from Athens for thirteen years, returning in 335 at forty-nine years of age, to found a new school. The next twelve years, until Aristotle left Athens as an exile the year before his death, were the most productive of his entire career. Because most of his earlier writings have been lost, it is the work of these years that forms the basis for our knowledge of his thought. Despite the fact that this material was written at least twelve years after the death of Plato, it is so strongly permeated with the thought of the master that it is probably true that at least in Aristotle's philosophical works, as distinguished from his scientific ones, there is probably not a page which does not bear the impress of Platonism.

To suggest that in many essentials, and in ethics in particular, Aristotle was a Platonist does not detract from the greatness of his intellect, for a number of reasons. In the first place, he explored uncharted regions of philosophy that had been ignored by Plato and other fellows of the Academy. This was especially true in his development of logic and in his scientific research. Plato had a carefully thought-out logical method, but Aristotle was the first to describe explicitly the principles of deductive logic. In scientific investigations, directed toward descriptive classifications, he went beyond any other scholar of his time. Secondly, Aristotle's approach to philosophy was different from that of Plato in his "analytical" or "empirical" method. In ethics, even when he began with a Platonic point of view, there was a more exhaustive analysis of commonsense ethical data. Finally, Aristotle was not a person to accept important doctrines on hearsay or authority. He possessed an intellectual energy, so every important idea that came to him met the rigorous criticism and renewal of his mind. In ethics, as elsewhere, his major ideas came from Plato. Some of these ideas were the creation of Plato's mind; others had their roots deeper in the Athenian ethos. But here, too, Aristotle was no doctrinaire Platonist. His ethic possessed a uniqueness, a vitality, and a richness of its own.

Aristotle's background led him to accept, as basic presuppositions of his ethics, the assumptions of the Athenian ethos. He recognized the interdependence and therefore the inseparability of ethics and politics, of the individual with his community; he was certain that man had a purpose and that the description of this formed the clue to a knowledge of what was good for man. He believed that the good life must be a proper ordering of human functions, and he knew that rationality was a key ingredient and guide to moral good.

His major aim was to describe the supreme good for the individual, and the opening remarks, which formed the introduction for both the *Ethics* and *Politics*, introduced the basic theme of his teleological ethic:

> Every art and every inquiry, and similarly every action and pursuit, is thought to aim at some good; and for this reason the good has been rightly declared to be that at which all things aim. . . . If, then, there is some one end of the things we do which we desire for its own sake (everything else being desired for the sake of this), . . . clearly this must be the good, and the chief good. Will not the knowledge of it, then, have a great influence on life: Shall we not, like archers who have a mark to aim at, be more likely to hit upon what is right? If so, we must try, in outline at least, to determine what it is.[121]

Aristotle accepted the popular definition of the chief good as *eudaimonia*, or "happiness." Aristotle accepted the view of "both the multitude and the refined few" that happiness is the same as "living well" and "doing well."[122] But "living well" and "doing well" are vague terms, and to clarify precisely their meanings was, Aristotle thought, the essential task of ethics. What, then, is the meaning of *eudaimonia*?

In the first place Aristotle described it as final and self-sufficient: it is both "desirable in itself" and of itself; it alone "makes life desirable and lacking in nothing."[123]

The only satisfactory way to describe this final and self-sufficient good was through a discovery of the function of man. Aristotle's ethic was explicitly based upon a view of the nature of man with a threefold division of the self or soul: the "vegetative," with the functions of nutrition and reproduction which man shared with all living organisms; the "animal," with the activities of locomotion, appetite, and sense-perception which man shared with the nonhuman animals; and the "rational" soul, which was possessed by man alone. Human reason divided into two types: (i) the passive reason, essentially imagination and memory, and (ii) the active reason which included the making of conceptions, the passing of judgments, and the activity of inference. Since rationality was the distinctive fact about human life, the chief good would be characterized, in some way, by reason:

> Now if the function of man is an activity of soul which follows or implies a rational principle, . . . human good turns out to be activity of soul in accordance with virtue, and if there are more than one virtue, in accordance with the best and most complete.
>
> But we must add "in a complete life." For one swallow does not make a summer, nor does one day; and so too one day, or a short time, does not make a man blessed and happy.
>
> Let this serve as an outline of the good.[124]

This "outline of the good," as Aristotle describes his interpretation, characterized the final and self-sufficient good as consisting of four qualities:

(1) *Reason.* Throughout, there was the recognition of rationality as an essential part of the human good.

(2) *Virtue, or excellence.* The human good was "in accordance with excellence," which implied that the central category of the ethic could be neither "acts" nor "responsibility." There were two kinds of virtue: the excellence of "intellect," and the virtues of "character." The chief good would be in accord with the "best and most complete" of these types.

(3) *Activity.* While the initial definition eliminated the possibility of the human good as consisting merely of acts, it was an active life. The good man

is not the person who is potentially good; he is actively so. The emphasis was placed upon "being," and human being means activity. "For," said Aristotle, "we have practically defined happiness as a sort of good life and good action." Or "the happy man lives well and does well."[125]

(4) *Complete duration.* The chief good possesses the quality of completeness: it is manifested in a full lifetime.

There are two kinds of virtue: virtue of "intellect" (e.g., philosophic wisdom and prudence) and virtue of "character" (e.g., liberality and temperance).

"Intellectual" virtue is developed mainly by teaching. This "moral" virtue is the product of habit, or the repeated performance of good acts. We learn to play a musical instrument by playing it; so we learn to be just by doing just acts. From this Aristotle drew a conclusion which he thought especially important for the understanding of education:

> It makes no small difference, then, whether we form habits of one kind or another from our very youth; it makes a very great difference, or rather *all* the difference. . . . Hence we ought to have been brought up in a particular way from our very youth, as Plato says, so as both to delight in and to be pained by the things that we ought; for this is right education.[126]

The next task is to define "moral" virtue, and Aristotle accomplished this by a concise definition of virtue and by extended definitions and illustrations of particular virtues.

First, he described the requirements of virtue, that is, what elements must be present in a situation in order to call a person "good." There are three essential qualities: (1) the person must know what he is doing; (2) the choice must be deliberate and the act must be chosen for its own sake; and (3) the choice "must proceed from a firm and unchangeable character."[127] The first two conditions indicate that the act must be voluntary. By "voluntary" is meant that the origin of the action is in the agent and that he understands the circumstances of the action.

The third condition, that the agent have a "firm and unchangeable character," means that virtue is defined essentially as a "disposition" or "state of character." Courage, temperance, liberality, and modesty, for example, are fundamentally "states of character." While Aristotle discusses actions with their consequences, this is not his fundamental interest. His ethical point of view is directed toward personal character which, of course, will be reflected in acts that have definite consequences.

> Every virtue or excellence both brings into good condition the thing of which it is the excellence and makes the work of that thing done well; e.g. the excellence of the eye makes both the eye and its work good; for it is by

the excellence of the eye that we see well. . . . If this is true in every case, the virtue of man also will be the state of character which makes a man good and which makes him do his own work well.[128]

From this there followed the doctrine of the "mean." The mean is the midpoint between two extremes, e.g., six is the mean of the numbers two and ten. So the good life was thought of as coming between extremes. The essential point of this doctrine was the conviction Aristotle shared with Plato that there are objective standards for the good human life and these will consist in any given situation of "just right" qualities. Human life must involve a proportion, or balance, or harmony. But the so-called Golden Mean is not an absolute standard since individual requirements differ from person to person. Nor is the "mean" an infallible guide. There are some actions and emotions (e.g., envy or murder) for which the mean does not apply, but Aristotle still insists there is absolute certainty in ethical reasoning.

Virtue is a state of character concerned with choice, lying in a mean, i.e. the mean relative to us, this being determined by a rational principle, and by that principle by which a man of practical wisdom would determine it.[129]

There are certain practical hints that may be given in moral choice: (a) avoid the "more erroneous" extreme by "taking the least of the evils"; (b) take the opposite extreme from the unique individual temptations or failings; and (c) be on careful guard against pleasure, since "we do not judge it impartially." But, even if we follow these "rules of thumb," it is impossible to determine absolutely what is morally right:

Up to what point and to what extent a man must deviate before he becomes blameworthy it is not easy to determine by reasoning, any more than anything else that is perceived by the senses; such things depend on particular facts and the decision rests with perception.[130]

The only reliable guide to value-choices is practical reason, and even this guide is not infallible. Right choices and good actions imply the possession of both character and practical wisdom. Practical wisdom involves the ability to deliberate about "what sort of things conduce to the good life in general."[131] And since deliberation is concerned only with those things that can be altered by man's activity, practical wisdom implies the power to act as well as think: "Practical wisdom, then, must be a reasoned and true state of capacity to act with regard to human goods."[132] It is distinguished from the other four ways (or states of mind) by which we possess true knowledge: (1) "science," which involves judgments about what is "universal and necessary"[133]; (2) "wisdom in the arts," which is the ability to make something "involving a true course of reasoning"[134]; (3) intuitive reason, which refers to the power of grasping ultimate principles from which science starts; and (4) "philosophic wisdom," which, combining scientific knowledge and intuitive reason, is "knowledge of the highest objects,"[135] i.e., metaphysics. Of these five ways of knowing, "practical wisdom" combined with desire is important for the moral life. In a significant passage Aristotle describes man in terms of both desire and reason: desire directed by reason, reason motivated by desire:

> Intellect itself however, moves nothing, but only the intellect which aims at an end and is practical; . . . for good action is an end, and desire aims at this. Hence choice is either desiderative reason or ratiocinative desire, and such an origin of action is a man.[136]

Moral good is a combination and interaction of true reason and right desire. The moral dialectic, therefore, is "I desire a certain end; I judge by reason it is a proper end; I discover by reason the means to that end; I recognize that some of the essential means are within my power; I choose, accordingly, I act."[137]

Now, this moral good forms not only the satisfactory basis for the individual's life but also for his relations with others. These relations are of two sorts: (1) the relations that exist by virtue of being a part of the political community, and (2) the relations of personal friendship. Aristotle insisted that the self-sufficient quality of human good was not meant for a single individual living a solitary life, but for his parents also and children and wife, and, in general, friends and countrymen; for human beings are born for citizenship.

1. The relations of the political community

Political society is natural, for "man is by nature a political animal."[138] Human beings associate together in families and villages for the purpose of satisfying instincts and needs. But with the creation of the city-state (the type of political community that was normative for Aristotle), law based upon moral order was instituted. The purpose of this community was rightfully the well-being of the whole and each of the parts. Within the state there is both a unity and a division of labor, just as with a ship's crew.

There were three aspects of Aristotle's view of politics that were extremely influential in later thought and social policy, and which help to illuminate his moral theory. First was his rejection of a monied economy in his consideration of the problem of wealth. There are various ways to acquire wealth: through securing the products of nature, through barter, and through trade (exchanging goods for money, investment, and lending money for interest). The first two are natural to the extent that they are concerned with acquiring what is actually essential for life. But the third is unnatural: the economy is perverted when, in trade, the buyers and sellers fix prices and when, in investments and loans, the impossible attempt is made to let money breed money. The belief that money could create money was for Aristotle a monstrous, unnatural, and immoral doctrine.

Second was his attitude toward slaves in considering the problem of labor in the state. Aristotle considered a working man's labor degrading to human beings. Thus, in his ideal state he admitted only slave laborers. The slave is a mere instrument, a possession. According to nature he is naturally subordinate to other men: "For the slave has no deliberative faculty at all."[139] A man who is properly a slave does not possess any of the moral rights of free men. Aristotle accepted as a part of nature the social arrangement of Greece with which he was familiar. But he also was critical of that arrangement: slavery by conquest he detested; the master should (out of self-interest) treat his slave leniently; slaves should be given the hope of securing freedom. He even suggested that a master and slave might be friends. But despite these exceptions, Aristotle believed thoroughly in basic natural differences: some men are meant to be slaves just as some are meant to be masters.

Third was his consideration of the organization of the state. Opposed to radical reform, Aristotle thought the state must realize a "just mean," or harmonious arrangement, of its political structure. There are three natural types of government: kingship, aristocracy, and republic. There are equally three unnatural types: tyranny, oligarchy of wealth, and demagogy. The best type of organization would be an enlightened monarchy, the rulership of one man possessing philosophic wisdom. But because of the difficulty of finding the right type of man for such power, a compromise between oligarchy and democracy is considered the best.

In all his political theory Aristotle was concerned with the small city-state. No other political order was deemed capable of satisfactorily directing the social life of man. No other organization could make so fully possible the achievement of the supreme good for the individual.

2. The relations of personal friendship

Turning to personal relations, the motive that creates friendships, Aristotle asserted, was either the useful, the pleasurable, or the good. Friends may find each other useful, or they may derive pleasure from their relations, or each may love the other for his own sake and desire his good. This final form, the friendship of virtue, is the only genuine friendship. The friendship of those who are good and who wish good for one another alone possesses the requisites of friendship. For true friendship it is necessary, first, that persons have kindly feelings toward one another; second, that each wishes the other good, for his own sake; third, that the feelings are mutually known; and finally, that there be time and a continued intimacy for the friendship to deepen. But the friendliness of those who find each other useful or pleasant does not have these qualities. The politician who repudiates a friend because he is no longer of service, the lover and beloved who no longer find pleasure in one another—these confessed to being friends, but their friendship was broken because it did not possess an adequate basis.

> Perfect friendship is the friendship of men who are good, and alike in virtue; for these wish well alike to each other *qua* good, and they are good in themselves. Now those who wish well to their friends for their sake are most truly friends; for they do this by reason of their own nature and not incidentally; therefore their friendship lasts as long as they are good—and goodness is an enduring thing.[140]

Moreover, this kind of friendship is both useful and pleasant.

Goodness is, therefore, the only adequate motive for genuine friendship. There is a sense, then, in which friendship is dependent upon the love of a good man for himself. A proper self-love is indispensable if a man would love others, and a proper love of the self means, primarily, a love of the intellect. The good man

> wishes for himself what is good . . . and does so for his own sake (for he does it for the sake of the intellectual element in him, which is thought to be the man himself); and he wishes himself to live and be preserved, and especially the element by virtue of which he thinks.[141]

In this view of friendship Aristotle was moving toward his final and concluding position: the chief good of man, that is *eudaimonia* or happiness, is to be found in the intellectual life. Human excellence was described at the outset as being of two kinds, excellence of intellect and of character. But the achievement of a moral state of character is genuine good "in a secondary degree,"[142] since its function is to help the individual attain the most complete happiness that is to be found only in contemplation. Contemplation, associated with theoretic wisdom, is considered to be the highest human good because it is the product of reason, the noblest human faculty. It is self-sufficient, it can be engaged in more continuously than any other human activity, it alone is done for its own sake, and it is a life like the gods'. Since contemplation includes theology "therefore the activity of God . . . must be contemplative."[143] The supreme good is, therefore, available only to the contemplative person, and in so far as he does attain the supreme good it is because of the divine present in him.

But such a life would be too high for man; for it is not in so far as he is man that he will live so, but in so far as something divine is present in him. . . . But we must not follow those who advise us, being men, to think of human things, and, being mortal, of mortal things, but must, so far as we can, make ourselves immortal, and strain every nerve to live in accordance with the best thing in us; for even if it be small in bulk, much more does it in power and worth surpass everything. . . . For man, therefore, the life according to reason is best and pleasantest, since reason more than anything else *is* man. This life therefore is also the happiest.[144]

THE UNIQUE CONTRIBUTION OF THE GREEK MORAL PHILOSOPHERS

The world cannot too often remember that a man named Socrates once lived. That is also true for Plato and Aristotle. These three persons constitute a remarkable continuity of personal relations between student and teacher over a one-hundred-year period that has forever changed the way those of us in the Western world must live.

What each did, and what the three together did, was unique. They were unique in speaking and writing with a focused incisiveness as well as a breadth and depth of thought. This incisiveness gave to their thinking a clarity, so that once there is an adjustment to their individual styles it is usually easier and better to read what they themselves said rather than what others have said about them.

But, although unique, they were not the first to reflect seriously upon moral, that is, human life; not even in their own time were they alone. They could raise important questions because others had preceded them and because many of their contemporaries were asking similar questions. Their disintegrating society presented them with many problems, and its basic beliefs gave them the perspectives with which to begin thinking about these problems.

Still, it is important to ask: what significant contributions did Socrates, Plato, and Aristotle leave us?

(1) First, there was a general conviction that the most important questions of life are the ethical questions, and that human beings avoid asking and answering these questions only at the price of failing to become as fully human as possible. While often dealing with specific moral problems, they each never lost sight of the fact that the question of ethics is what it means to be and to become fully human in a human society. Nothing could be more important than that. The fact that all three had wide-ranging intellectual interests gives a special cogency to this conviction.

(2) They shared a second confidence. This was that there are truths which human beings, with discipline and effort, can discover. Ethical princi-

ples are among these truths. They were aware of and insisted upon the difficulties of finding these truths. They understood the lack of precision in ethical thought. They saw the ambiguities of moral language and experience, recognizing that individuals often have to live with uncertainty. Still, they refused to give up their cherished view that there *is* moral truth, and that ethical principles have as much objectivity as medical principles.

(3) Reason plays a central, dual role in moral thought. On the one hand it is the essential means to the discovery of moral truth, and on the other, once moral truth has been discovered, it is a major power in the ordering of life, in directing practical expression in behavior. The first implies, for Socrates, rational moral dialogue in search of the elements of a moral theory; and it implies for Plato and Aristotle rational thought in the development of a theory. The second, reason in the ordering of life, means rational analysis and construction in working one's way through and out of serious moral perplexities.

Aristotle was the first to distinguish between these two uses of reason, "theoretical science" and "political reason," but the realities were known by Plato and Socrates. In fact, the conscious importance of reason was the gift of the philosophers even before Socrates, the pre-Socratics. But for Aristotle "theoretical reason" was the essential means of creating an ethical theory, while "practical reason" was the essential means of creating an ethical life.

A corollary to the centrality of reason in moral life and thought is the purpose of reason. That purpose is to make human life better, that is, more completely human. This is obviously the case with practical reason. These men thought it would make no sense to struggle rationally with life's practical problems unless reason improved life. They felt similarly and as strongly about the study of ethics, for while one may properly study the theoretical sciences for the pure joy of knowing and with no intention of becoming a scientist, this is not true for the study of ethics. Here while there should be joy in the knowing, the real purpose for the study is to make use of what is learned to become a better person and to create a better society.

(4) But who is "a better person," what is "a better society"? To answer these questions there was initiated a set of ideas, a set of key terms, that have become, through the Greeks, permanent elements in Western ethics. Basic to these elements is the view that there is a structure to human life, both individual and social, and therefore there is a proper order which is to be realized in the individual and community. The order is to be realized in the individual for the individual's sake, though with its realization there is a responsibility to the community and to friends. This realization, in turn, reflects a number of important principles.

(a) If life has a structure it must have a goal. It was the Greeks who taught the West how to think consistently in terms of goals or purposes, who thought of the moral life primarily in terms of ends and means.

(b) The only valid good for humans is happiness. Here there is introduced a great spiritual healthiness, a respect, love, and expectation for life.

(c) This happiness comes with the realization of one's proper human capabilities. To approximate more to the ideal of what an individual should be it is necessary to actualize inherent potentialities. The ideal is individual realization.

(d) When this is achieved there will be created within the individual and community a balance and harmony of the diverse forces of life, and with this newly established active order of life there will be an accompanying sense of satisfaction.

Thus, the key words in the moral ideal given to the West by the Greeks were: structure and order, goals and purposes, happiness, potentiality and realization, balance and harmony. Thinking though the centuries in these terms, along lines initiated by Socrates, Plato and Aristotle, has helped create one of the dominant patterns in Western moral thought.

(5) There were a number of consequences to such thinking which had a significant impact upon further moral reflection. Two ideas especially have become historically important. In terms of society it is the idea of justice, discoverable, interpretable, and enforceable. In terms of the individual it is the idea of friendship as essential to a full life. Given the ethos of their time, their limited conceptions of human rights and of forms of love, neither the idea of justice nor of friendship was ever fully developed by the Greeks. But they introduced the ideas as of central importance for ethics, and, with varying emphasis at diverse periods, these two concerns have had continual importance in moral thought since that time.

(6) While reason is essential for the understanding and achievement of a genuinely human life, and as such has to be learned, there is an even more primal necessary force given with life itself. Even reason builds upon this force. This is eros: longing, aspiration. Everyone, these Greeks thought, naturally desires to know, everyone naturally desires to be. An ethic with this view has as a major part of its task to release the individual as far as possible from the frustrating inhibitions whether imposed by physical necessity, society, or the individual's lack of knowledge.

There are two final lasting contributions made by the Greeks to Western moral thought. The first is their unique form of thinking ethically, and the second is their unique intensity and breadth of experience.

The form was first the form of reason. They distanced themselves from their subject, attempting to be impersonal. They attempted to be objective, and while often this impersonal objectivity led to a certain abstractness in their moral thought, yet each kept close to actual human experience, and it is never difficult to trace the most abstract idea back to its origins in perceived empirical fact.

Second, the form of thought was that of conversation. Beginning with the actual conversations of Socrates, later reported or imagined by Plato, through Plato's dialogues, to the monologue lectures of Aristotle, they conceived conversation, real or implied, as the ideal way of discovering moral truth. (In noting that the conversational form becomes increasingly abstract it must not be forgotten that none of the many dialogues written by Aristotle has survived.) They apparently had no theory about the form of conversation as they did about objective reason; but their use of conversation as a primary means of finding truth about human life opened possibilities for ethics, including the possibility that later moral thought would often be an implicit conversation with previous thinkers. This has contributed to the continuity and community of Western moral thought.

Although in the attempt to be objective Socrates, Plato, and Aristotle tried to keep themselves out of their ethics, it is not difficult to perceive the intensity of their moral feeling, the depth of their experience, and the breadth of their thought. Though they solved the problem in different ways, with Socrates differentiating between the knowledge of man and knowledge of the natural world and Plato and Aristotle each viewing ethics as having relations to all that can be thought and is, still each saw its subject matter as wide as human life and as full as all a human being could experience.

But finally, while the intensity of their moral experience and the spiritual depth of their lives may be the most important matter of all, it is one that is the most difficult to assess, for there are no criteria by which to measure this intensity and depth. Yet, these men are their own measure, for they have left us not only their moral philosophy but the symbols of their lives. The depth, the intensity of their lives has never been fully explored, nor perhaps can it ever be. But whenever the serious attempt to explore has been made, new depths have been freshly discovered. So it is that each time we look at their thoughts and their lives, we rediscover our own. The world cannot too often remember that each of these three men lived and thought.

NOTES

1. Thucydides, *The Peloponnesian War,* trans. Rex Warner (New York: Penguin Books, 1978), pp. 116–23.

2. Thucydides, *The History of the Peloponnesian War,* ed. Sir Richard Livingstone (New York: Oxford University Press, 1943), p. 159.

3. Ibid., pp. 266–74 passim.

4. Author's paraphrase, *Nicomachean Ethics* 1094a.

5. Kathleen Freeman, *Ancilla to the Pre-Socratic Philosophers* (Cambridge, Mass.: Harvard University Press, 1966), p. 126.

6. Ibid., p. 125.

7. *Phaedrus* 230d, trans. R. Hackforth, in *The Collected Dialogues of Plato*, Bollingen Series LXXI, ed. by Edith Hamilton and Huntington Cairns (New York: Pantheon Books, 1964).

8. *Apology* 21d, trans. Benjamin Jowett, *The Dialogues of Plato,* vol. 1 (New York: Random House, 1937).

9. Ibid., 23b.

10. Ibid., 38a.

11. Ibid., 24a.

12. Ibid., 29e–30a.

13. Ibid., 41d–42a.

14. *Crito* 54c.

15. *Phaedo* 117b.

16. Ibid., 117d.

17. Ibid., 118a.

18. Ibid.

19. *Epistle VII* 7.325c–26a, trans. L. A. Post, in *The Collected Dialogues of Plato,* Bollingen Series LXXI, ed. Edith Hamilton and Huntington Cairns (New York: Pantheon Books, 1964), p. 1575.

20. Ibid.

21. *Gorgias* 484c, d; 485a, c, d, trans. W. D. Woodhead, in Hamilton and Cairns, pp. 267–68. The whole passage is worth reading as indicative of Plato's mind at the time of writing.

22. From the internal evidence it is impossible to ascribe a date when the supposed dialogue took place. The two possible extremes are the reference to the "recent death" of Pericles (503c), which took place in 429 and Socrates' assertion that "last year" he presided at the Council, which was in 405. Plato was surely aware of these and other ambiguities, and must have meant something by them, but what? For essential details and fuller discussions see Plato, *Gorgias*, translated with notes by Terence Irwin (Oxford: Clarendon Press, 1979), pp. 109–10; E. R. Dodds, *Plato: Gorgias*, text and commentary (Oxford: Oxford University Press, 1959), pp. 17f.; and A. E. Taylor, *Plato, The Man and His Work* (New York: Methuen, 1926), pp. 104f.

23. Some of Plato's moral views are found in the earlier dialogues, of course; but these contain mainly Socrates' views. Plato's own discoveries are made with the middle dialogues. His ethical reflections were continued in later writings, especially *Phaedrus, Philebus,* and *Laws*; but since these are not as important for his ethical creativity as the middle dialogues, they will not be considered here. The question of the order of Plato's writings has been thoroughly examined, and general agreement has been reached. For interesting discussions see Paul Shorey, *What Plato Said* (Chicago: University of Chicago, 1933), pp. 58–60; and Arthur Kenyon Rogers, *The Socratic Problem* (New Haven: Yale University Press, 1933), pp. 29–54.

24. *Gorgias* 519a, trans. W. D. Woodhead.

25. *Epistle VII* 7. 326a, b.

26. Ibid., 326c.

27. For the remaining half of his life the Academy was the center of Plato's interest. Taylor, *Plato, The Man and His Work,* suggests that the founding of the Academy was the most memorable event in the history of Western science. It was the first institution devoted to scientific study; and later, though Plato could not have known this upon its founding, the greatest scientists of the day came to the Academy to carry out their researches. The Academy, however, was primarily a school to train philosophic statesmen, and was thus the direct result of Plato's conviction that the only hope for the world was in the union of political power and genuine science, which begins with mathematics and ends with philosophy. Its establishment was therefore a way of justifying his desire to enter politics with his deepest beliefs. The school lasted for more than eight hundred years, a record that has not yet been reached by any European university.

28. *Gorgias* 485c.

29. *Lysis* 223b. *Plato's Dialogue on Friendship: An Interpretation of the Lysis with a New Translation,* David Bolotin (Ithaca, N.Y.: Cornell University Press, 1979), p. 52.

30. It is not too much to say that Plato's views of love expressed in *Symposium* had a significant bearing upon Western life and spirit, especially in religion, philosophical thought, and aesthetic attitudes, and, perhaps to a negative degree, in personal relations. The subject has not been sufficiently recognized as of central importance in Plato's ethic. It provides insight for that ethic as for the remainder of Plato's thought. Gregory Vlastos asserts that the essay in which he "learned the most about Plato in the course of writing and rewriting" was his essay on "The Individual as Object of Love in Plato." Gregory Vlastos, *Platonic Studies* (Princeton: Princeton University Press, 1973), p. ix.

31. *Symposium* 177d, trans. Michael Joyce in Hamilton and Cairns.

32. Ibid., 178c.

33. Ibid., 180b.

34. Ibid., 181b.

35. Ibid., 184d.

36. Ibid., 184c, 185b–c. The *Symposium* is primarily concerned, yet not entirely, with homosexual love. See Socrates' speech below. It is likely that Plato was not only accepting Athenian mores but was also coming to terms with his own homosexuality. Later in his life he had greater difficulties with this.

37. Werner Jaeger has emphasized the relation of Greek medicine to Greek ethics. See "Greek Medicine as Paideia," in *Paideia: The Ideals of Greek Culture,* trans. Gilbert Highet (New York: Oxford University Press, 1939, 1943, 1944), 3: 3–46. Plato's definition of justice in the *Republic* clearly has medicine as a major source.

38. *Symposium* 187d–e.

39. Ibid., 188b–c.

40. Ibid., 188d.

41. Ibid., 191a.

42. Ibid., 195e.

43. Ibid., 196e–97b.

44. Ibid., 197d–e.

45. Ibid., 201c.

46. Ibid., 203b.

47. Ibid., 203d.

48. Ibid., 204b.

49. Ibid., 205e.

50. Ibid., 207d.

51. Ibid., 209a.

52. Ibid., 209bc.

53. Ibid., 209e–10a.

54. Ibid., 210e–11a, d.

55. *Republic* 443d, trans. Francis M Cornford (London: Oxford University Press, 1941).

56. *Phaedrus* 279b, c, trans. R. Hackforth in *The Collected Dialogues of Plato,* ed. Edith Hamilton and Huntington Cairns (New York: Pantheon Books, 1964), p. 525.

57. *Symposium* 223d, trans. Michael Joyce in Hamilton and Cairns.

58. Ibid.

59. *Republic* 338c, trans. Allan Bloom (New York: Basic Books, 1968).

60. *Republic* 344c, trans. Paul Shorey.

61. *Republic* 345a, trans. Cornford. It was not typical of Socrates in the early dialogues to make a forthright statement about his convictions. The fact that here he asserts his belief without yet claiming conscious reasons for it suggests the primacy of the unconscious, or the unselfconscious eros, in Plato's ethic.

Because the *Republic* is the first full development of Plato's own views it is assumed here that the voice of Socrates speaks in the mind of Plato. As with any creative student who goes beyond his teacher it is not possible, or necessary, to know where Socrates ends and Plato begins. It is enough that the views are truly Plato's at the time of writing, whatever the source. In what follows, whenever the name "Socrates," is used the reference is not to the actual person but to the character in the dialogue. The name "Plato" will represent the actual person who wrote the dialogue and believed its ideas.

62. *Republic* 354b.

63. Ibid., 360c.

64. Ibid., 364d.

65. Ibid., 365a–b. Years later in the *Laws* Plato condemned these same three beliefs as increasing forms of impiety.

66. Ibid., 367c, d, e.

67. Ibid., 368–427b–466d. Plato at times uses "guardians" to refer to both Auxiliaries and Rulers; at other times guardians refers only to Rulers.

68. Ibid., 420b.

69. Ibid., 592b. This passage is one of the primary sources of the Christian ethical conception of the City of God.

70. Ibid., 431a–b.

71. Ibid., 429d.

72. Ibid., 427c.

73. Ibid., 434c.

74. If, under the influence of modern sociology and the huge bureaucratic nation-state, this assumption is rejected it must be remembered that Plato lived in a small community where the character and behavior of individuals had an obvious influence upon social groups and the state. Nor need a rejection of his assumption imply a rejection of his central ethical idea. The parallel of individual and state might be viewed as another Platonic myth (though he did not consider it such) that, in the midst of difficult intellectual complexities, excites reverie and leads to some truth.

75. *Republic* 441d–e.

76. *Phaedrus* 279b; *Republic* 443d. *Great Dialogues of Plato,* trans. W. H. D. Rouse (New York: New American Library, 1956), p. 244.

77. *Republic* 442a–43c, 444b.

78. *Republic* 444e, trans. Shorey.

79. *Republic* 445a–b, trans. Cornford.

80. Ibid., 449d. While Plato is clear about equal opportunities for women his mind and the

Republic are male-permeated. He speaks, for example, of the male rulers having "wives and children in common," but he does not speak of the female rulers having "husbands in common." Despite the male orientation of the writing and the acceptance of the mores about women (see, e.g., 431c, 549d, 579b) at critical points Plato is insistent upon the equality of women. When, for example, he has given his completed picture of the just individual Glaucon comments, "You have produced ruling men who are wholly fair." Socrates responds: "And ruling women, too. . . . Don't suppose that what I said applies any more to men than to women" (540c, trans. Bloom).

81. Ibid., 473d–e.

82. Ibid., 521b. One can read in this and other passages Plato's poignant despair that wisdom and power were never combined in his own life.

83. *Republic* 479d, 480.

84. *Republic* 486a, trans. Shorey.

85. *Republic* 485–87a, trans. Cornford.

86. *Republic* 487d, trans. Shorey.

87. Ibid., 491c.

88. *Republic* 491c, trans. Cornford, 491e, trans. Shorey.

89. *Republic* 492c, trans. Cornford.

90. *Republic* 494b, d, trans. Shorey.

91. Ibid., 494e, trans. Shorey and Bloom. Plato is obviously thinking about his experience with kinsmen and friends, and with Socrates, the gentle persuader. He could remember acts done, words said, private plots and, most of all, a public trial. What is most surprising is that in this he is taking a measure of responsibility for the death of Socrates. This makes more understandable the intensity of Plato's thought and writing.

92. *Republic* 496d, trans. Cornford.

93. Ibid., 500a.

94. *Symposium* 211c, d.

95. *Republic* 504a. In this definition of "the divine order" a remarkable transformation has occurred. Previously the definition of justice had been in the third person in relation to the Guardians, "he" and "they." Suddenly it becomes the first person plural, "we" and "us." Plato, as has been indicated, is "present" throughout the entire *Republic* but earlier he had been a hidden presence. Now he becomes involved, and we the readers with him. Even though, later in the dialogue, he returns to the third person there is then no doubt he is talking to us, and to himself.

96. The phrase is W. H. Auden's.

97. *Republic* 505a.

98. Werner Jaeger is the person most responsible for emphasizing the importance of *paideia* in Plato, in his great work, *Paideia*. Jaeger points out that the rich meaning of *paideia* cannot be translated by any one word, for it encompasses education, culture, and civilization. One thesis of this book is that it was the contribution of the Greeks in general and Plato in particular toward what became a central concern of Western ethics, viz., what it means to be and become fully human in a human and humane society.

99. *Republic* 508c. In a footnote to the term "dignity" Bloom points out that the Greek word means "age," so the meaning of dignity comes from the honor belonging to age. This has obvious significance for Plato's understanding of the transcendent Good.

100. Ibid. Or, "I'm afraid I must leave out a good deal," trans. Rouse.

101. Ibid., 509a. The first phrase is Shorey's translation; the second, Bloom.

102. Ibid., 510a, trans. Bloom.

103. *Republic,* trans. Cornford, p. 223. The term is Cornford's and corresponds to the Greek word *noesis.*

104. Ibid., p. 220.

105. Ibid., 517a.

106. Ibid., 515a, trans. Bloom.

107. *Republic* 517c, trans. Cornford.

108. Ibid., 518c–d.

109. Ibid., 550c.

110. Ibid., 557c.

111. Ibid., 566bc.

112. *Republic* 444c.

113. Ibid., 443a.

114. *Republic* 577d, trans. Shorey.

115. *Republic* 579a, trans. Cornford.

116. Plato is here concerned with the relations of philosophy and poetry.

117. *Republic* 588e–99a.

118. Ibid., 592a, b.

119. Ibid., 617d, e.

120. Ibid., 618c,d,e.

121. *Nicomachean Ethics* 1094a:1–26, in *The Basic Works of Aristotle,* ed. Richard McKeon and trans. W. D. Ross (New York: Random House, 1966).

122. Ibid., 1095a:19.

123. Ibid., 1097a:35 and 1097b:15.

124. Ibid., 1098a:6–20.

125. Ibid., 1098b:21.

126. Ibid., 1103b:24–26 and 1104b:11–13.

127. Ibid., 1104b:33–34.

128. Ibid., 1106a:15–23.

129. Ibid., 1106b:36—1107a:1–3.

130. Ibid., 1109b:19–23.

131. Ibid., 1140a:29.

132. Ibid., 1140b:20–21.

133. Ibid., 1140a:31–32.

134. Ibid., 1140a:21.

135. Ibid., 1141a:18.

136. Ibid., 1139a:35–36; 1139b:1–5.

137. Author's paraphrase *Nicomachean Ethics* 1111b:25–27.

138. *Politics* 1253a:2. In *The Basic Works of Aristotle,* ed. Richard McKeon and trans. W. D. Ross (New York: Random House, 1966).

139. Ibid., 1260a:12.

140. *Nicomachean Ethics* 1156b:6–12.

141. Ibid., 1166a:14–18.

142. Ibid., 1178a:8.

143. Ibid., 1178b:22–23.

144. Ibid., 1177b:25–1178a:8.

2

THE BIBLICAL ETHIC

We are children of the Greeks. And we are also children of Israel. In our living we resemble both sides of our family, the Greek and the Israelite. Indeed, much of our conflict and confusion in ethics stems from the fact that sometimes we think and act like the prophets or the priests of Israel and sometimes like the philosophers of Greece. Other societies, of course, have helped to shape our ethical outlook, and these later influences must not be minimized. But these later societies were themselves conditioned by the earlier. So it is important to remember that, in a sense, the entire story of our lives is one of the development of Hebraic and Greek viewpoints: the attempt, at times, to develop each in isolation from the other, and to interrelate the divergent approaches. Still, these two are the primary perspectives for Western ethics and it is perhaps helpful initially to distinguish between them.

The Greeks, as we have seen, thought of ethical life as they thought of other aspects of existence: as a natural, developing object. Here the important word is *object*. For this was the assumption that enabled the Greeks to approach the ethical life rationally, to put questions to it, to analyze the meaning of moral existence. You can look *at* a tree, or a dog, or any other natural object. You can define, analyze, classify, discover relations, and describe "laws" relating to the natural object. Man, to the Greek perspective, is an object: he is an animal, a rational animal, to be sure, but none the less an animal. His ethical life, therefore, can be approached objectively; it can be defined, analyzed, classified; relations can be found and "laws" discovered. All of this is to be accomplished by the rational, objective approach, *by looking at*.

The Israelites began from an entirely different perspective. They began from their experience of interpersonal relations. Now, while a sociological and psychological description of my family is one thing, my own experience—my actual relations with the members of my own family—is quite another. The Israelites started with a sense of that "family" or community, and their approach to the moral life was as participants, not as rational observers. This does not exclude reason and an objective approach, but both are placed in an entirely different context. Consequently, for the Israelite the understanding of the ethical life is a matter not of *looking at* but of *responding to*.

In order to comprehend the biblical ethic, therefore, it is essential to look *with* the prophets and not *at* them. In order to discover any meaning in what they see, it is necessary to make some sense out of their assumptions, that is, their viewpoint. It is also important to recognize the continuity of the Israelite perspective. There is a biblical point of view that is basically the same throughout the history of the "Old Israel" and into the creation of the "New Israel." Within this community and continuity of a way of seeing there were many disagreements, just as there were disagreements within a common framework among the Greek philosophers, but these disagreements developed within the same tradition.

It is impossible to date the beginning of the biblical point of view since the sources of this unique approach to human life go back beyond the ages of recorded history. It first appears in the historically dim figures of Abraham, Isaac, and Jacob, for whom there are no certain dates. The important fact about each was that he felt himself chosen by a god (a god not yet known by the name of "Yahweh") and that he and his god make a compact together:

> When Abram was ninety-nine, the Eternal appeared to Abram and said, "I am God Almighty; live ever mindful of my presence, and so be blameless; I will make my compact with you and multiply your descendants greatly . . . I have appointed you to be the father of my nation."[1]

The perspective develops into a clear focus with Moses and the departure from Egypt. This event, dated by various scholars to between the sixteenth and thirteenth centuries, was the real beginning of Israel proper. That beginning was marked by a covenant between Yahweh and his people.

> Then Moses went and told the people all the orders and regulations of the Eternal, and the people all answered, with one voice, "Whatever the Eternal has ordered that will we do." So Moses wrote down all that the Eternal had said; and next morning he erected an altar. . . . He sent the youth of Israel to offer the burnt-offerings of oxen to the Eternal, while Moses himself took half of the blood and put it into basins, splashing the other half on the altar. Then he took the scroll of the compact and read it aloud to the people who said, "Whatever the Eternal has ordered, that will we do obediently." Then

Moses took and splashed the blood on the people saying, "There is the blood of the compact which the Eternal has made with you on those terms."[2]

Following Moses the viewpoint became even clearer in the life of the people through the work of courageous *nabi* of the tenth and ninth centuries, men like Nathan, Elisha, and Elijah. *Nabi* means, literally, "spokesman" (like the Greek term "prophet"). The *nabi*, then, were the spokesmen for Yahweh; and, claiming themselves to be chosen by Yahweh as his "messengers" and "interpreters," they helped to develop and clarify the Israelite faith. But it was with the prophets of the eighth and seventh centuries that the full fruition and flowering of the Israelite faith came: men such as Amos, Hosea, Isaiah, Micah, Jeremiah, and the "Second Isaiah."

THE SOCIAL LIFE OF THE EIGHTH CENTURY B.C.E.

The social history of the Israelites involved transitions from a nomadic existence to an agricultural and small village life and then, about the beginning of the eighth century, to a society that consisted of large farms and large cities.

After the conquest of Canaan in the eleventh century Israel became a land of small farms and independent farmers. For the next three centuries the strength of the nation was in the free landowner who worked his own farm. The family, or clan, was thus the center of Hebrew life. The importance of this for the moral life was that relations were maintained on a personal basis so the individual felt a part of and responsible to the whole community. Within the life of the clan the head was supreme, holding authoritatively the power of life and death. His despotic power was checked by the rules that had been created by centuries of experience.

The Hebrew villages were controlled politically by the elders. Through the ninth century the villagers' world was the local community. There were no law courts, but the elders judged cases on the basis of traditional legal codes that reflected a relatively high ethic.

By the time of the prophets, the mid-eighth century, this entire social structure had been changed by an economic revolution. The peasant farmer all but disappeared under the impact of a more complex commercial society. The land was now parceled out in large estates, and it was owned mainly by absentee landlords who lived in the larger cities. The older unity of the society, of the clans and the villages, was shattered; a growing economic wedge separated the classes. It was in this revolutionary, disintegrating social situation that the prophets appeared.

THE INTERNATIONAL POLITICAL SITUATION

There were many reasons for this changing economic status among the Hebrews: the growth of commerce, heavy taxation, bribery of corrupt officials, and increasing debts on the land caused by inflation. But basic to all of these reasons was the international conflict in which the Hebrew nations were embroiled.

In the latter part of the eleventh century the process of invading and settling new territory, a process that had been continuing for several centuries, was completed and the clans were united under Saul. For less than one hundred years Israel was one nation. Following the death of Solomon in 933 the northern section revolted and became an independent country, Israel.

Israel in the north, Judah in the south, and other Semitic areas bordering the two countries were placed geographically in the center of the fertile crescent of the eastern Mediterranean. This central position meant that the Hebrew peoples were on the crossroads of the empires of Egypt and Assyria. By the ninth century the Assyrian empire was on the march westward, and the Semites became the buffer states in a position to be crushed between rival great powers. With the death of the powerful Assyrian ruler Shalmaneser III (824 B.C.E.), who had systematically conquered the West, forcing most of the smaller nations to pay him tribute, Assyria was left comparatively weak for almost one hundred years. During this time both Israel and Judah developed expanding economies: it was the high level of Palestinian prosperity through international commerce. This was the period of the growth of large commercial centers. Toward the end of the hundred years Assyrian strength was rebuilt, and, under strong leaders, the march to the western sea began again. In the face of this renewed threat the only hope for the Palestinian kingdoms was to cooperate against the invader, but instead the political areas engaged in insane internecine warfare. Israel, the northern kingdom, threatened to attack Judah. Facing this threat, Judah appealed to "protection" from Assyria. Tiglathpileser answered the appeal by invading Israel; Assyria secured tribute from Israel because it had been captured and from Judah because it had been protected. Ten years later the northern kingdom refused to pay the tribute. Assyria moved against the tiny obstinate nation, subduing the people so completely in 722 that Israel never again became an independent country. Twenty-seven thousand of the aristocracy were deported to Assyria.

In 701 a new Assyrian king, Sennacherib, set out to conquer the West. He reached the seacoast, then marched south through the fertile valley toward Jerusalem. By his own account he subdued forty-six cities in Judah on that march and shut up the king Hezekiah like a caged bird within Jerusalem, his royal city. He camped outside the city and was ready to march upon it when a disaster, explained by most historians as a plague, struck his army and he was forced to withdraw.

For seventy-five years there was comparative peace in Judah. Then in 626 hordes of barbarians broke into the fertile crescent from the north, devastating Judah and striking a mortal blow at the decaying Assyrian empire. By this time a new eastern kingdom, Babylon, with imperialistic ambitions, was increasing in power. The rivalry was now between Egypt and Babylon. It was Judah's fate to be crushed between the two world powers. In 608 Judah was defeated by Egypt, and then three years later the king of Egypt was defeated by the Babylonian king Nebuchadnezzar. Judah, along with other kingdoms, became a vassal state of Babylon. Dissatisfied with this relation, Judah revolted in 597 and again in 586; but both revolts were immediately suppressed and, following the latter rebellion, Jerusalem was destroyed. Only the impoverished peasants, the largest and least creative group, were left in the city. The next largest number of persons went into self-imposed exile to Egypt. The wealth and culture of Judah was taken to Babylon. "Old Israel" was destroyed as a political nation, but the unexpected significance for the future of Western culture was that it survived as a religious community.

THE PRESUPPOSITIONS OF THE PROPHETIC ETHICS

It was in this history that the specific point of view of Israel developed. Its perspective was shaped by its unique relation to Yahweh, its specific social and economic structures and events, and its contacts with other nations. But fundamentally, Israel's experience was the experience of faith, a faith that involved relations and actions between a community and its God. Within that faith-experience there were six presuppositions that were the ground of Israel's moral outlook.

1. "Yahweh has chosen us: we are his people."

In reflecting upon their own lives, the Israelites felt that what was most important about themselves was that they had been chosen by their god for a specific destiny. It was he who had called Abraham, Jacob, and Isaac; it was he who had brought them out of the land of Egypt. It was because of his call that they became one people. By the conviction that they had been chosen by Yahweh the Israelites were affirming the primacy of his action. Everything important in their religious faith and moral thought stems from this belief: Yahweh has acted and we, thus, are enabled to respond to his action.

2. *"We, thus, have a covenant with Yahweh."*

The idea of a covenant relation, of a special agreement made between God and a people, is the expression of a distinctive experience and faith that is determinative for the entire moral attitude of Israel. This is the real basis of that peculiar perspective, so un-Greek. The compact between Yahweh and his people, entered into freely by both sides, indicated that they were forever bound to one another. Each promised endless fidelity. But for an individual or community to be bound to a particular god means that they must live according to the will of that god. Human beings are not independent creatures; they cannot make themselves or their communities after their own image; they are no longer free to do anything they wish. Their true freedom is to be found in abiding by the desires of their god.

It is especially important to know that the covenant was first made by all of the people as a people and not as individuals. "*We* are his people: he is *our* God." There was no concept of individual self-realization or the development of individual personality. There was no suggestion that what was important was the value of the individual. Quite the contrary: the presupposition of the covenant meant a thoroughgoing theocentrism. God was important, not man; and in so far as man was important, it was not the individual but the whole community, which also meant the individual-in-community, that was significant. There was, on the basis of the covenant faith, an intense individual responsibility and individualism. But it was never the autonomous individual or the rational individual of the Greeks. Likewise, individual disloyalty was not just disloyalty to the self, or to abstract reason. It was a disloyalty of the individual, involving a disloyalty of the total community, to Yahweh.

3. *"The activity of Yahweh we see especially in history, but his activity is everywhere."*

The Israelites never argue *to* the existence of God. They think *from* their experience of God. They did not look at nature and ask if the vast universe of living creatures and inanimate objects was the manifestation of a first cause. They did not look at history and ask if the moral nature of human life was indication of a Divine Being. They did not see a pattern in nature and history and therefore believe in God. They had a religious faith, a personal-community relation with Yahweh, and therefore saw patterns in history and in nature.

Yahweh's activity was seen especially in history, both in the history of their community, and in the lives of its individual leaders, for example, a Moses or a David. There are indications that suggest that initially Yahweh was only a tribal deity: "Other nations have their gods, but our God is Yahweh." But with the prophets the assumption is made that Yahweh has revealed himself in all history, that he acts in the life of all peoples: "I brought up Israel from Egypt, yes, and Philistines from Crete, from Kir the Aramaeans."[3]

While the activity of God was most clear in history, his acts were manifest in nature as well. Since Yahweh was the only creator of the earth and the heavens, all of nature was subject to his control. Earthquakes, drought, eclipse—all natural events were the work of Yahweh.

4. "He makes his will known to us: it is in large part moral command."

Yahweh had a will for his people which touched upon every human activity. But essentially it was a will that his people, recognizing his sovereignty, worship him through a living dependence upon him and through the establishment of justice in human relations. The individual prophets described in detail their interpretation of the moral commands, but their interpretation was never expressed by rational analysis or by legal regulations. There was no attempt made to create a universal ethic. The interpretations were always made according to the particular requirements of the specific, unique occasion.

5. "It is essential that we respond to his activity: we must be obedient with our will and our action."

Here there was the logical extension of the primary presupposition regarding the personal relations of a community and its God, and the compact made between them. The clue to the meaning of this presupposition is to be found in those personal relations where a child arrives at self-consciousness through the consciousness of another person who has knowledge of the child and who acts toward him. The child is enabled to respond to the knowing and activity of the other. For the Israelites it was a part of their experience that God had created them, had knowledge of their lives, and acted in relation to their community. This prior relation of God required the response of imitative activity. That activity would mean a proper will directed toward God, and, because the Hebrews did not differentiate sharply between will and action, the proper will would include moral activity.

6. "When, failing to respond to Yahweh, we commit evil, he will act again toward us with a corrective punishment."

The activity of Yahweh was neither stereotyped nor random but was always relevant to the situation. If the Israelites broke their side of the compact with Yahweh, it was not supposed that he would automatically cancel the covenant, for he was God and not man. Nor was it supposed that he would continue to act toward his people as though nothing had happened. The punishment of history would follow the sin of the community. That punishment was never thought of as blind, historical fate but as a planned consequence. Swiftly and surely Yahweh brought doom upon a rebellious people. That punishment was always corrective, with the purpose of reestablishing the covenant.

These personal presuppositions of a living faith conditioned all of the prophets' activities. But because their assumptions did not consist of impersonal, rational propositions, their task was never that of developing systematically an ethical theory. Their entire vocation was to "hear the word" of Yahweh and to speak that word to his people. In all of this they believed that their interpretation was the only valid view, and they insisted that their understanding was not the product of their imagination or discovery but of their being discovered; it was Yahweh's imagination working in them. They felt that there was something unique about their work. Yet they did not think that what they said was new. It was a truth as old as the covenant made between Israel and Yahweh, and it went beyond the covenant ratified by Moses to the beginning of history. All the prophets were doing was to remind the people of what they, as a community, had known and had forgotten.

To understand their ethics it is necessary to look with some of the individual prophets to see how the presuppositions were a part of their lives and how, in particular situations, they developed inner coherent meanings from these assumptions.

AMOS

About 760 B.C.E. something happened to an obscure farmer in the southern kingdom of Judah that provided him with a new sensibility. It is impossible to know exactly what his experiences were, not merely because the inner life of everyone finally retains its secrets but chiefly because he was not concerned with what happened to him. Still, while little is known about his unique experiences, very much is known about his view of their meaning.

All that Amos told directly about himself was in the simple claim of his credentials:

> I am no prophet, no member of any prophets' guild; I am only a shepherd, and I tend sycamores. But the Eternal took me from the flock, the Eternal said, "Go and prophesy to my people Israel."[4]

The wilderness of Tekoa was twelve miles southeast of Jerusalem, a barren land marked by soil erosion and dotted with scanty vegetation. This country was the wild steppes of Judah, not at all a likely place for creative thought to develop. Through his refusal to be associated with the *nabi* Amos revealed his independent and isolated spirit. Through his complete lack of sympathy with city life, his denunciations of ease and pleasure, he revealed his approval of the simple and rugged life of the countryside. Through the vivid style of his writing, the clear outline, the pointed imagery, the crackling, rhythmical poetry he showed his burning convictions. Those convictions which he expressed were so deep that it is likely they matured over a long period of time as he brooded in the solitude of his work, and as he witnessed the corruption of city life when he marketed his wool and fig-like sycamore fruit.

In the account Amos has left, he first appeared not in his own kingdom but at Bethel, which was the national shrine of the northern kingdom. There he declaimed against the enemies of Israel. His introduction was based upon a keen insight into mass psychology that enabled him to secure an audience. Only when his hearers were enthusiastic about the fate he foretold for their enemies did he turn his attack upon Israel. Carefully, point by point, Amos made his charges:

> After crime upon crime of Israel
> I will not relent
> for they sell honest folk for money,
> the needy for a pair of shoes,
> they trample down the poor like dust,
> and humble souls they harry;
> son and father go in the same girl
> (a profanation of my sacred shrine!)
> they loll on garments seized in pledge,
> by every altar,
> they drink the money taken in fines
> within the temple of their God.[5]

Because of these evils he saw only destruction for the nation, and he foretold that destruction despite the prosperity of the times. It would come from an external foe, Assyria or Egypt, because the internal life had rotted the foundations of society: "The foe shall overrun the land, laying your forts level, plundering your palaces."[6] This prophecy was popular neither with the priests nor with the people and Amos had reason to believe that the chief priest, Amaziah, was an informant to the king, and it was Amaziah who turned his wrath upon the lone prophet: "Be off to Judah and earn your living there; play the prophet there, but never again at Bethel, for it is the royal shrine, the national temple."[7] Here for Amos was the final irony of the official religion, accusing him of "playing a prophet" while it used religion for its income, and referred to the religious sanctuary in nationalistic terms as "the royal shrine, the national temple." The reasons that caused this farmer to be the first prophet to write are not known, but some of those reasons may be bound up with this narrow justification of a state religion which forbade him to speak.

The message of Amos occurred within the framework of the prophetic presuppositions and was conditioned by his own specific calling and unique outlook. That message had four essential notes: (1) the affirmation of a moral will manifest in nature and history, (2) the specific charges that reveal the failure of Israel to meet the requirements of Yahweh, (3) the demands of a righteous God, and (4) the doom that Yahweh will bring to Israel.

1. The affirmation of a moral will manifest in nature and history

Amos insisted that the basic issue confronting individual and society was the religious issue of ultimate loyalty. Through his relation to Yahweh, the God of righteousness, Amos was convinced that all of human history rested upon moral choice. Not the impersonal working of a moral law but a personal moral will confronts human beings. That will, since it is the will of the One God, was inescapable, and no society, least of all a religious institution, could escape the judgment of that righteous will. The qualities ascribed to Yahweh had never been so pointedly presented. He is the one, universal God. He is inescapable. He is absolutely righteous.

2. The specific charges that reveal the failure of Israel to meet the requirements of Yahweh

Living with such a God Amos was sensitive to the corruption of his time and brought a specific bill of indictment against the community. Those evils were mainly economic, social, and religious. He professed a bitter scorn of the prevalent commercial practices and an indignation at the way the poor had become more impoverished:

> Listen to this, you men who crush the humble,
> and oppress the poor,
> muttering, "When will the new-moon be over
> that we may sell our grain?
> When will the sabbath be done,
> that our corn may be on sale?"
> (small you make your measures, large your weights,
> you cheat by tampering with the scales)—
> and all to buy up innocent folk
> to buy the needy for a pair of shoes,
> to sell the very refuse of your grain.[8]

He scorned the social life of the aristocratic families of Israel:

> Woe to the careless citizens,
> so confident in high Samaria,
> leaders of this most ancient race,
> who are like gods in Israel . . .
> lolling on their ivory divans,
> sprawling on their couches,
> dining off fresh lamb and fatted veal,
> crooning to the music of the lute,
> composing airs like David himself,
> lapping wine by the bowlful,
> and using for ointment the best of the oil—
> with never a single thought
> for the bleeding wounds of the nation.[9]

But with the most bitter invective of all Amos lashed out at the accepted religion: (speaking for Yahweh) he proclaimed,

> Your sacred festivals? I hate them, scorn them;
> your sacrifices? I will not smell their smoke;
> you offer me your gifts? I will not take them;
> you offer fatted cattle? I will not look at them.
> No more of your hymns for me!
> I will not listen to your lutes.[10]

3. The demands of a righteous God

The demand that Amos brought to Israel was as simple as it was revolutionary. The demand was for a religion whose dependence was upon the one righteous will and not upon external authority: "Seek me and you shall live, seek not Bethel, go not to Gilgal, cross not to Beersheba, seek the Eternal and live."[11] The basic demand was for the reestablishment of justice in the common life, to "let justice roll down as waters, and righteousness as a mighty stream."[12]

4. The doom that Yahweh will bring to Israel

Amos had no hope that the demands would be met, so he saw that an inevitable doom would fall upon Israel. As far as the kingdom of Israel was concerned his book ends in helplessness. Never has there been a more thoroughgoing pessimism than this. Most scholars agree that the last of the book (9:5–6, 8b–15), which expresses some hope for the future of the nation, was added by later editors. The major portion of the future as seen by Amos was all dark; the day of the Lord, as he said, was to be "pitch dark, with not a ray of light."[13]

He reported a series of visions which told of the coming doom. He saw destruction by locusts and by drought, the Eternal with a plumb line testing the people, the Eternal with a basket of ripe fruit indicating that "doom is ripe" for Israel, the Eternal standing beside the altar commanding that it be destroyed and all the people killed. It is impossible to know the nature of these visionary experiences. While mystical trances were rare among the prophets, and while a supernatural vision was out of keeping with the personality of Amos, the visions may have been akin to trances. But it is also possible that the visions as reported by Amos were nothing more (or less) than the poetic imagination at work. Here was a new sensibility like that of any great artist, a sensibility that took the common things out of the prophet's own experience and found in them meanings and messages undiscovered by any other man. Amos as a farmer knew the fear that came every year from plagues of locusts and drought; he saw, at the end of each season, baskets of overripe fruit that would spoil in a day; he had used a plumb line in trying to build a strong wall. Amos as a man of faith had been to the temple and, accepting the ancient tradition, had believed that this was the place of God: "I saw the Lord standing beside the altar."[14] But he saw each of these ordinary experiences in an entirely new light when he came to them with his faith.

Throughout his life as prophet Amos was not a visionary and not concerned with possession of mysterious, esoteric knowledge. He was a realist who saw the events of his time in the light of his faith and who, with his religiously motivated intellect, developed his understandings of those events to logical conclusions. In this he anticipated a later prophet in suggesting that Yahweh uses the corrupt forces of history to overthrow his own people. His attitude toward Yahweh shaped his view of ethics.

HOSEA

Perhaps twenty or thirty years after Amos, the second of the great prophets of Israel taught in his native northern kingdom. The initial message of Hosea was essentially the same as that of Amos in its main impact. He recognized that Israel was dealing with a universal, righteous will which harshly judged the prevalent evil, made demands upon the people, and would bring doom upon them. There were, of course, some repetitions of Amos as well as significantly different emphases in these convictions of Hosea. In his denunciation of the sin of Israel the list of social evils was much the same as that stated by Amos, though expanded:

> No fidelity, no kindness,
> no knowledge of God in the land,

> nothing but perjury, lying, and murder,
> stealing, debauchery, burglary—
> bloodshed on bloodshed. . . .
> Your daughters play the harlot,
> matrons commit adultery . . .
> The men themselves go off with harlots
> and sacrifice with temple prostitutes.
> This brings a senseless people to their ruin—
> liquor and lust deprive them of their wits.[15]

The condemnation of a religion concerned with ritualistic practices and unconcerned for the common welfare of the people was also present. But while Amos was particularly shocked by the economic oppression of the poor, Hosea was troubled by the intrigues of international politics; there was little in the former about politics; there was almost nothing in the latter about economic injustice. This change of perspective indicated the different personalities and occupations of the two men as well as the development of a more critical international situation. Here Hosea speaks of Ephraim, the most important of the northern tribes, which for him represent the chosen people.

> Ephraim allows himself
> to be mixed up with foreigners;
> Foreigners eat away his strength,
> unknown to him . . .
> Ephraim is like a silly, senseless dove,
> crying to Egypt, flying to Assyria . . .
> They set up kings, but not with my consent;
> they set up chiefs, but not with my approval . . .
> Ephraim herds the wind
> and hunts the sirocco,
> piling up fraud and falsehood daily,
> striking a bargain with Assyria,
> carrying presents of oil to Egypt.[16]

The demands of the righteous Yahweh were understood in much the same manner by Hosea and Amos: "Love I desire, not sacrifice, knowledge of God, not any offerings."[17] And the future for Israel and Judah, as Hosea saw it, would mean great suffering and widespread destruction:

> Ephraim shall be laid bare
> upon the day of punishment
> (true is the doom that I declare
> upon the clans of Israel) . . .
> for I am like a lion to Ephraim,

> like a young lion to Judah,
> I tear, I go my way,
> and none can rescue my prey.[18]

But while Hosea had essentially the same understanding in the beginning of his prophecy, the end was entirely different. Hosea reached his beliefs through suffering. In the introduction to his prophecies Hosea left a "diary of the writer" that provided the perspective for all of this thought. The meaning of these leaves from his notebook is not clear. Critics have long debated the interpretation of his diary, whether he wrote about his actual marriage experiences or whether he wrote in purely imaginative, allegorical style. It makes some difference for the understanding of Hosea which view is accepted, but in either case it is obvious that he went through intense spiritual suffering.

Hosea married a woman for whom he had a great love. Gradually he learned that Gomer was faithless to him, and then she left him for other men. Through debauchery and the indifference of her new lovers her condition gradually became intolerable until she was to be auctioned as a slave. It was then that Hosea learned he could not hate Gomer since the impulse to love was stronger than his bitterness. He viewed that impulse as having a divine origin, so he bought her at an auction; and then, with full legal rights over her, he kept her in solitude that she might recover. In his anguish Hosea came to believe that his experience with Gomer was parallel to that of Yahweh with Israel: if he, a mere man, somehow continued to love a faithless wife, how much more perfect and intense must be the love of Yahweh for his faithless people. Thus through a faith in the divine love he was led to affirm the mercy of Yahweh, a mercy that would punish to correct and forgive to restore. In his magnificent poem, unmatched in the history of religion, Hosea saw the history of Israel in the care of a God of forgiveness. He heard Yahweh:

> I loved Israel when he was young
> ever since Egypt I called him my son.
> But the more I called to them,
> the farther they went from me. . . .
> Yet I taught Ephraim to walk,
> holding them in my arms;
> with human cords I led them,
> I drove with a harness of love,
> but heeding not my care for them,
> they broke away from me;
> so I smote them on the face,
> I turned against them, overbore them.
> They must go back to the land of Egypt,
> or Assyria must be their king. . . .

> Ephraim, how can I give you up?
> Israel how can I let you go? . . .
>
> My heart recoils,
> all my compassion kindles;
> I will not execute my anger fierce,
> to ruin Ephraim again,
> for I am God, not man,
> I am among you, the Majestic One,
> no mortal man to slay.[19]

The Holy One of Israel brought to his people a righteous judgment and a merciful love. Insofar as it is possible to speak of beginnings, the great prophetic faith began with Amos and Hosea and their understanding of this judgment and love. And while both placed clear-cut demands upon the people, they did not attempt to universalize, rationalize, or define precisely those demands. Neither had a carefully thought-out ethic. They believed, rather, that the people themselves, if they fully comprehended the work of Yahweh, would be enabled both to see and to do what was required of them. The later prophets worked from the point of view created by these men. While it is impossible to examine the details of that development, it is important to understand some of the significant, newly created convictions. Only then can there be an inquiry into the meaning of the prophetic faith for ethics.

ISAIAH

The kingdom of Israel was destroyed in 721, perhaps while Hosea was still alive. The faith of Israel, if it was to survive, had to grow in the economically poorer and culturally less mature Judah. Isaiah, who accepted from his older contemporaries, Amos and Hosea, convictions about a God of judgment and mercy, was largely influential in preserving and deepening the purity of the prophetic faith. The first thirty-nine chapters of the book that goes by his name reveal him as a man of sensitive culture and profound religious faith. His deep feeling, his comprehension of ideas, his analysis of the political situation, and his mastery of language made him one of the greatest of the prophets. He was perhaps the most theocentric of all for he is most concerned with the activity of Yahweh and less interested in interpreting the ethical response of man.

Isaiah first dealt essentially with a description and condemnation of the inner life of Judah.

> Ah, sinful nation . . .
> from the sole of the foot to the head,

> no part is sound;
> nothing but bruises and gashes,
> and raw bleeding wounds,
> unsqueezed, unbandaged,
> unsoftened with oil.
> Your land lies desolate,
> your towns are burned,
> and foreigners ravage your soil
> under your very eyes.[20]

The fundamental reason for this disastrous condition was the corrupt internal life of Judah. The political, economic, social, and religious life was permeated by iniquity:

> Your rulers are unruly men,
> hand in hand with thieves,
> every one fond of his bribe,
> keen upon fees,
> but careless of the orphans' rights,
> and of the widow's cause. . . .
>
> What mean you by crushing my people,
> and grinding the face of the poor? . . .
> Woe to men who add house to house,
> who join one field to another,
> till there is room for none but them
> in all the land! . . .
> Woe to those who are brave—at drinking!
> mighty at—mixing bowl!
> who let off guilty men for a bribe,
> and deprive the innocent of his rights! . . .
> Their land so full of idols,
> no end to their images,
> they worship what their own hands make,
> things their own fingers fashion! . . .
>
> Woe to those who call good evil,
> and call evil good,
> who make out darkness to be light,
> light to be darkness,
> who make out bitter to be sweet,
> sweet to be bitter![21]

When he dealt with the internal life of Judah, Isaiah described the ethical requirements of Yahweh which the people must satisfy, the doom that was to befall them, and the restoration that would come in after days.

Following his concern with national life, Isaiah turned to international relations. He did not refer again to the inner unrighteousness. His gaze became fixed upon the foreign policies of Judah and the movement of the large empires. He wanted to discern the activity of the living Yahweh in foreign relations, and with his perspective he developed the beginning of an attitude toward history that became important in the West for ethics and a philosophy of history. Historical movements, he taught, have within them the impulse and shaping power of a divine action. The nation Israel, disloyal to Yahweh, was to be punished unless it changed radically its way of life. For the punishment Yahweh was to use an unrighteous expansive empire, Assyria, which, while it thought it was independent, was yet under the control of the righteous God. In this punishment some of the people of Israel would be turned toward a loyalty to Yahweh, and, through penitence and obedience, would abandon confidence in themselves and in human machinations, seeking him alone: "A remnant, a mere remnant of Jacob, shall come back to the mighty God."[22]

The message of Isaiah, therefore, in a time of trouble was not "renew your energy and accept national responsibilities." It was rather a plea that the people return to Yahweh through a thoroughgoing repentance and become obedient to him through submission to corrective punishment. The penitence was not for this or that superficial sin. It was a recognition that the people's trust had been placed in human power and pride and not in the Righteous One. The acceptance of punishment involved an understanding of what was being done with them. Following the penitence and acceptance there would possibly come moral activity, but nowhere does Isaiah describe what would be involved in that activity.

Thus it is that one of the greatest of the ethical monotheists was the least ethical. There are various reasons why this was the case. Isaiah was almost completely concerned with Yahweh, and Isaiah's only advice to the men of Judah was to "trust Yahweh," a trust he left unspecified and defined only as an inner intent and devotion. It may have been that the chaotic times did not allow him to say, in general, what actions were required, though, finally, it is likely that he believed that the responsibilities for any man could become plain to him only as he looked at his crumbling society and his disorganized life from the standpoint of recognizing the activity of the Holy One in the world.

JEREMIAH

In 701 the Assyrian army applied a scorched-earth policy to Judah, lay siege to Jerusalem, and advanced against Egypt. The invader was unable to capture Jerusalem and, after an unexpected catastrophe on the Egyptian border, returned to Assyria. Unfortunately for Judah, this was no victory since the land was ravaged, the treasury empty, the morale exhausted. A generation later another Assyrian king advanced into the West and Judah became a province of the empire. With this measure of security, reaction, both political and religious, set in, and the prophetic movement was driven underground. It reemerged about 621 with the "discovery" of a law book that became the basis of internal religious reforms and the nucleus of Deuteronomy. The document was the attempt to codify many of the moral and religious advances made by the prophets of the previous century. At the center of the reform of Josiah, who was then king, was the destruction of idol worship and the creation of one temple where the religion could be kept pure. The reformation failed. Not only did centralization of the religion take a nationalistic and legalistic turn, but the society became drawn into the vacuum created by the fall of the Assyrian empire and the rise of Babylon as the new world power.

It was in this situation that Jeremiah, the son of a village priest, lived his message. Because of his denunciation of his people, his prediction that the nation would be destroyed, and his opposition to the official military and political policy, he was bitterly hated and his life was often threatened. In reality, from the nationalist point of view Jeremiah was a traitor, and any loyal Judahite felt justified in advocating that he be put to death when he insisted that the city would fall to Babylon. "This man deserves the sentence of death, because he has prophesied against this city, as you have heard with your own ears."[23] He was acutely sensitive to the scorn cast upon him and he thus explored, subjectively, the inner recesses of his own consciousness more thoroughly than any of the other prophets. Throughout his writings were the influences of Amos, Hosea, and Isaiah. Jeremiah began with their principles of the just and merciful God who is sovereign over history, and he followed their development of these principles, even employing many of the same figures of speech which they used. But there was originality in his own response to the times. He revealed that the chaos and suffering as predicted by the earlier prophets was in his time present in Judah; he showed the intrigues and deceptions of power politics, the secularization and pollution of the religion. In all of this Yahweh was acting in his condemnation.

Jeremiah made his greatest contribution in stating explicitly what had been implicit in the earlier prophets: he saw the relation of Yahweh to his people as involving an inner and individual spirit. God had chosen his people; they had rebelled, breaking their covenant with him; he had punished them and was still punishing. What of the future?

> Behold, the days come, saith the Lord, that I will make a new covenant with the house of Israel and with the house of Judah; not according to the covenant I made with their fathers, in the day *that* I took them by the hand to bring them out of the land of Egypt; which my covenant they brake, al-

though I was an husband to them, saith the Lord: But this *shall be* the covenant that I will make with the house of Israel; After those days, saith the Lord:

> I will put my law in their inward parts,
>   And in write it in their hearts;
> And will be their God,
>   And they shall be my people.
> And they shall teach no more every man his neighbor,
>   And every man his brother,
> Saying, Know the Lord:
> For they shall all know me,
> From the least of them unto the greatest of them,
>   saith the Lord:
> For I will forgive their iniquity,
>   And I will remember their sin no more.[24]

It is not possible to say that with Jeremiah religion, for the first time, became concerned with the inner life of the individual. All of the prophets were concerned with the spirit of faith, the inner relation with Yahweh rather than the nature of ritualistic practice and with the individual-in-community. But no one before Jeremiah had stated with such clarity the role of the individual; and though all of them looked to the time when the covenant relation between Israel and Yahweh would be reestablished, not one of them thought of it in terms of a *new* covenant that would be unlike the old since it would be based upon Yahweh's action in relation to the inner life of the individual in Israel.

"SECOND ISAIAH"

In 586 Jerusalem was destroyed. In the face of the advancing Assyrians, refugees crowded the roads to Egypt taking with them, as captive, Jeremiah. Many more were taken as prisoners to Babylon. Nearly a half century passed and a new empire, Persia, arose in the East, replacing Babylon. The king, Cyrus, had no personal interest in the Jews in Babylon and thus allowed them to return to Palestine. Since most of the Jews had become satisfied in their new land, only a few who were interested in the restoration of Israel returned to Jerusalem. In their group was one of the greatest prophets of Israel; but he left only his magnificent poetry, nothing more about himself, not even his name.

If there was any prophet apparently unconcerned with ethics it was this man. His poetry was concerned with the One God and His ways with human beings, particularly with Israel. Yet underlying all of his work was the intense consciousness of responsibility which he had to his God and to the meeting of this responsibility he called his people. In one particular conviction his attitude, while not "ethical" in the usual sense of that word, involved the transformation of the entire life, including ethics.

This view was his understanding of the role of suffering in human life, and, in particular, the suffering of the "innocent," revealed most clearly in the last of the four "Servant of Yahweh" poems (Isaiah 42:1–4; 49:1–6; 50:4–9; and 53). There has been much debate as to the identity of the "suffering servant." Probably the view most often accepted by scholars is that the servant refers to Israel, to a true or ideal Israel that has never been faithless to Yahweh. At any rate, it was this innocent servant who, despised by men and wounded by a divine will for the sin of a rebellious people, accepted the humiliation and death thrust upon him for the sake of others and through his suffering is vindicated by Yahweh:

> Therefore shall he win victory,
> he shall succeed triumphantly,
> since he has shed his life's blood,
> and let himself be numbered among rebels,
> bearing the great world's sins,
> and interposing for rebellious men.[25]

This is the first clear appearance in Western culture of the conception of the willing suffering of the innocent for the sake of the guilty. It is a conception that in various times and various ways has radically transformed the entire ethical outlook and life.

IS THERE A PROPHETIC ETHIC?

With this anonymous poet of the returned exiles the prophetic faith reached a new height from which it fell into an abyss of shame. Many of the prophetic insights were transformed into the life of the people, but the articulated faith was not restored until Jesus placed himself in the line of the prophets. This does not mean that there were no later individuals and writings that continued to reveal the prophetic spirit, but none revealed the depth of faith and the comprehension of thought that can be found in the men from Amos in the eighth century to the unnamed prophet of the sixth.

There are other prophets in that two-hundred-year flowering of faith whom we have not observed; the two most important were Micah and Ezekiel. There are also many other prophetic writings to be found in the Bible. The Psalms and, indeed, the entire canon of the Old Testament is conditioned for the most part by prophets and their spirit. But none of the other prophets added materially to the prophetic view as expressed by Amos, Hosea, Isaiah, Jeremiah, and "second Isaiah." Their outlook became an enduring part of Western culture. But with all of the contribution of the prophets one question needs to be carefully answered: In what sense, if any, is there a prophetic ethic?

This question did not have to be asked about the Greeks. Not only is the question itself a "Greek" question, but from the start it was obvious that the ancient philosophers had an explicit ethical theory. However, it is by no means clear that the prophets developed a moral philosophy. Ethical thinking never existed for them except as a part of their living relation to Yahweh, the Holy One of Israel.

But if they did not think ethically and did not construct a moral theory, is there any sense in which it can be said that the prophets had an ethic? If by ethic is meant "the science of moral conduct," the answer to that question is clearly no. But such an answer cannot satisfy any person who is concerned with the history of ethics in the West, with the ancestry of personal ethical views and the development of an adequate ethical theory. The dissatisfaction with the answer may be because the prophets of Israel have had an influence upon ethical attitudes in the West that equals and perhaps surpasses the influence of the ancient philosophers; and they have had an influence upon ethical reflection that is scarcely less significant than that of the Greeks. Moreover, the dissatisfaction stems from the fact that the term "ethic" may properly refer to more than a theory of the moral life; it can refer to the moral life as well, or to an attitude that conditions and impels actual moral decisions. With this understanding of the word it is clear that there is a "prophetic ethic."

CONCLUSION: THE PROPHETIC ETHIC

While the prophets did not outline their moral philosophy or systematically answer ethical questions, it is possible, because of the similarity of their outlook, to discover their answers to some central moral problems.

1. What is the nature of human beings and society?

By observing how the prophets talked about human life, three generalizations may be made of their view of the nature of human beings and one conclusion about the nature of society. The first is a descriptive statement about the structure of human nature; the second and third are existential statements of human relations and activities.

(a) A human being is a unity.

The clearest way to interpret this unique view is by negative statements. The prophets had no conception of the immortality of the rational soul as is found in Plato for the simple reason that no entity such as the rational soul existed. The prophets would not have developed the problem of the relation of mind and body even if they had been philosophically minded, because they were incapable of thinking of mental and bodily structure or functions in isolation from each other. Consequently for them an individual was never thought of as an embodied soul but as an enlivened body: as a unity. An understanding of this unity can be grasped by recognizing the meanings of the Hebrew words that have been most frequently translated in English versions of the Hebrew scriptures as "soul," "spirit," and "heart." These three usually have a spiritualistic emphasis that has been almost exclusively the product of the peculiar ways Greek meanings have been incorporated into Western comprehension while Hebraic understanding has been ignored.

The Hebrew word *nephesh,* most often translated "soul," had as its primary meaning "breath," and it was sometimes so used in the Old Testament. But the term also meant "life," "self," and "human consciousness," especially the emotional aspects of consciousness. The *nephesh* thus referred to the "life principle." The necessity of breath for life provided the clue as to why this particular word was used. The breath principle also became connected with the blood-principle (blood, of course, also being essential for life), so that the *nephesh* (or life-principle) was thought to be in the blood. *Ruach,* generally translated "spirit," originally meant "wind"; it came to refer to the "spirit of Yahweh" that manifested itself in an unusual activity or person. In the late prophetic period the *ruach* was understood to be the life principle in all animate life, and this conception gradually developed into the notion of individual consciousness. The term for heart (*leb, lebab*) in the Old Testament referred most often to the intellectual or volitional aspect of being human, quite often to the whole personality, and much less frequently as a synonym for the vague term "heart," which may refer to emotions such as joy and sorrow.

This understanding of Hebrew words that have been translated "soul," "spirit," and "heart" is sufficient to indicate that the comprehension of the biblical conception of what is human has often been misleading because of typically Greek and Western spiritualized connotations. There was no thought of a soul, or spirit, or mind existing apart from the body since each individual is an organic unity. The Hebrew thought indicated that the *nephesh,* or *ruach,* or *leb* of an individual was dependent upon Yahweh and subject to infusions of "breath soul," or "spirit," or "heart." It was this very fact that the person was subject to influence from without that made the prophetic consciousness possible. But it was not merely a part of the personality that was influenced by Yahweh. It was not only the prophet's rational thought, or feelings, or choices, or physical activity; it was the unitary and total person that alone had existence. And it was the whole person that had a relation to Yahweh.

(b) A human being is a creature.

Every individual is a creature in the original meaning of the Latin term *creatura*: a created thing. For the prophets human beings were thoroughly a creature in this sense, and for them the notion conveyed two connotations: (i) every individual was created by Yahweh and (ii) every individual was completely dependent upon Yahweh for the fulfillment of creation. A human being was not thought of as a "thinking animal," or as a "tool-making animal," or as a "symbol-making animal," or as an "animal who can will." The human being was a "God-related animal." This relation was both of a general and a specific sort. The general Yahweh-relation applied to everyone, and there was little further said about the fact that every individual had been created by and was dependent upon Yahweh. The specific relation referred to the fact that the people of Israel had been chosen by Yahweh for a special destiny and special obligations. And it was this specific relation that was uppermost in the prophetic conception of man. Here, once more, was an illustration of how the prophets dealt with the individual and not with the universal. Yahweh had chosen his people to become Israel; therefore, these people could "image" this selection by choosing Yahweh. Yahweh dealt righteously (i.e., faithfully with justice and mercy) with Israel; therefore, the people of Israel, dependent upon Yahweh, were enabled to deal righteously with Yahweh and with one another. Yahweh chose freely; therefore, each individual was free to choose the god whom they would serve.

(c) A human being is a rebel.

"Creature" is a relational term; so, too, is "rebel." Without someone or something against whom an individual can revolt there could be no rebel. Once more the absolute theocentrism of prophetic consciousness manifested itself in the conviction that it was Yahweh against whom individuals revolted. Each person owed fealty to Yahweh alone. But individuals were not satisfied with their status as a created and dependent animal. Each desired to be the creator and to be independent. So each manufactured idols that they might express their absolute freedom and might worship themselves as creator. This was the reason that acts of immorality were believed by the prophets to be such heinous crimes. It was not merely that in these acts that individuals mistreated themselves, or that they mistreated other humans. Sexual infidelity, drunkenness, bribery, corrupt business practices, the accumulation of wealth, selfish political alliances—all were the expression of the attempt to replace Yahweh with other gods. All reflected a distorted creature who revolted against dependence upon Yahweh and turned to a dependence upon partial, limited, even demonic realities, and to one's own incomplete existence.

(d) The nature of society: society is an organism.

The conception of society was analogous to that of the individual. The individual person was a unitary being in both structure and function, yet each of the parts possessed a semi-independent activity. So society was considered an organism. The notion of a "corporate personality" was especially strong among the prophets. It was the society, Israel, that was called into being by Yahweh. That social being may have been personified later in an individual (Abraham, Isaac, Moses), but the compact was not between Yahweh and an individual person; it was between Yahweh and the total community. A society, therefore, was not merely the sum total of individual persons who came together by chance or mutual agreement. There was no conception of individualism. Yet, paradoxically, there was throughout the prophetic period a strong consciousness of individuality. God called individual men—Isaiah, Amos, Jeremiah—for specific tasks. Yahweh made demands upon individual persons—Hezekiah, the wives of wealthy officials, farmers—for righteousness. The individuals, however, always existed within a community context. The tasks, as well as the very being of the particular individuals, were conditioned by the community of Israel in which they lived.

Since there was a community personality there was recognition of common loyalty, common guilt, and common punishment. Individual responsibility was, in reality, thought to be responsibility for the whole; individual sin polluted the entire community; individual suffering was shared by all.

2. What is the ethical norm?

The ultimate basis for moral judgment was the activity of Yahweh. The ultimate basis for the norm was the character of Yahweh, which was his "righteousness." This righteousness was shown in faithfulness to the covenant which he made with Israel, his exercise of a judgment of justice upon the rebellious people, and his mercy that would renew the covenant. The absolute righteousness of Yahweh became the final norm, and this righteousness was normative for the response of the individual in that there must be absolute obedience. Humans must take with complete seriousness the covenant made with Yahweh. The demands of Yahweh were ultimate and must be recognized as such, and the obedience must be that of a responding righteousness.

3. How are ethical requirements known in a specific situation?

For the prophets the problem of how an individual can know in specific situations what is morally right or good did not exist. They were as unconcerned with such a practical question as they were unaware of a theory of knowledge with such problems as "What are the origin, the nature, and the limits of knowledge?" Yet an answer may be given for the prophets to the specific question "In practical life how would an individual know in a unique situation what is required of him or her, or what is morally good?" If the prophets had thought in these un-Hebraic categories they would have said clearly:

(a) The morally good or right cannot possibly be known (i) in advance of the unique situation and (ii) apart from personal involvement in the situation. While they would affirm that the ultimate norm does not change, the righteousness of Yahweh may differ in requirements to meet the confluence of time and place, unique situation, unique individuals, and unique community.

(b) The morally good or right can be known only to the people of Israel from the prophetic presuppositions. The prophets did not deny that other peoples might have moral standards. They were simply uninterested in those standards, since the morally right or good for Israel depended upon the only righteous Yahweh, who had special relations with Israel.

4. How are the ethical goods accomplished in a specific situation?

Again, while the prophets did not answer this question directly, since they did not ask the question in this form, an answer may be made from their conceptions of the relations between Yahweh and Israel.

(a) The people of Israel had to begin from within the covenant made with Yahweh, and by living within this covenant, they could discover what was required of their lives. (b) This vantage point, especially the recognition of the absolute obedience required, led to a self-criticism. When that self-criticism was made from the viewpoint of Yahweh (when a prophet could say, "Thus saith the Lord") there was a recognition of the rebellion of the people against Yahweh, which meant that Israel had been disloyal to its God. (c) This recognition required repentance, a turning again to Yahweh. The disloyalty revealed in misplaced trust in other nations, or in idols, or in ritual had to be replaced by a living trust, a return to the Holy One of Israel. (d) Following the repentance there had to be an acceptance of what Yahweh would do. This acceptance involved a response to the renewed divine activity. It was this response that enabled the people to do what was required of them. Just as every part of life was claimed by Yahweh, so every right action was dependent upon him.

THE ETHICS OF JESUS AND PAUL

Jesus and Paul thought of themselves as prophets of Israel, but the Israel in which they lived was not, of course, the same as the Israel of Amos and Isaiah. Yet they believed that they belonged to a people who, no matter how much they might seem to change, possessed a historical continuity. There have been differing views as to whether Jesus and Paul were correct in their particular, unique ideas of Israel and in their new faith-relation to God, but there can be no doubt that they were correct in placing themselves in the line of the prophets.

This means that as far as their ethic was concerned, they did not possess a moral theory apart from their faith-experience. For them, their ethics were dependent upon and inseparable from their religion. Yet in other ways these two men, who shared similar ethical convictions, could not have been more different. While there was probably not more than ten years separating their ages, it is doubtful whether Paul ever saw Jesus, and it is certain they did not know each other. Their separate childhoods and youth were literally worlds apart: one had been born in a tiny town of Palestine and the other in a large and important city of the Greco-Roman world. There were even wider differences between the experiences of the one who never traveled more than seventy-five miles from his home and who was brutally killed after he had worked for less than four years, and the other who was one of the most traveled men of his time and who died, an old man, thirty years after his conversion. There are also important differences in their religious experiences, as well as in their "theology" if, as is doubtful, Jesus can be said to have had a theology. Yet, in spite of these wide variances of experience and personality, there is a fundamental similarity in their ethical outlooks. Paul's claim that he had *the mind of Christ* was accurate as far as the moral aspect of that mind is concerned.

THE SOCIAL SOURCES OF THE ETHIC

1. The Political Order

Jesus lived in the small Roman province of Palestine; Paul traveled throughout a large portion of the Roman empire. They were thus subject to different cultural influences, and their teaching reflects in many ways the places where they lived. But more important than the places they traveled was the fact that Paul and Jesus were Jews. They belonged to Jewish history.

Following the destruction of Jerusalem in 586 by a Babylonian army under Nebuchadnezzar, Israel became a pawn in the power struggles of the empires. The condition of her political life depended upon the policies of the controlling nations toward conquered peoples. Babylon attempted to control Israel by deportation of the best citizens. The peasants left in Israel did not possess the power to continue the customs and ideology that give a clear identity to a people, and many of the exiles found new homes and new loves in Babylon. But there were a few, inspired mainly by the prophetic hope for a restored Israel, who were described by the Psalmist:

> By the rivers of Babylon there we sat down and wept
> When we remembered thee, O Jerusalem.[26]

A half century after the fall of Jerusalem Persia gained control of Babylon, and the policies toward defeated enemies were softened. Jews were allowed to return to Palestine; the temple in Jerusalem, the center of the religious community, was rebuilt; and for two centuries the Jews lived peacefully in Jerusalem while a mixed race, with whom the pure Jews refused to have any dealings, occupied all of the land outside the city.

The conquest by Alexander late in the fourth century did not immediately change the political situation. But the introduction of the Greek language, while it did not replace the traditional Aramaic, opened the way for the influence of Greek customs and thought. When, following the death of Alexander in 323, internal struggles for power divided and weakened the Greek empire, Palestine became a buffer state between Egypt and Syria ruled by the Seleucid kings, a dynasty (312–64 B.C.E.) founded by Seleucus Nicator, a general of Alexander. The Ptolemies of Egypt controlled Palestine until 198 B.C.E., and left the Jews alone, even encouraging the development of purely Jewish communities in Egypt. When the Seleucids gained power, there began a conflict between Hellenism and Hebraism: it was a struggle between Greek and Jewish culture which did not cease in Palestine until the complete destruction of Jerusalem in 70 C.E.

The Seleucid kings at first gradually impregnated the Jewish culture with Greek ideas. But one of the kings, Antiochus Epiphanes, became impatient at the slow Hellenizing of Palestine. So in 168 he directly attacked the religion of Judaism, offering pagan sacrifices on the temple altar and making the rites of Judaism—circumcision and Sabbath observance—punishable by death. The fire of religious loyalty stirred the common folk to open rebellion. The guerrilla warfare of the Maccabees (see below) was successful in conquering much of Palestine and establishing a practical independence that lasted until 63 B.C.E. when, following a Syrian alliance with Rome, Pompey invaded the country.

Palestine became the trouble-spot of the empire. For a time the land was kept under control by a clever and unscrupulous half-Jew, half-Arab named Antipater. Through brilliant intrigues he succeeded in having his son, Herod, named king. Herod was an administrator of great ability who, through brutality when he deemed harshness necessary, was able to establish peace by treating Jews and Greeks with relative equality. Upon his death the Romans divided the rule over Palestine between two of his sons, Herod Antipas (the Herod at the time of Jesus' ministry) and Archelaus. This latter son was a miserable failure; and, after his deposition in 6 C.E. Roman officials called "procurators" were sent to rule Judea and Samaria. In all of the divided land Jews and non-Jews lived side by side.

Although Roman power was dominant, extensive measures of autonomy were given to the conquered territories. So long as the provinces were able to control themselves peacefully and to become a working part of the empire, they were allowed a large degree of self-control. For both economic and political reasons an enlightened Roman leadership allowed persons living in the provinces to become citizens of Rome. But while the empire in the East was Roman in structure, it was essentially Greek in culture and its language was Greek. And with the language there entered into Galilee some bits of Greek culture, but the Hellenistic influence was quite limited in the predominantly agricultural region. The greatest influence of Greek life was felt in the large commercial centers of the empire, especially in Asia Minor. It was in one of these cities that Paul grew up, it was in this region that he did most of his teaching, and it was in this Hellenistic world that the early church made its first most rapid developments. These rapid developments were partly a product of the early church's geographical relation to Palestine, and partly the result of affinities between the cults of mystery religions, Stoic universalism and individualism, the Greek ideal of education, and early Christian ideas and practices.

2. The Intellectual and Religious Life of Judaism

The impact of Hellenism was strong within the early church, and that impact is reflected throughout the New Testament. The Greek influence is revealed especially in the language with which the faith was expressed, in some of the ideas, and in the ways of thought. (Particular examples of these influences are the use of the Greek word "Christ" for the Hebraic "Messiah," the Logos doctrine of the gospel of John, and Paul's way of thinking theologically, especially in his more systematic writing such as Romans.) But if Hellenistic influences are present, the basic ideas have their foundation in Judaism; and it is this fact that makes it possible for Paul to have *the mind of Christ* despite the wide disparity between their experiences and personalities.

During the lifetimes of Jesus and Paul Jerusalem was the center of Judaism, with strong elements of Judaism in all of the larger cities of the Mediterranean world. Paul, living in the Jewish community in Tarsus, in

Cilicia, was subject to many of the same intellectual and religious influences as Jesus, living in Nazareth, in Galilee.

Jewish thought and religion were singularly free from dogma. Wide latitude was given the individual believer in his interpretation of the basic faith. Judaism was founded upon three key ideas relating to God, the life of man, and hope for the future: (1) there is one God who, as creator and sovereign ruler, requires worship; (2) the will of God is revealed in the law; and (3) salvation will come to man from God. While the diverse understandings of the first key idea—the view of the nature of God, the meaning of his sovereignty, and the kind of worship required—were fundamental in all disagreements within Judaism during Roman rule, the interpretation of the law and salvation were the major points of open debate. To comprehend this debate and its influence upon Jesus and Paul, it is necessary to recognize the major groups within Judaism, all of which originated in the time of the Maccabees (ca. 166–161 B.C.E.).

(a) The *Sadducees* were the "temple party." With strength in Jerusalem the Sadducees belonged to the priesthood and the upper classes. They insisted upon the letter of the law and a scrupulous obedience to the requirements of ritual. Since they were professional religious and leisured people, there was both the time and the money for satisfying the literal law requirements. With their religious and economic status they were, of all Jewish parties, most sympathetic to Hellenism in nonritualistic matters and most cooperative with Roman rule. In their view of salvation there was no belief in resurrection or in the imminent coming of a Messiah, whether "religious" or "political."

(b) The *Pharisees* were the most influential group outside of Jerusalem. Originally Pharisaism began as a lay movement concerned to keep Judaism pure from Hellenistic tendencies. This purpose was accomplished mainly by an emphasis upon the law, with moderate interpretations attempting to relate the law to the common life. Before the destruction of the temple in 70 C.E. there were two predominant pharisaic schools, the "Shammai," which was the stricter group, and "Hillel," the more lenient.

The positive contribution of the Pharisees to Judaism was in their emphasis upon the spiritual as known through the law, the development of the synagogue, and the influence of religion on the home. But within the group, too, as attested by the self-criticism of Pharisaism in the Mishnah, there were legalistic Pharisees who considered themselves different from and superior to the common folk. And in their interpretation of the law, even though it was frequently liberal, there was left the clear implication that the ceremonial demands were primary and the requirements of man's relation to man only secondary.

The Pharisees had a belief in the resurrection of the dead. They had an implicit trust, too, that their God who was king would deliver his people from their foes. They thus looked toward the coming of a Messiah who would be both a political and spiritual king. But, for the most part, leaders of the Pharisees refused to clothe this hope with predictions of how and when the Messiah would come, and they refrained from any violent action that would assist or pressure the will of God in this regard.

(c) The *Zealots* were the religious and nationalistic activists. They were like the Pharisees in their love for the law, but unlike the Pharisees in that they read important sections of the law literally, so that they found it intolerable to obey the "flesh and blood" of Roman rule since God alone was king. Through rebellion against foreign rule they were trying to hasten the triumph of the Messiah; this messianic hope was, throughout, nationalistic.

(d) The *Essenes*, who existed from the second century B.C.E. to the first century C.E., were a communal group. Like the Pharisees and Sadducees they had arisen in response to the Maccabean rule, but unlike the former two, they rejected the secularization of Judaism. They refused to participate in public life and considered themselves a new Israel of the new and eternal covenant. They emphasized, as did the Pharisees, the law of Moses, the sabbath, and ritual purity. Estimated to have about four thousand members at the time of Jesus and Paul, the Essenes were scattered in their communal ownership of property throughout the villages and towns of Palestine, and they thus had an impact upon the society as models of the ideal of perfection in religious observance.

(e) The *Scribes* were not a group in the same sense as the previous four, and they had a more ancient lineage, having developed about the fifth century. They were a combination of lawyer and theologian, a respected class of teachers who interpreted the Torah and gave guidance for daily living. Persons from the other groups could be scribes. The fact that Jesus was often quoted as linking "the Pharisees and scribes" indicated the influence of these groups and the dominance of the Pharisees in religious teaching. Jesus, like the scribes, sat to teach; he gave guidance for living and opinions about the Torah; he debated, he had disciples, and he was addressed as "Rabbi." But he was clearly not one of their number: there is no indication he had careful training in the schools, that he wore the robe of a scholar, or that he sat in the place of honor in the synagogue.

(f) As in every society, so in Judaism there were unorganized groups that were important to the community. The most significant of these were the pious, unsophisticated religious folk of the small villages. They were closest to the Pharisees and many identified themselves with pharisaic beliefs and practices. But the differences between the pharisaic leaders and the poor of the land was evident most clearly in their different attitudes toward the Messiah.

All of Judaism looked toward the coming of the Messiah. With the Sadducees this belief was vague and placed so far in the distant future as to be of no practical importance. The Pharisees, Zealots, and Essenes were more definite with their hopes for a spiritual and political Messiah. But on the whole the leaders of these groups refused to predict the time or to picture the coming of the kingdom of God, though all prayed for the coming of the Davidic prince. This was not so with many of the religious folk who, through the years, had developed an apocalyptic hope. This hope was based upon the view that space and time are divided into two areas: (a) heaven and earth, and (b) the present age and the age to come. God allows evil kingdoms to rule on earth in the present age, but he has a plan for the near future, when he will send his emissary to judge and transform the present world. The details of this picture varied, but indispensable to apocalyptic believers was the conviction that the details of the world-shaking plan could be known to man. Those details were expressed by many writers in imaginative language that was taken with varying degrees of literal interpretation. Despite many differences in apocalyptic interpretation, this way of thinking, which was especially prevalent among the common folk, had a strong influence upon both Jesus and Paul.

ETHICAL PRESUPPOSITIONS

It was in this political and religious milieu that Jesus and Paul lived, and it was out of this society and the historical community of the prophets that their ethical presuppositions developed.

Jesus and Paul, despite their wide diversity in experience and personality, shared similar assumptions which underlay their ethical beliefs. Where there are differences between them, these differences can be explained by two facts: (1) the unique situation of each provided particular ways of thinking and speaking; e.g., Jesus was reported to have spoken of himself in messianic terms as the *Son of Man* while Paul thought and spoke of Jesus as the *Christ*, and (2) Paul had more of a Greek and theological temperament than Jesus. Despite this, the moral assumptions of Paul, like those of Jesus, were based upon the Hebrew prophets and not the Greek philosophers. Perhaps the best approach to the subject, therefore, is to state their presuppositions and ethics from their point of view and in their own words, condensing their presuppositions into three sets of beliefs.

1. "All the prophets and the law prophesied until John. . . . The law is holy, and the commandment is holy and just and good." [27]

This frequently expressed attitude toward the prophets and the law is a clear indication that Jesus and Paul accepted and transformed both the law and the meanings of the prophetic ethical presuppositions.

(a) In the earliest tradition of the church Jesus was remembered to have made apparently contradictory statements about the law: on the one hand he spoke of himself as being the continuation and fulfillment of the law and on the other he spoke as though he were replacing the law with something entirely new. The same apparent contradictions appear in Paul, although he was much more emphatic than Jesus in emphasizing the discontinuity with the Jewish law. They both claimed a relation with Israel, and at the same time insisted that something entirely new had been brought into Israel, something creative that superseded the old law. They both recognized the written and oral traditions and accepted the Torah as the revealed will of God for man, but they believed that the will of God had been given a new expression in the person of Jesus. Thus for the early church the experience of Jesus and the *mind of Christ* became the norm by which the law was both judged and understood.

(b) Placing themselves in the prophetic line, they accepted and altered the presuppositions of the prophetic ethic. (i) They felt that they, and their community, were chosen by God. However, the "elect" were no longer a nation, but had become the "church." Paul thought of the church, a new universal community that broke all boundaries constructed by man, as the chosen people of God. And while it is doubtful that Jesus used the term "church," his relations with his disciples represented his belief that theirs was a new and unique fellowship brought into being by God. (ii) Jesus and Paul accepted the idea of the covenant, but it was a New Covenant. In the earliest tradition concerning the last supper Paul quoted Jesus as speaking of "the new covenant in my blood,"[28] and in a way that Jeremiah had not anticipated the new covenant was believed to be "written on the heart" in the fellowship of the disciples and the Christian community. (iii) Like the prophets, Jesus and Paul saw God revealed in history. But their assumption about historical revelation involved a new selection of history. They were not primarily interested in the history of the nation but in the lives of individuals, especially the prophets, and the life of Jesus. Paul believed, too, that the activity of God was manifest in his own life and the creation and life of the church. (iv) They believed that God had a will for humanity that was, in large part, a moral demand. But the nature of the demand was conditioned entirely by their beliefs about God and their personal relation to God. (v) Like the prophets, they assumed that everyone must respond to God's activity with both will and action. The emphasis was shifted in that the will—an absolute trust—was made more dominant than in the prophets. (vi) Finally, with the prophets they assumed that when an individual does not respond properly, God will act again with corrective punishment. But the notion of punishment was radically altered to the idea of the suffering love of God. In all of this Jesus and Paul widened and deepened the basic beliefs of the prophets, but they did not bring to those beliefs anything new except their experiences.

2. "The time is fulfilled and the Kingdom of God is at hand: Repent, and believe in the gospel." [29]

Jesus and Paul spoke of the *kingdom* with three distinct, but not entirely separable, meanings: (a) the present rule of God in heaven, (b) the manifestation of God's sovereignty on earth, and (c) the future age in which this world would be transformed. The most important usage for ethics was the third, the reference to the coming kingdom.

Jesus and Paul expected the imminent end of the world and the establishment of the rule of God on earth. Their entire ethic was spoken against this background of belief. Neither was apocalyptic in the sense of predicting when and how the rule of God was to be established, but both were thoroughly eschatological in expectation that the final end of the old history was soon to come and an entirely new history would begin.

3. "The Son of man came not to be served but to serve, and to give his life as a ransom for many." [30]

With both Paul and Jesus there was a messianic consciousness (with Paul, of course, believing that "Jesus was the Christ") and a view of the significance of suffering for ethical attitudes.

While the concept of the Messiah was taken over from their lives in Judaism, the view of the Messiahship involved a thorough rejection of the nationalistic and political hopes of Israel. It was not through power but weakness, not through glorification but through suffering that the Messiah was made known. In this way the suffering love of the sovereign God became the basic presupposition of the entire ethical theory. It was this love that Jesus thought of himself as revealing, and Paul accepted this interpretation.

With these assumptions Paul and Jesus possessed (1) a will of God ethic, (2) a kingdom of God ethic, and (3) a Christ ethic. These three sets of beliefs form the presuppositions of their ethic, and it was the full implication of these beliefs as they were worked out in their unique experiences that produced their moral views.

THE EXPERIENCE OF JESUS

It is impossible to reconstruct in its entirety the life and the thought of Jesus. This is true partly because of the deficiency of the sources. The writers of the gospels were not primarily interested in biographical details or in teachings. They had a belief that Jesus was the "Christ," and it was this, rather than an orderly account of his life or a systematic study of his teaching, that they proclaimed. But while the sources for the understanding of Jesus leave much to be desired, the main reason for the difficulty is similar to that of an understanding of anyone whose moral theory and moral experience are inseparable. For this means that one's moral views depend upon one's experiences. And any person's experiences—the inner struggles, the anguish and joy, the attitudes, indeed the whole spiritual life—are largely private. Since the most important aspect of Jesus' ethic was not what he taught but what he was in his own inner life, and since he left no writing and could not reveal directly what those experiences were, all that is essential for a complete comprehension of his ethic cannot be reconstructed. As with Socrates, the prophets, Paul—and others since their time—sparse clues must be followed with sympathetic insight. Those clues are essentially the main outlines of Jesus' life, his conflicts with loyal Jews, shifting emphases in his teaching, and the account left of his death.

When he was about thirty-two years old, Jesus was baptized, apparently indicating his acceptance of the teaching of a man referred to as "John the baptizer." That teaching was in the prophetic tradition as influenced by more recent apocalyptic Judaism and its essential points were clear: it was a call to preparation for the imminent appearance of the kingdom of God and the Messiah who would judge all people by the rigorous standard of whether they have obeyed the law of God. "Repent, for the kingdom of heaven is at hand. . . . You brood of vipers! . . . Bear fruit that befits repentance."[31]

Following the baptism, Jesus withdrew from society for a period and then, according to the earliest gospel, when John was arrested, returned to begin his Galilean ministry with essentially the same message as John, "The time is fulfilled, and the kingdom of God is at hand; repent, and believe in the gospel."[32]

At first his work in the rural province of Galilee was encouraging and he had a measure of public success. This, no doubt, was the result of the political and nationalistic hopes for the coming kingdom, the deeply ingrained pious faith in God, and the healing activities of Jesus. But opposition soon developed: religious hostility by the Pharisees, who understood clearly the purposes of Jesus, and the political hostility of Herod Antipas, who saw the social consequences of the activity of Jesus.

The animosity of the Pharisees was caused by what they considered to be Jesus' fast and loose treatment of the law. From their viewpoint they were correct. While Jesus had respect for the law and apparently was scrupulous about keeping the commandments, his attitude to the law was unlike that of normative Judaism. The difference was apparent, for example, in the treatment of the Deuteronomic decree regarding divorce. The Pharisees accepted the law as final but gave it various interpretations. But Jesus, when asked about divorce, pointed to the law, interpreted its origin ("For your hardness of hearts"[33] this law was made); and then rejected the law, going back to his conception of the original intention of God for marriage. The point was that in marriage, as a divine institution, a question about divorce should never arise.

Again, the law of Sabbath observance was one of the most sacred institutions of Judaism. The purpose of the law was that the people of Israel properly recognize and relate themselves to God. This law forbade any work on the Sabbath, and it fell to the rabbis to define what was meant by work. In the time of Jesus their definition contained a list of thirty-nine different types of labor that were forbidden, from "sowing" through "making a knot" to "carrying from one tenement to another." If Jesus had merely disagreed as to what was illegal work the situation would not have been serious. But Jesus did not question the interpretations made by the Pharisees; he brushed away the law. "The Sabbath was made for man, and not man for the Sabbath."[34] Laws exist for the sake of human beings; human beings do not exist for laws.

The difference here was fundamental. It has existed throughout the history of institutions, and good men (as in the case of Jesus and the Pharisees) have honestly disagreed about the major point at issue. That basic issue was bound up with the legal and the prophetic mind at work, and their differences were:

(1) The Pharisees were interested primarily in their society and the religious community, and for them what made Israel a unique people was its religion. This religion was embodied in the law and, therefore, any social reform must come through changed interpretations of the law; whereas Jesus was not interested in the social reform that would come through a modernization of the law, but concerned with the individual and the internal reform of individuals. The Pharisees were not unmindful of the individual. Indeed, they gave moderate interpretations of the law so that the individual could keep it. But the emphasis was upon the law, not upon the person. Jesus was not unmindful of the community and its cults. He apparently kept the laws and advised his disciples to do the same. But his emphasis was upon the original intention of God for man, and, whenever the law obscured that intention, he transcended it.

(2) The Pharisees, concerned with legal observance, emphasized the external activities involved in keeping the law, whereas Jesus was interested primarily in the disposition of man. For him nothing else really mattered.

(3) The Pharisees, with their legal interpretations, were attempting to make generalizations that would apply for all persons, to treat each individual just as every other person would be treated, whereas Jesus was interested in the uniqueness of the individual.

The Pharisees saw what Jesus was doing: he was giving the law a kiss of death. To accept his interpretation would mean to undermine Judaism. It would replace the religion based upon the law of God embodied in the Torah with an entirely new religion. The Pharisees, concerned for the purity of Israel's faith, looked upon Jesus as an imposter.

The political hostility of Herod Antipas, on the other hand, was caused by the actual and potential disturbances produced by the teaching of Jesus. Herod's position depended upon keeping peace in the land. He was quite aware that the Jews expected a Messiah who would overthrow the constituted authorities, and his administration was troubled by the rebellious Zealots. It did not matter greatly to him whether or not Jesus thought himself to be a political Messiah. He knew that many of the followers believed just that, and he was a good enough ruler to know that the best way to quell a rebellion was to destroy the leadership before the movement gained too much momentum.

Herod's resolution to kill Jesus became publicly known, and this hostility of the ruler had an effect upon both the attitude of the masses and the actions of Jesus. The conflict between the political authority and Jesus intensified the belief among many people that he was the political Messiah. The combination of nationalistic popularity and official antagonism was reflected in the rapid journeys from town to town, the attempts to hide, and finally the trip to Caesarea Philippi, which was outside of Herod's jurisdiction. Jesus was troubled, too, by the effect of the events upon his disciples. Would they leave him when the danger from Herod increased? Would they forsake him when they understood thoroughly the attitude of the religious leaders? Or would they come to accept the popular view that he was a political activist?

The journey to Caesarea Philippi, free from the speaking and responsibilities to large groups of people, free, too, from the threats of Herod, marked a turning point in the ministry of Jesus and probably in his conception of his work. It was on this trip that he asked the disciples their opinion of him, and received from Peter the answer "You are the 'Christ.' "[35] This is the clear center of all of the synoptic gospels, and from this point on all was different. It is likely that in this period Jesus' own understanding of his life was clarified. The tensions and conflicts—the knowledge that his life was in jeopardy as long as he remained in Galilee, the open hostility of the best people of the region, the mass pressure for him to lead an armed rebellion, and the doubts about the loyalty of his closest friends—forced him to reexamine his understanding of God's will for his life.

(1) Jesus, for the first time, spoke to the disciples of the inevitable suffering that he foresaw. The synoptic authors all relate the profession of his Messiahship to his view that he must suffer: "From that time," said Matthew, "Jesus began to show his disciples that he must go to Jerusalem and suffer many things."[36] In view of the personal suffering through which he had already lived, his forecast that further intense suffering was ahead, and the events of his visit to Jerusalem, a unique attitude toward suffering came to have a large place in Jesus' ethical view.

(2) Following Peter's confession Jesus more frequently referred to himself in the presence of the disciples as the *Son of man* and, for the first time,

demanded not repentance but personal loyalty. The precise meaning of the phrase *Son of man* is debatable, but its general import is perfectly clear: it had a direct connection with the messianic consciousness. Jesus, then, began to express the belief that in his life the purposes of God were being manifest. Thus what was required of the disciples was not a vague relation to God but a responding loyalty to the kind of qualities he exhibited in his relation to God, his regard for others, and his suffering. The requirement that "Whoever would come after me must take up his cross and follow me"[37] referred to actual suffering that would come to those who were loyal to Jesus and his cause.

(3) Following Peter's confession Jesus' teaching was directed often to the inner circle of his disciples. Jesus did not create a philosophical theology or ethic applicable to all men in the sense that it merely has to be recognized as true. His teaching was directed to those who could respond to the forces working in and upon his life. He did not make the general statement "Whoever would be great must be a servant"; he spoke directly to the disciples, "You know that the rulers of the Gentiles lord it over them, and their great men exercise authority over them. [But] it shall not be so among you."[38]

(4) Jesus began to speak increasingly of men entering the kingdom of God. This shift in emphasis had a double significance: (a) There was the recognition that the kingdom was not merely future but, in some sense, already present. "But if it is by the finger of God that I cast out demons, then the kingdom of God has come upon you."[39] There was the explicit notion that through his activity the kingdom of God was becoming a part of history. (b) What was required for entrance into the kingdom was not merely repentance but allegiance to God, who was sovereign of the kingdom, and an acceptance of his realm as a gift. "Fear not, little flock," Jesus said to the despondent followers, "for it is your Father's good pleasure to give you the kingdom."[40]

(5) After the disciple's recognition of Jesus as the Christ there was a deepening of his own spiritual life. Jesus rarely if ever spoke directly of God as Father except to his disciples, and even when he began to speak to them in this way it was only after Peter's confession. God was spoken of as *Father* long before Jesus by the Jewish prophets, and the fatherhood of God was a familiar idea in contemporary Judaism. There was nothing new in this aspect of Jesus' concept of God. If there was anything new in this connection, it was in the quality of Jesus' experience. Beginning with the data available it is reasonable to suggest that here—in his experience—was a quality previously unknown to Judaism. (a) He spoke of God as *Father* primarily after his acceptance of himself as the Messiah, in conversation with his disciples, and in prayer. One's most valued experiences cannot be communicated to a large public; they can be expressed only to intimate friends, and even then they are not completely expressed since there is something forever private and secret about the spiritual life of an individual. So for Jesus: the faith in God as

Father was not a theological doctrine but an experiential fact. (b) The records suggest that there was a genuine sense in which Jesus did not want to obey God and yet he exhibited absolute trust and perfect obedience. The night before the crucifixion his disciples heard Jesus pray, in anguish, "Father, all things are possible to thee; remove this cup from me; yet not what I will, but what thou wilt."[41] In his relations with persons as well as his own death he exhibited an obedience and a caring that he believed revelatory of God. It was this selfless, concerned regard for others that his disciples found characteristic of Jesus' life; and that attitude was the direct consequence of his certainty of God as Father.

Jesus' ethic therefore was an ethic of the inner life: the intention, the character of the individual was all-important. Moreover, the fruits of the ethical life were made possible by the forgiveness of sins. Just as God forgave the sins of those who had been disloyal to him, so the spirit of forgiveness should become characteristic of interpersonal relations. The ethical life, then, requires suffering and self-denial, not for any ascetic interest whereby one might pay the entrance fee into another world, but solely as the result of a positive experience of God's love.

Only now, in this context, is it possible to recognize the full meaning of the fact that the ethic of Jesus rests upon the two commandments:

> Hear, O Israel; the Lord our God, the Lord is one; and you shall love the Lord your God with all your heart, and with all your soul, and with all your mind, and with all your strength. . . . You shall love your neighbor as yourself.[42]

It was this love that had brought him to be haughtily dismissed by the procurator, crudely beaten by the police, reviled by a mob, tortured, impaled upon rough wood between two petty criminals, mocked by one of the suffering thieves; and—was this not the worst?—completely forsaken by his friends. According to the earliest gospel, in the midst of his agony Jesus uttered but one cry, the famous and despairing opening phrase of the 22nd Psalm: "My God, my God! Why hast thou forsaken me?" But certainly for Jesus, in this his time of greatest need, in the midst of this suffering despair, it must have been possible for him in a moment of intense consciousness to be instantaneously aware of the whole of the psalm. For while the psalm begins with this terrifying question, and while it depicts the immense suffering of a man who has been "scorned by men, and despised by the people," a man whose life has been "poured out like water," a man surround by "evildoers . . . [who] have pierced my hands and feet . . . [and] divide[d] my garments among them," still the ancient poem ends with the certainty of God's presence: "For dominion belongs to the Lord, and he rules over the nations . . .

[and] men shall tell of the Lord to the coming generation, and proclaim his deliverance to a people yet unborn. . . ."[43] Nevertheless, whatever the uniqueness of his private inner experience might have been, it is certain that many of those about him heard only this: "Why hast thou forsaken me?"

PAUL'S INTERPRETATION OF HUMAN LIFE

It is possible that a young student, Saul of Tarsus, was in Jerusalem when Jesus was crucified. If he did not see Jesus, then he must have heard, from his fellow Pharisees, about a renegade Jew. Saul was, at the time, thoroughly convinced the punishment was justified, and he was pleased that the death sentence was legally executed by Roman authorities. Having gone to Jerusalem to study Jewish law under a leading pharisaic scholar, he was a completely loyal and extremely promising "Pharisee of Pharisees" as he himself later put it.[44] But Saul was also a Roman citizen, a status which gave him legal privileges many of the Jews did not possess, and he had been exposed to the best in Hellenistic culture. It was the combination of these three elements—Hebrew faith, Hellenistic culture, and Roman citizenship—that had significant consequences for his life and for the future of Western civilization.

After his education in Jerusalem Saul joined the group of loyal Jews who were intent on correcting the heresies caused by Jesus of Nazareth. First by persuasion, later by religious and legal pressure, they tried to bring into line the obstinate followers of the crucified political criminal. When these methods were not successful, they incited a mob to violence. About three years after the death of Jesus they charged a young man, Stephen, with blasphemy, rushed him outside the city, and stoned him. "The witnesses laid down their garments at the feet of a young man named Saul," says the historian Luke, perhaps indicating that it was Saul who gave the signal when the stoning was to begin. "And Saul was consenting to his death." As Stephen was being stoned, Saul saw him kneel and cry, in a prayer almost identical to that reported of Jesus at his death, "Lord, do not hold this sin against them."[45] It may have been the first time that Saul had seen the brutality of death by stoning; it was surely the first time he had witnessed a man die praying that his persecutors might be forgiven. But that emotional shock, and secret doubts about his own position, only intensified his patriotic defense of Judaism, until gathering in intensity the inner conflicts deepened and his loyalties were radically changed. Following what he knew as revelatory experiences that now led him to become one with those he had persecuted, he went into exile in Arabia, returned with a friend, Barnabas, to Jerusalem where he was scorned by the Pharisees and coldly received by the disciples, and then returned to his home in Tarsus. It was only some time later that Barnabas made a special trip to Tarsus to ask Saul (now called Paul) to come to Antioch to help the new church. There began a restless, energetic teaching activity that has probably never been matched.

The meaning of Paul's faith developed out of his personal experience, and it was worked out in his almost constant conflicts—conflicts with the disciples, with the churches he founded, with former friends in the synagogue, and with political authorities. The most important, and perhaps bitterest, of these conflicts was with the disciples and other Christians over the nature of the church. There was a powerful faction in the early church that thought of Christianity as a reformed Judaism, so the only way to become a Christian was through the Jewish law. This meant that Greek converts had to keep scrupulously the Jewish laws. They had to be circumcised, rigorously observe the Sabbath, and they could not sit down to a table to eat with non-Jews. But Paul had a different religion. He proclaimed complete freedom from the Jewish law in declaring that the Christian's sole authority was the spirit of the love of God, which had come in Jesus, who, for this very reason, was manifest as the "Christ."

After Paul had established the church in the province of Galatia, some Judaizers followed him to the region, preached a Jewish Christianity, and cast aspersions upon the man who was not even an apostle. Paul was enraged; his religious beliefs and his personal relation to God had been called into question. The white heat of his anger and the fervor of his faith is revealed in his letter to the Galatians. He called down the curse of God upon those who preached a gospel different from his own, he appealed to his own personal call by God and his life in the new faith, he argued in pharisaic fashion by commentary upon the scriptures, and he arrived at his enlarged view:

> The law was our custodian until Christ came, that we might be justified by faith. But now that faith has come, we are no longer under a custodian; for in Christ Jesus you are all sons of God, through faith. For as many of you as were baptized into Christ have put on Christ. There is neither Jew nor Greek, there is neither slave nor free, there is neither male nor female; for you are all one in Christ Jesus.[46]

Conformance to the law, therefore, meant absolutely nothing and worse than nothing since it blocked a living comprehension of the love of Christ. "For freedom has Christ set us free; stand fast therefore, and do not submit again to a yoke of slavery."[47]

Paul's interpretation of "freedom in Christ Jesus" was the door to his ethical life and thought: nothing matters but "faith working through love."[48] The freedom of the Christian, therefore, is not a freedom to do as one pleases but a freedom to be "led by the Spirit" and "through love be servants of one another. For the whole law is fulfilled in one word, 'You shall love your neighbor as yourself.' "[49] The entire law for Paul, as it relates to ethics, is "fulfilled," that is, completely stated and realized, in a law that is no law. For love cannot be commanded. A man can be forced to be circumcised, or to keep the Sabbath, or not to eat with those of another race, but a person cannot be forced to love. Love is rooted only in a free spirit, and it transcends all law.

Paul's ethic, therefore, was grounded in his life and has a religious base. (1) His views involved a new analysis of human experience. (2) They involved an interpretation of who Jesus was and what he did. (3) The ethic had its roots in humanity's faith-response to "God in Christ." (4) Its sole motivating and manifest spirit was "love."

(1) Paul's detailed interpretation of human life—the personal predicament of man and the activity of God—was something quite new. It was unparalleled in Greek thought. There are some hints in the prophets that bear similarities to his views, but the closest analogues to his views are in those parables of Jesus, like that of the prodigal son, which related obviously to man's sin and God's forgiveness.

For Paul, man is a helpless sinner. Through the law man has some comprehension of what is required of him, but he is incapable of living as he should. His incapability is the consequence of his sin, and his sin consists in no particular acts but the corruption of his will. It is an all-pervasive power that turns the creature toward a love of the self rather than the love of God, and it has its roots in the "works of the flesh" rather than the "fruit of the spirit."[50] His list of the specific ethical consequences of the free life "in Christ" was meant to be illustrative and not exhaustive: "The fruit of the Spirit is love, joy, peace, patience, kindness, goodness, faithfulness, gentleness, self-control; against such there is no law."[51] His examples of the "works of the flesh" apply to a specific time and place situation though, he would say, they may be typical of all times and all places: "immorality, impurity, licentiousness, idolatry, sorcery, enmity, strife, jealousy, anger, selfishness, dissension, party-spirit."[52]

Paul thought of sin as permeating the life of the individual and humanity. All persons are "under the power of sin."[53] This had been suggested in the prophets, but Paul went far beyond prophetic teachings and even farther than the remembered statements of Jesus in (a) his interpretation of the dire need of man for reconciliation and (b) his psychological analysis of the tragic situation of human beings. Paul thought of man as needing not only a forgiveness that would obliterate past sin, i.e., make the person "innocent," but one that reconciled man to God. The act of reconciliation could only come from the one who has been offended. Man cannot initiate the proceedings that would recreate his personal relations with God. To suppose that a person can take the necessary steps was to fail to understand the seriousness of the human condition:

We know that the law is spiritual, but I am carnal, sold under sin. I do not understand my own actions. For I do not do what I want, but I do the very thing I hate. . . . I can will what is right, but I cannot do it. For I do not do the good I want, but the evil I do not want is what I do. . . . For I delight in the law of God in my inmost self, but I see in my members another law at war with the law of my mind and making me captive to the law of sin which dwells in my members. Wretched man that I am! Who will deliver me from this body of death?[54]

(2) Man escapes from the tragic and despairing human maze only by an act of God: "God was in Christ reconciling the world to himself."[55] The full meaning of this was developed by Paul in complicated ways and in accord with the theology and legal philosophy of his time. But fundamentally he saw Jesus as the "Christ" who, obedient unto death, revealed the love of God. Man was reconciled to God "through Christ"; and this reconciliation produced, in man, a new creation.

(3) What was given to the person was a faith-response. This enabled one to trust God absolutely as it was previously impossible to trust; life could be turned toward God rather than toward the self. The faith-response was given, it was not something that man could create. This had far deeper implications than intellectual assent to a creed. Paul did not bother to work out the details of his view of faith as a gift of God and man's responsibility for receiving faith, but he was convinced grace and freedom belonged together. Paul merely emphasized that faith was a gift, and, at the same time, he thought of man as having responsibility for acceptance of the gift.

(4) From the side of man faith-response is primary. But the essential consequence is love. Paul's fresh conception of the moral life came from the fact that when he wrote his poem to love he was thinking of Jesus and of the kind of life Jesus exhibited.

If I speak in the tongues of men and of angels, but have not love I am a noisy gong or a clanging cymbal. And if I have prophetic powers, and understand all mysteries and all knowledge, and if I have all faith, so as to remove mountains, but have not the love of Christ, I am nothing. If I give away all I have, and if I deliver my body to be burned, but have not the love of Christ, I gain nothing. Jesus was patient and kind; Jesus was not jealous or boastful; he was not arrogant or rude. Jesus did not insist on his own way; he was not irritable or resentful; he did not rejoice in wrong, but rejoiced in the right. Jesus bore all things . . . he endured all things.[56]

It was the suffering, selfless love of Jesus that appealed to Paul. He considered that faith became effectual when the individual reached the point of sharing in Christ's sufferings, that is, when acting from the same spirit that had dominated the life of Jesus. The implications of this for his attitude toward the role in the ethical life of (a) the law, (b) natural law, (c) reason, and (d) pleasure became clear. (a) The law which formerly possessed mainly an informative value of suggesting what should be done is eliminated by a faith which, leading to suffering love, provides a deeper insight into what is required of an individual and the motive power to fulfill the obligations. The Christian is no longer limited by the law. Through faith in God a person is free to do whatever love allows. But this means that the person is bound by what love requires. (b) Paul took over the idea of natural law, apparently from the Stoics, and suggested that even the Gentiles have a law "written on their hearts." But his experience of "faith working through love"[57] goes far beyond what he conceived to be the demands of natural law. Like the Jewish law the natural law was a "custodian"; but the divine will known in the love of Christ replaced the natural law. (c) Reason was employed by Paul in his ethic, but it was reason in the service of absolute "trust in God," not reason that served a "trust in reason." (d) Pleasure, self-seeking are excluded "on the principle of faith."[58]

If the implications for the personal ethic of Paul followed directly from his attitude toward love, the implications for his social ethic were conditioned more by his eschatology and his view of political power than by his principle of "faith working through love." His political doctrine was expressed in his advice and assertion, "Let every person be subject to the governing authorities. For there is no authority except from God, and those that exist have been instituted by God."[59]

Paul's ethic was dominated by his attitude toward Jesus and by the common presuppositions he shared with Jesus. Thus in a moment of fervor he advised some of his closest friends:

> Have this mind among yourselves, which you have in Christ Jesus, who, though he was in the form of God, did not count equality with God a thing to be grasped, but emptied himself taking the form of a servant. . . . He humbled himself and became obedient unto death, even death on the cross.[60]

Paul did not claim to have attained the perfection that he saw in Jesus. Perhaps he was too aware of his temper, his inner and outer conflicts, but he did affirm simply, "We have the mind of Christ."[61] In justification of this affirmation he could point to his life and the sufferings that were the result of discipleship: the beatings, the imprisonment, the shipwrecks, the starvation, the scorn of the Jews, the opposition of some disciples, and the disloyalty of some friends. So Paul could say that he was the slave of Christ, that he tried to bring every thought and word under the subjection to the obedient love he saw in Christ, that he shared in the sufferings of Christ. "Henceforth let no man trouble me; for I bear on my body the marks of Jesus."[62]

THE ETHIC OF JESUS AND PAUL

The "ethic" of Jesus and Paul had a basic similarity to the prophetic ethic and simultaneously a fundamental disagreement with the prophets' view. Jesus and Paul, like the prophets, did not have an ethic in the Greek, and usual philosophical, meanings of the term. There was no development of a moral theory based upon reason or philosophical analysis. There was no interest in ethical generalizations that possessed the validity of universal truth. But the ethical views of the prophets, Jesus, and Paul were grounded in a specific religious faith. These faith-views determined both moral understanding and moral action. The understanding was an interpretation of what should be done in unique situations; the action implied the resources to fulfill real obligations. But there always had to be a return to the religious source. To attempt to divorce the ethical attitude from the religious faith would leave only a meaningless jumble of moral maxims.

But while Jesus and Paul were closer to the prophetic ethics than to the philosophers there was also a significant disagreement with the prophets. For they both were convinced that something new had happened which, they believed, deepened or fulfilled the prophetic view. God had acted again in history in his own unique way. This action did not come from the human discovery of a new philosophical truth, or with a new command or law. The new action was a new life. That life constituted the ethic.

In examining the answers of Jesus and Paul to some of the major questions of ethics it is well to remember that while neither consciously asked these questions, Jesus was farther away from looking at the questions in this form. Paul was not a philosopher, but he sometimes employed the language of Greek philosophy, and his thinking at times resembled the Socratic dialectics. He was, however, much more a pharisaic interpreter of the law than a systematic Hellenistic thinker. Jesus was even less philosophical, or rather not philosophical. Many of his clearest meanings are revealed by a simple story or assertion. Still it is possible to examine their views through exploring five significant ethical questions.

1. What is the nature of man and society?

Both Jesus and Paul accepted the Hebrew psychology. The human being was thought of as a unity, a creature of God, and a rebel against his creator. The statement of Jesus about loving God with all of one's "heart and soul and mind and strength"[63] was understood in the terms of Hebrew psychology. And the statements at the last supper, "This bread is my body—this cup is my blood,"[64] had a unique meaning in that, for the Hebrews, the body was the expression of the total personality and the blood was thought of as life and the locus of the spirit of life. Paul was especially susceptible of misinterpretation in his view of the nature of man. "Flesh" and "spirit" were, for him, primarily religious and not psychological (or even metaphysical) terms. They represented two different kinds of life. The conflict was not (as in Greek thought) between physical appetite and the rational mind. The body was not evil. He thought of the body as "corruptible," but so, too, was the human spirit, since, for example, "knowledge" and "prophecy" were imperfect and would be superseded by the perfect knowledge after the resurrection. Paul's belief in resurrection was not a belief in the immortality of the soul but an affirmation that the Christian would receive a spiritual body just as in this life he had a physical body.

For both Jesus and Paul the nature of man was understood fundamentally in relational terms. Man was man because he had been created by God. Apart from this relation to God the person would not exist, and apart from this relation it could not be understood. As a creature his basic dependence was upon God, and his primary loyalty belonged to God. But as a sinner the human shifted his allegiance from God to self. Jesus did not make any statements about the universality of sin. His attitude toward the righteous of his time and his recognition that all of the disciples would forsake him were indications that he recognized that the root trouble with most persons was their inability to love properly. But Paul expressly charged that "all men are under the power of sin";[65] and this sin involved a corruption of the will that man was powerless, of himself, to change.

Society for both Jesus and Paul was understood in a dualistic sense. In the first place they had a conception of the social-political order, mainly in terms of the Roman rule. Their interpretation of this rule was conditioned by a social realism involving the recognition of power and, in Paul, an appreciation of the advantages offered by an orderly government. More basic was the eschatological belief of both that the political order would soon be overthrown. It existed by the permission of God who had established its rules for his own purposes. Advisory statements about living with this order ("Render unto Caesar the things that are Caesar's and unto God the things that are God's,"[66] and "Pay all of them their dues, taxes to whom taxes are due, revenue to whom revenue is due, respect to whom respect is due, honor to whom honor is due"[67]) were spoken against the background of these beliefs and to a specific situation. The precise meaning of the words depended upon a knowledge of that situation, though neither the disciples nor the early Christians would know exactly what belonged to Caesar and who should be respected.

Finally, however, Jesus and Paul were not interested in the social-political order. They were much more concerned with the society made up of the disciples and the early church. With both there was the view that they thought of these living social organisms as the "remnant," or the "Israel of God."[68] This society was made of individuals who have a relation to one another because they possess a common loyalty.

2. What is the objective of the moral judgment?

A moral judgment referred fundamentally to the intentions or the will. This was the meaning of the replacement of the law by Jesus with his view of the purpose of God: "You have heard that it was said of old time. . . . But I say unto you—Do not be angry with your brother, do not lust in your heart, love your enemies, pray in secret."[69] The root evils were not the external actions of men, and the basic good was not the consequences of action. Good and evil reside in the inner life.

> For no good tree bears bad fruit, nor again does a bad tree bear good fruit; . . . The good man out of the good treasure of his heart produces good and the evil man out of his evil treasures produces evil; for out of the abundance of the heart his mouth speaks.[70]

This emphasis upon the intentions of man was also apparent in Paul's distinctions between "works of the flesh" and "fruit of the spirit."[71] Again, Jesus and Paul recognized that love was the ethical characteristic of the good person, and love was a matter of an attitude of the spirit toward others and not a mere means of keeping punctiliously the code of a polite society, or of obeying any rules. Genuine love for neighbor was an inner attitude that would have consequences for external action and would be manifest in the total personality.

3. What is the norm of the moral judgment?

(a) The ultimate norm of any ethical judgment was the will of God. The ethic was based exclusively upon the religious conception of God: God was a living presence in the individual's life as creator, sovereign ruler and judge, and merciful father. It was the character of the divine as it was expressed in Christ's activity of completely selfless and suffering love that became the root foundation of all ethical life and ethical judgment.

When moral judgments were made, Jesus and Paul did not intend to blame or approve. They were interested not in who was to blame but in the fact of an individual's serious condition that must be improved. Whenever there was moral disapproval, it was given to clarify what for them was the more terrible fact of a false religious faith. In speaking of the unethical men of his time Paul declared emphatically:

> Because they exchanged the truth about God for a lie and worshiped and served the creature rather than the Creator . . . therefore God gave them up in the lusts of their hearts to impurity, to the dishonoring of their bodies

among themselves. . . . And since they did not see fit to acknowledge God,
God gave them up to a base mind and improper conduct.[72]

Precisely the same view was shown in Jesus's harsh denunciation of the religious leaders as hypocrites and blind guides whose actions might appear
righteous but whose inner lives were directed toward wrong goals. The
wrong goals were that they had "taken away the key of knowledge," that they
had neglected "justice and the love of God," and that they knew "neither the
scriptures nor the power of God."[73]

(b) If the ultimate norm was the will of God, then the human moral norm
was love. But love was not a norm that could be defined. It could be spoken of
in negative terms as completely selfless, or disinterested. Love could be spoken
of, too, in positive terms as a genuine regard for the neighbor, a gift of the self
to the other to fulfill the other's needs. The neighbor was neither humanity in
general nor the one who lives in the next house. The neighbor was any specific
human person who was in need of what love could offer. The qualities of love
could be characterized, as in Paul's poem in his letter to the Corinthians, but finally, for Paul as for Jesus, love could not be defined. It could only be pointed
to, and illustrated. Paul pointed to Jesus and said, "There was love."

(c) Finally, for Jesus and for Paul there was a specific norm that was applicable to the life of the particular person. This was not a norm even in the
same sense that the will of God and love became moral norms. It was a standard that the individual, meeting certain conditions, could understand what
was required. There was the recognition that since persons were different, so
what love specifically required would also be different. Jesus illustrated this
point by the parable of the differing amounts of money given to various servants. The sharpest focus on this aspect of his thought was the report that
when, after the resurrection, he gave specific orders to Peter and Peter in-
quired about the commands for John, Jesus replied, "If it is my will that he
remain until I come, what is that to you?"[74] Paul's concept of differing voca-
tional responsibilities appeared in his view of the different abilities and,
therefore, requirements that are placed upon individuals in the church.

4. How is the moral good known in a specific situation?

For a person to be related properly to God, it was necessary for him to understand what he should be, and this relationship would let him know that he
must love. Nothing else was required. Paul and Jesus apparently had great
faith that the knowledge of specific requirements would come through a
proper relation of self to God's will and a comprehension of the human
events that posed the moral problem. But it was not evident that they indicated how one achieved a satisfactory comprehension of the meaning of the

events, or whether the situation might be so complex as to make impossible a certain knowledge of precisely what was required.

5. How is the moral good achieved in a specific situation?

The ability to achieve good in any situation was not a matter of a person's own will; it was not the product of rational thought or of love of virtue. It was supplied by God who alone was good. But this did not mean that nothing was required of an individual or that the achievement of the good would be easy. Quite the contrary. Everything was required. All had to be offered to God and all became at once more difficult and more simple. The individual's life became more difficult because it involved actual suffering, a sharing, as Paul put it, in the suffering of Christ. But all became simple, too, for through the sacrifice of the self-will there was the dependence upon another more inclusive, more intense will.

THE UNIQUE CONTRIBUTION OF THE HEBREW PROPHETS, JESUS, AND PAUL

There are a number of difficulties that face us in discussing the question "What new and lasting contribution did the Hebrew prophets, Jesus, and Paul make to the Western ethic?" First, to phrase the question in terms of individuals obscures the fact that behind the individuals was a community, and that within the community were other types of individuals with contending and legitimate points of view. This difficulty is partly overcome by recognizing that the prophets, Jesus, and Paul spoke for their community or, more accurately, for the authorities that transcended and made the community possible.

Second, we are dealing with time periods of different lengths and often with lengthy separations from one another. The lives of the prophets we have observed cover at least 250 years. Then, after more than five centuries, the active lives of Jesus and Paul encompass a scant thirty years. But here it is the Hebrews themselves who suggest how to deal with this difficulty, since they taught us to think in terms of the continuity of history, and so, if continuity can be found in the moral thought, the difficulty presented by the span of time is not a real one.

The third difficulty, however, is probably insurmountable. This is knowing how to place Jesus and Paul in relation to the prophets and, indeed, to each other. Historically even if Jesus and Paul have often been seen as existing within the prophetic tradition, all parties have also seen them as distinct from the prophets and from each other in thought, temperament, and self-conception. The question is whether these separations help us to understand their ethics or obscure the ways ethical truth has been discovered and given to

Western moral thought. Since there is no obvious solution to the "placing" of Jesus and Paul, the question must first be asked about the new, important contributions of the prophets to the Western ethic and only then, in the light of this answer, can we inquire about the contributions of Jesus and Paul.

So, what were the unique contributions of the Hebrew prophets?

(1) In the first place, the most important issues in human history, social and individual, were seen as religious issues. And although for the prophets religious experience and language could be immediately translatable into moral life, the religious dimension of life was never reducible to the moral dimension.

The religious issue is that of authority. What is the basic source for existence, especially of human life? What is the sustenance of human life? Who or what are the guides to life? These religious questions of authority were the questions important for the prophets, and in answering them they believed they also answered the moral questions. This uniting of religion and ethics in such a way that, if each is adequately understood they can be differentiated yet never separated, was a fateful insight destined to have repercussions throughout Western history.

(2) Life, which means moral life, is lived in a community whose authority is beyond itself. The prophets were not "individuals" and could not conceive of individuality, certainly not apart from community. If now they are thought of as individuals, the most that would be accurate to claim for them is "individual-in-community," with the emphasis on community. And just as an "individual" is dependent upon the community for existence, so is the community dependent upon the sacred unnamed One who brought it into being, sustains and guides it. This One, this Other becomes determinative for what the community, and individuals-in-community, should be and become, that is, for ethics.

(3) Basic, therefore, to the moral life is the fact of the covenant. It was believed to be a special choice of the Holy One of Israel, a special set of promises and expectations, a special bonding that brought Israel into being. This covenant became determinative for the content and form of the ethic, adding significantly to the ethic of the West. This covenant implies certain conditions:

(a) Promise-making becomes central in human life and, therefore, in ethics.

(b) This, in fact, means that the ethical life is grounded upon trust, upon trusting, and upon being trusted.

(c) Response and responsibility are recognized as key aspects of human life. The concepts of faithfulness, loyalty, and duty become consciously present in shaping the form of moral experience.

(d) Motives also become central in moral experience. Accomplishments and consequences in themselves are insignificant. It is not what the community or individual-in-community achieves that is morally significant, but what they intended to achieve or, more accurately, what they ultimately intended in the achieving.

(e) Freedom is also assumed as essential for ethics. This was not the freedom of the Greeks. Neither that concept nor the possibility of rational debate ever occurred to the prophets. It was, rather, the freedom to respond or not respond, to be responsible or not responsible.

(4) The fact that promise-making and promise-receiving is so important for human life implies the possibility that the promise may be broken. With the manifestation of a broken legitimate promise (sin) there arises the question of how to deal with violations of the religious-moral covenant. The answer is given in the immediate reality of forgiveness. That idea, introduced in various forms by the prophets, has been of great importance for moral experience in the West while it has also caused enormous difficulties for moral thought.

(5) Given the religious origin of the ethics, it follows that both justice and love are expected of human beings who participate in the basic covenant. At first these qualities extended only to the community of Israel, but with the more imaginative, morally sensitive prophets the expectation of justice and love was universalized. Once more, as with the idea of forgiveness, the prophets did not hesitate to introduce often contradictory concepts that would provide great tension in ethical experience and enormous problems for ethical thought.

(6) Along with this sense of justice and love was the awareness that fidelity to the covenant could also result in suffering. This suffering, often of an intense kind both for individuals and for the community, was also seen as part of the plan of the Holy One who continued to act in history as a partner to the chosen people. While each of the prophets accented the importance of this suffering in his own way, certainly, in a balanced depth and breadth the suffering servant songs of "Second Isaiah" go beyond anything previously known. Suffering itself becomes a part of the covenant, and a recognition of one of the essential aspects of love and justice.

(7) Finally, the prophets recognized that human life is life in history, at the same time that it is life related to the God beyond history. They taught human beings how to live in the present by living in two worlds at once, both beyond yet within the present. This lesson, whether true or false, has been continually relearned by many persons and has had profound effects upon moral experience and thought. The nature of moral experience is potentially given new breadth and depth by this larger context. And moral thought must now include the past as well as the mystery of the ahistorical other in its reflections.

In the light of these contributions of the Hebrew prophets to Western ethics the question can be raised about the contributions of Jesus and Paul. It is a question that is probably impossible to answer. There is no doubt that they have had a profound effect upon Western sensibilities and the ways persons have dealt with moral perplexities. But what contributions are directly attributable to them is uncertain.

One thing that is clear is that these are no new moral ideas in Jesus and

Paul that cannot be found in the prophetic or prophetically influenced writings. Whether Jesus gave the ideas a new unity cannot be known. There is no clear evidence that he did so. Certainly Paul gave no new unity to ethics even though he placed it in an impressive coherent theological framework.

If we are to look for the unique contributions of Jesus and Paul, we must look away from their words to their lives. Here there can only be imaginative conclusions based upon the scant evidence that is available. The most important bit of evidence is that Jesus gave some persons the impression that he embodied the prophetic ideals and that he was unself-consciously aware that he embodied them. Paul put this impression into theological language with the claim that "Jesus is the Christ," that is, the Messiah. Later, authors of the gospels confirmed the impression by associating Jesus with the Suffering Servant. Others recognized that Jesus embodied the moral ideals he taught; and it is clear that he consented to the way those ideals worked themselves out to his own destruction. The ethical ideals themselves had a depth and breadth, but their presence in the moral experience of Jesus may have given those ideals a new intensity and inclusiveness. Now moral ideals were not just ideals but had been given actuality in a life.

Paul was a vastly different person from Jesus in temperament and moral experience, and he was clearly aware of those differences. But he claimed to have *the mind of Christ* and inferred that mind was in control. He, too, embodied the moral ideas of the prophets and let those ideals work their way in his life with great personal loss and also to his own destruction. And certainly the man who wrote the Hymn to Love, as well as the many spontaneous moral admonitions, must have known such love as a living source of life itself.

SUMMARY: THE GREEK PHILOSOPHERS AND THE HEBREW PROPHETS

The essential task performed by the Hebrew prophets and the Greek philosophers for ethics in the West was the creation of a basic moral personality. Since their times, at least until the twentieth century, individuals and communities have been able to look back to persons in either or both of these ethical communities to say, "They established our identity." In establishing an ethical identity they also set the channels for further growth by setting down the presuppositions through which we would face the tasks that their work left uncompleted. Through arduous labors they received their ethical insights, insights which became ethical truths transmitted through their speaking and writing. But these truths were incomplete truths in a dual sense.

First, the conceptual truth not only contained errors and inconsistencies that required harmonizing and corrections, but the style through which the truths were expressed inevitably had limitations. All these limitations have helped create for us our moral problems. The Greeks focused upon specific aspects of moral experience, thinking in special ways. The aspects and the ways were legitimate. The Hebrew prophets also selected difficult elements of the moral life to examine, and they appropriated those elements with their own unique style. These elements and style were also legitimate. However, each style of thought and ethical perspective provided only partial truths that needed supplementing.

Second, the conceptual moral truths required enactment. Both the Greek philosophers and Hebrew prophets recognized that moral truth is a marriage of human becoming and being as well as human thinking and thought, of human acts as well as words. Ethical truth is confirmed by life as well as language, and without the confirmation of life it remains an uncompleted, even uncertain, truth.

All ethical experience and thought since the establishment of the ethical identity in the West has been related to Hebraic and Greek experience, though it is far from certain that this will be the case in the future. Thus, almost all later discoveries of truth in Western moral life and thought have been the development, elaboration, or modifications of the basic moral personality. There have been two primary ways this has occurred.

First, there have been new discoveries within the formulations provided by the Greeks and Hebrews. This has sometimes involved, in act or word, a clearer or more consistent realization of what was present in the earlier ethic. At times, this has been a more limited and narrowly focused clarity and consistency. At other times the discoveries have been of what was implicit but not evident in the previous ethic until fresh experience and thought brought it to light. Or again, in moments of ethical creativity, the new discovery built upon and then went beyond previously known moral truth. In every case the new truths overcame tensions and dissolved conflicts whether in the self or in the nascent Western ethical personalty.

Second, new discoveries have been made from outside the moral structure of the Greek or Hebraic thought. At least prior to the twentieth century, these discoveries had integral relations with that thought. Indeed, the categories of "inside" and "outside" are not strictly applicable. But what is certain is that these discoveries have presented serious challenges to Greek and Hebrew style and ethic. For example, even after three hundred years it is far from certain whether the ethics of science can be harmonized with the earlier, uniquely Western ethic, and after one hundred years it is even less certain whether the technological results of science can be tamed and controlled by that ethic. Nor is it clear whether the ethic of the late nineteenth century— that of Darwin, Marx, Nietzsche, and Freud—can be integrated into the Western ethical personality, or if it cannot, what significantly new metamorphosized moral style and concepts will shape human life in the future. It is also equally certain that our contemporary life will bring to the Western ethic new challenges from discoveries in anthropology, from intimate contacts with other non-Western cultures, and from the stimulus of the works of the imagination from around the world.

Consequently, there are reasons it may be appropriate to refer, with proper attribution, to the twentieth century as "The Last Western Century." Whether or not the Western ethic has a future, it certainly has a past which has been deeply woven into contemporary life. Whether these patterns are now antiquated it is impossible to know. It is certain, however, that we must continue to deal with the patterns of the Western moral personality, either through painful reflection or painful restructuring. To perceive how that personality developed in our past may provide new moral insights into our future and help prepare the way for the challenges to come.

NOTES

1. Genesis 17:1, 2, 5b, in James Moffatt, *A New Translation of the Bible* (New York: Harper & Brothers Publishers. 1935).
2. Exodus 24:3–8.
3. Amos 9:7b.
4. Amos 7:14, 15.
5. Amos 2:6–8.
6. Amos 3:11.
7. Amos 7:12–13.
8. Amos 8:4–6.
9. Amos 6:1–6.
10. Amos 5:21–23.
11. Amos 5:5, 6.
12. Amos 5:24 (King James Version).
13. Amos 5:20.
14. Amos 9:1a.
15. Hosea 4:1b, 2, 13b, 14b.
16. Hosea 7:8a, 9a, 11; 8:4; 12:1.
17. Hosea 6:6.
18. Hosea 5:9, 14.
19. Hosea 11:1, 2a, 3–5a, 8a, 9.
20. Isaiah 1:4a, 6, 7.
21. Isaiah 1:23; 3:15a; 5:8, 22–23; 2:8; 5:20.
22. Isaiah 10:20.
23. Jeremiah 26:11b (Revised Standard Version).
24. Jeremiah 31:31–34 (King James Version).
25. Isaiah 53:12.
26. Psalm 137:1 (Revised Standard Version) (free translation).
27. Matthew 11:13; Romans 7:12 (Revised Standard Version; all remaining citations will be to this translation).
28. See Acts, 20:28; Romans 5:9.
29. Mark 1:15.
30. Matthew 20:28.
31. Matthew 3:2, 7b, 8a.
32. Mark 1:15.
33. Matthew 19:8.
34. Mark 2:27.
35. Mark 8:29b.
36. Matthew 16:21a.
37. Mark 8:34 (free translation).
38. Matthew 20:25–26a.
39. Luke 11:20.
40. Luke 12:32.
41. Mark 14:36.
42. Mark 12:29–31.
43. Matthew 27:46 and Psalm 22:1a, 6b, 14a, 16b, 18a, 28, 30b, 31a.
44. Acts 23:6.
45. Acts 7:58b, 60b.
46. Galatians 3:24–28.

47. Galatians 5:1.
48. Galatians 5:6b.
49. Galatians 5:18; 13b–14.
50. Galatians 5:19, 22.
51. Galatians 5:22–23.
52. Galatians 5:20.
53. Romans 3:9b.
54. Romans 7:14, 18b, 19, 22–24.
55. 2 Corinthians 5:19a.
56. 1 Corinthians 13:1–7 (free translation).
57. Galatians 5:6.
58. Romans 2:15; 3:27.
59. Romans 13:1.
60. Philippians 2:5–7a, 8b.
61. 1 Corinthians 2:16b.
62. Galatians 6:17.
63. Mark 12:30.
64. Mark 14:22–24 (free translation).
65. Romans 3:9b.
66. Luke 20:25.
67. Romans 13:7.
68. Galatians 6:16b.
69. Matthew 5:21, 22, 28, 44; 6:6 (free translation).
70. Luke 6:43, 45.
71. Galatians 5:19, 22.
72. Romans 1:25, 24, 28.
73. Luke 11:52; 11:42; Mark 12:24.
74. John 21:22.

3

THE ETHICS OF MARCUS AURELIUS

The year 148 C.E. was the nine-hundredth anniversary of the founding of Rome. To celebrate its history and legendary origins the emperor Antoninus (who had been asked by the Senate to accept the name "Pius") had special medallions minted portraying Rome's founder, Aeneas, landing in Italy. Marcus Aurelius was twenty-seven that year. As a boy he had been granted special privileges by the emperor Hadrian. As a youth he had been adopted as Antoninus's son; had served twice as consul, the highest appointed office in the empire; and on December 1, 147, he had received the *imperium*, which gave him authority over the armies and provinces. Marcus was at a place and a time to be imbued with the traditions of Roman rule and history.

For the previous half century childless emperors, each adopting his successor, had developed a government of efficiency and idealism unequaled since Augustus. This was, claimed Edward Gibbon,

> the period in the history of the world during which the condition of the human race was most happy and prosperous. The vast extent of the Roman empire was governed by absolute power, under the guidance of virtue and wisdom. The armies were restrained by the firm but gentle hand of four successive emperors whose character and authority commanded involuntary respect. The forms of the civil administration were carefully preserved by Nerva, Trajan, Hadrian and the Antonines, who delighted in the image of liberty, and were pleased with considering themselves as the accountable ministers of the laws.[1]

The character of Rome had been described in 144 C.E. by the famous Greek orator Aelius Aristides. A citizen of North Africa, Aristides journeyed to

Rome to celebrate the empire in a beautifully crafted public oration which, for all its flattery, described the lineaments of a great civilization. He began by speaking of the vastness and universality of Rome, comparing it favorably with the great empires of the past and suggesting it had made the whole world like a "city-state," and in this Aristides was speaking from his own experience:

> Neither sea nor intervening continent are bars to citizenship, nor are Asia and Europe divided in their treatment here. In your empire all paths are open to all. No one worthy of rule or trust remains an alien, but a civil community of the World has been established as a Free Republic under one, the best, ruler and teacher of order; and all come together as into a common civic center, in order to receive each man his due.[2]

The government, Aristides explained, exists in a just, orderly fashion; the emperor is not a despot but exists in responsible relations with senate, magistrates, and people; the constitution embodies the best elements of democracy, aristocracy, and monarchy. There has thus been created what had once seemed impossible, a firmness of rule over a vast empire. The ideals of this empire are best realized in the "abundant and beautiful equality of the humble with the great and of the obscure with the illustrious, and above all of the poor man with the rich and of the commoner with the noble."[3] Most significant of all for Aristides was the conception of citizenship. "There is nothing like it in the records of all mankind [for] you have everywhere appointed to your citizenship, or even to kinship with you, the better part of the world's talent, courage, and leadership."[4]

Aristides singled out the army as the greatest single work of Roman perfection, exhibiting quality in its recruitment, training, and service. Indeed, the army was a civilizing force in second-century Rome. Less than half a million men defended a border of ten thousand miles from North Africa in the South to Arabia and Syria in the East; the Danube, Rhine, and Clyde in the North; and the Atlantic in the West. Well over half of the army was recruited from outside Italy, the sons following in their fathers' profession. But the Roman soldier was far more than soldier: he was a fighting man and an engineer, a farmer and a surveyor, a policeman, an administrator, and a judge.

The emperor was the head of the army, and for most emperors much time was given to leading its battles, directing its many public services, and reorganizing its leadership. Indeed, the entire civil service, that complex bureaucracy which enabled a great empire to function efficiently, was largely the creation of the emperors—and, it should be added, of the Roman senate and the local magistrates—of the first two centuries C.E. For the senate had enormous power and prestige, and it was characteristic of the "good emperors" to submit themselves to its persuasive influence. The cities which had been built throughout the empire, often to provide civilian services for an army unit, were given considerable freedom, so the local magistrates, like the regional governors, were stimulated to create their own staffs and civil servants were empowered to perform essential governmental tasks.

In the Roman tradition so praised by Aristides, the individual existed in responsible relations with family and friends, with city and empire, with nature and the "gods." All these relations were sacred. *Pietas* was a primary virtue, and it was extraordinary praise for Antoninus (and a lesson for his adopted son, Marcus) that the senate, linking him in memory with Rome's founder, should ask him to accept the name of "Pius," a term that symbolized a whole complex of prized qualities and actions, including honesty, patriotism, dutifulness, and holiness.

The oration of Aristides pointed to the achievements of Rome. It also, with its similarities to Pericles' funeral oration in praise of Athens, pointed back to the Greeks. For not only was Greek one of the two official languages of the empire (the *Meditations* of Marcus were written in Greek), but the Roman ethos has assumed the major assumptions of Greek ethics. The Romans "knew" in their daily experience that human beings have a structure and function; that the good life, whether of the individual or society, is the harmonization, the balancing of human activities; that the good life is known and achieved by reason; and that the individual and society are mutually interdependent.

All these perspectives are present in the Roman ethos and, therefore, in the ethic of Marcus Aurelius. But by the time of Marcus at least two additional assumptions had been added. On March 7, 161, Antoninus Pius, aware that he was dying, called together his family and officials of the government. Commending his rule in state and family to Marcus, he ordered that the statue of Fortune, traditionally enshrined in the bedroom of the emperor, should be moved to the bedroom of Marcus. Good fortune, with all its uncertainty and unpredictability, had become an essential presupposition at the basis of ethics.

Marcus accepted the statue, but, as a counterpoise, he added another assumption to the ethics, a perspective adopted from Plato which that philosopher had reached by arduous intellectual labor: that "States flourish if philosophers rule or if rulers are philosophers."

It is not certain how old Marcus was when he first arrived at this belief, but it clearly developed from his years with the imperial family and with philosophy. Born in 121, he was given the name of Marcus by his father, Annius Verus. His father died when he was three, but years later Marcus wrote of what he had learned: "From the reputation of my father and what I remember of him: self-respect and manly behavior."[5] His mother, who lived for another thirty-five years, never remarried. During all of this time mother and son seem to have been very close, and if all was known about their relations, it is likely that the influence of a strong and loving mother upon an impressionable son would be clearer and more substantial in our understanding of Marcus's life. In letters and his *Meditations* he wrote of her with affection, and while she was independently wealthy, he remembered that the real gifts to him were of another sort: "piety, generosity, to avoid not only evil deeds but evil thoughts; to live simply without any display of wealth. "[6]

It was through his grandfather, who helped to raise him, that Marcus early came to the attention of Hadrian. The elder Annius Verus, a close friend of the emperor, was consul for the second time the year of Marcus's birth; and five years later he was consul for the third time, equaling the record of the emperor. While it is not certain why Hadrian favored the child Marcus, it is not difficult to imagine justifiable reasons. The bust of the child Marcus, and the profile on coins of the teenage youth show a curly-headed, regular-featured, handsome boy. Moreover, from his earliest years he showed a religious quality; from his first schooling he was a serious student. All of this, with the close family friendship, appealed to Hadrian, who gave Marcus the nickname "Verissimus" (the superlative form of *verus,* that is "truthful"), a name that stayed with Marcus and was later placed on coins and inscriptions.

When Marcus was six, Hadrian enrolled him in the order of the royal horse guards, an unusual honor for one so young. The following year the emperor had him become a member of the college of royal priests whose function was to perform ritual dances in honor of Mars. His formal education began at about the same time. Two teachers gave him elementary instruction in reading, writing, and arithmetic, including instruction in Greek language and literature. A third teacher was his *educator*, that is, the one responsible for his moral development. In the last years of his life Marcus remembered this unnamed teacher with gratitude, noting that from him he had learned not to be partisan at games or gladiator fights and "to bear pain and be content with little; to work with my own hands, to mind my own business, to be slow to listen to slander."[7]

When he was twelve, his secondary education began. One of his teachers, a painting master, stimulated his lifelong love of philosophy. But for Marcus this philosophy was a way not merely of thinking but of living, and it was the austere life and idealism of the Stoics that especially appealed to him. Even when, toward the end of his life, he regretted that he had not become a philosopher, his regrets had to do with the moral life as much as with philosophical thought.

In 136, when Marcus was fourteen, he assumed the *toga virilis*, the symbol of manhood. It was this same year that Hadrian had him betrothed to the daughter of the emperor's adopted son, L. Ceionius Commodus, and it was through the Commodus family that the Stoic teacher Appollonius entered his life. By the betrothal it was Hadrian's will that Marcus would one day be emperor. Unfortunately, Commodus died on the first day of 138. Hadrian then adopted Antoninus as his son with the express condition that Antoninus adopt Marcus, which was done. Marcus moved into Hadrian's palace in Rome. When Antoninus became emperor in 138, one of his first acts was to persuade Marcus to cancel the betrothal and to become engaged to Antoninus's daughter, Faustina. Thus, the destiny of Marcus Annius Verus—now Marcus Aelius Antoninus Aurelius "Verissimus"—was established.

Marcus attended the imperial councils, acted as deputy to the emperor with wide-ranging responsibilities, and at the age of eighteen became consul with Antoninus. Since he was to be an Antonine emperor, his higher education continued. For the next six years his most important teacher was the well-known grammarian Cornelius Fronto, who taught him the clarity and grandeur of Cicero and Vergil, and of the earlier writers Cato, Plautus, Terence, Gaius Gracchus, and Ennius. It was Fronto, too, who convinced a ruler whose authority would be exercised in speech and writing how important words are. "My Caesar speech is gripping me with hooked claws," Marcus wrote as he prepared a senate address. "Now I finally realize what a task it is to shape three or five lines and to take time over writing something."[8] His letters reveal a good-natured, active youth, who could play with words as well as people: "I slept rather late because of my slight cold," he once wrote Fronto in accounting for his day.

> From the eleventh hour of the night [5:00 A.M.] until the third hour of the day I spent part of the time reading Cato's *Agriculture* and part in writing— not quite such miserable stuff as yesterday. Then, after greeting my father, I soothed my throat, rather than gargled (though the word *gargarisso* is found in Naevius and elsewhere I think), by swallowing honeywater as far as the back of my throat and spitting it out again. After seeing to my throat I went off to my father and accompanied him when he made a sacrifice. Then we went to have lunch. What do you think I had to eat? I only had a little bit of bread, while I watched the others tucking into beans, onions and herrings with plenty of roe. Then we worked hard at gathering the grapes, sweating away and merry and, as the poet has it "left some high-hanging survivors of the vintage." After the sixth hour we came home. I studied for a little bit and what I did hadn't much sense in it. Then I had a long gossip with my little mother as she sat on the bed. My conversation was as follows. "What do you think my Fronto is doing now?" Then she said, "And what do you think my Gratia [Fronto's wife] is doing?" Then I said, "And what do you think the little sparrow is doing, our tiny little Gratia?" [Fronto's daughter] While we were chattering away and arguing which of us loved one or the other of you two the more, the gong sounded, the signal that my father had gone to the bath-house. So we had supper after we bathed in the

oil-press room—I don't mean we bathed in the oil-press room, but we had supper there after the bath and enjoyed hearing the country people make jokes at each other. Then back here and before I turn on my side and start snoring I am doing my duty and giving an account of my day to my sweetest master—and if I could miss him more I would not mind tormenting myself a little more.[9]

Fronto was pleased with his student, coming to believe that in some ways the student surpassed the master, especially when it came to having learned about the nature and feelings of others. This understanding was undoubtedly related to Marcus's virtues, especially to Fronto's judgment of his greatest ability, that of making friends. In writing of Orpheus, Fronto thought of his student:

If ever anyone had power by his character to unite all his friends in mutual love for one another, you will surely accomplish this much more easily, since you were born to practice all the virtues before you had any training in them. For before you were old enough to begin education you were already perfect and complete in all noble accomplishments, before adolescence "a good man," before manhood "skilled in speaking." But of all your virtues this is the most admirable, that you unite all your friends in harmony. I cannot conceal my opinion that this is much more difficult than to tame wild beasts with the lyre.[10]

While Marcus pleased his teacher he did not always please himself, nor did it please Fronto to learn that his student was turning from literature to philosophy. In 146, when Marcus was captivated by philosophy, he explained the effect that Ariston, a disciple of Zeno, the founder of Stoicism, was having upon him. The teacher of literature could only have been dismayed that his beloved poets were being replaced by philosophers.

Marcus's formal education ended at about this time. Thereafter, he turned his attentions to his family (he had married Faustina the year before) and to the serious work of the empire. But his love of education and of teachers continued. Marcus's biographer reports that "he gave so much honor to his teachers that he kept gold statues of them in his private chapel, and always honored their tombs by personal visits and offerings of sacrifices and flowers."[11] His love of philosophy was so great that even after becoming emperor he attended the lectures of philosophers whenever he could and, upon going to a city for the first time, often gave lectures himself. He thought of himself as a teacher and, with a light touch, imagined how his fellow Romans would all breathe more easily after his death without this schoolmaster to lecture them.

For over thirty years family and empire took most of Marcus's attention.

His marriage was, evidently, moderately happy though it was marred by rumors of Faustina's unfaithfulness, some rumors reported during her lifetime, others surfacing only after her death. Most of the rumors have been proved false. All are unsubstantiated, and the truth of the charges will probably never be known. Faustina bore him thirteen children, only six of whom survived Marcus; and yet, when he reminds himself of all the persons from whom he had learned, Marcus does not mention his wife. However, at the conclusion of his varied list of things for which he is thankful (including his own sexual restraint and purity), he mentions, almost as an afterthought, gratitude for "my wife . . . so obedient, so affectionate, and so simple."[12]

In 161 Marcus became co-emperor with Lucius, son of Aelius Caesar who had died before becoming emperor. There were enough imperial problems for the work of two men: wars in the East (largely attended to by Lucius), administrative details of directing a great empire, military threats on the northern frontier, and in 167 the greatest crisis of all: the plague. It extended throughout the empire and the loss of life was widespread, especially in the cities and in the army. And then coincident with it, the tribes along the northern frontier became a serious threat. In January 169 the two emperors went to the North where Lucius died, and then following a half year in Rome, Marcus returned to lead the northern armies. Eight of the remaining ten years of his life would be spent in war with the northern tribes, including the Sarmatians. For Marcus these years meant failure as an emperor and as a philosopher. He died in Vindobona, i.e., Vienna, on March 17, 180, a month before his fifty-ninth birthday.

"TO HIMSELF": THE MEDITATIONS OF MARCUS AURELIUS

In the last years of his life Marcus wrote a series of "meditations." While the exact time of writing cannot be known with certainty, he indicates that he wrote some of the notes "among the Quadi" and "at Carnuntum," that is, on the northern frontier where he had gone for the first time in 168. "To Himself" was a private journal. This means that the "you," a pronoun which appears repeatedly, refers not to a reader but to the writer: it is Marcus writing to Marcus, an emperor, or rather a man, paradoxically certain of himself yet puzzled and perplexed, still trying to find the right direction for his life. On rare occasions the writer lapses into a "we" or "us," but this only means, from his Stoic view, the ideal commonwealth of human beings and not writer and reader.

While the journal is philosophical, it is not a philosophy. The emperor Marcus delighted in attending philosophical lectures and gave lectures, but he never thought of writing a philosophy as, at one time, he began writing a history of Rome and Greece. For Marcus was an emperor with daily responsibilities. He was a general on military campaigns as well as a man beset by personal and social problems. But in the midst of his turbulent life he reflected philosophically on matters important to him.

While the writing lacks a logical order essential for a philosophy, Marcus gave it a human order by asking, "From whom have I learned? What have they taught me?" In answering these questions he wrote one of the most remarkable documents that has ever introduced a philosophical writing. He identified his learning, whether of ideas or of moral qualities and relations, with specific individuals, and he recognized that the learning had come from their acts and words. It is clear Marcus did not feel that his life exhibited the human excellencies he describes, but at least they had been learned as ideals. When as a mature man he identified the persons who had shaped his life, he mentioned sixteen major individuals. Four were parents and grandparents; one a "brother" whose son married Marcus's daughter; one was the emperor who had adopted him; and ten were teachers. The four most important teachers whom he recalled were Stoics. These persons gave him a framework and basic convictions. But what Marcus Aurelius then saw from his perspective he discovered for himself. When he quotes philosophers, he often does so inaccurately. To quote seriously but inaccurately can only mean that the idea has become a living part of his thought, forged out of his own experience.

The qualities Marcus mentions are complex, and yet they form a pattern. It is not certain that he mentions first what he learned from his grandparents and parents because of either his respect for them or the importance of the qualities. Perhaps it was something of both, and although the persons disappear in the subsequent part of the book, the qualities loom large. Marcus's teachers, enabling him to recognize what he had experienced at home, built upon these qualities—such as piety, simplicity, kindliness, and self-respect. Thus he learned from Rusticus humility and simplicity: "not to write one's theories or preach one's little sermon, not to show off by posing as a trained philosopher."[13] Appollonius taught him the importance of Reason: "not to look to anything else but Reason even for a moment," "to be the same man always, when in great pain, at the loss of a child, or during a long illness."[14] In Sextus he saw that the doctrine of life according to nature meant "affectionate consideration for one's friend's feeling," "to be tolerant of those whose opinions are not thought out," "to show no trace of anger or any other passion, to be quite unperturbed and yet very affectionate."[15] And from Maximus he received the ideas of "strength of character, self-control, and sobriety."[16]

But it was not in a teacher but a friend, Claudius Severus, the father of his son-in-law, that Marcus saw qualities which became central to his life:

love of family, love of truth, love of justice; . . . to grasp the idea of a Commonwealth with the same laws for all, governed on the basis of equality and free speech, also the idea of a monarchy which prizes the liberty of its subjects above all things; from him also a vigorous consistency in the appreciation of philosophy.[17]

Still it was Antoninus Pius who taught Marcus the most, and in the context of what he learned, it is evident that the phrase of the adopted son, "my father," was written with affection. There was no division or clear order in his reporting of what he learned from the emperor, for matters relating to personal, interpersonal, and political life are all interwoven. Yet this evident lack of order was perhaps the most important thing that was learned, this interrelationship of the personal and the political.

In the remainder of his reflections Marcus identifies over forty virtues which parallel what he had learned from his mentors. While they are never described in order of importance, it is not difficult to recognize which ones mean the most to him. They are, first of all, the virtues he mentions most frequently: piety and rational life. This combination of religion and philosophy went back to his childhood as, indeed, it went back to early Greek philosophy. Then, next in number, are the virtues of kindliness, simplicity, and freedom; self-respect and the acceptance of one's lot; and social-mindedness and justice.

There are also those occasions when Marcus spontaneously enumerates lists of the most important human qualities. On his different lists there is no exact repetition of the virtues since he wrote in diverse moods and situations. Yet in those spontaneous outbursts the same virtues or family of virtues appear and reappear: "sincerity, dignity, endurance of pain, indifference to pleasure, contentment, self-sufficiency, kindliness, freedom, simplicity, common sense, and magnanimity";[18] "high-mindedness, freedom, simplicity and piety."[19] "Find joy in simplicity, self-respect, and indifference to what lies between virtue and vice. Love the human race. Follow the divine."[20] "Do not think that because you despaired of being a logician, or a natural scientist, you therefore despair of being free, self-respecting, socially minded and obedient to the divine."[21] Such listings are repeated again and again as though Marcus needed to remind himself of who he was and who he wanted to be. Although there is no perfect order or consistency in his lists, there is an implicit pattern rooted in his life.

A similar order is true of his total philosophy. Although Marcus did not write a philosophy in the sense in which that term has been understood since Plato and Aristotle, there is an implicit philosophy in his personal notes. Moreover, if one attempts to relate to him as he wanted to relate to his fellows, trying to "enter into [his] directing mind,"[22] returning again and again to his specific experiences and words, then the effort to give order to his notes to himself may lead to a fuller understanding of who he was and what he believed.

THE ETHIC

The musings of Marcus Aurelius are the reflections of a life struggling to shape itself. The notes "To Himself" were an essential part of the shaping of a centered yet multifaceted personality.

The center to which Marcus aspired was reason. This was the acceptance of a fundamental assumption of all Greek ethics mediated to him by his Stoic teachers. That center can be simply expressed: one's reason is able to understand the orderly universe and thus to control one's life through the "directing mind." All of the complex human relations which Marcus attempted to understand and order were administered from this center: his life in relation to the totality of things, to society, to other individuals, and to the self. The ethical system was complex in its manifestations as Marcus's life was complex. But in its center and centeredness it was simple. That simplicity was its greatest strength, making possible both a depth and clarity of relations which were the source of his great human achievements. At the same time the rational center, in giving order to life, limited what he could experience and become.

Fundamentally, however, this center of reason provided two sources for the ethic of Marcus Aurelius.

1. "That over-all unity which we call the universe" [23]

Nothing was clearer to Marcus than that the multiverse is a universe. All things are interrelated; all are parts of one whole.

> All things are interwoven with one another, and the bond which unites them is sacred; practically nothing is alien to anything else, for all things are combined with one another and contribute to the same order of the universe. The universe embraces all things and is one. [24]

However, although all things are connected, this order is not static but in process.

> Everything that happens is as customary and understandable as the rose in springtime or the fruit in summer. The same is true of disease, death, slander and conspiracy, and all things which delight or pain foolish men.
>
> What happens next is always intimately related to what went before. It is not a question of merely adding up disparate things connected by inevitable succession, but events are logically interdependent. [25]

For Marcus the bond of this order, whether of the rose in springtime or disease and death, is sacred, and his experience of the sacred is related to his recognition of the providential origins of the orderly universe. This providential order is never clearly elucidated, and although he sometimes suggests that nature is providence he generally asserts its transcendence:

> Providence started the process which culminated in the present orderliness of the universe; for Providence had grasped certain rational, creative principles of what was to be, and marked out certain powers generative of substance, changes, and things of the same kind to succeed them.[26]

There is, therefore, a chain of causes so that "whatever befalls you" (we must remember that the "you" refers to Marcus) "was prepared for you from eternity, and the interwoven sequence of causes was spinning your existence from all time, and this event as well."[27] This, in turn, implies a kinship of all natural things which must be understood, for "The man who does not know there is an orderly universe does not know where he is."[28]

Because of this providential order, then, the universe is understandable by reason since it is reason's function to understand the nature of things. And the good life, therefore, is a life according to reason, whose first principle is to "pay attention": "Give your full attention to what is said. Apply your mind to what is being done and to who does it."[29] But the power of reason for Marcus lies not only in the conclusions reason reaches, but also in its method. These together constitute the full and good life: "The man who follows reason in all things is both a person of leisure and prone to action, both cheerful and consistent."[30] These were qualities he had seen and admired in his father, Antoninus Pius.

A life according to reason is necessarily a life in accordance with the universe, including the "universe" of the self. "To live the good life to the end" is the stated theme of one of Marcus's later meditations.[31] This is to recognize that no difficulties which come to him are intolerable.

> If they are in accord with nature, rejoice in them and they will be easy to bear; if they are contrary to nature, find out what is in accord with your nature, and hasten to that, even if it brings you no fame, for every creature is forgiven if it seeks its own proper good.[32]

Thus, to act in accord with nature is to act not only in harmony with the universe but in accord with one's own nature, since it has been endowed with reason.

2. "The directing mind . . . is the principle of life."

Reason in Marcus leads him to extol his "directing mind" or "ruling faculty." The fact that an individual has a "directing mind" is the most important truth about him and is, in fact, the most accurate definition of man since the directing mind "is the source of speech, it is the principle of life; it is, so to speak, the man himself."[33]

As rational will the directing mind is the power by which the individual gives shape to and controls his own life. It is the principle of self-direction and self-control,

> it sees itself, it shapes itself, it makes itself such as it wishes to be, it gathers its own fruit, whereas the fruit of plants and what animals may be said to produce as fruit is gathered by others.[34]

Self-direction is the first consequence of the directing mind since it is the directing mind that makes life what it wishes it to be.

But it is not only that the directing mind actively shapes his life, it is also the means toward the achievement of a primary virtue of Stoicism, self-control. There are times when Marcus suggests that the task of self-control is onerous, but he then excuses himself for being a slow and dull learner. More often it occurs to him, once there has been the learning of how to live in accord with nature, that self-control is simple: "How easy it is to banish and blot out every disturbing or uncongenial impression from the mind and at once to achieve a perfect calm."[35] All that is required is a recognition and rearrangement of thought. "To banish," or "blot out," suggests that his prescription was to reject and not to repress or to work through the troubles which touched him. And this prescription, as we shall see, has a great bearing upon Marcus's relations with others, with himself, and with death.

The self-shaping and self-control present to Marcus the ideal picture of what his life should be.

> As a Roman and a man should, think at all times how you can perform the task at hand with precise and genuine dignity, sympathy, independence, and justice, making yourself free from all other preoccupations. This you will achieve if you perform every action as if it was the last of your life, if you rid yourself of all aimless thought, of all emotional opposition to the dictates of reason, of all pretense, selfishness and displeasure with your lot.[36]

This focus upon the directing mind causes Marcus to have an intense concern for the spirit within. He continually advises himself to look within, to dig down within himself. He rejects the prevalent longing that men have for retreats "in country places, on beaches and mountains" since, he reminds himself, "it is possible at any hour you please to find a retreat within yourself. For nowhere can a man withdraw to a more untroubled quietude than in his own soul. . . . Grant yourself this withdrawal continually, and refresh yourself."[37] What is it that you resent, he asks himself, that can prevent this withdrawal into the self? Human evil? Dissatisfaction with your lot? Physical desires, pains, and pleasures? Fame? None of these, if understood, prevents an inner direction, control, and quietude. "From now on keep in mind the retreat into this little territory within yourself. . . .The universe is change, life is understanding."[38] This turning of the directing mind to itself is, consequently, the way to order adequately the important relations of life: "If you esteem and reverence the mind within you, you will be at peace with yourself, in tune with your fellows, and in harmony with the gods."[39]

THE MORAL RELATIONS OF LIFE

"Yourself, your fellows, the gods:" thus did Marcus characterize the important relations of his life. Self, the social order (including individuals and society), the natural order and its ultimate sources constitute the fundamental realities to which he returns again and again, always trying to locate the fitting place for his life.

1. Moral relations with the universe and "the gods"

It is a basic fact for Marcus that the universe is "an over-all unity." This "fact" is the primary source for his ethic. Now it remains for him to draw out the implications of this for his life. He does this by logical steps though he does not describe those steps in order. There must be a vision of the whole. In this vision there must be recognition of the permeating fact of change. Within and behind all the change, however, there is purpose. With these understandings there can be the acceptance of the whole and of one's life.

Marcus saw that "the whole earth is only a point in space"[40] and turned both to the finite spaces of the earth and the far larger spaces of the universe. But wherever he turned his gaze, he found order, so he believed that the vision of the whole was essential to the moral life. "The nature of the Whole," "the advantage of the Whole," were phrases that continually reverberated in his mind; and he always saw "the Whole" from the standpoint of his own existence, believing that whatever the Whole brought was to be accepted as a gift. All individual things are related to the inclusive reality.

The Whole then exists, but within it change occurs.

> Time is a river of things that become, with a strong current. No sooner is a
> thing seen than it has been swept away, and something else is being carried
> past, and still another thing will follow.[41]

But it is not only that things are "swept away," but that even in their passing
they are in constant change.

> The task of the universal nature is to transfer things from one place to an-
> other to change them, to lift them hence and take them yonder. All things
> are in process of change.[42]

It is important to recognize this fact, for transformations are the way the universe preserves its youth and vigor. The mind, therefore, should be trained to
see and understand change, not for the sake of understanding only, but because, when the self applies this recognition to its own transformations, it
achieves an excellence of mind and act.

Underlying all natural change, Marcus believed, there was purpose. He
did not hesitate to speak of "the aim of nature"; however there is no indication that by the use of this phrase he meant that nature or even "Providence"
was conscious, but that every functioning natural being exists toward its inherent goal. And he believed this "purpose" should become conscious in him.

Marcus continually connected his own life to his vision of the whole, of
its constant change. This led him to advise himself to accept what the fates
held in store for him: "Surrender yourself willingly to Clotho to help her spin
whatever fate she will."[43] Here Marcus's strong sense of himself and his relation to the universe reaches its greatest intensity and inclusiveness. This
emphasis on consciousness has direct implications for his further moral attitudes and behavior as well as his relations with society and self.

2. Moral relations with others

Marcus placed both society and individuals at the center of his moral relations; but while it may have been natural for an emperor to see society as the
locus of primary relations, it is not as evident why an emperor should place
such a high value upon his relations with other individuals.

In seeing human beings as social creatures, Marcus remained within the
central tradition of Greek ethics and Stoic philosophy: "Now the good of a
rational creature lies in community, and it has long ago been shown that we
were born for association in a community."[44] This community is both particular and universal; Marcus reminded himself that he was both a Roman and
a man:

My city and my country, as I am Antoninus, is Rome; as I am a man, it is the world. Therefore, only the things which are beneficial to these communities are good for me.[45]

In terms of his immediate duties as emperor, the political city of Rome had priority. He believed, however, that his most important citizenship was in the universal city and that only through that citizenship could he, or any man, understand why he had duties and what duties he had in his political city. For man is "a citizen of that Whole, the greatest city of which other cities are but households."[46] The vision of the "city of the Whole" haunts him; so he returns to the image again: "The universe is, as it were, a city—for what other common government could one say is shared by all mankind? From this, the common city, we derive our intelligence, our reason and our law— from what else?"[47]

From this ideal of common good arises his sense of duty. A human being's first responsibility is social, to enhance the common good. It was a question that Marcus would ask himself daily. "Have I done something for the common good? . . . This thought you must always keep before you and never give up."[48] But the idea of duty also comes from the acceptance of his position as an integral part of the order of the Whole; so he says to himself, quoting Socrates from memory:

> For this, gentlemen, is the truth: Whatever post a man has himself taken up, thinking it to be best, or has been ordered to take up by his commander, there he must, I think, remain and face danger, without a thought for death or for anything else but the shame of flight.[49]

He takes his position in the city, whether that of Rome or of the universe, because his "directing mind," informing him that he is a social being, tells him to do so. But his directing mind—general in its understanding of universal duties, specific in its understanding of an emperor's duties—also tells him to relate to individuals, and in a remarkable way: "Enter into the directing mind of each man, and allow any other man to enter into yours."[50] As a philosophically reflective emperor there were limits to which Marcus could allow others to enter into his "directing mind." Limits were set, also, by the contemporary understanding of the self and of personal relations. But the spontaneity of Marcus broke through these limiting factors; he opened himself to the approach of others in the way his social situation allowed, by writing to himself, thus enabling others, later, to enter into his "directing mind."

Marcus was a rare political ruler in his attempt to "enter into the directing mind" of others that he might understand them, and in understanding, learn how to rule. He began with his own formulation of traditional Greek beliefs: "rational beings are born for the sake of each other, . . . tolerance is a part of righteousness, and . . . men do not sin on purpose."[51] This attempt to understand the other, whether he acts in ignorance or not, alone enables Marcus to relate properly to the other and to himself. Consequently, the first step in meeting another person is to ask, "What belief does this man hold about good and evil?" For once these fundamental beliefs are understood, his actions will also easily be understood.

Entering into the directing mind of another, into the real bases for his actions, is all the more important, Marcus reminds himself, when he has been wronged. Then, above all, it is important to recognize the motivating beliefs about good and evil:

> Realizing this, you will pity him, be neither surprised nor angry at him. For either you yourself have the same view of good as he, or one like it, and then you must forgive him; if, on the other hand you no longer view good and evil in this way, you will the more easily feel kindly to one who sees things awry.[52]

Marcus thought of all human beings as "kindred" and "friends." One must be careful, therefore, not to destroy kindly feelings toward them or to isolate oneself from them.

In Marcus's observation of others there was the realistic recognition that speech and behavior often conceal hidden motives. To a discerning eye, however, the hidden motives became evident. He was enough of a psychologist to see that beneath social politeness there could be hatred, and beneath an apparent gracious submission, fierce competition. He saw, too, the meaning of double-mindedness which claims to be integrity:

> How rotten and spurious is the man who says: "I have decided to be straightforward with you." What are you doing, fellow? You need not declare this beforehand; the facts will speak for themselves. It need not be stamped on the forehead. Honesty is at once clear from the tone of the voice and the look of the eyes, just as a loved one at once knows all from the glance of his lovers. . . . Calculated simplicity is like a dagger. Nothing is uglier than wolfish friendship. Avoid it at all costs. The good, simple, kindly man looks these qualities; they are seen at once.[53]

3. Moral Relations of the Self with Itself

The characteristics of such simplicity are plain: self-love, self-respect, self-authenticity.

Marcus finds contradictory characteristics in his attitude of the self toward itself. While he generally had a high ideal of his work as emperor, sensing its importance and struggling to meet its obligations, there were times when he was dissatisfied with his work and he saw that as a dissatisfaction with himself.

> You do not love yourself. If you did, you would certainly love your own nature and its purpose. Other men love their own craft and wear themselves out in the performance of it without bath or food. You love your own nature less than the metal worker loves the art of working metals, the dancer the art of dancing, the money-lover his money or the lover of glory his precious reputation. They, in their passionate eagerness, sacrifice good and sleep to promote the objects of their passion, whereas you believe public affairs to be less important and less deserving of devotion.[54]

Yet in spite of his feelings about himself, there is thus a valid self-love, associated with the love of one's proper work. There is also an invalid self-love. It is a love which lacks self-respect, and which seeks to define itself through the eyes of others. "I have often marveled that every man loves himself above all others, yet he attaches less importance to his own idea of himself than to what his neighbors think about him."[55] Thus self-respect for Marcus leads to self-authentication.

It is to love the self as it should be loved, a part of the Whole; to respect the self as it should be respected, related in kindness and justice to others. It is to make one's judgment for one's self and not to heed the judgments of others. One way to do this is to enter the directing minds of others which, at times, can lead one not to respect their judgments. "Find your way into their directing minds and you will see what kind of judges you fear, and what poor judges they are about themselves."[56] But the more important way is to look to the self for its own judgments: "How much ease he gains who does not look at what his neighbor says or does or thinks, but only at what he himself is doing that his own action may be just, pious and good."[57]

That one's actions may be "just, pious and good" means that while in terms of process the self authenticates its own life, from the standpoint of ultimate sources of human good the self can only be authenticated by the Whole. So, at the end and throughout the journey of his meditations, Marcus is where he began: the universe is an ordered Whole, and what is humanly good can only be achieved by the vision of that Whole and of one's life in relation to it. The final truth is the first truth.

> You must therefore welcome with love what happens to you, for two reasons: first, because it happens to you, is prescribed for you, is related to you, a fate spun for you from above by the most venerable of causes; second, because whatever comes to an individual is a cause of the well-being and the welfare, indeed of the permanence, of that which governs the Whole.[58]

4. The Ends of a Moral Life

In the *Meditations* rational order is pervasive. With that presence of reason the emotions are largely missing, even frequently suppressed. This leads one who would enter the directing mind of Marcus to sense an inner bleakness and melancholy, even at times a despair. It is a false sense. The bleakness, the melancholy, the despair exist, but they exist because Marcus was a serious man writing his journal to himself. The blank parchment called for him to be himself, that is, to be serious. He was serious in his life, but he was more than that. He was a man of joy, with a sense of beauty and of pleasure, a man of leisure who was at home in the universe. Most of all, despite the fact that he was plagued by his agnosticism (and willing to confess it in his own private pages whatever he did in his public life), he was a man of religious depth, awed by the Whole and by the fact of his own death.

He saw that different people find joy in different things. But he also had the self-understanding to know the sources of his joy:

> I rejoice if my directing mind is healthy, avoiding no man or anything that happens to men, looking upon everything with kindly eyes, accepting everything and dealing with each on its merits.[59]

He had enough self-respect to believe that his way of finding joy was in harmony with the Universe and that all men could find it so. He knew there were times he did not find joy in his life, so he had to remind himself to seek it in simplicity, to search for self-respect, and to love others. He had a simple formula for what to do when he wanted to rejoice: he merely had to think of his friends:

> When you want to rejoice, think of the good qualities of your associates: the energy of one, the spirit of reverence in another, the liberality of a third, some other quality in a fourth. For nothing gives as much joy as to observe manifestations of virtue in the character of one's associates, the more of them at once, the better. So keep them before your eyes.[60]

He spoke disparagingly of "the persuasive picture of the imagination" and of despising "the activities of the senses."[61] Yet the man who spoke in this way obviously took great delight in beauty. For the Roman emperor who could recognize that "small boys believe a little round ball to be a thing of beauty"; who could write of "sunlight making its way into a dark house through a narrow opening," noting that "it pauses there and does not glide off or fall off"; who could speak of "the rose in springtime or the fruit in summer" surely knew beauty.[62] But there is a longer passage where Marcus, seemingly the most unromantic of men, finds beauty in the simplest things in the universe which is, or is a manifestation of, the Perfect Being which is good, just, and beautiful:

> The incidental results of natural phenomena have charm and attractiveness. For example, when a loaf of bread is being baked, some parts break open, and these cracks, which are not intended by the baker's craft, somehow stand out and arouse in us a special eagerness to eat; figs, too, burst open when they are very ripe, and the very closeness of decay adds a special beauty to olives that have ripened on the tree. The same is true of ears of wheat as they bend to the ground, of the wrinkles of a lion's brow, of the foam flowing from a boar's mouth. . . .The man of feeling and deeper understanding of the phenomena in Nature as a whole will find almost all these incidentals pleasantly contrived. He will look with as much pleasure upon the gaping jaws of actual wild beasts as upon representations of them in painting or sculpture. He will see a kind of fulfillment and freshness in the old, whether man or woman. He will be able to look upon the loveliness of his own slave boys with eyes free from lust.[63]

He had admired the ability of his father, Antoninus Pius, to arrange his business so as to seem to live a life of leisure. But for Marcus this combination of action and leisure was reasonable; it was the same reason that enabled a man to be at home in the universe. And to be at home was to learn to be open to all: "How ridiculous and how much of a stranger in the universe is he who is surprised at anything which happens in his life."[64]

The sense of being at home in the universe is also linked for Marcus to the sense of piety that pervades his thought. Indeed, not to be at home in the world leads to human evil: "The tendency to wrongdoing, to licentiousness, to anger, grief and fear, belongs only to one who has separated himself from Nature."[65] For piety is accepting one's place, and prayer as one of its expressions becomes for Marcus a means to seek the genuine good for either oneself or one's society. The good for oneself is the control of life, and believing that the gods can assist in this achievement, he did not hesitate to counsel that prayer should be for internal direction or for social good. Such prayer was a prayer for all:

> A prayer of the Athenians: "Rain, rain, beloved Zeus upon the fields and the plains of the Athenians." Thus simply we should pray like free men, or not at all.[66]

Death is a theme to which Marcus returned again and again; however, his concerns were not for the death of others or for those who would be left behind. His concerns were exclusively directed to the meaning of death for his life, and he treats that meaning in various ways, all of them directed toward assisting him in the facing of his own death. He recognizes that all of life is a dying, but for Marcus a consciousness of the dying life is preparation for the final death.

> The cessation of an activity, the ending of an impulse and a thought is, as it were, their death. There is no evil in this. Turn your thoughts now to the periods of your life: childhood, adolescence, youth, old age, for every change in these too is a death. Was this a dreadful thing? . . . Neither, in the same way, is the ending, cessation and change of your whole life.[67]

The reminder that all of life is a dying admonishes him to see that "death, like birth, is a mystery of nature." The critical term in this view is "nature," for this means that it is a part of the order of existence. Birth is "a joining together of the same elements into which the other is a dissolution."[68] There is, then, nothing to fear in death, for despite the fact that man is ignorant of its total nature, he does know its relation to nature. But, finally, death is acceptable to Marcus because he trusts his being to the gods.

> There is nothing terrible in leaving the company of men, if the gods exist, for they would not involve you in evil. If, on the other hand, they do not exist or do not concern themselves with human affairs, then what is life to me in a universe devoid of gods or of Providence? But they do exist and do care for humanity, and have put it altogether in a man's power not to fall into real evils.[69]

It is within a man's power not to fall into real evils. This lies at the core of Marcus's understanding, and his meditations to himself were his repeated attempts to discover how one can acquire this understanding. At the end of his life, having used his directing mind to understand and to act, he had come to terms with himself. His final words to himself, written out of a proper self-love and with self-respect, arose from his acceptance of his fate in the universe where he was at home:

> Mortal, you have been a citizen in this great city, what matter to you whether for five years or fifty, for what is in accord with the law is equal for all. What then is there to fear if you are sent away from the city not by a dictator or an unjust judge, but by the same nature which brought you to it, as if the magistrate who had chosen a comic actor were to dismiss him. "But I have not played the five acts, but only three." "You have played well, but in your life at any rate the three acts are the whole play." For he sets the limit who was at one time the cause of your creation, and is now the cause of your dissolution. You have no responsibility for either. So depart graciously, for he who dismisses you is also gracious.[70]

THE UNIQUE CONTRIBUTION OF ROMAN STOICISM

The Roman Stoics made unique contributions to the Western ethic both in content and in form of thinking. Part of this had to do with emphases they placed upon certain aspects of thought, part had to do with new elements they introduced into the thought. In most of his contributions Marcus Aurelius was a representative Roman Stoic, but he in turn went beyond normative Stoicism and added new elements out of his own experience.

(1) Like Roman Stoics generally, Marcus saw that the moral life is prescribed in terms of the relations of the moral agent, but he added a new element when he linked his relations as a moral agent to specific persons. In that remarkable introduction to his *Meditations*, which is unique in the history of moral thought, he reports how special persons taught him how to live ethically and think philosophically. The fact that he did not have a clear concept of the person or of the human personality prevented him from developing this line of thought, but this should not obscure the fact that the idea that ethics arises from the relations of persons is a potentially fruitful concept.

For Marcus, the fact that he could not think personally drove him to the opposite extreme: to the concept of the Whole. He thought of the moral life as a function of being a citizen of Rome, an emperor, a citizen of the world, an individual part of the material universe, or of "Providence." The relations became increasingly abstract and impersonal, and in fact it was one of the most abstract and impersonal, the relations of the human individual to the natural world, that became determinative for his ethics.

(2) "Life according to nature" became the very idea of the Stoic ethic. Thus, through Stoicism, the concept of natural law became a dominant idea in Western ethics. This idea is implicitly present in the Greek philosophers, with particular clarity in Aristotle, but the idea that nature can be the sole source of moral principles had never been enunciated prior to the Stoics. In fact, the Stoics can be said to have incorporated all of moral life into a simple, though obviously significant, formula: *The ethical life = life according to nature = life according to reason = life according to virtue.*

(3) The moral life, therefore, is preeminently a life of responsible relations with or to the universe. In this formula other intermediate responsibilities become important, but their importance is determined by the vision of the whole. The state exists in relation to the universe, so the individual has a responsibility to the political order. All humankind is part of the universe, so the individual has a responsibility to all of humankind. This note of cosmopolitanism, of a universal responsibility, is a distinctive characteristic of Stoicism, and it is especially strong in Marcus.

(4) This responsibility however is focused upon the individual, for it is

the individual who alone has a direct moral responsibility to the natural universe. The individual, then, becomes the focal point for ethics, and consequently the individual's duties to his or her own life is the critical moral problem. There are two sides to these ethical duties: the how and the what. Both, for Stoicism, have clear, simple guidelines in concept though they are not as simple when it comes to living the exemplary life.

(a) Reason is the sole means to moral life. It is reason that must clarify one's relations and direct one's activities, keeping all the dissident elements in order. For it is reason alone that can understand the natural universe. And it is reason alone that can control the irrational elements in the individual or in the political order. Consequently it is responsibility of reason not only to guide the passions or keep them in check, but to strictly control and extirpate them when necessary.

(b) This points toward the "what" of the ethics. The rational life, the life in complete control and indeed the life that directs the passions, becomes the morally good life. This means the moral life is one of equanimity, courage, determination, and nobility.

(5) It is also a life characterized by strict adherence to duty. Though it is difficult to express subtle moral distinctions, there was something new added to Western moral consciousness with the Stoic concept of duty. This newness had to do with the rational, impersonal context out of which the concept arises, giving an absoluteness and tautness to the demand. The Hebrews had the idea of responsibility out of which a notion of duty may develop, but this occurred in a personal and communal context giving a degree of flexibility, despite its imperative, to any developed concept of duty. For the Stoics the responsibility of the duty would often occur within the context of the personal and the communal, but the source of the duty lay elsewhere.

NOTES

1. Edward Gibbon, *The Decline and Fall of the Roman Empire,* ed. J. B. Bury (New York: Fred De Fau and Company, 1906), 1: 99–100.

2. James H. Oliver, *The Ruling Power: A Study of the Roman Empire in the Second Century after Christ Through the Roman Oration of Aelius Aristides* (Philadelphia: The American Philosophical Society, 1953), section 60. (Aristides's oration is cited by section number and the *Meditations,* below, by book and paragraph numbers. Since the numbers for each work are the same in all editions, the page numbers have not been included.)

3. Ibid., section 39.

4. Ibid., section 59.

5. Marcus Aurelius Antoninus, *The Meditations,* trans. G. M. A. Grube (New York: The Bobbs-Merrill Company, Inc., 1963), I:2.

6. Ibid., I:3.

7. Anthony Birley, *Marcus Aurelius* (Boston: Little, Brown and Company, 1966), p. 35.

8. Ibid., 90.

9. Ibid., 96.

10. Ibid., 101–102.

11. Ibid., 121.

12. *The Meditations of Marcus Aurelius Antoninus,* trans. A. S. L. Farquharson, with introduction and notes by R. B. Rutherford (New York: Oxford University Press, 1989), I:17.

13. *Meditations,* I:7 (Grube; all subsequent citations from the *Meditations* are in Grube's translation).

14. Ibid., I:8.

15. Ibid., I:9.

16. Ibid., I:16.

17. Ibid., I:14.

18. Ibid., V:5.

19. Ibid., V:9.

20. Ibid., VII:31.

21. Ibid., VII:67.

22. Ibid., VIII:61.

23. Ibid., VI:25.

24. Ibid., VII:9.

25. Ibid., IV:44,45.

26. Ibid., IX:1.

27. Ibid., X:5.

28. Ibid., VIII:52.

29. Ibid., VII:30.

30. Ibid., X:12.

31. Ibid., XI:16.

32. Ibid., XI:16.

33. Ibid., X:38.

34. Ibid., XI:1.

35. Ibid., V:2.

36. Ibid., II:5.

37. Ibid., IV:3.

38. Ibid., IV:3.

39. Ibid., VI:16.

40. Ibid., VIII:21.

41. Ibid., IV:43.
42. Ibid., VIII:6.
43. Ibid., IV:34.
44. Ibid., V:16.
45. Ibid., VI:44.
46. Ibid., III:11.
47. Ibid., IV:4.
48. Ibid., XI:4.
49. Ibid., VII:45.
50. Ibid., VIII:61.
51. Ibid., IV:3.
52. Ibid., VII:26.
53. Ibid., XI:15.
54. Ibid., V:1.
55. Ibid., XII:4.
56. Ibid., IX:18.
57. Ibid., IV:18.
58. Ibid., V:8.
59. Ibid., VIII:43.
60. Ibid., VI:48.
61. Ibid., VIII:26.
62. Ibid., VI:57; VIII:57; IV:44.
63. Ibid., III:2.
64. Ibid., XII:13.
65. Ibid., XI:20.
66. Ibid., V:7.
67. Ibid., IX:21.
68. Ibid., IV:5.
69. Ibid., II:11.
70. Ibid., XII:36.

4

AUGUSTINE:
THE FAILURE OF THE
CLASSICAL IDEAL

A s we have seen, the classical political ideal was expressed by Plato, who, reflecting upon his failure as a political adviser, arrived at the conviction that there was only one way a state could be satisfactorily ruled.

> Unless either philosophers become kings in their countries or those who are now called kings and rulers come to be sufficiently inspired with a genuine desire for wisdom; unless, that is to say, political power and philosophy meet together . . . there can be no rest from the troubles . . . for states, nor yet, as I believe, for all mankind.[1]

This tenet was an article of faith adopted by the Romans during their military and political victories in the Hellenistic world. With Rome's statesmen and emperors the classical credo became the basis for political activity in the attempt to build an "eternal Rome." But this credo also applied to personal life for the individual of true *virtus*, the Roman concept based upon the Greek *arete*, those qualities of excellence that make human life human. For it was only when the ruling power of life was guided by reason that the ideal person emerged.

This dual belief that a successful social and individual order must rest upon the combination of reason with power was itself based upon other Hellenic assumptions regarding the necessity for order in life, whether of a society or an individual, and upon reason as the sole guide to truth and order.

To these beliefs Rome added an element omitted in Plato and rationalized by other Greeks. This element was belief in the necessity of fortune. In the early empire there was created a religious cult that involved the popular

165

deification of "Luck."[2] The recognition of the Greek concept of *arete* as the basis for political and individual achievement had opened the way for the possibility of a rational interpretation of history, whether social or individual. But to introduce "fortune" as an additional essential principle was to raise doubts about the possibility of reason controlling life. It was to let the nose of the camel of irrationality into the tent of reason.

For years these principles were successful in the shaping of individual lives. They were also successful in enabling Rome to build an orderly empire, from the consolidating efforts of Augustus Caesar, the first Roman emperor (27 B.C.E.–14 C.E.), who declared his one ambition to be the establishment of a permanent republic on the foundations of an ideal constitution; and it continued through the Antonine rulers in the second century (Marcus Aurelius Antoninus, d. 180), an age described by Edward Gibbon as "the happiest and most prosperous period in the history of the human race."[3] But in the third century there was a catastrophic breakdown which

affected every aspect of Roman life. Politically, the situation may be judged from the fact that, of twenty-six reigning emperors, only one escaped violent death. In every section of the Roman world emerged war-lords (the so-called "thirty tyrants"); their rise and fall depending upon the caprice of the troops. The destruction of private quickly followed that of public law. . . .

Political anarchy was accompanied by acute economic and social distress. Plague and famine swept mercilessly across the provinces, depopulating vast areas. The inflation and flight of currency undermined the basis of municipal economy and shook the very foundations of the social system. . . .

The results were not less disastrous in the realm of spiritual and intellectual life. All efforts to maintain a *cordon sanitaire* about Italy finally collapsed; orientalism in its grosser forms broke in wave after wave upon the capital, and there now began in earnest that process of dilution whereby occidental values were to be overwhelmed. Meanwhile, the voice of Greek and Latin literature, which had been heard without interruption for centuries, was almost stilled; and the very silence testifies with eloquence to the wretchedness of the time. Such miserable records as survive point to an intensification of anxiety as the empire plunged into more and more hopeless confusion; and men began to anticipate the actual end of the world. . . .

The *débâcle*, however, was not merely economic or social or political, or rather it was all of these because it was something more. For what here confronts us is, in the last analysis, a moral and intellectual failure, a failure of the Graeco-Roman mind.[4]

The failure of the Graeco-Roman mind was the failure of the basic beliefs to provide an adequate foundation for individual and social life, but it was a century before that spiritual failure was recognized by Augustine

(354–430). The emperors of the fourth century saw that society was in disorder; and the greatest of them, each in his own way, tried to rebuild the republic. But they did not perceive the depth of the failure, nor did they have the inner resources to discover principles upon which a new social and individual life could be based. Constantine (emperor 306–337) attempted to introduce a new principle of integration into the empire by embracing the Christian faith; Julian (361–363) tried to return to the classical ideals; Theodosius (379–395) wanted to be a Christian prince and to create a theocratic state. Constantine and Theodosius were more important in that both tried to use Christianity in their attempts to reconstruct society, and both failed to achieve a synthesis of politics, culture, and religion. They failed because they tried to use Christianity to justify the empire. What Constantine saw in Christianity was a success story, and he attempted to use its success as a divine sanction to reorganize Rome. There was some social reform, but primarily he introduced a new Christian social etiquette while leaving the oppressive military, economic, and political machines to continue their destruction of the middle classes, the backbone of the empire.

Theodosius went further than Constantine in his use of the church as a tool. In the Edict of Thessalonica (380) he expressed the imperial "desire" that all Roman citizens should become Christians, the emperor

> adjudging all others madmen and ordering them to be designated as heretics, . . . condemned as such . . . to suffer divine punishment, and, therewith, the vengeance of that power which we, by celestial authority, have assumed.[5]

There was thus created the "Christian State." The policy of Theodosius, justified now by his belief in divine approval, became more thoroughly despotic than that of earlier emperors. The centralization of power was sanctified, the conscription of men and money in the interests of the state was complete. The heresy hunts ended with the confiscation of property and the defamation of character. The regimentation—economic, social, political, religious—was harsh; and though the measures were aimed at transfusing new blood into the life of a wounded society, the net result of Theodosian policies was to drain Rome of "the last reserves of moral and physical energy which it possessed."[6]

The year after the death of Theodosius, in 396, Jerome viewed the events of his time with shock and fear:

> The mind shudders to contemplate the ruin of our time. For the last twenty years, the blood of Romans has drenched the lands between Constantinople and the Julian Alps, where innumerable and ferocious tribes spread devastation and death. . . . The bodies of the free and noble, of matrons and vir-

gins have become the prey of lust. Bishops are imprisoned; churches plun-
dered; horses have been stabled at the altars of Christ; the bones of martyrs
flung out of their coffins. . . . Everywhere grief, everywhere lamentation,
everywhere the shadow of death![7]

Ten years later Gaul was invaded and permanently occupied by the Goths.
No longer was there a sharp division between the culture of civilization and
barbarism. In 410 Rome was conquered, "the light of the world was put out
and the head of the empire was cut off."[8] The invasion of Rome was symbolic
of the end of a civilization. The anguish of the good Roman was almost un-
endurable, particularly those Roman Christians who had viewed with hope
and joy the emperors' embrace of the faith. Augustine was one of those for
whom the destruction of Rome meant the destruction of that hope and that joy.

AUGUSTINE'S LIFE AND POINT OF VIEW

Augustine, who had assumed the Roman empire would forever maintain its
mastery of the world, felt the sack of Rome as a disaster. He had been partially prepared for the event by his observation of social trauma as a provin-
cial bishop responsible for civil society, but that scarcely lessened his shock
and dismay. He had been more prepared for the meaning of the débâcle by
his own personal disasters years before.

Augustine made a genuine attempt to build his life on the classical ideal
inherited from Greece. He struggled for years to base his thinking and life
upon the truth of the assumption that reason could create an ideal human
order. That attempt ended for him in abject failure. Neither his experiences
nor the resultant philosophy can be understood apart from a recognition of
the seriousness with which he had tried to accept the bases of classical
thought and his interpretation of his failure. He was not convinced rationally
of the inadequacy of the classical assumptions. There were, rather, the two
painful experiences, both occurring over a number of years, that forced him
to give up the perspectives of Greece and to find new presuppositions for his
life and thought. These were the personal failure of his inner life, including
his relations with others, and the social disaster of his times.

Augustine's childhood in North Africa was uneventful, with the usual boyhood escapades and distaste for school. When he was nineteen he was inspired
to study philosophy by reading Cicero's (now lost) *Hortensius*. "This book,"
Augustine said, "changed my affections," and it was significant for his moral
experience that he spoke first of changed affections and not ideas. There began
an insatiable longing for truth:

I was stirred up and enkindled and set aflame to love, and pursue, and attain and catch hold of, and strongly embrace not this or that sect, but wisdom itself, whatsoever it might be.[9]

His aim was that of the philosophers, to possess truth and to live the good life by the light of that truth.

He was successful, as his fellows measured success, in both attempts. In his search for a satisfactory metaphysical and ethical system he went to Manicheanism, a materialistic dualism that involved universal conflict between light and darkness, goodness and evil. For about ten years Augustine was a member of that dogmatic sect, but he finally left because neither his intellectual nor moral self found satisfaction. (Later he was to say, "I despaired of making progress in that false doctrine."[10]) He embraced skepticism for several years, only finding his way out of that despairing faith when he studied Plotinus, who had proclaimed a spiritual monism with a place for the rational, aspirational spirit of human beings; and Plotinus remained central for his beliefs. In his personal life Augustine was, by prevailing social standards, a good citizen. But while appearing successful to his friends, he could not hide from himself that he had failed miserably to reach either truth or goodness. Platonism was an important part of his philosophy throughout his life; yet he found it deficient as an interpretation of the world, an explanation of how individuals reach truth, and a guide to the good life. In his early thirties he felt the greatest defect in Platonism to be the same as that in all classical philosophy: reason alone could not provide an intelligible interpretation of and an adequate motive to live toward an ultimate good. It thus failed to satisfy his deeply felt personal needs. Augustine was dismayed that, while possessing philosophical wisdom, he could not control his feelings, and that indeed he was morally inferior to many ignorant monks who possessed self-control. He was disquieted by his discovery that his professed desire for truth was not sincere since, vain and proud, he sought popularity and social approval.

In retrospect, perhaps twenty-five years after it happened, a simple event in Augustine's boyhood became symbolic of his whole existence. The way he analyzed that experience, turning it this way and that, looking at its outer manifestations and ruthlessly examining his motives, was typical of Augustine's way of thinking, a way that possessed both self-conscious intensity and philosophic sophistication. When he was sixteen he, with some friends, took great pleasure in stealing and wantonly wasting some pears from a neighbor's orchard. In reflection he found in that experience the human fascination which evil possessed, that he loved sin "for the sin's sake," and that this enjoyment was produced by the company of his fellows.[11] This discovery of the socially conditioned will to sin became a permanent part of his life-view.

When he was thirty-two, in 386, discouraged with his inability to reach truth and a satisfying life, Augustine had an experience that was a turning point for his life. The experience itself was but the culmination of a long process of inner doubts, of philosophical perplexity, and moral self-despair. The impact of the moral courage and intelligence of Ambrose, then bishop of Milan, was crucial in leading to his conversion. (It was typical of Augustine that persons and affections preceded ideas in his transformations and growth.) In Ambrose Augustine found a moral authority that could defy the Roman emperor, an intelligence that was the equal of contemporary philosophers, and an attractive personality. No matter what the complex causes of his conversion were, there can be no doubt about the effects, which were psychological, philosophical, and religious. His psychological interests were redirected, his philosophical perspective was altered, and both these changes were intense because the new orientation was religious. It was religious not merely because it was connected with a historical religion, but primarily because Augustine was grasped by a new comprehension of what, for him personally, was an ultimate, an inescapable truth. The worship of this persuasive God became the basis for ways of living and thinking, with transformations of his old passions and thoughts.

The assumptions of that viewpoint can be stated with simplicity, but their consequences were exceedingly complex.

1. God is the ground of truth.

God was conceived of as pure being and spirit. What happened to Augustine in the acceptance of his new first principle was that he accepted the classical ideal of the objectivity of truth but rejected the notion that reason was sufficient to reach that truth. The causes through which he felt it necessary both to accept and reject the classical ideal were plain.

The assumptions of the philosophers regarding reason had led, historically, to schools of dogmatism and skepticism. Augustine, at different times, had belonged to each school. He had accepted the dogmatism of the Manichees only to find that he could not make progress in it either intellectually or personally. In reaction he had adopted skepticism, that all "knowledge" lacked certainty and was, at best, only probable. But to be skeptical this far was equally impossible since to say "all knowledge possesses only degrees of probability" was to say much more, for there could be no meaning to probability unless there was a standard by which the mind could have certain knowledge. For how could one say, "This is more probable than that" unless one had knowledge of a criterion with which the "this" and "that" might be compared? This standard, which might be only implicit and which Augustine contended cannot be defined, was God, who thus became the ground of truth.

Again, to the skeptics, who pointed out the inaccuracy of sense-perceptions and the illusions of some mental operations, Augustine replied that he was absolutely certain of the truth of his existence, his knowledge of his existence and of his will.

> I am most certain that I am and that I know and delight in this. In these truths I am not at all afraid of the Academicians who say, What if you are deceived? For if I am deceived, I am. For he who is not cannot be deceived; and if I am deceived by this same token I am . . . . Since, therefore, I, the person deceived should be, even if I were deceived, certainly I am not deceived in this knowledge that I am. And consequently, neither am I deceived, in knowing that I know. For in knowing that I am, so I also know this, that I know. And when I love these two things, I add to them a certain thing, namely, my love, which is of equal moment. For neither am I deceived in this, that I love, since in those things which I love I am not deceived; though even if these were false it would still be true that I *loved* false things.[12]

Since Augustine knew that he was not autonomous, his knowledge, just as his being and will, must have an ultimate standard and source, and for him this was God, the ground of truth. Moreover, Augustine believed that this dialectic led to the knowledge of God. For when the mind made distinctions between true and false, that was to admit that there was something objective to and superior to the mind. This was God.

Augustine never supposed that the relation of the mind to God as the principle of truth was solely intellectual. He did not see knowledge as existing for its own sake but only for life's sake. In both living and knowing the will held primacy over reason, and the conviction that he had to believe in order to understand meant basically that there first had to be trust that alone made possible insight into truth.[13] The trust that there was truth to be known and lived, the confidence in a ground of truth was essential for the discovery of knowledge. From the outset reason had to have an ally in the will. Those who did not arrive at knowledge may have made errors in their reasoning, or they may have had a deficient will (that is, they may not love the truth enough), or they may have been defective in both their reasoning and their love. This was true for knowledge in any area, but it was seen as especially true for knowledge in those areas such as theology and ethics where there could be no absolute certainty.

This primary principle of Augustine had two significant implications. First, there was the combination of Greek and Hebrew motifs in his recognition of God as the ground of truth, and second, there was a radical reorientation of the understanding of philosophic reason, or of the roles of reason and faith and of reason and insight. This latter point led to the view that, as God is the ground of truth, so God illumined the mind. Augustinian "illumination" was not a mysticism in the sense that through a unique experience one attained ineffable knowledge. It was, rather, the view that the rational, objective approach of classicism was deficient for two reasons. First, that approach could not be viewed as purely rational since it required a proper will; and, second, the subject-object approach was insufficient since it failed to take in large areas of crucial human experience. It could not, for example, deal adequately with human values. Objective reason could describe and analyze values, but it could not provide the basis for valuing values. For that the affections, the will, the love of the person was required as well as an object of these with whom the self could enter into inquiring relations. Thus, God as the ground of truth led to the second and third perspectives of Augustine.

2. God is the supreme good.

As the supreme good, God was thought of in terms of being and will. Here, once more, there was the synthesis of Greek and Hebrew thought. The objectivity of good was recognized, and with this recognition the possibility of developing, at least partially, a philosophic ethic, but the major emphasis was placed upon the Hebraic aspect of will.

If God was the supreme good, then the classical assumptions became distortions of the truth. Reason could not control the dissident elements in individual and social life, and reason and power together, even when fortune was added, could not create a good society or individual. Some greater influence and a more personal factor were required. That influence and factor clearly came to Augustine through his interpretation of the Christian faith.

In his theology Augustine did not develop a careful Christology. He accepted the Nicene formula though he had difficulties with it, attempting to make the Trinitarian concept intelligible by reference to the inner life, and while in his theological treatises he did not make detailed statements about Jesus as the Christ, in his prayers and sermons it was quite otherwise. They are permeated with references to Jesus as Christ, and when he thought of God as the sovereign good, it was the God he first glimpsed in Platonism but had come to comprehend in the church through the memory of the Hebrew faith and of Jesus. This personal way of comprehending led to a third basic presupposition.

3. God can be found in the inner life.

Augustine's interpretation of God as the ground of truth and as the supreme good formed the major assumptions for all of his mature life and thought. ("It is good for me to cleave to God" was the theme of his life.[14]) But there was another presupposition that, related to the first two, shaped Augustine's method of thought, providing both him and his readers the possibility of feeling and understanding his ideas. It was the original notion that *the inner life provides the proper clue to the most complete understanding, religious and philosophical.* Thus the unique experiences of the individual became both a model for and response to the divine being and activity, and that inner life pointed toward a valid interpretation of what actually happened in the world.

The results of this outlook were astonishing. For Augustine it freed the mind from preoccupation with things (though the delight in things remained) and turned it toward an interest in the inner life. There was a self-consciousness in Augustine that was unknown by any of the classical philosophers or Hebrew prophets. This self-consciousness led to a new view of the significance of selfhood and to a unique analysis of moral experience.

There was no dichotomy between Augustine the man and Augustine the philosopher, for both were grounded in a God who had disclosed himself as the sole satisfying basis for life. From this perspective Augustine's famous prayer: "Thou has formed us for Thyself, and our hearts are restless till they find rest in Thee,"[15] can be seen as beginning with God or, from his viewpoint, with a God who had begun with him. Every event was then related to this Being. Every event and every object therefore had a divine truth and a divine value. It was the task of a life to search diligently for both the truth and the worth.

Augustine was willing to make the search according to any method he could find that was allowed by the problem. Thus in his search he employed sense perception, rational analysis, inference, and objective interpretation. However, no matter how much he might intertwine them, he did not substitute one method for another, and he was especially insistent that being, loving, willing, and knowing could not be reduced to, or explained away, by any amount of objective description. He developed rationally the implications of his basic assumptions for understanding human life and the world; he compared, again by rational analysis that included much sensory perception, this understanding with the contemporary condition of human life in the world; he explained the discrepancies between the two by rigorous examination of his inner experience, checking to see whether his experience corresponded with that of others; and he developed his hopes for the future on the basis of the conflict between the present actual life and his basic assumptions.[16]

Augustine created two types of writing, subjective and objective. The two are never entirely distinct, for there was always much philosophical thought in his most personal expressions and he, as a person, was never far removed from his most abstruse reflections. The first type of writing was characterized by such books as the *Confessions* and *Soliloquies* (he coined the term "soliloquy" and the style of inner dialogue), the latter by *The City of God* and *On the Trinity*. His ethic was primarily his life, and, therefore, to understand his ethic it is necessary first to examine that expression of his life, the *Confessions*. It will then be possible to ask objective questions interpreting his ethic, questions that can only be answered from various sources since, though he had a coherent philosophical ethic, he never brought his rational ethic adequately together in one writing.

THE ETHICAL LIFE OF THE *CONFESSIONS*

Augustine's dramatic conversion was in 386 when he was thirty-two years of age. He was made bishop of Hippo in 395, and the *Confessions* were written between 397 and 400, eleven to fourteen years after the conclusion of the final events they describe. The first five chapters are reflections occurring at the time of his writing. The remainder of Books I through IX was his autobiography from infancy to his conversion, and to the death of his mother who had been so crucial in his life. The remarkable Book X contains his present reflections on events now more than a decade old, and the last three books are theological and philosophical observations.

Augustine's primary ethic was his life; and the *Confessions*, especially the first ten books, presents that moral life in a way that no previous autobiography had. When he was seventy-four Augustine said of the *Confessions*, which had been written thirty years previously, "they still move me, when I read them now, as they moved me when I first wrote them."[17]

He wanted to discover, to remember, to declare all that he had felt and done that had been his essential self. "Bear with me I beseech Thee, and give me grace to retrace in my present remembrance the circlings of my past errors."[18] The search was one continual prayer, for which Augustine had been prepared by previous philosophers, especially Plotinus with his view of the self's aspiring, striving, and remembering. "In venturing an answer," said Plotinus, "we first invoke God himself, not in loud words but in that way of prayer which is always within our power, leaning in soul towards Him by aspiration, alone towards the alone."[19] The natural striving of the soul to reach its source was because the soul "is a partial thing, isolated, weakened, full of care, intent upon the fragment."[20] The soul can return to its source only by remembering. But the soul's journey that was for Plotinus wordless, mystical, and with a general memory of metaphysical origins became for Augustine filled with words, and the specific memories of an individualized self in relation to a Being that was personal. The journey for Plotinus had been metaphysical; for Augustine it was historical. Augustine was probably the first person to recognize and believe that "there is no history but that of the soul, no peace but that of the soul."[21] Consequently for Augustine, the history of the soul is the history not only of its thoughts but far more of its feelings. The story of the heart is the truest autobiography, and the life of feeling is the most real life of the self. If there will be the transformation and growth of the self it must be the transformation and growth of feeling.

For Augustine this understanding of the inner life was the key to truth. Yet that inner life could never be fully known. "There is something further in man which not even that spirit of man which is in him knows."[22] It was that "something further" that Augustine always sought to know, and this restless wanting and searching was a primary characteristic of his moral life, this yearning to take the heart deep. This continual growth of depth in the heart was at the center of what it meant to be human. To find that depth, to explore it with God, to share that depth with others and to encourage it within their own lives were the basic reasons for the *Confessions*.

But for whom was the *Confessions* written? First, for Augustine's friends.

> But what I am at this time, at the very moment of making my confessions, divers people desire to know, both who knew me and who knew me not— who have heard of or from me—but their ear is not at my heart, where I am whatsoever I am. They are desirous, then, of hearing me confess what I am within, where they can neither stretch eye, nor ear, nor mind. . . .
>
> But for what fruit do they desire this? Do they wish me happiness when they learn how near, by Thy gift, I come unto Thee; and to pray for me when they learn how much I am kept back by my own weight. To such I declare myself. . . . Let the fraternal soul . . . which, when it approves me, rejoices for me, but when it disapproves me, is sorry for me; because whether it approves or disapproves it loves me. To such I will declare myself.[23]

His audience had been prepared for his writing by popular "religious autobiography," but that audience had never seen anything like what Augustine gave them. He was conscious of their presence and how they might react, using the familiar terms for them as *servi Dei*, "servants of God," and *spiritales*, "spiritual ones"; and he was aware, too, that the autobiographies with which they were familiar, originating among Greek and Roman philosophers and then taken over by Christian writers, consisted of highly stylized challenges, temptations, wanderings, thoughts of death, and triumphs. He knew his search and writing, though based upon tradition, broke with it: "Thy spiritual ones blandly and lovingly smile at me if they shall read these my confessions."[24]

Augustine was relaxed in thinking of such friends, for he loved conversation with them and he had an extraordinary ability for friendship. In his youth he was deeply shaken by the death of a friend, and by that death hated all things he saw because his eyes could no longer "say to me, 'Behold, he is coming,' as they did when he was alive and absent. I became a great puzzle to myself."[25] He referred appreciatively to Faustus, the Manichean teacher, whom he liked despite great disagreements. He admired Ambrose (though he was "less lively and entertaining" than Faustus),[26] and was profoundly influenced by his learning and life; although he was puzzled by many of Ambrose's actions, still he was convinced that "whatever his motive in so doing, doubtless in such a man was a good one."[27] He wrote at length of Alypius, a boyhood friend who later became a lawyer, judge, then bishop, and of their long friendship. In fact, it was in the presence of Alypius that Augustine was "converted." And he omitted no disclosure, however painful or pleasant, of conflicts and companionship with his mother with whom, after a deep conversation shortly before her death, he shared a vision, "that moment of understanding, for which we sighed."[28]

Augustine's friendships, then, were an essential part of his moral life, for they were the expression of feeling that was his core moral experience. His understanding of friendship was his ethic. He had great delight in the pleasure, in the companionship of friends, and in the satisfactions they gave. But he knew that, "If souls please thee, let them be loved in God; for they also are mutable, but in Him are they firmly established."[29] This meant for him the friend had to be loved in his or her relation with God, that is, in terms of the real self. The friend must be loved unselfishly, wanting the good of the other, giving freedom to the other. With such a friend, in sharing the best cause for life, devotion to God, to truth, to *caritas,* Augustine's daily life was transformed and renewed. It was for such friends that he wrote the *Confessions,* thinking of them as "brothers," "fellow citizens in that eternal Jerusalem," and "fellow pilgrims":

> Such is the benefit from my confessions, not of what I have been, but of what I am, that I may confess this not only before you in secret exultation with trembling and in secret sorrow with hope, but also in the ears of believing sons of men, partakers of my joy and sharers in my mortality, my fellow citizens and pilgrims with me, and those who follow me, and those who are companions on my journey. They are your servants, my brothers, whom you will to be your sons; my masters, whom you have commanded me to serve if I would live by you.[30]

Friends, in whose companionship Augustine delighted all of his life, were the most obvious audience for the *Confessions,* but the deeper audiences were God and the self. It was to God that he wrote, and for God. Augustine yearned for an intimate relation with God that he might both know and adore Being as truth and good. These he could find only by addressing God. "Lord, grant me to know and understand which is first, to call upon you or to praise you, and also which is first, to know you or to call upon you."[31] Augustine always had difficulty with his loves, and it was only through his speaking to God, with the accompanying knowledge and adoration, that his loves could be, again and again throughout life, reordered aright. This meant that he was his own audience, that the *Confessions* were written to himself and for himself. The writing was a long series of acts of therapy.[32] But the crises Augustine faced in his middle years were different from those that led to his conversion more than ten years previously. Moreover, during this time the therapy was occurring outside as well as within the writing, for, as Augustine believed, there was always activity in the recesses of the soul, and the moral task of enlarging and ordering life was never completed.

But why, more than a decade after his conversion, did Augustine continue to need guidance and motivation? Clearly it was because at the time of his writing his life was still not under control. Earlier he had the classical expectation that reason could control his unruly desires and feelings giving order to life. Those expectations had failed, and were replaced by the expectation that Christian faith could order his passionate life. After his conversion the first words he read, "as if before a peaceful light streaming into my heart," were those of Paul:

Not in rioting and drunkenness, not in chambering and impurities, not in strife and envying; but put you on the Lord Jesus Christ, and make not provision for the flesh and its concupiscences.[33]

The concupiscences, modified and driven inward, continued in the form of the three lusts of the flesh, the eyes, and the pride of life.[34] Augustine had given up his mistress and the possibility of marriage, yet in his memory "there still live images of such things as my habits implanted there," and he was troubled that he still had sexual dreams so that the images in sleep "assail me not only so as to arouse pleasure, but even consent and something like the deed itself."[35] He disciplined himself in eating and drinking, yet "sometimes gluttony creeps upon your servant."[36] The eyes took delight in "fair and varied forms and bright and beauteous colors," but the lust of the eyes was to love such beauty too much; and such a love he had so that the sunlight which "beguiles me while engaging in some other task" so filled his life that "if it is suddenly withdrawn, it is sought for with longing, and if it is long absent, it causes mental depression."[37] The lust of the eyes also led to delight with frivolous observations. But it was the pride of life that was most troublesome.

But, O Lord . . . hath this third kind of temptation left me, or can it leave me during this life? The desire to be feared and loved of men, with no other view than that I may experience a joy therein which is no joy. . . .[38]

This need for praise, the enduring problem of living with others while having pride in himself, was perplexing to him. "For in other kinds of temptations I have some sort of power of examining myself, but in this hardly any."[39] More than a decade after his conversion, Augustine had lost the illusion that either reason or faith could provide a perfect control of life or a clear perception of truth.

> Whoever thinks that in this mortal life a man may so disperse the mists of bodily and carnal imaginings as to possess the unclouded light of changeless truth, and to cleave to it with the unswerving constancy of spirit wholly estranged from the common ways of life—he understands neither what he seeks, nor who he is who seeks it.[40]

Augustine saw his life, and that of his spiritual companions, as a pilgrimage, but midway in life, indeed, throughout his life, he needed guidance and motivation to continue his inner and outer moral journey. What, then, were his purposes in writing the *Confessions*? And what was the ethical life reflected in and created through the *Confessions*?

Some answers to these questions have been suggested. Augustine wanted to find guidance for his life, he desired to help his friends, he yearned for truth and for God. But the most urgent reason was that he wanted to bring his life together, he longed for an order that provided fulfillment and peace. In the process of satisfying this need he made his greatest moral discovery, that the highest human ideal is the creation of a moral self, a creation that occurs only through the interaction of God, other persons, society, and the individual. This, for Augustine, was the most important human responsibility and gift. And the most complete moral self would be the unifying, the integrating of the self with its past, present, and future as well as the harmonizing of the self's inner and outer life.

Augustine's most basic human want was for happiness, and he thought this true of all persons.

> Nor is it I alone or a few others who wish to be happy, but truly all; which unless by certain knowledge we knew, we should not wish with so certain a will ... so do all men agree in their wish for happiness, as they would agree, were they asked, in wishing to have joy—and His joy they call a happy life.[41]

Yet most persons fail to recognize how this happiness can be achieved. It could only come through a concern for the self and its fullness of life.

> A great admiration rises upon me; astonishment seizes me. And men go forth to wonder at the heights of mountains, the huge waves of the sea, the broad flow of the rivers, the extent of the ocean, and the courses of the stars, and omit to wonder at themselves.[42]

Only through memory can the self's past and present be known, reconciled, shaped into one self that can live toward the future, its outer and inner worlds ordered harmoniously. When this highest moral ideal is realized—never perfectly, never completely, always in need of deepening and reordering—happiness and God are reached simultaneously.

> For when I seek you, my God, I seek the happy life. . . . Wheresoever I found truth, there I found my God, truth itself, and since I first learned the truth I have not forgotten it. . . . Too late have I loved you, O Beauty so ancient and so new, too late have I loved you! Behold, you were within me, while I was outside. . . . You were with me, but I was not with you.[43]

There were clear consequences of this wanting, and living, and writing. For the *Confessions* do not present a philosophical ethic; they express and contain a moral life. There were five primary new qualities of that life. While they had their roots in the philosophical and religious past, their particular creation was unique in Augustine.

(1) There was a recollection of life in the religious sense of achieving wholeness through memory. The full self was harmonized: the total self of past, present, and anticipated future; of unconscious and conscious; of inner and outer; of feelings, thoughts, and actions. With that deep remembrance of self new energies were released, fresh directions were found.

(2) There was the discovery of the self, that is, of personality. The inner life was that self's abode. The "I," the "me," the "my," and "mine" became important. Yet there was not in Augustine a morbid preoccupation with self because his attention was focused not upon the self but through the self upon God. It is in the self where God and truth reside; it is here they were to be found. With this discovery of the self a new emphasis, unknown in previous thought, was given to individuality.

(3) There was the discovery of other persons, of interpersonal relations. For what is characteristic of other persons is that they have their own inner and outer worlds, worlds that are unique to each self, yet worlds that can be shared.

(4) There was the discovery of social power, that social institutions and groups have enormous influence over the life of the person, an influence often for evil.

(5) There was the more ambiguous rediscovery of the passionate beauty of the world. It was ambiguous because Augustine never overcame his fear of being overcome by beauty, of loving the world too much rather than God. But his sense of beauty, including the nostalgic love for his mistress, was ever-present throughout his reports of his experience.

These new elements were woven together in Augustine's moral life, and that life became the basis for his attempts to develop a religious and philosophical ethic.

AUGUSTINE'S RELIGIOUS AND PHILOSOPHICAL ETHIC

Augustine's ethic centered around a group of questions, the first of which is the most important: What is the nature of human beings and society? The others are: What is the norm for a moral judgment? How is the moral good known in a specific situation? How is the moral good achieved?

1. What is the nature of human beings and society?

Augustine's ethical thought developed from his interpretation of God, and it cannot be understood apart from the ultimate theological presuppositions. From his comprehension of God he arrived at an understanding of human nature basic for his ethics. He presented both structural and functional definitions of the individual human being, that is, he described human beings in terms of their metaphysical nature and the existential consequences of that nature, thus providing an analysis of what an individual is and does.

First of all, human beings are made in the "image of God." This religious terminology appears to be a definition of what a human being is, but Augustine uses it ambiguously to refer both to what human beings are and what they do. It thus provided a unique synthesis of basic Greek and Hebraic ideas.

(a) The "image of God" refers to the human possession of reason, and it is this that distinguishes a human being from the animals.

> We behold the face of the earth furnished with terrestrial creatures, and man, created after Thy image and likeness, in that very image and likeness of Thee (that is, the power of reason and understanding on account of which he was set over all irrational creatures).[44]

Now in common usage, an "image" can refer both to a reflection and to an object. In the first case, the reflection of an image in the water or in a mirror depends solely upon the presence of the thing which creates the image. In the second, where the object is a picture or a sculpted work, the image can exist independently of its creator. Augustine interpreted human beings in the "image of God" in both senses; he thought of the two views as complementary, and neither, for him, could be properly understood apart from the other.

(b) To the possession of reason Augustine added, with characteristic originality and extreme importance, the will. Thus, it is not merely "the power of reason and intelligence" that distinguishes human beings but the rational will, i.e., their active reasoning and choosing.

> But the character of the human will is of moment; because, if it is wrong, these motions of the soul will be wrong, but if it is right, they will be not

merely blameless, but even praiseworthy. For the will is in them all; indeed, none of them is anything else than will.[45]

With this definition it is obvious that both Greek and Hebrew ideas were combined, and that for Augustine human beings were the "image of God" both structurally and existentially. He thought that human beings were basically good because they possessed being, and although this concept was typically Greek, Augustine did not define "being" in the predominantly Hellenic category of rationality. For him human beings were valued as good because they possessed rational will and therefore they could respond to God's activity. Essentially, therefore, human beings were good both in their being and in their capacity for active relations with the ultimate Being.

While Augustine began his view of humanity with this combined Greek-Hebrew outlook, the Hebraic perspective was much more important for his ethic. This is revealed through the next steps in his comprehension of human life. Those steps refer to (i) the proper objects of the human rational will; (ii) the distortion of the rational will; and (iii) his view of human freedom.

(i) Human beings are made to love. The possibility of love is found in the rational will. The proper objects of love are God, the neighbor, and (although Augustine said it in a peculiar sense) the self.

There are two diverse factors that motivate individuals to love properly: (*a*) The first is by responding to the example of Christ and the command of God.

> For so we should be prepared also to die profitably for our brethren, as our Lord Jesus Christ taught us by His example. For as there are two commandments on which hang all the Law and the prophets, love of God and love of our neighbor; . . . he who loves God must both needs do what God has commanded, and loves Him just in such proportion as he does so . . . he who loves his neighbor must needs also love above all else love itself. . . . Therefore he must needs above all else love God.[46]

(*b*) But Augustine also thought of love as arising from the needs of the individual who loves. This was the Greek *arete*, the Roman *virtus,* which included a noble regard for the self. Love arises from the needs of the self; love is therefore directed ultimately toward the self. But Augustine never thought of the self's real needs in terms of selfishness, and the ultimate object of love for him was never the self.

> Neither let that further question disturb us, how much of love we ought to spend upon our brother, and how much upon God: incomparably more upon God than upon ourselves, but upon our brother as much as upon ourselves; and . . . therefore we love ourselves so much the more, the more we love God. Therefore we love God and our neighbor from one and the same love;

but we love God for the sake of God, and ourselves and our neighbors for
the sake of God.[47]

The needs of the self can only be met not by self-conscious seeking but by
"love of love itself" which would be living for the sake of God. Only in this
way, thought Augustine, would people's thoughts and loves toward themselves and their neighbors be properly ordered.

(ii) While the real needs of human beings cannot be met by a self-conscious seeking for the good of the self but only by a regard for the neighbor
and, ultimately, a love for God, the will of an individual invariably chooses to
love the self. There is thus a distortion of the rational will. Its love, originally
good, dependent upon God, and directed toward God through proper love, becomes improperly turned to the self, thus attempting to declare its independence from God and so becomes corrupted. In this interpretation Augustine
added a singularly new point of view. The rational will of human beings is
good, but the rational will chooses wrongly. It is the very best in human life
that fails and the highest powers of human beings that are corrupted.

It is through the desire for independence that the rational will prefers the
wrong object. In recognizing this about human nature,

> Augustine was the first real psychologist for he was the first to see the basic
> fact about human nature, namely that the Natural Man hates nature, and that
> the only act which can really satisfy him is the *acte gratuite*. . . . His ego
> seeks constantly to assert its autonomy by doing something of which the re-
> quiredness is not given, that is to say, something which is completely arbi-
> trary, a pure act of choice. . . . In addition to wanting to feel free, man wants
> to feel important, and it is from the immediately given feelings with which
> he identifies himself that the natural man derives his sense of self-impor-
> tance. In consequence he is in a dilemma, for the more he emancipates him-
> self from the given necessity, the more he loses his sense of importance and
> becomes a prey to anxiety.[48]

The consequences of the human desire for independence and choice of
the self were thought of by Augustine as psychological, moral, and metaphysical. Psychologically the choices of an individual become vitiated, so the
individual (*a*) becomes unable to love what is good. This is because all action arises from the rational will, and when the root source of action is corrupted the individual cannot, by effort or thought, transform the will and
change its action. Placing the self in the center also means that the individual
(*b*) is unable to know what is good. The moral vision is distorted by a false
perspective. Along with this lack of knowledge (*c*) there is continuous dissatisfaction. With insatiable desires only partially capable of being fulfilled
the individual oscillates between groundless naive joy and absurd anxiety.

Morally diseased, the will by itself cannot understand, choose, or strive for good. Metaphysically, the distortion of the will (*d*) involves a loss of being. Originally good, the rational will had a place in the metaphysical scheme of things, and it retained its status as long as it reasoned and loved from its goodness. But the evil will is deficient, and this means that its metaphysical status has been changed.

Augustine maintained that in order to break these psychological bonds, to transform the moral corruption, and to recover the essential metaphysical status, a fresh creative act is required. It must be a genuine creation, and, therefore, though it may occur in human beings it is not created by them. God must do for an individual what, alone, an individual cannot perform for herself.

(iii) Augustine's concept of freedom was related to these first two existential stages. Freedom may be thought of as: (*a*) *absolute self-determination,* that with a metaphysical indeterminism the self is able to make unlimited decisions, even the decision to become a different kind of person; (*b*) *limited self-determination,* that within a given metaphysical system the self can control its desires; (*c*) *psychological desire-realization,* which means that with certain desires having been given and certain choices having been made, the self is able to satisfy those desires and choices; and (*d*) *individual autonomy,* meaning that within society the self is not limited by improper external compulsion. For Augustine (*a*) absolute self-determination never existed, and it is precisely the attempt to assert its existence that gets the self into trouble. (*b*) A limited self-determination exists so long as the desires are properly ordered. When the choice is made to be unlimited in desire, that is, when the self wills to be autonomous loving the self, the freedom of even limited self-determination is lost. (*c*) Such destruction of freedom affects the psychological desire-realization though this is in part retained. (*d*) But Augustine believed there should always be individual autonomy, the right to the freedom from improper external force.

These interpretations of freedom were woven into the fabric of Augustine's ethical views and have had a significant impact on Western ethical life. First, freedom, rightly understood, is always a good. Every individual originally possesses the important types of freedom, and it is only by this freedom that the self can remain truly human properly valuing human individuality. Second, there is no such thing as unlimited freedom. There is a certain givenness to human nature and human beings must live and choose within the framework of what is given. Central to this givenness is the fact that their freedom is limited by their love or loyalty. If human love is appropriately directed toward God it is limited by the object of that love. Third, Augustine's view of human freedom gave creative impetus to the life of the person in thought, in personal relations, and in politics. Human beings cannot be circumscribed by human authoritarianism.

> Being renewed in his mind, and beholding and apprehending Thy truth,
> man needeth not man as his director. . . . Thou [didst] form the living soul
> of the faithful, through affections ordered by the vigor of continency; and
> afterwards, the mind subjected to Thee alone, and needing to imitate no
> human authority, Thou didst renew after Thine image and likeness.[49]

There was thus present in Augustine the revolutionary doctrine that the sole loyalty of human beings is to God, which means to truth; to love that no human institution, philosophical dogmatism, religious authoritarianism, or political power can replace. Augustine thought that loyalty to the absolute alone was the source of freedom.

The general concept of society and the specific notion of a political community derived from Augustine's conception of human nature. Individuals are social beings. The human good is sought within society, and a particular society was thought of as a group of persons united by common loyalties.

> A people is an assemblage of reasonable beings bound together by a
> common agreement as to the objects of their love . . . [so] in order to dis-
> cover the character of any people, we have only to observe what they love.[50]

With this comprehension of the nature of human beings and society, natures described in both structural and dynamic terms, the remaining essential points in Augustine's ethic can be described with relative simplicity.

2. What is the norm for a moral judgment?

In his interpretation of the criteria of ethics Augustine combined Greek with Hebraic elements, but the latter were far more influential. Thus, in *On the Morals of the Catholic Church,* written shortly after his conversion, he spoke in terms of the traditional Greek virtues, but the conception of these was drastically altered along Hebraic lines.

> I hold virtue to be nothing else than perfect love of God. . . . Temperance is
> love giving itself entirely to that which is loved; fortitude is love readily bear-
> ing all things for the sake of the loved object; justice is love serving only the
> loved object, and therefore ruling rightly. . . . The object of this love is not any-
> thing, but only God, the chief good, the highest wisdom, the perfect harmony.[51]

God thus was the final standard, and this meant that a right love was the ethical norm by which everything should be judged. The right will is well-directed love, and the evil is ill-directed love.

But Augustine had another norm that was related to his metaphysical conceptions, and it was similar to the classical ideal of justice.

The peace of the body consists in the duly proportional arrangement of the parts. The peace of the irrational soul is the harmonious repose of the appetites, and that of the rational soul the harmony of knowledge and action. The peace of the body and soul is the well-ordered and harmonious life and health of the living creature. Peace between man and God is the well-ordered obedience of faith to the eternal law. Peace between man and man is well-ordered concord. . . . The peace of all things is the tranquillity of order. Order is the distribution which allots things equal and unequal, each to its own place.[52]

3. How is the moral good known in a specific situation?

The knowledge of good in a specific situation is provided by a proper faith-relation to God, and an understanding of the facts of the case. The first provides insight or wisdom, the second practical judgment.

If therefore this is the right distinction between wisdom and knowledge, that the intellectual cognizance of eternal things belongs to wisdom, but the rational cognizance of temporal things to knowledge, it is not difficult to judge which is to be preferred or postponed to which.[53]

The moral dialectic requires the use of both "the intellectual cognizance of eternal things" and "the rational cognizance of the temporal."

This dialectic does not make possible absolutely certain judgments in most moral situations, for certain knowledge must be founded upon the proper disposition of the knower's will (upon the right faith-relation) and, given the inveterate self-prejudices of human beings, that proper disposition is a state exceedingly difficult to attain and difficult to know when it exists. However, even given a correctness of will there is still no simple correspondence between "eternal things" and "temporal things." It is, therefore, impossible to unite the two as would be required for an infallible solution of a moral problem, though whatever insights may be obtained, the source is always God.

I will speak the truth, Thou inspiring me as to what Thou willest. . . . For by none other than Thy inspiration do I believe that I can speak the truth, since Thou art Truth. . . .

The intellectual mind is so formed in its nature as to see those things, which by the disposition of the Creator are subjoined to things intelligible in a natural order, by a sort of incorporeal light of an unique kind.[54]

4. How is the moral good achieved?

The moral good can be achieved only after the individual, through the activity of God, has comprehended the weakness of "the flesh and of the mind," and has been led to discover "what ought to be done." Then and only then is it possible to enact what has been discovered.

> He [God] not only exhibits truth, but likewise imparts love. For it is thus that God teaches those who have been called according to His purpose, giving them simultaneously both to know what they ought to do, and to do what they know.[55]

Such an achievement is not a human achievement. Human beings reach the good only so far as they receive it from God. Every possession of good, moreover, is partial. This was the final moral lesson that Augustine had to impart. He referred to the "stupid pride of these men who fancy that the supreme good can be found in this life."[56] They are stupid because they cannot see that complete moral achievement or ethical perfection is impossible for human beings. It was a lesson he had learned painfully, through a long life of striving. The extent of human goodness could only be the extent of the gift of God which the individual is enabled to accept. Human pride prevents the person from accepting those gifts completely and graciously.

The final conflict of Augustine with classicism was at just this point. Classical ethics sought the supreme good in the life of reason and wisdom; Augustine insisted that such a good could never be reached by the individual in this world. The classical ideal sought to establish an eternal Rome; Augustine believed that no human government was permanent. Security and peace could be attained by the individual and society only by the perfect ordering of love toward God. But this perfection is not possible for any person or any society. God remains the Creator and Redeemer. The eternal good enters into the temporal world and can be experienced, in part, by human beings. But that good in the world is only one part of genuine good, and the experience of even that part is always partial. The eternal good is forever the inspiration of moral thought and action, the lure for human effort, and the common judge of all of the noblest human ethical achievements. It is never completely experienced.

THE UNIQUE CONTRIBUTION OF AUGUSTINE

Augustine was the first person in history who combined in a significant way the ethical perspectives of the Greeks and the Hebrews, but this combination was not so much an intellectual construct as it was a sense of living experience. For Augustine did not merely repeat the earlier ideas, but he found in his experience of living them new insights and implications that had never before been perceived. These new insights had a number of different facets.

(1) Augustine brought to ethical reflection and to ethics generally an exuberant love of existence. This meant not only, of course, a love of life and of his experiences but also a love of what he experienced. His extant writings were written after his conversion, and they reflect clearly his love of friends and companionship, of places and natural beauty, of language and music. All are intensely enjoyed though somewhat muted because his deepest love had become God, the principle of being in which all these realities are grounded. Muted, too, are certain exuberant joys known before his conversion, especially those of sex; but the way he writes about his mistress and their life makes clear his love for her and the sexual pleasures they had together. He thus brought to moral experience, and therefore to ethics, a wider and deeper love of existence than previous moral philosophers.

(2) It was, moreover, Augustine who was the first to teach with clarity that moral experience is the basis for ethics, not ethics the basis for moral experience. The ethical life is not one that takes a code of ethics and then lives by it. Augustine tried this with various codes and it did not work for him. He had to struggle through his own way. These struggles became the bases for his moral thought; for then, reflecting philosophically upon the struggles, he developed moral concepts that then qualified and gave direction to his experience.

(3) Augustine was driven to find all kinds of connections that had importance for ethics. This is suggested in his soliloquy when the soul asks the self, "What do you want to know?" "God and the soul." "Nothing more?" "Nothing more." Yet he did want to know more, for he wanted to know all that came between God and the soul and how they were all related. This compulsion to find unexpected connections freed both his reason and his imagination. It enabled him, for example, to see that his own personal failure had relations with the failure of Rome. In both there was the inner failure of adequate belief and spirit, a failure that was pride and self-centeredness. These become key ideas in ethics.

(4) There was the recognition that life has a pattern, either a pattern imposed by the self or one created by God. There is the possibility, then, of the comprehensive ordering of life, and for Augustine this became the moral problem of his and every life. Past, present, and future all needed to be understood in their relations with each other and in their more fundamental relations with the nontemporal. It is through this view that memory and imagination, especially memory, became so important for Augustine. Memory not so much of external events (though that memory is important), but the memory of the inner meaning of the external events becomes the passageway to moral understanding.

(5) The inner life, then, the life of personal valuing, becomes the clue to the understanding of ethics. This means, in turn, that there is need for a method by which to comprehend the inner life. Here is where memory and

imagination are important, and also faith and love. These four are not only the method by which Augustine thought an ethical theory could be developed but they are fundamental elements in the moral life itself.

(6) Faith, as both belief and trust, becomes the essential basis for ethical as all other understanding. Reason, too, is essential for understanding, but reason is a means and not the beginning, nor the end, of the process. Both beginning and end require something more fundamental, and this is feeling, and this feeling is both a belief about and a belief in.

(7) Love becomes an even more fundamental basis for ethics, both as ethical understanding and ethical life. Without love in its most legitimate form, an understanding of anything is impossible. One has to give the self to the other in order to know the other. But love is even more essential for the creation of the moral life. Because for Augustine there is a first principle of truth and of being and of goodness (and all are intricately related), he accurately affirms that the primary rule of ethics is "Love God, and do as you please." By this rule one will find sufficient truth, will achieve a full being, and will arrive at real goodness, though it must, of course, be the real God who is the source of truth and being and goodness.

(8) Earlier moralists had dealt with friendship in their ethical views, but lacking Augustine's view of the self, their treatments had been objective or vague. Augustine was the first to see interpersonal friendship as central in the moral life. It is central in that it is both a necessary cause of the moral life and a necessary consequence.

When Augustine's unique contributions to Western ethics are interpreted in this way it is clear that it was not so much new concepts that he contributed as it was a new intensity of moral experience and new forms of moral thinking. It is true that his concepts—frequently vague or ambiguous and sometimes contradictory—became the basis for interpretation and development throughout Western history. And it is also clear that the nature of his concepts makes it difficult to find in Augustine a consistent, coherent, clear ethics. But with the intensity of his experience and the form of his thinking there is clarity. That clarity, together with the view that the best ethical theory is based upon the deepest moral experience, has stimulated persons again and again to try to find the man that Augustine was within and beyond his words. But if this were all, the process would be of interest but of not great importance. What is important is that Augustine has taught Western ethics to keep moral theory close to moral life. When this has been forgotten it has been because the intensity of life and forms of thought which Augustine brought to ethics have been ignored.

NOTES

1. Plato, *The Republic of Plato,* trans. Francis M. Cornford (London: Oxford University Press, 1941), 473c.

2. Charles Norris Cochrane, *Christianity and Classical Culture* (Oxford: Clarendon Press, 1980 [1940]), p. 158.

3. Edward Gibbon, *The Decline and Fall of the Roman Empire,* quoted in Cochrane, *Christianity and Classical Culture,* p. 144.

4. Cochrane, *Christianity and Classical Culture,* pp. 153–54, 157.

5. Ibid., p. 327.

6. Ibid., p. 337.

7. Jerome, Epistle 60, 16. Quoted in Cochrane, *Christianity and Classical Culture,* p. 351.

8. Christopher Dawson, *A Monument to St. Augustine* (London: Sheed, 1970), p. 37.

9. Augustine, *The Confessions of St. Augustine,* trans. John K. Ryan (Garden City, N.Y.: Doubleday, 1960), III.4; pp. 81–82.

10. Ibid., V, X; p. 126.

11. The account and interpretation of this event takes nine chapters in the *Confessions,* Book II.

12. Augustine, *Confessions,* V.10 (trans. Ryan, pp. 68–69).

13. The classical statement of this position was given by Anselm of Canterbury in his *Prosologium:* "For I do not seek to understand that I may believe; but I believe that I may understand. For this also I believe—that unless I believed, I should not understand" (p. 7). There is great ambiguity in this *Credo ut intelligam* perspective that derives from the dual interpretation of "believe" as "to believe that" or "to believe in." The more basic ambiguity is in the understanding of faith as belief ("faith that") and faith as trust ("faith in"). Augustine gave primacy to the trust or will aspect of belief and faith. St. Anselm, *Proslogium; Monologium; An Appendix in Behalf of the Fool by Gaunilon; and Cur Deus Homo,* trans. Sidney Norton Deane (Chicago: Open Court Publishing Co., 1930).

14. *The Basic Writings of St. Augustine,* vol. 1, ed. Whitney J. Oates (New York: Random House, 1948), "On the Morals of the Catholic Church," XVI, p. 332.

15. Ibid., I.1 (ed. Oates, p. 3).

16. This method employed by Augustine was never followed rigorously, simply, or consistently. In particular, he made appeals to authority, his fundamental authority being the scriptures which he believed were infallible in the Vulgate though he was not adverse to using an occasional appeal to the authority of Platonism.

Again, Augustine's method was obscured by his devotional, loquacious, and polemical writing. He passed rapidly from devotional to philosophical prose; and since the symbols of worship and rigorous thought are not applied with the same meanings, these abrupt transitions are confusing. His winding ways sometimes seem endless; so it is a rare reader of Augustine who, in accord with his own suggestion, has not had to forgive him for thinking he says too much. Many of his treatises were pamphlets addressed to the times and this, too, obscures the existence of his method.

Nor are these the only difficulties in discovering a sensible pattern and content in his thinking. His belief in the infallible Vulgate is troublesome enough. His pre-evolutionary conception of Adam and original sin, his literal hopes for the end of the world and the bodily resurrection, his trust in miracles, both of the Bible and his own time, his thoroughgoing faith in angels and demons: There is much in this that the modern individual thinks crass and superstitious and, therefore, confusing. Yet within the welter of these beliefs and ways of writing there is a method and a spirit that in philosophical rigor and religious fervor is the equal of the best creative thought produced in the West.

17. *Retractiones* II.32. Quoted in Peter Brown, *Augustine of Hippo: A Biography* (Berkeley and Los Angeles: University of California Press, 1967), p. 165

18. Augustine *Confessions* IV.1 (ed. Oates, p. 42).

19. Plotinus, *The Six Enneads*, trans. Stephen Mackenna and B. S. Page (Chicago: Encyclopaedia Britannica, Inc., 1952), V.1, 6, p. 211.

20. Ibid., Fourth Ennead VIII:4 (trans. Mackenna and Page, p. 202).

21. St. John Perse quoted in Dag Hammarskjöld, *Markings* (London: Faber and Faber, Ltd. 1964), p. 130.

22. Augustine, *Confessions* X.5 (trans. Ryan, pp. 232–33).

23. Augustine, *Confessions* X.3–4 (ed. Oates, pp. 148–49).

24. Ibid., V.10 (p. 69).

25. Ibid., IV.4 (p. 46).

26. *Confessions* V.13 (trans. Ryan, p. 130).

27. Ibid., VI.3 (ed. Oates, p. 76).

28. Ibid., IX.10 (trans. Ryan, p. 222).

29. Ibid., IV.12 (ed. Oates, pp. 51, 49). On friendship see *Confessions* IV.9.

30. Ibid., IX.13; X.4 (trans. Ryan, pp. 228, 232).

31. Ibid., I.1 (p. 43).

32. See Brown, *Augustine of Hippo*, p. 165, and E. R. Dodds, "Augustine's *Confessions*: A Study of Spiritual Maladjustment," *Hibbert Journal* 26 (1927–28): 459–73.

33. *Confessions* VIII.12 (trans. Ryan, p. 202).

34. Ibid., X.30 (p. 256).

35. Ibid.

36. Ibid., X.31 (p. 258).

37. Ibid., X.34 (pp. 262–63).

38. Ibid., X.36 (ed. Oates, p. 176).

39. Ibid., X.37 (p. 177).

40. Quoted in Brown, *Augustine of Hippo*, p. 147.

41. *Confessions* X.21 (ed. Oates, p. 163).

42. Ibid., X.8 (p. 154).

43. *Confessions* X.20; X.14; X.27 (trans. Ryan, pp. 248, 253, 254).

44. Ibid., XIII.32 (ed. Oates, p. 253).

45. *Basic Writings of Saint Augustine*, ed. Oates, vol. 2: *The City of God* XIV.6 (p. 245).

46. Ibid., *On The Trinity* VIII.7 (pp. 783–84).

47. Ibid., VIII.8 (p. 786).

48. W. H. Auden, "Squares and Oblongs," in *Poets at Work: Essays Based on the Modern Poetry Collection at the Lockwood Memorial Library, University of Buffalo*, ed. Rudolf Arnheim et. al. (New York: Harcourt Brace and Co., 1948).

49. *Confessions* XIII.22; and XIII.24 (ed. Oates, 1: 244, 255).

50. *City of God* XIX.24 (ed. Oates, 2: 503).

51. *The Morals of the Catholic Church* XV (ed. Oates, 1: 331-332.

52. *City of God* XIX.13 (ed. Oates, 2: 488).

53. *On the Trinity* XII.15 (ed. Oates, 2: 825).

54. *The Confessions* XIII.25 (ed. Oates, 1: 248), and *On the Trinity* XII.15; (2: 824).

55. *On the Grace of Christ* XIV (ed. Oates, 1: 592–93).

56. *City of God* XIX.4 (ed. Oates, 1: 476).

5

THE ETHICS OF
MEDIEVAL CHRISTENDOM

The ethics of Western Christendom, which came to full flower in the twelfth
and thirteenth centuries, took centuries to grow. The seed took root in the
hearts of men and women on the day, long before, that a carpenter was crucified in Jerusalem. The ethic had grown in the lives of many individuals, the
simple and the wise, and by the time of Augustine there had been many graft-
ings upon this new Christian plant from the flowering of Greek thought.

But before the rose of the faith matured in the experience of Abelard and
Héloïse, in the life of Francis of Assisi, or in the thought of Thomas Aquinas
(whose lives spanned two great centuries), the soil out of which it grew was
nourished by the lives and deaths of Romans, barbarians, and Christians. The
sack of Rome in 411 was indeed the outward and visible sign of an inward
and spiritual decay; yet Roman institutions continued to be influential for
years, especially in Italy, Spain, and Gaul, as though there existed some law
of historical inertia. Of even greater importance was the fact that the glory of
Rome had been imaged by its great creators in architecture, poetry, philosophy, law, and history. So, in a later day, when individuals became perplexed
as to how life should be ordered they could return to that glory. The barbarian
tidal waves did not destroy the visible city of Rome overnight; nor, when the
institutions of the empire disappeared, did the barbarian flood of the dark
ages destroy these images of Rome. Indeed, "barbarian" and "dark ages" are
misleading terms since they dehumanize the persons and destroy the vitality
of the life of those days. The Byzantine and Moslem cultures, during the
"dark ages," were rich in the colors and tones of the human spirit. The barbarians were the possessors of a vigorous folk culture. And when, after the

191

tenth century, the barbarian waters receded, the rich silt of that powerful folk life remained to nourish the rose of Christendom.

Nor must it be forgotten that the rose was the flowering of the church, that institution which alone of all institutions during these turbulent centuries grew steadily stronger. During the "dark ages" it was the church, as it disappeared from society into the monasteries and as it appeared in the lives of the priests, especially the missionaries, that continued to strengthen the strain of seed that one day would become a Bernard, a Bonaventura, a Hildebrande, to say nothing of the countless other Christians of the twelfth and thirteenth centuries whose names we have forgotten but who live yet in the music and poetry of the cathedral and mass.

In the twelfth and thirteenth centuries the forces most significant for the ethic were (1) feudalism, which, though decaying, was influential through the ethos it had created; (2) economic and social developments in the new commerce, especially the rise of the towns, and the growth of the universities; and (3) the political struggles between the empire and the papacy that ended in the triumph of the church. These forces largely molded the basic assumptions shared by all those who developed a Christian ethic in that age.

1. FEUDALISM

Feudalism arose from the need for an ordered life in specific social and economic settings. Built upon the foundations of a simple agricultural economy, it presupposed social relations of dominance and subservience, and of responsibilities arising from social status. Thus feudalism was primarily a political institution, and because, for a time, it so successfully ordered human life by placing authority in those who controlled the land, it developed social relations into class and caste groups, and it developed economic life into an organized agriculture. We can see how this happened by observing more closely some of the major elements in the feudal arrangement of life.

Feudalism proper started in the eighth century, when there was a union of property relations and personal relations. The property relations went back, through the usage of barbarians, to the late empire when tracts of land, together with necessary tools and servants for production, would be granted to individuals for personal use as long as the donor permitted. This was a *beneficium*, a benefit or favor. Because the whims of the donor made the security of the beneficiary too precarious, the *beneficium* gradually developed into a right for life or as long as stipulated services were performed. The personal relations stemmed out of the individualism of the Germanic tribes in which a warrior freely chose and pledged himself to follow his chieftain to victory or to death. Such a pledge, however, was not binding for life but for only so long as was mutually agreeable, and obviously it could exist only where there was mutual respect and mutual honor. Until the eighth century these two economic and tribal human relations developed separately. When, through political necessity created by the splintering of kingdoms, the property and personal relations were indissolubly joined in vassalage, feudalism began. Feudalism was the right of a vassal to control lands in return for military service. As such, feudalism had two levels: the upper level of the warriors and the lower level of the peasants. The former was the relation of vassal to lord which, in general, was one of equality with mutual respect and mutual obligations. The latter was the level of master-servant relation in which there existed an unbridgeable caste chasm.

The vassal promised his lord certain services. At first these were limited to military comradeship, vaguely defined. Later financial obligations became important, and these obligations were made more specific. In return, the lord not only granted the land to his vassal, but he also promised justice and protection from aggression. A vassal, for example, was tried by his peers (or *pares*, that is, equals) according to the accepted customs of the land.

It was from this warrior class that there developed the chivalry so important to the medieval ethos. *Chevalerie* at first referred to mounted troops, but the warrior who could afford to own a horse and all the necessary accoutrements for battle was so obviously superior to the poor footsoldier that the *chevalerie* class became a superior caste. Chivalry thus became a guild with its standards of admission and its recognized rules of behavior. A man had to earn his knighthood through years of training in the art of war and the accepted etiquette of the nobility and presumably through valor on the field of battle. Originally a man of the lower class might become a knight through the acquisition of a fief (land held under a lord) or by an unusual act of bravery. But by the thirteenth century chivalry had become the exclusive institution of a rigid caste; the law made it impossible for peasants to secure a fief and required that all knights be of noble birth. The knight had responsibilities toward those within his class, but outside the borders of his class the rules did not apply, and so the knight, who possessed all the refinements of polite society, felt it proper to massacre the peasants of his enemy, to live by the violence of warfare, and in victory by the brutality of rapine.

The church chastened the warfare of chivalry in two ways. First, in the late tenth century the "Peace of God" was introduced, by which the church forbade the warring parties to destroy church property or to attack women, children, or merchants, and by the mid-eleventh century the "Truce of God" outlawed warfare on three days of each week and during the planting and harvesting seasons. Second, through the effort to permeate chivalry with religious ideals, the church "baptized" chivalry, making of knighthood a vocation in which the warrior was called to the defense of the faith. The religious rituals that became connected with knighthood symbolized this conversion of secular chivalry, and the crusades were the most notable expression of the effort to direct warfare toward "Christian" ends.

However, during the later years of this same period new secular influences were at work. In the twelfth and thirteenth centuries the "Courts of Love," in which the poets sang the ways of love, achieved popularity. Here, chivalry became the protection of beautiful women and love the highest service and joy of life. In some of the courts this ideal became a reality. Religious men recognized its power, and they tried to convert the passionate love of a lady (or a knight) for the pure devotion of love for the Virgin (or Christ). However, this attempt was not always entirely successful. Meanwhile, the sharp distinction between nobleman and commoner and the deep social cleavages continued to form. A medieval rhyme stated that

> God hath shapen lives three:
> Boor and knight and priest they be.[1]

The boors (peasants) far outnumbered the knights and priests, and, until the development of town life, most of the peasants were serfs. A person became a serf through birth or the acceptance of land-tenure, and most serfs were bound to the land until death. In addition, the serf was liable to heavy taxes. It has been estimated that in Germany the payments amounted to two-thirds of the product of the land. This estimate did not take into account irregular payments that the master, depending upon his humaneness, exacted from time to time. The most bitterly resented of the taxes were those imposed at marriage and at death, for both meant that the serf had to begin or continue a family at the lowest level of poverty.

The serfs were bound to their land, to the manor where they lived, and to their fellows. This binding was the source of labor and suffering, but it was also the source of much happiness, for, if nature and a small community were hard task-masters, they also supported human life. The serf had to labor incessantly, particularly on the lands of the church which were more efficiently operated than secular manors. But no work could be done on Sunday or on holy days, and there were the pleasant interruptions of markets and fairs to attend as well as of troupes that came to the manor. Meaning was given to life by the intimacy of a small community.

But in the twelfth and thirteenth centuries serfdom began to decline. Many complex social causes were at work, but two factors were of special significance: the rise of the towns and the development of trade and commerce. Trade began to compete with agriculture and the new exchange economy introduced market-farming. There was no longer the need for large numbers of serfs for subsistence farming. Further, the towns became a refuge to which the serfs could go for a new life. It is not surprising that it was in the vicinity of the towns that freedom first became the ideal and the reality.

These developments, together with the centralization of political power in empire and church, were the harbingers of a new day that meant the destruction of feudalism, though its ethos continued to be influential. What, then, were some of the qualities imparted by feudalism, qualities that would be transmuted into the ethic of Christendom?

In the first place, feudalism was inclusive, from the soil turned by the peasant's hoe to the throne of God in heaven. Second, inclusiveness meant unity and the harmony of proper relations; all relations were ordered, and inevitably the task of the ethical life and thought was that of discovering a human being's *dignitas*, his proper rank or station in the inclusive unity. Third, observed from the life of the knights and priests, an individual's rank meant personal obligation. The ethos contributed the idea of individual responsibility. Fourth, feudalism involved the localization of authority. Beginning as the need for ordered social relations, it solved this problem in terms of relatively small units. It could not avoid the problem of individuality and authority, and its solution was along the lines of a community of persons. Fifth, in the localization of authority, at least among the nobles, respect for the individual and the law was emphasized. From this moral, albeit rudimentary, ideal of justice there developed the implicit ethic of liberty and the rights of man.

> Feudalism carried within it the germs of liberty: the principle of the liberty of the subject, of the right of man to be tried by his peers, the right not to be deprived of life or property without due process of law, the responsibility of those who rule to do justice under penalty of deposition . . . were all inherent in the feudal theory of government.[2]

Finally, chivalry embodied ways of behavior in the light of an ideal. Despite the fact that the behavior exhibited contradictory tendencies toward crudity and overrefinement, the chivalrous life was capable of transmutation into a new, spiritualized ideal.

2. THE NEW ECONOMY AND SOCIETY: TRADE, TOWN, AND UNIVERSITY

For centuries the communities of Europe were isolated commercially. Europe was encircled by the Moslems in Spain, North Africa, and the Eastern Mediterranean; by the Byzantine Empire in the Southeast; and by the Slavs and Hungarians in the East. Even without these unbridgeable moats, the internal instability and the localization of authority in small rival kingdoms ruled by warring lords made commerce precarious. In the tenth century the invading Norsemen, a trading folk, opened the northern seaways, and in the following century the Hungarian acceptance of Christianity built a bridge for commerce to the East. The developing feudalism, during the same years, created an order that made trade secure. With the expansion of commerce and growth of an exchange economy the foundations of the subsistence agricultural economy, centered in the manorial life, were destroyed.

The most momentous development accompanying the increasing trade was the birth and growth of the town in the twelfth century. It is impossible to know the exact origins of the towns, but this new birth, more than any other factor, presaged the death of the Middle Ages and the beginning of the modern world.

> This movement was an economic revolution . . . more important than any later revolution, even than that of the Renaissance, with the invention of printing and the discovery of the compass, or than that of the nineteenth century and all the revolution in industry which flowed from it. For both these later revolutions are but secondary consequences of the great economic and social transformation of the twelfth and thirteenth centuries.[3]

As the captains of commerce were drawn together by common interests, as they developed in a haphazard fashion into communities, they became aware of the need for control and protection. Thus they were led to make requests of the feudal lords. If the requests were denied, the impulse of economic and social forces soon led to demands for recognition and a self-governing community that would promise fealty to the lord, usually in the form of taxes. If these demands were denied, the impulsive forces led to open rebellion. The new class of burghers appealed to the principle of contract so important in feudal life, and to them nothing could seem more natural and right than this appeal. But two simple facts in the appeal were revolutionary and meant that the world would never be the same again: a new class of bourgeoisie had arisen, which, through restless energy and insatiable ambition, would so largely shape the modern world, and the request to apply agricultural principles to the towns was a request to recognize that a nonfeudal world was in the making. The new burghers wanted self-government.

Everywhere there was the same successive development of the town, though there were as many local variations on the theme as there were towns. First, there was a community of citizens, dominantly commercial men, who through daily interactions came to have similar emotional and intellectual attitudes. Then there was established a chartered town which, at first, had only a vague government. Later came the creation of a town government and of guilds, including the universities. From the outset there was a tendency for wealth to control the government, but it was not until the fourteenth century that the wealthy burghers controlled the government for their own benefit.

Originally there was no distinction between local and "foreign" merchants, or between those who lived by selling or by making. But by the twelfth century there was a division of labor. This added to the variety in the social composition of the town. But in all that variation, although there was never social equality, there was equality before the law. This freedom before the law was a new thing in the European world, and it helped the legal condition of the serf. The more ambitious serfs escaped to towns since, after a year's stay, they were granted full freedom. Some cities went so far as to promote emancipation and to encourage liberation of people behind the feudal curtain.

In trying to imagine this time, it is important to note that the towns were towns and not cities. They were large enough that a new communal ethos was created, but they were not so huge that the individual was lost in the masses. Late in the eleventh century the greatest towns had, at the most, two or three thousand persons. And even after the towns ceased rapid growth in the fourteenth century (an unusual growth that would not begin again until the nineteenth century), most towns were exceedingly small.

> Toward the close of the fourteenth century, really important towns, such as Frankfort, Nuremburg, or Hamburg, York, Norwich, or Bristol, may be assigned from 6–12,000. Such towns were few. More representative of fourteenth-century England is a town like Liverpool which in 1375 had about 1,000 inhabitants.[4]

There were some few exceptionally large towns, of course: London, in 1292, had about 20,000 persons; Bruges, about the same time, had perhaps 50,000; and Paris had between 130,000 and 200,000.

In these small towns that promoted individual freedom and yet retained the flavor and fellowship of the countryside, there arose the need for cooperation in common interests. In this way there arose the guilds which, by the thirteenth century, dominated the economic life with a strong influence upon political control and social relations. The guilds were of two types: merchant and craft. The general purpose of both was the same, the welfare of the persons forming the guild. The merchants established a monopoly to prevent outside competition; they set prices and trading hours, and they had thorough inspections of each merchant's business in accord with established standards for goods and weights. The craft guilds, created for the security and equality of the master craftsmen, established a monopoly in the labor supply. In this way the masters limited the number of persons who could enter the trade, as well as made the law for hours, wages, and prices. Because the members of a guild

had to unite for political action, they became a direct power in town government; and because the members, with a carefully controlled hierarchy of relations, lived in the same section of town, they became a potent social force.

The universities, at first, were a particular kind of guild, concerned for
the regulation of the new craft and for protection from outside interference.
Paris and Oxford formed a guild of masters; Bologna was a guild of scholars.
The differences arose out of the diverse origins of the schools. In the twelfth
century, a time of growth in the intellectual life, the domination of thought
passed from the monastic to the secular clergy. In the North, where theology
and philosophy were eminent, the universities grew out of the cathedral
school; in the South, where the lay professions of medicine and law were preeminent, the universities were not so closely connected to the church. The
significance of the university was that it provided the intellectual life for the
town. The insatiable drive for gain that marked the new burghers was paralleled in the universities by the insatiable thirst for understanding. The town
made possible the university, and the university embodied an intensive intellectual life that made possible the construction of the medieval ethic.

It is impossible to glance at the changing life of the twelfth and thirteenth
centuries in commerce, the towns, and the universities without recognizing
something of the effect upon the medieval ethos. For here there was the impetus toward achievement, a division of labor that retained a unity and a relation of diverse functions, cooperation that gave place to the individual
spirit, freedom and fellowship in the setting of a developing order of law, and
that restless pursuit of the truth that stimulated the development of Christian
ideas and ideals.

3. The Militant Empire
and the Church Triumphant

During the same period as the origin of the town there was a drive toward
centralization in both the large political and religious institutions. In the tenth
century there developed the "Holy Roman Empire." As the "emperors"
grasped political power and became an influence moving from feudal lords
to larger units, the church, too, was moving from a territorial system, in
which control was left largely to the power of local bishops, to a "Holy
Catholic Church." It was inevitable that the two institutions would clash.

The conflicts between the church and empire were replete with human
drama that had an influence upon the spirit of the thirteenth century: the
wresting of control over the election of bishops from the feudal lords; a penitent king forced by the pope to kneel in the snow for three days before he
was granted absolution; a pope forced by the king into exile and death; a

papal delegate at the coronation of a new king claiming that the pope was granting the king a "benefice"; the rebellion of the free Lombard cities against the emperor; and kings excommunicated and forced to go on crusades on behalf of the church they despised. What was important for the ethics of Christendom were the instruments of belief employed by the church in the warfare and the fact that the church won the struggle, becoming in the process a new kind of institution.

In the impulsive movement of the church, individuals and small groups of men made three astounding and, for many, unbelievable claims. The three claims were consolidated into dogma in the twelfth and thirteenth centuries. First, the papacy is absolutely preeminent in the church. This was the belief in the universal supremacy of the pope, and by this belief the church was led into an authoritarian unity by the claim that the papacy was continuous with the divine in human history. Second, the spiritual "sword" is superior to the temporal in all religious matters. Because it was the church that made the decision as to what matters were "religious," this was the claim for the control of the state by the church. Third, the seven sacraments are essential to salvation. This was the claim that the church had control over the life of each individual in society. The sacraments accompanied each person from birth to death and were the sustenance of life, as necessary as food and drink. It was because of the triumph of these dogmas in the minds of the people that the claims of the papacy to power in the church, in the political life, and in society became, for a time, realized fact. Life was permeated with Christian ideals.

The victory of ambitious ecclesiastics who knew that their cause was the cause of the one true God was all the more remarkable since, though they had many diplomats and spies, they had no military power, neither that of a large army nor of secret police.

> History records no such triumph of intellect over brute strength as that which, in an age of turmoil and battle, was wrested from the fierce warriors of the time by priests who had no material force at their command, and whose power was based alone on the souls and conscience of men.[5]

THE PRESUPPOSITIONS OF THE MEDIEVAL ETHIC

In the twelfth and thirteenth centuries many persons tried consciously to order all of life through the acceptance of inclusive, ennobling, and controlling principles. In this task they assimilated the assumptions and many of the basic beliefs of earlier societies. Thus, strands from classical civilization, from Hebraic culture, from the gospels and the early church, and from the Augustinian cities of God and the world met in the spirit of men and women of the time and, interwoven with newer strands from their contemporary culture, were transformed into the assumptions of the ethic of Christendom.

1. In all created existence there is a meaningful unity and ordered dignity which is discoverable.

This faith asserted that the oneness of nature, which was everywhere the same, was made up of individual parts united in an ordered whole. To have believed in unity without diversity would have been to see the oneness of creation without recognizing its variety. To have observed diversity without unity would have been to see the details without noting that they were details of a meaningful whole.

But this assumption was more than the simple recognition of unity and order. For the medieval mind, a metaphysical or factual judgment always included a value judgment. The scholastics, those thinkers who taught the medieval European universities, accepted without question that creation had a positive value, a meaning, and that the place of any created thing was determinative for its value. Nor was it only that there was a union of metaphysical and value judgment. It was always assumed that the unity and order was "discoverable." This epistemological assumption was integral to the basic faith, even though there were real disagreements as to how human beings attained knowledge of the world and its worth. Those disagreements could be seen in the intensity of the debates concerning reason and faith, rational knowledge and revealed knowledge, and in the vital differences in the variety of ethical lives.

This faith was symbolized in the Gothic cathedral. Anyone entering the medieval cathedral experienced it as unity and order, and it was probably impossible for a person then to enter a cathedral without instinctively making a value judgment about the meaning of the whole and the dignity of the parts. But for such a person, this discovered knowledge of the cathedral always pointed beyond the building itself to the intentions of those who in religious passion and devout patience conceived and constructed it. All the elements—the spire, the nave, the stained glass representations of biblical persons and events, the altar, the crucifix, the Virgin—directed attention beyond the cathedral to the supernatural, indicating clearly that the only adequate principle of meaning for the universe was spiritual.

2. The only adequate principle of meaning for the universe is spiritual.

This assumption was implicit in the first presupposition since, for the medieval mind, to believe in a "created existence" implied faith in an eternal existence that was not created. The universe, then, could only be understood properly as the creation of God, and the natural life required for its understanding a knowledge of its relation to the supernatural. While the sophisticated medieval mind warned itself that the supernatural could be spoken of only by analogy, yet the belief in the actuality of the supernatural was its most fundamental presupposition. And it was, of course, possible for the supernatural to penetrate into the natural. This had happened in the past in Christ and the gospels, and it happened continuously in the church.

3. Christ, present in the gospels and the Church, is the way and truth of life.

Many persons found that the first two assumptions of the medieval ethic made sense to human reason. This third assumption made sense to human faith or trust. But it was only by such faith that one was able to understand the Christ of the gospels. This same Christ was present in the church, and it was the acceptance of the Christ of the gospels, of tradition and the church that explained those who, in their lives, dared "the imitation of Christ." It was that same acceptance that accounted for the fact that most worthy life and thought in Western Europe in the twelfth and thirteenth centuries occurred in the framework of the church so that simple peasant and profound philosopher alike lived and thought in its spiritual climate.

4. Social and individual order and freedom depend upon the recognition and the realization of the nature of created things, their relations to each other, and their dependence upon the supreme spiritual reality.

This presupposition was the corollary of the first three assumptions. It included them all, made them specific in terms of human life, and pointed toward what was required for an adequate human existence. The life of society, as of individuals, can be as it should only when persons see beyond the facade of daily happenings to the meaningful unity and ordered dignity of life, when they note that the parts are all interrelated, and that each and all are related to the church, to Christ, and to God.

5. A universal Christian civilization is a present reality.

The truth about life was felt to be possible because the truth had been realized in contemporary civilization. Unlike the early church, unlike Augustine, persons in the middle ages did not approach life with the attitude that there was an inescapable conflict between church and world. To them the world had become a universal Christian society. This was one of the most remarkable facts about the assumptions of the medieval ethic, and without a recognition of this fact it would be impossible to understand that ethic.

The Church was able to permeate and unify society because society was ready for the permeation and was already unified by forces that did not know they were operating toward a Christian civilization. However, the fact of a "universal Christian civilization" does not mean that the civilization had perfect order or that the church had absolute domination in the world, rather that in the twelfth and thirteenth century the principles of Christianity had become the foundation of the society and that very foundation created new problems that could be solved only because society was then receptive to further Christianization.

6. The human person is an embodied soul with an eternal destiny.

It is often very difficult for persons to understand the basic assumptions of those who lived in a previous age. The "acids of modernity" have so corroded the human spirit that it is nearly impossible for many, even those who profess a faith in "immortality," to comprehend the true spirit and real force of this once living attitude. Yet it is essential to understand imaginatively this assumption if there is to be any comprehension of the medieval ethic.

The human being was not mind *and* matter, nor was the soul thought of as being imprisoned in the body. The person was an embodied soul. He or she was a child of two worlds. This "fact" was as commonplace to medieval men and women as that each was a child of two parents. Life, then, consisted in living toward eternal life thought of as both a "time" and a quality of existence. Salvation was the major theme of ethics as it was the dominant theme of religion. There followed the aspiration, the ceaseless longing for the vision of God. The longing was ceaseless in this life; for while one could make progress toward that vision, most Christians assumed that the vision would not become clear until the person reached the supernatural world after death.

The presupposition of the eternal destiny of the self accounted for the fact that salvation was all-important. It accounted, too, for the centrality of the person in the medieval ethic. One continuous belief that undergirded all ethical thought of the time was the belief in the absolute value and imperishable life of the individual, which is simply another way of affirming that the human person was an embodied soul with an eternal destiny.

The richness of life in the twelfth and thirteenth centuries was represented by the fact that these assumptions were worked out through a variety of means and in intricate details in individual lives, in theology, in poetry, and in social institutions. In the moral life and thought some of that variety was expressed in the experiences of Peter Abelard and Héloïse, Francis of Assisi, and Thomas Aquinas.

ABELARD AND HÉLOÏSE (1079–1142 AND 1101?–1164?)

The mutilation of Peter Abelard on a night in 1118, when he was thirty-eight, was also the mutilation of the life of Héloïse, his wife, who was seventeen. From that act, and all the complex circumstances surrounding it, there was the religious and moral transformation of two lives in both outer behavior and inner meaning.

We are indebted to Abelard for his story. In a letter subsequently titled *Historia calamitatum: Abelard to a Friend: The Story of His Misfortunes*, Abelard wrote the most complete autobiography of the twelfth century. As an *epistola consolatoria,* or letter of consolation, it had a recognized purpose and familiar rhetoric. The purpose was to persuade either an actual person or imagined individuals how to survive calamities in life, and the formula was traditional: "You have troubles, I have had more; and if you hear the story of my life you should be able to live your story." Given this purpose and form it is possible that Abelard embellished his story, but his account has the ring of authenticity, and its major facts are confirmed by other witnesses.

We are also indebted to Héloïse for her story. It is difficult to believe her initial assertion that "*by chance* someone brought me the letter of consolation you had sent to a friend,"[6] but it is not difficult to read between the lines of her letter that she felt she should have been the friend to whom his *epistola consolatoria* was addressed. Her first letter to him also had a recognized purpose and traditional style, the purpose being to persuade the recipient to respond to a request. The pattern followed was to make clear that what was asked was reasonable, that the addressee was able to meet the request, and that the writer had the right to have what was asked.

Héloïse writes to Abelard as "her master, or rather her father, husband, or rather brother" and considers herself "his handmaid, or rather his daughter, wife, or rather sister,"[7] identifying the various psychological relations they had with each other. For all these relations there were customary forms of letter writing, and Héloïse expresses surprise that in his first letter to her Abelard had broken with custom and "the natural order" in putting her name before his, so "we have woman before man, wife before husband," and other disorders.[8]

Both wrote their letters according to customary styles, and this accounts for some of their emphases. Both also broke through the familiar patterns to reveal individualized lives. Similarly, they lived within the customary lifestyles of their day yet broke with expected patterns. This combination of tradition, unique experiences and their reflections upon both ultimately created Abelard's *Scito te ipsum* (*Know thyself*) which "is an original treatise on moral philosophy, more valuable and interesting perhaps than anything which the Middle Ages produces after the recovery of the *Nichomachean Ethics*."[9] We can understand the ethic by a review of their lives, remembering the social context in which they lived and their assumptions; by an interpretation of their relations as reported in the letters, emphasizing the ethical interpretation Héloïse gave of the events; and by an interpretation of Abelard's ethical writings.

The Lives of Abelard and Héloïse

Abelard was born in 1079, Héloïse about twenty-one years later, in 1100 or 1101. It is uncertain when they first met, but they were married, against her best judgment, in 1117/18. In 1118 they separated, and both entered monastic orders in which they spent the remainder of their lives. Abelard died in 1142, Héloïse in 1164.

From an early age Abelard felt the calling of philosophy though little more is known of his childhood. Born in Le Pallet, two hundred miles southwest of Paris, as the eldest son to a knight, he was heir to his father's vassal rights, but at an early age he renounced his inheritance.

> I preferred the weapons of dialectic to all the other teachings of philosophy, and armed with these I chose the conflicts of disputation instead of the trophies of war. I began to travel about in several provinces disputing, like a true peripatetic philosopher, wherever I heard there was keen interest in the art of dialectic.[10]

After perhaps five years as a wandering scholar, Abelard arrived in Paris in 1100 to study with William of Champeaux (ca. 1070–1121), the champion of realism and the most famous philosopher of the time. Although Abelard was welcomed at first as a student, there soon developed intellectual disagreements which grew into personal conflict and enmity. This became a pattern in his relations with other thinkers. "This was the beginning of the misfortunes which have dogged me to this day," Abelard wrote in 1133, "and as my reputation grew so other men's jealousy was roused."[11] The deeper reasons for the continual conflicts were what he recognized as his "volatile temperament" and his consciousness of his intellectual superiority.[12]

Following the break with William, Abelard established his own school in a town near Paris when he was twenty-three. His fame as a schoolmaster and teacher began, and in the history of education there has rarely been a teacher more popular with many students and more disliked by others. Instead of the familiar *lectio*, in which the teacher commented upon the grammar and meaning of passages of scripture, he used the new method of *disputatio*, presenting a problem and proposing, by rational argument and quotations from church fathers, alternative solutions, finally deciding for one answer. It was through his teaching and scholarship that Abelard was the primary forerunner of the University of Paris and of the scholastic method that matured in Thomas Aquinas.

Abelard was at the height of his fame as a teacher when he met Héloïse. Nothing is known of her parentage, though it is assumed she was born in or near Paris. Only a few facts are known about her early life, but they are significant. Her guardian, an uncle named Fulbert, was a canon of Notre Dame, and he was assiduous about her education. Before she met Abelard, Héloïse's fame as a scholar was widespread. According to Abelard's testimony, prior to meeting her he had been singularly free from sexual entanglements, but he consciously set out to seduce her, persuading her uncle to trust him completely as her tutor.

> Two factors especially kept him from suspecting any wrongdoing, namely his fondness for his niece and my own reputation in the past for chastity.
>
> What was the result? We were first together in one house and then one in mind. Under the pretext of work we made ourselves entirely free for love and the pursuit of her studies provided the secret privacy which love desired. We opened our books but more words of love than of the lesson asserted themselves. There was more kissing than teaching; my hands found themselves at her breasts more often than on the book. Love brought us to gaze into each other's eyes more than reading kept them on the text. And the better to prevent suspicion, I sometimes struck her not through anger or vexation but from love and affection which were beyond the sweetness of every ointment. No sign of love was omitted by us in our ardor and whatever unusual love could devise, that was added too. And the more such delights were new to us, the more ardently we indulged in them, and the less did we experience satiety.[13]

The consequences came quickly. Abelard necessarily began to neglect his studies and teaching, repeating from rote. Instead of philosophy he wrote love songs to and in praise of Héloïse which became popular. His students became disenchanted and saddened by the deadening of his teaching. And, inevitably, Fulbert discovered the lovers and reacted violently. About this time Héloïse found she was pregnant, and Abelard sent her to his sister's in Brittany. Abelard thought that Fulbert's anger could be assuaged by marriage, which he promised if it were kept secret to protect his reputation. Héloïse, seeing that marriage would not satisfy her uncle and that it could only lead to disaster, argued eloquently against it, but finally yielded to Abelard's promise to Fulbert and demands upon her.

The real problems began with the marriage itself. Fulbert broke his promise and made known they were married; Héloïse angrily "cursed and swore that it was a lie"; Fulbert abused his niece; Abelard sent her to a convent for protection; and Fulbert, thinking greater disgrace resulted from

Abelard's attempt to get rid of her, broke into Abelard's lodgings one night with his kinsmen and castrated him.[14] Shortly thereafter, at Abelard's direction, she became a nun, he a monk.

The factual remainder of their lives can be briefly reported, although the meaning of their experiences, as it bears upon the creation of their ethics, is a more difficult exploration.

Abelard moved from monastery to monastery, at one time becoming an abbot, a position in which, given his temperament and the outrageous behavior of the monks at the time, he was a miserable failure. He gave himself to teaching and writing, but his writings had too much reason and too many questions for traditionalists, including the saintly Bernard of Clairvaux (1090–1153). Twice Abelard's writings were examined by church councils; twice elements of his thought were declared heretical; twice his books were burned. Despite his rebuffs he continued in his loyalty to the church, and late in his life affirmed simply, "I do not wish to be a philosopher if it means conflicting with Paul, nor to be an Aristotle if it cuts me off from Christ."[15]

Héloïse became an abbess. Her fame for good works and sanctity became greater than her previous renown for scholarship. (What she thought of that fame has an important bearing upon her ethics.) When her nunnery was in need of a place to relocate, Abelard provided his property, known as the Paraclete, that had previously been his place of solitude and, later, teaching. Both the nuns of the Paraclete and he recognized he had a special relation with their convent, but he had no personal relations with Héloïse except for the letters his *Historia calamitatum* instigated. These letters reveal that the personal relation which she needed and wanted to recapture was mainly one-sided. Whatever Abelard may have felt within, he kept the relation distanced and impersonal, transforming their love into a religious and even institutional relation.

Héloïse: The Ethic of Pure Human Love and Intention

It is important to recognize that Abelard and Héloïse have left to history not their experiences but their memories of the experiences sixteen years after the events; and that these memories are doubtless affected not only by the literary devices they used but by how each felt about the self, the other, and God as well as by what each wanted of the other. But behind each sentence of the personal letters there exist real persons: Héloïse is revealed by her words, Abelard hidden by his. Héloïse is open to her experience and range of feelings; Abelard is largely closed to his. Yet out of their experiences there emerges for each an ethic of intention, an ethic first and most incisively stated by Héloïse, and later stated and interpreted more fully by Abelard.

Héloïse candidly presents herself as a self-controlled and self-contained woman in great need. She is a scholar who readily quotes classical authors as illuminating her condition. She is a thinker who loves paradox ("a holy error and a blessed delusion"; "merciless mercy"; "Wholly guilty though I am, I am also, as you know, wholly innocent").[16] She saw clearly, far more so than Abelard, what she was doing, and she remembered more clearly. She had a literary and psychological mastery of letter writing. She knew when to say "we" and "I," she knew how far (and was unafraid) to press a point no matter how personally painful, and, when she saw that Abelard would not respond to her thinking, she submitted to his will in her letter writing as she had in her sexual and religious life. At the same time she communicated the impression that both within and outside this submission she remained true to herself. Throughout all of her experiences, including those in the writing of letters, she had a self-consciousness that enabled her to develop a theory of her life: she knew that she was living, and had lived, by pure love and moral intention.

It is impossible to know but not difficult to imagine Héloïse's feelings when she read Abelard's letter of calamity about his sufferings and hers, about their secret, private relations, and about her arguments made to him and to him alone for continuing their love without marriage, arguments which she felt had not been reported accurately. "But you kept silent about most of my arguments for preferring love to wedlock and freedom to chains."[17] But whatever her own private feelings she began her letter to him with "we" to express the honest anxiety of all the nuns at the Paraclete who had a special relation to Abelard, though soon she had to change to "I," for the necessity of telling him once more of her personal love and need, which was the whole point of her writing. She moved to the "I" deftly, pointing out that the way to repay his debt to the community was by paying his debt "to her who is yours alone."[18]

What was that debt? It was not simply that his mutilation, "that supreme act of flagrant treachery [which] robbed me of my very self in robbing me of you"; it was not just that by entering the nunnery she had "found strength at your command to destroy myself."[19] It was not the loss of herself that pained her; it was her loss of him. As always Héloïse wanted him, what he alone could give. She explicitly said that she wanted his comfort which, ever since their entry into religious orders ("which was your decision alone"), he had never given her.[20] What she really wanted was Abelard's confirmation of what she never doubted, that her love for him had been and was a valid love, that it had been and continued to be the most important thing in her life; that his love, which they both had always known had begun in his lust, had developed into his response of deep human affection.

> Surely the greater the cause for grief the greater the need for the help of consolation, and this no one can bring but you; you are the sole cause of my sorrow, and you alone can grant me the grace of consolation. You alone

have the power to make me sad, to bring me happiness or comfort; you alone have so great a debt to repay me, particularly now when I have carried out all your orders so implicitly that when I was powerless to oppose you in anything, I found strength at your command to destroy myself. I did more—strange to say—my love rose to such heights of madness that it robbed itself of what it most desired beyond hope of recovery, when immediately at your bidding I changed my clothing along with my mind, in order to prove you the sole possessor of my body and my will alike. God knows I never sought anything in you except yourself; I wanted simply you, nothing of yours.

She had pleaded with him for his own sake to avoid marriage. She had failed to persuade him; and sixteen years later she, a chaste abbess, wrote to him, an abbot, both of whom had vowed lifelong celibacy:

> I looked for no marriage-bond, no marriage portion, and it was not my own pleasures and wishes I sought to gratify, as you well know, but yours. The name of wife may seem more sacred or more binding, but sweeter for me will always be the word mistress, or, if you will permit me, that of concubine or whore.[21]

Héloïse's first appeal to him, that he recognize her as the person of love and respond to her personally, ended on a religious note.

> And so, in the name of God to whom you have dedicated yourself, I beg you to restore your presence to me in the way you can—by writing me some word of comfort, so that in this at least I may find increased strength and readiness to serve God. When in the past you sought me out for sinful pleasures your letters came to me thick and fast, and your many songs put your Héloïse on everyone's lips, so that every street and house echoed with my name. Is it not far better now to summon me to God than it was then to satisfy our lust?[22]

Abelard either could not or would not respond to her. He ignored her personal writing and replied to all the nuns at the Paraclete, first suggesting that if they needed his instruction "in matters pertaining to God" they should tell him what they wanted; and then, in the remainder of the letter, and before they asked, he gave his instruction in such matters. Such obtuseness in Abelard, such religious irrelevancies, angered Héloïse. She chided him for the way he addressed her, and, intentionally or unintentionally, she said things that could only hurt him. She spoke of her "rage against God," of God's cruelty to her, of her hypocrisy, of the fact that it was Abelard's command and not any love of God that made her a nun, and of her present misery. It was, as he pointed out in reply, her "old perpetual complaint against

God,"[23] but that fact made it no easier for him. Most of all, she was simply honest with her feelings. She knew she should repent but could not since her mind was still "on fire with its old desires."

> In my case, the pleasures of lovers which we shared have been too sweet—they can never displease me, and can scarcely be banished from my thoughts. Wherever I turn they are always there before my eyes, bringing with them awakened longings and fantasies which will not even let me sleep. Even during the celebration of the Mass, when our prayers should be purer, lewd visions of those pleasures take such a hold upon my unhappy soul that my thoughts are on their wantonness instead of on prayers. I should be groaning over the sins I have committed, but I can only sigh for what I have lost. Everything we did and also the times and places are stamped on my heart along with your image, so that I live through it all again with you. Even in sleep I know no respite. Sometimes my thoughts are betrayed in a movement of my body, or they break out in an unguarded word.[24]

Héloïse's intention in recounting past pleasures and present longing must not be misunderstood. She was not extolling a life of pleasure, but was remembering the past and accepting the present in the attempt to understand and interpret honestly her moral and spiritual life. She was well aware that Abelard was beyond their pleasures shared. She thought the reason for this was his mutilation, and she, like him, gave that a religious significance. But all this did not mean that she was beyond the memory and desire for pleasures or that there had come to her a religious solution.

> Where God may seem to you an adversary he has in fact proved himself kind: like an honest doctor who does not shrink from giving pain if it will bring about a cure. But for me, youth and passion and experience of pleasures which were so delightful intensify the torments of the flesh and the longings of desire, and the assault is the more overwhelming as the nature they attack is the weaker.[25]

She was a woman of thirty-two when she wrote this, remembering her youth of seventeen.

The ethic she learned from her experiences is simple. But the ethic, manifest in the moral life, had its paradoxes, and of these she was well aware. The basic paradox and ethic are contained in two sentences:

> Wholly guilty though I am, I am also, as you know, wholly innocent. It is not the deed but the intention of the doer which makes the crime, and justice should weigh not what was done but the spirit in which it was done.[26]

She knew that she was morally innocent because of the intention with which she had done everything. And what was that? It was, at base, the intention of his good and his good alone. He was a scholar and a philosopher, already the most renowned of his time. He was a man. She admired and trusted him, she loved his "every grace of mind and body"[27]; and she wanted him to become and to have everything that properly belonged to a scholar, a philosopher, and a man. She knew that he understood the purity of her love. "What my intention toward you has always been, you alone who have known it can judge. I submit all to your scrutiny, yield to your testimony in all things."[28]

Wholly guilty through the acts, wholly innocent through the intention. She applied these judgments both to the act of marriage and to the acts of love, indeed to the totality of her relations with Abelard. For in the ethic of pure intentional love the emphasis is upon the inner experience. It is an ethic of inner life. This is why Héloïse reported so honestly her secret experiences, experiences that were at times even secret from herself as in her sleep and dreams. Abelard was her intention, Abelard her final court of appeal. She was not afraid of him; she could and did live by her own judgments. But she wanted from him, and felt she had the right to receive, the recognition of her innocence, and the purity of her intention.

Yet morally she was still uneasy. "Wholly guilty": this was because her intentions had another judge than Abelard or her conscience.

> Men call me chaste; they do not know the hypocrite I am. They consider purity of the flesh a virtue, though virtue belongs not to the body but to the soul. I can win praise in the eyes of men but deserve none before God, who searches our hearts and loins and sees in our darkness. I am judged religious at a time when there is little in religion which is not hypocrisy, when whoever does not offend the opinions of men receives the highest praise. And yet perhaps there is some merit and it is somehow acceptable to God, if a person whatever his intention gives no offence to the Church in his outward behavior. . . . And this too is a gift of God's grace and comes through his bounty—not only to do good but to abstain from evil. . . . Both are vain if not done from love of God.[29]

This love of God she, an abbess, professed she did not have, and had never had.

> At every stage of my life up to now, as God knows, I have feared to offend you rather than God, and tried to please you more than Him. It was your command, not love of God which made me take the veil.[30]

She pleads with him to understand her inner life: to recognize her hypocrisy, her weakness. "Do not suppose me healthy and so withdraw the grace of your healing. Do not believe I want for nothing and delay helping me in my hour of need." She begs him to stop praising her since his "praise is the more dangerous because I welcome it."[31]

Abelard had been, and still was, her "God." "Up to now": Her ethic of intention and the inner life, her ethic of pure love, was being intensified and enlarged through her honest acceptance of suffering as she had been, and doubtless continued to be, honest in her acceptances of joys.

The Ethic of Abelard

In his letter to Héloïse and, from her reports, in his conversations with her, Abelard did not meet her expressed moral needs. He refused to be drawn into personal ethical relations on her terms and did not respond to the requests in her letters. It cannot be known whether this was because he could not, given who he was, or because he would not, believing that the comfort she wanted was not for her welfare or believing that the guidance he could provide was not in her best interest.

Abelard gave advice. He was ever the teacher, and instruction was his purpose in writing the personal letters to Héloïse as it had been in his *History of My Calamities*. But when Héloïse did not receive the replies she wanted, she made another request that Abelard write both a history of nuns and a rule for the Paraclete order. This Abelard could do, and he wrote two letters of direction far longer than all of the other letters combined. His concern was the church and the purity of its life. This concern had a bearing upon his ethic, and, indeed, the final third of his *Ethics* was given to an understanding of penitence and confession, and their proper ordering in the church.

It is not difficult to understand some of the reasons Abelard was led to this concern and the connection of his ethics with it. The reasons have to do with Abelard's initial relations with Héloïse, the painful sundering of those relations, the transformation of his inner self and with it the transformation of his love for Héloïse.

Abelard became a monk primarily out of shame at his castration, but he had not long been a monk when he took a further, and unnecessary, step of becoming a priest. This marked a new development in his life, a new love of God and of the church. His life from this point on was given to administration, in which he was not successful, and to teaching and to writing. He and Héloïse corresponded and saw each other; she encouraged his writing, and some of it was written specifically for her or the Paraclete.

About eight years after the letters were exchanged, Abelard wrote his *Ethics,* which he titled *Scito te ipsum,* or *Know Thyself.* It is a strange title, especially for one who probably had in mind Augustine's *Confessions* when he wrote his *Historia calamitatum.* For there is in *Scito te ipsum* none of the

specific memories of the inner life that are in Augustine. Indeed, in his autobiography and *Scito te ipsum* Abelard does not reveal the richness of his inner
life as Héloïse does in her letters. His writing is philosophical and abstract so
that even his vivid illustrations, frequently dealing with sexual behavior, are
general. But he does have a specific theme, the theme that was first presented
by Héloïse, that "it is not so much what things are done as the spirit in which
they are done that we must consider," since "it is not the deed but the intention of the doer" that is important.[32]

The argument is straightforward and clear. Morals are defined as "the
vices or virtues of the mind that make us prone to good or bad works."[33]
There is, at the outset, a clear double aspect to ethics. First, and primarily,
Abelard's *Ethics* are an ethic of the interior life of the person, and, though
this idea was not new with him, in his emphasis he was reaching toward a
new understanding of the self. Second, the ethic is concerned with what is
"fitting," that is, with behavior. This aspect of the ethic is clearly subordinate
in Abelard's thought, and, in fact, in his uncompleted book he does not deal
with it adequately, scarcely touching upon the subject.

Intention, then, is everything in the moral life, and evil intention is interpreted as "consent to what is not fitting."[34] There are, in addition to consent, four elements in an act: desire, will (or choice), act, and, accompanying
the act, pleasure. Some moralists thought that there could be moral evil in
each of these, and that, proceeding by stages, each subsequent evil added to
the moral guilt. Thus, an evil will is worse than evil desire; and an evil act
compounds the evil of the will; and pleasure known in an evil act adds to the
sum total of moral wrongness. Not so, insists Abelard. None of these taken
by itself is morally evil, for the only moral evil is the intention, that is, the
consent to the unfitting desire, will, act, or pleasure.

All this, of course, was interpreted within a religious ethic, that is, in relation to the judgments of God. God, it was obvious to Abelard, "considers
the mind rather than the action when it comes to a reward, and an action adds
nothing to merit whether it proceeds from a good or a bad will."[35] Even desires are not to be condemned: we are taught not to fulfill lusts and yet it is
not evil to have them.

> The former is vicious, but the latter [that is, to have no lust] is not possible
> for our weakness. So sin is not lusting for a woman but consenting to lust;
> the consent of the will is damnable, but not the will for intercourse.[36]

So with other familiar "vices" such as gluttony. A man who sees fruit belonging to another will have desires to eat the fruit. "He represses his desire;
he does not extinguish it, but because he is not drawn to consent, he does not
incur sin."[37]

Nor is an act or the pleasure associated with an act the same as sin. For an individual may be forced to an act unwillingly, or to perform an act in a way as to be "brought to pleasure," but in neither case would the individual, without express consent, be considered to have moral fault.[38]

> For God thinks not of what is done but in what mind it may be done, and the merit or glory of the doer lies in the intention, not in the deed. In fact the same thing is often done by different people, justly by one and wickedly by another, as for example if two men hang a convict, the one out of zeal for justice, this one out of hatred arising from an old enmity, and although it is the same act of hanging and although they certainly do what is good to do and what justice requires, yet, through the diversity of their intention, the same thing is done by diverse men, by one badly, by the other well.[39]

The exclusive focus upon intention Abelard generally held throughout his ethic, and it led to some radical, yet rationally consistent, conclusions. The criteria of reason and of intention apply to God as well as to man: God, too, is to be judged by intentions. For it is not inconsistent for God to command what is unfitting, as long as his intentions and consent are good. So God's command to Abraham to kill Isaac was not the ordering of a fitting act but had as its intention the testing of Abraham's obedience that would remain as an example.[40]

Abelard's basic moral belief also led to the consistent conclusion that those who act from ignorance through no responsibility of their own (for example, children or those who have not heard of Christ) are not to be blamed for their sins. Pushing this argument to its logical conclusion for a Christian, he concludes that those who crucified Christ, if their intentions were good, did sin in deed (they did what was not fitting) but were not morally evil in the true definition of sin. There are, therefore, acts which are evil in themselves which are not seriously evil. In terms of concepts familiar in the twelfth century of venial and mortal sins, Abelard's position was that there are no acts that in themselves are mortal sins.

Perhaps of greater significance is the fact that the most trivial venial act can easily become a mortal sin. Abelard took as his examples eating and dressing. Normally overeating or extravagant dressing are light moral evils since they are done with little or no thought of their moral implications. But if one consciously overeats beyond what is necessary or knowingly dresses out of vanity, the trivial venial sin becomes a mortal sin. However, there was also for Abelard the more subtle fact of forgetting or remembering. When a person "forgets," Abelard insisted, the moral evil is less. In his insistence upon the critical importance of knowledge and memory in the moral life, Abelard in his rational analysis was leading ethics farther into the interior life, and because knowledge and memory are both illimitable and often obscure, he was developing ethics in the direction of the intensification and depth of moral thought.

This same kind of careful rational analysis caused Abelard to inquire about punishments and rewards for moral evil. The problem was whether the punishment and rewards are of God or man. If the former, Abelard agreed with Héloïse that intention is all. Human beings, however, cannot understand the inner intentions or consents of another and must, therefore, direct their moral judgments to deeds. But this human way of determining moral culpability is inevitably erroneous, for two reasons: first, because it is not and cannot be a judgment of intentions which would be the true moral quality, and second, because the outer judgment refers primarily to the public and not the individual good.

The facts that the important moral qualities are inner and not outer, that they have to do with the person and not the act, that the only true judgment is by God and not man, and that the consent to evil breaks the relation of a person with God mean that the question of reconciliation had central importance in Abelard's ethic. This required an interpretation of repentance and confession. These themes were so important to Abelard that over one-third of his *Ethics* was given to their consideration, and the ethical development he made here was an advance in moral thought and a major achievement of medieval ethics.

Repentance is the first way of reconciliation for moral evil, and the beginning of repentance is "sorrow of the mind over what it has done wrong."[41] But such sorrow, if it is to be effective, cannot be because of social attitudes or pressures, as it often is. Nor can it come from fear of punishment. Only that repentance is fruitful that is based upon the love of God and the hatred of sin. Those who "repent healthily" are moved only by "love of him." Though Abelard had not been previously clear on this point, it becomes evident at this stage in his argument that love of God and his goodness is not merely the only valid motive for repentance but also the only satisfactory motive for the moral life. "Would that we would do or endure as much for God to whom we owe all as for our wife or children or any mistress!"[42]

With such an attitude, there comes after a moral failure and with recognition of the failure a "sigh and contrition of heart which we call true repentance." Nothing more is needed. "In this sigh we are instantly reconciled to God." Through this sigh of love the person is made, by the reconciliation, "what he is not yet worthy of being."[43]

Confession, then, is not always necessary. Tears are enough. Abelard quoted a moving passage by Ambrose about Peter's weeping:

> I do not find what he said; I find that he wept. I read of his tears; I do not read of his satisfaction. Tears wipe away a wrong which it is disgraceful to

confess with one's voice and weeping guarantees pardon and shame. Tears declare the fault without dread, they confess without prejudicing shame. Tears do not request pardon but deserve it. I find why Peter was silent, namely lest by asking for pardon so soon he should offend more.[44]

There are times, too, when confession can be put off, especially if fore-thought causes one to think that more harm than good may come from the confession. Generally, however, it is morally good that individuals confess for a number of reasons. There is, first, the simple need to be helped, and this can happen only when there is the frank communication of moral faults and failures. Then there is the fact that "in the humility of confession a large part of satisfaction is performed."[45] Finally, confession exists that priests might impose penance that will lead to correction: "he who seeks medicine for a wound . . . must show it to a doctor that an effective cure may be applied. The priest in fact occupies the place of a doctor."[46]

However, when a person is in need of moral reconciliation, it is impor-tant to choose carefully the person to whom to confess, for just as there are unskillful doctors so there are inauthentic priests who are "neither religious nor discreet, and moreover liable to disclose the sins of those who confess, so that to confess to them seems not only useless but also ruinous."[47] Such persons are a scandal to the church, and Abelard's anger with incompetent prelates is personal.

Before he wrote the *Ethics* Abelard's writings had been condemned, and while he had not been excommunicated, he knew what it meant to be ostra-cized by an unjust judgment. He was, then, imaginatively carrying his own experience one step further when he argued that only one with an infallibly true judgment, that is, God, had the power to excommunicate.

> In fact, anyone bound is bound unjustly when he incurs excommunication which he has not merited and is separated from the Church, with the result that the fellowship of the faithful is not allowed to him. But God breaks those bonds of the anathema because he makes this decision of the pastor invalid, so that it does not exclude from grace him whom the pastor has sep-arated from the Church.[48]

Some of the unusual ideas of the *Scito te ipsum* caused the fateful clash of Bernard of Clairvaux with Abelard, though they were not as important as the doctrines of the *Theologia,* Abelard's major theological work, and the *Liber sententiarum*, a garbled student account of Abelard's teachings falsely attributed to him. There were many other protagonists in the controversy, but the focus centered upon Bernard and Abelard.

It was clearly not a battle between moral good and evil or between a man of faith and man of reason. It was not a dispute between theology and philosophy, or between mystical and rational theology. As with many moral disputes, it had more to do with temperament and with two separate and opposing visions of the place of education in the world, between Bernard's defense of the monastic tradition of the cloister and Abelard's championing of the more open Cathedral schools, between a looking back to a simple asceticism of the past and Abelard's desire to open the theological traditions to public discussion. Certainly Bernard, with his profound love of Jesus, was deeply offended by Abelard's assertion that those who crucified Jesus committed an unfitting act but did not sin, and with his creedal faith was greatly troubled by doctrines of God and the atonement which seemed to deny the truths by which he lived.

Bernard, encouraged by others, charged Abelard with specific heresies. The two men met but could not resolve the conflict. Through the intervention of Abelard's students arrangements were made for the two men to engage in a *disputatio* at Sens in 1141. Bernard, unskilled in public disputation, was at a disadvantage, but at the last minute, for unknown reasons, Abelard refused to debate. He, instead, appealed his case directly to Rome. The Council of Sens met, considered Abelard's writings, and declared many of them heretical. A report was sent to the pope and, in addition, Bernard personally asked the pope to condemn Abelard. Pope Innocent III declared Abelard's writings heretical, and they were publicly burned in Rome. Abelard, sixty-two and ill, began a journey to Rome to appeal directly to the pope.

Peter the Venerable, the abbot of Cluny and an ardent supporter of scholarship, who was not on the best terms with the abbot of Clairvaux, invited Abelard to stay at Cluny. The abbot of Citeaux suggested a reconciliation between Abelard and Bernard; so Peter urged Abelard to visit Clairvaux and "to curb his language." Both were done; and upon Abelard's return, Peter the Venerable wrote the pope, indicating that peace had been made and asking that Abelard be allowed to spend "the remaining days of his life, which will perhaps not be many," at Cluny.[49] This was permitted.

The final portrait of Abelard at Cluny is vastly different from any previous description of him. It was, to be sure, written shortly after his death by an abbot known for his kindness, and it was sent to Héloïse. (This fact, in itself, suggests the closeness of their relations to the end.) But there is the ring of authenticity about Peter's portrayal.

> The nature and extent of the saintliness, humility and devotion of his life among us, to which Cluny can bear witness, cannot briefly be told. I do not remember seeing anyone, I think, who was his equal in conduct and manner. ... And although at my insistence he held superior rank in our large community of brothers, the shabbiness of his attire made him look the humblest of

them all. I often marvelled, and when he walked in front of me in the usual processional order, I almost stood still in astonishment that a man who bore so great and distinguished a name could thus humble and abase himself.[50]

He was frugal, content with only what was necessary. He read continuously, he prayed, he was silent except in sermons or personal conversation. "His mind, his speech, his work were devoted to meditation, to teaching and to profession of what was always holy, philosophic and scholarly."[51]

This letter must have been read and reread countless times by Héloïse with profound feelings, unfathomable to any other, of hurt and healing. Abelard's consent to poverty, particularly the poverty of the senses and spirit, was not the Abelard she had known and loved. He had not been a success in the church, and he now rejected fame. She had wanted both for him. She knew he had been a success and that he was rightly famous. But what she had most wanted he possessed to the end: "His mind, his speech, his work were . . . philosophic and scholarly."

That was her ethic—interior, intentional, consenting—and not this one of acts which was revealed to her at the end. Her ethic has rightly been called "the ethics of pure love."[52] That love was not only expressed directly but testified to indirectly by her pleas, her anger, her despair, which revealed her conviction that her love, which was her ethic, had not received the response from Abelard which it deserved. It is evident from their writings that Héloïse had the greater moral sensitivity. She possessed more moral depth, insight, and vision than did Abelard. She knew both the ideals and practicalities of morality better than he. Though, unlike Abelard, she did not write an ethic, she, aware of specific moral realities and not abstractions, lived far more effectively, and possibly more painfully and joyfully, than he. This ethical life, centered at first upon him and toward truth beyond him, was in time transformed in her life. Strangely, others recognized this before she did, for she was at first unwilling to admit that there could be any love, any life better than that which she had known and lost.

Still, it was not entirely lost, and for all of her complaints to Abelard, Héloïse must have understood that. For he who had not responded to her requests did respond, in his own way, with one of the final acts of his life, and in that response he revealed something of the self he had hidden. For he sent her, "once dear to me in the world now dear in Christ," his final confession of faith, "to banish fearful anxiety and all uncertainties from the heart within your breast."[53] That act was surely also the expression of an ethic of pure love.

And she responded. After Abelard's death in 1142 she asked that his body be sent to the Paraclete for burial. When that was done she asked Peter the Venerable to send her "under seal an open document containing the absolution of our master, to be hung on his tomb" and requested that "for the love of God" he give assistance to their son Astrolabe.[54] Her final request relating to Abelard, a request that revealed her moral intention and consent, was that at her death she be buried beside him, "her master, or rather her father, husband, or rather brother."[55] This request was granted.

FRANCIS OF ASSISI (1182–1226)

Assisi was a small village in central Italy. At the foot of the town was a vast plain, six hundred feet above sea level; above Assisi towered a four-thousand-foot mountain. In this town, where nature united a broad valley, large plain, and jutting mountains, an infant, christened Giovanni, was born about 1181. His father, Pietro Bernadone, was a prosperous cloth merchant who, from his mercantile travels, brought to Assisi news of happenings in the world, especially the world of religion. He also brought home a knowledge of the French tongue and the songs of the troubadours. He taught both to Giovanni who, because of his father's love for the French language and the lays of chivalry, was also given the name of Francesco. Little is known of his mother. It has been conjectured she was originally from Provence, and, if so, Francis would have learned the love of song and life from her as well as from his father. It is clear that she was devoutly pious, for once when chided about her son's escapades, she answered, "What are you thinking about? I am sure that, if it pleases God, he will become a good Christian."[56]

It is reported that as a child Francis had a love for play and for music, and that as a youth he had a love for comrades and for life. He was a ringleader in festivities with his companions and had an ambition to become a great hero. It was the ideal of chivalry that appealed to him. He wanted to pledge his allegiance to a noble warrior, to risk his life in great battles, and to return home a conquering knight. This ambition, shared with friends, was confused in his mind with all sorts of chaotic religious notions. They were unavoidably chaotic because he had never received any education beyond that of learning to read. So his ideas of religion came from his life in the small village; from listening to his parents' conversation and the talk of their townsfolk; from hearing the priests reading the Bible, preaching, and saying mass. Yet the moral ideals of the religion touched him early. Once, in his youth, when Francis was selling goods for his father, a beggar entered the Bernadone shop. Francis, busy with a well-to-do customer, dismissed the beggar gruffly. After the customer left, what he had done flashed into his mind. "If that poor beggar had come to borrow money representing some noble among your friends you would have been proud to have given it to him. How have you dared to dismiss one whom the King of Kings sent you?"[57]

But it was the secular ideal of nobility that appealed to him in his youth.

In that spirit, in his early twenties Francis fought a battle for Assisi against Perugia, was taken captive, and was in prison for perhaps a year.

> As he lived like a noble it was with the knights that he had been imprisoned. While they lamented their lot he laughed at his chains and never ceased to be gay. "Art thou mad," his companions said to him, "that thou makest a joke of the state we are in?" "Why should I be miserable," he answered "when I think of the future that awaits me, when I know that one day I shall be the idol of the whole world?"[58]

After his release he continued to dream of becoming the idol of the world, but in a serious illness he began to have doubts about his ambition. The return of health brought the return of ambition, so when he was twenty-five and still dreaming of military glory Francis persuaded his father to furnish him with armor and horse that he might once more leave Assisi to battle against the enemies of his town. He never reached the battlefield. Doubts about his ambition, working below the level of his consciousness, erupted in a dream in which a questioner asked who could do better for him, the servant or the Lord. "The Lord," said Francis. "Why then," came another question, "are you seeking the servant instead of the Lord?" Inwardly perplexed, Francis renounced his military ambition and turned back to Assisi to wait with troubled thoughts, not knowing what he was waiting for.

Soon the festivities were renewed, but the old pleasures no longer satisfied. Once, when Francis appeared preoccupied in the midst of conversation with his companions, they reproached him, "What is the matter with you? Are you thinking of getting married?" "Yes," Francis told them without yet knowing the meaning of his answer, knowing only a new life was emerging, "Yes, I am thinking of taking a wife more beautiful, more rich, more pure than you could even imagine."[59]

In his twenty-fifth year he spent many hours alone. In his solitude, as his mystical spirit began to mature, as the creative and imaginative conversation with his God deepened, Francis gradually came to a new consciousness of his own life and of how he should live. He had heard the gospels read and in them he had seen a man who owned no property, who lived simply, who gave freely of all that he had. From them he had memorized words of that man, words that greatly affected him. "He that loveth father or mother more than me is not worthy of me. Go, sell what you have and give to the poor and come, follow me."[60] His mind was transformed by what he did with his solitariness. He would sell what he had, wed Lady Poverty, and follow Jesus.

One day, when he was twenty-six, Francis entered a decrepit chapel of St. Damian near Assisi as he had so often done in the past. He knelt before the simple masonry and, gazing at the crucifix, prayed earnestly, "Great and glorious God, and thou, Lord Jesus, shed abroad your light in the darkness of my mind. Be found in me, Lord, so that in all things I may act in accordance with thy holy will." In his perplexity, from that inner dialogue there came the reply, "Francis, repair my house which, as you see, is falling in ruins."[61] Looking about he saw the cracked walls, the broken timbers, and he understood his task to be the restoration of the chapel in which he prayed. It was only later he gradually discovered the simple command "repair my house" had a larger meaning.

During the time he was rebuilding St. Damian, his father began to question the ways of his son, and not without reason. Francis in his strange renunciation was not realizing his father's ambitions. Nor was this all. In the single-mindedness of his new work Francis, who had always had access to his father's wealth, sold goods from the shelves of the Bernadone store to buy materials for St. Damian. His fellow citizens in Assisi openly called him a "madman," and this disrespect for the family name, together with his strange actions, was more than his father could tolerate. The clash of wills between father and son intensified until the father, attempting to restore his son's sanity more than the goods he had taken from the shop, made legal charges against Francis. The case was tried in public with the people of Assisi assembled, father facing son, the bishop seated between them. When he had heard the charges and received the evidence, the bishop ordered Francis to give all the money he had secured from his father back to its rightful owner. Francis, moved with emotion, entered the bishop's palace and reappeared a moment later, his clothes wrapped in a bundle in his hand. These, with what little money he had, he placed at the bishop's feet, and turning to the crowd, said,

> Listen all of you, and understand it well. Until this time I have called Pietro Bernadone my father; but now that I desire to serve God I return him not only his money, but the clothes, too, that I had from him. From henceforth I desire to say nothing else than, "Our Father, who art in heaven."[62]

He was taking the words of the gospel literally. His vocation had begun. Francis left the town, taking nothing with him, and retired to the mountains. There, for more than two years, he lived alone or in the seclusion of a monastery. Toward the end of 1208 he decided he should return to St. Damian to complete the task that had been assigned to him of repairing the church. It was there, probably on February 24, 1209, that he listened to the priest read the command of Jesus to the first disciples and he became aware this was a new command for him.

> Go, preach, saying that the kingdom of heaven is at hand; heal the sick, cleanse the lepers, freely you have received, freely give; provide neither gold

nor silver nor brass in your purses, nor scrip for your journey, neither two coats, nor shoes, nor yet slaves, for the workman is worthy of his meat.[63]

Francis reported years later that this was the day it was revealed to him what he should do, namely, that he must live according to the words of the gospel, and that he responded with joy: "This is what I desire, this is what I have been looking for, this I long with all my inmost heart to do."[64] He kept only his tunic, encompassed by a rough cord, and the next day he returned to Assisi to preach. His words, spoken by a man without learning and from the depths of his heart, touched many people, and it was not long before there were those who wanted to follow him. A rich citizen, Bernard, impressed by the bearing of Francis, asked what a wealthy man who wanted to follow Christ should do with his money. When Francis told him it should be given back to the persons from whom it had come, he replied that, desiring to be with Francis, this would be done. With a third friend they went to a church, at the suggestion of Francis, to find in the gospels what they should do. Francis opened the gospels three times. First he turned to the account of the rich man who had come to Jesus and read the command, "Go, sell what you have and give to the poor." Second he found the words of Jesus that had so impressed him a few days previously, "Take nothing for your journey, neither slaves, nor scrip, neither bread, nor money; neither have two coats apiece." Finally, he turned to the explicit words of Jesus to those who would follow him, "If any man will come after me, let him deny himself, and take up his cross and follow me."[65]

THE ETHIC OF FRANCIS

The ethic of Francis was his life. To understand his ethic, therefore, requires an understanding of the deepest motives of his actions and speech. This is not a difficult task intellectually, though to comprehend his motives emotionally requires an imitation, at least imaginatively, of his experience. Still, the fundamental beliefs that permeated all of the life of Francis stand out in bold relief. They were the assumptions of the ethic of medieval Christendom, though in Francis they were apprehended with a unique simplicity and intensity.

He lived with the ever-present conviction that God is absolute sovereign, that the entire creation is his kingdom, and that God and his creation met in Jesus, so that Jesus became liege lord and the image of what human creatures should be. To have God as his sovereign meant that there was meaning in life and that meaning was spiritual. All of creation was related, all had dignity and was to be reverenced. Jesus was the clue to this meaning and dignity, and Francis had the compulsion to shape his life directed by the words and life of Jesus. To follow Jesus meant to take his words literally, never forgetting, in all the joy of the created world, that at the end of that life there had been a cross. There was no escape in supposing that one could leave society because it was not Christ-like, or to live in society as though its standards had already become Christian.

These three—God, the order of the created world, and Christ—caused Francis to understand in new ways the nature of created things and their interrelations as well as their more basic relations with the supreme spiritual reality. The ordinary social norms and classifications were gone. Human beings should be responded to in terms of their needs to realize their beings, not in terms of their social status. And natural beings, the entire world of nature, should be responded to as no less the creatures of God than human beings. Francis was enabled to live in this spirit because of his certainty that Christian civilization was a present reality, an actual eternal order within and beyond the social order. Because that order stretched from heaven to earth, from the eternal "moment" to the time of each day, Francis also knew that the most important fact about the life of each person was his or her destination. But his entire ethic would be distorted if one believed that Francis was concerned with the eternal salvation of individuals, for his belief in eternal life was not an isolated item of faith but was woven together with all his basic convictions in which each belief implied the others.

These beliefs led to the ethical experience of a unique individual who "did the hardest thing in the world in the perpetual conviction that it was the easiest, and that all men, if they tried, would find it so."[66] His moral experience was that of an individual under authority, under the authority of his personal relation with God. In the testament left to his followers Francis reminded them that "after the Lord gave me brothers, no one showed me what I ought to do, but the most high revealed to me that I ought to live according to the model of the holy gospel."[67] The most dramatic revelation of his personal relation to God as the source of his individuality and authority occurred nine years after the establishment of the Franciscan Order. There had developed a strong tendency to forget the vow of poverty and make it another monastic movement. Some discontented friars spoke to a cardinal about persuading Francis to modify his rules of simplicity and poverty and to accept the rules of Benedict, Augustine, or Bernard. When the cardinal tactfully introduced the subject in a private conversation, Francis was deeply hurt. He took the cardinal to the assembled friars and spoke to all:

> My brethren, my brethren, the Lord has called me into the ways of simplicity and humility. He has shown me this way of life in truth for myself and for those who desire to believe and follow me. Do not, then, come speaking to me of the rule of St. Benedict or St. Augustine or St. Bernard, nor any other way except this which God in his mercy has seen fit to show me. And God has told me that he would, by its means, make a new covenant with the world, and he does not will that we should have any other.[68]

With this individuality, seeking to base his life upon the authority of the personal truth found through his relations with God, the ethic of Francis became that of devotion, renunciation, and purification.

1. Devotion

The devotion of Francis was a readiness to perform whatever the will of God required. It was a devotion to God that led to a love of all of God's creatures. In this love Francis found an exuberant joy in nature and in the social life as he identified himself with the creatures of God. That love, that joy, that identification led him to the service of humanity and the natural world.

The love Francis had for nature—for mountains and lakes and forests, for waterfalls, for tree and flower, and for all animals—and the joy he found in all being is one of the most familiar facts about his life. His was a joyful identification. He preached to the birds, released animals from traps, returned fish to the lake, and kept a plot of earth in his vegetable garden for "our sisters the flowers." His feeling for nature was expressed in a poem he composed a year before his death.

> O most high, almighty, good Lord God, to thee belong praise, glory, honor, and all blessing!
>
> Praised be my Lord God with all His creatures, and especially our Brother the Sun, who brings us the day and who brings us the light; fair is he and shines with a very great splendor; O Lord, he signifieth to us thee!
>
> Praised be my Lord for our Sister the Moon, and for the Stars, the which He hath set clear and lovely in the heaven.
>
> Praised be my Lord for our brother the Wind, and for air and cloud, calms and all weather by which Thou upholdest in life all creatures.
>
> Praised be my Lord for our sister Water, who is very serviceable unto us and humble and precious and clean.
>
> Praised be my Lord for our brother Fire, through whom thou givest us light in the darkness; and he is bright and pleasant and very mighty and strong.
>
> Praised be my Lord for our mother the earth, the which doth sustain us and keep us, and bringeth forth divers fruits and flowers of many colours, and grass.
>
> Praise ye and bless ye the Lord and give thanks unto Him and serve Him with great humility.[69]

His delights in the natural world did not lessen his love for human beings, nor did it weaken his trust in God. The contrary was the case. All were woven together in the fabric of existence so that love for one creature intensified love for all others as it matured trust in the creator. This elemental truth was manifest by the addition of two stanzas that Francis made to his "Canticle."

In 1225 there was a bitter feud in Assisi between the bishop and the chief magistrate. Francis invited the two antagonists, with all the townsfolk, to hear his canticle as he intoned each stanza and as each was then sung in unison by the friars. The people assembled, and Francis began. All listened reverently to the singing of the man, now blind, who could no longer see the world he celebrated. When the canticle was completed Francis added an unexpected stanza, and everyone understood he was singing to his God for the bishop, the magistrate, and all persons everywhere.

> Praised be my Lord for all those who forgive for love of thee,
> and who endure weakness and tribulation; blessed are they who
> persevere in peace, for thou, most high, shalt give them a crown.[70]

Love where human beings are present meant forgiveness. It meant identification with the lives of those in need, and service to them for the love of God. Francis had a sensitivity toward persons early in life, but it was only through personal struggle that he was able to enter into the actual experiences of others. It was this desire to know the life of others intimately that led him, in the year of his transformation, to become a beggar on the steps of St. Peter's in Rome, for only in this way did he believe he could comprehend how poverty felt to a beggar. It was this same desire to understand others that led him to embrace lepers. His entire mature life was identified with the poor and the dispossessed. The dominant motif of Francis's ethic was devotion to God in the love of all creation and in the joy of identification with nature and other human beings. That trust in God and sense of the eternal destiny of humanity was revealed in the final stanza he added to the "Canticle." In his last sickness, when he was forty-three, Francis asked his physician about his condition. When an evasive answer was given, Francis insisted upon the truth. Informed he had only a short while to live, Francis raised his hands to heaven, "Be welcome, sister death." Then he began to sing and sent for the friars to join him. His mind turned to his hymn in praise of all creation; and when he had sung, "Praised be my Lord for all those who forgive," he added the final stanza:

> Praised be my Lord for our sister, the death of the body, from
> which no man escapeth. Woe to him who dieth in mortal sin!
> Blessed are they who are found walking by thy most holy will,
> for the second death shall have no power to do them harm.
>
> Praise ye and bless the Lord and give thanks to him with great
> humility.[71]

This trust and ethic of devotion were possible only through an ethic with elements of renunciation and purification.

2. Renunciation

There were two elements in Francis's renunciation of socially esteemed life and values. The first was the acceptance of "Lady Poverty." This determination to be rid of money and property was stimulated by the desire to imitate Jesus, who did not have "a place to lay his head."[72] But it was also the result of what a young man, raised in a well-to-do family, observed of what a concern for this world's goods did to persons. Indeed, it had probably more than once made him mistreat a fellow human, as when he dismissed the beggar, failing to see who he was in actuality. The acceptance of Lady Poverty, then, was his desire for liberty, freedom from the oppressive burdens of body and spirit that the ownership of material goods usually imposed upon individuals. There was also in his acceptance of poverty the view that whenever an individual would serve the poor he must become one of them; so a church or monastery endowed with the wealth of the world was a poor instrument to proclaim to impoverished human beings the gospel of him who said, "Blessed are the poor."

While the renunciatory ideal of Francis was that of poverty, he also had the ideal of work.

"As for myself," he said in his last Testament,

> I worked with my hands as I am resolved still to do and I urge particularly all my Brethren to work at some honest labour. Let those among them who have no craft learn one; and this not in order to earn money, but to set a good example and avoid idleness. And if it should happen that we do not earn the wherewithal to live in exchange for our labour, let us have recourse to the table of the Lord in going from door to door for alms. It was also the Lord who revealed to me the salutation we should use; May the Lord give you peace.[73]

3. Purification

The devotion to God and love of neighbor led to the purification of the self in the form of a continual self-mastery and self-refinement. This purification was for the sake not of self-realization but of God and neighbor. The renunciation of wealth, the acceptance of poverty, the willingness to work all contributed to this purification. But the major means of creating a single self were prayer and identification with the suffering Jesus.

Francis was a mystic. This accounted for the zeal in his life. He was a mystic whose inner life of prayer was directed toward the Jesus of the gospels. This accounted for the direction of his life. His identification with Jesus culminated in the reception of the stigmata of the crucified upon his hands, and feet, and body. Precisely what happened in the stigmatization and how it happened have been disputed, but there was no doubt that Francis's hands and feet were discolored as with the holes made by nails, and that a wound was opened in his side. Francis, at the time, was ill; he knew that he did not have long to live, and with a single-minded fervor that illness sometimes brings he prayed,

> Lord, I ask two graces of thee before I die: to experience myself, as far as possible, the sufferings of thy cruel passion; and to have for thee the very love which caused thee to sacrifice thyself for us.[74]

In the solitude of the hours he made this prayer the stigmata appeared. It was a visible culmination of his attempt through the years to engage in a continual purging, a continual purification in identifying himself with Jesus and in following literally his master.

Francis was inspired to live as he did, embodying his ethic, because he believed there was already present a universal Christian society that still needed to be impregnated with the spirit of Christ. He did not, then, retire from society into a monastery, nor did he live conservatively within the established church. He lived in society, he participated in social and political struggles because he saw all of creation kin to him since all was the creation of God. He found ways to recognize the meaningful unity and ordered dignity of the natural world, including the world of humans. He lived daily with the conviction that his life and that of all persons had its most important destiny beyond this life. So in his life he developed an ethic expressed in the Franciscan prayer:

> Lord, make me an instrument of your peace; where there is hatred, let me sow love; where there is injury, pardon; where there is doubt, faith; where there is despair, hope; where there is darkness, light; and where there is sadness, joy.
>
> O Divine Master, grant that I may not so much to seek to be consoled as to console; to be understood as to understand; to be loved as to love; for it is in giving that we receive, it is in pardoning that we are pardoned, and it is in dying that we are born to eternal life.[75]

THOMAS AQUINAS (1225?–1274)

There have not been many persons in history that justly deserve the definition of the philosopher as one "whose thought can contemplate all time and all existence,"[76] but Thomas Aquinas is one of those persons. His writings are a system in the root meaning of that word, "an organized whole." No matter what may be thought of the system, the magnitude of the writing is an impressive monument to the spirit of Thomas and to the medieval mind. For the life of Thomas, too, was "an organized whole"; and, if there was little drama in his public life, it is because the vigor and depth of his personal experience were manifest in thought and words rather than deeds.

The externals of his life can be briefly related. Thomas was born in 1225 in the kingdom of Naples to a noble family of Aquino. At fourteen he went to the University of Naples. Attracted by Dominican friars he planned to enter the order, but because his family objected to his becoming a monk, he was kidnapped by his brothers and imprisoned for over a year while his family tried to dissuade him and while Thomas studied. Upon his release he took the vows of the order, and, when he was nineteen, he traveled to Paris, where he studied with Albertus Magnus, one of the greatest teachers of the century, following him to Cologne in 1248. Thomas became a priest when he was twenty-five, and the following year began teaching. The remainder of his life was a continuation of his prayer, discipline, and studying; and to this was added preaching, teaching, and traveling. Thomas soon was in demand throughout Christendom, for his abilities were directed by his passion to explain and defend the truth of Christianity. When, in 1265, the Archbishopric of Naples became vacant, he begged to be excused from the appointment since he felt he had not yet completed his work of writing.

This writing includes tracts and commentaries interpreting and defending the Christian philosophy, commentaries on Aristotle, as well as the major *Summa contra Gentiles* and *Summa Theologiae*. The former was the attempt to meet non-Christian philosophers on the common ground of reason and to argue that even on this basis, all the truths revealed to faith aside, Christian thought is the most adequate philosophy. The *Summa Theologiae* was written "by its author's own confession, like . . . a very little rule for beginners"[77] although it was a rule that ran to some 3,800 pages. With his judicious temperament Thomas tried to examine relevant ideas and to face all difficulties. In the *Theologiae* he perfected the scholastic method, stimulated by Abelard's *Sic et non*, of presenting alternative answers to a question. He announced his major topic (the "question") for interpretation, stated each thesis for discussion under the topic in the form of other questions ("articles"), introduced objections to the thesis, making use of extensive quotations from church fathers, scriptures, philosophers, and theologians; stated succinctly the alternative view to the objection, interpreted his solution to the problem; and finally described the implications of this solution, usually by explanation of the inadequacy of the original objections.

This method was not merely a matter of a traditional scholastic style. It was Thomas's way of thinking, the morality of his mind. It is one of the most impressive facts of intellectual history that over a long period of years one man's daily life was the asking of questions in a clear order in which he saw opposing positions that enabled him to develop his own answer that was usually clear and often subtle with inventive characterizations and reconciliations. It is also significant that through this style Thomas engaged in conversation with thinkers of the past. Philosophers and theologians, as well as the writers of scripture, were treated as contemporaries with whom he could respectfully dispute. Through this process Thomas created an intellectual community for himself, and by his work a visible community was developed and, through the years, expanded.

The writings of Thomas obviously were not restricted to ethics. Yet in the writings there emerges an interpretation of the moral life, central to Thomas's thought, that is rooted in a philosophical-theological system. Indeed, there is more writing about ethics in the *Summa Theologiae* than about any other subject.

The entire work of Thomas was based upon the acceptance of the principles of the Christian faith that he learned in his early training, so his moral theory rests upon the assumptions of the medieval ethic. His task was to make vague presuppositions more definite, to harmonize ill-defined, contradictory principles, and to extend the meaning of the assumptions to logical conclusions. These tasks he performed in his ethic by beginning with the view that the human mind, through reason and faith, can discover the meaningful unity and ordered dignity throughout all created existence which has its origin in a transcendent God, the source of all things and all value. It was in his inaugural lecture as Master of Theology at Paris that, at the age of thirty-two, Thomas stated the basic principles that would guide all of his work:

> The King and Lord of the heavens ordained from eternity this law: that the gifts of his providence should reach to the lowest things by way of those that lie between.[78]

Since this is so, the achievement of individual and social good depended upon the recognition and realization of the nature of created things, their relations to each other, and their dependence upon the supreme spiritual reality. The fundamental task of Thomas as an ethicist, then, was to study the place and the nature of human beings in the order of the created world: what can we know about the person as an individual and in society?

But before an ethic can be properly developed, Thomas thought it necessary to ask: How can we discover any truth? What do we discover as the truth about reality? This means that the ethic is grounded in a philosophical and theological view. While it is possible to interpret the ethic independent from its grounding, it is important to recognize that, for Thomas, this is to take the moral life out of its necessary context. Indeed, deeper than the philosophical and theological ideas is a religious attitude, as expressed in Thomas's prayer:

> Thou who makest eloquent the tongues of little children, fashion my words and put upon my lips the grace of Thy benediction. Grant me penetration to understand, capacity to retain, method and facility in study, subtlety in interpretation, and abundant grace of expression.
>
> Order the beginning, direct the progress, and perfect the achievement of my work, Thou Who art true God and Man and reignest forever and ever. Amen.[79]

It was in this spirit that Thomas wrote, grounding his ethic in a theory of knowledge and reality. Before asking about his ethics, therefore, it is important to ask about the pathways to truth, the pattern of reality, and, because ethics concerns human experience, the nature of human beings.

1. The ways to truth: reason and faith

Reason and faith are complementary means to the truth. Reason deals with the materials provided by the natural world and the truth discovered through reason is primarily a truth about this world. With this knowledge, however, it is possible to infer both the existence and some of the characteristics of God. Faith, mediated by the church, deals primarily with the materials of the supernatural world, so its truth is mainly a truth of revelation inaccessible to reason alone. These truths revealed by reason and by faith can never contradict each other, and it was this conviction that enabled Thomas to enter any inquiry and engage in any dispute without anxiety. But neat cleavages between reason and faith, while basically sound, should not be understood as static complementary relations or watertight compartments. For one person will believe by faith what another will discern by reason, and the same person may believe a truth by faith that will later be understood through reason.

In any case, knowledge of this world, whether known by reason or faith, is realistic, literal knowledge, but this is not so of the understanding of God. Here Thomas develops the cardinal methodological principle of "analogical reasoning." In any accurate speaking about God there is always a valid analogy of meaning. This is to say that language about God (e.g., that he is merciful, loving, just) is not equivalent to the speech normally used in the human world. Nor are such references to God "univocal" with a rigid identity of meaning as words frequently are when they are applied to the natural world. Human speech about God is analogical. There are, as Thomas expresses it, "various proportions" of meaning.[80] This principle of knowledge prohibits both skepticism and excessive claims to final truth. Yet the truth that is known is truth. Human beings do have real knowledge of God and genuine relations with God. But humans are human and not God.

It is precisely these facts of real yet limited knowledge, real yet limited being, that set the conditions for human life. Applied to ethics, therefore, analogical reasoning prevents both moral skepticism and absolutism. But it does more: it enables Thomas to make subtle distinctions and ingenious connections in his ethical theory, for it underscores the fact that the moral life is richer than the moral thought for which it is the basis. Thomas exhibits his typical good sense and practical manner of thinking that, however complex, is never far from the actualities of experience. "For St. Thomas all being and truth and goodness is kin, and wherever they are found there is some unity by analogy."[81]

2. The pattern of reality: the world and God

There are two realms of being: nature and supernature. The former is contingent and is, in Aristotelian terms, a dynamic compound of "matter" and "form." It is arranged in a hierarchical order from inanimate matter to plants to animals to human beings. Each of the lower levels of being (and Thomas does not hesitate to think in terms of "lower" and "higher") is a preparation for the higher which, however, is separated by a real discontinuity from the lower.

Nothing within this order of the created natural world would have existed without God, the Creator. Nothing in this contingent world would continue to exist without God, the necessary being. Nothing in these hierarchical degrees of being would have value without pointing toward God, the perfect value being. Nothing in this order of change would have reality without God, who is pure Being. All of nature, therefore, was created by and points toward supernature.

All of Thomas's theories about knowing and reality emerge from two basic assumptions of medieval thought, viz., that "in all created existence there is a meaningful unity and an ordered dignity which is discoverable by human beings" and that "the only adequate principle of meaning for the universe is spiritual."[82]

3. The nature of human beings

Thomas adopts the Aristotelian view of human beings, refinishing and enlivening that view from his Christian perspective. In human life three levels are present: the vegetative with the capacities of nutrition and reproduction; the animal with characteristic activities of locomotion and sense perception; and the rational with the intellectual functionings of imagination and memory, conception, and judgment. These levels form a unity in which there is an interrelation of activities, the "lower" activities, in particular, furnishing the materials for the "higher" and the latter, in some cases, directing the former. There can be no functioning of the intellect, for example, without sense perception since all reasoning is dependent upon the materials provided by the senses. The will, too is constituted of materials provided by the animal functioning (emotion, desire, appetite) as these are guided by the intellect. The will is, therefore, properly called "rational appetite."[83]

The human individual is a unity of soul and body. The soul is the "first principle of life" which cannot belong to material things since, if it did, all matter would be alive. The soul of each individual is incorporeal, and, because the individual is "real," the soul is "subsistent." The intellect is the soul, though this intellect must be conceived as the totality and unity that is the source of all intellectual activities and not as theoretical reason alone. Such a soul in union with the body constitutes the real life of the person. For this soul is not "entombed in, but endowed with, a body"[84] and it has an eternal destiny.

It is now possible to observe Thomas's view of the preconditions of morality in human experience, and to understand his ethics in terms of the characteristics of good acts, of a morally good person, and of the good in society.

THE PRECONDITIONS OF MORALITY: A THEORY OF ACTION

The essential preconditions of morality are found in the human experience of acting and in the realities toward which all actions occur. It is important, therefore, to recognize the purpose of all human acts, and the structure of a human act, noting specifically the roles of knowing and loving in human life (intellect and will) and the specifically ingrained moral guides in all experience.

1. The purpose of acting: happiness

Only those acts which are in the control of the person can properly be called "human," and "all human acts must be for the sake of an end."[85] There is a connaturality of the self and good, for the self naturally seeks what is desirable, and it is only the good that is truly desirable.

What all individuals want and seek is happiness, i.e., "a certain ultimate completeness, and since different kinds of things mount to various degrees of perfection, the term [happiness] admits variations of meaning."[86] Happiness can be found only when there is one proper ultimate goal, and it is impossible for a person to have more than one ultimate goal. Happiness is also to be found in the things and experiences that lead to the proper goal. Thus, hap-

piness does not lie in riches, honors, fame, power, health, the pleasures of
sense, or in any created good; though all of these, rightly ordered, produce a
kind of happiness and may be an accompaniment of genuine happiness.
There are "two stages in happiness, complete and incomplete. In the first the
true meaning of happiness in the fullest sense is realized, in the second happiness is shared in by some particular likeness."[87] Each "particular likeness"
to a human characteristic that satisfies the self constitutes a real happiness,
though not one complete in itself.

Happiness is an individual's activity, "the full expansion of his being." It
becomes "so much the greater as our activity grows more single-minded and
less distracted."[88] There are certain conditions that make happiness possible.
Some are preconditions, others accompanying conditions, or consequences,
and there is some variation, of course, depending upon whether the happiness
is "incomplete" or "complete." The most important requirement is that "a
right good will is required, both beforehand and during happiness."[89] Comprehension is an accompaniment, not a prerequisite, of happiness; and the
same is true of pleasure. In the present life, health, external goods, and
friends are essential for incomplete happiness. Thomas's remarks about the
individual's need for friends is typical of his balanced attitude:

> It is not that he makes use of them since he is self-contained, or because he
> finds them pleasant, since he finds his pleasure in the activity of virtue, but
> that he needs them in order that he may act well, namely that he may do
> them good, that he may take delight in seeing them do good, and also that
> they may help him in his good works, for he needs their support in both the
> active and the contemplative life.[90]

While subjectively happiness is sought by all individuals without exception, objectively it is a real good that is sought, and it is the relation with a
real good that alone can provide any form of happiness. It is an actual good,
not simply an imagined or thought good that is wanted. Here Thomas's practical realism is evident: human happiness depends upon the right relation
with that object that alone makes happiness possible. A person's "final end is
a good outside himself, and this is God."[91] But other lesser goals and goods
also are objectively real; so they, too, are to be sought, properly related to (at
times possessed) and enjoyed. And in the seeking of all objective goods, especially the ultimate good, the individual is in fact seeking to fulfill his or her
total nature:

> For the will wants, not only its own immediate object, but also all that cor-
> responds to each of the other powers, and to the whole man. By nature he
> wills all that matches his entire ability, not just his will, for instance to know

the truth, to be, to live, and so forth, indeed all that relates to the integrity he was born to have: the universal object of will embraces all these as so many practical goods.[92]

2. The structure of a human act

Human beings, then, always act for a purpose: objectively for a real being that is a good, subjectively for happiness. In every act there is a determinate structure. After the act is over it is possible to discern its logical constituent steps. In the act itself the situation is far more complex, for human life may be understood but it does not proceed by a logical order. Thus what is logically prior may be chronologically subsequent; and, in fact, there can be two or more factors, sometimes conflicting factors, occurring simultaneously.

The logical structure of a human act is as follows:

HUMAN ACT

Mind		Will
	immanent activity in 'order of intention'	
	about end	
1. Perception		2. Wish
3. Judgment		4. Intention
	about means	
5. Deliberation		6. Consent
7. Decision		8. Choice
	practical action in 'order of execution'	
9. Command		10. Application
	11. Performance	
	12. Completion[93]	

Yet every act, like every self, is a whole, a unity, and it is not to be broken into discrete, unrelated parts. There is in an act a living web of interrelations, and, at times, the most delicate touch of one part of the web has profound repercussions upon logically near and distant parts.

There are three fundamental points about this structure. The first is profound involvement in every act of the intellect and will, of knowing and loving. The second is that at each stage of the act matters can go awry, or they can go right. The third basic point is that for an act to be moral or immoral it must throughout be voluntary. To be voluntary means that the source of action is within the person and the person acts with requisite knowledge, including a knowledge of the purpose. In a limited nonmoral sense nonrational animals act voluntarily, but only a being with deliberating reason which can lead to choice is fully voluntary. Moreover, voluntary activity is essential for moral praise and blame. These considerations lead Thomas to the questions whether fear and lust, violence and ignorance, cause an act to be involuntary. The essential answers are that an act is voluntary even in the presence of fear and lust (unless the lust, and by implication the fear, "swamps knowledge entirely"[94]), but an act is not voluntary if compulsion and ignorance are present. "Accordingly voluntariness in its full sense is a quality of human acts."[95]

3. Intellect and will in the moral life: knowing and loving

Since a moral act is a voluntary act and a voluntary act is an act that is not determined by ignorance or compulsion, the intellect and will become central to the moral life. Thomas accepts Aristotle's definition of man and moral choice as "an intellective appetite or an appetitive intellect"[96] or, in Aristotle's words, "either Intellect put in a position of Will-ing, or Appetition subjected to an Intellectual Process."[97] He recognizes that "Aristotle leaves it open to doubt whether choice is appetitively cognitive or cognitively appetitive,"[98] that is, whether knowledge or will is primary. Under the influence of his experience Thomas alters the terms to the active experiences of knowing and loving.

What "the Philosopher" refrained from deciding, Thomas does not define with a simple answer, yet he makes subtle distinctions that Aristotle missed. And, at the last, there is no doubt where his sympathies lie in the relative importance of knowledge and love in the moral life. At the first there is a balance of significance between the two since both are required. "The will's desire starts for an end, but it is reached by becoming present to us by an act of mind, and then, when it is already gained, the delight of the will rests content with it."[99] Will is the instigator of the moral act of life, but intellect is necessary for its completion. "Love ranks above knowledge as an impulse towards an object, but knowledge is above love in holding it."[100] Knowledge gives clarification and understanding to love; love instigates and, to a degree, shapes knowledge.

4. The moral guides in all experience

As a precondition for moral experience there are essential factors present in human individuals and the world. There is, first of all, in every individual the faculty of recognizing that good is not the same thing as evil just as every person recognizes that truth is not the same as error, that black is not the same as white. This is called by Thomas *synderesis*. It is the indispensable root faculty of all moral experience, and it cannot be mistaken.[101]

In addition human beings recognize differences between particular goods and particular evils (*conscientia*).[102] All persons possess this faculty and in all it is fallible. This is because the conscience of the individual is developed over time and is not an innate, infallible guide. Individuals judge good and evil in terms of their own experience, and moral experience can be limited and distorted. When a person judges something as morally good in itself or good to be done, it is judged in terms of objective qualities, that is, of whether it is fitting, which is to say in terms of reason or "measure" or law. There is, then, an objective factor in the "world" or nature of things that is a precondition for moral experience, and this is law.

However, the ultimate objective measure is the Eternal Law: "the goodness of a human act depends principally on the Eternal Law" so that "whenever, therefore a human act goes out to an end according to the order of reason and of the Eternal Law, then it is right, but when it goes awry then it is termed a sin."[103] The Eternal Law in the mind of God cannot be known directly by human beings but can be inferred from other valid laws which "in so far as they partake of right reason, are derived from the Eternal Law."[104]

Various types of law are derived from the Eternal Law. There is the "Divine Law," the decrees of God stated in the Scriptures, in both the Old and New Testaments, which are different from each other not in kind but in degree of perfection. There is natural law which defines human rational and moral nature; therefore, it is a law about which persons, rightly ordered in intellect and will, can agree. Human law if genuine is based upon natural and ultimately upon eternal law, and it is of two kinds: the universal law of humankind that, though not necessarily codified, is found as the intention of the particular laws in all societies since these laws form the basis of social life; and civil law, the particular code of each political society. A civil law is defined by Thomas, following earlier scholastics, as "an ordinance of reason for the common good made by the authority who has care of the community."[105] In these elements he incorporates the ends to which human action, intellect, and will, *synderesis* and *conscientia*, must be directed.

In summary, the preconditions for morality exemplified in a theory of action indicate that moral good (1) related to being, is (2) something to be done, (3) by a self-directing person, (4) in terms of what is fitting, that is, of measure and norm or law.

THE CHARACTERISTICS OF MORALLY GOOD ACTS

Thomas had a consistently strong sense of reality in which he not only focussed upon objective facts but wanted to see them in their complex totality, leaving nothing out, nothing unexamined. This is evident in his conclusion that the moral worth of a human act depends upon four qualities: (1) the extent to which it has "active reality," (2) the propriety of the objective to which it is directed, (3) the adequacy of its circumstances, and (4) the quality of the end. Each of these requires interpretation.

(1) It is a cardinal principle that an act is good to the extent that it has the "full reality a human act should possess," that is, in its voluntariness, its reasonableness, and fittingness in the total context.[106] Integrity of the act, "a meaningful unity and an ordered dignity" exhibiting a fullness of being, is the moral standard.

(2) The basic goodness of a moral act is "provided by the befitting objective on which it is set," an objective being the material with which an act deals and the immediate purpose at which it aims. The act's materials and immediate goal must be fitting as a human act. An objective may also be an effect of an act when the effect is a necessary consequence, "so that although the goodness of an action is not caused by the goodness of its effect, nevertheless, an action is called good because it is conducive to a good effect."[107]

(3) A human action is not good solely by its own inherent qualities of having "full reality" or by its "befitting objective," but is also made good or bad by its circumstances and its adequate or inadequate adjustment to those circumstances. For all moral activity, "its full goodness as a whole is not constituted by what kind of act it is, but all filled out by additions which are like its qualities; such are its due circumstances."[108] Moral acts are never isolated events but always exist in a larger context, and their goodness depends upon an appropriate relation with that context.

(4) When thinking of an act's reality, objective, and circumstances, Thomas is thinking of the specific, actual act, but he recognizes that the goodness of an act depends upon something beyond itself and immediate nature. For human acts, besides having "a strain of goodness which is theirs considered in themselves," ultimately depend for their goodness upon their final cause, that is, upon the quality of the intended ultimate end.[109]

Unless an act has all four qualities, it is not genuinely good, although it may be partially good in possessing any combination of the four. For Thomas it is true that while acts and persons can be separated for analysis, good acts and good persons cannot be ultimately separated, and a human being, like a human act, is good to the extent that fullness of being is achieved.

THE CHARACTERISTICS OF A MORALLY GOOD PERSON

Thomas emphasizes a distinction between outward acts and the will's inner activity. The self's inner and outer activity are related in experience, but the morality of an act and that of the will are different, for the moral goodness of an act—or its evil—is sometimes identical in the interior and exterior sides of an act "and sometimes distinct."[110] The completion of a deed, moreover, does not add anything to the moral quality of the intending will though it may reveal more clearly that quality, and it subsequently affects the will for further good or evil.

A good act depends upon its fullness of being, its fittingness, and circumstances. A good person is primarily defined by "good acts of willing" and ultimately the acquirement of human virtues. "A good act of willing is one that accords with virtue" and "its good comes from this, that what a person wills is good."[111] Thus, "moral good and evil [in willing] derive from the objective alone, not from circumstances." This means that the goodness of a person is found in the ultimate intention because in the act of willing "the goodness deriving from the objective does not differ from the good deriving from the end."[112] The individual's intention should be happiness, "the full expansion of his being" which comes only through the exercise of virtue which unites the person, in service, with another being and "with uncreated good, his ultimate end."[113]

1. The virtues of the good person

Thomas Aquinas follows Aristotle in his initial identification of the virtues, but he makes significant additions and modifications in that description. There are two types of human virtues, intellectual and moral, related to the two principles of human action, reason and appetite. If a virtue "perfects man's speculative or practical intellect in order that his activity may be good, it will be an intellectual virtue; whereas if it perfects his appetite, it will be a moral virtue."[114] The theoretical intellectual virtues are understanding ("a firm and easy quality of mind which sees into principles"), science ("the demonstration of conclusions from principles"), and wisdom ("which considers the highest and deepest causes" judging all other science "with respect not only to their conclusions but also to their premises").[115] The practical virtues are art and prudence ("art is right judgment about things to be produced, while prudence is rectified judgment about things to be done").[116]

The moral virtues can exist without science, wisdom, and art, but not without understanding and prudence. (Except for prudence the intellectual virtues can exist without moral virtue.) The moral virtues are characterized by a right disposition, an ability to make a right choice, and a tendency to the good as an actuality and not merely an idea.

Moral virtues deal with either passions or actions, and the more perfect a virtue is, the more it causes feeling, so "Virtue overcomes inordinate passion, yet it produces ordinate passion."[117] Those virtues that deal with passions relate to either a pleasure or a good difficult to achieve (the concupiscible and irascible appetites). Thomas accepts Aristotle's listing of ten virtues relating to passion: courage, temperance, liberality, magnificence, magnanimity, love of honor, gentleness, friendliness, truthfulness, and playfulness. He adds justice that deals with actions. Following Cicero and Augustine (and he might have said Plato), he identifies four principal virtues:

> Thus they are called principal as being common to all virtues. For instance, any virtue that causes a good judgment of reason may be called prudence: every virtue that causes actions to fulfill what is right and due may be called justice: every virtue that restrains and tames the passions may be called temperance: every virtue that strengthens the mind against any onset of passion may be called fortitude.[118]

These are the chief human virtues not only because they are essential characteristics of a good person, but also because they can be achieved by human effort.

There are, however, other excellencies characteristic of a good person that cannot be achieved by human effort. These are the theological virtues which can only be infused by God into the life of the individual. Quoting a familiar definition of virtue, Thomas suggests it applies accurately to both the natural and theological virtues except for the final phrase: "Virtue is a good quality of the mind, by which we live righteously, of which no one can make bad use, which God works in us without us."[119] Love cannot be constructed by mere thought and will, no matter how arduous the effort; nor can a person argue or discipline the self into faith and hope. These theological virtues can only be given, and they "shape a man to supernatural happiness in the same way as his natural bent shapes him to his connatural end."[120] Supernatural happiness does not await another life though that, too, is an essential part of its meaning. It is a happiness that can be known here and now, yet imperfectly.

It was the work of Jesus Christ to bring the virtues of faith, hope, and love to human beings. Jesus was, in truth, the incarnate God. In him God and human life were united in such a way that he became for all teacher and priest as well as mediator and reconciler. Through him, rightly apprehended, the individual is freed from moral guilt and from the penalty of moral guilt. These gifts are within the province of the church to dispense, and this is an essential meaning of the sacraments.

In all his description of the moral virtues Thomas places the human person and freedom at the center of his thought. In asserting the possibility of the human achievement of the natural virtues he is emphasizing human dignity and reinforcing human effort. In describing how other virtues are infused by God he is careful to retain human freedom and responsibility, reason and will, which are the core of what it means to be a person. Moreover, the human virtues constitute an ordered meaning. Implicit in Thomas there is the clear understanding that the natural virtues no less than the theological are Christian virtues, but by being Christian virtues they become more than the classical natural virtues. Prudence, justice, temperance, and courage, when accompanied by faith, hope, and love, take on a fuller meaning and depth than before.

It is now possible to see how the first two assumptions of the medieval ethic have dominated the thought of Thomas, viz., (1) that in all existence there is a meaningful unity and an ordered dignity discoverable by persons; and (2) that the only adequate principle of meaning of life, for the individual as for the universe, is spiritual. It is evident, too, for the understanding of the nature and achievement of individual goodness that Thomas's thought stems from the presuppositions that (3) Christ, present in the gospels and the church, is the way and truth of life and (4) individual good depends upon the recognition of the nature of created things, their relations to each other, and their dependence upon the supreme spiritual reality.

To understand Thomas's view of social good these assumptions must be present and to them added a fifth: a universal Christian civilization is a present reality. This perspective not only provides a view of Thomas's social ethic but explains the absence of advocacy of fundamental social reform.

SOME CHARACTERISTICS OF THE GOOD IN SOCIETY

1. The family

The family is the original form of social life, and it is based upon natural law. The purpose of the family is to produce and to educate children, and this purpose leads to monogamy, private property, and the right of inheritance. While sexual relations are prohibited outside of marriage, even within the family they are restricted as far as possible since sexual relations are not the purpose of marriage. While the family is the symbol of the unity of love, there is also present a dominant patriarchal motif.

2. Property and the economic life

Thomas grew up in a series of small cities near Naples, surrounded by the agricultural seas, and his view of property and commerce arises from this fact. All property belongs to God, but the necessity of property for family life and the incentive which ownership stimulates justifies some limited ownership. Slavery is justified by the Natural Law and by the Fall, though the rights of slaves must be protected.

In business, an individual should not trade for a profit though he or she may trade at a profit. Income from the lending of money is not morally permissible. There can be no attempt to gain wealth by speculation, but an individual may rationally plan business enterprises and, if there is a profit, may share in the profit. In the sale of products, of course, there must be no misrepresentation of goods.

Two facts stand out here: (a) Thomas viewed property and the economy as ministering to the needs of individuals, and neither existed for the sake of one person's making a profit at the expense of another. (b) Thomas saw economic life in terms of an exchange economy dominated by agriculture and trade. There was no hint that a surging commerce and industrialism would destroy the ordered society of his time.

3. The state

Thomas did not believe that the church possessed "two swords," that it was both a spiritual and a political institution. Yet because of his view of the relation of nature and supernature, the church, possessing complete spiritual power, had an effective authority over the political state.

The purpose of the state is to maintain peace and order, and to insure that each individual will share in the common good. In keeping with the patriarchal temper of Thomas's thought there is a tendency to prefer a strong central power in the state, usually a monarchy. The monarch is under law, so his subjects may rebel if he is tyrannical and if there is some chance that the rebellion will lead to a more just order. Warfare between states is limited to "just warfare," that is, when the warfare is provoked by injustice or when it is for the sake of a good that can be achieved in no other way.

In all of these attitudes there is not the slightest tendency toward reform of the social order. This is because the existing order parallels in all essential respects the natural order. Similarly, there is in Thomas little of that creative, self-searching criticism because, in the nature of humanity, the environment, and the grace of the church, all the objective essentials necessary for the good life are present.

But if there is no notion of radical reform of society, if there is little of the intensive inner criticism of the self, there is evident a clear moral vision of the life of the individual in community. There is the attempt to understand the importance of the social, political, economic, and religious community in which the individual lived and, at the same time, to give due significance to the life of the person. In all of this, "The Kingdom of nature becomes the portal of the Kingdom of Grace."[121] That Kingdom of Grace is the final goal of human life. For each individual is a soul with an eternal destiny. In no slavish or selfish way did Thomas view an individual's struggle for eternal life, since, in this aspiration, each individual is living toward the destined end, to finally achieve the vision of God and properly return this life to the Creator.

This final end of humanity, this vision of God, can be approached, but it cannot be achieved in this life. In 1273, before he had completed the writing he had planned, Thomas approached, in hours of solitude and in celebrating the mass, that contemplation of God which he had, for so long, held before others as their ultimate goal in life. It was the kind of experience that he felt crowned his life, for he learned that no matter how many words he wrote, his philosophy would remain forever incomplete. "I can do no more," he said. "Such things have been revealed to me that everything I have written now seems to me rubbish."[122] The following year he died. He was not yet fifty years of age.

THE UNIQUE CONTRIBUTION OF MEDIEVAL CHRISTENDOM

The garden of the Middle Ages was not a patch of loosely tilled soil almost ignored in the shadows behind the manor house. Rather it was a carefully cultivated area that was enhanced by competent and gifted hands, and lovingly tended by many anonymous gardeners. It was a plot of land that expanded over time, extending its borders. Its flowers were varied and variegated, rich in colors and hues, diverse in complexity and kind, and yet for all its great diversity, it was an ordered tract—carefully conceived, thoughtfully fashioned.

Looking back we can see now that it was a time when contradictions were paradoxes, when dichotomies were complementary. We can see now how the extremes were linked together, and glimpse into a time that seems all the more remarkable for its great unity in diversity. For what now appear to be polarized forces were then laid out in the same sunlit plot of land. On the one hand, it was a time of the growth of the secular world. The medieval monasteries were dissolving, towns were forming, trade was flourishing, and the universities were opening. It was a time when the vernacular tongues were beginning to challenge the universal Latin as a form of literary expression. On the steps of the cathedrals the theater was ready to emerge, and already in the streets there were love songs and ballads, and troubadours to sing them.

And yet simultaneously the sacred encompassed all. The church had never been more vibrant and prospering. In Matthew Arnold's words: "The Sea of Faith/Was once, too, at the full, and round earth's shore/Lay like the folds of a bright girdle furled."[123] In the midst of a growing materialism, then, there was still the dominance of the spiritual, and the immanent sense that the destined life was not of this world but designed for the appreciation of eternity.

On the one hand, it was a time of the increasing importance of the individual. Individual artists were beginning to sign their own works, and yet the works were almost all still in the praise of God and the love of Christ. The created world was increasing its significance, and yet it was significant because God had created it. For the first time there was a hierarchical community of faith that encompassed everyone, an intensity of life in a religious setting, a shared sense of meaning, an overarching order that gave each individual a sense of his or her own place and value. All lived in harmony with God and the church.

But from a distance this disciplined and ordered way of life easily conceals another paradox equally significant, and that is the rich diversity of each flower in the garden, for while the effect of the whole is the sum of the parts, the beauty of the whole also resides in the delight in the particular.

All four representative individuals we have looked at were unique in their accomplishments, and yet (though Héloïse would not admit it) all four did what they felt God had called them to do. Two of them lived, and thought as they lived. Two of them thought, and tried to live as they thought. But for all of them, morality was life, and life was moral: a living unity of thought and action. All four had a great respect for reason, and yet individually the core of each of their lives was vastly different. For Abelard the driving force was a philosophical ethic of pure intention, while for Héloïse it was a living ethic of pure love which embraced her feelings and remained rooted in them. For Francis life was renunciation and purification, but more centrally it was devotion: a life lived from the heart. And for Thomas, the core was an honest intellectual endeavor, an ordered discipline which included a moral effort of the highest mind and which was no less a service to God than the others.

These four gardeners toiled on their own plots, labored in love, and left us richer for their efforts. Collectively and as representatives of the great medieval seeding of faith, they helped make four significant contributions to the way that ethics have been conceived and thought about ever since.

(1) For all four there was an inclusiveness to life. The feudal ethos had carried over, consciously and unconsciously, into the town, into trade and the

church. All four had a sense not only of their own place in society, but of how the individual and society were related to historical time and to eternity. Conversation, disagreement, and dialogue were important, but they took place in a larger world that was not questioned, not doubted. Theirs was an implicit faith in what later would be called the Great Chain of Being, and this sense has stayed with us—this sense that every event has meaning, not only in itself, but in how it is included in the whole. There is a sense of higher and lower, of purpose and destiny, and for the medieval mind, underneath and dwelling in everything was the sense that God had made all of this possible.

(2) At the same time, this order in God's world could be apprehended by the use of reason. If faith was somehow always more than reason, there was still a faith in reason. Faith and reason were not contradictory but mutually supportive, and while there was a respect for the limits of reason, its faculty was a gift from God in order that human beings might more naturally and authentically glorify his name and his creation, and more authentically rejoice in his world and in their own lives.

(3) There was also a value in purity. While there was a respect for diversity and individuality, there was a greater respect for purity, for discovering an inviolate and individual singleness of purpose and meaning. This purity could be the theological purity of Abelard, the emotional purity of Héloïse, the physical purity of Francis, or the intellectual purity of Thomas. But for each what was important was to find the essence, the rose without weeds. This purity was a goal, a means, and an end: a complex but unambiguous center—an inviolate sense of the self.

(4) And finally, this faith in reason which examined the inclusiveness and this search for purity which sought to glorify ended in a process of increasing interiorization. The heart of mystery was becoming an inner reality which was ultimately ineffable. To look at a cathedral without the eyes of faith was to see a hollow shell, at best a work of art, an artifact. But with the eyes of faith, the cathedral became a garden, and the colors sifting through the stained glass led to an inner experience that was beyond thought.

It is easy to overlook this crucial fact in all four of our medieval figures. It is easy to overlook the underlying intention of love which was the real life for each of them, for what was important for each was an experience of faith that cannot be seen. Just as actions do not always reveal our real intentions, so ultimately there is a mystery in the source of our lives, a mystery in the source of our "devotion," a mystery in the source of our "will."

If reasoning about God for Thomas was ultimately analogical, then what was ultimate was beyond words, but not beyond experience. Yet we are impressed by what we see. We are impressed by these four individuals, by the quality of their lives and the profundity of their thoughts, but they in turn were the most impressed by what they could not articulate, by the inner experiences for which words, at their best, were weeds, for the flower they could see and experience in all its sensual beauty could not be described. It was for them a paradox, for us, perhaps, a contradiction: the garden they saw impoverished the garden they had created. Life was more than they could say; more, perhaps, than we can see though what they said. For each of them the way is inward, and, finally, each of them leaves us with a silence that is as full as the individual experience of faith was for each of them alone.

NOTES

1. James Westfall Thompson, *The Middle Ages* (New York: Alfred A. Knopf, 1931), 2: 721.

2. Ibid., p. 699.

3. James Westfall Thompson, *An Economic and Social History of the Middle Ages, 300–1300* (New York: Century Co., 1928), p. 765.

4. John Harold Clapham, "Commerce and Industry in the Middle Ages," *The Cambridge Medieval History*, Vol. 6: *Victory of the Papacy* (New York: Macmillan Company, Cambridge University Press, 1929), pp. 493–94.

5. Loren Carey MacKiney, *The Medieval World* (New York: Farrar & Rinehart, Inc., 1938), p. 408.

6. Héloïse, "Epistle 1," in *The Letters of Abelard and Héloïse*, trans. Betty Radice (London: Harmondsworth, Penguin, 1974) 109; italics added. (Hereafter referred to as Radice.)

7. Radice, p. 109.

8. Ibid., Epistle 3, p. 127.

9. Hastings Rashdall, *The Universities of Europe in the Middle Ages* (Oxford: Clarendon Press, 1936), 1: 65 n. 1.

10. Abelard, *Historia Calamitatum*, in Radice, p. 58. Another translation with notes is in J. T. Muckle, *The Story of Abelard's Adversities: A Translation with Notes of the "Historia Calamutatum,"* preface by Étienne Gilson (Toronto: Pontifical Institute of Medieval Studies, 1964).

11. Radice, pp. 58–59.

12. Ibid., pp. 57–58.

13. For Abelard's account of his life as a teacher see Radice, pp. 58–65. On his sexual liaisons with Héloïse, see Muckle, *The Story of Abelard's Adversities*, p. 28; for another translation, see Radice, pp. 67–68.

14. Muckle, *The Story of Abelard's Adversities*, pp. 38.

15. "Abelard's Confession of Faith," in Radice, p. 270.

16. Radice, Epistle 1, pp. 114–15.

17. Ibid., p. 114.

18. Ibid., p. 112.

19. Ibid., p. 113.

20. Ibid., pp. 112–13; quote is on p. 116.

21. Ibid., p. 113.

22. Ibid., pp. 117–18.

23. Ibid., Epistle 3, p. 128; Epistle 4, p. 137.

24. Ibid., Epistle 3, pp. 132, 133.

25. Ibid., p. 133.

26. Ibid., Epistle 1, p. 115.

27. Ibid.

28. Ibid., pp. 115–16.

29. Ibid., Epistle 3, pp. 133–34.

30. Ibid., p. 134.

31. Ibid., pp. 134, 135.

32. Ibid., Epistle 5, p. 175; Epistle 1, p. 115,

33. *Peter Abelard's "Ethics,"* trans. with notes and introduction by D. E. Luscombe (Oxford: Clarendon Press, 1971), p. 3.

34. Ibid., p. 5.

35. Ibid., p. 13.

36. Ibid., pp. 13, 15. (Since this edition has Latin on the left page,with English translation on the right, alternate page numbers indicate a continuity in the text.)

37. Ibid., p. 15.

38. Ibid., pp. 19, 21.

39. Ibid., p. 29.

40. Ibid., pp. 69, 73ff.

41. Ibid., p. 77.

42. Ibid., p. 87.

43. Ibid., p. 89.

44. Ibid., p. 101.

45. Ibid., p. 99.

46. Ibid., p. 101.

47. Ibid., p. 105.

48. Ibid., p. 123. In the remainder of the *Ethics* Abelard argues that one should submit to the judgement of any church authority whether he considers it just or not. This section is found only in the fourteenth-century Balliol manuscript. Other extant manuscripts end book 1 just prior to the above quote.

49. Radice, "Peter the Venerable: Letter (98) to Pope Innocent II," pp. 275, 276.

50. Radice, "Peter the Venerable: Letter (115) to Héloïse," pp. 281–82.

51. Ibid., p. 282.

52. Étienne Gilson, *Héloïse and Abelard* (Ann Arbor: University of Michigan Press, 1960), see chapter IV, pp. 47–65.

53. Radice, Abelard's "Confession of Faith," p. 270.

54. Radice, "Héloïse: Letter (167) to Peter the Venerable," p. 285.

55. Radice, Epistle 1, p. 109.

56. Paul Sabatier, *Life of St. Francis of Assisi* (New York: Scribners, 1894), pp. 8–9.

57. Omer Englebert, *Saint Francis of Assisi* (New York: Longmans, Green, and Company, 1950), pp. 44–45.

58. Ibid., pp. 52.

59. Sabatier, *Life of St. Francis of Assisi,* pp. 22–23.

60. Englebert, *Saint Francis of Assisi,* p. 59.

61. Sabatier, *Life of St. Francis of Assisi,* p. 55.

62. Ibid., p. 61.

63. Ibid., p. 69.

64. Ibid.

65. Ibid., pp. 75–76.

66. C. G. Coulton, *Two Saints: Saint Francis and Saint Bernard* (Cambridge, Mass.: Harvard University Press, 1955), p. 104.

67. H. O. Taylor, *The Medieval Mind* (Cambridge, Mass.: Harvard University Press, 1949), 1: 457.

68. Coulton, *Two Saints,* p. 102; Sabatier, *Life of St. Francis of Assisi,* p. 220.

69. Englebert, *Saint Francis of Assisi,* trans. Matthew Arnold, p. 289.

70. Sabatier, *Life of St. Francis of Assisi,* 328.

71. Englebert, *Saint Francis of Assisi,* p. 307.

72. Matthew 8:20 (Revised Standard Version).

73. Englebert, *Saint Francis of Assisi,* pp. 303–304.

74. Ibid., pp. 280–81.

75. Cited in William Short, *The Franciscans* (Wilmington, Del.: Glazier, 1989), p. 143. This is a quote commonly attributed to St. Francis because it is in the likeness of his spirit, but it is probably not his.

76. Francis MacDonald Cornford, *The Republic* (New York: Oxford University Press, [1945] 1973), p. 191.

77. Kenneth E. Kirk, *The Vision of God: The Christian Doctrine of the Summum Bonum* (New York: Longmans, Green, and Co., 1931/1937), p. 393.

78. Richard Niebuhr, *Christ and Culture* (New York: Harper & Row Publishers, 1951), p. 137.

79. Jacques Maritain, *The Angelic Doctor* (New York: Dial Press, 1931), p. 300.

80. Robert Lowery Calhoun, *Lectures on the History of Christian Doctrine* (New Haven: Yale Divinity School, 1948), 2: 308–309.

81. Saint Thomas Aquinas, *Summa Theologiae,* trans. Thomas Gilby (New York: Mc-Graw-Hill Book Company, 1964), 18: 133. Hereafter cited as Gilby.

82. Calhoun, *Lectures on the History of Christian Doctrine,* 2: 308–18. The quoted passages are the author's paraphrases.

83. Gilby, 17: 51. Modernization of "rational appetition."

84. Kirk, *The Vision of God,* p. 384.

85. Gilby, 16: 5.

86. Ibid., p. 65.

87. Ibid., p. 79.

88. Ibid., pp. 63, 65.

89. Ibid., p. 99.

90. Ibid., p. 113.

91. Ibid., p. 55.

92. Ibid., 17: 85.

93. Ibid., p. 211.

94. Ibid., p. 29.

95. Ibid., p. 9.

96. Robert Goodwin, *Selected Writings of St. Thomas Aquinas,* Everyman's Library edition (New York: Bobbs-Merrill Educational Publishing, 1954), p. 128.

97. John Alexander Smith, *The Nicomachean Ethics of Aristotle,* trans. D. P. Chase (London: J. M. Dent & Sons Ltd., 1911), p. 132.

98. Gilby, 1: 127.

99. Ibid., 16: 71.

100. Ibid., 1: 73.

101. Ibid., 11; *synderesis* is discussed on pp. 187, 189, and 196.

102. Ibid., 11; *conscientia* is discussed on pp. 191, 193, and 195.

103. Ibid., 18: 105, 107.

104. Ibid., 28: 59.

105. Ibid., p. 17.

106. Ibid., 18: 7.

107. Ibid., p. 13.

108. Ibid., p. 15.

109. Ibid., p. 17.

110. Ibid., p. 91.

111. Ibid., p. 49.

112. Ibid., p. 53.

113. Ibid., 16: 63, 65, 71.

114. Gilby, 23: 71.

115. Ibid., pp. 43, 45.

116. Ibid., p. 51.

117. Ibid., p. 95.

118. Ibid., p. 123.

119. Ibid., p. 11.

120. Ibid., p. 143.

121. Ernst Troeltsch, *The Social Teaching of the Christian Churches,* trans. Olive Wyon (New York: Macmillan Company, 1950), 1: 283.

122. Maritan, p. 62.

123. Matthew Arnold, "Dover Beach," in *The Norton Anthology of Poetry* (New York: W. W. Norton & Co., 1975), p. 850, lines 21–23.

6

THE ETHICS OF THE RENAISSANCE AND REFORMATION

L anguage may obscure as well as reveal. The words we use to describe our lives may, if they are not carefully chosen and properly understood, hide from us what our lives have been. The terms "Renaissance" and "Reformation" are such words, since they imply a completed process, a finished product. But for the men and women in those times (roughly from the fourteenth to the seventeenth centuries) life and work was a ceaseless, restless activity. There was no process that was completed nor a product that was finished.

These terms "Renaissance" and "Reformation," moreover, are used with reference to the intellectual and spiritual activities of separate segments of society, and they point to the completion of the divorce proceedings initiated long before between partners in the cultural marriage of secular and religious life. Unfortunately, in obscuring the full range of human activity and in ignoring the interactions between the two movements, this divorce misconstrues the facts of life of those years, for many of the same forces at work in an individual of the Renaissance were often at work in the individuals of the Reformation.

In the attempt to understand the ethics of the Renaissance and Reformation, then, we shall look at four men who lived at the end of the fifteenth and beginning of the sixteenth centuries: Pico della Mirandola and Niccolò Machiavelli of Florence, Martin Luther of Germany, and John Calvin of Geneva. In order to summarize the ethic of the era we shall ask: What was the society of these men like, what were their major ethical assumptions, and what were the unique experiences and views of each?

THE SOCIETAL INFLUENCES UPON THE ETHIC

There are, of course, vast differences between the immediate societies of Pico
and Machiavelli on the one hand and Luther and Calvin on the other, but beneath the specific differences, which will be noted later, were those general
similarities that helped give to their ethical thought striking similarities. First,
of transcending and permeating influence, there was the breaking up of *corpus
Christianum*, the corrosion of that unity of civilization that had meant so much
to the age of Abelard and Héloïse, Francis and Aquinas. The cathedral of civilization was not destroyed suddenly, but to all clear-sighted persons it was evident that the changes in the political, economic, social, and religious foundations had destroyed it beyond the possibility of a complete restoration.

This dismantling of the *corpus Christianum* meant that the old authorities were disappearing and that the familiar institutions and beliefs had lost
their spiritual power. In such a situation, individuals often inherited the old
beliefs but without the unifying order that had supported them. Many individuals, of course, were not fully conscious of the revolutionary time in
which they were living, though some, like a Machiavelli, had a partial rational insight of what was occurring, and others, like a Luther, had a partial
emotional grasp of what was happening. But all thoughtful individuals knew
that change was becoming a permanent condition, and that no new philosophy or theology worthy of the name would find a widespread legitimacy
until some new unifying order could be created. To understand the individuals who were living in the midst of this upheaval one must ask: what happens to someone when their world begins to fall apart? Those who feel suddenly released from the burdens of the past often attempt to forge a new
order. Others, who have loved their world, often attempt to rebuild the old,
not by the reflective development of a theory but by a feverish activity. So it
was with the ethical ideals of the Renaissance and Reformation. And if we
would understand the turning of the wheel of history at this moment, then
perhaps the dominant activities of the age can provide us with an initial useful
image. For essentially this was a time of exploration, discovery, and conquest, and these realities can be seen as both facts and symbols of that time.

Certainly, there had been exploration and discovery by other societies,
notably the Chinese, the Mohammedan, and the Viking, but these had not
been followed by conquest leading to further exploration. That development
was the product of European Christendom with its unique combination of
factors, including the peaceful continuation of the crusading spirit, the desire
to strive for an unseen goal, the appropriation of Arabian cartography and
mathematics, the adoption of the Chinese compass, the political and economic desires of a new class of individuals, and a sense of personal courage
and love of adventure.

Added to these factors in the fifteenth century was a shift from the land exploration in the East to the adventure across unknown Western waters with the desire to reach the East. There was also a shift in the motive of the exploration: previously dominant in its religious overtones, it now became dominantly secular, with both political and economic gain in view. This combination of aims is clearly seen, for example, in 1469, when, in the year of Machiavelli's birth, the Portuguese government granted a Lisbon merchant a monopoly on trade with Guinea on the condition that each year he explore at least one hundred leagues (about 300 miles) beyond the last outpost. The result was that in the next half century Portuguese expeditions discovered the Congo (1484), sailed around the cape of Good Hope (1488), sailed around Africa to India (1498), and on to Malacca (1511), Canton (1516), and the Liu Chin islands (1518). Toward the West the European explorers reached the West Indies (Spain: 1492); Newfoundland, Nova Scotia, and New England (Great Britain: 1497–98); Newfoundland and Brazil (Portugal: 1500); and Florida and the Pacific Ocean (Spain: 1512–13). In 1519–1522 the Spanish expedition of Magellan sailed around the world. The discoveries of the British were not followed immediately by conquest, but those of Spain and Portugal were. By the time of the death of Calvin, in 1564, these two countries had claims to or trading posts in the Americas (North, Central, and South); on the African coast; and in India, the East Indies, and Japan.

The new explorers discovered lands without knowing what they had found and made inaccurate maps of their discoveries; they conquered new territories without knowing whether or by what means their control could be retained. And all of this was symbolic of the society at large. In politics and in economics, in social changes and in the intellectual-spiritual realm there were shifts to unknown, undiscovered, unexplored ways of life; there were ceaseless activities in these realms, and even after the discovery and conquest, there was often ignorance of what had happened and uncertainty about the future.

1. Exploration, discovery, and conquest in the political world

The major political changes influencing the ethics of the Reformation and Renaissance were the weakening of the power of the church and the developing of a variety of new, untried political divisions.

The shift of power was symbolized by the decisions of the church in May and September 1493 by which Pope Alexander VI, the viceroy of God, drew a line across a map of the world, granting half of the unexplored territory to the Spanish crown and half to the Portuguese. Previous papal bulls (1454, 1481, and 1484) had given Portugal the right to all lands as far as the Indies and south of Capes Bojeajor and Nun. In 1493 Columbus, returning from his first voyage on behalf of Spain, landed at Lisbon and he reported first to the king of Portugal. The king, believing his rights had been violated, wrote to the Spanish crown, and this led to an appeal to the pope which produced the famous edicts of 1493. The weakening of the church and the strengthening of secular powers were revealed not only in the futile act of the papacy drawing a line across the map of the earth and granting domain to secular governments, but by the more significant fact that the terms of the papal bull had been suggested by the Spanish government. The pope was being used by the king. The political power of the church was shifting to the secular governments.

In other areas, too, the authority of the church was declining. In arbitration between states the power of the pope to adjudicate disputes was increasingly being transferred to direct dealings between the political disputants; in taxation the power of the church to receive revenue declined, particularly in the northern regions of Europe; and in canon law the legal authority of the church was increasingly being replaced by laws of particular lands.

As the political power of the church weakened new political divisions were being created, although it was by no means clear what type of effective political control might develop. The nation-state was not yet in existence. There were small, compact associations (for example, the city-states of Florence, Milan, and Venice) which had an effective control over their own territory and, because of the compactness of power, were a real force in the total complex of European political conflict. There were the states attempting to consolidate their power on territorial bases (for example, in Scandinavia, Hungary, Bohemia, and Portugal; in Navarre, Castile, and Leon and Aragon). All of these were in the process of the political exploration, discovery, and conquest of territories. There were also the dukedoms that retained power primarily by the claim for loyalty to the individual (for example, the dukes of Burgundy and Brittany). And finally there was the old empire which was gradually being destroyed by the revolts of the Germanic princes.

But, with the obvious exception of some of the small city-states, the bond that was molding persons together in common loyalties was neither to the land nor to history but to individual sovereigns. Peoples were not yet bound by having shared a common soil: the territorial states were not yet a reality. There was not yet a national history, and the only common thread that ran through all the political events was the shattering of the power of universal church and empire, and the grasping at the pieces by the new political divisions.

2. Exploration, discovery, and conquest in the economic world

The Renaissance and Reformation was the era of the "commercial revolution." This revolution in trade was linked with the overseas lands. In 1497 Vasco da Gama led an expedition of four ships to India. He returned more than two years later with only two ships but with a cargo worth sixty times the total cost of the expedition. Such success would not be lost upon new entrepreneurs; therefore, stimulated by both government and private initiative, overseas trade grew rapidly, although during this period, trade within Europe was still far more important than that of commerce outside the continent. There were many factors which stimulated this burgeoning trade. The development of banks aided financial transactions throughout the continent. New techniques of bookkeeping made possible a more systematic planning of business affairs. (One of the first publications on double-entry bookkeeping appeared in 1494.) And the desire for and initiative in capital accumulation on the parts of merchants stimulated the commercial revolution.

There was also a steady development in industrial organization. By far the largest numbers of persons were engaged in agriculture or in work as individual craftsmen. These craftsmen had been organized into guilds which had become increasingly monopolistic. They rigidly limited the number of persons who could enter the crafts, and they attempted to control prices and production. But cracks appeared in the guild system through the industrial development in textiles, shipbuilding, mining, and printing. In these fields the chief marks were a rational organization of the industries and a clear division of labor. These changes in industry were slower than changes in commerce, yet the industrial changes were significant enough to be an effective agent in the breakup of the medieval economy. With the growth of the towns and of population there arose the need for larger food supplies, changing agriculture. In many places this need was met by developing single-crop cultivation, and such development affected the total land-human complex. Land enclosure also developed during the fifteenth and sixteenth centuries, and although initially it involved only a small proportion of the land, still, like those developments in industry, it had a significant effect upon society and ethical thought.

The old order was changing and a new, unknown economic world was acting as a major catalyst in the continuing activity.

3. Exploration, discovery, and conquest in the intellectual-spiritual world

As the power of the church waned and the new economic and political order brought new possibilities into the world, so, too, there were changes in the intellectual-spiritual realm. The traditional ideas and ideals were losing their formative power. This is not to say that the religious culture, in particular scholastic thought, disappeared. The Reformation was dependent upon religious ideas, and most Renaissance learning and art were based upon and permeated by religion. Scholasticism, moreover, had many capable defenders, particularly in the universities. But the religious culture as it had been known in the scholastic mode no longer had the power to command the instinctive loyalties of individuals. The individuals were religious, but they were not scholastics. Indeed, Renaissance and Reformation joined forces at this point to war upon scholasticism.

If the question is asked as to what ideas and ideals replaced the traditional thought, the individuals of that age provide their own answer. A Florentine scholar, Leonardo Bruni (1370–1444), borrowed a term from Cicero to describe the new learning as education that is worthy of the dignity of human beings: *humanitas*. It was this many-faceted humanism that reflected the ethics of the Renaissance and that, joining with earlier thought, prepared the materials and the minds of individuals for the ethics of the Reformation.

Humanism was not primarily a philosophy, though it rested upon an implicit ethical outlook and it implied a philosophy. Humanism was essentially the conception of an individual's nobility, and it appeared first in scholarship, in civic life, and in art. Its basic stimulus was the creative individual, whether scholar, artist, or patron, and its fundamental resource was the printing press and the library which, almost invariably, were controlled not by the universities or even by the church but by individuals. Its most important materials were the written documents of the past—the Greek, classical Latin, and biblical—which were reintroduced into the life of the present. For essentially it was the movable type of the printing press that transformed the history of Western civilization. Its most immediate effect was upon scholarship, suddenly making the work of many scholars widely available to all, and the printing establishments themselves often became research centers. New libraries were created, frequently built by the demand for authentic manuscripts of antiquity.

Secular scholarship was blossoming. In the past the scholar had usually been in the employ of the church, but now various patrons gave the scholars and artists ample scope to express their own individual abilities and visions. This shift in the role both of the patron and of the scholar or artist was of great importance for humanism in general and for ethics in particular. A new worldview was being fashioned. There was an acceptance of the natural world and of history, and with this acceptance, although there was not a rejection of the Christian faith, there came a rejection of conservative scholasticism which had been preoccupied with the supernatural.

This new learning, with the positive values given to nature and history and with the emphasis centering upon the dignity of the individual, was in the employ of persons who desired, through their learning, to reform society and the church. And it was just at this point that the humanism of the Renaissance was related to the Reformation.

4. Social classes in the changing political, economic, and spiritual world

The changes in the late fifteenth and early sixteenth centuries were initiated primarily by individuals who had just recently emerged in the new upper bourgeoisie. There was, then, a decline in the significance of nobility and clergy accompanied by an increase in the importance of merchants and merchant politicians. The nobility had become a hereditary caste whose functions of supplying protection for the lower classes was disappearing with the rise of new political divisions, just as the power of the clergy was decreasing as the influence of the church weakened.

Into the social order there was an ingression of those persons who had gained economic wealth and political power through conquest in the commercial revolution. This class came into increasing conflict with the older orders of clergy and nobility. But within the class itself the conflict was as great, or perhaps greater. There was antagonism between the merchant-politicians—whether they were the international financiers or the political leaders—and the smaller merchants. The former were the innovators, the venturesome explorers; the latter were more cautious.

The merchant-politicians constituted perhaps 2 to 4 percent of the total population, but they were far more significant than their numbers would indicate. They were, indeed, a primary creative force in society. The bulk of the population consisted of craftsmen or common laborers in the towns, with even more peasants in the agricultural areas. There was much tension and unrest in and among these groups which played significant roles in the expression of the Renaissance and Reformation ethic, but the day when these merchant-politicians would be at the center of the stage of history was still far in the future.

THE PRESUPPOSITIONS OF THE RENAISSANCE AND REFORMATION ETHIC

In the life of the late fifteenth and early sixteenth centuries there developed a common ethical outlook. Despite the diversity of experiences there were a number of basic ethical assumptions which were shared by the individuals of the Renaissance and Reformation. These assumptions enabled those with different beliefs to argue profitably with each other and gave to the ethic of the period a greater degree of similarity than is ordinarily supposed.

1. The traditional unity of life is changing.

The church continued to preach a unity of civilization and continued to claim it was the bearer of this unity. Because this preaching and these claims had been made for generations, they were generally accepted. But any clear-sighted observer knew (or, at least, felt) that the preaching was empty, the claims false. The changes were taking place at a faster rate than could be comprehended, and it was obvious that in all areas of life the unity fashioned by the church was disappearing.

The social order that had existed in the status of clergy, noble, and serf was being transformed by the new merchants. The philosophical order that existed in the relations of nature and supernature had been distorted by too great an emphasis upon supernature and now was challenged by emphases upon the natural world. The political order that had existed in the unity of prince and thrall, all giving final fealty to the pope, was disrupted by new political divisions. The economic order of an agrarian society was destroyed first by the guilds and then, when they had been assimilated into a new order, by the commercial revolution. The intellectual order of reason and faith, with theology as the supreme science, was challenged by new scholarship and loyalties. In every realm of life that had previously known the unity of Christian civilization there were disordering elements that made it evident to any sensitive observer that the unity of life was in rapid process of change.

2. Given this change, there is a need for each individual to establish a new order.

A strong sense of personal vocation and responsibility was characteristic of the individuals in this period. The significance of the individual was being given preeminence, and the old religious concept of vocation was being extended into secularized possibilities. For many, there was the sense that either the old unity, in some unknown way, had to be reestablished or that a new unity had to be created; and those persons alert to what was happening knew that this task could not be thrust upon the institution of church or empire. The dissolution of unity and power of both were essentially the problem. They could not also be the solution. Since there were no other existing institutions that could establish an order of life, this left but one possibility for many individuals, the sense that: "I must help establish the new order: Providence (or Fortune) has given this task to me."

This new order was to be essentially human.

3. Human life can be ordered only through the discovery of the genuine authority of order.

In the late fifteenth and early sixteenth centuries life was changing in its essentials. The disorder was deep; the fundamental beliefs had altered. The ultimate authority of the traditional Christian civilization no longer possessed power in the hearts and minds of many individuals. This breakdown in the ultimate principle of order meant that no superficial solution for the ills of contemporary life would cure the disease. That cure, that reordering of life—whether of the individual, the church, the state, or the total society—could only come through the discovery of a genuine authority of life. There was a restlessness present here at the end of the medieval period that was the accompaniment of guilt, there was a creativity that was the accompaniment of the search for perfection, and a rational planning that was the accompaniment of the desire for power. And all these characteristics—anxiety and guilt, the search for perfection and the desire for power—indicated both that there was disorder in life and that the ultimate authority of order was no longer fully known or accepted. Therefore, to break through to an ordered existence no palliatives, no moralisms would be sufficient. There had to be a discovery of the ultimate authority of order. This authority might be a renewal and reinterpretation of an old order, or it might be a new authority as yet unrecognized. But the old order was no longer sufficient.

4. The ultimate authority for order can be found through a return to ancient tradition and the combination of novel developments with that tradition.

The cry of the age was "Back to the past!" Or more accurately, *"Back through the past to the future!"* But this cry was no mere call to antiquity. There was not a concern with the Greeks or Rome of the republic for their own sake, nor a concern with early Christianity for the sake of an intelligible literalism. The individuals of the time had developed a sense of history. They, therefore, believed that since they belonged to history, their past had something to teach them. The return to classical and Christian culture was based upon the supposition that the purity of the early tradition could purify contemporary life.

However, the return to ancient tradition was not, in actuality, what to a later age it might appear. It was not a conservative traditionalism. Such conservatism was the program of the scholastics of the universities. The humanists and Reformers returned to the past only that they might introduce its vitality into the present and, combining ancient tradition with new experience, reestablish true and final principles for life.

5. The order of life can be created only by that individual (or social arrangement) in whom the genuine authority of life is operative.

The principle of authority was a personal principle. The ultimate authority had to operate through the individual (or social arrangement). This was true no matter whether that authority was conceived as a personal God, as the state, or as the unity of truth. This assumption, related to the earlier, existential sense of vocation, enhanced the sense of individualism that was characteristic of both Renaissance and Reformation. The individualism might be experienced in different ways: as individualism of the elite (in politics, art, and scholarship) or of the new authority (as in Lutheranism), or of the elect (as in Calvinism).

6. A human being is an individual who is forever active, ceaselessly seeking a meaningful order and an ordered meaning for life.

The exploration of the age had turned from overland travel to the East to the dangerous waters of the unknown West. This same kind of shift occurred in the individual's exploration of the world and of the self. Individuals were no longer content to adjust passively to the scheme of things, to be individuals in a familiar society. The limits of the familiar had been cracked, opening new vistas toward an unknown future. Confronted with the lure of this strange openness, all activities became intensified to the point that action itself became an essential characteristic of being human.

Yet still there remained the belief that there was a meaningful order for life and that there should be an ordered meaning to life. The old social order—with its institutions, graded social classes, economic relations, and political authority—was to the outer eye in disarray. Yet beneath this exterior appearance of an increasingly chaotic decentralization there was, many felt, a principle whereby a new meaningful order for life could become a reality. The first disturbances had already appeared in the natural order, but these were not familiar to many (Copernicus's theories were not published until after his death in 1545). The old spiritual order had also been blasted, but here, also, there was the implicit trust that life could and should be organized according to an ordered meaning within.

The assumption, usually too deep for words, of the continuous active search for order was in actuality the intensity of a moral focus inherited from the past which the explicit thought was seeking to recover. For here was the Platonic Good and *eros*, which having been of importance in earlier mysticism, was now turned toward other and unknown realms. Here was the Hebraic sense of traveling in time and in history toward an order that was both the greatest reality and yet waiting to be realized. Here was the Roman sense of order that permeated the life of the state and of man. And, throughout, here was that deeply ethical drive whereby each individual, no longer protected by the stable bounds of a known world, was thrust on his or her own, driven to inquire with a moral passion, "What must I do to be the person I was destined to be? What must I find and become in order to know the meaningful order and the ordered meaning that is meant for human beings?"

These assumptions were the starting point of the ethical exploration of the individuals of the Renaissance and Reformation. That ethical search took many forms. It appeared in the work of a scholar and in the thought of a religious zealot, in the life of a political leader and now in the creations of an artist. It is necessary to see the variations in the ethics as the moral issues appeared to four different individuals.

THE ETHIC OF THE RENAISSANCE

The entire creative vitality of the Renaissance was motivated by moral ideas and ideals. There was, however, no systematic philosophical statement of the ethic, but two individuals: Giovanni Pico della Mirandola and Niccolò Machiavelli can be said to sum up the Renaissance ethic. Both were citizens of the European world, and the lives of both were united with Florence. Giovanni Pico, a native of an Italian province of Mirandola, found refuge in Florence as an exile from Rome when he was twenty-four. Niccolò Machiavelli, a native of Florence, was exiled from his city in 1513 when he was forty-four. For both Florence was crucial to their development, and an understanding of that great city offers some clues to their ethics, for the city to which Pico came was the Florence of the humanists, while the city Machiavelli loved was the Florence of political leadership.

The city of Florence itself was small in size (about 75,000 in the late fifteenth century), but it was home to many of the great Renaissance leaders, and within its walls—on its streets, on the bridges across the Arno, in its houses and public buildings and cathedrals, in its gardens and on its hillsides—many individuals renowned for art and for learning were nurtured. In the fourteenth century it was the home to Dante Alighieri (1265–1321), Giotto (1266–1337), Boccaccio (1313–1375), and Petrarch (1304–1374). In the fifteenth century, Masaccio (1401–1428), Donatello (1386–1466), Filippo Brunelleschi (1379–1446), and Ghiberti (1378–1455). In that same century Florence produced historians who were the contemporaries of Machiavelli and of whom it has been said, "Whoever looks about to discover another city or nation which within the spread of approximately half a century harbored an equally brilliant array of historians will be put to a long and probably futile search."[1] This was the city of Leonardo da Vinci (1452–1519) and Michelangelo Buonarroti (1475–1564). This was the city of the Medicis, and since greatness responds to greatness, it is not surprising that Pico journeyed to Florence with longing and that Machiavelli lived in and then looked back to Florence with love. For theirs was a time and theirs a city conscious of its past glory and its present greatness.

The Florence that was the home to so many of the great Renaissance figures was made possible by the order established by its political leaders and its merchants. A Florentine merchant wrote in triumphant tones of the economic wealth of his city in 1472. During this period, he exclaimed, there were in Florence two hundred and seventy woolen factories, eighty-three silk factories, fifty-four stonecutters, eighty-four cabinet-making establishments, forty-four goldsmiths and jewelers, sixty-six apothecary shops, seventy butcher shops, thirty-two textile warehouses, and thirty-three banks. Florentine products, he noted proudly, were exported to every part of Italy, to Antwerp, London, Turkey, and the East. And to this Florentine merchant who spent his life in commerce, "the thought never occurred that his city had begun to decline or had ceased to be what to his mind it had been for generations past, the hub of the universe."[2]

During three decades, beginning in 1434, Cosimo de' Medici ruled and led Florence behind a continuing democratic facade. That small city-state had the tradition of democratic structure, but it was a structure manipulated by an oligarchy: at the height of political participation in the fifteenth century there were no more than three thousand persons active in political processes. In particular, the regions outside the city walls, a territory the size of Massachusetts, had no voice in the government, and the people who lived there were, in reality, a subject population. Moreover, the area of Cosimo's effective power extended beyond Florence to all of Italy since it was in his interests both as a citizen and a merchant that there should be peace throughout the peninsula. After Cosimo's death in 1464, Lorenzo, his grandson, became ruler. Lorenzo de' Medici ("The Magnificent") ruled in Florence from 1469 to 1492. Lorenzo inherited the political order, power, and prestige created by Cosimo.

> In Italy as a whole, Medicean diplomacy was able, for a time and in a measure, to satisfy the desire for unity without running counter to separatist instinct. With Florence, Medicean personality made possible the rule of an individual under the forms of a republic. Such a system had in it all the elements of impermanence and compromise. Its achievement was to give, to Florence and to Italy, an interlude of peace in which the spirit of man was set free to create for itself a wonderland of beauty, more enduring than the political framework from which it sprang.[3]

The Medicis, in the interest of economic wealth and in the process of building a personal banking and commercial empire, not only contributed to a political order that made spiritual creativity possible, but shared in the new developments in learning and in art. Cosimo created the famous Platonic Academy; Lorenzo participated in its Platonic discussions. Both were enthusiastic patrons of the Florentine artists.

It was not surprising, then, that when he was exiled from Rome in 1486, Giovanni Pico della Mirandola should turn to the city of Florence.

GIOVANNI PICO DELLA MIRANDOLA (1463–1494)

The ethical assumptions of the Renaissance manifested themselves fully in the life and thought of Giovanni Pico, Count of Mirandola. He was richly endowed in mind and body, and he also possessed the inheritance of wealth and nobility. At the age of fourteen he was sent to the University at Bologna. For the next seven years he studied at Bologna, Padua, and Paris, steeping himself in the languages and lore of the past. "Not the cunning of all philosophy was able to make him proud," wrote his nephew in praise, "not the knowledge of Hebrew, Chaldee, and Arabic language, besides Greek and Latin, could make him vainglorious; not his noble blood could blow up his heart, not the beauty of his body. . . ."[4]

By the time he was twenty Pico sensed the cultural disease of his time, and he proposed a startling remedy. The disease was spiritual disorder. The remedy was prescribed when, in 1486, he found a harmony in the diverse thoughts of all times, presenting this unity in the form of nine hundred theses with "An Oration on the Dignity of Man" which expresses the ethical enthusiasms and convictions of his age. These theses struck the dry tinder of ecclesiastical thought. Some of his propositions, after official inquiry, were declared heretical; others were deemed suspect. Pico was forced to flee Rome, returning to Paris. There he was arrested by the ecclesiastical authorities and imprisoned until he escaped to Florence.

His searching mind was given further impetus by personal qualities. Pico's biographer wrote in an enchanting passage that

> The comeliness of his body with the lovely favor of his visage, and therewithal his marvelous fame, his excellent learning, great riches and noble kindred, set many women afire on him, from the desire of whom he not abhorring (the way of life set aside) was somewhat fallen into wantonness.[5]

But, explained his nephew, "Women's blandishments he changed into the desire of heavenly joys."[6] This interpretation offered a narrower religious meaning for his life than is justified.

There were three essential themes underlying Pico's ethic: freedom, the ceaseless search for truth, and the harmony of truths; and the unique ways he stated these three themes constitute his development of the basic assumptions of his time.

THE ETHIC OF PICO

Pico sensed a breakup of the order of life of Christendom, and for the reestablishment of order he turned not to politics, nor to the church, nor to traditional philosophical or theological dogma. Pico turned to the individual and to the individual's dignity (from the Latin *dignitas,* meaning rank). For him this was the source of the nature of being and truth. In his desire for a meaningful unity of life Pico was led to a new form of individualism in which the individual was given only a starting point but no static position. The discovery and then transformation of the self was the individual's right and responsibility; the search and then the recognition of the harmony of all truth should be the individual's desire and duty.

1. The freedom of the individual

In asserting individual freedom Pico was not simply repeating the theme of the freedom of the will, that the will was able to choose this or that particular action. This freedom was more inclusive. Every individual has a decisive role in creating the self. The determinate structure of being human is the indeterminate nature of being human. Each individual's fate is to be free, and the only fundamental constraint is inescapable creativity. Pico heard the Creator addressing the creature:

> Neither a fixed abode nor a form that is thine alone nor any function peculiar to thyself have we given thee, Adam, to the end that according to thy longing and according to thy judgment thou mayest have and possess what abode, what form, and what functions thou thyself shalt desire. The nature of all other beings is limited and constrained within the bounds of laws prescribed by Us. Thou, constrained by no limits, in accordance with thine own free will, in whose hand We have placed thee, shalt ordain for thyself the limits of thy nature. We have set thee at the world's center that thou mayest from thence more easily observe whatever is in the world. We have made thee neither of heaven nor of earth, neither mortal nor immortal, so that with freedom of choice and with honor, as though the maker and molder of thyself, thou mayest fashion thyself in whatever shape thou shalt prefer. Thou shalt have the power to degenerate into the lower forms of life, which are brutish. Thou shalt have the power, out of thy soul's judgment, to be reborn into the higher forms, which are divine.[7]

"Thou mayest fashion thyself in whatever shape thou shalt prefer": here was faith in freedom. Pico's vision was fastened on the uniqueness of the individual and for Pico the only way to attribute value to this unique individual was to recognize that being is the process of becoming. Each individual is responsible for his or her own creation. If one were to ask Pico to interpret his meaning, perhaps he would have found an analogy in the creative explorations of the Florentine artists, who, with the materials of a physical world, fashioned and formed new worlds of the mind and spirit. That was the result of freedom. The new form, genuinely new, was the creation of a human self.

To be human was to become human. To be human was to be assigned no fixed place, and yet, in Pico's figurative language, to be human was to be "set at the world's center." By this phrase Pico conveyed several ideas central in his thought. One key notion was that a human being, alone of all beings, was able to observe the unity of all things and of all thought. But a human being was also "set at the world's center" in the sense that this indeterminate being was related to all determined beings. In being human there were "the seeds of all kinds and the germs of every way of life."[8] What each individual becomes, then, is according to the seeds that are nourished from within, which the individual, who can know in many ways, knows best when they have withdrawn into the center of their own unity.

This self-transformation is never completed; to become human is never finalized in a finished form of being human. Creativity continues. When he thought of a human being as being made in the image of God, Pico thought of a spiritual creativity that manifests itself in a unity of spiritual and physical realities. Pico's theme of a human being as one who is forever active, forever seeking a meaningful order and ordered meaning, is described by Ernst Cassirer:

> The freedom of man consists in the uninterrupted creativity he exercises upon himself, which can at no point come to a complete cessation. . . . But to man, security is denied. He must be forever seeking and choosing his own path: and this path carries with it for him a perpetual danger. But this uncertainty, this perpetual peril of human existence—not in the physical but in the moral and religious sense—at the same time constitutes for Pico man's real greatness. Without it he would not be what his destiny demands he should be.[9]

2. The search for truth

Pico was a scholar *par excellence*. Like his fellow humanists his work was motivated by a moral drive. He was not interested in research for its own sake; he did not turn back to the past for antiquarian interests. The fundamental belief for his work was the conviction that through impartial scholarship and the recovery of the ideas of the past an individual would be enabled to approach the truth to life.

Two aspects of the search for truth were emphasized: purpose and method.

The purpose was ethical, to establish a unity in the self and a harmony of the self in all its relations. Pico mentioned a passage in which Empedocles "makes complaint that he is being driven into the sea, himself goaded by strife and discord into the semblance of a madman and a fugitive from the gods," and he commented, "Surely . . . there is in us a discord many times as great; we have at hand wars grievous and more than civil, wars of the spirit."[10] He spoke, too, of how through philosophy an individual can "sometimes descend, with titanic force rending the unity (of nature) like Osiris into so many parts."[11] The way to overcome the disunity in the self, in society, and in nature is through the search for truth:

> we shall fly up with winged feet, like earthly Mercuries, to . . . that wished-for peace, most holy peace, indivisible bond, of one accord in the friendship through which all rational souls not only shall come into harmony in the one mind which is above all minds but shall in some ineffable way become altogether one. This is that friendship which Pythagoreans say is the end of all philosophy. . . . Let us wish this peace for our friends, for our country. Let us wish it for every home into which we go; let us wish it for our own soul.[12]

Unity must first be established within individual persons. This was the reason for his own search for truth. Pico criticized those philosophers who "do not embrace the very discovery of truth for its own sake" and added his personal testimony:

> I shall grant myself this and blush not at all to praise myself to this extent that I have never studied philosophy for any other reason than that I might be a philosopher; and that I have neither hoped for any pay from my studies, from my labors by lamplight, nor sought any other reward than the cultivation of my mind and the knowledge of the truth I have ever longed for above all things. . . . Philosophy herself has taught me to rely on my own conscience rather than on the opinions of others, and always to take thought not so much that people may speak no evil of me, as, rather, that I myself may neither say nor do aught that is evil.[13]

The method of the search was first to study all available thought of the past. Pico specifically mentioned moral philosophy, dialectic, natural philosophy, and theology. These were to be examined in diverse cultures—Greek, Chaldean, Hebrew, early Christian, medieval, Roman. At the age of twenty-four Pico stated matter-of-factly, "I have so prepared myself that, pledged to the doctrines of no man, I have ranged through all the masters of philosophy, investigated all books, and come to know all schools." He continued,

And surely it is the part of a narrow mind to have confined itself within a single Porch or Academy. Nor can one rightly choose what suits one's self from all of them who has not first come to be familiar with them all. Consider, in addition, that there is in each school something distinctive that is not common to the others.[14]

This method of study culminated in an inquiry into the personal self. Philosophy enabled an individual to climb "the steps of the ladder, that is, of nature." But Pico did not climb those steps since he was not personally interested in any objective study of nature. While having respect for the objective approach, he believed that there was another way of understanding nature.

> The saying "Know thyself" urges and encourages us to the investigation of all nature, of which the nature of man is both the connecting link and, so to speak, the "mixed bowl." For he who knows himself in himself knows all things.[15]

In this way Pico turned his attention inward and exemplified that characteristic of the Renaissance in which the individual self, as a self, had universal significance. For each individual "contains the seeds of all kinds." Within the self, therefore, each individual could discover and create a unity like the universal order.

Here Pico returned to his basic theme of a human being's dignity. This search for truth leading finally to an entrance into the dark recesses of the self, where one is "confined to the inner reaches of the mind," was an expression of each individual's self-transforming, creating freedom. For every person has the capacity to penetrate "all things from center to center," and expressing the hidden unity of his own individual creativity each person can, at last, perceive and participate in the unity of all things.

> Let us be driven, Fathers, let us be driven by the frenzies of Socrates, that they may so throw us into ecstasy as to put our mind and ourselves in God. Let us be driven by them, if we have first done what is in our power. For if through moral philosophy the forces of our passions have by a fitting agreement become so intent on harmony that they can sing together in undisturbed concord, and if through dialectic our reason has moved progressively in a rhythmical measure, then we shall be stirred by the frenzies of the Muses and drink the heavenly harmony with our inmost hearing. Thereupon Bacchus, the leader of the Muses, by showing in his mysteries, that is, in the visible signs of nature, the invisible things of God to us who study philosophy, will intoxicate us with the fullness of God's house, in which, if we prove faithful like Moses, hallowed theology shall come and inspire us with a double frenzy. For, exalted to her lofty height, we shall measure therefrom all things that are and shall be and have been in indivisible eternity; and, admiring their original beauty, like the seers of Phoebus, we shall become her

own winged lovers. And at last, roused by ineffable love as by a sting, like burning Seraphim rapt from ourselves, full of divine power we shall no longer be ourselves but shall become He Himself Who made us.[16]

3. The unity of truth

Each individual's freedom and search were linked in Pico's mind with another basic idea, the unity of truth. Recognizing that the traditional unity of life was destroyed and that the universal Christian civilization was disordered, Pico sought to recover a unity for life. This burden he imposed upon each individual that, by searching for the truth, a meaningful coherence could be found. To be sure, each creation of coherence would always be fragmentary, since no search could ever end in a complete discovery. Yet the incomplete order—the fragmentary creations, the partial discoveries—were sufficient because they were the expressions of a perfected unity. The unity of "Being itself" could be manifested only in partial, obscure, fragmentary ways. There could be no final philosophy or theology because no individual could ever complete his or her own freedom. At the same time, all philosophies—even those considered by theologians to be most heretical—contain something of value and are the dim expressions of the complete truth that is beyond human grasp.

In this antidogmatic, inclusive spirit Pico was no mere eclectic who saw all thought as equally good. The denial of a completed Christian dogma was not a denial of Christian theology. It was, rather, to purify Christian theology and to harmonize it with non-Christian thought that Pico developed his nine hundred theses and presented to the intelligentsia of the church a challenge to debate. "There is nothing either great or extraordinary about me," he told them in explaining why he desired debate.

> However great the burden I may have taken on my shoulders, therefore, it was not because I was not perfectly aware of my own want of strength but because I knew that it is a distinction of contests of this kind, that is, literary ones, that there is profit in being defeated . . . seeing that he who yields receives no injury but a benefit from the victor, in that through him he returns home even richer, that is, wiser and better equipped for future contests.[17]

Pico believed that beyond the discordance of thought there is unity, just as beyond the "solitary darkness of God" there is the light of truth. For him it was the responsibility of each individual to seek that unity and to know that truth. "Let a certain holy ambition invade our souls," pleaded Pico, "so that, not content with the mediocre, we shall pant after the highest and (since we may if we wish) toil with all our strength to obtain it."[18]

Pico enlivened the assumptions of the Renaissance and Reformation ethic. He knew that his basic task was to recover an order for life and that for this order to exist there must be a unique place for human beings as individuals, since of all creatures, only human beings could seek the real power which can invade and encompass a life and give it a unity of meaning.

Shortly before his untimely death and for reasons that are not clear, Pico turned to religious and political-social interests. Was the religious mysticism simply the development, the maturing of his own earlier beliefs? Did the social-political interests arise because he came to believe, in stressing the absolute freedom of the individual, that he had omitted some important facts of human life? In any case, it was largely due to his influence that Savonarola gained political power in Florence in 1494; and that same year Giovanni Pico, scarcely thirty-two years old, died. Perhaps it was well that he died before the four-year dictatorship of his friend produced evidence that a meaningful unity of life, which included the freedom of the individual and the search for truth, cannot be imposed by political power. Neither in Florence nor in all of Europe were the times to be controlled by Pico's optimism, by his development of the ethical assumptions of the time. His biographer wrote of him, "Liberty above all things he loved, to which both his own natural affection and the study of philosophy inclined him."[19] But there was to be no place in the social realities of the sixteenth century for the kind of liberty Pico espoused. Those realities were to be controlled by the leading ideas in the ethic of Machiavelli, Luther, and Calvin.

Niccolò Machiavelli (1469–1527)

On April 16, 1527, two months before his death, in a letter to a personal friend, Machiavelli confessed a love that provided a clue to all of his mature life and thought: "I love my native land more than my soul."[20] For a child of the church, even an indifferent child like Machiavelli, to say this about his own soul was to say something important. His whole life had been given to the service of the state. He confidently expected that through the political order he saw emerging a new unity would be formed. But this breakup of an ordered life and the determination to refashion it with distinctly new patterns were not just imagined by Machiavelli. He had experienced it personally, and had also written about it in his *History of Florence*: "Nations, as a rule, when making a change in their system of government pass from order to disorder, and afterwards from disorder to order, because nature permits no stability in human affairs."[21]

The relative stability that the Medicis had been instrumental in bringing to Florence and governments of Italy during the fifteenth century, a stability that Machiavelli had known in his youth, began to disappear following the death of Lorenzo in 1492. Looking back upon that event more than thirty years later, Machiavelli wrote, "For as soon as Lorenzo de' Medici was dead there sprung up those fatal seeds, which soon accomplished the downfall of Italy, and which, none knowing how to destroy, will perpetuate her ruin."[22] The fatal seeds were those of dissension within the city of Florence and disagreements between the independent governments of Italy in how to meet the foreign invaders. Machiavelli saw the reality of this dissension as an essential theme of his *History*:

> If any reading can be profitable to citizens who may be called upon to govern republics, it is that which reveals the causes of hatreds and dissensions in a state, so that, learning wisdom from the perils of others, they may maintain themselves in unity. . . . If ever the dissensions in a republic were remarkable, those of Florence have been the most remarkable, for most other republics of which we have any knowledge have been content with one division; . . . but Florence, not content with one, has had many. . . . In Florence the dissensions were at first among the nobility themselves, afterwards between the nobles and citizens, and finally between the citizens and the plebeians.[23]

This sense of civil strife was intensified for Machiavelli because of its dominance during his mature years. From 1492 until that fateful day in 1530 when, forced to submit to pope and emperor and "the spirit or genius or soul of Florence . . . took its departure,"[24] the city exhibited the excesses which were the product of unreconciled conflicts within Florence, Italy, and Europe. The will and power to live as a great community were enervated by the pressures of economic competition, the lifelessness of an imitative humanism, the disadvantages of geographical location, the stifling of a reactionary religion, and the oppressive powers of ambitious states. But to a sensitive participant, such as Machiavelli, the fatal flaw appeared as an inner division that, with moods oscillating between a frenzied fear and a foolish overconfidence, produced governmental indecisiveness.

Through bitter partisan politics the aristocrats in Florence exiled the Medici in 1494. That same year further troubles came from within and without. Pisa, a Florentine community, revolted, and the French invaded Italy. Constitutional debates followed these crises, and apparent democratic reforms were introduced. But for the next four years the city was, in reality, dominated in all phases of its life by the thundering Dominican monk and reformer, Girolamo Savonarola (1452–1498). His execution in 1498 (the same year Machiavelli received his first political appointment) did not resolve the difficulties. The fortune of Florence was linked with shifting alliances and warfare between the major and minor Italian powers (the papacy, Naples,

Milan, and Venice belonging to the former; many others, including Ferrara, Mantua, and Lucca, to the latter), and from the powers that had designs upon Italian territory (the emperor, the Spanish, the French, and the Swiss).

In 1495 a League against France was organized by the pope, the emperor, Venice, Milan, and Ferdinand of Aragon. In 1508 the Cambray League against Venice was created by the emperor, France, Ferdinand, the pope, and minor Italian principalities. In 1511 the Holy League against France was organized by the pope with the collaboration of Spain, Venice, and England. The waves of the future broke upon Florence with the shifting of political winds. Florence supported the French (Machiavelli made official visits to France in 1510 and 1511); and, following the victory of the League in 1512, Florence was punished for this policy with the restoration of the Medici. As the Medici were linked with the greatness of Florence in the fifteenth century, so they were joined with her demise in the sixteenth. After 1512 the Medicis had effective power over Florence with Medici rulers on the papal throne and in the city. However, this did not mean that their power was secure and their policies successful. Indeed, in 1527 they were again exiled and the republic was reestablished. Once more divisiveness, indecision, and the wrong decisions ruined the republic. With France and Spain competing for the Italian peninsula, Florence continued to support France. The Medicean pope, exhibiting an astute neutralism, leaned at the proper time toward the emerging victorious Spain. In 1530 the combined powers of the pope and the emperor defeated the Florentines and the Medici returned to the city to rule over a spiritual corpse.

THE POLITICAL ACTIVITY AND PERSPECTIVE OF MACHIAVELLI

Machiavelli was thrust into this political maelstrom when, at the age of twenty-nine, in 1498, he was appointed to the Florentine secretariat. For fourteen years, until his exile in 1512, he engaged in the feverish activity of a capable and trusted civil servant, and with the full knowledge of the city's affairs, he traveled as envoy to the important governments and participated in shaping policies. He was a sensitive observer. With a love for politics which was his life and a longing for an ordered unity which was his hope, Machiavelli claimed to see below the surface storms to the deeper dark waters of human life and political history: "I have found nothing among my possessions that I cherish more or value higher," he said in his dedication of *The Prince*, "than I do of my knowledge of the actions of great men, gained from long experience in modern affairs and the continual reading on ancient ones."[25]

When he was exiled from his beloved Florence, Machiavelli had the time to reflect upon what he had learned. Had it not been for that enforced leisure and increasing poverty the books that were in him would probably have remained unwritten. In a delightful letter to a friend he described his style of life out of which *The Prince* was created:

> I am living on my farm. . . . What my life is now I shall tell you.
>
> In the morning I get up with the sun and go out into a grove that I am having cut; there I remain a couple of hours to look over the work of the past day and kill some time with the woodmen. . . .
>
> When I leave the grove, I go to a spring, and from there into my aviary. I have a book in my pocket, either Dante or Petrarch or one of the minor poets, as Tibullus, Ovid, and the like. I read about their tender passions and their loves, remember mine, and take pleasure for a while in thinking about them. Then I go along the road to the inn, talk with those who pass by, ask the news of their villages, learn various things, and note the varied tastes and different fancies of men. It gets to be dinner time, and with my troop I eat what food my poor farm and my little property permit. After dinner, I return to the inn; there I usually find the host, a butcher, a miller, and two furnace-tenders. With these fellows I sink into vulgarity for the rest of the day, playing at *cricca* and *trich-tach*. . . .
>
> In the evening, I return to my house, and go into my study. At the door I take off the clothes I have worn all day, mud spotted and dirty, and put on regal and courtly garments. Thus appropriately clothed, I enter into the ancient courts of ancient men, where, being lovingly received, I feed on that food which alone is mine and which I was born for; I am not ashamed to speak with them and to ask the reasons for their actions, and they courteously answer me. For four hours I feel no boredom and I forget every worry; I do not fear poverty, and death does not terrify me. I give myself completely over to the ancients. And because Dante says that there is no knowledge unless one retains what one has read, I have written down the profit I have gained from their conversation, and have composed a little book *De principatibus*, in which I go as deep as I can into reflections on this subject, debating what a principate is, what the species are, how they are gained, how they are kept, and why they are lost. . . . I am dedicating it to His Magnificence Guiliano [de' Medici]. [26]

While Machiavelli was writing *The Prince* he was also working on *Ten Discourses on Livy*, a rambling commentary upon political topics. These two, with his letters, constitute the essential material for an understanding of his thought, though other of his extensive writings (especially the *History of Florence* and *Discourses on Reforming the Government of Florence*) also throw light upon his views.

THE ETHIC OF MACHIAVELLI

The first question that has to be clarified is: "In what sense is there an ethic in Machiavelli's writings?" Nothing is clearer than that Machiavelli has been frequently misunderstood and misrepresented in this matter by a moralistic Western audience. That which has fascinated political realists and idealists alike has been his recommendations of how a ruler should conduct himself. For the most part these recommendations occur in five short chapters of *The Prince* (chapters 15–19), running to twenty pages, and these proposals have often been accepted as proof of Machiavelli's political immorality. Nothing could be farther from the truth. Machiavelli was not writing ethical but factual statements; he was presenting not political morality, but political description. He himself was clear as to what he was doing, and, for Machiavelli, the way his purposes have been distorted would be further confirmation of his low opinion of human beings. In introducing his discussion of the ruler's person and policies he was careful to describe his feelings.

> And because I know that many have written on this topic, I fear that when I too write I shall be thought presumptuous, because, in discussing it, I break away completely from the principles laid down by my predecessors. But since it is my purpose to write something useful to an attentive reader, I think it more effective to go back to the practical truth of the subject than to depend on my fancies about it. And many have imagined republics and principalities that have never been seen or known to exist in reality. For there is such a difference between the way men live and the way they ought to live, that anybody who abandons what is for what ought to be will learn something that will ruin rather than preserve him, because anyone who determines to act in all circumstances the part of a good man must come to ruin among so many who are not good.[27]

The break with the principles of predecessors does not refer to a moral but to a stylistic difference. Machiavelli proposed to write about "what is," not about "what ought to be."

Yet beneath the factual statements there were ethical judgments, as beneath the descriptions there were valuations and conceptions of human life and good. In a passage in which he was thinking about his method, Machiavelli provided the clue toward a proper understanding of his work when he compared the "prudent man" in politics to a physician:

> The physicians say that at the beginning the disease is easy to cure and hard to diagnose, but if it is not diagnosed and treated at the beginning, and a long time elapses, it grows easy to diagnose and hard to cure. So it is in matters of state, for if the ills of a policy are recognized early (something that

can be done only by a prudent man), they are soon cured; but when, not being diagnosed early, they are allowed to increase in such fashion that everybody recognizes them, no remedy can then be found.[28]

In medical practice the immediate prescriptions of a physician are not ethical. They are simply the factual application of knowledge of general principles in a specific situation to restore the health of the patient, or, if restoration of health is impossible, to keep the patient alive. This is what Machiavelli intended to do in *The Prince*, to apply his knowledge of principles to a specific situation. But every physician's scientific art is based upon his ethical judgments, e.g., a valuation of human life, a belief that pain is bad, a desire for personal wealth, and a sense of service to the individual and God. Similarly there were moral judgments that were at the base of Machiavelli's work, and the main problem in understanding Machiavelli is to unite the ethical and the factual.

Underlying and pervading all of his work was an acceptance of the assumptions of the Renaissance. He knew that in the presence of all the forces working for disunity his own personal vocation was to help establish order in life. Through his experience in politics and his observations of life he was convinced that the ultimate authority for an ordered life had to reside in the state; and, within the state, it had to be expressed through those possessing political power. To find the way in which genuine authority of order should be manifested Machiavelli returned to ancient tradition, combining that tradition with novel developments of his own time. Undergirding all his views was a conception of the individual as an active, life-molding being and a conception of the state as the chief material upon which the creative person might impress the order of his personality.

In building upon these presuppositions the main door to Machiavelli's thought was the primacy of political order. Requiring a force powerful enough to give coherence to the disorder in life, he turned to the authority he knew best, the state. Apart from his personal involvement in political life there were positive and negative reasons for recognizing the state as the authentic authority for human order. Negatively, Machiavelli was simply unable to find an effective agency for order either in the individual's intellectual freedom to search for the truth, or in the traditionalist's return to the ecclesiastical institution, or in the experience of the sovereignty of God. Positively, Machiavelli believed that human beings lived within the matrix of the state, and it was part of his genius that he foresaw that in the creation of new political entities human life would be increasingly conditioned by the state and new forms of polity.

With this recognition that political order is the door to Machiavelli's thought there are two levels to be observed. The first is the descriptive element, the ways political power is established and maintained. The second is evaluative, the reasons for using these methods to gain and maintain political power.

1. The methods for achievement of political order

The description of the ways to attain and keep effective political control in a state were clearly stated. Machiavelli's analyses rested upon the assumption that there were two fundamental types of government, a republic and a principate (or a democracy and a monarchy). In understanding a particular society one must ignore personal preferences to recognize actual possibilities.

> To set up a principality where a republic would work well, and to set up a republic where a principate would work well is a difficult thing, and because it is difficult, is inhumane and unworthy of anybody who wishes to be thought prone to pity and good.[29]

Of the two types of government Machiavelli's preferences were for a republic, but here he gave a less precise analysis of the way order was to be maintained in such a state. His main insistence was that the downfall of a republic always coincided with too intense a factionalism and, therefore, a successful republican government must avoid partisan policies and direct its affairs toward the common good.

The description of the maintenance of order in a principate was equally clear but more detailed. His reputation as a political realist is based on his description of securing and maintaining order in a principate, for this is the theme of *The Prince*.

First, he explicitly stated that, in *The Prince*, he is concerned only with principates.

> I shall omit any discussion of republics, because I have elsewhere dealt with them at length. I shall concern myself only with princely governments, and shall proceed to spin my web about the classes mentioned, and discuss how these princely governments can be managed and maintained.[30]

For the first fourteen chapters of the book Machiavelli discussed the topics outlined in his letter, "What a principate is, what the species are, how they are gained, how they are kept, and why they are lost." In those sections the analysis began with an interpretation of the principality, but the description moved toward the key importance of the individual ruler in inculcating the governmental policies. The recommended policies of these chapters were not extreme except by implication in pointing to Cesare Borgia as the model of a prince. There was nothing in the actions of Borgia that was to be censured—

not his cruelty, his deceptiveness, his severity—except his bad judgment in accepting as pope a man he had injured and who would continue to fear him.

The themes were clear: a prince with too scrupulous a regard for virtue will bring ruin upon himself and his state; political policies cannot be formulated on an exclusively ethical basis; a ruler should be morally good when he can get away with goodness, but he should not hesitate to resort to evil methods when they are required for his success. But Machiavelli provided his own theme with unforgettable images, the teacher of the prince "who is half beast and half man"; the prince who needs "to be a fox that he may know how to deal with traps, and a lion that he may frighten the wolves."[31]

Machiavelli was not unmindful of the desirability of virtues in a prince so long as the virtues did not lead to his own destruction:

> I mean that he should seem compassionate, trustworthy, humane, honest, and religious, and actually be so; but yet he should have his mind so trained that, when it is necessary not to practice these virtues, he can change to the opposite, and do it skillfully. It is to be understood that a prince, especially a new prince, cannot observe all the things because of which men are considered good, because he is often obliged, if he wishes to maintain his government, to act contrary to faith, contrary to charity, contrary to humanity, contrary to religion. It is therefore necessary that he have a mind capable of turning in whatever direction the winds of Fortune and the variations of affairs require, and, as I said above, that he should not depart from what is morally right, if he can observe it, but should know how to adopt what is bad, when he is obliged to.[32]

Machiavelli reasoned that immorality in a prince may at times be more moral than a careful observance of the virtues. Cesare Borgia, for example, was in his cruelty "much more compassionate than the people of Florence, for in order to escape the name of cruel they allowed Pistoia to be destroyed."[33] Thus it followed that

> a prince ought not to be troubled by the stigma of cruelty, acquired in keeping his subjects united and faithful. By giving a very few examples of cruelty he can be more truly compassionate than those who through too much compassion allow disturbances to continue, from which arise murders or acts of plunder.[34]

Further, Machiavelli's justification for a prince breaking his pledge of faith possessed, as subsidiary reasons, semimoral factors.

> A prudent ruler, therefore, cannot and should not observe faith when such observance is to his disadvantage and the causes that made him give his promise have vanished. If men were all good, this advice would not be

good, but since men are wicked and do not keep their promises to you, you likewise do not have to keep yours to them.[35]

The immorality of a ruler was checked by the effect it would have upon the successful execution of his policy, and this meant that, for Machiavelli, the moral ideals of the citizens prevented a successful prince from being a tyrant. The kind of fear and respect that a people had toward their ruler was an important element in his regime. "I blame any prince who, trusting in his castles, thinks it of little importance that his people hate him."[36]

Though Machiavelli gave a role to virtue in a prince the images of the half-beast, half-man and of the lion and the fox were present. In the official work of ruling a state morality is not the primary factor but always subsidiary to the end of ruling a state. That end, most simply put, is to continue ruling. It was Machiavelli's aim to teach the art of ruling by describing the facts of political life. These facts include treachery, cruelty, deceitfulness, harshness, and faithlessness; and he who would be a successful ruler must know when, how, and to what limits it is necessary to practice these arts.

2. The reasons for maintaining political power

For Machiavelli, the end of ruling a state is to continue ruling. Yet this was only a partial and not his entire answer to the question, since finally the question about basic purpose cannot be answered for Machiavelli with any certainty. Here, each interpreter must sort through the ambiguities in Machiavelli's writings in order to fashion his own view. The interpretation we shall now make will lead us to further insights into Machiavelli's thought, into his conception of what it means to be human, and into his understanding of the state. It will also help us see more clearly the situation to which he was directing his attention and the assumptions with which he thought.

In *The Prince*, except for the last passionate chapter, there was no indication of deeper reasons for ruling the state than simply to rule. If this means that Machiavelli did not suggest that the state existed for "the common good," it also means that the aim of the prince's power was not to satisfy personal ambition. This was consistent with Machiavelli's purpose. As a medical manual does not interpret why an individual should be healthy, neither does Machiavelli in *The Prince* say why a state should have order. But in the last surprising chapter, "An Exhortation to Take Hold of Italy and Restore Her to Liberty from the Barbarians," an answer was given to the question why a ruler should secure and maintain political power. The deeper purposes of power were for the unity of the state (specifically of Italy) and for the common good. The way Machiavelli introduced the theme was typical, and, like so much of his writing, it enabled a reader to see him thinking, even to participate with him in pondering and discovering new thoughts appearing on the surface of his mind. Machiavelli seemed surprised that his dispassionate political analysis should lead to the passionate plea for action that would lead to a unified Italy for the benefit of the people.

> Having considered all the things discussed above, I have been turning over in my own mind whether at present in Italy the time is ripe for a new prince to win prestige, and whether conditions there give a wise and vigorous ruler occasion to introduce methods that will do him honor, and bring good to the mass of the people of the land . . . so that at the present time, in order to make known the greatness of an Italian soul, Italy had to be brought down to her present position . . . without head, without government; defeated, plundered, torn asunder, overrun; subject to every sort of disaster.[37]

For the first time since the dedication, which was not an essential part of the book, Machiavelli wrote specifically for and to the Medicis, concluding with an urgent plea for uniting Italy.

> May your illustrious House, then, undertake this charge with the spirit and the hope with which all just enterprises are taken up, in order that, beneath its ensign, our native land may be ennobled, and, under its auspices, that saying of Petrarch may come true:
> > "Manhood will take arms against fury, and the combat
> > will be short, because in Italian hearts the ancient
> > valor is not yet dead."[38]

This plea for a unified Italy existing to "bring good to the mass of the people" harmonized with many valuations Machiavelli made regarding the state in other writings. Throughout his political discussions there ran the dual theme that disunity is the fatal flaw in states and that a political community should serve the interests of as many parties and persons as possible. "The reason why administrations in Florence have been defective," he stated in his recommendations for reforming the government, "is that reforms in them have been made not for the fulfillment of the common good, but for the strengthening and security of one party."[39]

If the primacy of the political life was the key to Machiavelli's ethic, then the conception of what it means to be human and the idea of the state was its foundation. In his view of human beings Machiavelli began with and developed the Renaissance theme that "a human being is an individual who is forever active, ceaselessly seeking a meaningful order and an ordered meaning for life." Everyone seeks this power in life, and seeks it so desperately that he commits all sorts of evil in trying to reach his personal goals. No person has painted a sharper, darker picture of humanity than Machiavelli: "one must say of men generally that they are ungrateful, mutable, pretenders and dissemblers, prone to avoid danger, thirsty of gain"; men are wicked and their promises are "broken on every occasion for the sake of selfish profit."[40] He took it for granted that everyone who observes the leaders of a society knows that they are evil, and that if ever they appear good there is a selfish motive hidden from view. "As all those who discuss civil life make clear," he pointed out in his *Discourses on Livy*,

> and as every history shows with many examples, it is necessary for anybody who organizes a republic and establishes laws in it to assume that all men are wicked, and that they are always going to make use of the malice of their spirits whenever they have a good opportunity to do so. If their malice remains concealed for a time, there is hidden cause for it.[41]

Can this evil be cured, or if not cured, how can it be curbed? At no place does Machiavelli give any indication that he believes the evil can be eradicated in either political or individual life. He nowhere considered the possibility that the individual could triumph over evil. Indeed, there was no reason in his total view of human life why an individual should make such an attempt to transform the self. He did not propose that education could remedy or religion cure the disease of human disorder. Christianity offered a kind of cure, but this only made the patient susceptible to other and worse diseases.

> It has taught that the highest good consists in humility, lowliness, and contempt for human things. . . . If our religion does ask that you possess some courage, it prefers that you be ready to suffer rather than to do a courageous act. It seems, then, that this way of life has made the world feeble, and given it over as a prey to the wicked.[42]

The new disease produced by Christianity was, he thought, the chief reason why there "are not so many republics in the world as in ancient times, and, as a result the peoples do not now have the love of liberty that they did then."[43]

Since the evil in human beings could not be cured, how could it be curbed? The answer was obvious. "Men are always wicked at bottom, unless they are made good by compulsion."[44] That compulsion must be provided by the state.

The propensity for evil was not, however, his total interpretation of what it meant to be human. Machiavelli also saw individuals, in the way so typical of others in his time, as creative, order-shaping, order-imposing beings. This view had particular application for the ruler, and it was the reason Machiavelli was able, in good faith, to appeal to a prince to rise to the challenges of the occasion. He knew that fortune (or fate or chance) played an enormous role in human affairs. Yet fortune leaves the control of half of an individual's affairs to the individual. For this reason no one should blame Fortune, but his own failures for the loss of power. "Only those means of security are good, are certain, are lasting, that depend on yourself and your own vigor."[45] Machiavelli always saw life in relation to its actual possibilities. "He is successful whose way of doing things is fitted to the time; but quite the other way, he is unsuccessful whose actions do not fit in with the times and the conditions of affairs."[46]

Machiavelli lived at the end of a political age but before a new era had made its full appearance. The city-states, including his beloved Florence to which he had given his life, were already outmoded. They could not hope to endure in a world of larger political divisions. Yet the world of nationalism was not yet formed. In another sense, too, night had fallen upon one age but dawn had not risen upon the next day; in the theoretical understanding of how a state should be ruled theorists had provided ethical prescriptions which, no matter how they fitted an earlier era, were totally unrealistic for the new political order. "Nobody had yet fixed a philosophical standard of fair play for rulers of tomorrow," writes one observer.

> Machiavelli, in his "famous" "immoral" counsels to *The Prince* respected tradition and traditional morality as far as possible, and between the two stools of private morality and political standard he was bound to fall into what *seemed* disrespect for any standard, whereas it was (possibly) a dim attempt at finding *some* standard (either the public standard under the rule of patriotism, or the personal standard of *virtù*, of a real capacity to rule for the common good) which had never been explored by former political writers.[47]

Machiavelli made the attempt to apply, from his own experiences, ancient ideals to a new situation. The attempt was the expression of a courage that tore the mask of political morality from a changing political structure. He dimly envisioned that the world of the future belonged to larger states, and that nationalism would become a dominant theme in human affairs. In theory he gave to political life an autonomy that in actuality would become increasingly significant. Throughout, he desired to find a way, what he believed was the only way to heal the disorder in human life. It was a disorder in the individual that was reflected in the dissensions in society. The individual disease could not be cured, but it might be controlled. The only way Machiavelli believed that this would happen was for the genuine authority of life, that is, the political community, to be so effective in the lives of its rulers that a social order in which the individual might live would be established.

THE ETHIC OF THE REFORMATION

In the sixteenth century two men emerged as the recognized leaders and advocates of a changing and rebellious Christianity. Since then the West has lived in the shadow of their lives. Whether the long shadow they have cast is understood as a stimulating refreshment or a darkening disorganization of life is likely to depend upon the attitudes of the observer. Even in their own day no one was neutral toward Martin Luther and John Calvin, and since that day praise and condemnation have continued. Were they the rebellious leaders of a tragic civil war that tore apart the Western family, or were they the courageous surgeons performing an essential operation upon a sick society?

Martin Luther, the prophetic leader, and John Calvin, the systematic organizer, were not the only important persons of the Reformation, but no others, in their time or since, have had so pervasive an influence. This means that while the full range of the Reformation ethic cannot be understood by looking only at Luther and Calvin, yet its qualities can be recognized by seeing them, and it cannot be understood apart from them.

Luther and Calvin were influenced by the same forces—political, economic, and intellectual—that affected others of the Renaissance, and the general assumptions of their ethic were the same as the Renaissance assumptions. They, too, recognized that the unity of life was destroyed. In this recognition they knew that they were called to a specific task of recreating the unity. This commission led them back to the past in order to discover the ultimate authority of order that they might incorporate ancient insights into new situations. They saw that human beings were active beings, forever shaping and reshaping the world.

However, to point to the similarities of their views with the Renaissance does not deny the profound differences, which will, in the end, become more significant than the similarities. One can observe this, for example, by noting how personal interpretations placed upon a key assumption can lead in diverse directions. For if the Renaissance position was that an individual was an active being whose essential characteristic is a will and an energy that is always searching and surging into the future, then Luther can be said to have been in general agreement: "The being and nature of man cannot for an instant be without doing or not doing something, enduring or running away from something, for, as we see, life never rests."[48] However, this view, coupled with religious attitudes, led the Reformers to a different outcome. They agreed that there was disorder in the society and in the church, but for them the source of the disorder came from a loss of trust. And, lacking a confidence in the power of institutions or individuals, they saw no way for institutions or individuals, under their own initiative, to restore the order or to transform the trust. And yet, from the realization of this impasse both action and a new ethic developed.

Another way of describing the primary differences between the ethics of the Renaissance and the Reformation is to say that the latter was based upon profound and personal religious experiences. Many other influences, especially political and economic, molded the course of the Reformation; but these played an entirely subsidiary role in the development of the life and thought of individuals. The ethic of both Luther and Calvin arose out of personal life; indeed, the ethic was a universalization of individual experiences. Because their lives were conditioned by religious beliefs, they turned to the Christian tradition. It alone enabled them to find a meaningful order. If we are to gain an insight into the ethic of Luther and Calvin, it is essential that we move beyond their doctrines back into their personal experiences in their social setting.

MARTIN LUTHER (1483–1546)

When he was twenty-one and a graduate of the University of Erfurt with both a bachelor's and a master's degree, Martin Luther, who had decided to become a lawyer, felt called to the monastic life. He was returning to the university following a brief vacation at home when a sudden summer thunderstorm darkened his journey and a flash of lightning struck him to the ground. That darkness matched the despair in his life, that lightning kindled the anxiety that had troubled him, and for one moment the flash illuminated his future. No matter how others might interpret the terrifying experience, he immediately responded to the voice of God in the wind and fire: "I will become a monk."[49] Two weeks later he fulfilled his promise, and, in view of his years of failure in the monastery, it is significant that he never felt he had been wrong in the understanding of his call.

Luther struggled to order his life, he aspired for perfection, and he tried to know a divine meaning in his life. He knew defeat, and years later confessed his failure many times.

> For more than twenty years in my cloister I experienced the meaning of disappointment. I sought God with great toil and with severe mortification of the body, fasting, watching, singing and praying. . . . The more I sought and the nearer I thought I was to him, the farther away I got.[50]

But Luther's failure was not evident to his fellow monks. So exemplary was his life that in 1510 he was sent as a representative from the Erfurt monastery on official business to Rome. There, in keeping with personal piety and in accord with the official faith, he climbed Pilate's stairs on his knees to save the souls of others in purgatory. Patiently he paused on each step to repeat a Pater Noster, fervently he kissed each holy stair. All was done properly according to the best practice and faith of the church. And as he stood at the top stair, when he should have felt an inner satisfaction, there welled up within him that anxiety, that uncertainty that plagued him: "I wonder if it is so!"[51] Who knows?

Doubt of official doctrine led to further doubt. Anxieties increased, and in his ascent Luther found no secure foothold. The claims of the church did not satisfy his needs, and his earnest efforts to find peace through the monastic life did not end in fulfillment, but in futility. When his superior noted this, he ordered Luther to study for a doctor's degree that he might teach and preach in the University at Wittenberg. Luther began the intense biblical study that, in the next five years, led him into a new understanding of life. First were the lectures on Psalms, then Romans and Galatians. Here he found no institutional faith but met individuals who, in their individual experience of a sovereign God, had come through agonizing despair to joyful trust. This was also his experience.

> I greatly longed to understand Paul's Epistle to the Romans and nothing stood in the way but that one expression, "the justice of God," because I took it to mean that justice whereby God is just and deals justly in punishing the unjust. My situation was that, although an impeccable monk, I stood before God as a sinner troubled in conscience, and I had no confidence that my merit would assuage him. . . .
>
> Night and day I pondered until I saw the connection between the justice of God and the statement that "the just shall live by his faith." Then I grasped that the justice of God is that righteousness by which through grace and sheer mercy God justifies us through faith. Thereupon I felt myself to be reborn and to have gone through open doors into paradise.[52]

The experience was clear and distinct. Luther was a man who longed for goodness and who labored to gain a meaningful order in his life. But the uncertainties, the inner disquietude thwarted his aspirations. The more he sought the true source of all good, the farther away it receded. This failure was nowhere more clearly seen than in his longing for goodness and for God. But the very longing separated him from both goodness and God, simply because it was *his*. The seeking self was, in reality, a self-seeking. For this disease he could not be his own physician. Paul enabled the impeccable monk to know himself as accepted as he was, not because of his correct beliefs, his proper loyalty to an institution, or his achievements. He felt himself accepted because Love is Love.

Through his struggles and study Luther arrived at a new understanding of

God and himself, though he did not see the full meaning immediately. He was driven to that meaning inexorably as he faced the official doctrines of the church. The first issue was that of indulgences, and it arose because of the church's dual attempt to secure funds and to honestly answer the question, "What, finally, provides security for a disordered soul?" But where the Vulgate had translated the biblical injunction, "Do penance," Luther's own reading was "Be penitent." In 1517 the controversy broke into the open with the posting of the ninety-five theses on October 31. The tumultuous days began.

In the eruption that split the church there were other seething forces than the religious that were at work. Chief among these was the political drive toward local power, which in the German provinces was an incipient German nationalism. Luther's own prince, Frederick the Wise, elector of Saxony, was not an ardent anti-Rome nationalist. He was a pious Christian, whose sincerity led him to defend the right of Luther to a fair hearing before German princes using scripture as the authority for judgment. Other knights of Germany went much farther than Frederick in trying to turn the rebellion against Rome into a fight for German nationalism. Luther, too, made appeals to the German people. He objected to the indulgences, for example, partly because they drained German money into Italian coffers; and in his "Address to the Christian Nobility of the German Nation" (1520) he argued that the temporal power did possess a limited jurisdiction over the spiritual.

The primary drive of Luther and the Reformation, however, was not political but religious. Luther began with his conviction of the unique relation between God and the individual, and step by step in his conflict with the church he was forced to stand upon religious positions he had not anticipated. First, indulgences would not save anyone from purgatory; second, if the pope said they would, obviously the pope could be mistaken; third, an official council of the church might also err; finally, some of the sacraments of the church are not real sacraments. What remained, then? God, the active Word of God, and the individual.

Luther testified to this faith at the session at Worms on April 17 and 18, 1521. He had already affronted official Christendom by the audacious, unforgivable act of publicly burning a sacred bull of the pope. Now, at Worms, he was asked to repudiate his beliefs: "Martin—answer candidly and without horns—do you or do you not repudiate your books and the error they contain?"

Since your Majesty and your lordships desire a simple reply, I will answer without horns and without teeth. Unless I am convicted by scripture and plain reason—I do not accept the authority of popes and councils, for they have contradicted each other—my conscience is captive to the Word of God. I cannot and I will not recant anything, for to go against conscience is neither right nor safe. God help me. Amen.[53]

This was the foundation of Luther's ethic: "My conscience is captive to the Word of God. To go against conscience is neither right nor safe. God help me." But this was only the beginning of the ethic that was painfully built through his continuing activity and frequent conflicts, both inner and outer, into which his principles and the events of the day led him. With Luther's experience as the basis for his ethic, two basic attitudes, pervasive throughout his mature life, were significant: his sense of mission and his sense of imperfection.

Luther, from first to last, felt himself called and led by God. "God has led me on as if I were a horse and he put blinkers on me that I could not see who came running upon me."[54] The awareness of a divine calling was basic to his ethic. In addition to his human sensitivity there was his interpretation that the calling came from the sovereign God and was mediated through the Bible. The content and intensity of Luther's ethic was indebted (1) to his conception of a living God who is creator and controller of all things, wrathful in his righteousness and merciful in his love, and (2) to his understanding that the Word of God was communicated through, rather than literally present in, the scriptures.

Luther's consciousness of imperfection was an anxiety, ever-alternating and commingling with his sense of assurance, that lasted throughout his life. This anxiety was the bond that linked his human self with the eternal God. It both separated him from the absolute, holy source of all being, and, through despair, united him with the sovereign Good. In a word: *Anfechtung.* Luther tried to communicate his despair and desperation and doubt, his faithlessness and failure, his deep intellectual-moral-religious uncertainty and unrest. The agonies of faith (*tentationes*) through which he went again and again lasted to the end of his life. Luther believed that these agonies were essential for himself and for anyone who would truly learn of the real God and the real self: "I did not learn my theology all at once," he said. "I have had to brood and ponder over it more and more deeply; my *tentationes* have brought me to it for one learns only by experience."[55] This awareness was important for his theology and ethic. A human being, forever active, forever incomplete, must always reappear before God and therefore must continually reexperience the meaning of acceptance. This pointed to the impossibility of an orthodox theology. There cannot be right belief in the intellectual sense; there can be only right faith (itself a gift) in the springs of personal life.

The ethical principles of Luther can be summarized in five statements: (1) Trust is the sole source of all moral life. (2) Human beings trust that which is not trustworthy and so entangle themselves in an inner bondage. (3) Trust of the trustworthy God is to be received as gift and personal experience. (4) While faith is the root of the ethic and freedom is its reward, love is its result. (5) The active relation of tension and release between a person and God, a person and the neighbor must continue through life at ever deeper levels.

1. Trust is the sole source of all moral life.

At the basis of all human activity is the reliance upon that which directs life. The fundamental ethical question, therefore, is not whether an individual will be moral or nonmoral just as the fundamental religious question is not whether to be religious or nonreligious. Individuals are inescapably moral as they are inescapably religious; and for Luther these two are forever bound together. "What is it to have a god, or what is God?" asks Luther. And he answers:

> To have a god is simply to trust and believe in one with our whole heart. The confidence and faith of the heart make both God and an idol. . . . For the two, faith and God, have an inevitable connection. Now, I say, whatever your heart clings to and confides in, that is really your God.[56]

"Whatever your heart clings to and confides in": this is the basis of the religious and moral life. Luther was perfectly clear on this point, stating that the individual who feels self-sufficient if there is sufficient money "surely has a god, called mammon, on which he fixes his whole heart," and also, "In like manner he who boasts great skill, wisdom, power, and influence, and friends, and honors, and trusts in them, has also a god."[57] These are the idols of an individual's making. But the greatest idol, with the most destructive power, is created when a person relies upon the virtues of the self as the real basis of life. The central problem for ethics is not "Shall I have trust?" but "In what shall I have trust?" Thus, if an individual would experience order in this life and this world it can come only through a proper trust that, deep within the self, provides a touchstone for order.

2. Human beings trust that which is not trustworthy and so entangle themselves in an inner bondage.

Individuals trust the idols of wealth and friends and popularity, the idols of the self's intelligence and power and virtue. With such trust the consequent direction of life is clear. By such trust individuals are bound within. There is the inner limitation of the evil individual who is motivated by malice, selfishness, or sensuality. There is also the inner bondage of the good individual whose consciousness of virtue is a wall separating him from the genuinely good. Luther, in the words of one commentator, referred to this as the

> "curving in upon itself" of human self-interestedness, that inversion which makes a man consider his own status and profit in everything that he does, be it the pursuit of truth, in the practice of charity, in worship, or the exercise of humility. The self curved in upon itself discovers that instead of loving God it is admiring or grieving over its own measure of love; instead of being con-

cerned for the neighbor, it is concerned about its acquisition of the virtue of neighbor-love; instead of being humble it seeks to excel in humility.[58]

This inner restrictiveness is an individual's problem, one that can be interpreted in theological, psychological, or ethical terms. It is the problem of an individual's basic trust in the ultimate being who can create order out of the chaos of life. It is the problem of an individual's discovery of an integrity of personality that there may develop a balanced direction for the frantic emotional life. It is the problem of an individual's devotion to genuine goodness that there might arise a consistent pattern out of the confused moral life.

Here was Luther's understanding of the problem of human freedom. This is not a question of determinism or indeterminism. "I wish that the word 'free-will' had never been invented," he said. "It is not in the scriptures, and it were better to call it 'self-will.' "[59] The problem of freedom as it actually concerns an individual practically is the question of how an individual might be freed from inner restrictiveness.

This inner bondage appears in many forms. It is present in those habits of behavior that cannot be overcome by self-will. It appears, too, in the foolish fears, in the continuing petty worries, in the vain hopes, as well as in the repeated acts of compulsive behavior. The inner disorder also expresses itself in personal anxiety and a sense of guilt. In all these ways, thought Luther, God is at work, unknown by the consciousness of the individual, for at the point where an individual feels guilt, God is the most active, leading to penitence.

3. Trust of the trustworthy God is to be received as gift and personal experience.

The sovereign God of justice and love does for the individual what the individual cannot do alone. This insight came to Luther as, with his *Anfechtung*, his anxiety and guilt, he tried to understand the work of a holy and righteous Will. The resolution of his despair was influenced when reading the Psalms, "My God, My God, why hast thou forsaken me?"[60] he was reminded of Christ on the cross. Luther thought this cry of despair to mean that Christ had known *Anfechtung*, even at the moment of his final sacrifice. This must have been because, in the words of Paul, "he humbled himself." The life and death of Christ, then, was not first of all a model to be imitated but a redeeming Word spoken and acted for human beings. God acts always in this reconciling way, a way whereby the individual is reconciled to the self, to the neighbor, to the world, and to God.

> Learn then what takes place when God begins to make us godly, and what the first step is in becoming godly. There is no other beginning than that

> your king comes to you and begins to work in you. . . . You do not seek him,
> but he seeks you. You do not find him, he finds you.[61]

The One God continuously acts and what is essential for each person is to recognize this truth, to understand the loving activity, to receive and respond to the gracious acceptance. For this understanding and receiving and responding, preparations can be made and much effort is required. But, paradoxically, the preparations are not the individual's preparations.

At this point Luther's individualism enters. The trust that alone can remold life must be experienced by the person. This was the meaning of "the priesthood of all believers." That doctrine never implied for Luther that one might believe anything individuality led one to believe. No priest has such freedom. A priest must believe a truth mediated by the Word and that Word always speaks directly to the person.

Luther was also clear about the nature of the faith that must be a personal experience:

> We should note that there are two ways of believing. One way is to believe
> about God, as I do when I believe what is said of God is true; just as I do
> when I believe what is said about the Turk, the devil or hell. This faith is
> knowledge or observation rather than faith. The other way is to believe in
> God, as I do when I not only believe that what is said about Him is true, but
> put my trust in Him, surrender myself to Him and make bold to deal with
> Him, believing without doubt that He will be to me and do to me just what
> is said of Him.[62]

The first, immediate consequence of this kind of trust in God is the release from the dominant frustration and futility of the inner bondage. For so long as such faith is present the individuals are able to perform whatever work is required. They can lose themselves in the cause they serve, in the truth they seek, in the beauty they create.

4. While faith is the root of the ethic and freedom is its reward, love is its result.

Luther was led to proclaim the central paradox of this ethic: "A Christian man is the most free Lord of all, and subject to none; a Christian man is the most dutiful servant of all, and subject to everyone."[63] The relation of the individual to God is direct. No authority can create or control that bond. When any institution, whether church, state, or social custom, interferes with that relation, then the Christian is free from and no longer subject to the institution. But this personal freedom leads to responsible bondage to persons. The essential principles of his ethic were "personal freedom, grounded in faith, and social, communal responsibility based upon love."[64]

5. The active relation of tension and release between a person and God, a person and the neighbor must continue through life at ever deeper levels.

An individual is not made perfect by trust because trust is never perfect. He never approaches the holy God as a perfected person but ever appears knowing penitence and forgiveness, guilt and gratitude, conscious of his own inner disease and of God's healing. The continual forgiveness, gratitude, and healing make the individual more sensitive to the incompleteness of trust.

Continuing tension is a necessary characteristic of the Christian.

> There will ever be in us mingled purity and imperfection; we must be conscious both of the Holy Spirit's presence and of our sins—our imperfections. . . . Let no one think, "Here is a man who possesses the Holy Spirit; consequently he must be perfectly strong, having no imperfections and performing only worthy works." No, think not so; for so long as we live in the flesh here on earth, we cannot attain such a degree of perfection as to be wholly free from weakness and faults.[65]

The main characteristics of Luther's ethic were clear. The fundamental active principle is the relation between God and the individual. And the content of this relationship presupposes an ethic of response rather than rational self-affirmation, of motive rather than consequences, of responsibility rather than aspiration, of the equality of all vocations rather than the superior worth of some.

(a) An ethic of response

An adequate moral life must be lived in continuing response to God. In this response Luther did not despise reason, but reason by itself could neither begin nor complete the understanding of God and God's demands.

> God's actual divine essence and his will, administration and works—are absolutely beyond all human thought, human understanding or wisdom; in short, that they are and ever will be incomprehensible, inscrutable and altogether hidden to human reason. When reason presumptuously undertakes to solve, to teach and explain these matters, the result is worthless, yea, utter darkness and deception.[66]

Reason is able to comprehend a natural moral law which requires the simple acts of human decency. But reason cannot fathom the full requirements God demands, nor can it develop an adequate ethic. "A good deed rarely issues from planning, wisdom, and cleverness; it must all happen in the vagaries of ignorance."[67] An individual, then, must respond to God; and while it is not a rational response yet within it reason will be present. Technical knowledge, the understanding required by any individual who is confronted with a specific job, is essential; but no amount of technical knowledge can determine what should be the goal of life.

(b) An ethic of motives

In the ethic motives rather than outer acts are primary. "Good works do not make a good man but a good man produces good works."[68] The good individual is one in whom the motive of love, undergirded by faith, is present:

(c) An ethic of responsibility

Responsibility is dominant. By no quality and quantity of aspiration can an individual achieve the goodness that is required, nor did Luther suppose that there was any way to move, solely under one's own initiative, from self-love to realize the love of God.

(d) An ethic of vocation

Luther arrived at an ethic of vocation in which the call of God was linked with the call of culture, the work of God with the work of society. He railed against the notion that there were special religious vocations that had a superior worth in the sight of God. The only distinction between the priest and the peasant, the monk and the magistrate, or a Mother Superior and a mother of a family was one of function. Any work necessary for the best human life is a work to which God calls the individual.

With this conception of vocation Luther ennobled the total life of human beings in society. The average life was given a new dignity. Yet as this understanding of the divine call to work mingled with other experiences in Luther's life, there developed a conservative attitude toward social institutions and enterprises.

The year 1525 was crucial for the statement of Luther's social ethic. The Reformation by that time was in full progress. The first martyrs had been killed, the monasteries in some areas were being emptied, priests and nuns were putting into practice Luther's view that marriage is to be preferred to the monastic life, political battles were being waged with knights against church and empire, and the peasants began to rebel. Luther heard in the complaints of the peasants a kindred voice. They, too, were anti-clerical and evangelical. But, in addition, they demanded congregational authority over the minister, the development of common lands, the elimination of burdensome taxes, and the abolition of serfdom. Luther tried to mediate between the extremes of the peasants and the princes, but his temperament led him to oppose rebellion and to espouse political authority and order. When peasant rebellion broke out, Luther wrote, in May 1525, the most conservative and vitriolic of his political tracts, *Against the Murderous and Thieving Hordes of Peasants*, in which he said:

> If the peasant is in open rebellion, then he is outside the law of God, for rebellion is not simply murder, but it is like a great fire which attacks and lays waste a whole land. Thus, rebellion brings with it a land full of murders and bloodshed, makes widows and orphans, and turns everything upside down like a great disaster. Therefore, everyone who can, smite, slay, and stab, secretly or openly, remembering that nothing can be more poisonous, hurtful, or devilish than a rebel. It is just as when one must kill a mad dog; if you don't strike him, he will strike you, and the whole land with you.[69]

At this same time, Luther, then forty-one, indicated that he planned to marry, and his marriage with Katherine von Bora, formerly a nun, took place on June 13, 1525. While at first he indicated that the marriage was to confirm his teaching and to satisfy the hopes of his father for grandchildren, he later, living with his wife, their six children, and others who formed part of the household, came to recognize other reasons for marriage, though romantic love was never one of them.

The family existed, first of all, to provide for an orderly continuation of the race and to curb an individual's inordinate desire. Patriarchal in type, the husband and father should have authority over his wife and children. While romance had no place in the relationship, yet there was opportunity enough for the continuing pleasures of love. "The first love is drunken. When the intoxication wears off, then comes the real married love."[70] Basic to the relations of husband and wife is trust:

> When a man and woman love and are pleased with each other, and thoroughly believe in their love, who teaches them how they are to behave, what they are to do, leave undone, say, not say, think? Confidence alone teaches them all this and more. They make no difference in works: they do the great, the long, the much as gladly as the small, the short, the little and vice versa; and that too with joyful, peaceful, confident hearts, and each is a free companion of the other.[71]

In the economic and political ethic Luther's conservatism was manifest. His vision of society was that of an orderly, agricultural economy. Individuals should work for their living, they should "share in bearing and suffering the community's burdens, dangers, and injuries," and there should be no investing or lending of money for interest.[72]

In political ethics the important distinctions were made between individuals acting on their own and acting on behalf of society. Individuals were called of God to social responsibilities. The magistrate was ordained of God, and the soldier also is called to perform the righteous work of preserving order. The work of the political ruler and soldier is a Christian calling; yet it cannot be performed with Christian standards. There was also a difference between personal and social life, between the ethical possibilities open to an individual and to an institution. Since order is needed in society the only way to insure that order is through the use of force in the hands of the authorities who have been "ordained of God." For this reason the individual is to be obedient to the established magistrates.

> It is in no wise proper for anyone who would be a Christian to set himself against his government, whether it acts justly or unjustly, but a Christian ought to endure oppression and injustice, especially at the hands of his government.[73]

There are some limits to this obedience. If ever an authority "should urge a subject to do contrary to the Commandments of God, or hinder him from doing them, there obedience ends."[74]

So at the last, as at the beginning, faith is the source of the ethic. It is a faith that, providing spiritual freedom, leads to a joyful love and the joy of service.

JOHN CALVIN (1509–1564)

The moral convictions of John Calvin were based upon the same assumptions as the ethic of Martin Luther. Indeed, Calvin often expressed his debt to the earlier Reformer and in 1543 proclaimed that "God raised up Luther and others, who held forth a torch to light us into the way of salvation."[75] Because of the similarity in the assumptions of these two men it is surprising to find their ethical conclusions so different. Those differences, significant for later history, were due to the diverse experiences and social situations of the two men and to their distinct personalities.

John Calvin was the son of a well-to-do, moderately influential lawyer of Noyon, near Paris. Young Calvin attended the University of Paris in preparation for the priesthood; but while he was there, his father, in 1528, decided that the law was a preferable profession. John left Paris to study law at Orléans and later at Bourges. In his university training he came under the spell of humanist scholarship, and his first book, written when he was twenty-three, was a commentary on Seneca's *De clementia* (1532). Here there was that lucidity of style and thought which characterizes all of Calvin's writing, together with a passion for moral and political order that dominated his life. His interest in contemporary religious thought appeared for the first time in the rectorial address that Calvin prepared for delivery by Nicholas Cop on November 1, 1533. In this there were the influences of Erasmus's idea of a "Christian philosophy," the New Testament, and Luther's conception of grace and faith.

It is probable that in this year, when he turned from Seneca through Erasmus to Luther, Calvin achieved a new perspective. However, there can be no definite dating of this major change in his life, for it is characteristic of Calvin (and so unlike Luther) that in his writings his emotions are insignificant and his inner life is hidden. He did state that "God by a sudden conversion tamed and made teachable my mind,"[76] but he never described or dated that conversion. The closest he may have come to a description of his inner experience was cast in impersonal terms when he wrote, in 1539,

> I, O Lord, as I had been educated from childhood, always professed the Christian faith. . . . When, however, I had performed all these things [which the Church required] though I had some intervals of quiet, I was still far from true peace of conscience. For whenever I descended into myself or raised my mind to thee, extreme terror seized me which no expiations or satisfactions could cure. The more closely I examined myself, the sharper the stings with which my conscience was pricked; so that the only solace which remained was to delude myself by obliviousness. Yet as nothing better offered, I was pursuing the course which I had begun, when a very different form of doctrine started up, not one which led us away from the Christian profession, but one which brought it back to its original purity. . . . Being exceedingly alarmed at the misery into which I had fallen, and much more at that which threatened me in eternal death, as in duty bound I made it my first business to condemn my own past life, not without groans and tears, and to accept thy life.[77]

This was characteristically Calvin. There was a sense of sin but not of guilt; there were "groans and tears," but they were more the result of a self-critical understanding of his situation than of an emotional experience. Above all the whole passage (as all of Calvin's later life and thought) reflected that assurance, that certainty of one who knows his status before God.

Through his conversion Calvin was committed to the radical reformation of the church. His life was endangered by the reaction to the rectorial address, and for three months he fled from town to town in France until, early in 1535, he went to Basel as a refugee. There he continued his scholarly work and, in 1536, at the age of twenty-seven, wrote one of the most influential books in religious history. The first edition of the *Institutes of the Christian Religion* had only six chapters, and they indicate that he was led into theology through ethics. "The first edition of the *Institutio* is distinguished from all later editions by the emphasis it lays, not on dogma, but on morals, on worship, and on polity."[78] The final edition published during his life was expanded to eighty chapters.

Later in 1536, returning to Switzerland from a visit in France, Calvin was prevailed upon to settle in Geneva with a view toward assisting in directing the affairs of the church. The remainder of his life was associated with that city, which both shaped and was shaped by his thought.

Geneva, a city in which church and state were interwoven, had for centuries exhibited democratic tendencies. The bishop, elected by the clergy and endorsed by all the citizens, was the political and judicial authority. Major military and police powers were vested in an official of the church. The citizens, through a variety of councils, had final authority for establishing laws, conducting economic policies, and developing alliances. This threefold division in which church and state were separate yet intertwined was the setting for the growth of Calvinistic republicanism. The rebellion against the established Catholicism prepared the way for Calvin. On May 21, 1536, two months before he arrived in Geneva, the citizens replaced the Mass with the evangelical faith and replaced the bishop with a council.

In July 1536, Calvin began his labors with Genevan leaders in trying to establish a holy community. The exacting discipline produced reaction among the 13,000 inhabitants. If they did not want a native bishop with dictatorial tendencies, neither did they desire a French clergyman to control their lives, and in March 1538 Calvin was exiled by vote of the council.

From September of that year until September 1541, Calvin lived as a refugee in Strassburg. He became minister of the French-speaking church and a teacher in the theological school, he continued his scholarly work with a study of the New Testament, he married (1540–1549), and he wrote an eloquent defense of the Reformed Faith. Cardinal Sadolet had pleaded with the Genevan citizens to break with the new heresy and to return to Catholicism. Though Calvin no longer had any official connection with the events in Geneva, he felt a moral compulsion to reply to Sadolet. He wrote a letter that, urbane on the surface yet bitter beneath, was a superb expression of his life and ideas. There could be no sharper statement of his revolutionary point of view than the simple assertion that "the salvation of that man hangs by a thread whose defense turns wholly on his constant adherence unto the religion handed down to him from his forefathers."[79] Or, again,

Christian faith must not be founded on human testimony, not propped up by doubtful opinion, not based on human authority, but engraved on our hearts by the finger of the living God, so as not to be obliterated by any deceitful error. There is nothing of Christ in him who does not hold the elemental principle, that it is God alone who enlightens our minds to perceive his truth, who by his Spirit seals it in our hearts, and by his sure testimony of it confirms our conscience.[80]

In September 1541, at the invitation of the council, Calvin returned to Geneva, and there he remained as its most influential citizen until his death in 1564. His first act was to persuade the council to appoint a committee, including himself, that should draft a program of reform. The *Ordonnances Ecclésiastiques* were adopted on November 20, and through the years they remained as the framework through which Calvin tried to build the New Jerusalem on the shores of Lake Geneva. He created a ministry that was both called of God and disciplined by training, and this made necessary an extensive education of clergy and laity. He established a "consistory" with responsibilities of guarding the morals of the community and with the power to excommunicate, which led to intolerance and persecution.

The achievements of Calvin's program of a trained ministry and universal education have often been obscured by an abhorrence of the harshness and pettiness of Calvinistic discipline. The pages of Genevan records are filled with punishments for continued absence from church, the singing of profane songs, playing cards, criticizing ministers, swearing, dancing, frequenting taverns, Catholic practices, adultery, and heresy. Criticism of Calvin, refusal to attend church, and adultery were crimes subject to banishment; witchcraft and heresy led to the death penalty. Between 1542 and 1546, fifty-eight persons were executed and seventy-six exiled.

How is it possible that the Reformation faith, which claimed to be rooted in the New Testament, led to these extremities? An answer to this question helps to provide an understanding of the ethic of Calvin.

It is of primary importance that the context of Calvin's acts of petty and extreme discipline be recognized. He did not create the system of penalties for moral and religious misbehavior; those penalties were established in Geneva before he arrived. Moreover, if his punishment was harsh, it should be remembered that he lived in a harsh age. In 1534 and 1535 twenty-three persons were put to death in Paris for heresy; in 1546 fourteen Reformers of Meaux were burned because they celebrated Holy Communion. Throughout France, as in other parts of Europe, severe punishment for heresy was a generally accepted procedure. The experiences Calvin had known of opposition to his doctrines and person caused him to see that he, with Geneva, was at war with the enemies of the new faith. Punishment of heretics was self-defense and defense of the true religion. How could beleaguered Geneva survive the attacks of her opponents if the core of her resistance was weakened by false preaching and immoral practices?

If the events and spirit of the time provided the context for Calvin's harsh discipline, it also derived from his vocation, his personal religion, and his thought. These, moreover, reflected the assumptions of his ethic and clarified his moral thought.

In vocation, John Calvin knew that he was chosen to glorify God by building a holy community on the basis of revealed truth. He was aware of the disorder within and about him, and he knew that the proper order of life could come only by serving the sovereign God. He did not hesitate to stand in the presence of God: "Always, both by word and deed, have I protested how eager I was for unity. Mine, however, was a unity of the Church which should begin with thee and end with thee."[81]

The full details of Calvin's personal religion are not clear, but he made repeated references to two aspects of the religious life: the struggles of conscience before conversion, and the assurance of salvation afterward. "You have too superficial a theology," he said to a cardinal of the church, "as is almost always the case with those who have never had the experience in serious struggles of conscience."[82] After the enlightenment by the Spirit there is "that full and firm assurance commended by Paul, which, as it leaves no room for doubt, neither hesitates nor wavers among human arguments as to which party it ought to adhere, but maintains its consistency though the whole world oppose it."[83] In his defense of religion Calvin was callous and vindictive toward his opponents, and yet he did not have a personal animosity toward them because he felt he was merely the agent of the righteous God who judged all impartially.

Calvin's theology made his attitude toward discipline consistent. Here all the assumptions of his ethic became apparent. His thought began and concluded with the one sovereign God, who as Holy Will was the source and end of all things. The Will of God was lucid in the scriptures and in Christ. Through the scriptures and through Christ it was evident that God selected individuals to glorify him and to establish a holy community under his sovereignty. All of the Reformation's elementary ethical assumptions were present: an awareness of disorder and a vocation to establish order, God as the true principle who can be known only through a return to the purity of ancient tradition, and the individual as that being whose ceaseless activity can be engaged to serve the sovereign God. Throughout there was the certainty not that one possesses the truth but that one is possessed by the truth.

In Calvin's thought there was no place for self-seeking. Even the desire for salvation placed first in life is an unworthy desire. In an affirmation that constituted the theme of his thought he says,

It is not very sound theology to confine a man's thoughts so much to himself, and not to set before him as the prime motive of his existence zeal to show forth the glory of God. For we are born first of all for God, and not for ourselves. As all things flowed from him and subsist in him, as Paul says, they ought to be related to him.[84]

The sum of Calvin's ethic, then, can be compressed into the following statement: (1) The perfect God confronts the perverted individual, (2) reordering the lives of the ones he selects toward life's proper goal, (3) thus creating lives of obedience and (4) establishing a holy community.

1. The Perfect God confronts the perverted individual.

While Calvin's ethic rested upon the Protestant doctrine of "justification by faith," he did not begin with an analysis of the faith as experienced by the individual but of the God who is sovereign over all. "Our wisdom, in so far as it ought to be deemed true and solid, consists almost entirely of two parts: the knowledge of God and of ourselves."[85] These two are interdependent, but the proper order is to begin with the knowledge of God.

At the beginning of the *Institutes* this theme of the perfect God and the imperfect person was introduced.

We always seem to ourselves just, and upright, and wise, and holy, until we are convinced, by clear evidence, of our injustice, vileness, folly and impurity. Convinced, however, we are not, if we look to ourselves only, and not to the Lord also—He being the only standard by the application of which this conviction can be produced. . . . If, at mid-day, we either look down to the ground, or on the surrounding objects which lie open to our view, we think ourselves endued with a very strong and piercing eyesight; but when we look up to the sun, and gaze at it unveiled, the sight which did excellently well for the earth, is instantly so dazzled and confounded by the refulgence, as to oblige us to confess that our acuteness in discerning terrestrial objects is mere dimness when applied to the sun. Thus, too, it happens in estimating our spiritual qualities. So long as we do not look beyond the earth, we are quite pleased with our own righteousness, wisdom, and virtue; we address ourselves in the most flattering terms, and seem only less than demigods. But should we once begin to raise our thoughts to God, and reflect what kind of Being his is, and how absolute the perfection of that righteousness, and wisdom, and virtue, to which as a standard, we are bound to be conformed, what formerly delighted us by its false show of righteousness, will become polluted with the greatest iniquity; what strangely imposed upon us under the name of wisdom, will disgust by its extreme folly; and what presented the appearance of virtuous energy, will be condemned as the most miserable impotence. So far are those qualities in us, which seem most perfect, from corresponding to the divine purity.[86]

But when any individual attempts to approach the knowledge of this perfect God, there are three topics that become important for ethics: (a) the purposes of the knowledge, (b) the ways to knowledge, and (c) the nature of God.

(a) The purposes of knowledge

The prime purpose of the knowledge of God is its practical influence upon life,

> *first,* to teach us reverence and fear; and, *secondly,* to induce us, under its guidance and teaching, to ask every good thing from him, and, when it is received, to ascribe it to him. . . . For this sense of the divine perfection is the proper master to teach us piety, out of which religion springs.[87]

(b) The ways to knowledge

This knowledge of God is gained through universal human experience, beginning with the realization that "a sense of Deity is indelibly engraven on the human heart."[88] There is, however, a distinction for Calvin between inadequate knowledge (from emotion and reason) and adequate knowledge (individual apprehension through the scriptures and the Spirit) that has implications for the religious and moral experience.

(c) The nature of God

The nature of God is perfection, in both Being and Action. He was understood first as that active will which sustains the universe throughout time. This is Providence,

> a special Providence sustaining, cherishing, superintending, all the things which he has made, to the very minutest, even to a sparrow. . . . God is deemed omnipotent. . . . because, governing heaven and earth by his providence, he so overrules all things that nothing happens without his counsel.[89]

The perfection of God refers also to moral qualities.

> The attributes which it is most necessary for us to know are these three: Loving-kindness, on which alone our entire safety depends; Judgment, which is daily exercised on the wicked; . . . Righteousness, by which the faithful are preserved.[90]

In terms of the individual, there are two ethical possibilities: either to become the essential (perfect) person that is possible or to remain the existen-

tial (perverted) person that one is. Or, in Calvin's use of then familiar terminology, to either become the individual as "made in the image of God," or to
remain the individual after "the Fall."

The "image of God" referred mainly to the soul, that is, to an individual's
mental, emotional, and spiritual faculties, but since he ascribed goodness to
all of creation, Calvin also saw the image of God as reflected in the human
body:

> By this term is denoted the integrity with which Adam was endued when his
> intellect was clear, his affections subordinated to reason, all his senses duly
> regulated, and when he truly ascribed all his excellence to the admirable
> gifts of his Maker. And though the primary seat of the divine image was in
> the mind and heart, or in the soul and its powers, there was no part even of
> the body in which some rays of glory did not shine. . . . At the beginning
> the image of God was manifested by the light of the intellect, rectitude of
> heart, and soundness of every part.[91]

But this image has become perverted. In attributing the distortion to
Adam and in making the disorder hereditary, Calvin was expressing his view
of the historical unity of human life as well as affirming his belief in the universality of evil. Individuals no longer exist in "the image of God" (though
that image has not been "utterly effaced and destroyed,"[92] but are naturally
depraved so that "the hydra lurks in every breast."[93] But what was the cause
of this depravity, and what were its characteristics and consequences?

The fundamental evil is that each individual has refused to accept his
true status. This evil is not sensuality, a notion that Calvin calls "childish." It
is, rather, infidelity to the individual's assigned station in the world, an unwillingness to recognize one's fealty to God, and a refusal to see one's finite
dependency upon God and instead claiming for oneself an infinite independence.

> Augustine, indeed, was not far from the mark when he says that pride was
> the beginning of all evil. . . . Infidelity was at the root of the revolt. From
> infidelity, again, sprang ambition and pride, together with ingratitude.[94]

Through an individual's faithlessness the whole life becomes disordered.
"Everything which is in man, from the intellect to the will, from the soul even
to the flesh, is defiled and pervaded with this concupiscence."[95] By "concupiscence" Calvin did not mean sensual lust, for that would make sensuality
the basic evil and this he expressly denied. He did mean that the total life of
man was pervaded by illicit desires, wrong desires or ambitions of the mind,
the will, and the body. "Man's natural gifts were corrupted by sin, and his supernatural gifts withdrawn."[96] The individual is by nature both a rational and

social animal, and it is such gifts as these that have been distorted by disloyalty. The individual still has, for example, a love of truth but now, through
self-centeredness, he is unable to arrive at the final goal of truth and so becomes vain; unable to pursue the right means toward truth, he becomes be-
wildered; unable to know what knowledge is really important, he becomes a
dilettante.

When the perfect God confronts the perverted individual, the plight of
the self becomes evident. Disordered by faithlessness, he is not able to re-
order life. With this theme Calvin reaches the ultimate meaning of depravity:

> When the will is enchained as the slave of sin, it cannot make a movement
> towards goodness, far less steadily pursue it. . . . Man, since he was cor-
> rupted by the fall, sins not forced or unwilling, but voluntarily, by a most
> forward bias of the mind; not by violent compulsion or external force, but
> by the movement of his own passion; and yet such is the depravity of his
> nature, that he cannot move and act except in the direction of evil.[97]

2. God reorders the lives of selected individuals

What we are unable to do alone, that is, to restore life's original integrity and
redirect life toward its proper goals, God does for us. Or, more exactly, God
does this for some of us.

> None but the elect have a will inclined to good. But the cause of the elec-
> tion must be sought out of man; and hence it follows that a right will is de-
> rived not from man himself, but from the same good pleasure by which we
> were chosen before the creation of the world. . . .
>   The first part of a good work is the will, the second is vigorous effort
> in the doing of it. God is the author of both.[98]

What is the principle of this new order? It is the gift of faith, but faith is
not to be equated with intellectual belief, creedal affirmation, or rational
knowledge. Faith is a living, lively confidence, and as it must be experienced
by the individual, so it must have its fruits in individual life. Such faith re-
stores the "true and substantial integrity"[99] of the individual.

3. The new life of obedience

The results of religious faith are both psychological and ethical. Psychologically there is a double consequence: the absolute assurance of one's present
status and ultimate salvation, and the motive power for continuous activity.
New trials, new troubles there will be, but all anxiety as to one's status before God or others is drowned in the sea of faith.

The pious man, how much soever it may be agitated and torn, at length rises superior to all difficulties and allows not its confidence in the divine mercy to be destroyed. . . . Doubtless it is a terrific thing to walk in the darkness of death, and it is impossible for believers, however great their strength may be, not to shudder at it; but since the prevailing thought is that God is present and providing for their safety, the feeling of security overcomes that of fear. . . .

Faith, apprehending the love of God, has both the promise of the present and future life, and ample security for all blessings.[100]

Now with renewed confidence the individual can intensify as well as redirect all of life's activities. "The highest wisdom, even of him who has attained the greatest perfection, is to go forward, and endeavor in a calm and teachable spirit to make further progress."[101]

The ethical effects of faith are as definite as the psychological, for the moral life, rooted in faith, has as its purpose the glory of God. Self-denial is the fundamental moral characteristic. It is the rejection of this cherished claim of the proud, ambitious self, and it is characterized by both inner and outer qualities of life. The self now sees and accepts its true condition, always dependent upon God, inevitably related to others. Humility becomes the inner ethical quality; love and liberty are personal ethical consequences.

These inner ethical motives are expressed in behavior. Love becomes the service of others. "All the endowments which we possess are divine deposits intrusted to us for the very purpose of being distributed for the good of our neighbor."[102] Christian freedom is also expressed in outward activity. It is not only that "consciences are exempt from all human authority,"[103] though this, as will be noted later, has far-reaching effects. The Christian is free to make use of and to desire the goods of the world. One side of this has often been noted because it was more fully developed in later Calvinism, the permission to seek wealth and honor so long as the desires are not excessive and are sought with honesty, sobriety, and frugality. The other side, not so frequently noted because it was later ignored in Calvinism, is the emphasis upon the freedom to enjoy the pleasures of life.

If we consider for what end he created food, we shall find that he consulted not only for our necessity, but also for our enjoyment and delight. Thus, in clothing, the end was in addition to necessity, comeliness and honor; and in herbs, fruits, and trees, besides their various uses, gracefulness of appearance and sweetness of smell. . . . The natural qualities of things themselves demonstrate to what end, and how far, they may be lawfully enjoyed. Has the Lord adorned flowers with all the beauty which spontaneously presents itself to the eye, and the sweet odor which delights the sense of smell, and shall it be unlawful for us to enjoy that beauty and this odor? What? Has he not so distinguished colors as to make some more agreeable than others? Has he not given qualities to gold and silver, ivory and marble, thereby rendering them precious above other metals and stones? In short, has he not given many things a value without having any necessary use?

Have done, then, with that inhuman philosophy which, in allowing no use of the creatures but for necessity, not only maliciously deprives us of the lawful fruit of the divine beneficence, but cannot be realized without depriving man of all his senses, and reducing him to a block. . . .

Certainly ivory and gold, and riches, are the good creatures of God, permitted, nay, destined, by divine providence for the use of man; nor was it ever forbidden to laugh, or to be full, or to add new to old and hereditary possessions, or to be delighted with music, or to drink wine. This is true, but when the means are supplied, to roll and wallow in luxury, to intoxicate the mind and soul with present, and be always hunting after new pleasure, is very far from a legitimate use of the gifts of God. Let them, therefore, suppress immoderate desire, immoderate profusion, vanity and arrogance, that they may use the gifts of God purely with a good conscience.[104]

The ethic of John Calvin was a religious morality of motives characterized by active love and freedom, the outer expression of the inner character. This moral life is given content through the recognition of the unique responsibilities of the individual, that is, through the calling of God.

The Lord enjoins every one of us, in all the actions of life, to have respect to our own calling . . . that in following your proper calling, no work will be so mean and sordid as not to have a splendour and value in the eye of God.[105]

This doctrine of vocation in Calvin, as in Luther, introduced a sacred character into the secular life. Since all proper work has a "splendour and value" to God, the individual finds meaning in life's labor. In Calvin, more than in Luther, there developed an intense individuality, an awareness of the dignity of one's own person. To be called is to be selected for salvation by God. The moral meaning of predestination is that one is enabled and privileged to glorify God through the service of others. This power and this honor make one aware of one's own worth as a person, a worth that is not of one's own making but that is bestowed by God. The personal experience of dignity enhances individuality.

4. The creation of the holy community

The individuals who are predestined by God are given a calling and a cause. The cause ultimately is to glorify God, but mediately it is to serve humanity's deepest needs, a service that can be accomplished only through the creation of a community.

Dismayed by the disunity of life, Calvin was led to the dominant aim of creating a unity of Christian civilization. In the building of unity different institutions, the state and church, and different individuals, the elect and the nonelect, are interrelated and interactive. There are distinctions between church and state as there are between individuals. But distinctions and differences do not divide the society or destroy its essential unity. All work together for the creation of that community that glorifies God.

> In man government is twofold: the one spiritual, by which the conscience is trained to piety and divine worship; the other civil, by which the individual is instructed in those duties which, as men and citizens, we are bound to perform.[106]

The church exists to mediate salvation to the individual and to develop moral character in individual and society. Salvation is accomplished through the sincere preaching and hearing of truth and through observance of the sacraments. The function of the church is fulfilled through the four orders of pastors, teachers, deacons (to serve those in need), and elders (to approve and discipline). The state has as its purpose

> to foster and maintain the external worship of God, to defend sound doctrine, and the condition of the church, to adapt our conduct to human society, to form our manners to civil justice, to conciliate us to each other, to cherish common peace and tranquillity.[107]

There is a positive value ascribed to the state, and no sharp distinctions, therefore, were made between secular morality as required by the state and religious morality as required by the church, nor between private and public morality. There are no contradictions between the laws of Nature, of Moses (the Ten Commandments), and of Christ. There are differences of clarity but not of validity. Yet the laws of society come under the divine purpose and they must be transformed by that purpose. Thus the way is open for individual Christians to act directly, as Christians, in social affairs, molding the life of the state into a pattern of a more perfect community, just as the Christian is active in the church helping to fashion, according to the larger plan, a *corpus Christianum*. The Christianizing of both church and state is the never-ending task of the elect. In this task they are sharing in the work of creating a holy community in which each individual, having fellowship with each other, is enabled to live for the glory of God.

THE UNIQUE CONTRIBUTION OF THE RENAISSANCE AND REFORMATION

The cathedral doors were opening. There was a new clarity of light shinning inside, exposing cracks, creating possibilities. The congregation was venturing forth, in and out through the archway. There were voyages of discovery into the mind and into the world. The borders of what was known were shifting and advancing with each year, and the explorers were returning with new products, ideas, and stories. Trade was flourishing, towns were prospering. There were possibilities for new relationships, new outlooks. The inner symbolic world was giving way to a natural realism. In art and sculpture there was a return to the human body, to a glorification of the individual body. But if the open doors brought the church out into the world, they also brought the challenges and conflicts of the world into the church. The old unity was shattered, the old certainties dissolved.

Everywhere there was disorder, confusion, and turmoil; but underneath the challenges that the voyages of discovery had brought, there was an incontrovertible confidence. There was a faith in the future, a belief that things could be made better, that a new kind of human being could be fashioned. For in the midst of the breakup of the medieval family, there was, as yet, no Descartian doubt, no deep despair or irony, no satire or sarcasm. There was little of grief. There were conflicts and arguments, disputes and threats, new allegiances and alignments. But for those who had stepped outdoors, it was a new dawn, and the victory could still be won.

Along with the confidence, there was also a new realism, a new naturalism: in art, in sculpture, in politics. Individuals were looking at the world, and they were trying to depict the world as it was, to map the world they saw, and what they saw was a world that had a human face, at times an idealized human face: the confidence of a young David in the midst of the challenges of Goliath.

Suddenly, outside, the church became only one ordering principle among others, and even inside the church there were rifts and challenges to the old doctrines, the old creeds. But if there were now multiple choices for meaning, then choice itself became important. And choice implied that the individual was important, that truth and commitment and action were to be grounded in the individual and not in a fixed structure residing outside the individual. This underlying commitment to choice did not yet imply that people ought to be free to make choices, that freedom in itself was a guaranteed right, but it did suggest that reason was central: that blind faith was blind, and that faith was meant to be received with knowledge.

In the midst of the disorder, then, there were multiple choices for a new order, and while there was no universal overarching meaning, the individual could still create meaning, and joining with other individuals, could posit this new meaning as a universal meaning. It was perhaps a strange new paradox that the old certitude and assurance of the crumbling faith were still present in the new faiths, and in fact the new faiths were often asserted with the dogmatism of the old order.

Yet, as different as the Renaissance and Reformation were, their underlying processes were similar. For Pico and Machiavelli, the ideal was (a) the (re)construction of the self or society (b) through creative thought and (c) continual action, (d) that required flexible responses and called upon all the varied powers and potentialities of the self. For Luther and Calvin, the ideal was (a) the reconstruction of the self (and in Calvin's case of the society), (b) through individual faith and trust. This new faith and trust would (c) lead to a life of continuing challenge and commitment, but always (d) blessed with the assurance of "salvation."

Thus what was common to all was the individual's thoughts, actions, and commitments. What was common was that something was clearly required of the individual, and what was required was a continual process. With the similarities in these two processes we can now see the four significant gifts that the Renaissance and Reformation have made to Western ethical thought.

(1) The central key is the creative activity of the individual. The times had called for a new response, not only from institutions, but more significantly from each individual. The burden and joy of faith was within reach of everyone.

(2) In positing as its crucial thesis the centrality of the individual, there was a series of corollaries. In the first place each person could be "called" to faith. The authority of the world resided in each person, and each could exist in a direct relationship to the truth.

(3) In addition, the sense of the good was radically extended. The doors of the church were opened outward, and there was an importance placed on the value of the created world. There was the possibility for sacredness in the secular world. God could call individuals to faith not only in the service of the church, but through the daily work of life.

(4) And finally, new communities were being formed. In the Reformation these communities, composed of individuals who had made free choices, were still grounded in God and were holy communities. In the Renaissance the new communities were often political, economic, or artistic. But what was central to all was the sense that salvation was still possible, that human beings could still create and respond to meaning, that the doors were open now and for all time, and that these open doors could bring with them a renewed hope for human lives as well as a renewed sense that the individual life could be improved.

NOTES

1. Ferdinand Schevill, *History of Florence from the Founding of the City through the Renaissance* (New York: Harcourt, Brace and Company, 1936), p. xviii.

2. Ibid., p. 402.

3. Cecilia May Ady, "Florence and North Italy," *Cambridge Medieval History* (New York: Macmillan Company, 1924), 8: 224.

4. Thomas More, *The English Works of Sir Thomas More,* ed. W. E. Campbell (New York: Lincoln MacVeagh, 1931), 1: 356.

5. Ibid., p. 353.

6. Ibid.

7. Pico, *The Renaissance Philosophy of Man,* ed. Ernst Cassirer (Illinois: University of Chicago Press, 1948), pp. 224–25.

8. Ibid., p. 225.

9. Ernst Cassirer, "Giovanni Pico della Mirandola, A Study of the History of Renaissance Ideas," *Journal of the History of Ideas* (New York: College of the City of New York, 1942), 3: 330.

10. Pico, *The Renaissance Philosophy of Man,* p. 231.

11. Ibid., p. 230.

12. Ibid., pp. 231–32.

13. Ibid., p. 238.

14. Ibid., p. 242.

15. Ibid., p. 235.

16. Ibid., p. 234.

17. Ibid., p. 241.

18. Ibid., pp. 225, 227.

19. More, *The English Works,* 1: 359.

20. Niccolò Machiavelli, *The Prince and Other Works,* trans. Alan Gilbert (Chicago: Packard and Company, 1941), p. 270.

21. Niccolò Machiavelli, *Florentine History,* trans. W. K. Marriott (London: J. M. Dent & Company, 1909), p. 183.

22. Ibid., p. 360.

23. Ibid., pp. 1–2.

24. Schevill, *History of Florence,* p. 517.

25. Machiavelli, *Prince,* p. 93.

26. Ibid., pp. 241–42.

27. Ibid., p. 141.

28. Ibid., p. 100.

29. Ibid., p. 84.

30. Ibid., p. 96.

31. Ibid., p. 148.

32. Ibid., p. 149.

33. Ibid., p. 145.

34. Ibid., p. 145.

35. Ibid., p. 148.

36. Ibid., p. 163.

37. Ibid., p. 177.

38. Ibid., p. 180.

39. Ibid., pp. 80–81.

40. Ibid., pp. 145–46.

41. Ibid., pp. 145–46.

42. Ibid., p. 295.

43. Ibid., p. 296.

44. Ibid., p. 171.

45. Ibid., p. 173.

46. Ibid., p. 226.

47. Mario Rosi, *Modern Language Review* 44 (1949): 424.

48. Martin Luther, *Works of Martin Luther* (Philadelphia: Muhlenberg Press, 1943), 1: 198–99.

49. Martin Luther, *Martin Luther: Selections From His Writings*, ed. John Dillinger (New York: Anchor Books, 1961), p. xiv.

50. Martin Luther, *A Compend of Luther's Theology*, ed. Hugh Thomas Kerr (Philadelphia: West Minister Press, 1943), p. 33.

51. Roland Bainton, *The Reformation of the Sixteenth Century* (Boston: The Beacon Press, 1952), p. 30.

52. Roland Bainton, *Here I Stand: A Life of Martin Luther* (New York: Abingdon-Cokesbury Press, 1950), p. 65.

53. Bainton, *Reformation*, p. 61.

54. Wilhelm Pauck, *The Heritage of the Reformation* (Boston: The Beacon Press, 1950), p. 16.

55. Ibid., p. 21.

56. Richard Niebuhr and Waldo Beach, *Christian Ethics* (New York: Ronald Press Company, 1955), p. 245.

57. Ibid.

58. Ibid., p. 237.

59. Martin Luther, *Works of Martin Luther* (Philadelphia: Muhlenberg Press, 1930), 3: 110.

60. Bainton, *Here I Stand*, p. 62.

61. Luther, *A Compend*, pp. 105–106.

62. Luther, *Works*, 2: 368.

63. Harry Emerson Fosdick, *Great Voices of the Reformation* (New York: Random House, 1952), p. 81.

64. Pauck, *The Heritage of the Reformation*, p. 11.

65. Luther, *A Compend*, p. 72.

66. Ibid., p. 39.

67. Pauck, *The Heritage of the Reformation*, p. 16.

68. Luther, *Works*, 2: 331.

69. Bainton, *Here I Stand*, p. 280.

70. Ibid., p. 302.

71. Luther, *A Compend*, pp. 194–95.

72. Ibid., p. 182.

73. Ibid., p. 230.

74. Ibid., p. 23.

75. John Calvin, *Calvin: Theological Treatises*, trans. Rev. J. K. S. Reid (Philadelphia: The Westminister Press, 1954), p. 185.

76. James Mackinnon, *Calvin and the Reformation* (New York: Longmans, Green, and Co., 1936), pp. 44–45.

77. Calvin, *Theological Treatises*, pp. 250, 251–52, 253.

78. *The Cambridge Modern History*, ed. A. W. Ward (New York: Macmillan Company, 1907), p. 357.

79. Calvin, *Theological Treatises*, p. 253.

80. Ibid., p. 244.

81. Ibid., p. 249.

82. Ibid., p. 243.

83. Ibid., p. 244.

84. Ibid., p. 228.

85. John Calvin, *Institutes of the Christian Religion*, trans. Henry Beveridge (Grand Rapids, Mich.: Wm. B. Eerdmans Publishing Company, 1953), 1: 37.

86. Ibid., pp. 38–39.

87. Ibid., p. 41.

88. Ibid., p. 44.

89. Ibid., pp. 172, 174.

90. Ibid., p. 88.

91. Ibid., p. 164.

92. Ibid.

93. Ibid., p. 251.

94. Ibid., p. 213.

95. Ibid., p. 218.

96. Ibid., p. 233.

97. Ibid., p. 253, 254.

98. Ibid., pp. 257, 259.

99. Ibid., p. 164.

100. Ibid., pp. 487, 488, 493.

101. Ibid., p. 471.

102. Calvin, *Institutes,* 2: 10–11.

103. Ibid., p. 140.

104. Ibid., pp. 32–33, 136.

105. Ibid., pp. 34, 35.

106. Ibid., p. 140.

107. Ibid., p. 652.

7

THE ETHICS OF THE RELIGIOUS
AND SCIENTIFIC REVOLUTIONS:
THE SEVENTEENTH CENTURY

When we remember our past life we do not recall all days with equal vividness. Some days can never be remembered. But there are other times that press upon our memories with a force and a meaning. The events of those days and our response to the events shaped our character. Such a day, for our common ethical consciousness, was the seventeenth century. Many of the ethical ideals that have become a part of our ordinary ethical consciousness in the West, particularly in the English-speaking world, were forged in the fires of the sixteen-hundreds. They are the moral ideals that perplex us today, not because we do not accept them but because we do not yet know how to make them a reality rather than merely a set of ideas in our own vacillating world. They are moral ideals now taken for granted, but many of our kin in the seventeenth century had to live and die for their radical beliefs of speech, religion, government of consent, and equality of rights.

The ethics of the century were intimately related to politics, and the political conflicts overflowed into ethical thought and tended to monopolize moral reflection. The main reason for this was that while the two other major revolutions of the time—the scientific-philosophical and the religious—were equal to the political revolution in intensity, they did not reach as many persons as the shifts of political power.

These three revolutions, then, account for the vitality of ethical expression in the seventeenth century. In politics the century began with what appeared to be an absolute sovereignty ("the Divine Right of Kings"), but by century's end the locus of sovereignty had shifted to Parliament. In science, it began with the martyrdom of Giordano Bruno, who was burned at the stake in 1600, but by the end Isaac Newton was recognized by almost all educated individuals as "the greatest genius who has arisen for the ornament of the human species." In religion, at the beginning of the century the principle that the religion of a people would be determined by the ruler was dominant ("cuius regio, eius religio") with no toleration for other faiths, but by the end the right of the individual conscience had been accepted in a limited form in England, the Netherlands, and New England.

The main achievements of the political revolution were that the government of the community was no longer subservient to an individual but to the law that was created by representatives of the people, and that was based upon a conception of human rights. The main achievements in science were not in the scientific discoveries themselves but in a changed attitude toward science and in the incentive toward scientific study.

The new science had its influence upon philosophy, too. Theology had declared its independence from philosophy in the sixteenth century. Now, in the seventeenth, philosophy agreed to the divorce. This divorce was the beginning of a widening gulf between philosophy and theology, science and religion. Philosophy, influenced by scientific, political, and economic changes, turned away from an interpretation of spirit and purposiveness (as found in the Greeks), from a concern with culture and personality (as expressed by Augustine), and from an interest in God and the created world (as in the philosophers of medieval Christendom) and became preoccupied with a metaphysics reflecting a scientific worldview, a theory of knowledge that justified scientific investigation, and a naturalistic ethics and political theory that reflected the ascendancy of science and the middle-class rise to power.

THE SOCIAL BACKGROUND OF THE PURITAN REVOLUTION

In religion there was a rapid proliferation of religious groups, and this development was especially notable in England and the Low Countries among those persons influenced by the Calvinistic view of Christianity. Having discovered the right of the individual judgment as this was expressed earlier in the battle cry "the priesthood of all believers," individuals began to exercise that right. The creation of groups, large and small, followed the question, "What must I do to be saved?" John Bunyan's pilgrim, grimly battling through the English countryside toward the light he dimly saw ahead of him, was typical of the fervent and determined religious individualism of the time.

Changes in the economic and social life were much less revolutionary than alterations in politics, science, and religion.

The harmony of the economic and social structure in the Stuart era was certainly one reason why England was able to survive the violent religious and political strife of the period, and arrive at a peaceable adjustment of those quarrels at the end of the seventeenth century.[1]

In the Elizabethan and Stuart periods the economy of England was primarily that of agricultural and personal industry, as it had been for centuries. Four-fifths of the population lived in the rural areas, and by far the largest number of these were engaged in the production of food and clothing. Those who worked at some trade other than farming labored, for the most part, in their own homes with their own tools and on their own looms or forges. There were no masses of propertyless wage earners; there was almost no large-scale production.

There was, thus, a basic harmony in the economic and social structure, and yet beneath this placid exterior a quiet fermentation was taking place. They were changes that created, toward the middle of the seventeenth century, a social and economic order that was the essential condition of the Puritan revolution. In the economic life there were four major developments: (1) the creation of new industries and new tools, (2) the development of "capitalism" in some key industries, (3) the development of banking, and (4) the rapid growth of foreign trade.

There was an extensive development of various types of mining. Coal came into widespread use in the late sixteenth century largely because of the needs of manufacture and the English households, and the depletion in the timber supply. Textiles, glass-manufacturing, and iron smelting engaged the labors of increasing numbers of persons. Many of these industries, particularly those of textiles and mining, were "capitalistically" owned. An individual or group of individuals would own and operate larger-scale industries than had previously been known in Europe. There was also a decay of the guild system, a system that, with its control of workers, restricted economic growth.

The development of merchant capitalism paralleled the growth of banking and foreign trade. With the removal of the age-old limitations which had been placed upon the use of credit and interest, deposit banking developed rapidly and, in London, there were the beginnings of the money market that was destined to dominate world trade until the First World War.

Foreign trade was stimulated by the needs of the government for more resources and by the adventurous spirit. The overseas trade was controlled by the government through the issuance of exclusive charters, but most of the calculated risks were taken by London companies. The results of the economic enterprise were not solely monetary: in India, North America, Africa, and other new lands, the entrepreneurs developed qualities of initiative, leadership, self-government, and self-dependence.

These changes in England occurred in the Elizabethan and Stuart periods within a stable though developing economic order. During the years of the Puritan revolution that stability was disordered first by the government's economic and land policies, and then by civil war. Both the Loyalists and the Independents had difficulty securing a sufficient revenue to raise and supply an army. Taxes steadily increased. The burden was upon all, but because of the hidden taxes on basic necessities, the burden was greatest upon the poor. During much of the decade of the forties there was widespread depression in London, southwest England, and the border counties, and the depressions were in those areas where Puritanism was strongest.

In 1650 there was a moderate revival of trade, but it was short-lived because the government had no positive economic policy. Instead of stimulating foreign trade so that British companies could compete with other nations, the Cromwell regime conducted senseless wars first against the Dutch and then the Spanish. The wars produced treaties favorable to England, but treaties instead of trade, and the costliness of the wars in commerce and ships lost made them Pyrrhic victories. The agrarian program favored the landowners, especially the new gentry, and the yeoman-tenants were not protected. During previous centuries the policy had been to grant tenure for years or even for life, but in the Puritan regime there was an increasing tendency to demand yearly rents. The failure to create a constructive industrial and agricultural policy in the next ten years was, indeed, one of the major factors that led to the return of Charles II in 1660. In the early years of the seventeenth century 3,300,000 of the approximately four million persons living in England lived in the countryside, and perhaps 400,000 more lived in the small towns of about five thousand. Those who live together in groups of such size, where each knows all the others by their first names, see life in a different way from the dwellers in large cities. For where there was poverty and suffering, it was always poverty and suffering shared, and in a living harmony with nature and the land.

But the cities were developing, too. At the beginning of the Stuart dynasty not more than four had a population of above 20,000, and of these four only London, with its 200,000 inhabitants, was a "tall town." But London was the center of power, politically and economically.

During Elizabeth's reign came the rise of a middle class; this was the class of the gentry (as distinguished from the lords of the manor) and of the business entrepreneurs (as distinguished from the aristocracy), and there was a decided shift of power to them. Many persons in this new class had been nourished upon the English legal tradition, and it was the rights found in that tradition that they turned to when first they sought freedom from new compulsions or freedom for new privileges. The union of these persons who had an interest in property with new religious forces was the earliest propulsive drive of the Puritan revolution, and Puritanism was strongest where the greatest economic and social changes had occurred, i.e., in London, and in the "industrial" centers, among the tradesmen, the free-workers, and the new gentry, as well as in the universities.

Those responsible for the policies of the government, James I and Charles I included, were not fully aware of the economic currents and religious winds. Whether wiser policies could have restrained the storm that was to engulf the people and release a movement and a spirit that has not yet spent its force it is impossible to say. But the actual policies adopted could hardly have been more helpful in establishing the results they were intended to destroy. For the government attempted to retain an absolute political power when the economic and social basis for that power had been eroded.

The defense that James I made of "the Divine Right of Kings" was an indication that the doctrine could no longer command the assent of the people. The battles of Charles I, who at twenty-five became king in 1625, with Parliament were more direct, and they were battles about money. The crown had an independent income, but centuries earlier Parliament had won the right to approve any new sources. Charles, however, was unable to rule within his means, and while the fault was not his own but arose because of the decrease in revenues and the increase in the costs of government, still in 1628 Parliament refused to approve taxes until Charles accepted a Petition of Right designed to prevent arbitrary imprisonment and taxation without Parliament's consent. So, in 1629 Charles dismissed Parliament, and for eleven years he tried to rule alone. His troubles during those years were mainly financial. Without a sufficient income from regular sources he improvised new methods of securing the necessary money, and thereby gave new power to the currents flowing against the king.

Added to the economic policy, one that attempted to maintain the tradition of absolute monarchy supported by a nobility, were attempts made to impose religious uniformity upon the people of Scotland as well as England. William Laud, one of Charles's major advisers, extended the demand for uniformity to include religious as well as political beliefs. Religious uniformity extended to censorship of the press. But in attacking the Puritans Laud was goading an untried and unknown power. The attack was a catalyst for the Puritan revolution; it helped to develop the Puritan movement which "eventually . . . was to subdue English civilization to an attitude of mind, a code of conduct, a psychology, a manner of expression, the vitality of which far outran the particular forms of religious life which sprang up from time to time."[2]

THE PRESUPPOSITIONS OF THE PURITANS

The Puritan was a man or woman who had given individual life away or, if not yet given, was a person poised, seeking the insight that would release the energies stored within. It is this that makes it so difficult to relive, in imagination, the life of the Puritan, for the Puritans' sensibilities were thoroughly theological and their loyalties were worked out in their own inner experience as they responded to the public events of the day and the unique events of their own lives. But basic to the inner life of each Puritan were assumptions that all Puritans shared.

1. "God the absolute sovereign Lord and King in heaven and earth . . . doth all things merely and only by his sovereign will and unlimited good pleasure."[3]

Belief in an "absolute sovereign Lord and King" was not, for the Puritan, a doctrine. It was an experience. The "absolute sovereign" had met them in their lives, and it was only by stating frankly what they believed had happened to them that they could make sense out of their existence. This presupposition, therefore, was not first of all the article of a new creed, though certain of the Puritans later attempted to make it that. The assumption was a fresh consciousness of power and of holiness, the power and the holiness. But the God to whom this assumption referred could not be a basis for the Puritan's life without a consciousness of relation with God. The Puritan's concern was not for philosophical truth but for a grasp of the truth by which every moment of life was lived so that there were further affirmations.

(a) "Men as men are corrupt and will be so."[4]

This view, the "doctrine of original sin" or "absolute depravity," was, again, not a doctrine for the Puritan but an experience. Many persons, to be sure, became interested in the interpretation of the doctrine, providing prescientific explanations of how it happened, but no matter how theoretical or fanciful the writers became, they never departed from the belief that each person is corrupted by sin, that the relations of each are poisoned by false loves, and that the thought of each is vitiated by thinking from the wrong point of view. Nor among many of the Puritans is there hope that all of the remnants of sin can be eradicated from the individual's life. "We are very apt, all of us," confesses Cromwell to his fellow Puritans, "to call that faith, that perhaps may be but carnal imagination, and carnal reasonings."[5]

(b) "God . . . works in us the power of acting freely, of which, since our fall, we were incapable, except by means of a calling and renewal." [6]

The Puritans' sense of the sovereignty of God was such that, when any one of them saw in the mirror of life their own corruption, they were led into a painful experience through which they became convinced that God, "by a calling and renewal," had worked in them "the power of acting freely." This was the doctrine of predestination when viewed from the side of its effect. There were among the Puritans conflicting interpretations of this central tenet of Calvinism, and the differences primarily involved the degree of God's activity in the "calling and renewal." Among the Puritan revolutionaries the disputes about "single" and "double" predestination (i.e., whether God chose only some for salvation or chose some for salvation and others for damnation), and the arguments about the roles played by God and the individual in the process rarely reached the level of precise theological statement. This was partly because few of the English Puritans had either the time or the interest for the niceties of theological speculation. But of far greater importance was the fact that these busy revolutionaries had realized the moral meaning of predestination in their own lives and were not interested in logical consistency or carefulness. What did it matter whether God did all the calling? Or what concern was it whether he merely refrained from calling others or shouted them toward death? All that really mattered was that their lives had been renewed and that they could not have been made new except by the activity of the sovereign God.

2. *"Christ by his spirit shall call and gather a people, and form them into several families, churches, and corporations."* [7]

The Puritan as a person "called and renewed" was unable to think of the self in isolation from others, though here the others were not the general social order but the society of the saints. This is the notion of "holy community" that formed the actual context for the Puritans' actions and thoughts.

This presupposition was developed in diverse directions by the Puritans, and it was the diversity of their interpretation of the relation of holy community to the political order that constituted one of the most obvious marks of the different Puritan groups. One position, destined to be less influential, was that the holy community was to rule the political and social life. This was the theocratic solution, and it was expressed most clearly in the continuation of the statement that

Christ "*by his spirit*" shall call and gather a people . . . which, when they are multiplied, they shall rule the world by general assemblies, or church-parliaments, of such officers of Christ, and representatives of the churches, as they shall choose and delegate.[8] (Original italics)

Another position, which became far more influential in the West, was that the holy community was completely separate from the political society. The Puritan development of this view, unlike that of the sect movements which arose out of Lutheranism, always produced a dynamic interrelation between the holy community and the secular order, even though in formal structure and function the two societies were distinct. Thus, the Puritan never escaped the presupposition that the individual was a part of the holy community called by God, and that, therefore, he, with that community, had a decisive role to play in the world. From this viewpoint the individual Puritan could always say with his fellow soldiers in Scotland in 1650, "And here give us leave (not in a boasting spirit, but in meekness and fear) to tell you that we are persuaded we are poor unworthy instruments in God's hand, to break his enemies and preserve his people."[9]

3. "Christ Jesus, whose is the kingdom, the power, and the glory, both in nature and in grace, hath given several maps and schemes of his dominions: . . . both of his great kingdom, the world; . . . and also of his special and peculiar kingdom, the kingdom of grace." [10]

The general distinction between grace and nature, the spiritual and the secular, church and state, was inherited from Calvin and the scholastics. The Puritans, under the duress of the situations they faced, worked out new relations between the two spheres, relations that had an effect upon the development of democratic politics in the West. Again, there was a diverse development of the presupposition. All Puritans began with the insistence that the state had no right to impose uniformity upon the church. The principle of "religious freedom for the saints" was not an idea developed by logical argument but an insistent belief with which the Puritans began. But since they had begun with this principle, there was the possibility that the Puritans would (1) insist upon the right of those who possess the truth (namely, the saints) to impose that truth upon all others, or (2) extend the right of religious freedom they claimed for themselves to all persons and to all fields. No matter how the presupposition developed, there was basic agreement that (1) the world, no less than heaven, is the "kingdom of Christ" and therefore contains positive value, and (2) there remains a direct relation between the faith of the Puritans and life in the world. The map of "his great kingdom, the world," was read primarily by reason. The map of that "special and peculiar kingdom, the kingdom of grace," was read in the scriptures and in experience. This fact led to a fourth assumption.

4. "I am verily persuaded the Lord hath more truth yet to break forth out of his holy word. . . . I beseech you to remember it is an article of your church covenant that ye be ready to receive whatever truth shall be made known to you from the written word of God." [11]

This assumption that experience and experiment are the only paths to truth, that there is still more truth to be discovered, that truth has not been "once for all delivered unto the saints" had a penetrating influence upon the thought and action of all the Puritans. The Puritan lived in a church that encouraged the free expression of all members. No longer was the priest or prelate or even presbyter listened to as though the individual alone possessed the word of God. All persons participated in the discussions and decisions of the church. In this way new ideas invaded the thinking of individuals, and the assumption was merely the recognition of that fact.

Though the Puritan appealed to experience, the Bible remained the basic authority for truth. But the Bible was interpreted in a unique way since God was still active, and therefore truth was to be discovered by new experiences and free discussion. Any view of the Bible was inevitably an interpreted view. "The scriptures themselves are but a sealed book except Christ by his Spirit speak in them, and by them, to our understandings and hearts." [12] Because the entire truth was not revealed by God on some remote day in the past, because truth was not static or dogmatic, and because God was still active, revealing yet more truth, there was the need for new experiences and for free discussion based upon those experiences.

The thirst after new understanding, and the belief that it was reached by the experiences of the individual and by free discussion with others, gave to the simplest Puritan a sense of personal significance and a determination to live by the dictates of conscience.

So, there was no single, doctrinaire development of these assumptions, nor was there always a logically consistent development. Many of the individuals in whom these ideas lived, and through whom the ideas brought a new ethical spirit to the West, are unknown and will remain forever unknown. But John Lilburne and John Bunyan are exemplary of the force of these assumptions.

JOHN LILBURNE (1614–1657)

About 1638 there was printed in London an engraving of a young man with an identifying inscription:

Mr. John Lilburne, a pious young gentleman of about 22 or 23 years of age, for suspicion of printing and divulging certain of Dr. Bostwick's and other books, as against Popish innovations, was censured in the Star-Chamber to be whipped at a Cart's tail from the fleet in Westminster, had thereby about 200 lashes with a whip, was then presently upon it set on a pillory with a gag in his mouth, was fined 500 and kept close prisoner in the fleet where day and night he lay in iron-shackles, and long time endured most barbarous and cruel usage.[13]

The inner meaning of that day led Lilburne to leadership and to suffering. For eight of the remaining nineteen years before his early death he lived in prisons. He was often brought to trial, first before the law courts of the king, then before those of the revolutionary parliament, and finally before those of Cromwell's government. He fought in the war with Cromwell, and then he fought bitterly against the Protector when he came to believe that Cromwell betrayed the principles of the war. He quarreled with courtiers and with prelates, with judges and with members of Parliament; and even some of those who once were his most intimate friends became his bitterest enemies. He was twice forced into exile from England, and returning twice without permission he was immediately arrested each time and brought to trial. It was the Puritan ethos that led him to explain his behavior, "My spirit was all on fire."[14]

While Lilburne enraged those who controlled the government, whether king, Parliament, or protectorate, he enlightened and inspired the common folk. Lilburne, reported one of his friends, was "a candle lighted, accommodating others, and consuming himself."[15] His life and his writings were the center of the democratic revolt. In 1647 it was reported that "the army had become 'one Lilburne thought.' "[16] His popularity was due in part to the fact that while other leaders spoke for the king or the aristocracy or the Parliament or even for the law, Lilburne spoke for the people and in their name. And he spoke in words that the people, disciplined by their reading of the Bible, understood. He was one of the people, expressing their feelings and aspirations.

Lilburne was not a consistent thinker. He did not handle ideas carefully as a philosopher who loves truth, but as a prophet outraged by injustice. The intensity, clarity, and lack of consistency in his thought are explained by the fact that his beliefs were not developed in the quiet of a library but in the isolation of prisons. His ideas were forged in sufferings in physical punishments and cells, in demands for personal rights in the lawcourts, in conversation with friends, in debates with Independents, in the turmoil of battle, on long evenings around army campfires, and above all in his inner experiences.

When, in 1638, this younger son of a well-to-do family was punished for assisting in the printing and sale of religious books critical of the church, every whip of the lash reached into the recesses of his life. Two years earlier, in 1636, Lilburne had been converted to a Baptist personal-experience faith. But it was the stripes, he said, that purged out his ignorance. Before that he was

> but a very idiot in the right ways of God, having muddy affections, but wanted inward principle, having fiery zeale, but it was without grounded spiritual knowledge; But now the Lord hath made known to me, by his spirit, the way wherein to serve and worship him.[17]

That day,

> I counted my wedding day in which I was married to the Lord Jesus Christ. . . . My soul was that morning exceedingly lifted up with spiritual consolation . . . . The executioner . . . tied my hands . . . which caused me to utter these words, "Welcome be the cross of Christ."[18]

Lilburne's first conflicts with the authorities were purely religious. But when he was refused the right to confess openly his religious beliefs, there immediately developed the demand for a larger freedom, for political rights. This, he felt, was the only justification for the war in which he participated as a daring, but unlucky, soldier.

In 1648 some of the men in the army, dissatisfied with the turn events were taking under Cromwell, wrote "The Case of the Army Truly Stated," which, in demanding redress of the soldiers' grievances and democratic reforms, was an answer to earlier statements written by the generals. These documents mark the beginning of a rift between the Independents and their more liberal allies, and in the course of events the rift soon became an impassable gulf. The Putney debates in the fall of 1648 between the two groups were filled with trivial arguments that often obscured the real problem, which was simply "Who shall have the right to elect the officials of government?" The Independents insisted that the right of voting be tied to the ownership of property. They feared that to grant every individual the right to vote would be to create anarchy. "All the main thing that I speak for," said Henry Ireton with a disarming frankness, "is because I would have an eye to property."[19]

The group opposed to the Independents insisted that voting privileges should be granted to all individuals, as argued by Colonel Rainsborough.

> I think that the poorest he that is in England hath a life to live, as the greatest he; and therefore truly, sir, I think it's clear, that every man that is to live under a government ought first by his own consent to put himself under that government.[20]

It was this proposal that led to the identifying name for the group, a name first spoken in scorn, "because all persons have an equality of right to choose and be chosen . . . the promoters of this way are not improperly called Levellers."[21]

Lilburne was not at Putney. He was in prison. But his influence was felt there, and he participated later in the "Agreements of the People." The series of "Agreements" were covenants which stated the democratic bases upon which a new government should be founded. The particular points in the different "Agreements" varied, but all of them were grounded in a view that government rests upon the consent of the people, that there must be a recognition of fundamental law, a respect for inalienable rights, and a delegation of authority.

It was about this time that a serious breach developed between Lilburne and Cromwell. On August 2, 1648, "on the second day of my freedom, . . ." Lilburne wrote to the general

> to demonstrate unto you that I am no staggerer from my first principles that I engaged my life upon, nor from you, if you are what you ought to be, and what you are strongly reported to be; although, if I prosecuted or desired revenge for an hard and almost starving imprisonment, I could have had of late the choice of twenty opportunities to have paid you to the purpose; but I scorn it, especially when you are low: and thus assure yourself, that if my hand be upon you, it shall be when you are in your full glory, if then you decline from the righteous ways of truth and justice; which, if you will fixedly and impartially prosecute, I am,
>   Yours to the Last drop of my heart bloud
>   (for all your late severe hand towards me)
>   John Lilburne[22]

On December 6 Colonel Pride purged the Royalists and their fellow travelers from Parliament. On January 30, 1649, following quasi-legal proceedings that deceived no one, the king was beheaded. Lilburne opposed the procedures by which Charles had been dethroned and destroyed. He left for Scotland, determined to stay out of politics. But when he became convinced that Cromwell was a new tyrant, he returned to England, where he was arrested immediately. When he had been dismissed after questioning by the Council and before he was taken back to the Tower, Lilburne heard Cromwell through the barred doors, "very loud, thumping his fist upon the Council Table til it rang. . . . 'I tell you, Sir, you have no other way to deale with these men but to break them in pieces. . . . If you do not break them, they will break you.' "[23]

For the next four years Lilburne was in prison and in exile. He returned from exile in 1653, was arrested, and brought to trial. Before the trial began he insisted that the public be admitted, and he won his point. To the jury and the public he argued that he was being tried solely because he demanded rights that belonged to him as a freeborn Englishman. As his custom had always been in previous trials, Lilburne demanded that he be tried by due process of law and he refused to testify when he might make incriminating statements against himself. The jury pronounced a verdict of "Not Guilty." When the verdict was announced the people assembled "gave such a loud and unanimous shout, as is believed, was never heard in Yeeld-Hall, which lasted about half an hour without intermission."[24]

In Lilburne the sense of religious duty was primary, not the claims for rights. But his Christian duty led to demands for religious freedom which, forced by the pressures of the time, were expanded to include claims for personal political rights. This claim was immediately enlarged to include the rights of all true believers, and soon the rights of all the English people. The cause was religious, and so it remained, and yet it became open to secular influences.

THE ETHIC OF LILBURNE

Lilburne's thought was grounded upon the presuppositions of the Puritans. The sovereign God was the starting point for his thought and action, and it was God who was the source of all human equality. He provided an excellent summary of his basic position in a postscript to "The Free-man's Freedom Vindicated" (1646):

> God, the absolute sovereign Lord and King of all things in heaven and earth, the original fountain and cause of all causes, who is circumscribed, governed, and limited by no rules, but doth all things merely and only by his sovereign will and unlimited good pleasure, who made the world and all things therein for his own glory, by his own will and pleasure gave man, his mere creature, the sovereignty (under himself) over all the rest of his creatures and endued him with a rational soul or understanding, and thereby created him after his own image.[25]

God created first Adam and Eve who became

> the earthly original fountain . . . of all and every particular and individual man and woman . . . in the world since who are, and were, by nature all equal and alike in power, dignity, authority, and majesty, none of them having by nature any authority, dominion, or magisterial power one over or above another. . . . And unnatural, irrational, sinful, wicked, unjust, devilish, and tyrannical, it is for any man whatsoever, spiritual or temporal, clergyman or layman, to appropriate and assume unto himself a power, authority, and jurisdiction, to rule, govern or reign over any sort of men in the world without their free consent.[26]

This equality was the equality of right to political self-determination. The sole power of government basically resided in the people governed: "No man can binde me but by my own consent."[27] But political self-determination was based upon more than the principle that all the people should choose the government officials. That principle, Lilburne conceived, was meaningless without more fundamental rights to freedom of religious belief, freedom of expression, and freedom to live under a common law.

The equality of individuals largely determined the method, not the purposes of government. That was determined by sin. Lilburne quoted with approval the view that

> whosoever meanes to settle good laws, must proceed in them with a sinister opinion of mankind, and suppose that whosoever is not wicked, it is only for want of opportunitie."[28]

He believed that "man is naturally ambitious and apt to encroach and usurp the liberty" of other individuals.[29]

The purpose of government was primarily to limit power and to protect the rights of the people. Those rights were not conceived in economic terms. Nowhere in the Levellers was there expressed the view that private property was to be tampered with and distributed equally to all. Such a position was held by the radical sect of "Diggers," and Lilburne and the Levellers viewed destruction of property rights with abhorrence.

Many times during tumultuous controversies, Lilburne tried to rationalize his views of God, the equality of man, human evil, and government. The rationalization developed through the use of law as a central concept. Government was by law and not by individuals. The law was the law of nature and of God, and the two, never clearly distinguished, melded into each other. Others had appealed to God and nature in claiming that Parliament, and not a king, had the sole right to create laws. But Lilburne was yet more radical. He first appealed to the law of God and natural law in claiming rights for Parliament against the king; but later (and this was the startling innovation), he appealed to the same laws in claiming rights for the people against Parliament.

For knowledge of the "law Eternal and Natural" Lilburne appealed to scripture, to history, to reason, and finally to the personal experience of the individual. No law, of course, could be properly a law if it violated the precept of scripture, but Lilburne soon discovered that the precepts of scripture could be variously interpreted, so he did not make this appeal to the Bible the sole basis for knowledge of law. He turned, and increasingly so in later years, to English history, particularly to the Magna Charta and the popular histories, largely mythologized, of the primitive Saxon communities. This appeal, too, was not final:

Whatever our forefathers were: or whatever they did or suffered, or were enforced to yield unto; we are men of the present age, and ought to be absolutely free from all kind of exorbitancies, molestations, or *arbitrary power*.[30] (Original italics)

The knowledge of just law, then, became possible through reason. But because reason at times led in different directions, the final authority for just law became the appeal to personal experience, particularly the personal experience of the true believer. The proper view of political law, however, was not restricted to the saints. Lilburne accepted the view that

there is law written in the heart of every man, teaching him what is to be done, and what is to be fled . . . and therefore against this law [neither] prescription, statute, nor custom may . . . prevail.[31]

When individuals have appealed to the "Law Eternal and Natural" as the ground of their proper rights, the appeal has usually been in the interest of individualism. The importance of law for the Puritans can hardly be overemphasized: For in "the sects the idea of Law is substituted for the idea of the Church as the organ of Grace and Redemption."[32] It was the individual who was redeemed, who received grace just as, with Lilburne, it was the individual who finally must judge what a proper law is. Those concerned for order in the land, those in positions of political authority, the new landed gentry who had a stake in a stable society, and those in commerce and in industry viewed this individualism with horror as a threat to the existence of society. They firmly believed that the individualism proclaimed by the Levellers was subversive of all order. The cry of Cromwell to break them in pieces was a defense not of personal power but of political order.

This reaction of fear was based upon a misunderstanding of the individualism of Lilburne. For his radical individualism was held in check by the presuppositions of Puritanism and by further beliefs which were to be the heritage of the eighteenth century. The individual, to be sure, was the final judge of right and wrong, but it was not an individual judgment. The individual was not autonomous and judgments were not the product of arbitrary whims. The individual must judge according to the demands of his conscience. The conscience was the voice of reason and of God, rooted in nature and scripture. Lilburne argued that there could be nothing more objective and less subject to the manipulation of the peculiarities of an individual's personality than conscience. Nor was this all. The logic of Lilburne's position should have led him to conclude that it was only a member of the holy community who could properly judge. That he did not take this step was due to the difficulty he shared with most other Puritans in identifying the citizenship of that community. But despite the failure to take this step explicitly the ideal of the holy community as reality and as goal restricted the limits of individualism and prevented an anarchistic view of society.

Lilburne was fundamentally an optimist. It was also his optimism that held his view of individualism in check. He could not believe that when individuals realized their proper nature in exercising the judgments of their separate consciences, the result would be an endless conflict and mutual destruction. Through loyalty to his basic faith Lilburne conceived that there should, and would, develop a society so ordered that it would grant to the English their just rights of freedom and equality. The freedom was fundamentally a freedom of the spirit. In religious beliefs, and in the expression of opinions, no one should be molested by any authority. But such freedom was not the entire story. The individual had an equality with others both before the law and in electing the officials who should govern by just laws.

Oliver Cromwell broke Lilburne in pieces. The Protector effectively quenched the fire by which "Free-born John" claimed political rights. Cromwell had Lilburne imprisoned and he would undoubtedly have died in chains but for his conversion to the Society of Friends. His earlier life had not been devoid of a kind of love. Indeed, the scars on his body and spirit were testimony of his devotion to his principles and to others. But love as forgiveness and reconciliation had never been a part of Lilburne's principles or his practice. This was opened by an inner light. Henceforth he renounced revolutionary activity and looked upon his earlier feverish battles for justice as fruitless. When, in 1652, Cromwell was convinced that the "troubler of England" had been converted to the views of George Fox and thus would no more threaten the order of society, he pardoned Lilburne. But the candle had already burned low. John Lilburne, a young man of thirty-six, died within a year after his release from prison.

JOHN BUNYAN (1628–1688)

John Bunyan was born in 1628, so by the time of his life-shaping experiences in the 1650s the Puritan battles for political power had been temporarily won. When he wrote his autobiographical account of those experiences in the mid-sixties the Puritan battles, especially those for political power and religious freedom, had been lost. Prior to Bunyan the primary focus of the Puritan ethic had been social, with emphases upon religious freedom and toleration, freedom of speech, and government by consent. The social ethic had its source in the inner experience of the believer; but in persons like Lilburne it was the social effects of the inner life, and not the inner life itself, that was of major interest. John Bunyan was one of the persons who turned the Puritan ethic inward, and in no other person does the inwardness of the ethic appear more clearly. When Bunyan was arrested in 1660, following the return of the monarchy and the restrictions imposed upon religious sects, he could have turned the issue into one of religious toleration, since he had been arrested for continuing to preach in his unlicensed fashion out of the jurisdiction of the Church of England. Instead, he used the occasion of his imprisonment not to fight political battles, but to report his inner struggles, first in autobiographical then in allegorical form, and to insist that the most important battles are those of the inward self, the most important history that of the individual soul.

The inner moral struggles of the individual which preoccupy Bunyan occurred in the framework of Calvinistic theology. Bunyan's ethic, then, is a religious ethic of a particular kind. Yet the ethic is misunderstood if it is viewed as limited by its theological boundaries. Bunyan transcended his theological beliefs as every creative moral thinker must go beyond his or her initial intellectual origins. But his theological ideas provided him a framework for his thinking and enabled him (1) to recognize the moral problem confronting him; (2) to deal with that problem emotionally and intellectually, that is, with practical reason; and (3) to deal with the problem artistically which, surprisingly, became another way of dealing with it ethically.

(1) The essential human problem for Bunyan was the achievement of salvation for the next life *in this life*, and it was the last phrase "in this life" that made it a moral problem. Negatively the essential moral problem for Bunyan was that of overcoming destructive forces in the self, the forces of sin and guilt, but even more that of anxiety which arises from the first two. Positively, the moral task was the achievement of wholeness as a person, an achievement that can come only as a result of struggle and effort. In this way of recognizing the problem, Bunyan made a major contribution to ways of thinking about human life in terms of the spiritual and moral struggle to become a self.

(2) The theological framework also provided him with a stimulus to deal with the moral problem both emotionally and with practical reason. Here certain assumptions of the Puritans were significant, especially those that recognized God as sovereign, the "power of acting freely . . . by means of a calling and renewal," and the granting of "maps and schemes of his dominions."[33] In the initial struggles (which in some senses lasted throughout his life) as well as in the memory of his struggles, Bunyan was given the courage to be honest with his tempestuous, debilitating feelings. And in his examination of the "maps and schemes" he used his best reason to discern directions for life. While he made use of religious language he also often translated that language into moral terms.

(3) The theological context also helped to enable Bunyan to take a further highly significant step to put his moral experience into artistic form.

Driven to find a wholeness for his life, he was a person who, throughout his experience, had to rediscover and reshape that wholeness. Thus, he was stimulated first to write his autobiography, *Grace Abounding* (1666). It became a model for many similar writings in the seventeenth and eighteenth centuries, an autobiography that dealt almost exclusively with his inner life. Later Bunyan wrote allegories, the best by far being the fictional *Pilgrim's Progress* (1678, 1684), for which he used as a justifying epigram the verse from Hosea, "I have used similitudes."[34] Both styles of writing were moral acts for Bunyan in which he not merely reported but continued to give moral shape to his life, and since his time (though he, of course, was not solely responsible for this fact) both autobiography and fiction have been ways of dealing ethically with experience.

Grace Abounding is an account of Bunyan's inner life. He scarcely mentioned external events; he did not report the names of his wives nor of his children, yet the love he had for them was obvious. His preoccupation was solely with his inward self. Much of its ring of authenticity derives from the fact that he remembered specific external factors that were tied to his inner experiences. In urging his readers to remember their inner history he asked, *"Have you forgot the Close, the Milk-house, the Stable, the Barn, and the like, where God did visit your Soul?"* (original italics)[35] He also associated physical things and occurrences with his mental states. In despair he heard a voice in his mind that was so clear he turned around to see who had spoken to him; in emotional discomfort he felt he was living on the cold side of a mountain, away from the sun.

There was also in Bunyan's writing an unpretentious honesty. The meaning he was seeking in its Puritan context was for salvation, that is, for eternal life, which must not be understood solely as life after death, though it included that. The demand for meaning was a demand for meaning in life here and now; and the meaning Bunyan was seeking at the deepest level was for the wholeness and health of his person.

By the time of writing Bunyan had come through his own inner moral struggles and had achieved some semblance of wholeness. *"I can remember my fears, and doubts, and sad months with comfort,"* he says; *"they are as the head of Goliath in my hand"* (original italics).[36] He had come through, and yet not entirely. One of the most remarkable facts about Bunyan's experience was that, while the transformation in his moral life was major, it did not transform his entire life. He was always in need of more moral conversions. Throughout his life Bunyan periodically wanted to blaspheme in the pulpit, or was tempted "to question the being of God, and the truth of his Gospel."[37] And in concluding his autobiography he confessed, "I find to this day seven abominations in my heart," including tendencies to unbelief, legalism, complaints about what he possessed and a presence of evil when he would do good.[38]

In remembering his life Bunyan reported the discovery of both structural and chronological patterns, though it is not evident he was self-conscious about either. Structurally his inner life was marked throughout by conflicting temptations to evil and to good. The temptations and succumbing to them produced a painful disorder. Chronologically he had sequentially a sense of guilt, then of anxiety and despair which, he at last discovered, was his major sin. The chronological pattern also required his repeatedly reviewing his inner torment, finding relief usually in an insight from scripture. ("The Bible was precious to me in those days.")[39]

While a child Bunyan had terrible dreams which he attributed to his moral evil, and when he was about nine or ten he was "so overcome with despair of Life and Heaven" that he wished he might be a devil, to be a tormentor rather than tormented.[40] That was the first expression of that lifelong desire of wanting to sin fully, which was a wanting of autonomy and, as he came to believe, a manifestation of pride. The struggle continued, and even when others saw him as "a new and religious man," Bunyan saw himself as "a poor painted hypocrite."[41] As a young Christian visiting the town of Bedford, he came upon "three or four poor women sitting at a door in the sun, and talking about the things of God."[42] Since he was "now a brisk talker . . . in the matters of religion" he listened to them. "And me thought they spake as if joy did make them speak."[43] Bunyan was impressed by what they said, "as if they had found a new world"; he was depressed that he did not live in that world in which they found joy.

Bunyan was tempted by the extremes of moral freedom and moral rigidity. What he wanted was truth that satisfied his emotional needs. How could one be certain? The uncertainties and doubts, the guilt, the anxieties, the despair continued. He would have brief respites that came from his own imaginative life, other persons, sermons, and scriptures; but none would last long. Once, deeply affected by a sermon on love, as he walked home there reverberated in his mind, "*'Thou art my love, thou art my love,'* twenty times together" and as it began to dwell in his consciousness he said to himself "with much gladness . . . surely I will not forget *this* forty years hence; but alas! within less than forty days I began to question all again" (original italics).[44]

Bunyan doubted whether his beliefs were true; he more seriously doubted whether they were true for him. He wanted to sin to assert his independence. His heart was "hard" and he could not shed a tear. The inner conflicts continued and he wanted opposite things for his life at the same time. In his struggle for an inner order, for a moral health of mind, he was driven more and more inward, taking on new intensity. There were alternating moods: "Now I began to conceive peace in my soul." "And *now* I was both a burthen and a terror to myself."[45] The reconciliation with himself came only when "one day, as I was passing in the field, and that too with some dashes on my Conscience, fearing lest yet all was not right, suddenly this sentence fell upon my soul, *'Thy righteousness is in heaven!'* " (original italics).[46] Bunyan was troubled by the fact that he could not find this sentence in the scriptures, but he found another that he reasoned proved its truth. So the words that arose in him and were his were the means of his release from the destructive inner conflict. If his righteousness was "in heaven," it was not moral evil as sin that was his problem. The problem was his despair, his sense of guilt, his inner disorder. Helpless to overcome by himself the despair and sense of guilt, helpless to create his own order, by placing moral goodness outside of himself Bunyan was able to have it introduced into himself.

> Now I could look from myself to him, and should reckon that all those graces of God that were now green in me, were yet but like those crack'd-Groats and Four-pence-half-pennies that rich men carry in their purses, when their gold is in their trunks at home: O I saw my gold was in my trunk at home! . . . Now could I see myself in Heaven and Earth at once; in heaven by my Christ, by my Head, by my Righteousness and Life, though on earth by my body and person.[47]

Only then, for Bunyan, could the true moral life begin and be created and renewed, and now, as he looked back, he saw that all along he had been engaged in moral struggle. He had begun with the basic assumptions of Puritanism. These inspirited him, giving him courage and determination to find truth in his experience. Throughout he dealt with himself honestly, accepting his sufferings, with determination to understand them. He refused the temptation to become abstract and to ignore the realities of the outer and inner worlds; he had an extraordinary will to morality, which was a will to health, to wholeness. He learned much about himself: of his sin, of his struggles to escape and to avoid the hard realities, of his despair that he painfully learned was his sin, of his acceptance by God which was also his acceptance of himself, of his transforming the disorder in his life by finding a meaning.

Throughout *Grace Abounding* the whole essential self of Bunyan, as he conceived it, was involved. In the *Pilgrim's Progress*, too, the whole Bunyan was present. Part I was the Bunyan of *Grace Abounding*. In Part II a new, more humane Bunyan emerged. The whole of *Pilgrim's Progress* was about what it means to be and become a human individual. Part I is about the soul's struggle to become a moral self; Part II concerns an individual in a community. It deals with the problems of living, that is, with moral problems. Like *Grace Abounding* it is a story of the inner life. The characters accompanying or confronting Christian, or Christiana, on their journeys are not simply other characters but primarily aspects of the self to be rejected or assimilated in the creation of a moral life. *"Relations are our second self,"* asserted Greatheart.[48]

However, it is not possible to translate *Pilgrim's Progress* into a rational, descriptive ethic, for the metaphor of the journey suggested the unpredictable, the unexpected qualities of life. Moreover, while the journeys in the two parts were over the same terrain, what happened to the persons on those journeys was so different as to imply different ethics, and while the different ethics of the two journeys can be suggested, neither can be delineated with precision.

The same structural and chronological patterns that were present in *Grace Abounding* reappeared in the pilgrimage of Christian. There were the conflicting temptations to evil and to good (although it is significant that in Part I there were almost four times as many temptations to evil as to good). Responding to the temptations produced a painful disorder even though the response was a mark of progress. Chronologically, there was anxiety and despair of varying degrees accompanying the sense of guilt; this would be relieved by a new moral insight or experience, only to return with a later threat.

Despair is the moral danger both at the beginning and at the end of the journey. It appeared first in a generalized form, as the Slough of Despond. It appeared toward the end in Doubting Castle as the specific Giant Despair. Indeed, despair appeared and reappeared on the journey.

Prior to the removal of the burden from his back, Christian had to reject obstinacy and pliability, worldly wisdom, moral legality and civility, and passion or impatience. He had to acquire goodwill and patience. ("As to the burden" of guilt and despair, "be content to bear it, until thou comest to the place of Deliverance."[49]) Bunyan did not explain how the burden was removed, but was content merely to report that there was a place where a cross stood and "just as *Christian* came up with the *Cross*, his burden loosed from off his Shoulders, and fell from off his back."[50] It was clearly an act of God, though in moral terms it was being accepted and self-acceptance.

Following the removal of the burden the moral problems for Christian did not decrease, but increased. Now he had many associations with moral evils that he had to reject: presumption, formalism, and hypocrisy; timorousness and mistrust; talkativeness and to "Saywell"; envy and superstition and currying favor ("Pickthank"); vanity in its many guises; love of money and "holding-the-world"; vain confidence; diffidence; ignorance (Christian "was learned"[51]); and flattery. There were also virtues in addition to goodwill and patience that were required for a full moral life. Among these were discretion; prudence, piety, and charity; faithfulness; hope; knowledge, experience, watchfulness, and sincerity.

Through the recollection and reshaping of his life in *Grace Abounding*, through the metaphorical reconstruction of his life in *Pilgrim's Progress*, Part I, Bunyan arrived at some important conclusions about an ideal life, about what it means to be a human individual.

(1) The moral life is a gift from others, and ultimately from God; yet it

is always uniquely individual, requiring throughout life personal struggle and responsibility.

(2) The ideal life is one lived in gratitude for the gift of life, but it is life lived toward a goal; and it is important to want that goal with all the intensity of one's being. (a) Religiously the goal is eternal life, which means both a quality of life beyond death and also a quality of life on earth. (b) Morally the goal is a longing for wholeness, for the accomplished unity of the self.

(3) In one's life it is essential to be honest about the self and the world. It is necessary to recognize the corruption and incompleteness in the self and so (in the light of a goal) to want the self's transformation and fulfillment. It is necessary to recognize the evil in the world, for it is a pervasive evil, and to refuse to succumb to it.

(4) The essential human problems are those of sin, guilt, and anxiety, and these all feed on each other. These problems, when honestly faced, in turn, lead to pride, excess confidence, and hypocrisy on the one hand; to lack of confidence and despair on the other.

(5) The essential ideal becomes the development of the right degree of confidence and trust. The possibility of finding an adequate self-image can only come from proper trust and confidence.

(6) The overcoming of guilt and anxiety (an overcoming that is a gift received) can lead to the achievement of the virtues. That achievement, however, is not automatic, but only comes with continual struggles accompanied by intense feelings, learnings, and sufferings.

(7) The moral life can occur only in community, or at least among friends. For Christian, life is not yet lived in a community. His inner pilgrimage is too much of a solitary journey for that. But there are friends who assist him, especially Evangelist, Goodwill, Interpreter, Prudence, Piety, Charity, Faithful, and Hopeful. Without their companionship the journey could not have been completed, the moral ideal life not achieved as adequately as it was.

But in Part II the individual moral life of Christiana was balanced by the moral life of the community. Christiana's task in her pilgrimage was not only to achieve a moral life for herself, but also to create and protect the moral life of the community, that is, the church. It is not fair to assert, as it has often been said, that "Christian goes on a pilgrimage, Christiana goes on a walking tour."[52] The journey she took followed the same map as his. But what she saw and experienced was unique because she was a different person with different companions.

Christiana had no heavy burden with which to begin her journey. While she used the Puritan language of sin, she did not experience it with inward intensity since she began with love for her husband, her children, and herself. When she reached the place of the cross, her experience was significant, yet vastly different from her husband's.

For though my heart was lightful and joyous before, yet it is ten times more lightsome and joyous now. And I am persuaded by what I have felt, though I have felt but little as yet, that if the most burdened man in the world was here and did see and believe, as I now do, 'twould make his heart the more merry and blithe.[53]

This meant that Christiana's moral struggle was not so much against evil as for good. Her task was to find "how virtue may be joined to the soul and so make it better."[54]

Her companions, too, were vastly different from those of Christian. In his solitary inner struggles he would not have tolerated some of the characters Christiana accepted and experienced in herself; but given who she was it was Christiana's task not only to tolerate the weak but to love them, since her moral achievement depended upon their living successfully. They were persons with whom one normally associates and personifications which live in the self which one must deal with: Master Fearing, Master Feeblemind, Master Ready-to-Halt, Master Despondency, and his daughter Much-Afraid. There were also the noble characters who assisted Christiana outwardly and within: her neighbor Mercy, old Honest, Master Valiant-for-Truth, and above all, Great-Heart. It may well be that Great-Heart was more a picture of John Gifford, the pastor of the Bedford Church who meant so much to Bunyan, than of the author; but he was surely a moral model of what John Bunyan would like to be. Great-Heart was a protector and guide for Christiana, and she, in turn, was an inspiration to him. Without her fineness of character the community would not have held together.

Christian's journey was that of a solitary soul in moral struggle; Christiana's was that of a healthy and companionate soul who relished the joys no less than the frustrations of life. Largely because she was merry and blithe, there was dancing and laughter and singing on the journey. (Upon arrival at Interpreter's House Mercy asked Christiana if she heard a noise and received the reply, "Yes, 'tis as I believe the Noise of Musick, for Joy that we are here." Mercy responded the way Christiana lived daily in the world, "Wonderful! Musick in the House, Musick in the Heart, and Musick also in Heaven, for Joy that we are here.")[55] And when Christiana and her companions arrived at the town of Vanity Fair they settled there. She, like Christian, knew that "the way to the Celestial City lies just through *this town*, where this lusty fair is kept, and he that will go to the city, and yet not go through this town, must needs *'go out of the World.'* "[56] But she knew more, that one must live in this Town of Vanity with its lusty fair. So, finding good neighbors, she remained there, for a time, and her sons were married there.

When Christian's pilgrimage began he was confronted by Worldly Wiseman who, proposing an easy way, directed him away from the path of

the ideal life. Christiana's journey neared an end when Stand-fast told the pilgrims about Madame Bubble, who was one of the most intriguing of all of
Bunyan's characters. She claimed to be mistress of the world, *"and men are
made happy by me."* Honest asked,

> Is she not a tall comely dame, something of a swarthy complexion? Doth
> she not speak very smoothly and give you a smile at the end of a sentence?
> Doth she not wear a great purse by her side, and is not her hand often in it
> fingering her money as if that was her heart's delight?

And Great-Heart commented, "She is always . . . at one pilgrim's heels or
other, now commending, and then preferring, the excellencies of this life."[57]
So *Pilgrim's Progress* ended as it began, with the dangers of worldliness.
It was necessary to "go through this town," to live in this world, but that
could be done successfully only if, with an eye fixed on the Celestial City,
and another pattern of life, one was sensitive every day to what would destroy the ideal life.

The ethic of John Bunyan was a profoundly religious ethic. It was a theological ethic arising from specific Puritan beliefs and experiences. Without
those beliefs and experiences it could not have been created. And yet the ethic
was not of another world but of this world. The pilgrim who would make
progress "from this World to That which is to Come" journeys in this world.
The world "which is to Come"[58] is in this world as well as beyond; and the ideal
life is not just an afterlife but life here and now, deepened and transformed.
John Bunyan, through his life and thought, reached his unique understanding
of what it meant to be a human individual in a human community.

> The sense of the eternal conveyed by the *Pilgrim's Progress* . . . is a sense
> of a dimension felt in earthly life. . . . For what makes the *Pilgrim's
> Progress* a great book, one of the great classics, is its humanity—its rich,
> poised, and mature humanity.[59]

THE PURITAN ETHIC OF THE SEVENTEENTH CENTURY

The Puritan spirit in the seventeenth century was embodied by individuals
who possessed a unique way of thinking and believing, seeing and feeling.
They did not set out to write an ethic; yet despite the fact that their sensibility
was never expressed in systematic terms, their experience molded a moral
perspective that possesses a clarity and vitality.

1. The nature of the individual and society

(a) The individual

The Puritans, of course, described the individual with religious symbols: everyone is a "creature of God," made in "the image of God," whose purpose is "to glorify God." The religious symbols can be expressed in moral terms as well: everyone is a being who is responsible, who possesses rights, and who has the ability to reason and to love. This is the essential nature of being human.

No Puritan could have arrived at these beliefs by looking at most of the people around him. For when the Puritans saw human beings as they were and acted, they saw persons whose responsibility was limited, whose rights were curtailed, and whose ability to reason and to love was weakened. This was the existential human being, existing in the natural state.

Each individual, then, is a divine creature who through the self-violation of his own essential nature becomes ensnared by his existential nature. Here, obviously, the Puritans were insisting upon the truth of original sin as they had found that conception (though not always by that name) in Paul, Augustine, and Calvin. But, influenced by the pressure of their times, they made significant shifts in interpreting the consequences of the individual's perverseness in rejecting the religious and moral demands of God. The results were always viewed in social and political, as well as in personal, terms. Hints of this viewpoint were present in the Puritan's theological ancestors; but the permeation of thought with problems of politics had never before been so dominant in Christian thinkers. Sin sharply delimited the freedom and responsibility of the individual in the social as well as the personal world. Sin destroyed the living tissue that knit together individuality and community.

However, the essential nature of a human being is not entirely destroyed by sin. The individual's responsibility is limited, but the individual still possesses responsibilities. The ability to reason and to love is weakened, but it is still possible to do both. It is through the possession of natural responsibilities, rights, reason, and love that one is able to establish a political society with order and justice, and to create a tolerably meaningful life as an individual.

But to say that the natural human being can establish a decent political community does not mean that human beings are not in a deplorable condition. For those elements of life which have been destroyed are the valuable elements of human life. The natural individual cannot possess that most important of all freedoms, an inner freedom that arises only from a proper responsibility to one's own genuine being and to God. The natural individual is able to hate the consequences of sin, but is unable to hate sin itself; is able to love his friends, but not his enemies; and is unable to love his friends for the right reason.

In addition to the natural (existential) human being there is also the recreated individual. In theological terms this is one of the "elect." In metaphysical terms this is the one who has been restored to his own essential nature; in practical religious terms this is the one "active and ready at the commands of God"; in ethical terms this is the one with an inner freedom who lives with a consciousness of the temporary—through real—value of "this world's goods" and of the needs of others. By his genuine love for God then, and for others, this person recognizes others of like nature, and in this way the holy community is brought into existence.

(b) The nature of society

Just as there are two kinds of individuals, natural and recreated, so there are two societies: natural and redeemed, the civil and the religious. The English Puritans lived in a society which already possessed a glorious history. Their frequent appeal to that history and to their participation in battles that would give birth to a more just society reveals the awareness of the extreme importance of political society. The state existed to establish order and to protect the rights of individuals to believe, to think, and to express in words their ideas, as well as the right to participate in the processes of government. Political society, the most important branch of civil society, was established by the people and for the people.

But the Puritan was also a member of a religious community. How is this society, the holy community, related to the political order? Or, in other words, how is the theological ethic of the elect related to the ethic of the natural individual? There were three answers given to these questions.

The first answer, that the holy community is absolutely separate from civil society, suggests a cleavage between the church and state, between theology and politics, a religious and a natural ethic. The second, that the holy community can control the political, suggests an identity of church and state, of theology and politics, but it solves this problem on the grounds of eliminating all secular politics. These positions lead either to renunciation of all political responsibility or to a totalitarian acceptance of all authority. Yet paradoxically, both of these approaches influenced the rise of democracy and a democratic ethic. How was this possible? There are two major reasons. First, in the course of historical events the devotees of both views were forced to insist upon their rights to belief. Antidemocratic in intent, they united with others to help give birth to the very political structure and ethics they, in theory, opposed. Second, in their claim for rights they were led to argue, by analogy, that just as there was equality and liberty in the holy community (in grace), so there should be equality and liberty in the state (in nature); and just as the elect have a covenant with God, so a political covenant among individuals is the foundation of all government.

It is the third main answer, that the holy community is separate from yet responsible for the state, that established a direct relation between the church and society, theology and politics, a Christian and a natural ethic. This type of Puritanism based political democracy upon theology. Similarly, particular policies were brought into politics from the theology. These policies would not conflict with those of non-Christian rational and moral policies because natural (though unregenerate) reason and morality is divinely established. But the Christian also brought something more to politics, and this was a new motive, new ways of acting, and a new point of view about the ultimate aim of the political order.

2. What is morally good?

There were two sides to the Puritan's interpretation of moral good: the vision of new individuals and a new community, and the recognition of the limited value and rights of existent individuals and societies.

(a) The new vision

The vision of individuals redeemed and a holy community did not refer to everyone, nor was it projected entirely into the future. The vision included those individuals and that society whose sole purpose was "to glorify God."

For the redeemed individual this meant a consciousness of being an instrument in the "hands of God" for the realizing of righteous purposes. There was a fusion of the Puritan's existential and essential being. The consciousness of having a vocation had, first of all, ethical consequences for the personal (or inner) life of the individual. Fundamentally, it provided a perspective in which the individual's status in relation to all that existed could be clearly recognized. That recognition elicited a temper of gratitude for what had happened, a dependence for further happenings, a continual self-examination which led to penitence and humility, and a devotion to God. Such obedience and love required a service to humanity.

The redeemed community was understood to be the corporate life of those who, as individuals, had recognized their election and had covenanted together. The good of such a community would be found in its common worship of the true God and in making it possible, through social order and discipline, for the individual to live properly.

The conception of good realized in the community and in individuals stimulated a creative ethic and religion. It was the mark of the Puritan to be restless.

(b) The limits of individuals and communities

The saints and the holy community have special worth and privileges, but all individuals and political societies possess both values and rights because all are creatures of God. Individuals have the rights of a personal freedom of belief and a social-political equality. They are considered morally good when, living by reason, they exercise these rights properly. A society is considered good when it establishes order and protects basic individual rights.

The Puritan had a vision of a community of grace and a society of nature, with individuals who had an active citizenship in one or both societies. It was just this dual vision that led to conflicting moral consequences. Those whose lives were dominated by the vision of the holy community that would be (at least, in part) realized on this earth were led to a reformist temper. Hopeful for the future and afraid of the people, these persons could abide a dictatorship in the interests of the common good. But those possessed by the ideal of individual inner freedom and political equality could not tolerate any procedure but a democratic process. Because of this fundamental conflict the Puritan concept of moral good cannot be simply stated. While there was basic ethical agreement among all the Puritans, when a particular definition of moral good was presented, it had to be related either to the social reformers or to the social democrats.

3. How is the moral good known in a specific situation?

For all individuals reason is an indispensable means toward knowledge of moral good. This term, frequently used by the Puritans, was never given a precise definition. Nor did they believe that it needed one. The structure of the world and of human beings is such that observation and thought reveal the obvious about natural moral relations.

Those individuals whose ethical experience is qualitatively different from that of natural human beings require other ways of recognizing what is ethically good or right. They arrive at moral knowledge by means of scripture and special providence. The scriptural basis is inescapable for all Puritans: none of them would have thought to justify a course of conduct without appeal to biblical authority. Such authority was usually illustrative and explanatory of a proper action or it led to a comprehension of the divine basis for a specific moral decision. The special providence was to be found either in the inner experience of the individual or group, or in the occurrence of an event that opened possibilities for action or disclosed new meanings. In the first alternative the Puritans moved in the direction of a personal or corporate piety and mysticism, such as they found in John Bunyan and the Quakers. In the second method there developed an emphasis upon social activity, always with a sense that the particular activity must be motivated by and must enter into the divine direction of the historical process. Either method could lead to a cult of the miraculous and superstitious; and while such elements may be found in seventeenth-century Puritanism, the fact that the mainstream was not diverted into the vagaries of the occult indicates the effective presence of other factors in ethical judgment.

Two of those factors, reason and scripture, have already been mentioned. But the most important was the conception of experience of the individual. This experience was demarcated by the Puritan beliefs and the Puritan community: in particular by the scriptural basis, the understanding of God, the view of Jesus Christ, the real hope for the Holy Spirit, the historical community of Christians, and the living presence of other individuals who had been transformed. There was also the sense that there is always new truth yet to be discovered.

While there were clearly certain modes by which the Puritan knew what was good in a specific situation, and while there were certain means by which this knowledge might be checked, there was no final, objective authority by which a moral truth could be known. The saint might be redeemed but the saint was not infallible. Cromwell was speaking for all the Puritans when he addressed with solemnity his fellow saints: "My brethren, by the bowels of Christ I beseech you, bethink you that you may be mistaken."[60]

4. How the moral good is achieved

Once more the dichotomy between grace and nature appears. The natural man or woman achieves such good as is available by the use of reason and the capacity to strive as an individual and to cooperate for certain social ends. But the achievement of the highest good does not come in such a manner as pursuing a goal. The best life, rather, is the result of God's choice of the individual, and the individual's response to the obligations to God made possible by a spirit (or power) that has been given by God. Even when the ceaseless moral activity so characteristic of the Puritan seems to be in pursuit of a goal it is, in reality, the propulsion of a person who is possessed by the knowledge of divine destiny and responsibility. That such an exalted sense of one's own significance and obligations did not more often lead to megalomania is, again, an indication of the kinds of checks present to the Puritan consciousness.

When we remember these complex forces present in the Puritan life and thought, we can recognize that the Puritans were making an attempt to hold together their inheritance from the Greeks, the Hebrews, the medieval and Reformation thinkers, and to extend their heritage in their own pressing times. With many of them there was also the attempt to weave the many-colored cloth of the Renaissance into the tapestry of their history. The fact that they drew upon diverse historical streams is apparent from their social status as well as their writings. The Puritan leaders were educated in the universities of Renaissance England; many of them arose from a rising economic class whose members had contacts with distant places in the world, and with the best in the contemporary culture; all of them were "people of the Book," and that book they knew intimately.

If it is true that they tried to reconcile conflicting cultures, the Puritans gave no indication that they were conscious about what they were doing. That lack of self-consciousness was doubtless caused by their singleness of vision and of devotion that steadied their lives through all those tumultuous years. "We bless God," wrote four of them from their captivity in the Tower of London in declaring "An Agreement of the Free People of England,"

> We blesse god that he hath given us time and hearts to bring it to this issue, what further he hath for us to do is yet knowne only to his wisdome, to whose will and pleasure we shall willingly submit; we have if we look with the eyes of frailty, enemies like the sons of Anak, but if with the eyes of faith and confidence in a righteous God and a just cause, we see more with us than against us.[61]

THE ETHIC OF THE SCIENTIFIC REVOLUTION

In the seventeenth century in England and on the continent some individuals had a new vision of the world. The vision of scientists has transformed the world, and its transforming power has not yet spent its force. There is scarcely an event, social structure, achievement, or cataclysm of our time that does not have direct relation to what happened in the minds of scientists over three hundred years ago. And every person who lives in the twentieth- or twenty-first centuries has the difficult task of relating that vision of science into his or her own moral perspectives.

What was the cause of this scientific revolution? Various accompanying factors can be identified which clarify but do not totally explain the development of modern science: the social changes in the rise of cities and the growth of universities, economic changes in the development of incipient capitalism and a new class of entrepreneurs, religious reforms that split the ancient institution of the church, political changes into national units and the overt demands for political freedom, geographical discoveries and new inventions, and—through it all—an increasing shattering of the unity of culture into segregated segments of life that led to the independence of the parts from each other (e.g., theology divorced from philosophy, art from religion, science from politics), to a secularization of all of the parts so that each existed for its own sake. But it was essentially a new vision; so to abstract in this manner does not explain the scientific revolution, nor recognize what was involved in the new vision.

"A new vision" implies a newness both in the ways of looking and in what is seen. So it was in the revolution of the seventeenth century. There were changes in the ways of thinking and what was thought; there were new sensibilities and new explanations of nature. Not the least startling fact about this creative vision is that, at the time, it was not startling. It was a quiet revolution. The scientists fought no wars, they deposed no kings, they reformed no church, they founded no new government. The revolution was in the mind and few persons had any awareness of what was happening.

The scientific view was immediately carried into ethics by Thomas Hobbes (1588–1679) and Benedict Spinoza (1632–1677), and from ethics it was taken into a theory of politics. The moral ideas of each man began with presuppositions found in the new perspectives of scientists. Their ethical method and their conceptions of nature (including human nature), which are the bases of their ethics, were the results of the scientific revolution.

It would be difficult to find two men more diverse in temperament than Hobbes and Spinoza, and there were corresponding diversities in their ethics. Yet both were alike in the consistency with which they applied scientific assumptions to ethical inquiry. They were alike, too, in initiating that train of scientific ethical thought that runs throughout the modern world. Scientific ethical theories have exhibited a remarkable development and diversity since the seventeenth century, just as rational ethics have changed since Plato and Christian ethics since Jesus and Paul. Yet the basic approach and assumptions of a scientific ethical thought were present, clear, and precise in Spinoza and Hobbes. To understand their ethics it is essential to examine the new sensibility and the new explanations of the vision of scientists in the seventeenth century.

The most fundamental revolution was not in the actual discoveries that were made but in the new viewpoint that made those discoveries possible. This was *a vision of nature as a mechanism that can be explained by experiential mathematical methods.* There were two equal parts to this way of looking at things: (1) the understanding of nature as a mechanical order, and (2) the idea that nature can only be understood by an experiential mathematical approach.

1. Nature has a mechanical order.

Basic to the new vision was the belief that nature was both ordered and orderly. In this respect seventeenth-century scientists would not seem to differ from medieval philosophers who also viewed nature as forming one vast order. But for the earlier thinkers nature was ordered but not naturally orderly. God could disrupt the order of nature by miracles, and spiritual "intelligences" were the ultimate explanations of most natural events. The order was thus imposed; it was God's order and not nature's. For most early scientists, too, the order was given by God, but once given it was not removed. The orderliness involved an interrelation of parts and functionings, a similarity of individuals of the same class, and a uniformity of causes. This was made clear by a historian's reference to Robert Boyle (1627–1691), one of the great scientists of the seventeenth century:

> A man would be a dull fellow if, when he wanted an explanation of a watch, he was to be satisfied from being told it was an instrument made by a watchmaker—true though it is. An intelligent man, Boyle thinks, would want to know how the spring and balance and wheel and hands cooperate to form a time-telling instrument. So he gives us his opinion that the world being once constituted by the great author of things as it now is, *I look upon the phenomena of nature to be caused by the local motion of one part of matter hitting against another.*[62] (Original italics)

With the stimulus of dominant images this orderliness became conceived as a mechanism. The mechanical clock had been in use since the thirteenth century, but it was in the first half of the seventeenth century that English clockmakers were incorporated and during the Restoration the English were among the foremost producers of clocks in the world. The clock became a dominant image of the age. Hobbes began his ethic by inquiring,

> For seeing life is but a motion of limbs, the beginning whereof is in some principal part within, why may we not say that all automata (engines that move themselves by springs and wheels as doth a watch) have an artificial life? For what is the heart, but a spring; and the nerves but so many strings; and the joints but so many wheels giving motion to the whole body?[63]

2. This mechanical order could be explained only by an experiential mathematical method.

Mathematics was the essential element, and the development of mathematics was stimulated in the seventeenth century by the belief that it provided the clue to nature, and that development, in turn, made possible the most notable advances in scientific thought.

"Philosophy," wrote Galileo,

> is written in that vast book which stands ever open before our eyes, I mean the universe; but it cannot be read until we have learnt the language and become familiar with the characters in which it is written. It is written in mathematical language, and the letters are triangles, circles, and other geometrical figures, without which means it is humanly impossible to comprehend a single word.[64]

The use of mathematics was coupled with the study of nature for its own sake. There had been observation and experiment in the Middle Ages, but it was in the framework of an Aristotelian cosmology that had religious significance. It was not until this crust of custom was shattered that individuals came to look at nature and not to look through Aristotle to nature or to God.

But it was not only that the power of nature enabled individuals to amass facts and to imagine surprising explanations. What was of greater importance was that the hypotheses were different in kind from those previously used. The scientist was interested not in *why* an event happened in personal terms but in *how* it happened. The hypotheses and consequent explanations were nonteleological, which is to say they were non-Aristotelian and non-scholastic. It was precisely this shift in viewpoint, this revolution within the mind, that was so startling and, for many, so absurd.

As nature came to have a value in and of itself, the scientists became more and more convinced that their belief in the orderliness of nature was thoroughly justified. The puzzling parts began to fit together in unexpected ways. The mind became satisfied with basic assumptions because they worked, and nature, too, seemed to possess this same characteristic of workableness. Every part of nature seemed to possess a marvelous utility. This recognition had an important effect upon the ethics of the scientific vision.

The way the scientists in the seventeenth century looked at nature was not a revelation that came with startling suddenness. At the beginning of the century the intuitions were formed in the hidden recesses of many minds; they were not fully expressed, nor were these individuals entirely conscious of their existence. The early scientists were individuals of faith who set out for a country not knowing where they were going, for there was as yet no map. And as individuals who leave one country for another take much of the old world with them (and not less so when they would prefer to leave old customs and habits of thought behind), so these individuals brought to the modern world many of the mental mores of the medieval country. Most of them believed in God. And, again and again, they fell back upon "personal" explanations that had satisfied their fathers. Nicholas Copernicus (1473–1543) was stimulated to his greatest achievements precisely because he believed that the sphere was the most perfect shape and uniform circular motion most natural. Bacon, that arch-foe of Aristotelianism, rejected the Copernican theory for that of Tycho Brahe, in which some planets rotate around the sun and this whole system moves around the central, motionless earth. William Harvey (1578–1657), who discovered the circulation of the blood, believed there were "vital spirits" in it. And Boyle, the *Sceptical Chymist* (1661), spoke of inanimate material possessing "aspirations" and "dispositions."

The new mathematical-empirical explanations were most successful in astronomy and dynamics. Copernicus tentatively adopted the theory of Aristarchus of Samos (310–230 B.C.E.) that all the planets, the earth included, moved about the sun. With circular motion, this view made a neater geometrical picture. Since there were apparent irregularities that could be explained only by resort to the Ptolemaic theory of epicycles, and since there were no mathematical interpretations of the regularities the neatness was largely illusory. It was Johannes Kepler (1571–1630) who, profiting from the careful observations of his teacher Brahe, adopted the Copernican theory and, stimulated by a Pythagorean-Platonic religious fervor, after many wild guesses arrived at the "three laws of planetary motion" in which (1) the planets move in ellipses around the sun (2) to sweep out equal areas of the ellipse in equal times and (3) in a time proportional to their distances from the sun.

Even with the regularities noted by Kepler the modified Copernican system was not universally accepted by scientists because, according to the prevalent theory of dynamics, there was no satisfactory explanation as to how the planets moved. That acceptance came only when a new theory of motion was developed and then applied by Isaac Newton (1642–1727) to the motion of planets as well as the motion of objects on the earth.

The major effect of the Copernican system upon ethics was to shift the attitude toward what it meant to be human. It was the dislocation of the human race. But that dislocation was not a simple unilateral movement in which the individual, no longer the center of the world, became insignificant in the vast infinity of the universe. When one looked at the universe Copernicus and Kepler opened before the eyes, it was true that the individual was but a tiny speck. But when one looked at Copernicus or Kepler unfolding a new universe, the individual possessed a grandeur found nowhere else. The various ethics of science have oscillated between the insignificance and the grandeur of what it means to be human.

While astronomy had an important general effect upon ethics, the effect of dynamics was of an entirely different sort and more far-reaching. Within the larger framework of the scientific vision, the theory of dynamics provided the basic assumptions for the ethics of Hobbes and Spinoza.

In developing the modern theory of motion Galileo (1564–1642) made the greatest discoveries. The way was prepared for him by a line of persons, who since the fourteenth century had been dissatisfied with the Aristotelian theory of motion that (1) motion, while present through nature, is unnatural in the sense that it is ultimately caused by the Unmoved Mover, (2) the movement of an object is always toward the center of the world with its tendency to "go home"; and (3) an object moves only because it is moved by an adjacent object. On this view when the object causing movement stops the motion would stop, and a constant mover would result not in accelerated motion but in constant motion. Galileo, imagining objects in Euclidean space, showed that bodies of different weights fell with the same speed and plotted mathematically the rate of acceleration of falling bodies. René Descartes (1596–1650) formulated the laws of inertia and of action and reaction which were so directly influential upon the ethics of Hobbes and Spinoza and which later, in Newton, formed the starting point of most modern treatises on dynamics.

> The law of inertia: "The first law of nature: that each thing, as far as is in its power, always remains in the same state; and that consequently, when it is once moved, it always continues to move."[65]
>
> The law of action and reaction: "The third law: that a body upon coming in contact with a stronger one, loses none of its motion; but that, upon coming in contact with a weaker one, it loses as much as it transfers to that weaker body."[66]

The choice of the problem, that is, the view that motion needed to be explained, was important for ethics. This problem and its resolution assumed that objects were located spatially and temporally, and that motion was to be understood in mechanistic terms. The solution had an impersonal character. Of greater importance was that in the explanation some of the reaction of the human mind revealed qualities actually present in the object while other aspects of the human reaction were due solely to the mind. This was the famous distinction between primary and secondary qualities that has been no less significant in ethics than it has been in the metaphysics and epistemology. It was stated clearly by Galileo:

> No sooner do I form a conception of a material or corporeal substance, than I feel the need of conceiving that it has boundaries and shape; that relative to others it is great or small; that it is in this place or that; that it is moving or still; that it touches or does not touch another body; that it is unique, rare, or common; nor can I, by any effort of imagination, disjoin it from these [primary] qualities. On the other hand, I find no need to apprehend it as accompanied by such conditions as whiteness or redness, bitterness or sweetness, sonorousness or silence, well-smelling or ill-smelling. . . . Wherefor I hold that tastes, colours, smells, and the like exist only in the being which feels, which being removed these [secondary] qualities themselves do vanish. . . . I hold that there exists nothing in external bodies for exciting tastes, smells, and sounds, but size, shape, quantity, and motion. If, therefore, the organs of sense, ears, tongues, and noses were removed, I believe that shape, quantity, and motion would remain, but there would be no more of smells, tastes, and sounds. Thus apart from the living creatures, I take these to be mere words.[67]

All these views, by direct analogy that usually was unconscious, became important for the ethics of Hobbes and Spinoza. We can recognize how this was so by describing the common presuppositions of both ethicists, and the life and ethics of each man.

THE PRESUPPOSITIONS OF THE ETHICS OF THE SCIENTIFIC REVOLUTION

1. There is one order of nature in which each thing exists, moves, and has its being.

The vision of nature as a functioning and deterministic mechanism, in which everything that is has its place, is one of the three major bases that permeate and condition seventeenth-century scientific ethics. This and the second presupposition were related directly to the central ideas of scientific ethics as represented by Hobbes and Spinoza. The order of nature is all that there is, or—more precisely—it is all that is essential for human understanding and life. The God of some of the scientific ethicists was other than nature, but he was an Aristotelian and no Hebraic God, who was entirely irrelevant for scientific understanding and the moral life. This was not to deny that some of the scientists had a vital sense of a divine activity, but either that sense was kept in a separate compartment from their scientific and moral vision (as with Isaac Newton) or else they rejected the scientific assumptions as being entirely inadequate (as with Blaise Pascal).

The totality of things was conceived as a mechanism. They are impersonal, and they possess a given, determinate being. But the being of objects is characterized by motion and thus it possesses a dynamic existence. That mechanism of dynamic existence, moreover, is a mechanism that works. Universality, determinism, impersonality, dynamism, utilitarianism: all were present in this basic ethical presupposition.

2. Mathematical empirical reason is able potentially to explain this order, to predict its future, and, at times, to control its fate.

There was this faith in mathematical-empirical reason partly because, like the nature it sought to comprehend, it was impersonal. Such reason was concerned not with the individual and the unique but with general laws and uniformities. The faith also involved the conviction that there was no irreducible mystery in nature and the confidence in human ability to overcome all obstacles. A corollary of the faith was that there were no feelings, colors, sounds, or values in nature: "Nature is a dull affair, soundless, scentless, colorless; merely the hurrying of material, endlessly, meaninglessly."[68] This assumption, so central in ethical thought, developed partly because of the overwhelming and surprising success of science and partly because of the ambiguity of the word "nature," in which it meant sometimes the totality which included human beings and sometimes the totality which human beings observed.

If an individual could come to such a complete comprehension of nature, then it was possible to learn to predict and, within limits, control the future. There were two points important for ethics: (1) the explanation, partial prediction, and limited power to control referred to human life as well as other objects, and (2) the belief in any control introduced an implicit value-presupposition that affected scientific ethics.

3. The order of nature, including (the structure of) humans (with mathematical empirical reason) is good.

The scientific ethicists proposed the control of human life. They recommended one way of life rather than another. This clearly meant that a value judgment had been made. One way of life is better than another way; some acts are preferable to others. Such a simple fact had far-reaching effects in their ethics.

There was nothing inconsistent with scientific description and ethical prediction. This was to describe they ways in which individuals use ethical terms, make moral judgments, and act *and* the consequences of these activities. There was also no inconsistency between a belief in a rigid determinism and the recommendation of a way of life. The recommendation was a part of the cause-effect-cause deterministic process.

But when an individual is considered a part of nature there is a serious omission in suggesting that mathematical-empirical reason can explain and predict nature, and recommending one way of life. Such a recommendation required a value judgment and not merely a fact judgment. The only basis for this ethical judgment in scientific ethics was the implicit assumption that the determinate order is good. This was the essential third presupposition of scientific ethics.

The means by which this value assumption was reached was not difficult to understand. First, the scientific enterprise itself was based upon an ethical judgment, "Truth is good," just as it was based upon a metaphysical judgment, "There is an order of nature," and upon an epistemological judgment, "Inductive procedures are a path to truth." The ethical, metaphysical, and epistemological judgments were prerequisites for the scientific enterprise, and if prerequisite, then no scientific propositions alone could verify the truth of these essential judgments.

THOMAS HOBBES (1588–1679)

It was typical of Thomas Hobbes that he traced a dominant trait of his personality back to his parentage. John Aubrey, an indefatigable biographer, expressed the matter with characteristic brevity: "His extraordinary timorousness Mr. Hobbes doth very ingeniously confess and attributes it to the influence of his mother's dread of the Spanish invasion in '88, she being with child of him." One of Hobbes's ingenious confessions was that "in 1588 my mother gave birth to twin sons: myself and fear."[69]

When he was twenty, "Crow" Hobbes was graduated from Oxford. An indifferent student, he was able to excuse himself with the alibi that Oxford was the stronghold of Puritanism which he thoroughly despised. However, he was sufficiently promising as a scholar to be recommended as tutor to William Cavendish, the second earl of Devonshire. For the next twenty years he spent his time leisurely reading the classics and in continental travels, and he remembered those years as the happiest in his life.

Shortly after the death of William Cavendish, in 1629, Hobbes, in his early forties, had two experiences that shook and shaped his life. The first was his accidental discovery of geometry. "Being in a Gentleman's library," wrote Aubrey,

> Euclid's *Elements* lay open, and 'twas the 47 El. libri 1. He read the proposition, "By G—!" he said (he would now and then swear an emphatical oath by way of emphasis) "this is impossible!" So he read the demonstration of it, which referred him back to such a proposition, which proposition he also read. *Et sic deinceps* [and so as a result, it happened] that at last he was demonstratively convinced of that truth. This made him in love with geometry.[70]

The second experience occurred in a gentleman's drawing room. Not yet fully accepted in scientific circles, Hobbes listened while some learned men debated, "What is a sensation?" He was shocked by their failure to recognize what, to him, was an obvious truth: sensation is nothing other than motion, and if there were no motion there would be no sensation. Both experiences opened before him the new worlds of mathematics and science, and as soon as he had stepped into these worlds he became so confident of his capabilities that soon he was accepted by scientists in Paris, and within ten years he was arguing confidently against the renowned and versatile Descartes.

However, the events in England soon turned Hobbes's thoughts away from his newly discovered world of science to politics. In 1640 he published a book that, as he later recalled, "occasioned much talk of the author, and had not his majesty dissolved the parliament, it had brought him into danger of his life." The result was that "he went to France, the first of all that fled."[71]

In 1651 Hobbes published *Leviathan*, the primary basis for his fame and notoriety. Later the same year he returned to England. While he did not participate directly in the social struggles, he boasted, in 1656, of assisting the stability of Cromwell's government by having reconciled a thousand gentlemen to the new government, thus dissuading them from selling their property and fleeing the country. In 1662 he looked back and claimed he had persuaded "those thousand gentlemen" to remain in England loyal to the king, therefore making possible the king's return. With these different interpretations of the same event it may be that the timorous Hobbes, seeking security in different situations, was merely being Hobbesian. But his defensive explanations were not as contradictory as they appeared. Troubled by sectarian conflict he desired peace and so each time supported the power of the de facto sovereign. His persuasion of a thousand gentlemen was not as important as he thought, but it did serve to stabilize the economy of a tottering interregnum, and it did assist the orderly return of the king.

For the last thirty years of his life Hobbes engaged in public controversies that grew more bitter each year. Soon after the return of Charles II, the king's advisers recommended suppression of *Leviathan* and, by an act of the king, the book was banned. Hobbes, loyal to Leviathan doctrines, acquiesced in the censorship. But if he quietly submitted to the king, he was neither quiet nor submissive before bishops and university professors, both of whom he thought were obstructing science and progress. One of his most famous disputes was the debate with Bishop Bramhall on freedoms. Hobbes's denial of free will stated the case for scientific determinism. In another he made a vitriolic attack upon the leading mathematician at Oxford and, attempting to "square the circle," Hobbes neither understood nor accepted the mathematician's demolishment of his arguments.

But the most important disputes were stimulated by *Leviathan* and its apparently anti-moral, anti-Christian egotism. Hobbes thought his philosophy was quite moral; indeed, he went so far as to equate some of his basic tenets with Christian ethics. After all, he was charitable. Aubrey remembered one time when

> a poor and infirm old man craved his alms. He, beholding him with eyes of pity and compassion, put his hand in his pocket and gave him 6 d. Said a divine that stood by, "Would you have done this if it had not been Christ's command?" "Yea," said he. "Why?" quoth the other. "Because," said he, "I was in pain to consider the miserable condition of the old man; and now my alms, giving him some relief, doth also ease me."[72]

This experience was, in miniature, the life and ethics of Hobbes.

THE ETHIC OF THOMAS HOBBES

Hobbes's ethic was conditioned and permeated by his scientific view. Because, in his time, that view was dominated by physics, his ethic was dominated by a mechanism. The human being was likened to a machine. As a machine has a purpose and means of operation, so for the human being the basic end is self-preservation and the means are psychological.

Self-preservation requires power, "So that in the first place, I put for a general inclination of all mankind, a perpetual and restless desire of Power after power, that ceaseth only in Death."[73] The desire is not of power for the sake of power, nor is it, at this point, an insatiable selfishness. All desire for power is for the sake of life. Hobbes was merely pointing out that "the power of a man . . . is his present means to obtain some future good,"[74] and that the very attainment modifies human wants and needs. Human life was thought of essentially as change.

> For there is no such *Finis ultimus* [utmost aim], nor *Summum Bonum* [greatest good], as is spoken of in the books of the old moral philosophers. . . . Felicity is a continual progress of the desire from one object to another; the attaining of the former, being still but the way to the latter. The cause whereof is, that the object of man's desire, is not to enjoy once only, and for one instant of time; but to assure forever the way of his future desire.[75]

The primary want and need of the individual is self-preservation. But it is always a particular kind of self (or a self with particular desires) that exists. The available secondary wants of the individual are many: "Competition for riches, honor, command," "desire of ease," "desire of knowledge," "desire of human praise."[76] These are but a few of the possible desires available. But whatever the desire may be, thought Hobbes, it is always loved and is always a desire for good.

> Of the voluntary acts of every man, the object is some *good to himself.* . . . And for as much as necessity of nature maketh men to will and desire *bonum sibi*, that which is good for themselves, and to avoid that which is hurtful[77] . . . it is not against reason that a man doth all he can to preserve his own body and limbs both from death and pain.[78]

Thus, for any individual, there is an equivalence of desire and love, and a relation of both with good.

If existence and the satisfaction of wants are the aims of an individual, those aims can be attained only by the means of social-psychological determinism and associationism.

(a) "Associationism," because every effect must be directly related and contiguous to a cause. This is true for all motion, for moving objects on an inclined plane and for thoughts.

> For in a discourse of our present civil war, what could seem more impertinent than to ask (as one did) what was the value of a Roman penny? Yet the coherence to me was clear enough. For the thought of the war, introduced the thought of the delivering up the king to his enemies; the thought of that brought in the thought of the delivering up of Christ; and that again the thought of the thirty pence which was the price of that treason: and thence followed that malicious question; and all this in a moment of time; for thought is quick.[79]

(b) "Determinism," because, as a behaviorist before behaviorism, Hobbes insisted upon the unbroken chain of cause-effect sequences. Individuals are sometimes free to do what they will, but they are never free to will what to do. To will is the effect of antecedent causes. Or, as it might be expressed, individuals are sometimes free to respond to stimuli, but they are not free to choose the stimuli since the stimuli and the choice of the stimuli are the product of a confluence of causes, including prior stimuli. So the scientific assumptions provided Hobbes and Hobbes provided scientific determinism with a definition of freedom: "A free man *is he that in those things, which by his strength and wit he is able to do, is not hindered to do what he has a will to*" (original italics).[80] He added immediately that "*liberty* and *necessity* are consistent":

> as in the water, that hath not only a *liberty*, but a *necessity* of descending by the channel; so likewise in the actions which men voluntarily do: which, because they proceed from their will proceed from *liberty*; and yet, because every act of man's will, and every desire, and every inclination proceedeth from some cause, and that from another cause, in a continual chain (whose first link is in the hand of God the first of all causes) they proceed from *necessity*.[81] (Original italics)

(c) "Psychological," because the indispensable and basic means by which an individual satisfies desires (i.e., attains the good) are feelings and thoughts. Thus, feelings of pleasure and pain, and conceptions of truth and falsehood are the stimuli that help or hinder vital motion.

> *Pleasure* . . . is the appearance or sense of good; and . . . *displeasure* the appearance or sense of evil. And consequently all appetite, desire, and love is accompanied with some delight more or less; and all hatred, and aversion with more or less displeasure.[82] (Original italics)

Reason does not determine what is good but how to attain what is desired as good: "for the thoughts are to the desires, as scouts, and spies, to range abroad and find the way to the things desired."[83] It is reason, thus, that discovers "what conduceth to the defense and conservation" of the individual.[84]

(d) "Social," because, after a definition of the essential human being, Hobbes pointed out that it is only through life in an organized society that individuals possess the security to satisfy their desires.

The beginning of the ethic can be further summarized in this way: the scientific assumptions used by Hobbes led to an ethic of absolute individualism. (The ethic is more popularly called "egotistical," but this term, especially with its emotional connotations, is misleading.) "Absolute individualism" meant that all uncoerced activities of the individual are activities of the self and for the self. They are "of the self" in that they arise from the individual's desires, loves, pleasures, and pains. They are "for the self" in that they have self-preservation or some form of self-satisfaction as their sole aim. The individual, insofar as he has liberty, is, indeed, a self-winding clock that runs by its internal springs and balances for the purpose of running further (i.e., remaining a clock), and for the satisfaction of keeping correct time. Hobbes's meaning of absolute individualism was made perfectly plain by the definitions of love, charity, and pity.

Love is "the joy man taketh in the fruition of present good."[85] Sexual love, eros, is but one form of love:

> This is that *love* which is the great theme of poets: but notwithstanding their praises, it must be defined by the word need: for it is the conception a man hath of his need of that *one person desired*.[86] (Original italics)

Charity is the delight an individual has in using power to help others realize their desires; and it includes only the natural affection of parents or it extends to associates, "those that adhere to us."

> But the affection wherewith men many times bestow their benefits upon *strangers* is not to be called charity, but either *contract*, whereby they seek to purchase friendship; or *fear* which maketh them to purchase peace.[87] (Original italics)

Finally, there was one succinct definition that was the epitome of Hobbes's absolute individualism: "*Pity* is imagination or fiction of future calamity to ourselves, proceeding from the sense of another man's calamity" (original italics).[88]

This absolute individualism was a psychological determinism and hedonism. The determinism was not fatalism, and because of moral and intellectual pleasures, the hedonism was not the pleasure of the senses. Most important, the absolute individualism of a human self could be directed by reason. This role given to reason had important consequences. In the first place, Hobbes, without using the precise terminology, was giving expression to the idea of "enlightened self-interest" that was to become important later.

Nor was this the only result of reason's relation to absolute individualism. If reason ever had a serious conflict with basic human desires, either the individualism or the reason would have to be eliminated. Once more Hobbes developed ideas that became basic to the Enlightenment and that were integral to most moral and political thinking until the twentieth century. There is no final, destructive conflict between reason and pleasure (or feeling). There is not a radical disjunction between the individual and nature, nor, for that matter (though Hobbes's theological position is less clear than his naturalistic metaphysic) an inescapable cleavage between the activity of a human being and that of God. Nor is there a tragic disorder of the individual and society. While, for the essential human being, there is "a war of each against all,"[89] this did not mean there is an inevitable conflict between individuals, each of whom can act only for himself. For as soon as the essential human being is placed in a proper society, sword and shield are laid down and war is studied no more. Everything for Hobbes, when seen by the eyes of a faithful mathematical-empirical reason, is fundamentally harmonious. The mood of optimism, after the provisional pessimism, is pervasive.

The harmony and the optimism were present in the assumptions accepted from the new science. They became more explicit in the interpretation of the essential human being and the world. The optimism, the harmony, became the theme of the scientific ethics when Hobbes, having described the wants of the individual, revealed the only way individuals could achieve their desires. When this transition took place a strange metamorphosis occurred: the ethic which began as an absolute individualism became a social absolutism.

Social absolutism was the remainder of the story. The essential human being is the individual who is free, to the extent of anyone's capabilities, to get whatever is desired. However, the existential human being is ruled in actual life by a Sovereign who is the "essence of the commonwealth, that great Leviathan."[90] How did this transition take place? Why was it that when the winds of individualism and human freedom were rising in the seventeenth century, Hobbes's ethic of the scientific revolution took refuge in the ancient shelter of absolutism?

The steps were simple, and they were all made by the discoveries of reason. First, reason recognized that individuals in the (fictitious) "state of nature," i.e., the essential human being, could seek to satisfy all their desires. But this would lead to a ruthless competition. Second, reason recognized that in nature individuals are relatively equal in strength and intelligence, at least equal to the extent that they are able to kill each other. This meant that they did not have the power (i.e., the liberty) to get what was desired. Third, reason recognized that the only possible way individuals could recover part of this power was to satisfy these desires. A theoretical liberty must be sacrificed for an actual security, and the power of individuals must be given—completely and irrevocably—to a sovereign. Since the sovereign likewise wanted power to achieve desires as sovereign, it was justifiable for every individual to expect that all one's greatest individual wants would be satisfied.

It was all very simple. And philosophically it resulted from Hobbes's interweaving the scientific assumptions, his conception of the nature of the human being (especially the individual's desires), and his ideas of society and politics. Because the transition from individualism to absolutism was so simple it is imperative that the development be examined in more detail. In that examination three points are of particular importance: (1) the change from description to evaluation, (2) the laws of nature basic to the social (or moral) life, and (3) the nature of sovereignty.

1. From description to evaluation

In its interpretation of the essential nature of the human being Hobbes's work was descriptive. This was true to the point that Hobbes made his famous portrayal of "the time wherein men live without other security than what their own strength, and their own invention shall furnish them withal."[91] Here there were none of the benefits that come with society: there was no industry, no agriculture, no architecture, no science, no education—indeed, there was nothing at all except that "which is worst of all, continual feare and danger of violent death; And the life of man, solitary, poore, nasty, brutish, and short."[92] The world was not created good with a Garden of Eden: the real creation was the bite from the forbidden apple. As far as the essential nature is concerned this was Augustinian Christianity turned on its head. If Hobbes had been a theologian he would have replaced the doctrine of original sin, namely, that the individual, essentially good, inevitably yet freely chose evil, with a doctrine of original goodness, i.e., that the individual, essentially evil, inevitably yet freely chose good.

To say that, devoid of society, human life was "solitary, poore, nasty, brutish, and short" was to describe. But to add: "To this war of every man against every man, this also is consequent; that nothing can be Unjust"[93] was to evaluate. That evaluation continued when Hobbes described the discoveries made by reason of those "theorems concerning what conduceth to the conservation and defense of" individuals.[94]

The point at issue here was a fundamental one in the theory of Hobbes and in all scientific ethics. That point involved the nature of ethics. The alternative views are variants of two contradictory positions: (a) morality is imposed by fiat at the whim of capricious desires of beings that possess no determinate structure but only power, or (b) morality is imposed by human nature and the world. The issue was not the particular norm of morality that is valid but whether, in fact, moral principles have an objective or an exclusively subjective source.

Hobbes, interestingly, gave both answers. In the "state of nature" nothing is unjust; and this was answer (b) that morality is subjective. But the state of nature is a "state," and the individual is a part of it. Despite the wide variations between individuals, each is human and a human is, at least, a structural being that can be described. Whatever else a human being may be, he is the being that wants self-preservation. This was answer (a) that morality has objectivity. Two paths diverged in Hobbes's ethical forest. Hobbes wanted both, but finally took one, and that made all the difference in his ethic.

2. The laws of nature basic to the moral life

Reason discovers fifteen laws of nature, and the knowledge of these laws is "the true and only moral philosophy."[95] The laws arise from the individual's "fear of death; desire of such things as are necessary to commodious living; the hope by their industry to obtain them."[96] The first law was the consequence of all previous description and evaluation:

> *That every man ought to endeavor peace, as far as he has hope of obtaining it; and when he cannot obtain it, that he may seek, and use, all helps and advantages of war.*[97] (Original italics)

The second is that individuals make a covenant to live together:

> *That a man be willing, when others are so too, as far-forth as for peace and defense of himself he shall think necessary, to lay down this right to all things; and be contented with so much liberty against other men, as he would allow other men against himself.*[98] (Original italics)

It was the third law that Hobbes correctly recognized as most important for his entire ethical scheme. This was the law *"That men perform their covenants made"* (original italics).[99]

Hobbes saw order as the basis of society, but he saw no tendency to order *in* individuals. No one would intend to keep a covenant except that one was forced to keep it.

> Therefore before the names of Just, and Unjust, can have place, there must be some coercive power, to compel men equally to the performance of their

covenants by the terror of some punishment, greater than the benefit they expect by the breach of their covenant.[100]

If this is so, then ethics relates only to those matters a sovereign can control. Step by step the absolute individual moved toward social absolutism.

3. The nature of political sovereignty

A government with power to create and enforce law is essential for human security, for industry and culture. The government was created when the absolute individuals say, in effect, to each other:

> *I Authorize and give up my Right of Governing myself to this Man, or to this Assembly of men, on this condition, that thou give up thy Right to him, and authorize all his Actions in like manner.*[101] (Original italics)

From this time forward the delegated sovereign had complete power. The sovereign, preferably an individual, did not covenant with the people. The sovereign promised nothing. Rather the people covenanted together, each person with all others, that the sovereign should act as "the Person of them all."[102] The ruler, therefore, could do no injustice to the subjects since the ruler was given the authority by the subjects to do anything. The individuals could not ethically rebel, nor could they morally attempt to transfer political power to another sovereign. There was freedom of thought, so long as the thought is not expressed, and freedom of religion if the beliefs did not lead to an action:

> No human law is intended to oblige the conscience of a man, unless it break out into action, either of the tongue or other part of the body.[103]

The individual did not have the right to defend another person against the government, not even if that person was innocent of the crime for which he was being punished because "such liberty takes away from the Sovereign the means of Protecting us; and is therefore destructive of the very essence of Government."[104]

But the individual, even if guilty, does have the right to resist the sovereign if existence itself is endangered since the reason for accepting the creation of the sovereign was security.

Here was totalitarianism. Yet there are fundamental differences between the totalitarianism of Hobbes and that of the twentieth century. (a) Authority, for Hobbes, was founded upon the individual and existed for the sake of the individual. (b) There was a natural harmony between what was good for individuals and what was good for the sovereign. (c) The purpose of the totalitarian authority was peace.

> For such commonwealths, or such monarchs, as affect war for itself, that is to say, out of ambition, or of vain-glory, or that make account to revenge every little injury, or disgrace done by their neighbors, if they ruin not themselves, their fortune must be better than they have reason to expect.[105]

BENEDICT SPINOZA (1632–1677)

The ethical beliefs of Benedict Spinoza were permeated by the fundamental assumptions adopted from the new science. The other major ethical defender of the ethical scientific faith in the seventeenth century, Thomas Hobbes, was forty-four years old when Spinoza was born, and when the naturalized Dutchman died, the Englishman still had two years to live. There was no indication that Hobbes or Spinoza had any influence upon each other, yet in their political theories and their ethics there are some basic similarities.

Any similarity, however, must not obscure the real differences between the philosophies of the two men. They represent diverse types of scientific moral philosophy, and each is so exemplary a representative of the type that the most important interpreters of scientific ethics in modern thought wear the eyeglasses of either Hobbes or Spinoza. Hobbes appealed to the realistic empiricist, the individual who wants the facts and nothing but the facts, the modern individual who is impatient with vagueness and with dreamy philosophizing and sentimental nonsense. Spinoza reached through the mind of other scientific ethicists to the heart which has reasons of its own, but the mind is able to find reasons that satisfy the longings of the heart. This type of moral thinker, who is no less a scientist than the tough-minded empiricist, is a romantic. This thinker wants the facts to be painted into a picture of nature that will give significance to all of life.

Variations upon the same theme: this summarizes the general relation of the ethics of Hobbes and Spinoza. Those variations will be seen more clearly if it is recognized that they are largely the results of different types of mind, dissimilar experiences of life, and diverse individual responses to social experiences.

Spinoza had a mind that was synoptic and self-conscious; the mind of Hobbes was analytic and object-conscious. These characteristics must not be understood as denials that Spinoza had an interest in analysis or that Hobbes had a synoptic view. The former's analysis of the emotions, the latter's metaphysical materialism disprove such conclusions. But the differences in the inner lives of the two men were as striking as their diverse types of mind.

There was little of the poet in Hobbes. His only writing that conveys a poetic feeling were the passages depicting the bestiality of the human being in the state of nature. But Spinoza, particularly in his moral conclusions, was often unable to restrain a poetic language that obscured philosophic clarity. Their attitudes toward religion were also illustrative of their personal lives. Hobbes took the communion of the Anglican Church with the nonchalance of an individual who cared little for his eternal salvation but who knew what was good for peace with his orthodox neighbors. Spinoza had no religious home, but his entire life and thought were one continual act of piety and devotion.

The peculiar social experiences of the two men and the unique response of each also had direct relations to the variations between their ethics. The Spanish Armada that Hobbes maintained was influential for his life was also fateful for Benedict Spinoza. The destruction of the Armada and the weakening of Spain's military power made it possible for the Jews, bludgeoned by the Inquisition, to escape that country and Portugal. Holland, in 1579, had declared that every citizen shall be able to worship freely. Scarcely hoping to believe that this would apply to Jews as well as to Christians, some Jews, in 1593, sailed in secret from the Iberian peninsula without making arrangements for their reception by the Dutch government. Because they were given asylum in Amsterdam and despite the fact that for many years they had no legal status in their new country, the refugees of 1593, including Spinoza's father and grandfather, were the first of many Jews to find a home in the Low Country.

Thirty-nine years later, Baruch d'Espinosa was born in Amsterdam. His father, a respectable merchant, gave his only son all the advantages of a Jewish education in the synagogue school and a secular education by private tutors. By the time his father died in 1654, Baruch, then twenty-two, showed promise of being a great Jewish scholar. He also showed dangerous tendencies toward being unorthodox. He was much influenced by the history of Jewish thought, especially by the criticisms of Judaism made by medieval scholars revered by the orthodox, and by contemporary critics excommunicated by the orthodox. When he expressed such views that there was nothing in the Bible to support the opinions that God has no body, or that there are angels, or that the soul is immortal, and when he refused a bribe to keep his beliefs to himself, Spinoza shared the fate of his contemporary Jewish radicals. On August 6, 1656, the eldest and most revered rabbi in Amsterdam stood before a hushed congregation in the synagogue and read,

> The lord of the spiritual council do you to wit that they, having been long aware of the godless words and sentiments of Baruch Spinoza, have endeavored on various occasions and with promises to turn him from his evil ways. But since they could do nothing with him, but, on the contrary, had daily greater experience of the frightful errors which he manifested by word

and deed, and of his shameless utterances in truth of which they had a number of trustworthy witnesses, who in his presence gave their testimony, and brought these things home to him therefore they have resolved, in the presence of the Rabbis and with their concurrence, to pass this sentence of excommunication on this Spinoza and to expel him from the people of Israel under the following anathema. According to the judgment of the angels and of saints, we, with the full approval of the spiritual tribunal, and with the consent of every holy community, in the presence of the holy Books, with the six hundred and thirteen precepts therein contained, banish, expel, condemn, and curse Baruch Spinoza, with the curse which Joshua pronounced over Jericho, with the curse wherewith Elisha cursed the children, with all the curses which are written in the Book of the Law. Let him be cursed by day and cursed by night. Let him be cursed when he sleeps, and cursed when he rises up. Let him be cursed in his going out and cursed in his coming in. May the Lord never forgive him. May the Lord cause his anger and jealousy against this man to burn, and visit him with all the curses that are written in the Book of the Law. Let his name be destroyed under heaven, and let him be separated to his destruction from all the tribes of Israel, with everything that is cursed in the Book of the Law. But you, who hold to the Lord your God, we greet you this day. See to it that no one of you address him, either by word of mouth or in writing, let no one of you show him any kindness, let no one of you be under the same roof with him, let no one remain standing within four yards' distance from him, let no one read anything that he has composed or written.[106]

The anathema transformed the life of Baruch. On the surface the transformation was marked by a change in his name from the Jewish Baruch to the Latin Benedict and by a permanent separation from his former friends. Beneath the surface the transformations were far greater, far more painful. The anathema imprisoned Benedict Spinoza in solitary confinement. In a time when the young thinker was trying to work out his own beliefs, the supporting props of his tradition and his institution were taken away. He was forced to find, alone, the new foundations for his life. During the next four years of mental torture and perplexity it often seemed that the curse had come true for his inner life. In 1661 Spinoza recalled those days:

> I saw myself in the midst of a very great peril and obliged to seek a remedy, however uncertain, with all my energy: like a sick man seized with a deadly disease, who sees death straight before him if he does not find some remedy, is forced to seek it, however uncertain, with all his remaining strength, for in that is all his hope placed.[107]

And he remembered how he had freed himself:

> The whole happiness or unhappiness is dependent on this alone: on the
> quality of the object to which we are bound by love. . . . The love towards
> a thing eternal and infinite alone feeds the mind with pleasure, and it is free
> from all pain; so it is much to be desired and to be sought out with all our
> might.[108]

The remainder of his life Spinoza spent in seclusion. He boarded with
friends and he earned enough money for his ascetic life by tutoring and
making lenses for telescopes and microscopes. This latter work, requiring
great skill and a thorough knowledge of optics, was indicative of his scientific interests.

During these years he maintained a detailed correspondence with many
persons, especially theologians and scientists. The most important letters
were answers to inquiries by Henry Oldenburg, the secretary of the British
Royal Society, and it was largely through these letters that Spinoza's reputation as a scientist and philosopher grew in some few circles in his lifetime.

In 1670 Spinoza published his political philosophy. It was immediately
denounced, particularly by the Calvinistic clergymen, as having been "forged
in hell by a renegade Jew and the devil."[109] That denunciation of the *Tractatus
theologico-politicus* dissuaded him from allowing any more of his writings
to be published until after his death. When, in 1673, Spinoza was invited to
the chair of philosophy at the University of Heidelburg with the promise that
he would have freedom to teach, he refused the offer, explaining that he
would not be able to continue his own studies if he had to teach, that he had
a love of quietness, and that he did not know the limits of the academic
freedom that had been promised to him.

So he continued to live what he called his "quiet lonely life." And "as
Spinoza lived, so he died; quietly and peacefully, and free from all the fears
and terrors of death."[110]

THE ETHIC OF BENEDICT SPINOZA

When, in his days of personal inner suffering, Spinoza discovered that the
whole of happiness depended upon "the quality of the object to which we are
bound by love," the direction of his life and love became definite. The object
to which he became bound by love was "a thing infinite and eternal," the
whole of nature. It was in this love that he found his own deep and abiding
happiness, and so he became convinced that "the greatest good . . . is the
knowledge of the union which the mind has with the whole of nature."[111]
Such love and such knowledge could not be reached easily. Spinoza knew
that his life work was the creation of a new philosophy for the scientific age,

and in this understanding he was thoroughly conscious of the aims, the method, and the problems of his philosophical tasks.

He saw the goal of philosophy as human salvation.

> I wish to direct all sciences in one direction or to one end, namely, to attain the greatest possible human perfection: and thus everything in the sciences that does not promote this endeavor must be rejected as useless, that is, in a word, all our endeavors and thoughts must be directed to this one end.[112]

The method of philosophy was a rigidly objective method, the mathematical empirical method of the new science.

> That I might investigate the subject matter of this science [i.e., politics] with the same freedom of spirit as we generally use in mathematics, I have labored carefully not to mock, lament, or execrate, but to understand human actions; and to this end I have looked upon passions such as love, hatred, anger, envy, ambition, pity, and the other perturbations of the mind, not in the light of vices of human nature, but as properties, just as pertinent to it, as are heat, cold, storm, thunder, and the like to the nature of the atmosphere.[113]

This was to consider "human actions and desires in exactly the same manner as . . . lines, planes, solids."[114]

An objective inquiry revealed that there were three kinds of knowledge: (1) "opinion" or "imagination" was the result of the vague experiences of ordinary life, or perhaps the result of casual reading or hearsay; (2) "reason" referred to the generalizations of the scientist which involved "common notions and adequate ideas of the properties of things"; and (3) "intuition" was the philosophic insight into the "essence of things" in their concreteness, individuality, and relations to the whole of nature.[115]

Motivated by the aim for salvation and using a method of objective understanding that culminates in *scientia intuitiva,* Spinoza recognized that, to achieve his goal, his philosophy must describe the universe and the individual's place within "the whole of nature."

In understanding the ideas of Spinoza, it is necessary to give careful attention to his definition of key terms. Spinoza used familiar words in quite unfamiliar ways, and so to understand Spinoza—especially his conceptions of God, nature, substance, eternity, mind, and body—it is essential to replace familiar ideas with his definitions.

God is "a being absolutely infinite." Through intricate reasoning God was identified as the only possible substance ("that which is in itself and is conceived through itself"), as eternity (which is "existence itself"), and as the whole of nature.[116] Nature was viewed in two ways: nature as cause (*natura naturans*) and nature as effect (*natura naturata*). The first is to see nature as a dynamic process; the second, to see nature as an interrelated structure.

God = substance = eternity = nature: this is the totality of reality, this is the order of all that is, this is ultimate being. The possibility of employing such terms meaningfully was dependent upon Spinoza's theory of knowledge. There was no possibility of the individual's having an image of God constructed from perceptions: "We cannot imagine God but we can, indeed, conceive him."[117] This conception of God as absolute totality and unity of reality led Spinoza to claim, "Like Paul . . . I assert that all things live and move in God."[118] "Whatever is, is in God, and nothing can exist or be conceived without God."[119] But while he made his claim in the same words as Paul, Spinoza's meaning was not that of Pauline theology. It was closer to the Stoics whom Paul was quoting in the statement that "in him we live and move and have our being."[120] The God of Spinoza was not a transcendent being revealed in history and in personal life more than in nature. Properly speaking, the God of Spinoza was not "immanent" in the natural world or "transcendent" to the world. Notions of transcendence and immanence involve "otherness." God can be transcendent to or immanent in nature only if God is different from nature and the totality of reality. But for Spinoza there was a sameness of God and nature, though nature had an expanded meaning. These identifications of God, nature, substance, and eternity were the foundation of his philosophy.

It is important to see how he discovered these foundations and to comprehend the importance of the ideas for his ethic. Many complex elements were combined in vague relations in Baruch d'Espinosa's early experiences. In the indefiniteness with which his experiences were assimilated he was no different from any other person. The differences were, at first, in the elements of his life. Even as a child who was a refugee in a strange land, his knowledge of the Bible, his living within the community and cultus of Judaism, his love for the critics of orthodoxy, his discovery of Descartes and the new science helped to weave the personality of the young intellectual. Then there came the personal moral shock. Excluded from his tradition, cut off from his friends, cursed by the leaders of his people, he was brought to the one existential question, "What shall I do to be saved?"

It belonged to the greatness of Spinoza that he did not stop with the question. He was not content with asking only what he must do. He saw that there was no way out by action without knowledge. This was the result of an inner metaphysical shock, the shock that came when he asked the basic question, "What is ultimate being?" Spinoza answered the question of the ultimate by saying "God," "substance," "the whole of nature," "eternity." This, he thought, was the necessary presupposition of all thought. This was the reality that must be if there could be any existence at all. "Nothing can exist or be conceived without God."[121] Thus the presupposition of the ethics of science was pushed back by Spinoza to be a presupposition of science and of all particular existent being, "There is one order of nature in which each thing that exists moves and has its being."[122]

To the questions "Why does anything exist?" "What is ultimate being?" Spinoza, therefore, gave two answers that referred to existence and to thought: (1)

> God [or nature, or substance, or eternity] necessarily exists; he is one alone; he exists and acts merely from the necessity of his nature; all things are in God, and so depend upon him that without him they could neither exist or be conceived; all things are predetermined by God, not through his free or good will, but through his absolute nature or infinite power.[123]

(2) "It is not the nature of reason to regard things as contingent but necessary."[124]

And these two, necessary existence and the mind which thinks in terms of necessary causation, belonged together. They were the essential assumptions for existence and for philosophy.

The whole of nature was characterized by attributes, "which the intellect perceives as constituting the essence of substance."[125] Two attributes, thought and extension, are known to the individual. God is not a particular extended object but the whole of space and objects in spatial relations. The attributes could be further defined in three statements.

1. The attributes are the intellect's perception of what is essentially a unity.

In his view of thought and extension as it appears in the mind and body of the individual, Spinoza insisted upon the unity of the human being. In this insistence he was influenced by the Hebraic view of the indissoluble unity of personality.

> The mind and body are one and the same thing which, now under the attribute of thought, now under the attribute of extension is conceived.[126]

2. There is no interrelation of cause and effect between mind and body.

There is a co-relation in that "mind" and "body" are the essences of a unity, and they always accompany each other.

> The body cannot determine the mind to think, nor the mind the body to re-
> main in motion, or at rest, or in any other state. . . . All modes of thinking
> have God for their cause, in so far as he is a thinking thing and not in so far
> as he is explained through another attribute. . . . Absolutely everything
> which arises in a body must have arisen from God in so far as he is consid-
> ered as affected by some mode of extension, and not some mode of
> thinking.[127]

The two were conceived as always accompanying each other, as co-related. Thought and extension are not interrelated for they cannot affect each other; they are not even parallel, for this would make them entirely separate. They are co-related aspects of the unity that is the whole of nature.

3. The attributes are expressions of a deterministic order.

The chain of cause and effect extends through all existence. There is no freedom in the sense of indeterminism or creativity; there is no possibility that anything in a given present could be other than it is.

These views led to an understanding of the human being, a "mode" which is "a modification of substance or that which is in something else through which it may be conceived."[128] A human being, like other modes of nature, is a unity in which there is a co-relation of mind and body, a unity that is strictly determined. A human being has no freedom to will and no freedom to think. Both willing and thinking are part of a determined series, and, in-deed, the will and the intellect are the same thing. The only important ques-tion is whether the will of an individual is the expression of vague experience or of intuition. If there is no freedom to will there can be no moral blame. A traitor to a country can be called evil, but there is no justification in blaming the traitor any more than in blaming one who is born tone-deaf for singing the national anthem in a monotone.

For Spinoza the most significant fact about the nature of a human being was the self-maintaining quality of the individual. This was the first law of motion, the law of inertia which in the seventeenth century cast a new light upon all philosophy. For the law of inertia was generalized and applied to every existent thing and to every possible way of existing.

> Everything in so far as it is in itself endeavors to persist in its own being.
> . . . The endeavor wherewith a thing endeavors to persist in its being is
> nothing else than the actual essence of that thing.[129]

The striving (*conatus*) to be what one essentially is, is the most important char-acteristic of an individual, and it is crucial for an understanding of human perfection. In human beings the striving is accompanied by conscious desire (*cupiditas*). As the striving, or desire, is expressed, external or internal causes effect changes in the individual. When those changes produce an increased power of action (i.e., a successful persistence in one's being) the individual feels pleasure; and, contrarily, when there is a decreased power of action there is pain. From these elemental facts about the human self the entire behavioristic structure of Spinoza's subtle analysis of the emotions was built.

Human striving is always for a "good." But the "good" is not an ideal that causes purposive striving. It is whatever is useful to the individual, and because it is desired it is called "good."

> It may be gathered from this, then, that we endeavour, wish, desire, or long for nothing because we deed it good; but on the other hand, we deem a thing good because we endeavour, wish for, desire, or long for it.[130]

This point of view seemed to lead to an ethical relativity since whatever the individual desires is called good. Spinoza, in one sense, encouraged this view of the relativity of morals.

> As for the terms good and bad, they indicate nothing positive in things considered in themselves, nor are they anything else than modes of thought, or notions, which we form from the comparison of things mutually. For one and the same thing can be at the same time good, bad, and indifferent. E.g., music is good to the melancholy, bad to those who mourn, and neither good nor bad to the deaf.[131]

But the essential point was that good is relative. It was relative to human nature and to the individual's situation.

Now the relation between the metaphysics and the ethics became clear. At this point Spinoza was led into a basic value judgment as to what was good and into an interpretation of how metaphysical and moral value were brought together. "Reality and perfection," explained Spinoza, "I understand to be one and the same thing."[132] The entire order of nature was considered good, and so was the essential nature of the human being, or any other mode of being. Since this was so, then,

> to act absolutely according to virtue is nothing else in us than to act under the guidance of reason, to live so, and to preserve one's being (these three have the same meaning) on the basis of seeking what is useful to us.[133]

To live ethically is to live not by the passions but by reason. In this alone can human freedom and salvation consist. All individuals are "slaves of God"[134]; but there is a vast difference between the individual who blindly submits and the free individual who opens his eyes to his determined place in the universe. Humans and nature are made for each other, but the only satisfactory bond that can bind a human being to this object is intellectual love. "The greatest good of the mind is the knowledge of God and the greatest virtue of the mind is to know God."[135] This is the "third kind of knowledge" (intuition, "the union of the mind with the whole of nature"),[136] and possessing this knowledge the individual lives by reason. To live by the intellectual love of God is true human blessedness.

> Blessedness is not the reward of virtue, but virtue itself: nor should we rejoice in it for that we restrain our lusts, but, on the contrary, because we can rejoice therein we can restrain our lusts.[137]

This was the truth at which Spinoza arrived; this was the truth for which he tried to live. "Let those who will," he cried, "die for their food so long as I am allowed to live for the truth."[138] But truth, by its very nature, cannot be a private truth. It must be for all. And Spinoza saw that truth by its very nature is neither simple to find nor simple to follow.

Such truth, thought Spinoza, confers great benefits upon others. (1) It offers the individual peace of mind, true liberty, and the only genuine happiness in the knowledge of God. (2) It teaches the individual how to respond to those things that are not in the individual's power, "that we should expect and bear both faces of fortune with an equal mind." (3) It enriches the life of the individual in society because it reveals there is no reason to hate or ridicule other persons and that there is reason to help others, not from pity but from the guidance of the intellect. (4) Finally, it is beneficial to politics, for it shows that the purpose of the state is the freedom of the citizens.

In his political writings Spinoza insisted that "the true aim of the government is liberty":

> The ultimate aim of the government is not to rule, or restrain, by fear, nor to exact obedience, but contrariwise, to free every man from fear, that he may live in all possible security; in other words to strengthen his right to exist and work without injury to himself or others.[139]

But because few individuals live by the intellectual love of God the origin and structure of the state was almost identical to Hobbesian political theory. Spinoza did plead for freedom of thought and speech. But there was not a complete freedom of religion. The sovereign legislates the kind of religion as the sovereign decrees the type of actions permitted.

Few individuals live by the intellectual love because such a life, binding the individual to the whole of nature, is exceedingly difficult to achieve. This

Benedict Spinoza had found to be true in his own life; so it was from the depths of personal striving and suffering that he wrote the last words of his *Ethics* conveying a sense of quiet triumph.

> If the road I have shown is very difficult, it can yet be discovered. And clearly it must be very hard when it is so seldom found. For how could it be that it is neglected by practically all, if salvation were close at hand and could be found without difficulty? But all things excellent are as difficult as they are rare.[140]

SCIENTIFIC ETHICS OF THE SEVENTEENTH CENTURY: A SUMMARY

Thomas Hobbes and Benedict Spinoza were among the intellectuals of the seventeenth century whose imaginations were captivated by the new world of science. They believed the universe to be an order of objects that operates mechanically and that can be known, and in part controlled, through mathematical-empirical reason. Motivated by the faith that truth is good, they had the belief—a belief not clearly defined—that the natural order is good. Their ethical perspective was conditioned by the predominate interests of the contemporary scientists in motion and in the success which the scientists had in discovering laws of motion.

These ideas coalesced with other aspects of the experience of each man, and the result was the development of two main types of scientific ethics, the empirical and the empirical-intuitive. Hobbes and Spinoza did not agree in specific ethical conclusions, but they did agree in general ethical beginnings. They asked questions from essentially the same points of view, and, at times, they arrived at similar answers.

1. Human nature

Human beings were thought of as part of a vaster world of nature, and they were to be understood through the laws of the larger universe. Thus, the individual is recognized as an object (a) existing among other objects, (b) which has a given order or unity, (c) that is determinate in structure and functioning. Human beings, as everything else in nature, are understood only when they are viewed as determined by an unbreakable chain of cause and effect.

Since nature (including human nature) was seen in this way as mechanically ordered, a major category of ethics became the useful. The remarkable thing about a machine is that it works. Whatever was useful to the individual, what enables the individual to work as an individual, became the criterion of moral good. That nature was largely conceived through the general notions of the scientific view and through specific ideas derived from the new attitudes toward motion and the law of inertia. A human being was observed as the object that, above all else, tended to preserve itself or to persist in its being. This is the origin of the ceaseless desire for power which is never an end in itself but always a means toward self-preservation (Hobbes). It is the source of defining pleasure as that which accompanies the increase of vital activity and pain as the accompaniment of the decrease of vital activity (Spinoza).

But when an individual desires self-preservation, she must also desire to preserve a particular kind of self. As a matter of actual fact different individuals desire to preserve many different kinds of selves, e.g., the selves of honor, pleasure, wealth, political power, strength, and scientific knowledge. Because the individual, like everything else, has a structure, it is possible to say that real essence can be discovered no matter what the actual and particular desires happen to be. It is in this interpretation of the human self that reason was recognized as an essential part of the individual's structure.

Beginning with the notion of a human being as an object, causally determined, the scientific ethics assumed an absolute individualism. Here, Hobbes would assert, the individual is a part of nature, since all of the universe is reducible to discrete particles of matter in motion. The person for Spinoza was an individual mode. For both, the individual was the material out of which a society is constructed.

2. The nature of society

Human beings cannot realize being (i.e., desires) alone. The individual was thought of as an object, and society was the totality of objects regulated in the interests of the individual object. Society was the political order that existed to provide security for the individuals that they might secure the good for their beings.

The origin of society was rooted in the absolute individualism which required mutual agreements that the extremes of individualism could be controlled if they were not to end in mutual destruction. An individual's inordinate desire to persist in being and reason were the basis for political sovereignty. Reason saw the end result of an unlimited absolute individualism, and reason discovered the means to curb a disordered individualism in the interests of an ordered society and ordered individuals.

The structure of the society rested upon the complete power of the sovereign. This power, it was supposed, would be rationally employed by the sovereign's own interest. There should be a minimum of government, for if the disruptive elements of life were kept under control the individuals would function properly. There thus developed the night-watchman theory of the state. Hobbes and Spinoza had little interest in the civil rights of the individual because it was not supposed that there would be a real conflict between the rights of the individual and those of the sovereign. Thomas Hobbes granted the individual no rights except to think as she wished so long as those thoughts were not revealed. Spinoza insisted upon the right of free thought and speech. But the difference between the two men was not primarily a difference in principle. Both asserted that the government should extend only to those areas of life which it could control. Hobbes believed the sovereign was able to control speech, Spinoza thought the government was not able to control the expression of ideas.

Living as they did in a time of civil and international warfare, Hobbes and Spinoza could not but recognize the conflict existing in society. But this social conflict, as well as any individual disorder, they attributed to a simple cause, the failure of persons to recognize and accept the proper shape of nature. If individuals saw the centrality of reason in life, they would not be disrupted by the passions. If individuals recognized that a strong sovereign was in their own interests, they would support a centralized authority who would grant them their basic need of security that they might be free from external limitations. In short, throughout their views of the individual and society was the pervasive belief in harmony.

3. The object of moral judgment

The ethics of Hobbes and Spinoza were directed toward a judgment of (a) persons and their achievements and (b) the consequences of actions.

These objects can be clarified by negative statements. There was no judgment in their ethics of motives of persons if such a judgment implied blame or praise. The moral judgment of an individual is a purely factual statement about individual characteristics in relation to a norm. The consequence of this position was that moral responsibility was explained in nonmoral terms, which meant that moral responsibility was explained away. And just as there could be no uniquely ethical responsibility, so there was no ethical blame.

In the ethics there were no basic criticisms of the state, or of any human activity, unless it did not work. This followed from the facts that the object of moral judgment were acts with consequences and that, based upon a vision of an orderly nature, the scientific ethicists could not conceive of a disruptive fundamental conflict between the state and the individual.

4. The norm of moral good

Moral good was what is useful to the individual. This meant that whatever enabled the individual to be an individual was good. These factors were (a) power, in the sense of the capability of achieving individual being; (b) reason, mathematical-empirical and intuitive, that made possible knowledge of the individual and the world; and (c) a society that provided security so that power and reason might operate. From another perspective the individual who realizes being was thought good. From this view the norms of good were: (a) a relatively self-sufficient individual, determined by desires and directed by reason and not by external forces or forces alien to the individual's nature, and (b) the individual who realized the order of essential being.

5. How is the moral good known in a specific situation?

The answer to this question was apparently simple. When confronted by an ethical problem, the individual discovered the solution by reason. A moral problem was to be solved by the same method as an intellectual problem. Because scientific problems are answered by the mathematical-empirical method, ethical problems will be resolved in the same way. Science informs of uniformities, and the important uniformities for ethics are those that describe the human being. When mathematical-empirical reason comes across a discrepancy between an actual human being or activity and the uniformity it has revealed the individual to be, there will be the further rational step of pointing out how the disordered individual can become an ordered being.

Spinoza was not satisfied with the prevailing emphasis upon mathematical-empirical reason which revealed, he argued, only generalities or uniformities. What was needed was the linking of the general law to the unique in two directions, the unique particular and the unique whole of nature. There was thus the need to go beyond the purely mathematical-empirical to the intuitive in order to see every individual thing in relation to the whole of which it is a part, which would be to see everything "under the species of eternity."[141]

For Hobbes the recognition of the ethical good in any particular situation was a relatively simple matter for those who had a sufficient knowledge of mathematics and science. Spinoza emphasized the difficulty of attaining the perspective from which moral truth could be recognized. For him, this attainment required strenuous intellectual effort and emotional discipline. Only some persons have the capacity to achieve this.

6. The achievement of the moral good

The answer to this question was precisely the same as the answer to the question, "How is the moral good known in a specific situation?" To know the good would be to achieve the good. This followed from the psychology of the scientific ethicists. The will was not a separate entity; it was nothing other than the intellect.

But another side of the answer to this question was that the moral good could be achieved only when society freed the capable individual to seek the truth which, given the moral assumption of seventeenth-century science, would be to seek the good.

THE UNIQUE CONTRIBUTION OF THE SEVENTEENTH CENTURY

The ethics of the seventeenth century is obviously filled with conflicting views. Individuals disagreed with each other, and they not only disagreed intellectually but at times literally fought over moral issues. But in addition to conflict there are also extremes in convictions. For these reasons it is intellectually difficult and emotionally exhausting to try to keep the ideas of these individuals in mind at the same time. It is like inviting friends who are incompatible with each other to a Saturday night party. Argument there would be, disagreement also, but I would like to entertain the idea that if these persons could talk with each other long enough, they would discover that there was less fundamental conflict than they had initially thought.

I would like to explore the view that each of the individuals we have looked at in this century have made a significant contribution to moral truth, and that contrary to what this century may seem, the history of ethics is the history not of individuals quarrelling endlessly over problems that cannot be solved, but of the discovery and expanding of ethical truths, truths that are often difficult to discern and decipher. I would like to examine the prospect that each of these individuals was right in some of the most important areas he affirmed, but often wrong in matters of secondary importance or in what he denied. I would like to imagine that each of them adds a significant element to our understanding of what ethics is about and what the content of ethics is; consequently, if we are to develop an adequate personal ethic for ourselves, we need to be aware of their views and their points of viewing, building facets of their perspectives and positions into a consistent, comprehensive ethic of our own. If all of this is possible, then it may not be such a bad Saturday night party after all.

It is impossible to define briefly the perspective of each of these four persons and to say this constitutes their essential moral philosophy. They were each too complex, their interests too far-ranging for that. But having said it is impossible I want to identify the basic perspective of each person and then say, "These perspectives do not necessarily conflict. They are simply different. And each is needed in ethics."

Lilburne and Bunyan wanted to locate the self in the world religiously, that is, in relation to God, the one by a political thought that would lead beyond politics, the other by a story or metaphorical thought that would lead beyond metaphor. Hobbes and Spinoza were interested in locating the self philosophically in the world, the one attempting to do it empirically (and perhaps psychologically), and the other metaphysically (and perhaps psychologically). Lilburne and Bunyan were interested in a religious insight and motivation, while Hobbes and Spinoza were interested in a metaphysical vision and motivation. All four were interested in a moral agent living in a moral society.

However, if we look beyond these individuals to seventeenth-century Puritanism and science in general, some of these initial overlapping areas and concerns begin to diverge, and the guests at our party begin to drift off into separate rooms. In Puritanism itself we can note four important traits.

(1) The first is the centrality of direct experience. What was crucial was the journey, the pilgrimage toward a real (and yet ultimately unknown) goal. It was a journey that took place in the here and now and would continue after death. It was a journey that involved the individuals engaged in it in a restless creation of a holy community. This community stressed the importance of discipline and hard work.

(2) But if experience was central, the nature of that experience was equally central, and that experience was ultimately of sin and grace, of the fallen individual and his or her possible redemption and justification. Consequently, for the Puritan, the world was often sharply divided into "good" and "evil," though what was more important was that the good had the authority to order personal life in a renewed and vital way.

(3) In their search for truth and in their sometimes rigid division of the world, the Puritans, paradoxically perhaps, also helped significantly advance human rights. For theirs was a search which stressed the freedom of conscience and toleration, of speech and of writing; it stressed equal rights, the right to representational government and the right of property. It was a search which stressed most significantly the centrality of the moral life, and the individual's responsibility for improving the self.

(4) Finally, and perhaps this is the most important gift of the Puritan search, for the first time the ordinary person became the "reason" of history. The focus of the journey, the ceaseless creation of the holy community, the attempt to face sin and create the good: all this was done for the individual, that humanity might under God's grace receive a fuller and more complete life.

If there were four traits that distinguished Puritanism, it is also possible to elucidate four traits that distinguished seventeenth-century science:

(1) If the initial Puritan accent was on direct experience, this was equally true, though in another fashion, for the scientist. Here direct experience becomes a mathematical-empirical method. Here objectivity becomes a conscious principle, and the commitment to an objective truth becomes para-

mount. Certainly the Greeks had focused on objectivity as one of their own tenets, but in the seventeenth century, the scientists did not merely rediscover this Greek principle. They expanded it and went beyond it, enshrining truth and objectivity, and using this viewpoint for further exploration.

(2) Truth was to be discovered not merely for its own sake, but for the "goods" it could bring. Initially there was the belief in an authority that could be known by a mathematical-empirical method. That confidence expanded into the knowledge of authority through a metaphysical reason. But in both instances the aim was to control nature, whether it was the nature of the natural world or human nature. Nature itself became a good and simultaneously an essential means for achieving the good.

(3) In this desire for control there was already implicitly a nascent behaviorism. There was the belief that the individual self was a machine, self-maintaining and self-preserving, and that with the proper understanding of the parts, the good of the self could be created.

(4) In this assumption the ideal of science manifests its magnificence and simultaneously its superficiality. For the ideal of objective truth reconceived by the seventeenth-century scientists has had a profound effect on ethics, but this effect has been more indirect than direct, has been more in the created objects of science than in its metaphysics, more in its viewpoint than in its ability to make specific pronouncements about ethics.

Still, if we step back from the voices in the party, it is possible to see some of the commonality of their individual neighborhoods, for in the broad strokes seventeenth-century Puritanism and science share four views in common: In each (1) there is a belief that truth exists, although it is not finally possible to say what that truth is. In each, however, (2) what is crucial is the search, and in that search (3) reason plays an instrumental part. And using reason in the search for truth, there is the profound joint belief that (4) life can be controlled, the good can be achieved, and the individual human life can be improved.

As we listen to the voices in the party, observing for the time being that they have drifted into two separate groups, two final questions need to be addressed:

1. In the seventeenth century, what is the relation of religion to ethics, that is, how does one locate oneself with ethical religion in the world?

Religion, so various in human history, is difficult to define; but as trust in and loyalty to what most essentially is—such as it seems to have been for persons like Lilburne and Bunyan—it provides two qualities for ethics: vision and motivation. Religion gives in multiform ways a sense of something permanent in a transient existence, of something solid in an insubstantial world, of something valuable in the midst of relativities. The vision has been a reality for many persons who have portrayed it in history, but it has never become a reality. It is a vision of what is and could be but is not and, so far as the evidence goes, cannot be. The vision provides a model, intense, real, yet indefinite, of a moral person and a moral society.

And the experience of trust and loyalty, aided and abetted by what is known of adoration and gratitude, longing and forgiveness, provides a motive power, a stimulus.

Both vision and motivation combined confirm what is known by reason: aesthetics, public life and private endeavor, and moral experience. That is, to be a person in a human world is essentially to be a power, a will, an authentic author of one's life, living among and being sensitive and responsive to other persons, that is, to other powers, other wills, other authorities of existence.

2. In the seventeenth century what are the relations of science and metaphysics to ethics, that is, how does one locate oneself with moral rationality in the world?

Science is both a limiting and an enabling factor for moral rationality. On the one hand the believed and recognized "facts" and "truths" of science set the limiting conditions of the world in which reason must exist. On the other, scientific "knowledge" provides multidimensional maps of a world in which one makes one's way. Science for any one individual is always incomplete and imperfect, so the limiting conditions and the map are only provisional, although they provide essential provisions for the time being.

And this is, I believe, what the moral thinkers of the seventeenth century were pointing to, each in his own way, from their separate rooms at the same party.

NOTES

1. George Trevelyan, *Illustrated English Social History* (New York: Longmans, Green and Co., 1930), p. xi.

2. William Haller, *The Rise of Puritanism* (1938; Philadelphia: University of Pennsylvania Press, 1972), p. 18.

3. A. S. P. Woodhouse, *Puritanism and Liberty* (Chicago: Chicago University Press, 1951), p. 317.

4. Ibid., p. 42.

5. Ibid., p. 8.

6. John Milton, *De doctrina Christiana,* in *The Works of John Milton* (New York: Columbia University Press, 1933), 15: 357.

7. Woodhouse, *Puritanism and Liberty,* p. 245.

8. Ibid.

9. Ibid., p. 477.

10. Ibid., p. 247.

11. Ibid., p. 45.

12. Ibid., p. 263.

13. W. Shenk, *The Concern for Social Justice in the Puritan Revolution* (London: Longmans, Green and Co., 1948), p. 21. The quote itself is a reprint of an engraving by Hollar.

14. William Haller and Godfrey Davies, *The Leveller Tracts 1647–1653* (1944; New York: Columbia University Press, 1964), p. 18.

15. Schenk, *The Concern for Social Justice,* p. 24.

16. Haller and Davies, *The Leveller Tracts,* p. 11.

17. D. B. Robertson, *The Religious Foundations of Leveller Democracy* (New York: King's Crown Press, 1951), p. 14.

18. William Haller, *Tracts on Liberty in the Puritan Revolution 1638–1647* (New York: Columbia University Press, 1933), 2: 10, 7.

19. Woodhouse, *Puritanism and Liberty,* p. 57.

20. Ibid., p. 53.

21. Haller and Davies, *The Leveller Tracts,* pp. 1–2.

22. Ibid., p. 414.

23. Ibid., pp. 20–21.

24. Ibid., p. 31.

25. Woodhouse, *Puritanism and Liberty,* p. 317.

26. Ibid., p. 317.

27. Robertson, *Religious Foundations of Leveller Democracy,* p. 73.

28. Ibid., pp. 94–95.

29. Ibid., p. 94.

30. Ibid., p. 115.

31. Haller and Davies, *The Leveller Tracts,* p. 42.

32. Robertson, *Religious Foundations of Leveller Democracy,* p. 59.

33. Woodhouse, *Puritanism and Liberty,* pp. 39–40.

34. John Bunyan, *Pilgrim's Progress,* ed. James Wharey (Oxford: Clarendon Press, 1928), p. xxvii.

35. John Bunyan, *Grace Abounding to the Chief of Sinners* (Oxford: Clarendon Press, 1962), p. 3.

36. Ibid., p. 3.

37. Ibid., p. 102.

38. Ibid., pp. 102–103.

39. Ibid., p. 17.

40. Ibid., p. 6.

41. Ibid., p. 13.

42. Ibid., p. 14.

43. Ibid., p. 15.

44. Ibid., pp. 29–30.

45. Ibid., pp. 44–45.

46. Ibid., p. 72.

47. Ibid., p. 73.

48. Bunyan, *Pilgrim's Progress*, p. 292.

49. Ibid., p. 28.

50. Ibid., p. 38.

51. Ibid., p. 108.

52. Roger Sharrock, "Spiritual Autobiography in Pilgrim's Progress," *Review of English Studies* (1948): 101, n. 1.

53. Bunyan, *Pilgrim's Progress*, p. 212.

54. Arthur Kenyon Rogers, *The Socratic Problem* (New Haven: Yale University Press, 1933), p. 77.

55. Bunyan, *Pilgrim's Progress*, p. 222.

56. Ibid., p. 89.

57. Ibid., pp. 300–302.

58. John Bunyan, *The Pilgrim's Progess* (New York: New American Library, 1964), p. 298.

59. F. R. Leavis, *The Common Pursuit* (New York: George W. Steward Publisher, 1952), p. 206.

60. Alfred North Whitehead, *Science and the Modern World* (New York: Mentor Book, 1925), p. 23.

61. Haller and Davies, *The Leveller Tracts,* p. 320.

62. F. S. Taylor *A Short History of Science and Scientific Thought* (New York: W. W. Norton and Co., 1949), p. 135.

63. Thomas Hobbes, *Leviathan* (New York: E. P. Dutton Co., 1914), p. 1.

64. R. G. Collingwood, *The Idea of Nature* (Oxford: Clarendon Press, 1945), p. 102.

65. René Descartes, *Principles of Philosophy,* trans. Valentine Roger and Reese Miller (Holland: Reidel Publishing Company, 1983), p. 59.

66. Ibid., p. 61.

67. Charles Singer, *A Short History of Science: To the Nineteenth Century* (Oxford: Clarendon Press, 1941), pp. 209–10.

68. Whitehead, *Science and the Modern World,* p. 55.

69. Oliver Lawson Dick, *Aubrey's Brief Lives* (Ann Arbor: University of Michigan Press, 1957), p. 156.

70. Ibid., p. 150.

71. Thomas Hobbes, *The English Works of Thomas Hobbes of Malmesbury* (Darmstadt: Scientia Verlag Alen, 1966), 4: 414.

72. Dick, *Aubrey's Brief Lives,* p. 157.

73. Thomas Hobbes, *Leviathan* (New York: J. M. Dent & Sons, 1928), p. 49. All subsequent quotes from the *Leviathan* are from this edition.

74. Ibid., p. 43.

75. Ibid., p. 49.

76. Ibid., p. 50.

77. Ibid., p. 68.

78. Dick, *Aubrey's Brief Lives*, p. 83.
79. Hobbes, *Leviathan*, p. 9.
80. Ibid., p. 110.
81. Ibid., p. 111.
82. Ibid., p. 25.
83. Ibid., pp. 35–36.
84. Ibid., p. 83.
85. Hobbes, *English Works*, p. 48.
86. Ibid., p. 48.
87. Ibid., p. 49.
88. Ibid., p. 44.
89. Hobbes, *Leviathan*, pp. 67, 64.
90. Ibid., p. 89–90.
91. Ibid., p. 64.
92. Ibid., p. 65.
93. Ibid., p. 66.
94. Ibid., p. 83.
95. Ibid.
96. Ibid., p. 66.
97. Ibid., p. 67.
98. Ibid.
99. Ibid., p. 74.
100. Ibid.
101. Ibid., p. 89.
102. Ibid., p. 90.
103. Hobbes, *English Works*, p. 172.
104. Hobbes, *Leviathan*, p. 115.
105. Hobbes, *English Works*, p. 220.
106. Fischer Kuno, "Life and Character of Baruch Spinoza," in *Spinoza: Four Essays,* ed. W. Knight (London: Williams and Norgate, 1882), pp. 103–104.
107. Baruch Spinoza, *Spinoza's Ethics and "De Intellectus Emendatione"* trans. A. Boyle (New York: E. P. Dutton and Co., 1910), p. 229. All quotations are from this edition unless otherwise noted.
108. Spinoza, *Ethics*, p. 229.
109. Leon Roth, *Spinoza* (London: Ernest Benn Ltd, 1929), p. 178.
110. Kuno, "Life and Character of Baruch Spinoza," p. 308.
111. Spinoza, *Ethics*, p. 230.
112. Ibid., p. 231.
113. Benedict Spinoza, *Writings on Political Philosophy*, ed. A. G. A. Balz (New York: D. Appleton Century Company, 1937), pp. 81–82.
114. Ibid., p. 84.
115. Spinoza, *Ethics*, p. 68.
116. Ibid., pp. 1–2.
117. Ibid.
118. Baruch Spinoza, *The Correspondence of Spinoza,* ed. Abraham Wolf (New York: The Dial Press, 1927), p. 343.
119. Spinoza, *Ethics*, p. 11.
120. Acts: 17:28 (Revised Standard Version).
121. Spinoza, *Ethics*, p. 11.
122. Roth, *Spinoza*, pp. 145–46.

123. Spinoza, *Ethics,* p. 30. Some words have been added to enhance the meaning.

124. Ibid., p. 71.

125. Ibid., p. 1.

126. Ibid., p. 86.

127. Ibid.

128. Ibid., p. 1.

129. Ibid., p. 91.

130. Ibid., p. 92.

131. Ibid., p. 143.

132. Ibid., p. 38.

133. Ibid., p. 158.

134. Ibid., p. 118.

135. Ibid., p. 159.

136. Baruch Spinoza, *Ethics,* ed. James Guthman (New York: Hafner Publishing Co., 1949), pp. 272, 254.

137. Ibid., pp. 223–24.

138. Spinoza, *The Correspondence,* p. 206.

139. Spinoza, *Writings,* p. 65.

140. Spinoza, *Ethics,* p. 224.

141. Ibid., p. 216.

8

THE ETHICS OF THE ENLIGHTENMENT

In the seventeenth and eighteenth centuries new ideas and social forces battered the walls of the established order in society and the entrenched orthodoxy in the minds of those who were alive at that time. In economic life, the walls of mercantilism and the landed gentry were attacked; in the political order, those of monarchy and aristocracy; and in the minds of many, the walls of theological and philosophical dogmatism. The fires of the Enlightenment burned away old ideas and old institutions; and in those same fires the ideas which were to justify the institutions and permeating spirit which shape our lives were molded: political democracy, capitalism, a technological society, a scientific temper, nationalism, and humanitarianism.

These revolutions, with their origins in the past, were not always observable at the time. Yet we can look back and see in the transformations major fuming points in our lives. In the eighteenth century the significant revolutions were economic, political, and philosophical. The economic development of mercantilism, based upon a dynastic nationalism, reached a point of no return; the steady and slow political changes built to an eruption in the American and French revolutions; the scientific advances were justified by Hume and Kant in ways that would shape all later life.

We can easily misinterpret the changes, but we can scarcely overestimate their importance for our lives. That importance is this: our lives are dependent upon those institutions created by the Enlightenment, but we have forgotten the basic ideas which were the formative power for those institutions. We are the heirs of the Enlightenment, heirs who have spent the inherited capital and are living on the dwindling interest. Retaining and defending institutions given to us, we have lost the justifying reasons—the ethical faith and the confidence in natural order—by which those institutions were established. To change the metaphor, we live in houses built upon the foundations of the faith and ideas of specific individuals; but the rivers of time have washed away most of the foundations. We can no longer easily believe what men and women in the eighteenth century believed.

It is, therefore, of greatest importance that we understand the ideas and the persons that built our institutions, and that we question carefully what, if anything, of the faith of our past we can believe in the present. What, then, was the Enlightenment? What were the assumptions of the ethical faith of the eighteenth-century revolutions? What were the social conditions of those transformations? And what were the leading ethical views of those changing times?

WHAT WAS THE ENLIGHTENMENT?

In 1784 Immanuel Kant asked this same question: "Was ist die Aufklärung?"

> Enlightenment is man's release from his self-incurred tutelage. Tutelage is man's inability to make use of his understanding without direction from another. Self-incurred is this tutelage when its cause lies not in lack of reason but in lack of resolution and courage to use it without direction from another. *Sapere aude!* "Have courage to use your own reason!"—that is the motto of the enlightenment.[1]

Here is the basic faith of the Enlightenment: it is a moral faith that individuals with determination and courage can be self-reliant and self-governing. By the determined use of their understanding, individuals can comprehend the world and their place in it, and with this new understanding, by courage, they can master the world and control life for human good, creating a genuine community.

It is not surprising that those men of the Enlightenment who met in Philadelphia in 1776 should have affirmed a "respect for the opinions of mankind," "declare[d] the causes" of their action, maintained some "truths to be self-evident," and insisted that they ought to be and were "free and independent," concluding: "For the support of this declaration, and with a firm reliance on the protection of Divine Providence, we mutually pledge to each other our lives, our fortunes, and our sacred honor."[2]

Understood in this way the Enlightenment was not merely an eighteenth-century movement. A moral faith, with confidence in the individual and in human reason, the Enlightenment overflows the neat limits that are established for the periods of history. The Enlightenment did not begin in 1689 with John Locke and end in 1804 with the death of Immanuel Kant. As a faith, the elements in the Enlightenment go back beyond the boundaries of modern times to the Middle Ages and antiquity. In modern times its beginnings are to be found in the Reformation with its religious individualism and moral fervor, and in the Renaissance with its rationalism and humanism. The creation of natural science was a direct manifestation of the scientific temper of the Enlightenment, as the Puritan revolution was an indirect expression of the moral drive and individualism of the Enlightenment. Seventeenth-century scientists and Puritans had one foot in the door of the Enlightenment.

In the following century many persons forced the door open, and there was one development and three major revolutions that provide the basis for identifying the eighteenth century and the Enlightenment. The development was the further discovery of nature with the extension of scientific principles to the human world, to social and historical existence. This development made possible social science and social control.

The three major revolutions—economic, political, and philosophical—incorporated much of this new outlook. While most of the leaders in those revolutions castigated Hobbes and Spinoza, they accepted their essential insights, viz., the ideas of (a) the order of nature, including the human, (b) the possibility of reason comprehending this order, and (c) the beneficence of the natural order. Most of the leaders of the revolutions ignored the theological subtleties of the Puritans, but they did incorporate into their lives the moral fervor of their devoutly religious fathers. The religious attitude of the Enlightenment was the real foundation of this-worldly, anthropocentric humanitarianism. The men and women of the Enlightenment are often described as antireligious, as believing that human beings had no need of supernatural assistance, as possessing the confidence that the heavenly city would be built by human hands. Many, especially in France, were anticlerical and, in an age of progress, with good reason; many delighted in public expression of skepticism; many were indignant at the idea of miraculous supernatural aid; many had hope for the future. But few were fundamentally antireligious utopians. If you went into the childhood homes of the leaders of the Enlightenment, you would often find devout parents, and such leaders were unable to escape completely their childhood. They had, for the most part, lost the theological faith of their fathers, but those who lost the theology found an ethic.

So, if the Enlightenment, and its significance for our lives, is to be understood, we must examine the ethical assumptions of the time, the events that had a bearing upon the moral beliefs, and the lives and ethics of some men who both created and were symbolic of the revolutions of the era.

THE PRESUPPOSITIONS OF EIGHTEENTH-CENTURY ETHICS

The assumptions of the ethical theories which justified the revolutions of the eighteenth-century Enlightenment can be described in six propositions. From these presuppositions all of the dominant moral thought of the time developed.

1. Human beings are moral beings.

The proposition, so simply stated, has a double significance. First, all moral ideas must begin with a conception of the nature of what it means to be human. Ethical belief must, therefore, be grounded in matters of fact about this being. Second, an ethic discovered through a proper understanding of human nature will be universally valid, possessing a validity for all times and places. Human nature and morality are made for each other.

The belief that each individual is a moral being is not so much the kind of assumption that leads to a specific ethical theory as a motive for the creation of a moral theory. It does, however, eliminate the possibility of developing one type of ethics. The faith that "human beings are moral beings" makes it impossible to develop an egotistical ethical philosophy. But fundamentally the general perspective implies that an ethical view was part of the thinking of the time. Having lost the satisfaction of participating fully in a traditional religious faith, individuals in the eighteenth century created an ethical faith that enabled them to participate fully in the economic and political institutions.

The entire point of this basic assumption has been brilliantly stated by Ernst Cassirer: "The Enlightenment came more and more to set forth the self-sufficiency of morality as its fundamental postulate."[3]

2. As a moral being a human being is also a natural being.

Two forms of ethics become possible through the working assumption that individuals are a part of nature. First, there is the ethic of "inalienable right" (natural rights) and/or responsibilities, and there is a fundamental sense that these rights and responsibilities cannot be ignored. This is the eighteenth-century interpretation of an ethic of natural law.

From the view that human beings are natural beings there also develops an ethic that sees human activities in utilitarian terms. This was an extension of the scientific view that the natural world, like a machine, is orderly. Social institutions, if they are natural, must possess a basic order. It is not the superficial order of an apparent harmony or near harmony. It was just this apparent superficial order to which critics, especially late in the century, objected. But social institutions must exhibit a genuine order, and this order can be known only by the results of the working of the institutions. In particular, the economic and political life are known by their results.

3. Human beings can understand and control their own lives and society by comprehending the simplest parts and understanding how those parts relate to the whole.

This is a further effect of the scientific method which attempts to understand anything, say, the movement of the planets or of an arm, by breaking the activity down into its simplest parts and then by discovering how these parts fit together into a larger whole. In a comparable way, the ethics of the late Enlightenment were also based largely upon this kind of analysis. It was not *a priori* or theological, and this point of view made possible the development of political science, of economics, and of eighteenth-century sociology and associationist psychology.

But in extending the methods of natural science to the study of social and individual life something new was added. It was the attempt on the part of the most sophisticated thinkers of the time to comprehend the self and to find what makes the moral self possible. As we shall see, the empirical analyses of the British ethicists and the inquiries of Kant are attempts to describe the activities of the self and to discover the necessary structure that make possible a moral self.

In this extension of the methods of natural science the limits of those methods become clear. The adoration accorded Isaac Newton by the ethicists does not obscure from them the fact that their empirical interpretations of human behavior do not have the same precision as his mathematical-empirical interpretations of physical objects. Of greater importance is the fact that while reason is able to describe the goals of the moral desires and to direct individuals and societies toward these goals, pure reason of itself is not the source of moral judgments, nor are the methods of reason able to exhaust the meaning of the moral experience. Individuals may live by reason but not by reason alone. The nonrational factors are present in ethical experience.

4. In all things human the individual is the fundamental reality, and individual freedom is the key to social and individual moral achievement.

The individual is the simplest part of society. In the mechanical imagery of the time the state is an artificial person and the individual the only real person. The rights of society are thus to be determined by the conception of individual rights.

Since the individual is the fundamental reality with which moral judg-ments have to deal, the individual should be allowed to be an individual. Each person should be self-determining and self-reliant as far as this freedom from being controlled by others and independence from needing others is possible. But how far is this freedom possible? This is the question to which the eigh-teenth-century leaders thought they found satisfactory answers in their democ-ratic assemblies, in the pursuit of trade, and on the fields of battle.

5. Self-interest is a primary motivation for human behavior.

In the preceding century Thomas Hobbes had declared that a central fact about man was the "restless desire for power after power that ceaseth only in death." During the same period, at the time of the English civil war, the Pu-ritans asserted that "Man as man is corrupt and will be so."[4] This perspective continued among the Puritans, yet even with many of them it was comple-mented by a belief in natural human virtue. Among the non-Puritans the be-lief in "original sin" was secularized and softened. In Adam Smith self-in-terest was a dominant force, but, in certain aspects, it was morally neutral. In Joseph Butler self-love was a dominating factor, but he distinguished be-tween a legitimate self-love and an illegitimate selfishness. Yet generally the moral philosophers recognized there was in human life an endemic moral evil. Hume saw that all persons were guided by a natural preference for the self, and the philosopher who extolled human reason, Immanuel Kant, con-fessed that "there is something in the misfortune of my best friend that does not displease me."

6. A possible fundamental harmony exists for the individual and for society.

"Harmony" is one of the key words by which the Enlightenment is identified. There is good reason for the word, since faith in harmony pervaded the minds of these creative thinkers. The belief in harmony, and the power of human reason, was the basis for their optimism about human beings, human nature, and the future of humanity.

The leaders of the Enlightenment believed in harmony and were opti-mistic, but theirs was no naive faith or facile optimism. They were too deeply involved in the economic and political wars of their time to fail to see the re-ality of serious conflict. They were too close to human life to fail to observe the frequent pride, selfishness, and ignorance of men. Yet beyond conflict they believed, with faith in the order of nature, a harmony might develop. They recognized the pride and ignorance of human beings, but they also saw individual benevolence and understanding.

JOHN LOCKE (1632–1704) AND GREAT BRITAIN OF THE ECONOMIC AND POLITICAL REVOLUTIONS

John Locke has become the perfect symbol of eighteenth-century England. But Locke was in those days more than a symbol. He was a reservoir whose ideas, entering many streams of life, cut new channels in political and economic structure, produced new rapids in events of the century, and opened new lakes of philosophical thought. But since no century is the century of one person, so Locke must be understood as a symbol. No idea is perfectly original and pure, so the views of Locke must be seen as connected to his past as well as battle-slogans for the future. No philosophy, alone, is able to control life; therefore, the thought of Locke must be seen as it enters into the maelstrom of the social forces. But given these qualifications, the main point should be underscored all the more sharply that John Locke is the perfect symbol and a powerful fact in the life of eighteenth-century England.

A physician forced into retirement because of ill health, and in retirement driven to think and to write by his middle-class social position, his humane religious morality, and his insatiable curiosity, Locke is both symbol and fact in four main ways. First, he was defender of the new democratic faith of his social class. Second, his writings became the political Bible for the Whigs, the party in power during most of the eighteenth century. Third, his defense of the democratic faith includes revolutionary elements, elements that would be glossed over by a party in power but that would be perfectly plain to dispossessed men who wanted power. And fourth, he justified the ways of Newton to man. Locke attempted to develop a theory of knowledge that would validate the new science, and in this attempt he initiated that line of British empiricism in philosophy that has continued in importance in all fields of thought since his time.

In 1688 the new owners of property and business entrepreneurs, fearful of the power of the king, united with the landed aristocracy to elect a new monarchy under William and Mary. The effect of the Glorious Revolution was to make Parliament supreme as the maker of laws. Among the new laws passed immediately by Parliament was the Toleration Act of 1689, which granted religious liberty to all groups and, though it imposed political restrictions upon Catholics and Jews, gave social rights to the believers of all faiths. These developments were political acts. They were the product of adjustment and compromise between men, influenced by the moral attitudes of the individuals involved, and the results of expediency in the interests of new political forces. For those who initiated these developments there was no well-developed justifying philosophy, that is, there was none until it was produced by John Locke.

The subject of toleration was close to Locke's heart. It was the subject on which he first wrote and, at his death in 1704, he left unfinished a defense of toleration. The general basis for his plea was at once religious and philosophical: toleration is "so agreeable to the Gospel of Jesus Christ, and to the genuine reason of mankind." The specific argument he grounded upon the distinction between the church and the state, a distinction familiar to the toleration literature of the Puritans. So strongly did he maintain that radical belief in absolute freedom in religion that he insisted "neither pagan, nor Mahometan, nor Jew ought to be excluded from the civil rights of the commonwealth because of his religion."[6] However, Locke did feel that it was necessary to impose restrictions upon the rights of atheists because he argued it would be impossible to believe their oaths.

Freedom of religious belief extended to freedom of speech, and in a ringing statement Locke expressed the faith of the Enlightenment:

> The business of laws is not to provide for the truth of opinions, but for the safety and security of the commonwealth, and of every particular man's goods and person. . . . Truth certainly would do well enough, if she were once left to shift for herself. . . . If truth makes not her way into the understanding by her own light, she will but be the weaker for any borrowed force violence can add to her.[7]

In all his impassioned arguments for toleration Locke was holding to a central faith in the democratic balancing of liberty and equality: "The sum of all we drive at is, that every man enjoy the same rights that are granted to others."[8]

Political principles implicit in Locke's view of toleration are made explicit in the second treatise, "An Essay Concerning the Pure Original, Extent, and End of Civil Government." Government, Locke suggests, is the result of a contract made by men in the state of nature. We, naturally, "are born free, as we are born rational"[9] and indeed, "The freedom of man, and liberty of acting according to his own will, is grounded on his having reason, which is able to instruct him in that law he is able to govern himself by."[10] Man, then, with "a title to perfect freedom and uncontrolled enjoyment of all the rights and privileges of the law of nature . . . hath by nature a power . . . to preserve . . . his life, liberty, and estate."[11]

It is to make more secure these rights that men contract together to form a civil government. Such a government exists solely to guarantee the security and rights of property and person. If the government fails to meet its purpose the community may resist the violation of the fundamental contract.

The most basic right of the individual is the ownership of property. Again and again, with unmistakable clarity, Locke returns to this central point:

The great and chief end, therefore, of men's uniting into commonwealths, and putting themselves under government, is the preservation of their property.[12]

This right is not left without limitations by Locke, though the limitations may have been conveniently forgotten by his disciples. "As much land as a man tills, plants, improves, cultivates, and can use the product of, so much is his property."[13]

Insisting that the fundamental duty of the state was the protection of property, Locke also argued for a genuinely democratic government. He pleaded for a reform of the election laws extending the franchise. He urged that a people should protect themselves by division of the government into executive and legislative branches:

For he that thinks absolute power purifies men's blood, and corrects the baseness of human nature, need but read the history of this, or any other age, to be convinced of the contrary.[14]

Of greater importance was his plea for government by law and not by men:

Freedom of men under government is to have a standing rule to live by, common to everyone of that society and made by the legislative power erected in it.[15]

This work of John Locke was the handwriting on the wall of eighteenth-century England: defending the recent past he could not have prophesied with greater accuracy the future.

The political party controlling Parliament accepted the gospel according to Locke. The Whigs found two doctrines particularly comfortable: the idea that the people create a representative sovereign, and the view that the main purpose of government is the defense of property. From 1714 on there was no royal veto of any parliamentary action, and during the entire century, but especially until 1760, Parliament had prestige and power. During this time the main attempts of Parliament, emphasizing the two precious doctrines found in Locke, were to secure and extend the rights won in 1688, and to develop the colonial empire as well as foreign and domestic commerce.

But if Parliament had power, it was not a power derived from the people. During the century the electorate never totaled more than 85,000 persons out of a total population of six to nine million. Nor is this all. Shifting populations meant that some areas with no more than one or two voters, and occasionally with no voters, sent representatives to Parliament while the new heavily populated industrial towns had no representation at all. Locke had recognized and urged the reform of these "rotten boroughs." But a Parliament made up of merchants, lawyers, officers of the army and navy, and large landowners saw no need for self-reform. During the century, then, Parliament actually represented only a fraction of the nation, the landowners (who were dominant both in the Houses of Lords and Commons) and the merchants.

In 1779 one M.P. penned this marginal note on a trade paper: "No man shod be eligible to sit in the H of C that has not a competent knowledge in geography and the trade and manufacturers of Great Britain."[16] Parliament was, in this way, invaded by an economic spirit. The fiercest debates raged about economic policy, particularly the means to secure and expand commerce. All antagonists in these debates accepted the tenets of mercantilism, that economic system that was to be attacked by the economic revolutionaries. A portrait of mercantilism reveals clear personality traits: (1) the belief that money is the measure of wealth; (2) the insistence that trade is the chief means of accumulating money; (3) the view that there must be a favorable balance of trade; and, therefore, (4) the convictions that (a) colonies are essential and that (b) the colonies, existing mainly for the mother country, are to be controlled, as all commerce is controlled, by the state. Beneath these obvious traits the portrait of mercantilism reveals the inner character of the system to be a rising nationalism, a crass self-interest in which the merchant's profit is identified with the national good, and the absence of a belief in natural order.

The system was overcome by the economic and political revolutions. Those revolutions consisted of two parts: the ethical and economic ideas of individuals and the development of agriculture, trade, industry, and political relations. We shall observe in detail the ethical-economic and the ethical-political ideas of two leaders in those revolutions, Adam Smith and Thomas Jefferson.

THE ECONOMIC REVOLUTION

During the time that Adam Smith was creating his ethical and economic theories profound changes were occurring in agriculture, in trade, and in the social order. In the years 1740–1780 there existed a generation of men characteristic of the eighteenth-century ethos:

> A society with a mental outlook of its own, self-poised, self-judged, and self-approved, freed from the disturbing passions of the past, and not yet troubled with anxieties about a very different future which was soon to be brought upon the scene by the Industrial and the French revolutions. The gods mercifully gave mankind this little moment of peace between the reli-

gious fanaticisms of the past and the fanaticisms of class and race that were speedily to arise and dominate time to come. In England it was an age of aristocracy and liberty; of the rule of law and the absence of reform; of individual initiative and institutional decay; of Latitudinarianism above and Wesleyanism below; of the growth of humanitarian and philanthropic feeling and endeavor; of creative vigor in all the trades and arts that serve and adorn the life of man.[17]

In this period there were harbingers of the industrial revolution, but the impact of the changes in industrial organization was yet to be made when Smith wrote.

At the beginning of the century British agriculture was still essentially medieval. But about 1750, largely because of the gentleman-farmers who had the leisure to study agricultural problems, there began the widespread system of crop rotation, drill sowing, and cattle breeding that multiplied the farm product. In mid-century, too, the drive toward land enclosure was reintroduced and, for all practical purposes, completed. The effects of this policy were to improve agriculture and the profits of the landowner at the expense of the small farmer and the poorer classes.

Directly related to the land enclosure, as well as to the increase in trade and industry, was the rapid rise in population during the century. An increased population creates a need for increased necessities, and it was because England in the eighteenth century could provide those additional necessities and because of the improvement in health knowledge and conditions that the population grew so fast. There was no official census before 1801, but the estimates are that there were six million persons in England and Wales in 1700, six and one-half million in 1750, and nine million in 1801. As important as the population growth was the shift toward the industrial centers of the North and West, a shift that developed mainly in the last quarter of the century.

This population growth and change paralleled the changes in trade as evidenced by these startling figures of British foreign trade:

Year	Tonnage (in pounds)	Imports (in pounds sterling)	Exports (in pounds sterling)
1700	317,000	6,000,000	7,500,000
1725	450,000	7,000,000	10,000,000
1750	640,000	8,000,000	15,000,000
1775	840,000	14,500,000	17,500,000
1800	1,924,000	31,000,000	41,000,000

What was remarkable about the volume of trade during the century is that, apart from minor decreases during the brief war periods, there was a steady rise in foreign commerce until the last quarter of the century, when the trade volume skyrocketed.

These changes in trade accompanied changes in industry. During the century there were three major developments, especially in textiles and in the metal industries that, developing gradually in the first three quarters of the century, grew prodigiously in a few years: (1) the creation of new techniques (both mechanical and chemical) that made possible an increase in productivity; (2) the concentration of money and of enterprise in some industries and in commerce; and (3) the integration of production and trade, or the development of the merchant manufacturer. The results of these developments were an economic system that was essentially new and the growth of new social classes, especially those of the merchant manufacturers and the property-less wage earners.

In order to comprehend many of the ethical ideas of the nineteenth and twentieth centuries it is necessary to take into full account the detailed facts of these new creations. But when Adam Smith wrote, the new creations in trade and manufacture were still in the stage of germination: the flower and the later fruits had not yet matured. Even in the last quarter of the century the changes were so momentous and so complex that they could scarcely be understood by men living amidst those changes. It was part of the genius of Smith that, observing a seed that had never before been planted in human history, he envisaged something—certainly not all, but something—of what the flower and fruit might be if the seed were nurtured with the proper ethical and economic care.

Smith's life as a professor-citizen in Glasgow from 1751 to 1764 provided him with a unique sampling of the economic soil and the new seed. The ancient city of Glasgow (population in 1750: 23,000), with its medieval cathedral and university, became a modern city in those years as it grew into one of the leading centers of trade and industry. In 1724 Glasgow imported 4,100,000 pounds of tobacco from the New World; in 1771 it imported 47,268,873 pounds. The growth of the Glasgow textile industry had the same effects upon cotton imports. But this trade increase was not all, for added to the volume of trade was the variety of industry. The founding of new industries reads like a Chamber of Commerce brochure: 1742, tannery, linen printing and bleaching; 1747, copper and tin; 1748, pottery; 1750, carpet, silk, leather gloves, and the opening of the first bank. A few years later Smith helped protect James Watt within the wall of his college so that Watt might continue his experimentations with steam engines. Fully as important as the large trade and the variety of industry in influencing Smith's thought was the presence of enlightened merchants. In 1743 these merchants founded the first known "Political Economy Club" in history, whose members were pledged to examine the principles of foreign trade and to communicate their discoveries to each other. Shortly after he arrived in Glasgow as a teacher of belles-lettres and later of ethics, Adam Smith became a member of the club, read papers at its meetings, and became friends with the merchants and manufacturers. In this city and among these persons his ethical and economic mind was shaped.

THE ETHICAL THEORY OF THE ECONOMIC REVOLUTION OF ADAM SMITH

In 1776 Adam Smith published his Declaration of Independence. Like the other Declaration signed in Philadelphia, *Wealth of Nations* had an ethical basis. That basis was an ethical perspective and a view that had already been presented in great detail in Smith's *Theory of Moral Sentiments* (1759). But in comparison with the turbulent lives of many of the signers of the American declaration, Smith's life was dull and prosaic. On June 7, 1767, he wrote from his seclusion in Kirkaldy, Scotland, to an intimate friend, David Hume,

> My business here is study, in which I have been very deeply engaged. . . .
> My amusements are long solitary walks by the seaside. You may judge how
> I spend my time. I feel myself, however extremely happy, comfortable, and
> contented. I never was perhaps more so in all my life.[18]

Smith's life was one of serenity and of evenness of temper, the ideal life of the Enlightenment gentleman, scholar, and citizen of the world. It was un-ruffled except for his talking to himself and his lifelong absent-mindedness. Sir Walter Scott tells of how, when as a commissioner in Edinburgh Smith was given an official document to sign, he did not write his own name but copied carefully the signature of the commissioner who had signed before him. On another occasion, deep in conversation he absentmindedly rolled a piece of bread and butter in his fingers and dropped it into a teapot. A moment later he poured boiling water into the pot, and, when he drank the brew, pronounced it the worst tea he had ever tasted.[19]

The chronology of Smith's life, with its major turns, can be briefly related. In April 1723, his father, Adam Smith the elder, died; in June 1723, Adam the younger was born. This, and the fact that, disappointed in love, he never married, helps to explain the closeness of Smith's relation to his mother until her death.

When he was fourteen, young Adam, "a delicate child and already inclined to fits of absence of mind," went to study at Glasgow. There he came under the influence of the ethical and economic teaching of Francis Hutcheson (1694–1746), the renowned moral philosopher who was the originator of the phrase "the greatest good for the greatest number." In 1740, after three years' study at Glasgow, Smith received a scholarship to Oxford. The scholarship was granted on the expectation that he take orders in the church, but he did not find "the ecclesiastical profession suitable to his taste." While he studied for six years at Oxford he found little in the university teaching to appreciate, spending most of his time in reading. Despite frequent letters to his mother, little in detail is known of those years beyond such typical reports as the one written on November 29, 1743: "I am just recovered from a violent fit of laziness, which has confined me to my elbow-chair these three months."[20]

In 1748 Smith returned to Glasgow to lecture on literature for three years. When he was twenty-nine he was elected to the chair of moral philosophy in which he discussed natural theology, ethics, the political institutions based upon justice (jurisprudence), and the political institutions founded upon expedience (political economy). In 1759 he published *Theory of Moral Sentiments* and, says his biographer, "took his place, by almost immediate and universal recognition, in the first rank of contemporary writers."[21]

Smith lectured for the last time in 1764, after which he became the traveling companion of a young aristocrat. The position paid well. He received 300 pounds not only for each of the three years he traveled but also for the twenty-three remaining years of his life. In those three years of travel, mainly in France, Smith lived in the world of sophisticated intellectuals and was received in the best salons of Paris. He became close friends with many of the French philosophers, particularly the Physiocrats with whom he agreed in many basic economic ideas.

Returning to England in 1766, Smith spent six months in London reading in the British Museum. He retired to the family home in Kirkaldy to live with his mother, and until his death he left Kirkaldy only on rare occasions. Once in 1773 he went to London to discuss in detail the manuscript of *Wealth of Nations* with Prime Minister Horace Walpole and with Benjamin Franklin, the American elder statesman. When first published in 1776 the book had a quiet success. Gradually it became more powerful in its influence, so that the historian Buckle commented, "in its ultimate results [it is] probably the most important book that has ever been written."[22]

William Pitt, who gave credit to *Wealth of Nations* for new governmental policies, was speaking for himself and for history when Smith visited some dignitaries in London. All present rose when Smith entered the room, and the prime minister insisted that Smith be seated first "for we are all your scholars."[23] Now, "much with the ministry" and a close friend of Edmund Burke and other M.P.s as well as Pitt, Smith had become a brain-truster. A brain-truster and an economist, he was first and last the moral philosopher. In 1788, two years before his death, he revised the fifth edition of *Moral Sentiments,* though from his death-bed in 1790 he insisted that sixteen volumes of his unpublished manuscripts be burned.[24]

To understand the motifs of Smith's thought it is necessary to remember the social setting for that thought and the perspective of his mind. He lived during the commercial revolution but before the major industrial transformations and the development of corporate capitalism. He never escaped the Enlightenment belief that "human beings are moral beings." This ethical outlook places his economic writings in proper focus and provides the fundamental harmony in his thought.

Smith had a clear grasp of the problems he thought worth considering in ethics:

> In treating of the principles of morals, there are two questions to be considered. First, wherein does virtue consist, or what is the tone of temper and tenor of conduct which constitutes the excellent and praiseworthy character? . . . And, secondly . . . how and by what means does it come to pass that the mind prefers one tenor of conduct to another; denominates the one right and the other wrong . . . ?[25]

In solving these two problems his thought was influenced throughout by the ethical assumptions of the Enlightenment. The second problem is the analysis of how individuals make moral judgments, and here Smith accepts the viewpoint of scientific description. In the first problem, that of constructing a normative ethic, Smith attempted to incorporate the scientific perspective with other assumptions, viz., that human beings are moral beings and therefore ethics cannot be defined in nonmoral or immoral statements; that there is a natural order which provides the basic structure for a normative ethic; that the systems of the individual and society can be understood by analyzing the parts and how they should fit together to work properly; that the individual is the basic ethical reality; and that beyond all the real conflict is a possible harmony, a harmony that does not eliminate the conflict but gives it meaning.

1. Ethical analysis: How do individuals make moral judgments?

In his description of how individuals make moral judgments, Smith presented a psychological and sociological analysis. In that analysis he discussed moral judgments of two major kinds: those that refer to what is proper or improper (the judgment of approval or disapproval, that a character deserves praise or blame) and those that refer to merit or demerit (the judgment that a person should be rewarded or punished for his act). The first judgment is of persons, motives, and character. The second is of consequences. Two key terms, "sympathy" and "the impartial spectator," provide the clue to his theory.

"Sympathy" is the basic psychological principle of "fellow-feeling," of "feeling what another self feels." Smith used the term in a recognized eighteenth-century meaning and not with a twentieth-century definition, since he did not define "sympathy" as "pity," nor did he think of "sympathy" as a moral quality. Thus, the person who acts from self-interest acts on the basis of "sympathy" no less than the individual who acts from benevolence. The difference is that the two have a fellow-feeling of a different kind and with different selves: the one who acts from self-interest has a fellow-feeling with his interested self, the other who acts from benevolence has a fellow-feeling with his neighbor. Thus while sympathy is not the only means by which both other persons and the self are judged, it is an essential means of moral judgment, and understood in this way it is an important source-principle for interpersonal relations and for an individual's ethical life.

The "impartial spectator" is a moralized sympathy. There are two levels of sympathy: the first is the amoral fellow-feeling in which no value judgments are made; the second is the ethical fellow-feeling in which we can "entirely sympathize with" (i.e., morally approve) the motives or feelings of another. This second activity, that of the impartial spectator, implies that human beings are moral beings: that they not only can experience the feelings and motives of another self, but can also pass judgment upon the other. And this is true for self-judgment as well as for judging others:

> The principle by which we naturally either approve or disapprove of our own conduct seems to be altogether the same with that by which we exercise the like judgments concerning the conduct of other people. We either approve or disapprove of the conduct of another man according as we feel that, when we bring his case home to ourselves, we either can or cannot entirely sympathize with the sentiments and motives which directed it. And, in the same manner, we either approve or disapprove of our own conduct according as we feel that, when we place ourselves in the situation of another man and view it, as it were, with his eyes and from his station, we either can or cannot entirely enter into and sympathize with the sentiments and motives which influenced it. . . . We endeavor to examine our own conduct as we imagine any other fair and impartial spectator would examine it. If, upon placing ourselves in his situation, we thoroughly enter into all the passions and motives which influenced it, we approve of it by sympathy with the approbation of this supposed equitable judge.[26]

In this analysis of how persons make moral judgments Smith was not creating a normative theory but was attacking the basic positions of three types of normative theories. First, he was objecting to a rationalistic ethic: reason alone is not the basis for moral judgments. While he agreed with many of the moral principles of the rationalists (e.g., the sophists or Thomas Aquinas), he denied that reason led them to those moral principles or that reason alone can verify their moral views. Second, he was expressing opposition to those theories which base moral judgments upon individual preferences or emotion (e.g., the sophists or Thomas Hobbes). Preference and emotion are always present in a moral judgment and oftentimes, he pointed out, they distort the judgment. But no person can escape his impartial spectator, the moral alterego of the self. Third, Smith was objecting to all moral theories which had authoritative and precise definitions of the morally good. The impartial spectator is a living person and not a dead code, and what this spectator judges can only be known by actual sympathy with the impartial spectator. The moral good must be known in experience, not in definitions.

Ethical distinctions are valid, and this validity is guaranteed by the impartial spectator who is the rationalized and emotionalized representative of the ethical interpersonal society. All these factors combine in a specific case to produce a valid moral judgment: reason, emotion, the interpersonal society, objectivity, and ethical approval or disapproval.

> When we approve of any character or action, the sentiments which we feel are . . . derived from four sources which are in some respects different from one another. First, we sympathize with the motives of the agent; secondly, we enter into the gratitude of those who receive the benefit of his actions; thirdly, we observe that his conduct has been agreeable to the general rules by which these two sympathies generally act; and last of all, when we consider such actions as making a part of a system of behavior which tends to promote the happiness either of the individual or of the society, they appear to derive a beauty from this utility not unlike that which we ascribe to any well-contrived machine.[27]

This answer given by Smith to his initial inquiry, "How do individuals make moral judgments?" is enriched by a wealth of illustrative detail, unique insights into the workings of individual minds, and an urbane style of writing. The answer provides evidence of his serene life, and of his calm and careful observation of himself and other persons.

2. Ethical construction: What is moral good?

Smith's true character is revealed more fully in the answer given to the other question of ethics, "Wherein does virtue consist, or what is the tone of temper and tenor of conduct which constitutes the excellent and praiseworthy character?" The answer is that the impartial spectator will judge that act, motive, person to be "good" which is the expression of a proper prudence, benevolence, justice, self-command, or a correct combination of these characteristics. To understand this ethic we must recognize the meaning of each virtue.

When we consider the character of any individual, we naturally view it under two different aspects; first, as it may affect his own happiness, and secondly, as it may affect that of other people.[28]

"Prudence" is the result of a concern for our own happiness. "Benevolence" and "justice" are the products of an interest in the happiness of others. "Self-command" does not result from a concern for happiness but from "the sense of propriety," from a "respect for what are, or for what ought to be, or for what, upon a certain condition, would be, the sentiments of other people."[29]

(a) In recommending *prudence* as a great virtue Smith was recommending the familiar Scot prayer: "O Lord, give us a guid conceit of ourselves."

The care of the health, of the fortune, of the rank and reputation of the individual, the objects upon which his comfort and happiness in this life are supposed principally to depend, is considered as the proper business of that virtue which is commonly called prudence.[30]

The preservation and concern for the body are "the objects which nature first recommends to the care of every individual." Through training in childhood, that responsibility to the self extends to other areas than physical preservation and health. But prudence alone, "though it is regarded as a most respectable and even, in some degree, as an amiable and agreeable quality, yet it never is considered as one either of the most endearing or of the most ennobling virtues."[31]

Prudence, therefore, needs to be combined with many greater and more splendid virtues, with valor, with extensive and strong benevolence, with a sacred regard to the rules of justice, and all those supported by a proper degree of self-command. This superior prudence, when carried to the highest degree of perfection, necessarily supposes the art, the talent, and the habit or disposition of acting with the most perfect propriety in every possible circumstance and situation. It necessarily supposes the utmost perfection of all the intellectual and all the moral virtues. It is the best head joined to the best heart.[32]

(b) *Benevolence* is sometimes defined in negative terms, i.e., refraining from hurting others, and sometimes in positive terms, an active concern for the happiness of others.

A sacred and religious regard not to hurt or disturb in any respect the happiness of our neighbor, even in those cases where no law can properly protect him, constitutes the character of the perfectly innocent and just man; a character which . . . can scarce ever fail to be accompanied with many other virtues—with great feeling for other people, with great humanity and great benevolence.[33]

Benevolence, unlike justice, is "free and cannot be extorted by force." Sometimes it is based upon gratitude; sometimes it goes beyond gratitude.

(c) *Justice* is contrasted with benevolence in that it is a matter of law and not of freedom. It is, "upon most occasions, but a negative virtue and only hinders us from hurting our neighbor."[34] Justice in this negative sense is absolutely essential for society:

> Society however cannot subsist among those who are at all times ready to hurt and injure one another. . . . If there is any society among robbers and murderers, they must at least, according to the trite observation, abstain from robbing and murdering one another. . . . Justice . . . is the main pillar that upholds the whole edifice. If it is removed, the great, the immense fabric of human society, that fabric which to raise and support seems, in this world, if I may say so, to have been the peculiar and darling care of nature, must in a moment crumble into atoms.[35]

Justice thus presupposes individual freedom and individual rights.

> The origin of natural rights is quite evident. That a person has a right to have his body free from injury and his liberty free from infringement unless there be a proper cause, nobody doubts. But acquired rights such as property require more explanation. Property and civil government very much depend on one another. The preservation of property and the inequality of possession first formed it, and the state of property must always vary with the form of government.[36]

These interpretations of benevolence and justice are based primarily upon individualism and rationalism. Individuals and societies, however, are recommended to an individual's concern by their relations of importance. These are: the relations of the interpersonal life (e.g., the members of one's own family, or of those who are of service and whose personal qualities one can most easily sympathize with) and of social structure (e.g., the nation is the society most significant for every person).

But there is also a universal benevolence that arises, Smith believes, from a religious faith:

> The wise and virtuous man is at all times willing that his own private interest should be sacrificed to the public interest of his own particular order of society. He is at all times willing, too, that the interest of this order of society should be sacrificed to the greater interest of the state or sovereignty of which it is only a subordinate part: he should, therefore, be equally

willing that all these inferior interests should be sacrificed to the greater interest of the universe, to the interest of that great society of all sensible and
intelligent beings of which God himself is the immediate administrator and
director.[37]

(d) *Self-command,* the capacity to act from freedom with restraint, with
discipline that is self-rule, is the result of acting from a sense of propriety or
moral right. In some respects, particularly since it enhances the other virtues,
it is the greatest virtue of character, though it is not the greatest virtue in an
ethic of consequences.

> To act according to the dictates of prudence, of justice, and proper benefi-
> cence, seems to have no great merit where there is no temptation to do oth-
> erwise. But to act with cool deliberation in the midst of the greatest dangers
> and difficulties; to observe religiously the sacred rules of justice in spite
> both of the greatest interests which might tempt, and the greatest injuries
> which might provoke, us to violate them; never to suffer the benevolence of
> our temper to be damped or discouraged by the malignity and ingratitude of
> the individuals towards whom it may have been exercised, is the character
> of the most exalted wisdom and virtue. Self-command is not only itself a
> great virtue, but from it all the other virtues seem to derive their principal
> lustre.[38]

Smith frequently points to the difficulty of acting from self-command
and indeed the impossibility of achieving moral perfection, but these are a
part of the necessary discipline for character, and they enhance the worth of
moral achievement. Smith is aware, too, that the virtues may conflict with
each other. An individual must be willing to sacrifice self-interest for the interest of the society. The conflict between virtues, or between individuals and
societies, is an important but not a final conflict. The hope for harmony pervades all understanding of disorder.

This ethic developed in *Theory of Moral Sentiments* forms a necessary
window through which *Wealth of Nations* must be viewed. The main ideas of
the ethical and economic theories were developed at the same time, and after
he wrote his political economy Smith republished his ethic. To those who
find an irreconcilable conflict between the two writings, with the economic
theory based upon an immoral (or at best amoral) self-interest, four interpre-
tative facts may be stated. (1) Self-interest as understood by Smith is not to
be equated with selfishness. In economic life it may be an expression of prudence, though it is also evident to Smith that much economic self-interest is
quite different from prudence. (2) Political economy does not encompass the
whole life; so it is possible to have one area of life dominated primarily by
prudence (and other forms of expedience) and others dominated by other

virtues (and their corruptions). (3) Smith nowhere states that self-interest is the only motive in the economic life. What he does say in those famous sentences that have become the text for interpretations of his "immoral economic theory" is:

> It is not from the benevolence of the butcher, the brewer, or the baker that we expect our dinner, but from their regard to their own self-interest. We address ourselves, not to their humanity, but to their self-love, and never talk to them of our own necessities but of their advantages.[39]

He does not say that the butcher, brewer, and baker cannot have any benevolence toward us when they provide our food, though he clearly thinks that this would not be a sufficient cause for those actions. Their self-love is such an adequate cause. What is of greater importance is the assumption that they must satisfy the rules of justice in their economic self-interested activities. One passage from *Moral Sentiments* points toward the ethical basis of *Wealth of Nations*:

> In the race for wealth and honors and preferments, [each man] may run as hard as he can, and strain every nerve and every muscle, in order to outstrip all his competitors. But if he should jostle, or throw down any of them, the indulgence of the spectators is entirely at an end. It is a violation of fair-play, which they cannot admit of.[40]

(4) But evidence that the economic theory is based upon an ethical view is even more evident in *Wealth of Nations* itself. There are three kinds of moral judgments in that book: first, judgments concerning the purposes of economic activity; second, evaluations of the economic groups in society; and third, criticisms of the means for achieving social ends.

In describing the purpose of economic activity Smith comments that the moral basis is so clear that it scarcely needs to be mentioned:

> Consumption is the sole end and purpose of all production; and the interest of the producer ought to be attended to only so far as it may be necessary for promoting that of the consumer. The maxim is so perfectly self-evident, that it would be absurd to attempt to prove it.[41]

To make the interests of the consumer primary in an economic system is to make a moral judgment. It is to say that the needs of individuals, which can be met by consumption of goods, are basic. With this insistence that consumption is the ultimate end of economic activity, Smith is demonstrating an acceptance of the moral aphorism of his teacher, Francis Hutcheson, that the economic system should serve "the greatest good of the greatest number."

This is the expression of a basic moral individualism. But a society based upon a moral individualism must be concerned not with one class or with only some of the people. The concern of an adequate economy must be for all persons.

> Political economy, considered as a branch of the science of a statesman or legislator, proposes two distinct objects: first, to provide a plentiful revenue or subsistence for the people, or more properly to enable them to provide such a revenue or subsistence for themselves; and secondly, to supply the state of commonwealth with a revenue sufficient for the public services.[42]

The national real income is thought of in terms of per capita income. Smith's moral outlook, the fact that he was "vigorous and weighty in his denunciation of wrong," is so evident in *Wealth of Nations* that it is difficult to account for how the ethical perspective has been so frequently ignored except that "the father of capitalism" has been used to justify an economic system that he never envisaged and to defend an economic class of which he was deeply suspicious.

He was sympathetic to the wage earners and critical of the merchant-manufacturers.

> Our merchants and master-manufacturers complain much of the bad effects of high wages in raising the price, and thereby lessening the sale of their goods both at home and abroad. They say nothing concerning the bad effects of high profits. They are silent with regard to the pernicious effects of their own gains. They complain only of those of other people.[43]

The members of this group continually cooperate with each other in their own interests, so the government should carefully refrain from enacting legislation that would assist them in making trade agreements or in developing monopolistic practices.

> People of the same trade seldom meet together, even for merriment and diversion, but the conversation ends in a conspiracy against the public, or in some contrivance to raise prices. It is impossible indeed to prevent such meetings by any law which either could be executed or would be consistent with liberty and justice. But though the law cannot hinder people of the same trade from sometimes assembling together, it ought to do nothing to facilitate such assemblies, much less to render them necessary.[44]

The ethical criticism of the "merchants and master-manufacturers" does not stop at this point. The crux of the matter is that the interests of this group and that of society are often in irreconcilable conflict.

The interest of the dealers, however, in any particular branch of trade or manufactures, is always in some respects different from, and even opposite to, that of the public. To widen the market and to narrow the competition is always in the interest of the dealers. To widen the market may be agreeable enough to the interest of the public, but to narrow the competition must always be against it, and can serve only to enable the dealers, by raising their profits above what they naturally would be, to levy, for their own benefit, an absurd tax upon the rest of their fellow-citizens. The proposal of any new law or regulation of commerce which comes from this order ought always to be listened to with great precaution, and ought never to be adopted till after having been long and carefully examined, not only with the most scrupulous, but with the most suspicious attention. It comes from an order of men whose interests are never exactly the same with that of the public, who have generally an interest to deceive and even to oppress the public, and who accordingly have, upon many occasions, both deceived and oppressed it.[45]

The interests of the two other major economic groups, the landlords and wage earners, however, always parallel the public interests. Smith despised the landlords, as he despised all those who made a living without work, but he felt their interests were identical to those of society. This is true, too, for the wage earners, the group toward which Smith exhibited the most sympathy. Years of prosperity mean good times for landlords and workers but not necessarily for merchants and manufacturers, since the degree of profit in an industry or enterprise does not depend upon general prosperity. Smith argued that profits are usually high in poor countries and highest in societies "which are going fast to ruin."

The employees should receive fair wages, and Smith, in a succinct statement, marshals both economic and ethical arguments to support this contention.

Servants, laborers, and workmen of different kinds, make up the far greater part of every great political society. But what improves the circumstances of the greater part can never be regarded as an inconveniency to the whole. No society can be flourishing and happy, of which the far greater part of the numbers are poor and miserable. It is but equity, besides, that those who feed, clothe, and lodge the whole body of the people, should have such a share of the produce of their own labor as to be themselves tolerably well fed, clothed, and lodged.[46]

It is the description of how a society can best realize the purposes of its economy for which Smith has become most famous. This description involved an intensive attack upon the reigning economic system and an advocacy of the freedom of trade, "the simple system of natural liberty." In understanding this aspect of his thought, it is essential to remember that Smith wrote in terms of the concepts and situations of his time.

He attacked mercantilism with the arguments that the system was both immoral and unworkable.

> In the mercantile system the interest of the consumer is almost constantly sacrificed to that of the producer; and it seems to consider production, and not consumption, as the ultimate end and object of all industry and commerce.[47]

Nor, ethically, is this the only fault. The international consequences of the system that restricts trade through tariffs, monopolies, and other types of control must be recognized.

> Nations have been taught that their interest consisted in beggaring all their neighbors. Each nation has been made to look with an invidious eye upon the prosperity of all the nations with which it trades, and to consider their gain as its own loss. Commerce, which ought naturally to be, among nations as among individuals, a bond of union and friendship, has become the most fertile source of discord and animosity. The capricious ambition of kings and ministers has not, during the present and preceding century, been more fatal to the repose of Europe than the impertinent jealousy of merchants and manufacturers. . . . The mean rapacity, the monopolizing spirit of merchants and manufacturers, who neither are, nor ought to be the rulers of mankind, though it cannot perhaps be corrected, may very easily be prevented from disturbing the tranquillity of anybody but themselves.[48]

Economically, the system has not worked because it was based upon false ideas. It assumed that a nation's wealth consists in money, that nations can profit only at the expense of other nations, that government must regulate business and strictly control its colonies. Against these ideas Smith argued that a nation's wealth consisted in the consumable goods it produced, that nations could profit mutually by commerce, and that there should be a freedom of competition and trade.

He did not believe, however, that the freedom of trade would come easily, or that it would ever be complete. To expect a perfect freedom in trade would be as absurd as to expect a utopia. "Not only the prejudices of the public, but, what is more unconquerable, the private interests of many individuals irresistibly oppose it."[49]

The motto "laissez-faire" (a term which Smith did not use as descriptive of his economic theory) is likely to be misleading to those whose livelihood depends upon an economic system different from what Smith knew. For what Smith was trying to avoid with his new proposals was (a) an economic attitude directed exclusively to production or profits and not to consumption; (b) monopoly; (c) wage and price fixing by groups of "merchants and master-manufacturers"; and (d) legislation, especially tariffs and granting of monopolies, that restricted competition, the development of new industries and new trade. He was advocating a free competition between individuals. In one sense this might be thought of as Hobbes's "warfare of each against all"; but it was not nasty, brutish, and short because with an ethical basis it was a warfare of equals. Equality would prevent any one person or group from gaining absolute power. And the ethical basis was present in the fact that the economic competition must exist according to the rules of justice.

> All systems either of preference or restraint therefore being then completely taken away the obvious and simple system of natural liberty establishes itself of its own accord. Every man, as long as he does not violate the laws of justice, is left perfectly free to pursue his own interest his own way, and to bring both his industry and capital into competition with those of any other man, or order of men.[50]

Government has the responsibility of insuring justice in the society. This is to protect, "as far as possible, every member of society from the injustice or oppression of every other member." In addition, the government has two other functions: the protection of society from external enemies and the establishment of certain public services. The given services will benefit all the members of the society and are established because the profit from the service is likely to be insufficient to repay a private enterprise. These services are of two major types, those that benefit commerce and those that promote "the instruction of the people." In the former Smith would place the construction of roads, bridges, canals, harbors, and communication. In the latter he places public schools. Both were at the time radical proposals.

Apart from these public services the economic activities are to be the responsibility of free individuals. This is the natural order; this will produce the most beneficial results for society. For each individual, although often the action may not be intentional, helps to realize the good of the society:

> He generally, indeed, neither intends to promote the public interest nor knows how much he is promoting it. By the support of the domestic to that of foreign industry, he intends only his own security; and by directing that industry in such a manner as its produce may be of the greatest value, he intends only his own gain; and he is in this, as in many other cases, led by an invisible hand to promote an end which was not part of his intention.[51]

This belief in the beneficence and harmony of the natural order did not obscure for Smith the reality of conflicts in social life, nor did it lead him to a facile optimism for the future. He was writing a declaration of independence from an unjust and unworkable economic system. He was advocating, he thought, not a utopia, but a better economic system.

That "obvious and simple system of natural liberty" had an ethical foundation. It had its roots in the conviction that human beings and morality are made for each other. The nature of human beings and morality can be understood through analysis and reconstruction of the natural order, in which the individual is most important and has rights and social responsibilities, and in which there exists—if human beings will but recognize the truth and act upon this recognition—a pervasive harmony of life with life.

THE POLITICAL REVOLUTION AND THE AMERICAN ETHIC

In the American ethical autobiography 1775 to 1787 were years of trauma. During those days many lucid statements of the American ethic were made. The expressions might have been forgotten save that the words of freedom and equality were welded together with some redeeming deeds. It was such a linking of words and deeds that forged the first chain of the American ethic.

The words and deeds are not always easily identifiable since the revolution was not a battle of light against darkness, or American freeman against British tyrant, true patriot against disloyal Tory, good against evil. Such an interpretation would be false to the facts of revolutionary life. In the 1770s there were many persons in England who looked with alarm upon the governmental policy toward the colonies, and there were many in the colonies who believed that the radical revolutionists committed treason against their country and fomented trouble in the social order. During the early days of the war perhaps one-third of all the colonists remained loyal to the established British political authority, one-third were willing to sign away their lives with the members of the Continental Congress, and one-third were for minding their own affairs. Among the Tories there were many good men who wanted a decent society. And each true patriot who was willing to sign away his life was driven by various motives: some were professional agitators, some were debtors with nothing to lose, some were men with a lust for excitement, and some were merchants who wanted a freer and larger market. In fact, the conflict at first was mainly economic, and economic battles are frequently inflamed by self-interest.

Seventeen eighty-seven and the Constitution were possible only because of 1776 and the Declaration of Independence. But there were other years besides 1776 and 1787, and other events besides the signing of a Declaration and debating a constitution. All those years had their sources in the past, in earlier events of colonizing struggles and in the remote life of Greece and Rome, the communities of the Hebrews and early Christians, and Anglo-Saxon history. Nor was this relation of the present to the past vague for revolutionary leaders. Many were conscious not only of contemporary thought but of their history; so again and again they pointed back to Cicero and Socrates, to the prophets and to Jesus, and to Anglo-Saxon liberties.

THE COLONIES, THE REBELLION, AND THE SOVEREIGN STATES

When in the 1770s various parties began to look with greater interest at the British colonies in North America, what they saw depended in large part upon who they were and where they lived. To a British cabinet and king living in London the colonies appeared in the morning glow of empire, a glow that cast a new light upon the undeveloped possibilities of colonial possessions. The slow, gray dawning of empire had been long advancing. It had begun with exploration and settlement of new lands, and its gravitational pull had been mercantilism. These new lands had been settled for reasons religious, political, and economic, but the official policy came to look upon those settlements as means of directly exploiting new resources for the mother country. Those in London who were directly responsible for the colonies, the members of the king's Privy Council and the Board of Trade, were interested not in political control of territory but in economic profit. During the seventeenth and the first half of the eighteenth centuries, therefore, there was a double tendency of colonial expansion and centralization. The expansion was primarily the result of private initiative. In some cases no charter was given, but even in the granting of royal charters the government baptized the infant colonies into the national community, leaving it to the infants exposed to the rigors of life in the New World to work out their own salvation. But the time came when this patternless political expansion was threatened by an ambitious France with its neatly regimented economic and political policy. Thus, viewed from London, the drive toward centralization was inevitable if Britain was to profit from the colonies. Profit depended upon the security of trade and the trade routes, and this security required economic control and military defense. By 1763 Great Britain possessed more than thirty colonies in the New World, and of this number all but four (Pennsylvania, Connecticut, Rhode Island, and Maryland) had been brought under the direct sovereignty of the crown. All these colonies were governed by a common external plan no matter what vestigial or real remnants of local self-government remained, for all were legally responsible to the British political authority.

It was in this dual process of expansion and centralization that the world of Great Britain was turned in its orbit first by the pull of mercantilism and then by the force of imperialism. The slow, gray dawning of empire gave way, about 1763, to a bright morning light when, with a victory over France, Great Britain gained both security and territory. This double achievement changed tastes and increased appetites so that mercantilism gave way to imperialism. The aim remained the same, profit to the mother country, but the strategy was new. The mercantilist notion of investment for immediate return gave way to investing in enterprises that would bring a return at an unknown future date. Mercantilism had advocated casting colonists upon the waters only if profit would be brought home in returning ships. Desire was for wealth, not for territory. But imperialism wanted territory, though not just for its own sake but for the returning ships that would come later.

Still, whatever their motive, the policy of imperialism demanded the machinery of government to a degree not required by mercantilism. To a landowning member of Parliament, this policy seemed benevolence personified. Were not the colonies protected from French attacks, were not the Western frontiers defended against the Indians, were not the trade routes kept relatively free from piracy? The lives and livelihoods of the colonists were protected by the British crown. Why, then, in all justice, should not the colonists help to defray the costs of this benevolence by some fees for services performed (such as the Stamp Act of 1765) or some customs duties upon certain commodities shipped from Britain (such as the Townshend Act of 1767)?

But what appeared benevolence and justice to officials of the government living in London looked like folly and tyranny to radicals and merchants in America. They were individualists who saw themselves and their fellow colonists as persons who had risked their lives in an unknown land. From the small beginnings the colonies had developed into self-reliant, self-governing communities. The activist temper of courageous enterprise and steady labor had become characteristic of the colonists. The traditions of self-government, despite the curtailment of local authority by the crown and the limitation of the electorate by the colonies, were living realities. The colonists had never made strenuous objection to the principle of mercantilism, since the risks and the work seemed to produce enough for the colonists to share with the mother country. When, however, the policy of mercantilism developed into the territorial and restrictive trade policy of imperialism, it was time for objections from the New World.

The first objections to the Stamp and Townshend Acts were grounded in economic grievances, for those acts seriously affected trade and the cost of living. Then, because the economic grievances of men in America did not appear as valid in Britain, the colonists argued that the acts were illegal as well as economically disastrous. It was significant that at this time (1765–1769), even in radical propaganda, the illegality usually referred to the acts and not to the right to make acts, though some radicals were already using the emotional language of "the rights of man," "freemen or slaves," and "taxation without representation." The economic objections resulted in the parliamentary repeal of the acts because merchants in England as in America brought pressure upon the government. But the radical attitude that the acts were illegal had only a negative effect upon the parliamentary defenders of established government.

From 1770 until 1773 there was relative harmony between the colonies and the British government. Moderates were in control of policy and opinion on both sides of the Atlantic. These were the men who proposed patient conciliation and compromise rather than coercion. In America the moderates were ready to defend their economic rights, but they wanted justice with order, not revolution. They deplored the spirit of "The Sons of Liberty," who, suspicious of the motives of the British, found occasion in every new development to cry "oppression."

Two beliefs caused many of the moderates to move toward the radicals, distrusting every move of the British authorities. The beliefs were grounded in their long experience in the New World as this had been informed by the Puritan Revolution in England, the battles that removed James II from the throne, and the Glorious Revolution that placed William and Mary there. These were the dual beliefs that power and privilege are the great corrupting forces of all social life. Power was always seen as evil and was never to be trusted. Ways would have to be found to oppose it and to protect a society from its inevitable insidious effects. So, too, with privilege that accepted and emphasized distinctions among men, that built a society upon class differences, and that refused to recognize the principle of human equality and liberty.

In 1773 the British cabinet, with the sublime ignorance that sometimes combines with good intentions, committed a blunder that effectively dissolved the moderate group in America, so one had to be either loyalist or patriot. The act of the cabinet seemed to its members innocent and virtuous. The large East India Company had accumulated too much surplus stock and was in danger of bankruptcy. To protect the company Parliament granted it certain trade privileges with the colonies, which reduced the cost of tea in Atlantic ports by 50 percent. The colonial consumer could buy tea more cheaply, but if he did the American tea merchant would be financially ruined. Moderates now joined forces with radical patriots, for they did not know when other British companies would be granted similar privileges. It was only in Boston that mob rule triumphed in December 1773, with the violation of the natural right to property by the destruction of tea valued at 14,000 pounds. Other cities had their tea parties, too, but they were mild affairs in which the citizens merely refused to drink the East India brew, impounded it in warehouses, or returned it to England. Many colonists thought the Boston action extreme, but their fear of the violence of New England radicals was canceled by parliamentary coercive punishment against Boston. When delegates from all the colonies except Georgia met at the first Continental Congress assembled in Philadelphia on September 5, 1774, they agreed that their rights should be defended but disagreed as to the methods of successful defense. The conservatives wanted to send conciliatory proposals to Parliament; the radicals, to recommend that Massachusetts create a government independent of the established authority and that all the colonies create an "Association" agreeing that they would not import, consume, or export British commodities. In a compromising spirit the delegates approved both policies. The conservative resolutions were highly praised in Britain, but a British friend of the American colonies is reported to have declared, "There can be no doubt that every one who had signed the Association was guilty of treason."[52]

In Massachusetts the illegal government was organized and developed plans for military defense. The British authority recognized its duty to destroy the ammunition stockpiles. So, on April 18, 1775, there began the attack upon Concord, the rides of William Dawes and Paul Revere, and the battle of Lexington. News of Lexington and of Parliament's proposals of conciliation reached the delegates of the Second Congress shortly before it assembled in May 1775. Again the moderates were for sending a petition to the king; again the radicals were for action by raising an army that would support Massachusetts. And again the compromise ended with the acceptance of both proposals. In December the British government refused the petitions of the colonists. In April 1776, Congress opened the ports of "the free-people" of America to the world. The acts of independence were leading by irreversible steps to a declaration of independence.

> When one has made, with whatever reluctance, an irrevocable decision, it is doubtless well to become adjusted to it as rapidly as possible; and this he can best do by thinking of the decision as a wise one—the only one, in fact, which a sensible person could have made. Thus it was that the idea of independence, embraced by most men with reluctance as a last resort and a necessary evil, rapidly lost, in proportion as it seemed necessary, its character of evil, took on the character of the highest wisdom, and so came to be regarded as a predestined event which all honest patriots must rejoice in having a hand in bringing about.[53]

The revolutionists were forced, act by act, to find ethical rationalizations for their beliefs and decisions. The rationalizations were in part psychological and many colonists recognized them to be so. They wanted a better livelihood and a better trade, they craved a freedom to rule themselves, and they found moral slogans to justify these desires. But they also believed they were driven, by every new act and consequent shift in their arguments, to deeper truths about human life and society, and it was these truths that they thought were the valid ethical rationalizations for their actions. "We hold these truths"[54] they proclaimed, and for these revolutions these truths were the heart of the matter.

On July 2, 1776, after almost a month of debate, the Continental Congress adopted a resolution that

> these United Colonies are, and of right ought to be free and independent states, that they are absolved from all allegiance to the British Crown, and that all political connection between them and the State of Great Britain is, and ought to be, totally dissolved.[55]

Two days later the Congress agreed to "A Declaration by the Representatives of the United States of America, in General Congress assembled," which had been drafted by Thomas Jefferson, and modified in committee and in full session of the Congress.

The purpose of the declaration as political propaganda was stated with clarity and candor in the first paragraph:

> When in the course of human events, it becomes necessary for one people to dissolve the political bands, which have connected them with another, and to assume among the powers of the earth, the separate and equal station to which the Laws of Nature and of Nature's God entitle them, a decent respect to the opinions of mankind requires that they should declare the causes which impel them to the separation.[56]

Those causes were a list of general grievances against the king, an account of the colonists' side of the argument to prove that they were completely innocent and that the king was to blame for the whole affair. The causes appeared in the contexts of their understanding of the relations of the colonies to Britain and of the Enlightenment's natural rights philosophy. The view of relations between the mother country and the colonies implicit in the declaration revealed how far the Americans had come in their practical political ideas. The thought had moved steadily toward the justification for independence, from the time when the colonists generally recognized the authority of Britain, to the argument that certain parliamentary acts were illegal, to the contention that Parliament had no power to legislate for the colonies. Now the colonists maintained that their legislatures were the equivalent of Parliament, that their allegiance had been only to the king, and that even this allegiance had been entered into voluntarily. This voluntary allegiance meant that the king had no coercive power, and it was his repeated indignities of compulsion that, because of the truth of natural rights, provided just cause for renouncing allegiance to the British crown. It was precisely this shift in the poles of thought that John Adams had in mind when he pointed out that the American Revolution ended before the first shots were fired at Lexington.

But if the Revolution had ended before the war began there were many who, unfortunately, did not know this to be the case. The six years of war, for soldiers and civilians on both sides, had its moments of heroism and its hours of homesickness, daring acts of courage and patient endurance of suffering, sacrifice and sympathy. There was also often the wanton violation of persons and property, even though many did not participate in the conflict directly, or only for the briefest time.

What did the Revolution accomplish? How was political life different in 1781 from what it had been in 1776 or 1767? The Revolution was not fought to make the world safe for democracy, nor to establish a Bill of Rights, nor to create a democracy. The fundamental political issue was one of political power, whether the political authority over the colonies was to be external or internal: "these united colonies are and ought to be free and independent States."[57] They united against a common enemy, but they declared that they were free and independent from each other as well as from Britain. The Articles of Confederation written in 1777 and completely ratified in 1781 granted to the Confederation government certain general powers such as that of making war, establishing a postal service, coining money, and adjudicating boundary disputes. But there was no power to tax and no direct relation of this government to the individual. The sovereign states were indeed sovereign.

The writing of a constitution in 1787 was the culmination of the years of failure of the independent states. Few of the delegates who went to Philadelphia in 1787 had any idea that they would transform their governments. They had been called together to propose amendments to the Articles of Confederation, not to create a new nation. Yet what the delegates

> actually did, stripped of all fiction and verbiage, was to assume constituent powers, ordain a constitution of government and of liberty and demand a plebiscite thereon over the heads of all existing legally organized powers. Had Julius or Napoleon committed these acts, they would have been pronounced coup d'état.[58]

The author of much of the new constitution, James Madison, argued that it was not so much an addition of new powers to the federal government as the invigoration of original powers inherent in the Articles of Confederation. Since the original powers were intentionally limited by the sovereignty of the states, they could be invigorated only by the destruction of state sovereignty.

This was the accomplishment of the convention of 1787. And it was achieved by placing the individuals in direct relation to the federal government in matters of defense and taxation and by declaring that

> This Constitution, and the Laws of the United States . . . shall be the supreme Law of the land, and the Judges in every State shall be bound thereby, anything in the Constitution or Laws of any State to the contrary notwithstanding.[59]

The main dispute in the convention was the controversy between the large and the small states. This dispute, like many a lesser disagreement in the convention, was resolved by the compromises involved in equal representation in the Senate and popular representation in the lower house.

On economic matters there was scarcely need for compromise, since the delegates were representative of the middle class. The landowners, merchants, and manufacturers were well represented, but the small farmers, workers, and debtors were without representation. If they had been present the debate would have been more heated when economic policy was discussed, especially when the convention forbade the states to issue paper money and in the vote that the new government should have the power to discharge the debts previously made by the individual states. James Madison explained that one of the aims of the Constitution was to protect property against radical state legislatures:

> To secure the public good and private-rights [against interested majorities] and at the same time to preserve the spirit and the form of popular government is the great object to which our inquiries are directed.[60]

In ratifying the Constitution some of the states acted with the proviso that a Bill of Rights would be written immediately into the new document. There had been no serious objection to the adoption of such articles at the Constitutional Convention, but most moderates assumed that they formed the evident premises of government and did not require expression in the laws relating to the structure of government. The easy adoption of the Bill of Rights in 1789 did not complete the shaping of the American ethic. This is what Benjamin Rush had in mind when, in 1783, he had said, "The American war is over, but this is far from being the case with the American Revolution. On the contrary, nothing but the first act of the great drama is closed."[61]

THE ETHICS OF THE DEMOCRATIC REVOLUTION: THOMAS JEFFERSON (1743–1826)

It is not difficult to account for the fact that Thomas Jefferson never wrote a philosophical ethical theory. He was not a philosopher. The ethic of Jefferson must be discovered in his letters, political documents, and life.

At the age of eighteen he had an intellectual awakening much like that of many students in college. The year before he left home on the Virginia frontier to study at William and Mary. His father willed him 2,750 acres, and the income from the estate was to pay the cost of education. At the end of a frivolous freshman year of house parties, dancing, hunting, and cards, young Jefferson felt so remorseful that he wrote his guardian asking that the debts be paid by sale of some property rather than by income from the estate. It was in his sophomore year that Jefferson's personal age of enlightenment began. He tells what happened in his *Autobiography*:

> It was my great good in fortune, and what probably fixed the destinies of my life, that Doctor William Small of Scotland, was then Professor of Mathematics. . . . He, most happily for me, became soon attached to me, and made me his daily companion when not engaged in the school; and from his conversation I got my first views of the expansion of science, and of the system of things in which we are placed. Fortunately, the philosophical chair became vacant soon after my arrival at college, and he was appointed to fill it *per interim*: and he was the first who ever gave, in that college, regular lectures in Ethics, Rhetoric, and Belles-Lettres.[62]

William Small was a young man of twenty-six who, three years before Jefferson arrived at Williamsburg in 1760, had graduated from Aberdeen. In the eighteenth century the Scottish universities were in advance of the English in giving attention to science, both natural and moral. Francis Hutcheson at Glasgow and Adam Smith at Edinburgh and later at Glasgow established the style and content for moral philosophy throughout universities in Scotland. In both their popular lectures (carefully copied by students since until 1730 books were chained to library shelves) and writings their thought carried into all Scottish and American universities. Francis Hutcheson's *Short Introduction to Moral Philosophy* (1747) was the text for a required course at William and Mary, Columbia, Yale, and Harvard. (It was not required at Princeton only because John Witherspoon, who taught the culminating course in ethics to all seniors, plagiarized the book for his lectures.) When Dr. Small came to William and Mary, he brought with him in natural sciences Isaac Newton and in moral science Hutcheson and Smith. It was in opening up to Jefferson these two systems "of things in which we are placed" that he "probably fixed the destinies" of that young man's life.

In significant ways the destinies of Jefferson's life were fixed, for, from that time on, his life was motivated by a fundamental moral drive and insatiable curiosity. There began at this time, too, the rigorous self-discipline that led him to study, according to some reports, fourteen hours a day. Yet there was time for house parties, fox-hunting, and falling in love, though Jefferson's first attempt in proposing was not entirely successful.

> Last night, as merry, as agreeable company and dancing with Belinda in the Apollo [Room of the Raleigh Tavern] could make me, I never could have thought the succeeding sun would have seen me so wretched as I now am. I was prepared to say a great deal [between dances, but the result was] . . . a few broken sentences, uttered in great disorder, and interrupted with pauses of uncommon length.[63]

In the second attempt a week later he remembered the legal brief he had prepared, but Belinda accepted the proposal of another suitor who, not aware of Jefferson's feelings, asked him to be best man at the wedding.

For the next eight years Jefferson managed his estate, studied law, and became a lawyer. During this period his self-disciplined study led him to write his "Commonplace Books" which were daily entries from the authors who influenced him most. It was his era of religious doubts and ethical affirmations.

On January 1, 1772, Jefferson married, and he took his wife to the unfinished Monticello and to a life in the western settlement. Already one of the wealthiest in his county, he expected that he would spend his life nourishing his own estate, his own culture, and a new civilization, but the events of his time did not leave him alone. Swept into the maelstrom of the political struggles, Jefferson, with his moral convictions, was one of the individuals to create a revolution and to give it direction. In 1774, as a member of the Virginia legislature, he felt which way the political winds were blowing. He wrote "A Summary View of the Rights of British America," in which he rested his case upon an appeal to natural rights and the view that the colonies had, as free men, left the king when they had left England, so that their rights in America rested upon discovery, conquest, and occupation. To the other delegates at the Virginia convention the statement was too extreme to be adopted.

In June 1775, Jefferson attended the Congress in Philadelphia, and he was immediately accepted by the Massachusetts radicals. John Adams years later recalled that Mr. Jefferson

> brought with him a reputation for literature, science and a happy talent of composition. . . . Though a silent member of Congress, he was so prompt, frank, explicit and decisive upon committees and in conversation—not even Samuel Adams was more so—that he soon seized upon my heart.[64]

Appointed to the committee to draft a "Declaration of the Causes for Taking up Arms," Jefferson wrote the last four paragraphs of the statement adopted by the Congress; in those paragraphs there was a clarity of thought, moral and historical justifications for warfare, a determination and confidence, as well as a miswriting of history:

> Our cause is just. Our union is perfect. . . . We fight not for glory or for conquest. We exhibit to mankind the remarkable spectacle of a people attacked by provoked enemies, without any imputation or even suspicion of offense. They boast of their privileges and civilization, and yet proffer no milder condition than servitude or death. . . .
>
> In our native land, in defense of the freedom that is our birthright, and which we ever enjoyed until the late violation of it; for the protection of our property, acquired solely by the honest industry of our forefathers and ourselves, against violence actually offered, we have taken up arms. We shall lay them down when hostilities shall cease on the part of the aggressors, and all danger of their being renewed shall be removed, and not before.[65]

Without his knowledge of what was happening, the "Declaration of Independence" was being prepared in Jefferson's mind and heart. Meanwhile, this preparation in his inner life was also being affected by personal suffering. His second child died in September 1775 when she was seventeen months old. Shortly after her death Jefferson returned to Philadelphia and for more than six weeks, because of poor postal conditions, he had no news of his sorrowing wife and his sick mother. "The suspense under which I am is too terrible to be endured," he wrote. "If anything has happened, for God's sake let me know it."[66] He left for Monticello late in December and did not return to Congress until May 14, so he missed much of the deliberation leading to the momentous events of June and July. While he was home Jefferson was occupied with official responsibilities for the defense of Virginia which, for years, he referred to as "my country." Of greater importance for the emotional intensity of the Declaration was the anguish caused by the death of his mother and the serious illness of his wife. The reserve with which he always expressed his personal feelings underscored the sense of anxiety over his wife that appeared when he wrote to a friend, "every letter brings me such an account of the state of her health, that it is with great pain I can stay here."[67] Appointed on June 10 as one member of a committee of five to draft a statement defending the "Resolution of Independence," Jefferson conveyed these personal sufferings and anxieties indirectly through the emotional impact of his draft of the declaration.

The statement written by Jefferson was presented by the committee on June 28, with slight modifications, to the Congress. Debate on Richard Henry Lee's "Resolution of Independence" had been going on intermittently since

June 10, and Congress spent only four days revising the "Declaration." In Jefferson's draft there appeared a criticism of the king for official conduct of the slave trade, the assertion that the colonists had achieved their present status without any help from the king, and an attack upon the official policy of sending "Scotch and other foreign auxiliaries" to suppress the American people. These were deleted by Congress. There were also some minor changes in wording. But it was not necessary to make other significant changes because Jefferson had so thoroughly assimilated the vague feelings of the revolutionaries, and in his statement had given shape to those feelings, though many felt that the thought of the Declaration was not new with Jefferson. Richard Henry Lee later charged that Jefferson had copied the Declaration from John Locke; and John Adams, in 1822, insisted that "There is not an idea in it but what has been hackneyed in Congress for two years before."[68]

But Jefferson himself recognized that his responsibility was not to create but to express the faith of his fellow men,

> not to find out new principles, or new arguments, never before thought of, not merely to say things which had never been said before; but to place before mankind the common sense of the subject, in terms so plain and firm as to command their assent. . . . Neither aiming at originality of principles or sentiments, nor yet copied from any particular and previous writing, it was intended to be an expression of the American Mind. . . . All its authority rests then on the harmonizing sentiments of the day, whether expressed in conversation, in letters, printed essays, or the elementary books of public right, as Aristotle, Cicero, Locke, Sidney, etc.[69]

"To be an expression of the American mind" was its real importance for the American ethic.

By the time that, in solitude, he completed the first draft, Thomas Jefferson's ethical faith had become definite. It was the faith to which he was to give varied expression the remainder of his life, defending and extending the articles of his moral credo. In this first draft he created a compact ethical outlook:

> We hold these truths to be sacred and undeniable; that all men are created equal & independent; that from that equal creation they derive in rights inherent & inalienable, among which are the preservation of life, & liberty, & the pursuit of happiness. . . .[70]

These were the two polar stars that guided Jefferson: the rights of the individual because "all men are created equal," and the freedom of the mind because "all men are created independent."

When viewed as a whole, there were four main periods of ethical activity in Jefferson's life. The first encompassed his work as legislator, governor, and author in his own country, Virginia. On July 8, 1776, he stated that he would not accept reappointment to Congress, and in September he returned to Virginia. As a member of the legislature Jefferson introduced four major laws. The first two, both of which were passed, dealt with the land problem, namely the abolition of entail whereby lands remained in the landowner's family, and the abolition of primogeniture by which land was inherited by the eldest son. Both prohibitions, central to his ethic of equal and independent persons, were essential if a neofeudalism of landed aristocracy was to be prevented. The third law, introduced for religious freedom, would prevent taxation to support any church and would offer complete liberty of belief, thus emphasizing the individual's independence. This act was not passed until 1786, after Jefferson had left the legislature. The fourth bill, and one that he considered a keystone of democratic government, was for public education. Only education would enable the people "to understand their rights, to maintain them, and to exercise with intelligence their parts in self-government."[71] It was fundamental to Jefferson's ethic that freedom should be available only to those capable of using it. The intent of this bill was not adopted by Virginia until the following century.

As governor for two terms, 1779–1781, Jefferson was not a success. Essentially a reticent person, he lacked the decisiveness required of an administrator during time of war; and, always a poor speaker, he did not possess the public flair that inspired enthusiastic support. Indeed, there was a move in the legislature to impeach the wartime governor, and there was an investigation of his administration following his retirement, though this ended in a public apology to Jefferson.

The *Notes on Virginia,* written largely in 1781, were a potpourri of description and opinion, ranging from agriculture to advocacy of the emancipation of the slaves, to descriptions of the country and judgments of its laws. Throughout there was expressed the spirit of a man of the Enlightenment, driven by a moral credo and possessing an insatiable curiosity about everything that impinged upon human life.

In 1781 Jefferson retired to Monticello, expecting to spend the remainder of his life with his family and in improving his estate. For thirteen years he had been a public servant, and for the government to demand all of the life of any citizen would be tyranny indeed. In September he wrote to a friend, "I have taken my final leave. . . . [I] have retired to my farm, my family, and books from which I think nothing will evermore separate me."[72] Five months later an infant daughter died, and less than a year after that Jefferson was crushed by the death of his wife. Marina, his eldest daughter, later described those days of travail:

For four months that she lingered he was never out of calling. . . . A moment before the closing scene, he was led from the room in a state of insensibility. . . . He kept his room for three weeks. . . . When at last he left his room, he rode out, and from that time he was incessantly on horseback, rambling about the mountain, in the least frequented roads, and just as often through the woods. In those melancholy rambles I was his constant companion—a solitary witness to many a burst of grief.[73]

A man who linked individual dignity with privacy of inner life, Jefferson concluded a simple epitaph with a quotation from the *Iliad*:

> If in the house of Hades men forget their dead
> Yet will I even there remember my dear companion.

After his own death forty years later there was found a worn paper which had been carried in a wallet since the days of grief, "There is a time in human suffering when exceeding sorrows are but like snow falling on an iceberg."[74]

On November 12, 1782, James Madison jotted a note in his journals of Congress,

> The reappointment of Mr. Jefferson as Minister Plenipo: for negotiating peace was agreed to unanimously and without a single adverse remark. The act took place in consequence of its being suggested that the death of Mrs. J. had probably changed the sentiments of Mr. J. with regard to public life.[75]

New years of public service began for Mr. Jefferson.

Jefferson reached France in 1784, a despondent and homesick American. After six months in Paris he wrote, dejectedly, "I am savage enough to prefer the woods, the wilds and independence of Monticello, to all the brilliant pleasures of this gay capital." The following year his mood had not changed: "Lazy and hospitable countrymen I often wish myself among them as I am burning the candle of life without present pleasure, or future object."[76] As he was welcomed into the best Parisian salons and intellectual circles, became familiar with French art and science, and observed the autocratic government and class society, gradually he learned to love French culture and to despise its government. The years from 1784 to 1787 were an interim in direct ethical activity; they were years of preparation for later crusades.

The second period of moral activity, a concern over the proposed Constitution, was very brief, and it was a skirmish that led to the war, fought with increasing ferocity, with the Federalists. Jefferson received news in Paris about the Constitution proposed by the Convention of 1787 to the states for their ratification. While approving the strengthening of the Federal government, he wrote letters of alarm to influential friends. The Constitution might become a document of tyranny without a bill of rights and a limitation set upon the term of the president.

> A bill of rights is what the people are entitled to against every government on earth, general or particular; and what no just government should refuse, or rest on inferences. The second feature [about the Constitution] I dislike, and greatly dislike, is the abandonment, in every instance, of the necessity of rotation in office, and most particularly in the case of the President.[77]

Once more Jefferson expressed the American mind, for the Bill of Rights was adopted with popular acclaim in 1789.

The same year Jefferson returned to America he found a request from President Washington that he become Secretary of State. Reluctantly the appointment was accepted without awareness that the acceptance would place him in the center of political conflict. The Secretary of the Treasury, Alexander Hamilton, was a leader of those who, fearing the unruly people, wanted to centralize political power. It was doubtful that the brilliant Hamilton supposed his country could become a monarchy or hereditary aristocracy, but on political principle and because of personal ambition he was nationalistic, desiring an authoritarian government controlled by men of property and unlimited by the whims of the masses. Jefferson by moral outlook and temperament was opposed to any government tinged with aristocratic authoritarianism.

The Federalist-Republican controversy reached its climax in the years 1798–1800. Twenty-two years after the affirmation, in the Declaration of Independence, that government rested upon the will of the people, the Alien and Sedition Bills were passed in July 1798. By the former the president was authorized to deport "all such aliens as he shall judge dangerous to the peace and safety of the United States," and by the latter citizens were forbidden to print, write, or say anything "false, scandalous, and malicious . . . against the government of the United States, . . . either house of Congress . . . or the President." A Vermont Republican was sentenced to jail because he referred to President Adams's "continual grasp for power" and "unbounded thirst for ridiculous pomp, foolish adulation, and selfish avarice," and a Vermont editor who decried the punishment was summarily punished. An illiterate veteran spent more than two years in prison because he helped erect a liberty pole with the treasonable motto, "No Stamp Act, No Sedition." If the Alien and Sedition Acts had been isolated events, they would not have been of primary importance, but they were important because they were a part of the Federalist pattern in the power struggle. They became a rallying point for the Republican attack, which, rooted in the rights of individual citizens, developed a strategy of states' rights. The Kentucky and Virginia resolutions, written largely by Jefferson and Madison, proclaimed that natural rights were to be protected by the states, and that the Alien and Sedition Bills were an infringement of these individual and state rights. Until the presidential campaign of 1800 Jefferson had almost invariably been the reluctant candidate, but now he felt wedded to another cause, the defeat of encroaching absolutism. He always referred to his election as "the great revolution of 1800."

Jefferson's expression and embodiment of the democratic ethic appeared in his personal attitude as well as in official acts during his two terms as president. There were many personal acts that revealed the integrity of his character, but none was more typical than his response to scurrilous attacks made by his enemies. One day a foreign visitor to the White House, Baron von Humboldt, noticed on Jefferson's desk a hate-sheet containing a character assassination and absurd lies. Shocked by such an attack upon the leading official of a country, von Humbolt asked why the President did not have the paper suppressed and the writer punished. Jefferson reached for the paper, reread the defamation of his character, and handed it to his visitor:

"Put that paper in your pocket, Baron," he said, "and should you hear the reality of our liberty, the freedom of the press questioned, show them this paper—*and tell them where you found it.*"[78] (Original italics)

When he retired from the presidency there began the fourth period of Jefferson's ethical activity. While continuing an interest in politics in advising Presidents Madison and Monroe, most of the remaining years of his life were spent in agricultural improvement, scientific investigation, architectural planning, and—most important of all—the creation of educational opportunities. He believed in education because he believed in people and in what the individual, through education, might become. He helped to reform the curriculum of William and Mary. Aware that other states had established public universities, Jefferson began the University of Virginia, placing the imprint of his personality in its charter and curriculum, as in the architecture and landscape of the campus. His own estimate of his life, written shortly before his death, was carved on his tomb and in the life of America: "Here lies Thomas Jefferson, Author of the American Declaration of Independence, of the Statute of Virginia for Religious Freedom, and Father of the University of Virginia."

He became ill for the last time in June 1826. One night in his sleep he returned, in his mind, to the struggle of the Revolution, for, sitting up in bed, he whispered, "The Committee of Safety must be warned." On July 3, he awoke about seven o'clock, and seeing his physician by his bedside, he spoke for the last time: "Is it the fourth?" The next day he died. It was fifty years after the revolutionists had adopted as their own his statement of the American mind.[79]

The American Ethic of Thomas Jefferson

The ethical attitude of Jefferson led him to participate in the struggles of the American political revolution, and by that participation his moral views were clarified. Whenever he attempted to state personal ethical convictions, the statement inevitably expressed the assumptions of the Enlightenment. But the spirit of the age—the belief in man as a moral being, the conception of a natural order ethic, the confidence in reason, the exaltation of the individual, and the hope for harmony—was a field that magnetized his life. These ethical assumptions were present in his descriptions of the American ethic. They provided the vitality for the important paragraph of the Declaration:

> We hold these truths to be self-evident: That all men are created equal, that they are endowed by their creator with certain inalienable rights; that among these are life, liberty, and the pursuit of happiness; that to secure these rights governments are instituted among men, deriving their just powers from the consent of the governed; that whenever any form of government becomes destructive of these ends, it is the right of the people to alter or to abolish it, and to institute new government, laying its foundation on such principles and organizing its powers in such form, as to them shall seem most likely to effect their safety and happiness.[80]

The moral values are self-evident truths. Despite the language, the self-evidence was not so much a theory about truth as an emphasis (evident to all as innate truths) upon the significance of human rights and how these rights are recognized by individuals. Jefferson had first written that the truths are "sacred and undeniable," but in the rough draft presented to Franklin Jefferson crossed out these words and substituted "self-evident."

Although the Jeffersonian statement of the American ethic emphasized moral rights and not moral responsibilities, Jefferson was not untypical of many fellow Americans in that his life was a response to duty. Further, in the Declaration it was affirmed that when tyranny is committed upon a people, "it is their right, it is their duty" to rebel. He often spoke, too, of moral duty as when, in 1820, he wrote:

> We exist and are quoted, as standing proof that a government, so modeled as to rest continually on the will of the whole society, is a practicable government. Were we to break in pieces, it would dampen the hopes and the efforts of the good, and give triumph to those of the bad through the whole enslaved world. As member, therefore, of the universal society of mankind, and standing in high and responsible relation with them, it is our sacred duty to suppress passion among ourselves, and not to blast the confidence we have inspired of proof that a government of reason is better than one of force.[81]

Yet it is true that most of Jefferson's writings on ethical subjects referred to human rights and not to duties. The rights of man, viewed as the privileges of man, were the dominant theme of his ethic. The American cause was a demand for rights that were denied or threatened by men in power. The spirit was that of "Give me liberty!" The consciousness of duty was present in this cry, and, as men together voiced their claims they became compelled by a final loyalty: "And for the support of this declaration, with a firm reliance on the protection of divine providence, we mutually pledge to each other our lives, our fortunes, and our sacred honor."[82] But human rights were primary because the individual life was primary, and from this valuation of man and his rights came the experience of obligation, of human right.

But how did Jefferson think of (1) this individual, "man," and his rights; (2) how government should be established and with what purpose; (3) the nature of moral good; and (4) the way good is known and achieved in life?

1. An ethic of the natural rights of the person

In ethics the individual human being was recognized as the basic reality. Human rights come from each individual's responsible and inviolable inner life and the possibilities of what that individual might become. Since the individual is the fundamental reality, each person has a right to life and its necessities. "A responsible and inviolable inner life" meant that everyone should find his own values and discover his own beliefs, and that there should be no forcible intrusion upon or violation of his inner life. "The possibilities of what the individual may become" pointed to the thrust of life into the future in that the individual might try to realize all his potentialities. When in the Declaration of Independence Jefferson, with a knowledge of the classics, used the word "happiness," he probably had in mind the Greek word *eudaemonia,* that is, "well-being" or "self-realization" rather than "pleasure." In this sense individual possibilities implied the right of "the pursuit of happiness," of individual well-being and self-achievement.

This was social atomism. Because the individual was the basic reality there was a theoretical equality among individuals. Thus, the social atomism suggested individual equality and individual freedom or, what amounted to the same thing, social equality and social freedom. These notions of equality and freedom of essential status and opportunity were elemental in Jefferson's ethic.

The rights of the individual were conceived as "inherent and inalienable" and as natural rights. Their origin derived from the fact that a human being was a human being, and not from the fact that the individual was a member of a particular society or a child of God. To say that the rights were granted by nature was not to say that they were rights which individuals had in a state of nature, although this was often asserted in the Enlightenment. The fundamental point about natural rights was that each individual, by nature, had rights; or that there was a structure of human life that in and of itself was of worth; or that every individual was a moral being and the fact of this morality came with its own natural origin. Jefferson frequently expressed his ethic in theistic terms, but he did not appear to have any particular awareness of the presence of God. In any case, his ethic did not consciously require God. Man, by nature, has a law pertaining to himself.

Jefferson was one of those who, throughout Western history, used the word "man" in ambiguous, even contradictory, senses. By this term it is often thought that he meant "human beings," but he really meant men of a certain type. His ethic did not extend to women, or to blacks, or to the propertyless urban workmen.

In his attitude toward women Jefferson was probably a typical Virginian landholder. Women were to be treated with respect and to be cared for with gentleness, but there was no place in his plans for university education for women. Books should be for them only a pastime, "filling up the chinks of more useful and healthy occupations."[83] And there was clearly no place in politics for women since "the tender breasts of ladies were not formed for political convulsion."[84] When he was president and it was suggested to him that women might be able to hold public office, he said that the notion was an "innovation for which the public was not prepared," making clear that he agreed with the public.[85]

Jefferson's attitude toward blacks and slavery was much more complex and often contradictory. In his draft of the Declaration of Independence he condemned the king for the slave trade, but there was no evidence he objected when the condemnation was removed. Like many other Virginians he frequently expressed his dislike of slavery:

> Indeed, I tremble for my country when I reflect that God is just; that his justice cannot sleep forever; that considering numbers, nature, and natural means only, a revolution of the wheel of fortune, an exchange of situation is among possible events; that it may become probable by supernatural interference! The Almighty has not attributes which can side with us in such a context.[86]

Jefferson also spoke of his willingness to accept any adequate plan for freeing the slaves; but, in all of his long life, he took no steps to free his own slaves although there were other slaveholders who did take such steps. In 1779 he proposed a bill for Virginia dealing with slavery, "that no persons shall, henceforth, be slaves within this commonwealth, except such as were so on the first day of this present session of Assembly, and the descendants of the females of them." Even those who were free or to be freed were required to leave the commonwealth within a year or "they shall be out of the protection of the laws."[87] Moreover, he was convinced that when the slaves were freed they would have to be deported.

> Nothing is more certainly written in the book of fate, than that these people are to be free; nor is it less certain that the two races, equally free, cannot live in the same government. Nature, habit, opinion have drawn indelible lines of distinction between them.[88]

Jefferson's views were grounded in his many deep prejudices about the natural inferiority of blacks, and he recognized those prejudices, at least in others:

> Deep-rooted prejudices entertained by the whites; ten thousand recollections, by the blacks, of the injuries they have sustained; new provocations; the real distinctions which nature has made; and many other circumstances, will divide us into parties, and produce convulsions, which will never end but in the extermination of the one or the other race.[89]

He was also sensitively aware of the corrupting effect that owning slaves had upon the slaveholder and upon his children.[90]

But there was a more serious reason than social mores or racial prejudice why Jefferson did not apply his ethic of human rights to women or to blacks. This was because he believed the rights of equality and freedom should be available only to those persons independent and capable enough to make use of the rights. As he looked at the social status and abilities of both women and blacks, he did not believe they were qualified to make use of the human rights.[91]

2. The establishment of government and its purpose

Individual men create and continue their government. The political society, therefore, rests upon the agreement of the individuals with one another; and this agreement must always be a living compact that is expressed by actual contact, by rebellion, or by participation in political processes. The Declaration, the war, the struggles for power with the Federalists, as well as voting, were all legitimate ways that individuals kept their compact with each other a vital thing. Because there are always threats to human rights, and because each individual, in every generation, possesses rights, there must be continual affirmations of the democratic faith and possible transformations of the governmental structure, even to the point of rebellion.

> The Creator has made the earth for the living not the dead. . . . A generation
> may bind itself as long as its majority continues in life; when that has dis-
> appeared, another majority is in place, holds all the rights and powers their
> predecessors once held and may change their laws and institutions to suit
> themselves. *Nothing then is unchangeable but the inherent and inalienable
> rights of man.*[92]

In referring to the Declaration of Independence and the Revolution Jefferson
commented, "God forbid that we should be seventy years without such a revolution in this country."[93]

Jefferson believed in extending the franchise (though not to women or
blacks) because he had an unbounded faith that individuals, properly informed, would choose the right leaders to guide them. He conceived democracy to rest upon two "hooks": the educational system and local self-government. And he thought that "that form of government is the best which provides the most effectually for a pure selection of those natural *aristoi* into the
offices of government."[94]

The purpose of government was to secure the individual's rights. Jefferson is one of the clearest advocates of what has been called "the night-
watchman theory of the state." In his first inaugural address he described the
purpose of government as the preservation of civil liberties (the freedom of
religion, press, habeas corpus, trial by jury) and the securing of equal and
exact justice for all citizens. These goals could best be achieved by preserving the right of election by the people, the dominance of the civilian over
the military authorities, an economical administration, peace and the extension of foreign commerce, secure military defenses, the support of state governments, and the encouragement of agriculture. Distrustful of urban life,
Jefferson thought that Americans would keep their democracy as long as they
remained a rural people, "but when they get piled upon one another in large
cities, as in Europe, they will become corrupt as in Europe."[95]

3. The knowledge and achievement of moral good

Jefferson adopted the moral sense theory of ethics. His reasons for that adoption were based not upon philosophical analysis, but upon his belief in the
moral judgment of the individual. Advising his nephew about college education in 1787, he spoke of "Moral Philosophy," commenting,

> I think it lost time to attend lectures in this branch. He who made us would have
> been a pitiful bungler, if he had made the rules of our conduct a matter of sci-
> ence. For one man of science there are thousands who are not. What would have
> become of them? Man was destined for society. His morality, therefore, was to
> be formed to this object. He was endowed with a sense of right and wrong

merely relative to this. This sense is as much a part of his nature, as the sense of hearing, seeing, feeling; it is the true foundation of morality. . . . The moral sense, or conscience, is as much a part of man as his leg or arm. It is given to all human beings in a stronger or weaker degree. . . . It may be strengthened by exercise, as may any particular limb of the body. This sense is submitted, indeed, in some degree, to the guidance of reason; but it is a small stock which is required for this; even a less one than what we call common sense. State a moral case to a ploughman and a professor. The former will decide it as well, and often better than the latter, because he has not been led astray by artificial rules. In this branch therefore read good books, because they will encourage as well as direct your feelings. . . . Above all things lose no occasion of exercising your dispositions to be grateful, to be generous, to be charitable, to be humane, to be true, just, firm, orderly, courageous, etc. Consider every act of this kind, as an exercise which will strengthen your moral faculties and increase your worth.[96]

The moral sense may be "strengthened by exercise." This is the reason for Jefferson's emphasis upon discipline, and it follows that there are occasions when the good can be discerned only by individuals whose discipline has led to an adequate moral sensitivity.

The supposition is that individuals can achieve moral goodness as long as they are socially free because there is both a fundamental harmony among individuals in society and a harmony among the various functionings of the individual self. The problem of a conflict of interests, whether between people in society or between activities of an individual, was never seriously considered. Perhaps this was because Jefferson thought that social conflicts had been settled harmoniously with the victory over Great Britain and the triumph of republicanism, and because with an integrated personality he had no sense of sin or chaotic inner struggles. He may have vacillated on the matter of harmonizing of interests and optimism for the future. The man who could cry exultantly "as long as we may think as we will and speak as we think, the condition of man will proceed in improvement," also looked at Napoleon and sighed, "I fear from the experience of the last twenty-five years that morals do not of necessity advance hand in hand with the sciences."[97]

4. The definition of moral good

From his political ethic it is plain that Jefferson would conceive moral good in terms of individual and social achievement. There is a basic utilitarianism, both individual and social, in his ethic. We have observed his descriptions of individual and social good, and the fact that the two, far from being in conflict, required each other and advanced harmoniously together. Jefferson, believing in some moral absolutes, thought the good would be achieved in diverse ways by various individuals and societies.

> ... [N]ature hath implanted in our breasts a love of others, a sense of duty to them, a moral instinct. ... When [the moral sense] is wanting, we endeavor to supply the defect by education; by appeals to reason and calculation, by presenting to the being so unhappily conformed other motives to do good ... nature has constituted utility to man the standard and test of virtue ... the same act ... may be useful, and consequently virtuous in one country which is injurious and vicious in another differently circumstanced. I sincerely then believe ... in the general existence of a moral instinct. I think it the brightest gem with which the human character is studded, and the want of it as more degrading than the most hideous of the bodily deformities.[98]

While he thought most often of individual and social achievement as the primary criteria of moral goodness, Jefferson also placed stress upon motives. It was the emphasis placed by Jesus upon the inner dispositions that attracted him to the Christian ethic. In comparing the Greek and Jewish ethic with that of Jesus he maintained that, despite deficiencies in our knowledge of Jesus and the corruption of his thought by the theologians, the ethic of Jesus was superior to all other moral systems:

> His moral doctrines, relating to kindred and friends, were more pure and perfect than those of the most correct of the philosophers, and greatly more so than those of the Jews; and they went far beyond both in inculcating universal philanthropy, not only to kindred and friends, to neighbors and countrymen, but to all mankind, gathering all into one family, under the bonds of love, charity, peace, common wants, and common aids. A development of this head will evince the peculiar superiority of the system of Jesus over all others.
>
> The precepts of philosophy, and of the Hebrew code, laid hold of actions only. He pushed his scrutinies into the heart of man; erected his tribunal in the region of his thoughts, and purified the waters at the fountainhead.[99]

Jefferson, too, had an ethic that encompassed a concern for all humankind and he also "pushed his scrutinies into the heart of man." He believed in freedom of the person, and this led him both to intensive political activity and to his advocacy of religious toleration and of universal education. Tyranny over the mind can come either from external compulsion or from internal restraint. His ethic, therefore, is best summarized in his own quiet affirmation, "for I have sworn upon the altar of God, eternal hostility against every form of tyranny over the mind of man."[100]

ETHICS OF THE PHILOSOPHICAL REVOLUTION: IMMANUEL KANT (1724–1804)

Most of the philosophers of the Enlightenment were men of affairs. It was not so with Immanuel Kant, the greatest philosopher of the age. The externals of his life were as simple as the interior of his study, a room with bare walls except for the solitary picture of Rousseau. Born in Königsberg, in East Prussia, he lived his entire life within the borders of his native province. He was a traveler only in the realm of the intellect, and the man who wrote the first systematic geography never saw a mountain or a sea.

Kant's parents had a profound influence upon his ethic and, indeed, his entire life. They had little money but, as Pietists, much religion. So in the Kant home, as in the anticlerical movement begun in the seventeenth century, there was the expression of a simple and direct relation to God, a spirit of quiet faith, good works, moral responsibility, and a scorn of religious ritual and dogma. Such was the life of the young Immanuel Kant, and, though he came to despise a fossilized Pietism, he always remembered the religion of his parents with respect.

> People may say of Pietism what they will. Those in whom it was sincere were worthy of honor. They possessed the highest thing that man can have—the quiet, the content, the inner peace, which no suffering can disturb. No need, no persecution could disturb them: no quarreler could move them to anger or hate. In a word, even the mere onlooker must against his will have been compelled to respect them. I remember a dispute which broke out between the harness makers and the saddlers, in which my father suffered pretty severely. But, nevertheless, my parents behaved in this dispute in such a spirit of reconciliation and love to their opponents that, though I was only a child at the time, the memory of it has never left me.[101]

At sixteen Kant began his studies at the University of Königsberg, one of the poorest of the German universities. The small faculty was mediocre except for the professor of logic who inspired Kant with a love of science that was so influential in his later thought. During the six years that he was a student, the decade he was a family tutor, and the fifteen years he was a lecturer in the university until he was appointed a professor in 1770, Kant knew little but poverty and work. In his early years of teaching he wrote a few inconspicuous scientific and speculative treatises, and he lectured never less than sixteen and sometimes as much as twenty-eight hours a week on logic, ethics, metaphysics, mathematics, physics, and anthropology. Since Kant was a man who loved company (he had worked his way through the university by regular winnings at billiards and cards) and conversation, his friends feared that social distractions would keep him from his philosophical work. He became a popular lecturer and he communicated his love of thinking to others as a student later recalled: "By his own example and by a pleasant compulsion he made us think for ourselves: despotism was alien to his nature." And another student commented:

> He was always warning his students against mere repetition. "You will not learn from me philosophy, but how to philosophize—not thoughts to repeat, but how to think. Think for yourselves, inquire for yourselves, stand on your own feet," were expressions he was always using.[102]

The years of teaching and study until his late fifties were the formative years of Kant's life. These were the years that the intellectual influences worked their way deep into his life, the influence of Newton and Leibniz and the British psychological ethicists. But, as Kant pointed out, it was Rousseau who changed his life by pushing into full consciousness the latent moral beliefs he had learned early in life from his parents. He was thirty-eight when he discovered Rousseau, and the discovery directed his life into a new sense of the primacy of morality. Two years after the discovery Kant wrote:

> I am myself by inclination a seeker after truth. I feel a consuming thirst for knowledge and a restless passion to advance in it, as well as satisfaction in every forward step. There was a time when I thought that this alone could constitute the honor of mankind, and I despised the common man who knows nothing. Rousseau set me right. This blind prejudice vanished; I learned to respect human nature, and I should consider myself far more useless than the ordinary workingman if I did not believe that this view could give worth to all others to establish the rights of man.[103]

A few years after Rousseau corrected his dogmatic prejudices, the reading of Hume awoke Kant from, as he put it, his "dogmatic slumber."[104] Just as Rousseau opened before him the question of value, Hume opened the question of truth, and it was a part of Kant's greatness that he saw both questions as aspects of the same problem. The issue of moral worth was, for Kant, a question of truth and not of opinion or emotions, and Hume, he believed, had irrefutably proved that neither ethical truth nor scientific truth could be established by the widely heralded empiricism. It was in the analysis of the possibilities of science and ethics that Kant charted his map of the interrelated lands of epistemological and ethical thought. In those discoveries he reached the border of the promised land of metaphysics. He viewed that land from afar, he reported how it made possible such worlds of truth and morality as human beings could see, but he denied that any philosopher could ever cross the borders of that impenetrable and unchartable country. This remarkable system of thought was published from 1781, when Kant was fifty-seven, until 1790, in a series of volumes: *Critique of Pure Reason, Prolegomena to Any Future Metaphysic, Fundamental Principles of the Metaphysic of Morals, Critique of Practical Reason, Critique of Judgment, Metaphysical First Principles of Natural Science,* and a number of short treatises.

All of these books were written rapidly with a sense of urgent compulsion, and this may help to account for their difficulties of style and apparent inner contradictions. In 1778, three years before he produced any notable book, Kant had been offered a professorship, with a much larger salary, at the greatest university in East Prussia, Halle. He was urged by many friends to accept the position because it would give him an opportunity for a greater influence. But he had never been physically strong, and both the health and established orderliness of the bachelor who was so methodical that fellow citizens set their watches when they saw him on his afternoon walk, caused him to decline the offer.

> All change makes me anxious even when it seems to promise the greatest improvement of my condition. I believe I must heed this instinct of my nature if I am to draw a little longer the threads which the Fates spin very thin and brittle for me.[105]

When he was seventy Kant ran headlong into difficulty with political authoritarianism. Immediately the philosopher of freedom who viewed with admiration the American and French Revolutions bowed to his sovereign and backed out of the trouble. In 1792 the official censor forbade him to publish parts of *Religion within the Bounds of Reason Alone* on the grounds that the writing "attacked Biblical theology." Kant completed the book, and then, after the approval of the theological faculty at Königsberg and the philosophical faculty of Jena, he published it. In October 1794, he received a royal order:

> Our highest person has for some time seen with great displeasure how your philosophy is misused to misrepresent and depreciate many of the chief and fundamental principles of Holy Scripture and of Christianity, how you yourself have done this in your book. . . . We had hoped better of you, as you must be aware what little responsibility you have shown of your duty as a teacher of the young. . . . We demand of you the most conscientious fulfillment of your duties, and inform you that on pain of our highest displeasure you commit no offenses of this kind in the future, but rather so use all your thoughts and talents that our sovereign intention may be more and more realized. If, on the contrary, you persevere in your behavior, you have infallibly to expect disagreeable consequences.

Kant defended, with deep feeling, his responsibility in teaching; but he concluded,

> As for the second point that I am not in the future to let myself be guilty of any of the perversion or depreciation of Christianity of which I am accused: I think that the safest way to avoid the least reproach on that head is, as your majesty's most loyal subject, solemnly to declare that I will abstain in lectures or in writing from all public discourses on religion, whether natural or revealed.

About the same time that the sick, seventy-one-year-old philosopher sent this official letter he wrote a personal memo justifying his act:

> To recant or deny one's convictions is contemptible, but to be silent in a case like the present is the duty of a subject; and though all that one says must be true, it is not necessarily one's duty to say in public all that is true.[106]

During the last decade of his life he wrote little; and for many of those remaining years he was confined, as an invalid, to his chair. After his death in 1804 he was buried in the cathedral, with the simple inscription from his writings carved into his stone,

> The starry heavens above me
> The moral law within me.[107]

THE ETHICS OF THE ENLIGHTENMENT: PHILOSOPHICAL REVOLUTION

The ethics of Immanuel Kant were conditioned throughout by his thorough acceptance of the assumptions of the Enlightenment. The content of his ethic was affected by his acceptance of the tenets that every person is a moral and natural being, that the individual is the basic reality, that individual freedom is the means to human achievement, and that a fundamental harmony pervades existence. The method of his ethical inquiry resulted from his agreement with the presuppositions of empiricism that it is possible to understand and control life by comprehending the simplest parts of human existence and their organization into the individual and social system. It was in his unique interpretations of these assumptions that he made the major contribution to the ethical philosophical revolution.

The more important development began with the assumption regarding understanding through analysis of the simplest elements of human existence.

Kant understood this assumption in a new way radically different from that of the empiricists. The "simplest parts" referred to the structure of the knowing and willing self and not, as the empiricists supposed, to the objects of knowledge. The empiricists' interpretation of this same assumption, Kant's reading of Hume led him to believe, made both knowledge and morality impossible. For them knowledge was the passive assimilation of the objects of experience, and morality was the acceptance of given desires. But empiricism could find no necessary connection between the objects of experience, and thus it could account only for isolated impressions which were certainly not knowledge. Empiricism in ethics with the acceptance of given desires could discover no human obligation, and thus inevitably developed a utilitarianism of desires which, for Kant, was not morality. The attempt to comprehend the simplest parts, therefore, had to be understood in a new way. It was this fresh approach that constituted the methodological side of the philosophical revolution of Immanuel Kant. His task in ethics, as in science, was to inquire into the structure of the experience and the self to find the necessary conditions that make morality, as science, possible.

Kant's metaphysical conclusions were developed from his epistemological and ethical presuppositions. The definition of moral worth required, for its truth, some essential realities, and the existence of these realities was affirmed by the possibilities of human knowledge and will and value.

It was in these ways that Rousseau, Newton, Leibniz, and Hume met together in Kant. His philosophy began when he accepted the validity of both science and morality, and when his restless love of truth forced him to justify this acceptance.

1. What is the ethical structure of the valid moral experience?

An acceptance of the validity of the moral experience was at the base of Kant's inquiry. His task was to analyze that experience to discover its ethical structure and to disclose its necessary metaphysical conditions. His aim was to explain the moral experience and not to explain it away. The complete discovery of the ethical structure of the valid moral experience was nothing other than to arrive finally at "the supreme principle of morality."[108] How did Kant make this journey?

His travels of ethical discovery began with a striking motto that pointed from the origin to the end of the philosophical journey: "It is impossible to conceive anything at all in the world, or even out of it, which can be taken as good without qualification, except a *good will*" (original italics).[109] The origin of this statement was to be found in Kant's acceptance of the ethical assumptions of the Enlightenment. Kant was writing from moral faith to moral faith. It was as though he were saying, "Anyone who begins this journey with me must accept, as presupposition, the fact that there is a valid moral experience; and examining their own inner ethical experience and that of others they will be able to find nothing that, of itself, can be called 'good' except a good will. Other qualities of mind and character—intelligence, wit, perseverance, courage—or of external possessions—wealth, power—are generally good; but the real goodness of all these is dependent upon a good will since an evil will can corrupt their worth. But the goodness of a good will is dependent not upon anything else but solely upon itself."

The distinctively ethical experience, thought Kant, was an experience of obligation, so the characteristics of a good will could be seen only by an analysis of the concept of duty. First, a moral will acted "from duty" and not merely "in accord with duty." The point here was a simple one. There are many beneficial acts in which a person can find inner satisfaction; for example, the acts of a kindly disposed man who delights in being generous. These acts are, no doubt, good, but they do not possess moral goodness. Such acts "deserve praise and encouragement but not esteem."[110] No matter what inclinations are present, whether social or antisocial, a good will is one that acts from a recognition of duty.

This meant, second, that a good will is characterized by the fact that "an action done from duty has its moral worth *not in the purpose* to be attained by it but in the maxim according to which it was decided upon."[111] Moral worth is a characteristic of motives and not of desires or intentions. It is the inner motive cause of the act and not what the act intends to produce or actually produces that is ethically important.

Third, a good will is further clarified by the fact that "*duty is the necessity to act out of reverence for the law*."[112] This statement is misleading since it suggests a moral legalism and such legalism would be a denial of Kant's central ethical belief. "Respect for the law" must be understood as respect for the moral law. The moral law is not a rigid code but the true ground of an individual's inner, free being.

What has Kant done in these three definitions of duty which is the characteristic of a good will? Positively, having begun with the common moral experience, he has insisted that the basic moral fact is the rational will of the individual. This insistence was determinative for his entire ethical analysis and construction. Negatively, he has stated his implacable opposition to empiricism, utilitarianism, and legalism in ethics. Ethical empiricism, which he rejected, was concerned with the psychological inclinations of action. With a deterministic conception of the individual, inclinations would necessarily be evaluated in terms of their consequences, that is, how they affect the passive individual or society. Thus, the method of empiricism in viewing the individual as passive object vitiated its ethical interpretations, for, in Kant's view, its assumptions prevented it from reaching a conception of absolute worth. In this emphasis on psychological inclinations the individual was viewed as an object who is acted upon. However, the individual is not passive, but rather is to be seen as an active, rational will. Any approach that could not incorporate such an understanding in its categories was necessarily doomed to ethical inadequacy.

Kant's anti-utilitarianism had a related objection. The consequences of action can affect what happens to an individual, but, since each individual is essentially rational will, no consequences can determine what an individual is or wills. The strictures against utilitarianism did not mean that Kant thought a person should make no consideration of consequences in the decisions to act. Such a view would have been absurd since actions without relation to consequences are impossible. The point involved in the anti-utilitarianism was that the moral worth of an ethically good action resided not in the consequences, intended or realized, but in the motive.

This attitude toward consequences also destroyed legalism in moral life. Legalism required the punctilious performance of required actions. Goodness resided in the fact that there has been a proper achievement of consequences demanded by the moral code. Thus, Kant's respect for the law was antilegalistic in that it was farthest removed from a respect for a moral code or social conventions.

But what kind of law could this be, a law that can become the principle of an absolutely good will? Here we arrive at the familiar Kantian notion of imperatives. An imperative is a command "so far as it constrains a will."[113] All imperatives are expressed to the individual by "ought" and the imperatives are of two types. The "hypothetical imperative" (an "if . . . then" command) is dependent upon the particular desires or individual characteristics of persons. These imperatives command conditionally, and they are counsels of skill ("If your musical talent is to be developed you ought to practice regularly") or counsels of prudence ("If you would achieve happiness then you ought to choose carefully your vocation"). "The hypothetical imperative says only that the action is good to some purpose, possible or actual."[114] The categorical imperative does not rest upon the specific situation of a particular individual, but is dependent upon the general condition of individuals. It is thus valid for everyone and in all time, for it presupposes not unique desires or situations but the universal rational will. The categorical imperative is an unqualified "ought." It has no reference to intended consequences but solely to the moral motive. "What is essentially good in it is the intention, the result being what it may. This imperative may be called the imperative of morality."[115] But can this imperative of morality, this "ought" that confronts every human will, be further characterized? Kant thought that it could and he offered three statements of the categorical imperative.

First, "Act only according to that maxim by which you can at the same time will that it should become a universal law."[116]

Second, "Act so that you treat humanity, whether in your own person or in that of another, always as an end and never as a means only."[117]

Third, "So act as if you were always through your maxims a law-making member in a universal kingdom of ends."[118]

The first formula emphasized the *universality* of the *moral principle*. The second pointed to the *basic value*, or *end*, of *moral existence*. The third suggested the *autonomy* or *creativity* of *moral action*, and the participation of the free moral individual in a *kingdom of ends*.

Kant arrived at "the supreme principle of morality" from his analysis of what is involved in the ordinary moral experience. This supreme principle is not three different principles. All statements of the categorical imperative form a unity. For a motive can be universalized only when it arises from a free individual who shares life with other individuals and when it incorporates the valuation that all persons, by virtue of the rational will, are "ends-in-themselves." Or the interpretation might begin from the second statement. I can treat humanity as a basic value only when my motive can be universalized and when my action is the result of my creativity and universal community-of-persons membership.

The practical application of the categorical imperative was made by four illustrations. The moral issues involved could be clarified by reducing the illustrations to questions: (1) When an individual's future threatens more evil than good can the individual, with moral justification, commit suicide? (2) May a person in need morally borrow money with the promise to repay knowing that the promise will not be kept? (3) May an individual ethically neglect the cultivation of his talents for the sake of pleasure? (4) May a person refuse on principle to help others in need? In each case Kant found that the motive of the action, as he described it, could not become a universal law without self-contradiction; that the motive was a denial of humanity as an end-in-itself, and that the action could not therefore arise from a "law-making member in the universal kingdom of ends."

At the outset Kant insisted that the moral principle to be valid must be *a priori*, the product of the pure practical reason. By *a priori* or pure reason he meant that it should be universal (true for all time and all persons) and necessary (not derived from experience but the ground of experience). We can now see in what sense the categorical imperative is *a priori*. It is true for all rational beings; the categorical imperative confronts every human individual. And it is not derived from moral experience but is the essential condition of the ethical experience. Moreover, it is a principle of reason and not of the emotions. The influence of the principle over the will, rather than any influence solely over the intellect, makes the principle a matter of "practical reason" rather than "pure reason."

2. What are the necessary conditions of the valid moral experience?

The categorical imperative as the necessary condition of the moral life has been described. But the imperative itself required for its existence human freedom. The reality of human freedom was the keystone of the Kantian ethic. His task was (a) to demonstrate freedom's actuality, (b) to define its meaning, and (c) to indicate its possibility.

(a) The actuality of freedom is the existential presupposition required by every moral action. Without human freedom the universal experience of obligation would be an illusion. Since the validity of the experience was a basic assumption, this possibility could not be seriously considered by Kant. Moreover, for him, ethical experience as a facade that hides human determinism would destroy what every human person knows most surely to be of worth, that is, human dignity. "I ought," if it has any legitimate meaning, "implies 'I can.' "

(b) The concept of freedom was arrived at by a logical analysis of the ethical life. Human freedom meant that the rational self, or will, had the power to produce effects. "Will is a kind of causality belonging to living beings so far as they are rational."[119] The law, or principle, of behavior of a free being is self-imposed or spontaneous. It arises from what a person is and not from what happens to him.

(c) The possibility of freedom had been reached by the metaphysical results of Kant's epistemological inquiry, "How is scientific knowledge possible?" Freedom is possible because of the nature of the knowing self. Kant made a frontal attack upon empiricism that had reduced the self to a "bundle of perceptions," or to a behavioristic stimulus-response activity. In his view the self, including the rational will, is a substantial reality that cannot finally be analyzed. We can, by empirical investigation, recognize external forces acting upon a human agent and we can discover the self's senses, emotions, images, concepts, and desires. But this causal analysis does not explain the "self" since (i) the concept of self is an essential presupposition making possible the analysis and (ii) the analysis fails to account for the experience of being a self. Therefore, since the self cannot be completely explained in the causal terms of natural science, it must be thought of as a "cause-of-itself."

Kant believed that he had an explanation as to why the methods of science could not explain the self (and so explain it away), and how it was possible for the rational will to be self-caused. That answer was the result of his epistemological inquiry in which he had discovered a distinction between the phenomenal and the intelligible worlds, the worlds of appearance and of nonempirical reality. The world of appearance is knowable because it is accessible to the forms and categories which the knowing mind brings to it, for example, the spectacles of time and space, such categories as cause and effect, quantity and quality. But the intelligible world is not accessible to the rational mind. The human mind in its explorations can reach the point of asserting of the intelligible world that it is, but reason can never describe what it is. The limits of empiricism make impossible a complete rational metaphysics and make possible religion and morality. "I have therefore found it necessary to deny *knowledge,* in order to make room for faith. The dogmatism of metaphysics . . . is the source of all that unbelief, always very dogmatic, which wars against morality" (original italics).[120]

Thus, the human self cannot be analyzed because it is at once partially accessible to the categories of reason yet ultimately beyond those categories. The self is both an appearance and a reality-in-itself, a citizen of both the phenomenal and the intelligible worlds.

> A rational being counts himself, *qua* intelligence, as belonging to the intelligible world, and solely *qua* efficient cause belonging to the intelligible world does he give to his causality the name of *"will."* On the other side, however, he is conscious of himself as also a part of the sensible world, where his actions are accounted as mere appearances of this causality. Yet the possibility of these actions cannot be made intelligible by means of such causality, since with this we have no direct acquaintance; and instead these actions, as belonging to the sensible world, have to be understood as determined by other appearances—namely, by desires and inclinations. Hence, if I were solely a member of the intelligible world, all my actions would be in perfect conformity with the principle of the autonomy of the pure will; if I were solely a part of the sensible world, they would have to be taken as in complete conformity with the law of nature governing desires and inclinations. . . . *But the intelligible world contains the ground of the sensible world and therefore also of its laws*: and so in respect of my will, for which (as belonging entirely to the intelligible world) it gives laws immediately, it must also be conceived as containing such a ground. Hence, in spite of regarding myself from one point of view as a being that belongs to the sensible world, I shall have to recognize that *qua* intelligence, I am subject to the law of the intelligible world—that is, to the reason which contains this law in the Idea of freedom, and so to the autonomy of the will,—and therefore I must look on the laws of the intelligible world as imperatives for me and on the actions which conform to this principle as duties.[121] (Original italics)

Here the limits in the explanation of freedom, the will, and the intelligible world were reached. They were required by the moral experience and were made possible by the metaphysical results of the epistemological analysis. But philosophy can go no farther than this, for philosophy is limited to experience. The intelligible world and freedom are presuppositions of experience, but they are not themselves experienced nor, given the structure of human reason, can they possibly be experienced.

> And so we do not indeed comprehend the practical unconditional necessity of the moral imperative; yet we do comprehend its incomprehensibility, which is all that can be fairly demanded of a philosophy which in its principles strives to reach the limit of human reason.[122]

Here, then, was the essence of Kant's ethic: the understanding of the free moral individual who considers himself to be a creative member in the universal community of rational persons. In retrospect it becomes evident that this ethic was stimulated by Kant's deep and abiding ethical perspective and that it was based upon his conception of the nature of human beings. In the announcement for his lecture of 1765–1766 he stated,

> I shall make clear the method by which one must study . . . the abiding *nature* of man and its unique position in creation.[123]

"The abiding nature of man and its unique position in creation": this was the dominating idea in Kant's life. To describe man's abiding nature and unique nature was the aim of his critical philosophy. Kant had a profound sense of mission to "establish the rights of man," and no matter how intricately abstract his philosophy may appear to others, at least in his own mind it was always intimately connected with his vocation.

> If there is any science man really needs it is the one I teach, of how to occupy properly that place in creation that is assigned to man, and how to learn from it what one must be in order to be man. Granted that he may have become acquainted with the deceptive allurements above him or below him, which have unconsciously enticed him away from his distinctive station, then this teaching will lead him back again to the human level, and however small or deficient he may regard himself he will suit his assigned station, because he will be just what he should be.[124]

In interpreting Kant's view of man's nature and the rights of man it would be impossible to improve upon Ernst Cassirer's comment upon this passage:

> For Kant man's "assigned station" is not located in nature alone; for he must raise himself above it, above all merely vegetative or animal life. But it is just as far from lying somewhere outside nature, in something absolutely other-worldly or transcendent. Man should seek the real law of his being and his conduct neither below nor above himself; he should derive it from himself, and should fashion himself in accordance with the determination

of his own free will. For this he requires life in society as well as an inner freedom from social standards and an independent judgment of conventional social values.[125]

THE UNIQUE CONTRIBUTION OF THE ENLIGHTENMENT

Just as it brought an explosion in population and the creative expansion of a mercantile class, so the Enlightenment also brought with it a new confidence. For there was an indispensable optimism in the eighteenth century, an optimism which existed almost as an oxymoron alongside the travails and birth pains of the times. For there was a sense that revolutions could be successful: in economics, in politics, in overcoming the established orthodoxies. There was a sense that greater liberty would bring a greater freedom, and this freedom in turn would, almost reflexively, bring a release of the human spirit, the creation of a new individual who would act more morally, more humanely.

There was also a confidence in the individual, a deification almost of the individual's unique ability to unite reason and a new kind of feeling and to forge a new human identity. There was a confidence in nature, in natural laws. But these laws, as they touched on ethics, were not codes, commandments written in stone or carved on the outside of buildings, but "inalienable" and "self-evident." Perceived by reason, they were enacted by the faith of feeling that each freeborn male was entitled to them, equally.

Born out of this confidence, the Enlightenment created new institutions which embodied these ideas and nourished the individuals who helped create them, as they continue to support us today. It was a century that required courage, that believed that the method of knowing moral "truth" was in itself an ideal and a paradigm of that truth. This courage implied action, not just sedentary thought, implied that these "self-evident" ideas were worth dying for as much as they were worth living for.

Conceived out of confidence and optimism, born out of social and scientific revolutions, embodied in its new institutions, the Enlightenment brought into Western ethics four new perspectives which it had made its own.

(1) Human beings are basically good. While the leaders of the Enlightenment were aware of the reality of evil, and of the culpability of human beings in dealing with evil, still they felt that essentially human beings were good. They felt that if you added self-love to benevolence you would create justice. They felt that there was a proper self-love, a proper self-interest, and that if the restraints were removed and human beings were left to their own initiative they would instinctively follow their natural feelings, and that these feelings were grounded in benevolence, in the "impartial spectator's" ability to express good will.

(2) There was a trust, then, that human beings are basically good because the genuine human emotions are inherently good. The Enlightenment brought to the surface of life a new way of feeling and experiencing. At its core was a sense of sympathy, of fellow-feeling. There was the sense that this good will was essential for the achievement of human good, and the creation of human communities—that it was natural to the individual and if the individual were left alone it would seek its own expression.

(3) There was also the sense that along with this natural goodness, there are natural human rights. These rights were believed to be universal and to transcend political boundaries. The keystone of the rights was the inherent worth of each individual as an individual. And in order to protect the integrity of the individual, it was necessary to make freedom accessible and available for all. At first this freedom, embodied in an American bill of rights, sought to grant freedom to individuals. But equal to this gift and guarantee of freedom was the concomitant sense that something was required of individuals as well: a duty, a responsibility to others and to the self, a responsibility above all to be tolerant and to seek tolerance. This double-sided freedom then brought to and required of each individual the recognition that all individuals were equal, not in their possessions or achievements, but in their essential worth, in their individual humanity.

(4) Finally there was the sense that a new kind of moral life was being forged. Born in the fires of revolution, hammered on the anvil of freedom and liberty, enshrined in the life of each individual, there was the underlying sense that morality, not religion, was what was important in life. The accent was on this world, on the life of the individual in this world, in the economy and politics of the time. It was an anthropocentric humanitarianism and it stressed two things: motives and action. It was less interested in the ends than in the motives that would dictate those ends. And fundamentally and finally it was interested in action itself, and the aim of all action was to increase freedom and good will whether in others or in the self. There was the inherent belief that the community was made of individuals acting freely for their own best interests and thereby in the best interests of all.

NOTES

1. Immanuel Kant, "What Is Enlightenment?" in *Foundations of the Metaphysics of Morals,* trans. Lewis White Beck (Indianapolis: Bobbs-Merrill, 1959), p. 85. Beck's footnote translates "*sapere aude*" as "Dare to know!"

2. See Carl Becker, *The Declaration of Independence,* 2d ed. (New York: Alfred Knopf, 1942), p. 192.

3. Ernst Cassirer, "Enlightenment," in *Encyclopaedia of the Social Sciences*, ed. Edwin R. A. Seligman (New York: Macmillan, 1931), 5: 552.

4. Thomas Hobbes, *Leviathan* (Cambridge: Cambridge University Press, 1991), p. 70.

5. John Locke, "A Letter Concerning Toleration," in *Works of John Locke,* Thomas Tegg, et al. (London, 1823; reprint Darmstadt: Scientia Verlag-Aalen, 1963), 6: 9.

6. Ibid., p. 52.

7. Ibid., p. 40.

8. Ibid., p. 51.

9. Locke, "An Essay Concerning the Pure Original, Extant, and End of Civil Government," in *Works,* 5: 372.

10. Ibid., p. 373.

11. Ibid., p. 387.

12. Ibid., p. 412.

13. Ibid., p. 356.

14. Ibid., p. 391.

15. Ibid., p. 351.

16. L. B. Namier, *England in the Age of the American Revolution* (London: Macmillan and Co., Limited, 1930), p. 38.

17. George M. Trevelyan, *Illustrated English Social History* (London: Longman's, Green, 1949–1952), 3: 47.

18. John Rae, *Life of Adam Smith* [1895], introduction by Jacob (New York: Augustus M. Kelly, 1965), p. 242.

19. For absent-mindedness see Rae, *Life of Adam Smith,* pp. 330–31, 237–38.

20. Ibid., p. 25; for the years 1731–1759 see ibid., pp. 9–152.

21. Ibid., p. 141; for the years 1764–1776 see ibid., pp. 174–294.

22. Ibid., p. 288.

23. Ibid., p. 405.

24. Ibid., p. 424, 434.

25. Adam Smith, *The Theory of Moral Sentiments,* ed. D. D. Raphael and A. L. Macfie (Oxford: Clarendon Press, 1976), p. 265.

26. Ibid., pp. 109–10.

27. Ibid., p. 326.

28. Ibid., p. 212.

29. Ibid., p. 263.

30. Ibid., p. 213.

31. Ibid., pp. 212, 216.

32. Ibid., p. 216.

33. Ibid., p. 218.

34. Ibid., p. 82.

35. Ibid., p. 86.

36. Adam Smith, "Lectures on Justice, Police, Revenue and Arms," in *Moral and Political Philosophy,* ed. Herbert W. Schneider (New York: Hatter, 1948), p. 286.

37. Smith, *Theory of Moral Sentiments,* p. 235.

38. Ibid., p. 241.

39. Adam Smith, *An Inquiry into the Nature and Causes of the Wealth of Nations,* 2 vols. (1776), ed. R. H. Campell and A. S. Skinner (Oxford: Clarendon, 1976), 1: 26–27.

40. Smith, *Theory of Moral Sentiments,* p. 83.

41. Smith, *Wealth of Nations,* p. 660.

42. Ibid., p. 428.

43. Ibid., p. 115; see also p. 599.

44. Ibid., p. 145.

45. Ibid., p. 267.

46. Ibid., p. 96.

47. Ibid., p. 660.

48. Ibid., p. 493.

49. Ibid., p. 471.

50. Ibid., p. 687.

51. Ibid., p. 456.

52. Carl Becker, *The Eve of the Revolution* (New Haven, Conn.: Yale University Press, 1918), p. 220.

53. Ibid., p. 246.

54. Becker, *The Declaration of Independence,* p. 8.

55. Ibid., p. 3.

56. Ibid., pp. 185–86.

57. Ibid., p. 53.

58. J. W. Burgess, *Political Science and Comparative Constitutional Law, Sovereignty and Liberty* (Boston: Ginn, 1898), p. 8.

59. Constitution of the United States, Article VI, 2.

60. *The Federalist,* ed. Benjamin Fletcher Wright (Cambridge, Mass.: The Belknap Press of Harvard University Press, 1961), p. 132.

61. D. F. Hawke, *Benjamin Rush: Revolutionary Gadfly* (Indianapolis: Bobbs-Merrill, 1971), p. 341. Quoted in Edmund S. Morgan, *Challenge of the American Revolution* (New York: W. W. Norton, 1976), p. 198.

62. Thomas Jefferson, Autobiography, Memorial Edition, I, in *The Writings of Thomas Jefferson,* Memorial Edition, ed. Andrew A. Lipscomb (Washington: Thomas Jefferson Memorial Association, 1903), 1: 3. Also in Gilbert Chinard, *Thomas Jefferson: The Apostle of Americanism* (Boston: Little, Brown, 1989), p. 11.

63. Letter to John Page, October 7, 1763, in *Papers of Thomas Jefferson,* vol. 1, 1769–1776, ed. Julian Boyd (Princeton: Princeton University Press, 1950), p. 11.

64. Quoted in Chinard, *Thomas Jefferson,* p. 59.

65. Ibid., pp. 60–61.

66. Ibid., p. 65.

67. Jefferson to John Page, July 30, 1776, in *Papers,* 1: 483.

68. Becker, *Declaration of Independence,* p. 24.

69. Ibid., pp. 25–26; Jefferson, *The Writings of Thomas Jefferson* (1869 edition), 7: 407.

70. Jefferson, *Papers,* 1: 423.

71. Albert Jay Nock, *Jefferson* (New York: Harcourt Brace, 1926), p. 42.

72. Jefferson to Edmund Randolph, September 16, 1781, in *Papers,* 1: 118.

73. Chinard, *Thomas Jefferson,* p. 137.

74. Ibid., p. 138.

75. James Madison, notes on "Debate in the Congress of the Confederation," in Gailard Hunt, *The Debates in the Federal Convention of 1787* (Westport, Conn.: Greenwood Press, 1970), 1: 207–208. Quoted in Adrienne Koch, *Jefferson and Madison: The Great Collaboration* (New York: Alfred A. Knopf, 1950), p. 6.

76. Letter to Baron Geismer, September 6, 1785, in *Papers*, 8: 500; Letter to Mrs. Trist, December 15, 1786, in *Papers*, 10: 600.

77. Jefferson to Madison, December 20, 1787, *Papers*, 12: 440.

78. Quoted in Claude Bowers, *Jefferson in Power: The Death Struggle of the Federalists* (Boston: Houghton, Mifflin, 1936), pp. 50–51.

79. Thomas Fleming, *The Man from Monticello: An Intimate Life of Thomas Jefferson* (New York: William Morrow, 1969), p. 384; *The Jefferson-Dunglison Letters* (Charlottesville: University of Virginia Press, 1960), p. 69.

80. Becker, *Declaration of Independence*, p. 8.

81. *Writings*, 15: 284. Also in Chinard, *Thomas Jefferson*, pp. 489–90.

82. Becker, *Declaration, of Independence*, p. 17.

83. In Edmund S. Morgan, *The Meaning of Independence* (Charlottesville: University of Virginia Press, 1975), p. 61.

84. September 21, 1788, Boyd, 13: 623. In Morgan, *The Meaning of Independence*, p. 61.

85. To Albert Gallatin, January 13, 1807, Ford 9: 7. In Morgan, *The Meaning of Independence*, p. 61.

86. From Notes on Virginia, Query XVIII, 1785, in John S. Pancake, ed., *Thomas Jefferson: Revolutionary Philosopher, A Selection of His Writings* (Woodbury, NY: Barron's International Series, 1976), p. 317.

87. A Bill Concerning Slaves, 1779, ibid., p. 304.

88. Autobiography, 1821, ibid., p. 306. See below for the strong prejudices of Jefferson.

89. Notes on Virginia, Query XVI, 1785, ibid., p. 309.

90. Notes on Virginia, Query XVIII, 1785, ibid., p. 316.

91. See Morgan, *The Meaning of Independence*, p. 69.

92. Paraphrased in C. E. Merriam Jr., "The Political Theory of Thomas Jefferson," *Political Science Quarterly* 17: 428; for quote see *Works*, 5: 115.

93. Merriam, "The Political Theory of Thomas Jefferson," p. 27.

94. Jefferson to John Adams, October 28, 1813, in *The Portable Thomas Jefferson*, ed. Merrill D. Peterson (New York: Viking, 1975), pp. 534–35.

95. Merriam, "The Political Theory of Thomas Jefferson," pp. 40–41.

96. Letter to Peter Carr, August 10, 1787, in *Papers*, Boyd, 12: 14–15.

97. Ralph H. Gabriel, "Thomas Jefferson and Twentieth-Century Rationalism," *Virginia Quarterly Review* 26, no. 3: 332.

98. Letter to Thomas Law, June 13, 1814, in *The Portable Thomas Jefferson*, pp. 542–43.

99. "Syllabus of an Estimate of the Merit of the Doctrines of Jesus, Compared with those of Others," in a letter to Benjamin Rush, April 21, 1803, in *The Works of Thomas Jefferson*, ed. Paul Leicester Ford (New York: G. P. Putnam, 1905), 9: 462–63.

100. Chinard, *Thomas Jefferson*, p. 367.

101. Quoted in A. D. Lindsay, *Kant* (London: Ernest Berm Limited, 1934; reprint The Folcroft Press Inc., 1970), p. 2.

102. Ibid., p. 8.

103. Ernst Cassirer, *Rousseau, Kant, Goethe*, trans. James Gutman, Paul Oskar Kristeller, and John Herman Randall Jr. (Princeton: Princeton University Press, [1945] 1970), pp. 1–2.

104. Quoted in Friederich Paulsen, *Immanuel Kant: His Life and Doctrine*, trans. J. E. Creighton and Albert Lefevre (New York: Scribners, 1902), p. 97.

105. Ibid., p. 42.

106. Lindsay, *Kant*, pp. 11–12.

107. *Immanuel Kant, Groundwork of the Metaphysics of Morals* First Section, in *The Moral Law*, trans. H. J. Paton (London: Hutchinson, 1976 [first published 1948]), p. 29.

108. Ibid., p. 29.

109. Ibid., p. 59.

110. Ibid., p. 64.

111. Ibid., p. 65.

112. Ibid., p. 66.

113. Immanuel Kant, *Foundations of the Metaphysics of Morals,* trans. Lewis White Beck (Indianapolis: Bobbs-Merrill, 1959), p. 30.

114. Ibid., p. 31.

115. Ibid., p. 33.

116. Ibid., p. 39.

117. Ibid., p. 47.

118. Immanuel Kant, *The Categorical Imperative, A Study of Kant's Moral Philosophy,* trans. H. J. Paton (New York: Harper and Row, [1947] 1965), p. 129.

119. Ibid., p. 107.

120. Immanuel Kant, *The Critique of Pure Reason,* trans. Norman Kemp Smith (London: Macmillan, [1929] 1968), p. 29.

121. *Moral Law,* trans. Paton, pp. 113–14.

122. *Foundations,* trans. Beck, p. 83.

123. Paul Schillp, *Kant's Pre-Critical Ethics* (Evanston, Ill.: Northwestern University, 1938), p. 76.

124. Cassirer, *Rousseau, Kant, Goethe,* p. 23.

125. Ibid., p. 23.

9

THE ETHICS OF ROMANTICISM

Among the most significant moments of life are those when we become aware that something new and important has been added to our experience. They are moments "Of present pleasure, but with pleasing thoughts/ That in this moment there is life and food/For future years."[1] These "spots of time" come to us in both our individual and social history. When this happens we know that something unique has been added to life.

Such a momentous period in our ethical history happened at the end of the eighteenth and the beginning of the nineteenth century through the movement that was self-styled "Romanticism" and that has been so identified since then. It has long been obvious that Romanticism changed poetry and prose fiction, music and painting, so that these art forms have never been the same since. What has not been obvious is that Romanticism was essentially an ethic. It manifested itself primarily in aesthetic modes, and it also had its philosophical and political expressions. But at its base Romanticism was an ethic.

To be sure, Romanticism was not an ethic in the sense that the major Romantics, even those who were philosophers, asked the usual ethical questions. They did not make the same inquiries as the moral philosophers of the Enlightenment or earlier periods, such as "How do human beings make moral judgments?" "What is the structure of a valid moral self?" "What is justice?" "What is the meaning of self-fulfillment?" "What is the role of reason in the moral life?" or "What is an ethical will?" Yet, while they did not ask the traditional questions in a philosophical fashion, they did delve, sometimes more deeply, into the history of moral reflection to ask implicitly

440

that question which is at the source of all Western ethics: "What does it mean to be and to become a human individual in a human society?"

If the Romantics did not ask the formal philosophical moral questions, they also did not give their answers in philosophical style. The Romantics lived their ethic. This, however, does not mean that they were moral in the generally accepted mores of their time, but that they embodied their unique ethics in their lives, though not always with full success. They, at the same time, struggled to express their moral understandings in poetry and other art forms that they might be given a new embodiment in experience. For one historical moment in European life there arose the ideal and reality of the individual in his or her uniqueness, with potential and realized richness and depth. And here the "her" has to be emphasized, since in ways unprecedented in previous moral history there were many women who publicly and/or privately expressed the primary Romantic qualities. Each of these individuals broke previous rational limits and discovered new ways of feeling and thinking. In each there emerged new perceptions of what life essentially was and might be. Romanticism, then, was essentially a moral vision, a vision of what it means to be and to become more fully human.

Romanticism at its best constituted one of the most important ethics in Western history. The Romantics were the major heirs of Western moral history and, at their time and place, the culmination of the Western moral outlook. Without always consciously intending to do so, they wove together much of the ethical thought of the past, in particular the three dominant motifs of the Greeks, the Hebrews, and the eighteenth-century British moralists. They thus contained in their thought, with varying degrees and tensions, the goal-oriented, purposive, self-realization ethic of the Greeks; the motive, responsive, spiritual, inner-life ethic of the Hebrews; and the feeling, sympathy, interpersonal and societal style of making moral judgments of the British moralists. In addition, they incorporated into their experience much that was of importance to other major moral thinkers and they did this not always conscious of the sources of their experience.

They were the culmination of the Western experience in attempting to experience the moral life as a whole and in its particulars, as life could and should be lived. They wanted to break the dichotomies which previous ethics had emphasized and to reach a unity. While they initially saw the basic choice of a full moral life as an either/or, once that decision was made they saw life itself as a combination of both/and: both end and motives, goals and intentions; both pleasure and duty, happiness and obligation; both self-realization and responsibility.

The Romantic moral experience has been far more important for our lives than has been noted in ethical study. That moral vision and expressive style had obvious profound effects upon later nineteenth-century ethical thinkers such as Charles Darwin, Karl Marx, Friedrich Nietzsche, and Sigmund Freud. But perhaps even more significant than all this is the fact that Romanticism contributed to moral consciousness a new perspective that has been pervasive for two centuries.

THE PRESUPPOSITIONS OF THE ROMANTIC ETHIC

Romanticism has usually been interpreted and the Romantics themselves seen as being in opposition to the Enlightenment, and while there were significant differences between the two, in ethics the Romantics were clearly the heirs of the Enlightenment. All but one of the fundamental assumptions of Enlightenment moral reflection were built into the lives of their Romantic descendants. However, that one rejection did modify all the acceptances and led to two additional basic perspectives. The acceptances, the rejection, and the new beliefs, then, were the foundation of what was unique and lasting in the ethic.

The ethical thinkers of the Enlightenment knew with a knowledge beyond the necessity for explanation or defense that human beings are moral beings and natural beings. By the first half of this statement they understood not that human beings are morally good but that their lives are inevitably lived in terms of moral judgment and worth. Human beings make judgments of value as naturally as apple trees make apples. It is in this sense that they are natural beings. The moral self follows laws of human nature analogous to the laws of the physical world.

Basic to Enlightenment ethics were additional beliefs that in human affairs the individual is the fundamental reality, that individual freedom is central to moral experience, and that there are possible harmonies in life whether within the individual, among individuals, among societies, or among whatever relations humans might have with other realities. The focus upon the individual, associated with the development of democracy, was a primary eighteenth-century perspective in thought and experience. Previously, the individual occasionally had important roles in diverse contexts in European history, but the emphasis upon the person gained newness and strength in the Enlightenment. Freedom, too, achieved a new dimension. The ideal of freedom had frequently been associated with Western thought, but the insistence upon freedom as belonging to and the responsibility of the individual, as one of the essential human rights and the major human right, was distinctive. Finally, the possibility of harmony had a long past, but previously it had been a harmony painfully achieved through the difficult work of reason or love. Conflict had been thought of as natural to human beings. Basic to the Enlightenment faith was to turn these concepts around. It is not conflict but harmony that is natural. Even though the motivation may be self-interest, it is by cooperation (often a concealed cooperation) that society develops; even though the driving force may be survival, it is by mutual support that the human world evolves.

The Romantics accepted all these beliefs, and their experiences were profoundly affected by those acceptances. But those experiences could not have developed as they did had the Romantics not rejected another major belief upon which the Enlightenment was built, replacing it with a new image and, as a consequence, modifying the old assumptions by adding two new ideas. Central to the Enlightenment moral experience had been the conviction that rational analysis and construction could provide all necessary knowledge of the individual and society. This concept had developed out of mathematics, physics, and chemistry, the dominant sciences of the seventeenth century, and out of the technologies which those sciences had made possible. The idea was one of clear comprehension by reason; the faith was in objective, logical thought. The image was of a machine, for a machine can be understood and controlled by comprehending its parts and their organization.

But what if human beings are not machines? What if society is not a machine? What if nature is not a machine, not just something to be analyzed and manipulated, but a reality with a life of its own to be understood in other ways than by rational, scientific thought? These were questions that were troubling persons at the end of the eighteenth century, just as biology was gaining ascendancy as a science. For many the struggle ended in the rejection of the idea and image of "man the machine." This meant the rejection of a basic Enlightenment belief that human beings can understand and control themselves and society by comprehending the organization fitting the individual into the social system. This was replaced by the image of the self as an organism which biologically is divided into separate functions which are nevertheless mutually dependent. It was a revolution of the European mind against thinking in terms of a static mechanism and instead perceiving of the mind as dynamic.

This change in perspective from the mechanical to the organic subtly changed the interpretation of all other basic beliefs. The acceptance of human beings as moral beings in the light of being organically alive meant that the central moral concern was being human, since the moral life was not to be analyzed and described, but lived and reflected symbolically. Humans as natural meant that persons were not thought of so much in terms of natural laws as the fact that they were a part of nature, thus opening new ways of relating to nature and to other natural realities. Friendship, whether with nature or other persons, became of primary importance. The individual as the fundamental reality became the self-creating and self-created individual. Freedom was not so much a matter of freedom from social restraints as freedom to become and to be a self. Harmony was not merely a possibility for human life but a present actuality, although often hidden, within the structure of organic life.

The presupposition that life is essentially organic created two new perspectives. The first was the belief that the means to the achievement of a life or art is imagination. "Creative imagination" was the dominant theme of Romanticism. Imagination "has been our theme," asserted Wordsworth in reporting the "growth of the poet's mind."[2] "The imagination," wrote the painter Sir Joshua Reynolds in 1786, "is the residence of truth."[3] The Romantics lived with the conviction that imagination, not reason (though there was a kind of reason in imagination), was the way to truth. Creative imagination thus became the primary element of Romanticism,

> the way to unify man's psyche and, by extension, to reunify man with nature, to return by the paths of self-consciousness to a state of higher nature, a state of the sublime where senses, mind, and spirit elevate the world around them even as they elevate themselves.[4]

The senses, mind, and spirit: imagination was recognized as a compound of feeling, intuition, and will. These three elements were present in earlier eighteenth-century philosophy, but they were experienced by the Romantics in new combinations and with new emphases.

The final basic assumption was a pervasive attitude more than an ideal, it was the experience of a longing. The longing was for no small thing but for the infinite, a feeling and a yearning that was to be realized through finite small things. This led to much thought and contemplation. The thought and contemplation should begin with a particular reality directly experienced, with something seen, touched, and heard, whether in the past or here and now. If in the past it was to be remembered vividly and thought about. Poetry, said Wordsworth, "takes its origin from emotion recollected in tranquillity: the emotion is contemplated. . . ."[5] If the particular reality was encountered in the actual or imagined present, what was experienced was meditated upon and thought through. In either case the thought and contemplation should last until the finite yielded its secret of infinite meaning and was encapsulated in an organic whole, perhaps a poem, or a life. As John Keats said:

> I am certain of nothing but of the holiness of the Heart's affections, and the truth of Imagination. What the Imagination seizes as Beauty must be truth —whether it existed before or not. . . . The Simple imaginative Mind may have its rewards in the repetition of its own silent Working coming continually on the Spirit with a fine Suddenness—to compare great things with small, have you never by being surprised with an old Melody, in a delicious place by a delicious voice, *felt* over again your very speculations and surmises at the time it first operated on your soul? . . . Even then you were mounted on the Wings of Imagination. . . . What a time![6]

There was something revealing about human nature in this process. Beginning with the definite contemplation of a finite particular did not lead immediately to infinity but to the indefinite and the ambiguous. It was this very indefiniteness and ambiguity that intensified the feeling of longing which existed at the beginning. Indefinable meaning increased the yearning. Coleridge affirmed that poetry was best when not clearly understood. The real, yet indefinite fulfillment of the first longing led to a further longing, a deeper feeling, and far more intense yearning for the infinite.

The beginning longing was not merely for the infinite, which itself would be no small, if indeed, possible achievement. It was a longing for the realization of the infinite in the finite, the perfect in the imperfect, the eternal in time. It was the yearning for the organic whole to be present in the part, the individual self. It was the longing for the creation of a work of art. That longing was to be realized through the participation of the self in and with the other, through the free development of one's own personality, through the awareness of an organic whole that was manifest in, or as, nature and history. And it was the creative imagination as feeling, intuition, and will that alone could fulfill this yearning.

These were the major assumptions of ethics, but they alone did not constitute an ethic. The fundamental question thus becomes, "How did these basic moral beliefs develop in individual persons into ethics?"

The first response to the question must be that there was no one way the developments occurred. Since individualism was a primary characteristic of Romanticism, it was not possible that varied individuals should develop identical ethics. Indeed, "Romanticism" itself is an abstraction with no simple unity. It has been denied that any such reality existed, and even those who believe the abstraction points to a cultural and social reality usually agree there was not one but several Romanticisms. To understand the Romantic ethic, therefore, it is essential to discover how it was developed in the lives of individuals and then reflected in their cultural expressions. Many persons could be examined to provide this understanding. No one person expressed the total ethic, though there were differences in the quality of moralists just as there were in the quality of artists. Individuals were representative or typical in their acceptance of the basic assumptions, but no single individual was "representative" as though he or she spoke for a group of similar persons.

A remarkable fact about the various Romantic ethics is that they frequently developed within the circle of friends, and among such friends women almost invariably made essential contributions without which the ethic, or the art, would not have existed. Women, too, gained a new importance in the creation of an ethic or art, but cultural limitations restricted the possibility of a woman's expression and recognized contribution. Historically, of course, a woman had often been the inspiration for a man's creation, but it had been the image of the woman, whether actual or imagined, in the mind of the male and not the woman in her total reality. In the late eighteenth century, woman as an intellectual and emotional equal to man became evident. So while the final expression of experience continued to be dominantly male, it oftentimes would never have developed without the explicit contribution from the experiences of a specific woman or women. In a similar fashion, while moral reflection in past history had often occurred among friends, now friendship in the late eighteenth century took on a new quality and intensity. These new friendships with deeper feelings and emotional communications often make it impossible to know who was the actual source of a specific expression. The individual who put the expression in symbolic form was obviously a creator, but not infrequently he or she received the image or idea from a friend.

Finally, the ethical assumptions developed into an ethic within the social context. The Romantic creators were especially sensitive to the society in which they lived. It was recognized at the time as an age of revolutionary change. John Stuart Mill in 1830 wrote a series of essays on "The Spirit of the Age," in which he asserted that this was "an age of transition." [7] Thus, the societal characteristics of the Enlightenment—the rapid growth of population and of cities, the increasing technology, the changing economic patterns which were to result in the later nineteenth century in industrialism, capitalism, nationalism, and science—continued to dominate the late eighteenth and early nineteenth centuries. It was the increasing awareness of these forces that helped forge the Romantic vision and gave a new Romantic perspective in ethics.

THE SOCIAL SOURCES OF THE ROMANTIC ETHIC

The major events that affected the cultural creators of the age were political revolutions in America and especially France. In 1818 the perceptive critic William Hazlitt asserted that "the whole Lake school of poetry had its origin in the French Revolution, or rather in those sentiments and opinions which produced that revolution." [8] Later, in writing of Wordsworth's poetry of the *Lyrical Ballads,* Hazlitt remarked:

> It partakes of, and is carried along with the revolutionary movement of our age: the political changes of the day were the model on which he formed and conducted his poetical experiments. His Muse (it cannot be denied, and without this we cannot explain its character at all) is a levelling one. [9]

These same claims could be made for most of the artists and their creations in various media. Wordsworth said as much about his and Coleridge's work in the original "Advertisement" to *Lyrical Ballads* which "were written chiefly with a view to ascertain how far the language of conversation of the middle and lower classes of society is adapted to the purposes of poetic pleasure."[10] He was even more explicit about his experience at the beginning of the French Revolution,

> Bliss was it in that dawn to be alive
> And to be young was very heaven![11]

This was because of the hopes for a new world that came with the event.

> The dread Bastille
> With all its chambers in its horrid towers
> Fell to the ground—by violence overthrown
> Of indignation; and with shouts that drowned
> The crash it made in falling.[12]

The optimism for a world made new, for the perfectibility of human society and human individuals which had characterized much Enlightenment thought, came to fruition with the earliest revolutionary victories, especially in the French Revolution. Suddenly the old seemed to be swept away, and a new vision promised a regeneration of the human spirit. Within the next decade, however, that optimistic vision gave way to despair for most of those with a moral sense of life, the despair arriving at different times with the excesses of the Revolution or with Napoleon's use of power.

Many individuals, first in England and on the Continent, then in the New World, embodied and revealed a Romantic ethic, but no persons possessed in their lives the aspiration for such an ethic more clearly than William Wordsworth, Dorothy Wordsworth, and Samuel Taylor Coleridge. None expressed the ethic more incisively and dramatically in their writings than Wordsworth and Coleridge. William, born in 1770, and Dorothy, born one year later, had an intimate friendship from his eighteenth year until her mental breakdown almost fifty years later, and even after that for fifteen years William cared for her with an extraordinarily patient love. Coleridge, born in 1772, first met the Wordsworths in 1795, and for sixteen years, until the tragic rupture in their friendship, the three were on the closest terms, corresponding with and seeing each other as often as possible.

The two poets contributed so much to each other in the form of ideas for poems, suggested phrases, and graphic images that during the period of their friendship it is often impossible to know what belongs to whom. This was even more true for Dorothy, who had clearly the most lasting influence upon Wordsworth, and who had continuing impact upon Coleridge until 1811. While her facility for language was not as great as that of her brother or their friend, she was their equal in intellect and was possibly more sensitive to sights and feelings. Again and again there occur in her journal descriptions of the natural world or her response to it that would later recur in her brother's poetry. The greatest impression she made upon Thomas de Quincey when he met her was of

> the exceeding sympathy, always ready and always profound, by which she made all that one could tell her reverberate to one's feelings by the manifest impression that it made on *hers*. The pulses of light are not more quick or more inevitable in their flow and undulation than were the answerings and echoing movements of her sympathizing attention . . . . I may sum up her character as a companion by saying that she was the very wildest (in the sense of the most natural) person I have ever known; and also the truest, most inevitable, and at the same time quickest and readiest in her sympathy with either joy or sorrow, with laughter or with tears, with the realities of life, or the larger realities of the poets.[13] (Original italics)

Wordsworth was fully conscious of what his sister had done for him as well as why she had been able to do it. In his period of deepest depression it was Dorothy who "Maintained for me a saving intercourse/With my true self."[14] Earlier in life he had known that he was "a dedicated spirit,"[15] but it was she who, in his darkest hours, confirmed him in his vocation.

> She, in the midst of all, preserv'd me still
> A Poet, made me seek beneath that name
> My office upon earth, and nowhere else.[16]

He maintained not only that Dorothy saved him to be a poet, but that she shaped his imagination which, apart from her, had been too stern.

> > Thou didst soften down
> This over-sternness; but for thee, sweet friend,
> My soul, too reckless of mild grace, had been
> Far longer what by nature it was framed,
> Longer retained its countenance severe,
> A rock with torrents roaring, with the clouds
> Familiar and a favorite of the Stars;
> But thou didst plant its crevices with flowers,
> Hang it with shrubs that twinkle in the breeze,
> And teach the little birds to build their nests,
> And warble in its chambers.[17]

Coleridge, too, saw the reasons for her great influence upon both Wordsworth and himself.

She is a woman indeed! in mind, I mean, and heart; for her person is such, that if you expected to see a pretty woman, you would think her rather ordinary; if you expected to see an ordinary woman, you would think her pretty! but her manners are simple, ardent, impressive. In every motion, her inmost soul outbeams so brightly, that who saw would say,

> Guilt was a thing impossible in her.

Her information various. Her eye watchful in minutest observation of nature; and her taste, a perfect electrometer. It bends, protrudes, and draws in, at subtlest beauties, and most recondite faults.[18]

Because, during the years of Wordsworth's and Coleridge's greatest poetic activity, the three persons were so intermingled in mind and heart, there will follow, first, an exploration of the ethic of the *Lyrical Ballads*; second, a description of the developing ethic of Wordsworth and Coleridge in the poems written by the two in response to each other; third, an interpretation of Wordsworth's ethic as revealed in his greatest poem, the autobiographical *Prelude*; and finally, an explanation of the mature ethic of Coleridge created after the break in his relations with the Wordsworths.

THE *LYRICAL BALLADS*

On November 13, 1797, Dorothy, William, and Coleridge, then living in southwest England, started "pretty late in the afternoon" on a walking tour through the Somerset and Devon countryside. "The evening," wrote Dorothy Wordsworth, "was dark and cloudy: we went eight miles, William and Coleridge employing themselves in laying the plan of a ballad, to be published with some pieces of William's."[19] Wordsworth remembered the practicality of the idea, that since "our united funds were very small we agreed to defray the expense of the tour by writing a Poem."[20] The poem was "Rime of the Ancient Mariner," which, by the time they arrived home, had been well outlined with some of the stanzas written. Coleridge's poem became the first of the *Lyrical Ballads* written to trace "the primary laws of our nature" and published less than a year after the tour, on October 4, 1798. The final poem in the volume, not originally planned to be a part of the *Ballads*, "Lines written a few miles above Tintern Abbey," was also begun on a walking tour by William and Dorothy in July 1798.

I began it upon leaving Tintern, after crossing the Wye, and concluded it just as I was entering Bristol in the evening, after a ramble of 4 or 5 days, with my sister. Not a line of it was altered, and not any part of it written down till I reached Bristol.[21]

When the *Lyrical Ballads* are read as a moral document they reveal a clear picture of the ethical perceptions and intensities at that time of Dorothy, William, and Coleridge. The poets might well have intended to "defray the expense" of a walking tour, but each was so thoroughly imbued with the Enlightenment conviction that the human self is a moral being that their primary sensibilities were ethical and their writing revealed that. It is unlikely that whoever decided the order of the poems consciously planned that the "Ancient Mariner" would set dominant themes and "Tintern Abbey" provide a summarizing statement for all the poems. But they did provide a perfect frame for the ethical expression of the *Ballads,* and each within itself contained many of the ethical views of the whole. What were those ideas?

The fact that all but three of the poems are conversational has rich ethical significance. They are conversational poems in that a conversation occurs within the poem, or that the poet is speaking to a specific person, or that an individual is addressing the poet. This arose from the importance of interpersonal relations in the moral life, and especially the significance of friendship. It underscored further the centrality of imagination in understanding, since listening or speaking to another as the power of imagination works in shaping a poem or a life was dominant for Wordsworth and Coleridge. The fact that the poems were conversational also revealed that, almost certainly unconsciously, the poets had adopted the view of eighteenth century moral philosophers that "sympathy," the ability to feel as the other feels, is basic to human life.

The conversational poems suggested further the egalitarian nature of life, egalitarian not in the sense of ability but in the sense of worth, that the finest moral qualities may be found in any human being. And the poet is a person not of moral authority but of moral sensitivity who lives with and on the plane of other folk.

> What is a poet? . . . He is a man speaking to men: a man, it is true, endowed with more lively sensibility, more enthusiasm and tenderness, who has a greater knowledge of human nature, and a more comprehensive soul, than are supposed to be common among mankind; a man pleased with his own passions and volitions, and who rejoices more than other men in the spirit of life that is in him; delighting to contemplate similar volitions and passions as manifested in the goings-on of the Universe, and habitually impelled to create them where he does not find them.[22]

The poems possess conflicts, uncertainties, ambiguities, despair, failure, even contradictions, just as conversation and life contain these qualities. The simplest poems of the *Lyrical Ballads* are often deceptive, not least when they seem to have a clear didactic message containing strong yet unclear meanings and feelings below the obvious. The two poems that frame the whole are replete with disequilibriums. In "Tintern Abbey" Wordsworth had lived through the inner conflicts and despair, but even as he remembered the "darkness," the "joyless daylight," the "fretful stir unprofitable," "the fever of the world," he knew there would be further conflicts in the future.

The "Ancient Mariner," despite its didactic conclusion, contained all the literary and moral difficulties: conflicts, uncertainties, ambiguities, despair, failure, contradictions. It is as though Coleridge were saying that the person who can resolve these elements into a harmony with a simple, clear message is probably dealing falsely with the poem, just as anyone who can dissolve these factors in a tormented life is dealing falsely with moral experience. It was this danger that Coleridge years later had in mind in his statement that the problem with the poem was that it had too much of a moral "and that the only, or chief fault, if I might say so was the obtrusion of the moral sentiment so openly on the reader as a principle or cause of action in a work of such pure imagination."[23]

For the Romantics the moral life was the acceptance of these ambiguous qualities, though it did not end there. It was felt that life, as Coleridge thought of poetry, gives a greater pleasure when it is generally rather than perfectly understood. For an adequate understanding there were times when moral experience no less than literature required "the suspension of disbelief."[24] In accepting the ambiguities and conflicts of existence the poets were affirming what John Keats, having learned partly from them, described as the "quality [that] went to form a Man of Achievement," which was *"Negative Capability*, that is, when a man is capable of being in uncertainties, mysteries, doubts, without any irritable reaching after fact and reason."[25]

It was a characteristic of the moral self not to remain in a condition of "negative capability," but to move through conflict, failure, and partialities to wholeness. This was the experience Wordsworth reported in "Tintern Abbey." When five years previously he had visited the same place he had been in the greatest emotional trauma of his life. He had then known "the heavy and the weary weight/Of all this unintelligible world"; he had been

> more like a man
> Flying from something that he dreads than one
> Who sought the thing he loved.[26]

The "Ancient Mariner" had a similar theme of movement from ambiguity, uncertainty, conflict, and failure to wholeness. Neither the reader nor the mariner knows why he killed the albatross, nor what the process of regeneration was; indeed, the reader cannot be certain whether the mariner achieved wholeness. The fact that Coleridge's life at the time had an illusory unity may have no relevance for the mariner, but in the case of both the mariner and the poet life moved from the most profound frustration to the vision of wholeness. When the mariner approached his home port he first saw the familiar rock and the kirk that caused him to question, with joy, "Is this the Hill? Is this the kirk?/Is this mine own countree?" His final words to the wedding guest were of his sufferings and the understanding he reached:

> O Wedding-guest! this soul hath been
> Alone on a wide wide sea:
> So lonely 'twas, that God himself
> Scarce seemed there to be.
>
> O sweeter than the marriage-feast,
> 'Tis sweeter far for me,
> To walk together to the kirk
> With a goodly company!—
>
> To walk together to the kirk,
> And all together pray,
> While each to his great Father bends,
> Old men, and babes, and loving friends,
> And youths, and maidens gay!
>
> Farewell, farewell! but this I tell
> To thee, thou Wedding-Guest!
> He prayeth well who loveth well
> Both man and bird and beast.
>
> He prayeth best, who loveth best
> All things both great and small;
> For the dear God, who loveth us,
> He made and loveth all.[27]

It was the nature of the moral self to move toward wholeness, and it was the whole person in a whole context. The essential unity of the self was possible only with a unity of the self with the other, with "man and bird and beast." The context was interpersonal, social and natural, even extending beyond nature and this life while remaining within nature and life. It was "a sense sublime" of

> A motion and a spirit, that impels
> All thinking things, all objects of all thought,
> And rolls through all things.[28]

The community of wholeness extended beyond this life as well. When the poet asked a child how many were in her family,

> She answered, "Seven are we;
> "And two of us at Conway dwell,
> "And two are gone to sea.

> "Two of us in the church-yard lie,
> My sister and my brother;
> And in the churchyard cottage, I
> Dwell near them with my mother."[29]

Not all the obvious arguments of the poet could convince her that there were any less than seven in her family.

Almost all of the poems in *Lyrical Ballads* were founded upon the conviction that the moral life consists in moving from partialities to wholeness, from disorder to order, from conflict to resolution, from ambiguity and uncertainty to some clarity. Various poems reveal different aspects of that movement, some ending in fulfillment, others in a tragic human frustration. In the revelations the poems were answering three basic questions of ethics: How is the moral good known and achieved? What are the essential characteristics of an integrated human life? What are the felt consequences of the good life?

WAYS TO THE KNOWLEDGE AND ACHIEVEMENT OF MORAL GOOD

All the ways to ethical knowledge and achievement require an openness to experience of the world which involves an acceptance of the teaching of nature, a reliance upon feeling, the rejection of a rational analytical attitude, and a receptiveness to a simplicity like that of childhood with a readiness for natural development. When persons are responsive to the teaching of nature, whether of human nature or the natural world, they can find "a tale in everything,"[30] no matter how infinitesimal and insignificant the event or reality may be. Nature, in particular, pours "soft influences" on the "wandering and distempered" individual,

> Till he relent, and can no more endure
> To be a jarring and a dissonant thing,
> Amid this general dance and minstrelsy;
> But, bursting into tears, wins back, his way,
> His angry spirit healed and harmonized
> By the benignant touch of love and beauty.[31]

"Remembrance of Collins, Composed upon the Thames Near Richmond" pleads for the river to give moral shape to life:

> Oh glide, fair stream! for ever so,
> Thy quiet soul on all bestowing,
> Till all our minds for ever flow
> As thy deep waters now are flowing.[32]

But Nature can also "Bring sad thoughts to mind," giving "reason to lament/What man has made of man."[33] A twisted thorn seen on a mountain ridge stimulated Wordsworth to write, "The Thorn," an imaginative narrative of a woman's great suffering caused by false promises. The man she loved and had sworn to marry had left her for another, even though "she was with child." And so the child was lost or killed and twenty years later any traveler "must take care and choose your time/The mountain when to cross" or you will find her there sitting by the thorn and hear her cry:

> "Oh misery! oh misery!
> Oh woe is me! oh misery!"[34]

So when nature impinges upon human experience, it does so with the full range of possible human emotions, and in the individual there must be a ready responsiveness to receive whatever it may bestow. In inviting his sister to "Come forth and feel the sun," joining him in a day of idleness, Wordsworth asserted that "One moment now may give us more/Than years of toiling reason." Nature has its lessons to teach, so twice he urged her to come with him "And bring no book: for this one day/We'll give to idleness."

> Love, now a universal birth,
> From heart to heart is stealing,
> From earth to man, from man to earth:
> —It is the hour of feeling.[35]

In two related poems, "Expostulation and Reply" and "The Tables Turned," Wordsworth gave exquisite expression to the view that feeling must guide life with a necessary rejection of analytic reason.

> The eye, it cannot chuse but see,
> We cannot bid the ear be still;
> Our bodies feel, where'er they be,
> Against or with our will.
>
> Nor less I deem that there are powers,
> Which of themselves our minds impress;
> That we can feed this mind of ours
> In a wise passiveness.[36]

In that "wise passiveness" Nature is the best teacher, so books should be left to learn from her.

> One impulse from a vernal wood
> May teach you more of man,
> Of moral evil and of good,
> Than all the sages can.
>
> Sweet is the lore which nature brings;
> Our meddling intellect
> Mis-shapes the beauteous forms of things;
> We murder to dissect.
>
> Enough of science and of art;
> Close up those barren leaves;
> Come forth, and bring with you a heart
> That watches and receives.[37]

In the wise responsiveness of feeling there is the need for a childlike receptivity. In "The Nightingale" Coleridge writes about his son Hartley, then two years old. Six months previously he had been deeply affected when "Hartley fell down and hurt himself—I caught him up crying & screaming—& ran outdoors with him—The Moon caught his eye—he ceased crying immediately."[38] It was this sensitivity to a child that led the poet to observe him listening to a nightingale:

> My dear babe,
> Who, capable of no articulate sound,
> Mars all things with his imitative lisp,
> How he would place his hand beside his ear,
> His little hand, the small forefinger up,
> And bid us listen![39]

Moral growth, however, should come through a natural development and should not be rushed. This was Wordsworth's explicit intention in writing "Anecdote for Fathers" with the subtitle, "Shewing how the art of lying may be taught." His aim was to show the injurious effects of putting questions to children which life had not yet equipped them to answer.

There are no simple formulas for making a human life receptive to experience, especially to that of nature and of other human beings. Receptivity is natural, innate, and though it cannot be taught it constitutes the basis of all moral life. Every poem of Wordsworth and Coleridge constituted an effort to recapture that natural receptivity and to report what happened from it.

ESSENTIAL CHARACTERISTICS OF A GOOD LIFE

At the core of human achievement there is a profound self-consciousness. It is not a consciousness that focuses upon the self but one that is projected outward into things and events so that the self, reflecting the world, also makes its impress upon the world. Such a self-consciousness is not obtrusive in poetic creations and is often hidden from view, but it forms the vantage point for all the poems of *Lyrical Ballads*. Only later did the poets discover this quality in their lives. In Coleridge it came with his experience of the "Brocken Spector," when he was climbing a German mountain and with the light to his back he suddenly saw his own body, reflected, magnified, upon the mist in front of him. Wordsworth discovered the quality in 1804 when he reviewed his growth as a poet and described minds that are powers,

> and hence the highest bliss
> That can be known is theirs, the consciousness
> Of whom they are habitually infused
> Through every image, and through every thought,
> And all impressions.[40]

With such a self-consciousness there is a freedom to establish one's own "living calendar" and not to live by the "joyless forms" of the socially adopted schedule of months and days and hours. It is, through experience, to shape one's own mode of being. Paradoxically, accompanying this individual self-consciousness and freedom there must be the acceptance of the common virtues that bind life to life. It was the value of these virtues, such as gratitude, sympathy, friendliness, and kindness, that was fundamental to these poets; these virtues they found particularly in rural life, and it was largely their presence there that made that life so appealing. Conversely, Wordsworth hated the cities because there he considered its life was marked by "evil tongues," "rash judgments," "the sneers of selfish men," and "greetings where no kindness is."[41] So, for these poets, the common virtues that bind life to life and humans to nature were found in a common life among the common people.

With the acceptance of the common life and virtues there was an outrage at social injustice. Dorothy's journal reports again and again the vagrants on the country roads, men and women forced to wander and to beg because the social system gave them no work or place to live. She reported conversations they had with these unfortunates, which Wordsworth turned into imaginative poems. In "The Last of the Flock" there was bitter rejection of the system of poor relief that forced a shepherd attempting to be self-reliant into abject poverty. In "The Female Vagrant" there was denunciation of the wealthy landowner who caused the degeneration and poverty of those who had lived on the land:

> Then rose a mansion proud our woods among,
> And cottage after cottage owned its sway,
> No joy to see a neighbouring house, or stray
> Through pastures not his own, the master took.[42]

The worst thing about social injustice was the degeneration of the spirit it inevitably produced, the deterioration of the inner life whose strength and dignity alone made possible the moral life. "The Female Vagrant" concluded her sad tale with remorse that

> what afflicts my peace with keenest ruth
> Is, that I have my inner self abused,
> Foregone the home delight of constant truth,
> And clear and open soul, so prized in fearless youth.[43]

The poem makes it clear that it was not she but society that had abused her inner self and that caused her to lose the most precious possession a person can have, the idealism of youth. It was the spiritual loss more than the physical suffering, a loss caused by the suffering, that was most destructive. At the end of her story she

> weeping turned away,
> As if because her tale was at an end
> She wept;—because she had no more to say
> Of that perpetual weight which on her spirit lay.[44]

Accompanying these objective characteristics there were definite feelings that mark moral achievement. These were the "sensations sweet,/Felt in the blood, and felt along the heart,/And passing even into my purer mind/With tranquil restoration."[45] There was the feeling that the self lives in a moral universe where moral retribution and creation occur. It was

> to recognize
> In nature and the language of the sense,
> The anchor of my purest thoughts, the nurse,
> The guide, the guardian of my heart, and soul
> Of all my moral being.[46]

With such a feeling there was a consequent self-criticism and self-acceptance, since

> True dignity abides with him alone
> Who, in the silent hour of inward thought,

> Can still suspect, and still revere himself,
> In lowliness of heart.[47]

But the primary marks of moral achievement were the feelings of joy and of love, and the two were intertwined. In writing of the "deep'ning twilight of the spring/In ball-rooms and hot theatres" Coleridge exclaimed,

> My Friend, and my Friend's Sister! we have learnt
> A different lore: we may not thus profane
> Nature's sweet voices always full of love
> And joyance![48]

"True knowledge leads to love,"[49] and therefore it was not surprising that both the "Ancient Mariner" and "Tintern Abbey" concluded with an appeal to and confession of that love and joy which characterized the feelings of the moral life.

BEYOND THE *LYRICAL BALLADS*

In 1802 Wordsworth and Coleridge wrote poems responding to each other that clearly reveal the quality of moral experience of each at that time. The dialogue began in October 1800 with "The Mad Monk" by Coleridge and apparently ended with the completion of Wordsworth's "Ode" in 1804, though the real completion perhaps came on the night of January 8, 1807, after Wordsworth read his poem to Coleridge and the latter immediately responded with "To William Wordsworth." The poems of 1802 revealed the moral condition of each poet and presaged the moral development and life of each. The poems thus characterized a significant life span through which they were living and marked an important transition period for each.

To feel the significance of the poems it is important to recognize that Coleridge's and Wordsworth's respective situations, their moral relations with self, others, and nature, were vastly different from each other that year. Wordsworth had emerged from his years of debilitating depression and, through the ministrations of Dorothy, Coleridge, and nature, had gained a steadiness of life. He had already begun what Dorothy described as "the poem to Coleridge" or "the poem on his own earlier life." That poem itself was a substitute for a great philosophic poem he planned to write, *The Recluse, or Views on Man, Nature, and Society.* But he was not far into that writing before he had doubts about his capabilities for the task, and so he decided to examine the adequacy of his preparation as a poet. In beginning the search for self-understanding he compared himself with Shakespeare,

Milton, Chaucer, and Spenser. That justifiable comparison indicated a healthiness of mind and self-confidence.

Coleridge, at the same time, was desperate with self-doubts and despair. He had discovered that he was in a miserable marriage from which he could not escape. He had fallen in love with Sara Hutchinson, the sister of Mary, who was engaged to Wordsworth. He was plagued with illnesses which required, for minimum relief, increasing doses of laudanum and the dreadful addiction to that drug was already evident. Again and again Dorothy wrote in her journal about her friend. "O! how many reasons I have to be anxious for him,"[50] repeatedly calling him "Poor Coleridge."[51]

The difference in their situations also reflected fundamental differences in their personalities. The superficial differences were readily obvious, but the deeper distinctions were more difficult to discern. Perhaps the fundamental difference between the two was that while Wordsworth's imagination was essentially moral and he himself was a moralist, Coleridge's imagination was embedded with a sense of sin and suffering and he himself was ultimately religious. Certainly this was relatively true for the year 1802, but it ignores the fact that Wordsworth had also been a sin-sick soul; that he, too, was one of the twice-born, that there was always a religious dimension to his experience, and that Coleridge asserted that his own primary experience, like that of all human beings, was moral. So while the differences revealed in the poems of 1802 were more subtle in their experiences of nature, others, and the self, yet even with their differences both were ready for transformations in their lives.

The attempt to define and demarcate themselves and their moral perceptions began with "The Mad Monk." The poet heard a hermit on Mount Etna sing,

> "There was a time when earth, and sea, and skies,
>   The bright green vale, and forest's dark recess,
> With all things, lay before mine eyes
>   In steady loveliness:
> But now I feel, on earth's uneasy scene,
>   Such sorrows as will never cease;—
>   I only ask for peace."

Peace was not granted; and the mournful plaint of the hermit matched the plight of the poet, for after the voice ceased the poem concludes, "In deep dismay,/Down thro' the forest I pursued my way."[52]

Wordsworth picked up the theme later for his "Ode" but how different the moral expression in the first four stanzas which he read to Coleridge on March 28, 1802. The beginning parallels the monk's voice:

> There was a time when meadow, grove, and stream,
> The earth, and every common sight,
>   To me did seem
>   Apparelled in celestial light,
> The glory and freshness of a dream.
> It is not now as it hath been of yore;—
>   Turn wheresoe'er I may,
>   By night or day,
> The things which I have seen I now can
>   see no more.

And the poem at that time ended in despairing questions, "Whither is fled the visionary gleam?/Where is it now, the glory and the dream?"[53] Yet, strangely, even with the loss of vision the natural world still had its beauty. "Land and sea/Give themselves up to jollity," and the poet's heart was at this festival, "My head hath its coronal,/The fulness of your bliss, I feel—I feel it all." With such beauty it would be an evil day "if I were sullen," even though Wordsworth knew, for him, "That there hath passed away a glory from the earth."[54]

This optimism in the presence of loss was too much for Coleridge, and the happiness in the Wordsworth household was also too much. On April 4 he wrote a poem in reaction to Wordsworth, that he titled "A Letter to ——." He spoke directly to Sara Hutchinson, pouring out the feelings, agony, and hopes of his life and heart. He reported his imprisonment in his marriage,

>   of those habitual Ills,
>   That wear out Life, when two unequal minds
>   Meet in one House, and two discordant Wills—
>   This leaves me, where it finds!
>   Past Cure, and past Complaint! a fate Austere
>   Too fixed and hopeless to partake of Fear!

His home, he maintained, had given him no moral education by which he could bring to Sara and other friends life-giving encouragement,

>   my coarse domestic life has known
>   No Griefs, but such as dull and deaden me,
>   No Habits of heart-nursing Sympathy,
>   No mutual mild enjoyments of it's own,
>   No Hopes of it's own Vintage, None o! none—[55]

The poem revealed Coleridge's alienation from nature, from his past, from himself, and his potential alienation from others. It was these alienations that distinguished his moral experience from that of Wordsworth, though, at a deep level, they shared a common outlook.

Coleridge had the need for his experience of nature to be inward and intimate because he needed his life to be inward and intimate. He did not want merely to see the beauties of nature and he certainly did not want from nature thoughts or moral messages. He wanted feelings not *about,* but *of* nature, and it was the ability to feel that he had lost. He still saw, he could still describe and in detail, "And still I gaze—and with how blank an eye!" The stars and

> Yon crescent Moon, as fixed as if it grew
> In it's own cloudless, starless Lake of Blue,
> A Boat becalm'd! dear William's Sky-Canoe!
> I see them all so excellently fair,
> I *see*, not *feel*, how beautiful they are![56] (Original italics)

The alienation from his past was not that "The things which I have seen I can now see no more," but "They are not now to me the Things, which once they were." It was not that he asked, "Whither is now fled the visionary gleam?" but that hope and joy, which he had once known with nature, had disappeared from his life, and with their disappearance, what was worst of all, his poetic powers.

> There was a time when, tho' my Path was rough,
> This Joy within me dallied with Distress,
> And all Misfortunes were but as the stuff
> Whence Fancy made me Dreams of Happiness:
> For hope grew round me, like the climbing Vine,
> And Fruit and Foliage, not my own, seem'd mine.
> But now Afflictions bow me down to earth—
> Nor car'd I, that they rob me of my Mirth;
> But O! each Visitation
> Suspends what nature gave me at my Birth,
> My shaping Spirit of Imagination![57]

Coleridge's alienation from nature was also his alienation from his past of hope and joy and from the person he aspired to be.

There was also alienation from those he loved most with "fair Remembrances" of happiness in the Wordsworth home which he could no longer know:

> While ye are well and happy, 'twould but wrong you,
> If I should fondly yearn to be among you—
> Wherefore, O! wherefore, should I wish to be
> A wither'd branch upon a blossoming Tree?[58]

He suffered because he had written Sara a "complaining Scroll," to which she had replied with a self-abnegating "guileless Letter":

> And only this I learn—and this, alas! I know,
> That thou art weak and pale with Sickness, Grief, and Pain,
> And I,—I made thee so![59]

Coleridge's alienation was such that he could not then possess the foundations and the fruits of moral experience, but he could wish them for Sara, believing that in her goodness she possessed them.

> O Sara! we receive but what we give,
> And in *our* Life alone does Nature live—
> . . . .
> O pure of Heart! thou need'st not ask of me,
> What this strange music in the Soul may be,
> What and wherein it doth exist,
> This light, this Glory, this fair luminous Mist,
> This beautiful and beauty-making Power!
> Joy, innocent Sara! Joy, that ne'er was given
> Save to the Pure, and in their purest Hour,
> JOY, Sara! is the Spirit and the Power,
> Which wedding Nature to us gives in dower,
>   A new Earth and new Heaven,
> Undreamt of by the Sensual and the Proud![60]

Such joy, unfelt by himself, he wished for her and believed she possessed: "So may'st thou ever, evermore rejoice!"[61]

Wordsworth's experience of nature, of his past, and of himself and other persons was different. From nature he received not only feelings but also thoughts. He was always wanting to find in nature a moral message and a moral renewal. His loss of the past was not a loss of hope and joy but of a vision, and in the loss he typically found compensations. He was uncertain whether he was equal to his poetic tasks, but he was not uncertain about his divine mission as a poet and his poetic powers, for he had no sense of loss of his "shaping spirit of imagination."[62] He loved and was at home embraced by the love of his sister and his friends, and he was soon to be married.

Dorothy reported in her journal that on April 21, 1802, "Coleridge came to us and repeated the verses he wrote to Sara. I was affected with them, and was on the whole, not being well, in miserable spirits."[63] Wordsworth was affected, too, and, not understanding Coleridge's alienations as well as impatient with his irresolution, dependence, and self-abasement, on May 3 he began writing "The Leech-Gatherer" which he subsequently titled "Resolution and Independence." The poem was based upon an encounter, recorded in Dorothy's journal, with a beggar who no longer had the strength for his trade of gathering leeches. Upon hearing of Coleridge's plight Wordsworth recalled the incident. He imagined himself in something like Coleridge's state of mind:

> As high as we have mounted in delight
> In our dejection do we sink as low;
> To me that morning did it happen so;
> And fears and fancies thick upon me came;
> Dim sadness—and blind thoughts, I knew not, nor could name.

It was because of his "untoward thoughts," which included those of "Solitude, pain of heart, distress, and poverty," that he identified himself with his friend,

> We Poets in our youth begin in gladness;
> But thereof come in the end despondency and madness.[64]

In this Coleridgean frame of mind Wordsworth imagined meeting the old and decrepit beggar, romanticizing and transforming him into one who, against all odds, retained his dignity and was manfully self-reliant.

> I could have laughed myself to scorn to find
> In that decrepit Man so firm a mind.
> "God," said I, "be my help and stay secure;
> I'll think of the Leech-gatherer on the lonely moor."[65]

From Coleridge's perspective this completely misconstrued his difficulty. He knew that other human beings were worse off than he was, but that knowledge could not help him with the moral problem of his life.

Nor was he assisted in Wordsworth's conclusion to the "Ode." For having described his situation ("The things which I have seen I now can see no more") and asked his question ("Where is it now, the glory and the dream?"), Wordsworth provided his encouraging answer with a theory of human development. In that description he made reference to what Coleridge could only understand as his son Hartley, "A six years' Darling of a pigmy size!" In the natural growth of the self, despite all trials, there was joy to be experienced.

> What though the radiance which was once so bright
> Be now for ever taken from my sight,
>   Though nothing can bring back the hour
> Of splendour in the grass, of glory in the flower;
>   We will grieve not, rather find
>   Strength in what remains behind;
>   In the primal sympathy
>   Which having been must ever be;
>   In the soothing thoughts that spring
>   Out of human suffering;
>   In the faith that looks through death,
> In years that bring the philosophic mind.

And at the conclusion he found his moral message in nature, "To me the meanest flower that blows can give/Thoughts that do often lie too deep for tears."[66]

This form of the dialogue was over. Essential differences in Wordsworth's and Coleridge's moral views had been clarified and that left them with different moral tasks. Wordsworth had to discover and give shape to his life through the memory of his past. Coleridge had to find understandings of and ways to overcome his alienations. In meeting their tasks each made major contributions to the moral sensibility. They added new qualities to the ways of experiencing and thinking about human life.

Despite their differences which would erupt in the sad break in Coleridge's and Wordsworth's friendship, their contributions were complementary. This was because they began with shared assumptions. Since life was organic and not mechanical they did not engage, as most previous moral thinkers had done, in a rational analysis of that life. Human life must be lived and then reflected symbolically. For the deepest moral questions have to do not with the nature of human virtues, the principles of human obligation, or the procedures of making moral decisions. Rather, they deal with becoming and being a self in a human society. The most important moral problems are the discovery not of abstract principles but of finding a stance for life. In providing their versions of that stance, Wordsworth and Coleridge opened new ways of feeling and thinking, making the possibilities for life more intense, varied, difficult, fulfilling, and individual.

Each saw the essential ethical task as the creation, through imagination and longing, of the moral self. In meeting this task they had to find new ways to relate to nature and society and especially, in friendship, to other persons. They had to find the harmony that existed in the structures of life. And in engaging in self-creating the individual, they had to exercise their freedom to become and be a self. Theirs were the ethics of human development.

WORDSWORTH'S DISCOVERY AND SHAPING OF THE SELF

In 1798 Wordsworth began the search to find whether he had been prepared by "Nature and Education" to write the great philosophic poem he had planned, *The Recluse, or Views on Man, Nature, and Society*. The search took the form of "the poem on his own earlier life," which, during its composition and first manuscript of 1805, was referred to as the "poem addressed to S. T. Coleridge."[67] It is not clear whether Wordsworth found the answer to his initial question, since the complete planned philosophical poem remained unwritten, and we have only the fragments of a completed section titled *The Excursion* and the famous and powerful section titled *The Prelude*. But in writing these sections Wordsworth discovered what was more important, his self, and in that discovery he gave form to his moral life. For *The Prelude* is the greatest of Wordsworth's writings and one of the very great revolutions of the human spirit, opening new possibilities for the ethical sensibility and life.

In the history of the moral consciousness the most similar autobiographical writings were Augustine's *Confessions* and John Bunyan's *Grace Abounding*. Wordsworth's exploration of his inner life was in their tradition as well as that of the many Protestant "confessional" writings of the seventeenth and eighteenth centuries. But unlike Augustine's and other religious confessionals the poem was not addressed to God but to a friend, and this emphasized an essential way the moral life comes into being. Again and again in his writing Wordsworth spoke directly to Coleridge, sometimes to heighten his own excitement with his thoughts; sometimes it was to cement the bond of friendship ("we, by different roads at length have gain'd/The self-same bourne," that is destination); sometimes it was to ask for help ("O honor'd Friend!/ Who in my thoughts are ever at my side,/ Uphold, as heretofore, my fainting steps"); and sometimes it was to recognize Coleridge's quality ("Thy monument of glory will be raised").[68]

The poem was framed by the joy with which it began and by the hope, with which it ended, of being, along with Coleridge, an inspiration to others. The joy came from "this gentle breeze/That blows from the green fields," giving freedom and promises, including promises of "Pure passions, virtue, knowledge, and delight." Joy was at once the precondition and the consequence of the moral life, and experiencing joy as he began to write, one of Wordsworth's tasks was to find its sources.

> The earth is all before me: with a heart
> Joyous, nor scar'd at its own liberty,
> I look about, and should the guide I chuse
> Be nothing better than a wandering cloud,
> I cannot miss my way.[69]

The joy with which the poem began was individual yet shared, for Wordsworth was speaking to his friend. It ended with a shared hope that they might be "Bless'd with true happiness if we may be/United helpers forward of a day/Of firmer trust." So to the multitude of men who give up their freedom,

> we to them will speak
> A lasting inspiration, sanctified
> By reason and by truth; what we have loved,
> Others will love; and we may teach them how;
> Instruct them how the mind of man becomes
> A thousand times more beautiful than the earth
> On which he dwells.[70]

His task was not only to find the sources of joy but to find what was worth loving. To find these would be to discover what it is to become and to be human.

To discover this meaning Wordsworth felt he had to discover himself, and for this he used memory and imagination. The memory of his past life was, as with any autobiography, highly selective. Late in his journey he found that he was returning to those "spots of time" which appeared first and most conspicuously in childhood and which filled his life. They were the memorable moments or periods of time,

> Which with distinct pre-eminence retain
> A vivifying Virtue, whence, depress'd
> By false opinion and contentious thought,
> Or aught of heavier and more deadly weight
> In trivial occupations, and the round
> Of ordinary intercourse, our minds
> Are nourished and invisibly repair'd,
> A virtue by which pleasure is enhanced
> That penetrates, enables us to mount
> When high, more high, and lifts us up when fallen.[71]

From his memories throughout his life until he engaged in the arduous task of remembering, the spots of time were almost invariably associated with Wordsworth's moral sensibilities. From childhood until he became aware of his vocation as a poet, from his discovery while climbing the Swiss mountains of how imagination works and of what it means, from his lack of human friendships in London, from his transition of his "love of nature leading to love of mankind,"[72] from his years of depression which began during the French Revolution and his slow recovery, from his experience and reflections that showed him the place of imagination in human life, the ethical theme was present.

One evening when he was a boy in the Lake District, Wordsworth roamed to Ullswater and, finding a boat on the shore, rowed out onto the moon-lit lake "Of sparkling light." The ridges about him, the stars and grey sky, the oars dipping into the silent lake, the mountain echoes all penetrated the child's life because "It was an act of stealth/And troubled pleasure." Thus began his sense of the kind of human feeling that creates a life, addressing the "Wisdom and Spirit of the universe!":

> By day or star-light thus from my first dawn
> Of Childhood didst Thou intertwine for me
> The passions that build up our human Soul,
> Not with the mean and vulgar works of Man,
> But with high objects, with enduring things,

> With life and nature, purifying thus
> The elements of feeling and of thought,
> And sanctifying, by such discipline,
> Both pain and fear, until we recognize
> A grandeur in the beatings of the heart.[73]

He experienced the joys of youth, "when all knowledge is delight," and received from nature a "sublimer joy" which made him know that no matter how much being he achieved there was still more in life. It was those "fleeting moods/Of shadowy exultation" when

> the soul
> Remembering how she felt, but what she felt
> Remembering not, retains an obscure sense
> Of possible sublimity, to which,
> With growing faculties she doth aspire,
> With faculties still growing, feeling still
> That whatsoever point they gain, they still
> Have something to pursue.[74]

It was an important lesson of the worth of the self, of the necessity for life-purposes, and of the refusal to rest content with any goal that was reached.

It was while at Cambridge, but not from Cambridge, that Wordsworth learned "I was a Freeman; in the purest sense/Was free, and to majestic ends was strong." It was from nature that he recognized his "powers and habits," enabling him to look for the universal in the common things and causing him to discern a moral life in all things.

> To every natural form, rock, fruit or flower,
> Even the loose stones that cover the high-way,
> I gave a moral life, I saw them feel,
> Or link'd them to some feeling: the great mass
> Lay bedded in a quickening soul, and all
> That I beheld respired with inward meaning.[75]

With such a response to nature, when he was on a summer vacation at eighteen, Wordsworth experienced a spot of time that gave shape to the remainder of his life. He had spent "The night in dancing, gaiety, and mirth"; walking across the field the two miles to home the following morning was "More glorious than ever I had beheld." More than a decade later he told his "dear Friend" of his secret

> that to the brim
> My heart was full; I made no vows, but vows

> Were then made for me; bond unknown to me
> Was given, that I should be, else sinning greatly
> A dedicated Spirit. On I walked
> In blessedness, which even yet remains.[76]

Since Wordsworth knew that his vocation as a poet was as "a man speaking to men," this sense of dedication was his own, yet it meant that he thought that any person who would live fully must discover or be discovered by his life purpose.

Two summers after that discovery Wordsworth arrived at a great self-consciousness, including a beginning awareness of the process by which his life would be shaped. While climbing the Alps with Italy as their destination, he and a friend became lost. They met a peasant who, despite the speech barrier, made clear that they would have to retrace their steps to find the right road. Questioning him further, they discovered that unknowingly "we had crossed the Alps." That experience became for Wordsworth an image of the imagination, of how beginning with the sensory experiences of eye and ear imagination works unconsciously, transposing the experience from the physical to the spiritual, elevating the love of self, the foundation of all moral life, and illuminating its yearning for a good life and relations with infinity.

> to my Soul I say
> I recognize thy glory; . . .
> Our destiny, our nature, and our home
> Is with infinitude, and only there;
> With hope it is, hope that can never die,
> Effort, and expectation, and desire,
> And something evermore about to be.[77]

Imagination was the central theme of the poem as of life, and to this theme Wordsworth returned again and again; although he was never able to define it, he was always discovering new images and deeper meanings for it.

Wordsworth's four months in London in early 1791, where he pitched his "vagrant tent" and was a "casual dweller," confirmed the power of nature over his life. Knowing how much friendship and human interchange meant for his life he was baffled "how men lived/Even next door neighbours, as we say, yet still Strangers, and knowing not each other's names," and that "the face of every one/That passes by me is a mystery." He saw the city as a "blank confusion," where its citizens, living amidst trivial objects, conformed to such an extent so that even "the strongest are not free." This experience confirmed for him that the essential human need for "order and relation" came from nature, from "the mountain's outline" which "shapes/The measure and the prospect of the soul/To majesty," so that

> to him who looks
> In steadiness, who hath among least things
> An under-sense of greatest; sees the parts
> As parts, but with a feeling of the whole.

Even living among "transitory things," such a one arrives at "Composure and ennobling harmony"[78] which marks the moral life.

This experience prepared Wordsworth for his next major transformation, when human life gained preeminence over nature in his affections. This, he reported, happened no earlier than his twenty-third year, when his thoughts were "attracted more and more/By slow gradations toward human Kind/and to the good and ill of human life." What had begun years before as the sense of being "a dedicated spirit" was now fulfilled in the recognition that this was the demand to be as fully human as possible, to be concerned with what it means to be a human being. When Wordsworth's primary affections turned toward man often trembling with "guilt and wretchedness," he "thought of human life at times/With an indefinite terror and dismay." Under this pressure, he confessed,

> I essay'd
> To give relief, began to deem myself
> A moral agent, judging between good
> And evil, not as for the mind's delight
> But for her safety, one who was to *act*,
> As sometimes, to the best of my weak means,
> I did, by human sympathy impell'd;
> And through dislike and most offensive pain
> Was to the truth conducted; of this faith
> Never forsaken, that by acting well
> And understanding, I should learn to love
> The end of life and everything we know.[79] (Original italics)

THE UNIQUE CONTRIBUTION OF THE ROMANTICS

For Coleridge the "Brocken Spector" was a "spot of time" that radiated outward in multiple filaments. Certainly it was a moment of mystery, but equally it was another way of perceiving himself, of looking at himself, and what he saw both was and was not the self he knew. For certainly it is often true that we are most blind to the things that are the most familiar, those daily occurrences in the immediacy of our lives: the clothes that need cleaning, the lines on our hands, the follies and foibles of our own family history. Often we need distance in order to see the things that are the closest to us. So it is with the

Romantic movement. Since we are still pocketed in its "spot of time," it is difficult for us to get the proper distance in order to fully appreciate the unique contributions that the Romantics made to our lives. That is one reason that it has been difficult for individuals to see the profound shifts in our ethical views that the Romantics made, since those viewpoints still seem natural to us; it is the music we have grown up with.

But if the moral life consists (a) of goals and purposes, (b) of responsibility and duty linked in (c) an interpersonal method for making moral judgments, if any profound view of life is ethical, then Romanticism was certainly an ethic. It was a transposition of faith, and a grounding of a new vision of human life. It embodied, as it continues to do, a new humanistic ideal. Its essential characteristic is that the best life is one of self-development, a self-creating of the unique individual from the materials given. It added to Western history a new sensibility and a new perspective, a perspective which in its finest lineaments has four essential elements.

(1) The importance of feeling. This is the gateway into the Romantic ethic. There have been previous ethical communities that stressed feeling, but none with the throughgoing exploration and centrality of the Romantics. In the first place this was a feeling of longing for life and the infinite. But the experience of the infinite was in the here and now: "Eternity," the poet Blake said, "is in love with the productions of time."[80] This longing required of each individual that he remain open to the world, receptive and responsive, and along with this openness was a reverence for Nature. The natural world was the human world; the human world was the natural world. Nature was our home and not the constructions we had imposed on Nature.

So the Romantics began with feelings. But theirs was not the scientific eye looking objectively around the horizon, noting and calculating, but rather the body on a walking tour. The moral life was a life not of quantity, but of quality, and the essential ingredient of that quality was of the feeling, the intensity of the experience of the human world—a world rich in its manifestations and electric in its currents. It was a world in which suffering exists, and joy. And the Romantics did not try to exclude one in order to favor the other. At times they almost seemed to seek suffering, not for its knowledge as the Greeks might have done, but for the intensity itself, and because through that suffering it was possible to reach a new harmony. And so, along with the capacity to suffer was an equally generous benevolence—a sharing of beauty and joy, either in the recollection of things past or in the immediate experience of things present. The world exists because the individual can feel it, and while the danger was that the world could easily be reduced to the individual's sensuality, the Romantics, for the most part, steered clear of those shoals by always seeking a greater sympathy and intimacy—by always reaching out.

(2) If feeling was to be first element, then freedom was second, for the purpose of feeling was to free the individual. If there was conflict and inner failure in an individual's life, they were seen as a part of a pursuit of a greater wholeness, a larger world, and each enlargement of the world was meant to increase the individual's liberty and latitude. But there was a deeper aspect to freedom in the Romantic ethic, and this was in its emphasis upon the creative imagination. Feeling by itself has limits, but feeling in the service of the imagination is boundless. Suddenly the world is open, the dream can be explored, what is strange can be brought close, and what is exotic can be made exemplary. The natural and the supernatural can interpenetrate each other's domains. For the Romantics there was little sense that the imagination could be demonic. For them its free use restored what was lost as it discovered what might be. It was a guide, muse, counselor, and friend.

(3) Not since the Greeks had friendship received such a primal place in an ethic, and this was a friendship not only with nature and with the acts of the imagination, but more centrally with others. Friendship was the supreme good, not only in itself but in its gifts. The individual was free to become a friend, and here friendship took on dimensions that had not been noticed or accented before. There was a breadth of friendship here, an inclusion of all kinds of individuals and relationships. There was an equality between men and women, between humans and nature. There was not only a joy in Platonic friendships, but a delight in those that were romantic, and often an exultation in those that were sexual. There was a sense of the creative energy and vitality that was present in friendship, and the importance of commitment to each other—a commitment which did not diminish freedom, but expanded it.

(4) For this was the purpose of feeling, freedom, and friendship. These three were meant to help embody the development of the individual personality. The goal was self-realization. The good life was that which could embrace the opposites, touching both extremes at once, reconciling consciousness and unconsciousness, human beings and nature, individual and society, subject and object. The moral life was seen as one of "organic unity." It was a life of growth, a life lived in the garden again.

NOTES

1. William Wordsworth, "Lines Composed a Few Miles Above Tintern Abbey," in *The Complete Poetical Works of William Wordsworth,* ed. Alice N. George (New York: Houghton Mifflin and Co., [1904] 1932), p. 92.

2. Quoted in Raymond Dexter Havens, *The Mind of a Poet* (Baltimore: Johns Hopkins University Press, 1941), 1: 278.

3. Joshua Reynolds, *Discourse XIII,* quoted in James Engell, *The Creative Imagination: Enlightenment to Romanticism* (Cambridge, Mass.: Harvard University Press, 1981), p. 186.

4. Engell, *The Creative Imagination,* p. 8.

5. Thomas Hutchinson, ed., and revised by Ernest De Selincourt, *The Poetical Works of Wordsworth* (London: Oxford University Press, 1959), p. 740.

6. Letter to Benjamin Bailey, November 22, 1817, in Hyder E. Rollins, ed., *The Letters of John Keats* (Cambridge, Mass.: Harvard University Press, 1958), 1: 185.

7. John Stuart Mill, *The Spirit of the Age,* introductory essay by F. A. Von Hayek (Chicago: University of Chicago Press, 1942), p. 17.

8. William Hazlitt, "On the Living Poets," in *Lectures on the English Poets*, Introduction by A. R. Waller (London: J. M. Dent and Sons Ltd., [1910] 1955), p. 161.

9. Hazlitt, "Mr. Wordsworth," in *Lectures on the English Poets,* p. 253.

10. W. J. B. Owen, ed., *Wordsworth and Coleridge Lyrical Ballads 1798* (London: Oxford University Press, 1969), p. 3.

11. Ernest De Selincourt, ed., *Wordsworth The Prelude* (Text of 1805) (Oxford: Oxford University Press, 1970), Book X, lines 693–94.

12. William Wordsworth, "The Excursion," in *The Complete Poetical Works of William Wordsworth* (Boston and New York: Houghton Mifflin Co., [1904] 1953), Book III, lines 709–13.

13. In David Masson, ed., *The Collected Writings of Thomas De Quincey* (Edinburgh: Adam and Charles Black, [1889] 1964), 2: 239.

14. Wordsworth, *Prelude,* Book X, lines 341–42.

15. Ibid., Book IV, line 337.

16. Ibid., Book X, lines 345–48.

17. Ibid., Book XIV, lines 246–56.

18. In Ernest De Selincourt, ed., *Dorothy Wordsworth* (London: Oxford University Press, 1933), p. 75.

19. Ibid., p. 174.

20. James Butler and Karen Green, eds., *Lyrical Ballads and Other Poems: 1797–1800* (Ithaca, N.Y.: Cornell University Press, 1992), p. 4.

21. *The Complete Poetical Works of William Wordsworth,* ed. George, p. 91.

22. Hutchinson, *The Poetical Works of Wordsworth,* p. 737.

23. S.T. Coleridge, *The Table Talk and Omniana,* ed. T. Ashe (London: George Bell and Sons, 1909), p. 87.

24. S. T. Coleridge, *Biographia Literaria,* ed. J. Shawcross (London: Oxford University Press, 1907), 2: 442.

25. John Keats, "Letter to George & Thomas Keats, December 22, 1818," in *Autobiography of John Keats,* ed. Earle Vonard Heller (London: Oxford University Press, 1933), p. 62.

26. Wordsworth, "Tintern Abbey," ed. Owen, lines 39–40, 70–72.

27. Wordsworth, "The Rime of the Ancyent Marinere," ed. Owen, lines 598–617.

28. Wordsworth, "Lines Composed a few miles above Tintern Abbey," ed. Owen, lines 95, 100–102.

29. Wordsworth, "We are Seven," ed. Owen, lines 18–24.

30. Wordsworth, "Simon Lee, The Old Huntsman," ed. Owen, line 76.

31. Wordsworth, "The Dungeon," ed. Owen, lines 22, 21, 25, 30.

32. Wordsworth, "Lines written near Richmond, upon the Thames, at Evening," ed. Owen, lines 21–24.

33. Wordsworth, "Lines written in Early Spring," ed. Owen, lines 4, 23–24.

34. Wordsworth, "The Thorn," ed. Owen, xii: 7, vi: 10–11.

35. Wordsworth, "To My Sister," ed. George, lines 12, 25–26, 39–40, 21–24.

36. Wordsworth, "Expostulation and Reply," ed. Owen, lines 17–24.

37. Wordsworth, "The Tables Turned," ed. Owen, lines 21–32.

38. Herbert Hartman, *Hartley Coleridge* (London: Oxford University Press, 1931), p. 13.

39. Coleridge, "The Nightingale," ed. Owen, lines 91–96.

40. Wordsworth, *The Prelude,* ed. Ernest De Selincourt, Book XIII, lines 113–17.

41. Wordsworth, "Tintern Abbey," ed. Owen, lines 129, 130, 131.

42. Wordsworth, "The Female Vagrant," ed. Owen, line 39.

43. Ibid., lines 258–61.

44. Ibid., lines 267–70.

45. Wordsworth, "Tintern Abbey," ed. Owen, lines 27–30.

46. Ibid., lines 107–11.

47. Wordsworth, "Lines left upon a Seat in a Yew-tree," ed. Owen, lines 61–64.

48. Coleridge, "The Nightingale," ed. Owen, lines 36–37, 40–43.

49. Wordsworth, "Lines left upon a Seat in a Yew-tree," ed. Owen, line 56.

50. Wordsworth, *Dorothy,* ed. De Selincourt, line 129.

51. Ibid., line 95.

52. Coleridge, "The Mad Monk," in *The Complete Poetical Works of Samuel Taylor Coleridge,* ed. Ernest Hartley Coleridge (Oxford: The Clarendon Press, 1957), 1: lines 15, 46–47.

53. Wordsworth, "Ode: Intimations of Immortality," ed. George, lines 1–9, 57–58.

54. Ibid., lines 30–31, 41–42, 43, 18,

55. In Stephen Maxfield Parrish, ed., *Coleridge's Dejection: The Earliest Manuscripts and the Earliest Printings* (Ithaca, N.Y.: Cornell University Press, 1988), lines 242–47, 257–61 (pp. 31–32).

56. Ibid., lines 39–43 (p. 24).

57. In Earl Leslie Griggs, ed., *Collected Letters of Samuel Taylor Coleridge,* vol. II, 1801–1806 (Oxford: The Clarendon Press, 1956), p. 815.

58. Parrish, *Coleridge's Dejection,* lines 165–68 (pp. 28–29).

59. Ibid., lines 127–29 (p. 27).

60. Ibid., lines 295–96, 307–17 (pp. 33–34).

61. Ibid., line 339 (p. 34).

62. Coleridge, "Dejection: An Ode," ed. E. H. Hartley, line 86.

63. In Ernest De Selincourt, ed., *The Journals of Dorothy Wordsworth* (New York: The Macmillan Company, 1941), 1: lines 135–36.

64. Wordsworth, "Resolution and Independence," ed. George, lines 24–28, 53, 35, 48–49.

65. Ibid., lines 137–40.

66. Wordsworth, "Ode: Intimations of Immortality," ed. George, lines 87, 176–87, 203–204.

67. Wordsworth, *The Prelude,* ed. De Selincourt, original title.

68. Ibid., Book II, lines 453–54; Book III, lines 201–203; Book XIV, line 432.

69. Ibid., Book I, lines 1–2, 53, 15–19.

70. Ibid., Book XIII, lines 430–32; 435–41.

71. Ibid., Book XII, lines 209–18.

72. Ibid., Book VIII, heading.

73. Ibid., Book I; lines 394, 388–89, 428, 433–41.

74. Ibid., Book III, lines 88–89, 124–29.

75. Ibid., Book III, lines 130–35.

76. Ibid., Book IV, lines 332–338.

77. Ibid., Book VI, lines 598–99, 605–609.

78. Ibid., Book VII, lines 734–37, 771.

79. Ibid., Book VIII, lines 519–29.

80. William Blake, "The Proverbs of Hell," in *The Marriage of Heaven and Hell*, introduction and commentary by Sir Geoffrey Keynes (London and New York: Oxford University Press, 1975), plates 7–10, p. xviii.

10

THE LAST WESTERN CENTURY

The attempt to discover the sources and history of our ethical ideas is much like the first attempt to explore and to map a great river. There are only portions of the river that can be charted with accuracy, and within the depths of the waters remains a hidden, moving life. The origin of the river and its destination are not easily known. The sources are lost within impassable mountain chasms, and the mouth eddies in countless ever-changing streams that form a delta before the river flows into the sea.

So with our life. The sources of our ideas and ideals are lost in the distant recesses of the past. Then, about the eighth century in Israel and the fifth century in Greece, the ethical streams enter the plain of history and become navigable. From those times until the eighteenth century we can journey again and view again our past. To be sure, there are times when the stream disappears underground, there are places where rapids are rough for traveling, and there are always the deeper waters hidden from view. But for the most part, with patience and persistence, the stream is navigable. We can understand the history of our ethical ideas; we can see their relations to their own time and place. When we approach the last hundred years, however, we reach the delta. Here there can be no easy travels, no accurate mapping. Now there are eddies that run counter to the main stream of our past, and rivulets that change in importance as we move farther from them into the future. Most of all, there is an amazing complexity of actions and ideas that defies a simple mapping.

The ethical mapping of the last half of the nineteenth century is difficult enough, and for the twentieth it is a nearly impossible task. Yet the attempt to make the map must be made. For we are the inheritors of the last Western century, and we must live with, accepting or transforming, the institutions and ideas we have received. The late-nineteenth-century map reveals that those institutions and ideas of the past century exhibit both a continuation of and contradiction with previous structure and thought. On the one hand, there was a developing continuation of the Enlightenment and Romanticism with all that had gone before, both religious and secular, but on the other there was a fundamental rejection of essential earlier ideas and institutions. It was this rejection, coupled with worldwide technological developments, that made the period before the First World War the last Western century. The ideologies of the future cannot be exclusively Western; future history cannot be Western history. For those of us who live beyond the last Western century, one crucial test is the extent to which a Western ethical tradition can, without losing meaning and vitality, accommodate itself to and help create a new world situation.

To understand the nature of this test it is not only necessary to remember our ethical history. It is imperative that there be recognition of major creations of the nineteenth century that, arising from yet reacting to their past, have helped to transform values in our world. Life in the late twentieth century has been significantly influenced by the nineteenth-century work of men like Charles Darwin, Karl Marx, Friedrich Nietzsche, and Sigmund Freud. The ideas created by these men would have been impossible without the long history of thought before them, and, indeed, many of their assumptions relevant for ethics were drawn from the history of ethics. Yet, in significant ways, each man rejected the tradition he had received, and much of the result of the work of each contradicted the moral heritage of the West. Their contributions present to persons of the twentieth and twenty-first centuries a plain challenge, one not yet successfully met. How can there be an acceptance of their insights and, at the same time, an acceptance of the moral tradition which their insights appear to have destroyed?

In addition, the events and institutions of the last Western century that transformed life—industrialism, capitalism, nationalism, and science—possessed a similar duality of continuation and conflict with history. These events and institutions helped to provide the presuppositions of evolutionary, Marxist, Nietzschean, and psychoanalytical ethics. Therefore, before examining these ethics, it is essential to observe some of the major developments of the century and some of the major assumptions underlying these ethical views.

INDUSTRIAL REVOLUTION

The term "Industrial Revolution" was first used by the Frenchman A. Blanqui, who in 1837 looked back at the previous half-century and observed such changes that he believed an absolute transformation had taken place in European life. There have been attacks on the term based upon the facts that a long industrial development preceded Blanqui's "revolution" and that it is still in process over a hundred years later. But for all the deficiencies of the term, "Industrial Revolution" is sufficiently accurate to deserve retaining. It is at least as accurate as other general terms of history, for example, "Reformation," "Renaissance," "Enlightenment," and "Romanticism."

It was a period of radical change, and the essence of this change was that the life which had consisted primarily of personal and agricultural occupations with local markets was altered into one characterized mainly by industrial labor with worldwide commerce and an impersonal society. Thus, the "Industrial Revolution" meant changes in the nature of work, trade, and personal relations.

The work of producing and distributing the material goods of life was transformed first in England which, in the first half of the nineteenth century, became "the workshop of the world." The fundamental changes were few in number: the development of steam power, machine inventions (first in textiles), manufacture of machine tools, use of coal and iron, and changes in transportation. Each new development reacted from and stimulated the others, and the whole fused together in such a fashion as to create new ways of working and new works.

The combination of steam power with machinery was a fundamental development that drove civilization away from its old order. The "steam engine" became an image with which individuals in the nineteenth century naturally lived. Here was a power, inexhaustible and simple in origin, that erupted to move the mechanism of industry. At first the "steam engine," restricted to the simple mechanism of pumps, stimulated the mining of coal and iron ore. Then, in 1782, steam was yoked with rotary power and the wheels began to turn the machines of factories and later of transportation. The wheels turned slowly at first. In 1800 there were but 289 "steam engines" in England with a total of 4,543 horsepower. Moreover, because of the crudeness of the handmade machines, the wheels would often break down. However, toward the second and third decades of the century, with the invention of tools for making accurate machines, the momentum of industrialization gained speed. The tempo was increased in 1825 by the invention and improvement of the steam train. By 1840 there were almost 800 miles of railroad in England; by 1850 there were more than 6,000 miles; and in 1870, 15,000. The miles of track worldwide in the same years were 38,000 and 204,000. These railroads in turn stimulated the demand for coal and iron. In the hundred years between mid-eighteenth and mid-nineteenth centuries the mining of coal in Great Britain expanded fifteen times, from 4,700,000 to 64,700,000 tons. It was to increase another fourfold in the next half century.

Transportation by sea was behind rail transportation in use of steam power. The improvements in the sailing vessels in the mid-century made distant lands accessible, and later in the century oceansteamers replaced sailing ships. A new era of worldwide commerce began. There had been worldwide trade before, but it had been sporadic and sparse compared with that of the nineteenth century. With the linking of the continental islands of the world by ship, with the penetration into the hinterlands by rail, there came to the countries of Europe and America new goods and new peoples. There were the potentialities for use of the world's resources, and there were also the dangers, caused by the linking of industrial manufacturing and transportation with capitalism and nationalism, for destruction of those same resources.

New personal relations were introduced in part because of the mobility of persons from nation to nation. More important was the migration from farm to industrial city and the rise of the industrial-social classes. There was, in the first decades of the Industrial Revolution, real opposition to going into cities and factories, and this resistance was a reason for the slow development of industrial momentum. Moreover, the first factories were exceedingly small, even by the standards of previous centuries. As late as 1851 in England 457 firms employed less than ten men, 200 employed between ten and 350, and only fourteen employed more than 350. Even at the end of the century the average factory in London had 41 workers. It was not, then, the size so much that caused a change in personal relations as the new status of workers and the location of the factory. Previously the owner of a loom or forge worked side by side with his hired laborers. Often the worker ate and lived with the family of his employer, but gradually this system of work relations changed. The manufacturer was moving into a different class and he no longer worked with his employees. The location of the factory, too, caused a change in the human relations. With the coming of steam power the factories tended to locate near the sources of coal and iron or near the best points for distribution rather than in villages near the source of water power.

Thus while the development of industry was not the sole cause for the rapid development of cities in the nineteenth century, it was an important cause, and the fact remains that the "urbanization" of life was a major product of the nineteenth century, with an intensive impact upon the life and ethics of the time.

CAPITALISM

The economic structure that directed the developments of the Industrial Revolution was the system of "capitalism." The organization of capitalism had both its technical and human sides. The picture of London as the banking house of the world, or of London as the center of the rail system of England provided simple images for this organization. For capitalism was organized concentrically around the individual industry and the individual entrepreneur, and it was the position of the entrepreneur (a combination of inventor, discoverer, engineer, organizer, and merchant) that was largely determinative for human relations. For it was the entrepreneur who had access to the necessary capital and who controlled the industrial policies. Thus the structure was not built around the needs of the state, nor the landed aristocracy, nor the worker, nor the consumer. The individual with property-potential was the center of value. From such persons and property the technical and human organization of capitalism was constructed.

Basic to the building of the structure were the freedoms that made possible profitable enterprise. On its technical side the structure consisted of (a) expanding industrial patterns, (b) a free market where saleable goods (including labor) were exchanged, and (c) a separation and coordination of the essential industrial-commercial functions.

The human structure centered around the welfare of the middle-class entrepreneur. There were to be no restrictions placed upon his activity, but strong restraints, both legal and moral, were placed upon his workers. Apart from the important but weak humanitarian forces of the early industrial era the many were not considered in policy making or economic theory. The justification for this was found in the classical economic theories which were believed to be a statement of natural law. In T. R. Malthus's "theory of population," population was limited by subsistence and tended to increase in geometrical ratio when the means of subsistence increased. Population and essentials for life are kept in a rough balance through "moral restraint, vice, and misery." Because these forces do not work properly among the working class, the theory states that "they are themselves the cause of their own poverty; [and] that the means of redress are in their own hands, and in the hands of no other persons whatever."[1]

The classical economist David Ricardo (1772–1823) developed Malthus's population theory into a theory of wages. According to his view real wages will necessarily stay at about the subsistence level, since the rise of wages would introduce contradictory consequences. The size of families would increase, producing a surplus of labor and causing a fall in real wages. Necessarily wages would "enable the laborers, one with another, to subsist and to perpetuate their race, without either increase or diminution."[2] The entrepreneur, therefore, was not responsible for the subsistence livelihood of the worker, since this condition was controlled by inexorable economic law.

There was also a spirit unique to capitalism as well as its technology and organization. This spirit was not that of the workers but of the enterprising class. Permeating the ethos was (a) a spirit of freedom for capitalist organization and capitalist organizers. The demand for freedom was linked with a desire for profits, so (b) the acquisitive attitude was the second characteristic of the unique spirit of capitalism. But if acquisitiveness was the goal of economic man the spirit of (c) rationality and (d) competition directed the means toward the goal. Rational organization applied to the behavior of the individual industrialist and industry. It did not refer to rational planning by the state or by the workers. Competition involved a willingness to take risks. It was a competition with nature and in the market. Thus freedom, acquisitiveness, rationality, and competition marked the spirit of nineteenth-century capitalism. But there was a further notion present, too. It was the idea that these characteristic motives working together would result in (e) harmony and (f) progress. Something new was introduced in the world; it was the belief that economic man would necessarily create a good society.

NATIONALISM

The nationalism which was such an important ingredient in the life of the West in the nineteenth century included both the evolving of the nation-state and, more significantly, the spirit of a people in relation to their nation and destiny.

The realities to which the word "nation" refers cannot be precisely defined. In general a "nation" is a people unified on the basis of geography, language, religion, customs, institutions, and race, though each of these factors is not always operative in every nation. Such elements taken together, however, do not necessarily make a nation. There must be a unifying force, historical events that bring the nation into existence through making the people aware that they belong to one another.

> A nation is a body of men, inhabiting a definite territory, who normally are drawn from different races, but possess a common stock of thoughts and feelings acquired and transmitted during the course of a common history.[3]

The "common stock" usually includes religious belief, language, and "a common will." It was when the common wills of peoples became political wills that the modern nation-states were born. The course of development was that first the cultural unity of nationalities was linked with a political unity, and, later, the cultural-political unity was bound to an economic order.

For the cultural and political unities to be brought together the two doctrines of popular sovereignty and self-determination had to be widely accepted. Through political and intellectual developments both doctrines gained ground in the seventeenth and eighteenth centuries, particularly through the revolutions in England and America. But it was in France, where the ideological ground had been cultivated, that the doctrine of the nation-state achieved its clearest expression in the French Revolution, and it was through the "liberating" Napoleonic armies that the doctrine became firmly rooted in European soil.

The first period of nineteenth-century nationality, lasting until about 1870, was the development of the liberal nation-state. The spirit of nationalism that infused the dominant thought of this era was the spirit of a democratic and liberal ethos. This nationalism was stated clearly in an official report by the French revolutionary Lazare Carnot in 1793:

> Let us follow the law which is written on the heart of all men, and let us try not to abuse it; let only national honor and French generosity be for all peoples of the world the certain guarantee of the justice which you owe them and which you should render them; in breaking the chains of oppressed nations, let such sublime sentiments surpass their hopes and desires. . . . Every nation has the right to live by itself if it pleases or to unite with others, if they wish, for the common good. We Frenchmen recognize no sovereigns but the peoples themselves; our system is not at all one of domination, but one of fraternity.[4]

Under the impulse of this spirit the "cosmopolitanism of the Enlightenment was replaced by the nationalism of the Romantic movement."[5] Nationalism still involved an international outlook. There was the feeling that an individual's loyalty to one's nation was a loyalty to all human beings since the nations would, by free interchange with each other and by the development of their own destinies, progress in mutual accord. Throughout the Western world middle classes replaced aristocratic governments; the franchise was gradually extended; there was sympathy for the oppressed, culminating in the emancipation of serfs in various countries; and intellectual and industrial developments were shared among receptive nations.

During the first half of the century nationalism became associated with other major social forces. Industrialism stimulated nationalism through the development of large-scale industry accompanied by development of the middle class and the proletariat. Growth of the cities strengthened a loyalty to the nation-state, for as persons moved from farms into factories, new loyalties to the nation replaced the vacuum caused by the weakening of traditional home ties. Transportation and communication, often based upon national geographical areas, served to bind the nation within its borders, and more clearly demarcated one nation from another. Capitalist enterprises with their dominant drive for profits required the services and protection of the state. Economic rivalry thus continued between nations, intensifying the nationalistic outlook. Finally, the propagation of Darwin's evolutionary theories in mid-century was rapidly absorbed into justification of nationalistic struggles for survival and domination.

Romantic nationalism with its internationalism was replaced in the last half of the century by a realistic nationalism which, locating the source and center of value in the nation, emphasized the inevitability of conflict between states. As the cultural-political nation state became fused with the economic order, the conservative (often aristocratic) forces began to dominate the nationalities. Nationalism became imperialism. Scientific tariffs were introduced, coupled with a competition for overseas markets and the conquering of the "backward" peoples of Asia and Africa. Authoritarian, nonmoral, calculating nationalism conflicted with the earlier democratic, ethical, idealistic order.

> This realism has been the product of a variety of novel factors: absorption in the mechanical and utilitarian aspects of the industrial revolution; admiration for the "practical man" of big industry and big finance; acceptance of a mechanistic theory of the universe and of a materialist interpretation of human behavior; distrust of human reason and trust in pragmatism and human will; adaptation of the biological hypotheses of Darwin to support such conceptions as the inequality of races, the "struggle for existence" and the "survival of the fittest."[6]

SCIENCE

The social events of the Industrial Revolution, the development of capitalism, and the intensification of nationalism created the dominant ethos for the development of the late-nineteenth-century ethic. However, the fusion of science with these social events and with human ideals had a profound impact upon moral thought, and acted as a catalytic stimulus for evolutionary naturalism, communism, psychoanalysis, and existentialism. Indeed, while the assumptions of these varied ethical views were influenced directly by the social events of the time, the basic presuppositions were taken from a modification of Enlightenment views by nineteenth-century science, particularly from the new biology of organic evolution.

After Isaac Newton scientists had a primary goal toward which all lesser goals were directed, to discover unified principles that explain the operations of the universe. In the seventeenth century Newton had viewed the promised land of a "machine-world"; in the eighteenth century there were further reports of nature as a mechanism. And by the nineteenth century the mechanical metaphor seemed almost inevitable. Sir William Dampier in *A History of Science* described the fundamental outlook of the time:

Throughout the nineteenth century, most men of science, consciously or unconsciously, held the common-sense view that matter, its primary properties and their relations, as revealed by science, are ultimate realities, and that human bodies are mechanisms perhaps occasionally controlled or influenced by minds.[7]

For most scientists, however, the question was not whether nature was a mechanism but rather, "How shall we conquer the unified mechanical principles that control nature?" The answer to this question was made by the incessant activities of the scientists, geologists, chemists, physicists, biologists, and later the investigators in sociology and psychology.

The influential sciences for the ethos and ethic of the time were chemistry, physics, and, most important, biology. How did these sciences arrive at deterministic principles which became significant for ethics? The answer to this question in chemistry was in John Dalton's atomic theory; in physics it was in Thomas Young's and Augustine-Jean Fresnel's wave theory of light, in Michael Faraday's electromagnetism, and in J. P. Joule's and William Thomson's thermodynamics; and in biology it was in Charles Darwin's evolution. However, it is misleading to single out these men and events in isolation. The work of scientists and new scientific knowledge were dependent upon the cooperation of many individuals and the coalescence of many discoveries. But these individuals and their theories provide a rough indication of scientific influences upon ethics. Dalton found that all chemical substances are composed of discrete, minute particles of which there are only a limited number (he counted twenty-six). Young and Fresnel, demonstrating that light-rays "bend," accounted for this fact by a theory that light travels by "waves," and developed a quantitative measurement for these "waves." Faraday, building upon the work of Alessandro Volta, Hans Christian Oersted, and André-Marie Ampère pushed further the discovery that electrical phenomena are connected with magnetism to the point of demonstrating that electromagnetism can be a source of energy. Joule and Thomson in thermodynamics explained a relation between work and heat and found mathematical means to measure this relation. Darwin proposed a theory for "The Origin of the Species" and explained the possible natural principles by which this origin took place. Each of these developments had immediate social consequences in industry or in agriculture. Their importance for ethics was not in the theories or social effects but in the meanings seen in the theories.

That meaning can be suggested by the terms *matter, energy, process,* and *determinism.* The atomic theory in chemistry emphasized the material structure of all chemical substances. This reinforced the view that the universe ultimately consists of matter and that this mass remains constant throughout all transformations. The wave theory of light and electromagnetism suggested that physical events pervade all of space, for if light travels by waves there must be something to form the wave, just as, if electric currents are related to magnetism, there must be a physical medium through which the currents pass. Thermodynamics pointed to the importance and persistence of energy (conservation of energy) and the theory of evolution directed attention away from the structure to the process of life.

Throughout all these scientific discoveries mechanism was assumed. The contradictions that existed between the discoveries made in diverse fields were not apparent at the time, and a mechanistic determinism was widely believed to be basic to all new developments. It was not observed, for example, that an atomic theory which explained everything in terms of discrete particles of matter conflicted with a wave theory of light that recognized physical continuity throughout space. It was not noted that if energy was "one of the most important qualities" of matter, then the conception of physical matter was changed. Nor was it apparent that if living things were interpreted by organic process, then the notion of nature as a mechanism was no longer tenable. It was because these contradictions were not recognized and analyzed that the beliefs in the omnipresence of matter, energy, process, and determinism were so influential in ethics.

These developments of science, particularly the development of a theory of organic evolution, had specific, profound effects upon the ethos and ethics of the time. Both Marx and Freud were devotees of Darwin, and Nietzsche, though he claimed to detest Darwinism, was obviously influenced by evolutionary biological thought. Marx wanted to dedicate *Das Kapital* to Darwin. Freud, explaining his choice of a vocation wrote, "The theories of Darwin which were then of topical interest strongly attracted me, for they held out hopes of an extraordinary advance in our understanding of the world."[8] So, in a sense, Darwin was the first eddy, and it is appropriate to begin with him.

CHARLES DARWIN (1809–1882)

Charles Darwin's father was a physician who introduced and encouraged his son in scientific interests. His grandfathers were Josiah Wedgwood, a man of scientific ability and industrial interests, and Erasmus Darwin, a naturalist, philosopher, and, more doubtfully, a poet. However, it was Erasmus Darwin who caught a glimpse of the insight that was to be seen in its full significance by his grandson. "When we observe," he wrote,

> first the changes which we see naturally produced in animals after their birth ... secondly, the changes by artificial cultivation ... thirdly, the changes produced by climate, ... fourthly, the changes produced before

birth by crossing or mutilation, fifthly, the similarity of structure in all the warm-blooded animals, including mankind, one is led to conclude that they have alike been produced from a similar living filament.[9]

The evolutionary development he envisaged in his poem "The Temple of Nature":

> Organic life beneath the shoreless waves
> Was born and nurs'd in ocean's pearly caves;
> First forms minute, unseen by spheric glass,
> Move on the mud, or pierce the watery mass;
> These, as successive generations bloom,
> New powers acquire and larger limbs assume;
> Whence countless groups of vegetation spring,
> And breathing reels of fin and feet and wing.[10]

Some of the aspects of organic evolution had been noted by many naturalists before Charles Darwin. Theories of evolution to explain natural and social history had been offered by philosophers. Certain ideas of conflict and harmony, process and progress, determinism and environmentalism, basic to the first scientific evolutionary view, were familiar in the economic, social, and political life and thought of the Enlightenment. In order for a scientific theory of evolution to arise, there was need for the patient accumulation of factual data, the recognition of problems posed by the data, and the imaginative construction of a hypothesis to resolve the problems and explain the facts. The need was for a scientist with varied abilities rarely found in combination with each other. Charles Darwin met that need.

The patient accumulation of data was made possible when the twenty-two-year-old Darwin was assigned as naturalist to HMS *Beagle* on its journey around the world. The name of the ship aptly suited the young scientist. Darwin's hunting for natural data of all kinds was insatiable, and the bo's'n referred to him as "our fly-catcher," while other crewmembers nicknamed him "Philosopher." The "Philosopher" even pursued nonexistent animals. At midnight on April 1, 1832, he was awakened by the excited voice of a young officer, "Darwin! Did you ever see a grampus? Bear a hand, then." He rushed to the deck, scientific notebook in hand, to be greeted by laughter of the crew.[11]

On that voyage from 1831 to 1836 Darwin accumulated many facts and saw that some of these facts raised fundamental questions about geological and biological origins. In the land south of Buenos Aires he noted that two European plants, a thistle and artichoke-like cardoon, had completely obliterated native vegetation. Here was a dramatic example of a struggle for life. Elsewhere in South America he found the fossil remains of a horse; knowing that the discoverers of America had seen no signs of horses, he wrote,

> It is a marvelous fact in the history of Mammalia that in South America a
> native horse should have lived and disappeared, to be succeeded in after
> ages by countless herds descended from the few introduced by the Spanish
> colonists.[12]

Here was a struggle for life and similarity of mammalian structure. In the
Andes at a height of thirteen thousand feet he found sea shells. This was evidence of the slow processes of nature.

As Darwin saw with fascination the infinitely changing nature, questions
about the beginnings and development of life entered his mind; however, the
first most important clue to an answer did not come until two years after the
Beagle voyage.

> In October 1838 I happened to read Malthus on Population, and being well
> prepared to appreciate the struggle for existence which everywhere goes on
> from long continued observation of the habits of animals and plants, it at
> once struck me that under these circumstances favourable variations would
> tend to be preserved, and unfavourable ones to be destroyed. The result of
> this would be the formation of a new species. Here then I had a theory by
> which to work.[13]

Beginning with that reading of Malthus the theory on the formation of
new species slowly matured in Darwin's mind. But it required courage for
him to overcome the inner opposition of his own misinformation and the anticipated outer opposition of social misunderstanding, especially that of scientists and theologians. As late as 1844 he wrote to an intimate friend

> I have been now ever since my return engaged in a very presumptuous work
> and I know no one individual who would not say a very foolish one. I was
> so struck with the distribution of the Galapagos organisms etc., and with the
> character of the American fossil mammifers etc., that I determined to col-
> lect blindly every sort of fact which could bear in any way on what are
> species. . . . At last gleams of light have come, and I am almost convinced
> (quite contrary to the opinion I started with) that species are not (it is like
> confessing a murder) immutable.[14]

Darwin was hesitant to present his views even to scientists. He made
sketches of his theory in 1842 and 1844, but it was not until fourteen years
later that he was persuaded to have a paper read at a scientific society. At the
same meeting the secretary of the Linnean Society read a paper by Alfred
Russel Wallace, a British naturalist living in Malaya, who had developed a
similar evolutionary theory. The following year Darwin sent his manuscript
The Origin of Species to John Murray, who had already agreed to publish the

book before knowing its contents. As Murray read and began to understand the theory he became alarmed, thinking it "as absurd as though one could contemplate a fruitful union between a poker and a rabbit." After consulting with others Murray tried to persuade Darwin to forget the book and publish instead an account of his observations on pigeons with only a brief account of his theory; for after all, he said, "everybody is interested in pigeons."[15]

From Malthus and his own observations Darwin had learned that living things tend to increase in geometric proportions and that, on the whole, species remain fairly constant in numbers. From these dual facts he deduced that there is a struggle for survival continuously taking place throughout all nature. He noted, too, the wide variation of living things and concluded that "favored races" are preserved or, in the more famous phrase of Herbert Spencer, there is a "survival of the fittest."

The full title of Darwin's book revealed the influential elements of his theory: *The Origin of the Species by Means of Natural Selection or the Preservation of Favored Races in the Struggle for Life*. The phrase, "the preservation of Favored Races in the Struggle for Life" pointed to (a) the struggle for existence. "It inevitably follows from the high rate at which all organic beings tend to increase. It has truly been said that all nature is at war."[16] The phrase also suggested (b) the "survival of the fittest":

> Can we doubt . . . that individuals having any advantage, however slight over others would have the best chance of surviving and of procreating their kind? On the other hand, we may feel sure that any variation in the least degree injurious would be rigidly destroyed.[17]

The phrase "by Means of Natural Selection" meant (c) that the entire process operated by a natural determinism. The main title *The Origin of Species* referred to (d) the theory that species are not immutable, but that they arise and are modified according to natural principles. In the words of Thomas Huxley, who described himself as "Darwin's bulldog,"

> The suggestion that new species may result from the selective action of external conditions upon the variations from the specific type which individuals present and which we call "spontaneous" because we are ignorant of their causation is as wholly unknown to the historian of scientific ideas as it was to biological specialists before 1858. But that suggestion is the central idea of the *Origin of Species* and contains the quintessence of Darwinism.[18]

The theory of evolution as presented by Darwin was far from complete. But the essence of the doctrine was clearly formulated, and that formulation affected much of the nineteenth-century ethic. What, in brief, are some of the central motifs as these entered ethical thought? First, the environment or the events that happen to a species are determinative for its life. Second, life consists essentially of conflict, of a struggle to exist. Third, life is interpreted in terms of process, of historical process and of function, rather than explained primarily by structure. Fourth, any satisfactory explanation of life must be made in terms of origins. Fifth, the natural process is essentially progress in which species are "perfected by accumulation of innumerable slight variations."[19]

Sixth, determinism was assumed throughout, for throughout mechanism was accepted as the means by which process occurs. There was, seventh, the view that while the forces of nature relentlessly go their own way man is able to assist nature in directing the process for many animals and plants. "Man," wrote Darwin,

> does not produce variability; he only exposes beings to new conditions, and then nature acts on the organisation, and causes variability. But man can select variations. . . . He can influence the character of a breed by selecting, in each successive generation, individual differences so slight as to be quite inappreciable by an uneducated eye.[20]

Finally, Darwin shared with other scientists of his own time and of all time the faith that truth which is hidden below the surface appearance of nature is both desirable and possible to achieve. Truth is good. Scientific truth became a system that explained the inevitable, impersonal workings of the natural world which sustains the life and thought of man.

PRESUPPOSITIONS IN THE ETHICS OF MARX, NIETZSCHE, AND FREUD

Karl Marx was born in 1818 in the German Rhineland. Friedrich Nietzsche and Sigmund Freud were born, respectively, twenty-six and thirty-six years later, the former in the Prussian province of Saxony and the latter in Austria. Marx and Freud died in exile in London in 1883 and 1939. Nietzsche, insane for the last decade of his life, died in 1900. In the formative years of their lives all three were subject to the same influences of nineteenth-century capitalism, industrialism, nationalism, and science; and their basic ideas attest to these influences. They were the sons of liberal-bourgeois fathers, the students of German professors of the Enlightenment. Marx and Freud were the grandsons of Jewish rabbis. Nietzsche was the son and grandson of Protestant clergymen. These similarities in the lives of three men whose experiences were so diverse help to account for a fundamental similarity of outlook despite the great differences in their theories. All three men were the heirs of Western history, though all vigorously denied this fact. All three were the products of the

Enlightenment bourgeois mind, though all rejected much in the Enlightenment mentality. All were directly and deeply influenced by Romanticism. Indeed, in essential ways they were combinations of the Enlightenment and Romanticism, and, just as these two cultural movements were at war with each other, so there were unresolved inner conflicts in Marx, Nietzsche, and Freud.

The fundamental assumption in their lives that formed the basis for their arduous work was received from Western history through the Enlightenment and Romanticism. Permeating all of their work was a moral passion. This consuming passion consisted of two motive-forces, a concern for human good and a determination to know the truth.

In their hatred of middle-class moralism these three men denied that their own work was motivated by ethical principles, but the facts of their work belie the denials. Their recognition of disorder in human life and the demand for a reconstruction of society or the individual, reveal their roles as prophets and priests who desire the salvation both of the world and of individuals in the world. In this they were in the tradition of Western ethical thought. Their motivating concern was for what it means to be and to become fully human.

This concern for human good was, in their conscious thinking, subordinate to a desire to know the truth. Such subordination was possible only because they held tenaciously, unquestioningly to the belief that "truth is good." The statement made about Marx might have been written of Freud and Nietzsche, namely, that "all that men need, in order to know how to save themselves from the chaos in which they are involved, is to seek to understand their actual condition."[21] Their goal was a theory that would explain everything about society or the individual self.

In addition to this goal that constituted the basis of their work there were five specific presuppositions that provided a fundamental framework for their ideas. These ideological presuppositions were inherited from the Enlightenment and Romanticism, and modified by the nineteenth-century forces of industrialism, capitalism, nationalism, and science, in particular, Darwinian biology.

1. An individual is a natural, evolving being.

An individual here was understood as either a social or individual organism, and the difference between a sociological and a psychological perspective distinguished the thought of Marx from that of Freud and Nietzsche. However, for all three, there were two characteristics of societies or individuals that determined the possibilities and ways human life was to be understood: naturalism and evolutionism.

Naturalism implied that the order of nature is self-existent, self-operating, self-directing, and thus self-explanatory. Because this is true human nature can be known in the only way that any nature can be known, by scientific (i.e., empirical) discovery of the uniformities of behavior and by philosophic (i.e., rational) organization of these uniformities into explanatory theories.

Evolutionism pointed to the significantly pervasive fact that human nature, individual or social, like all other nature, is in process. Natural development is everywhere evident. Being human is to become human. An individual's life can be known as it is told, historically, for the story is history. Evolution requires a beginning, a processing, and an ending. Human beings, therefore, are to be understood genetically, historically, and teleologically. They are to be understood genetically in that the beginnings of life are the clues to the process and goals of life. They are to be understood historically in that the events of their development can be comprehended only as the representations of the historical patterns of their development. And, finally, they are to be understood teleologically in that the becoming leads to true being; the historical process moves to the end, in history, of process.

2. Life is essentially conflict.

An individual's life begins in conflict of forces and continues by conflict. Everywhere, always there is competition and a struggle for survival. To understand life it is necessary to understand the essential nature of the competition. To survive it is necessary to participate in the struggle.

3. The life of the individual is determined by primary, nonrational forces.

The life of each individual as social or as solitary person follows definite laws of behavior. This means determinism, but what determines human life are primary, nonrational forces. They are forces in that they have the power to mold life, either constructively or destructively. They are primary in that they are limited in number, and they are nonrational in that it is they and not reason that decide which forces shall motivate a human being.

4. Through knowledge of the life forces the individual is enabled to participate in shaping the future.

Reason plays a paradoxical role in the Marxian, Nietzschean, and Freudian drama. Their rejection of rationalism and the Enlightenment is manifest in that "the life of the individual is determined by primary nonrational forces." But it is not the entire truth to say simply that it is the primary forces motivating human beings which determine their capacity for reason. For the determination of the reason of some individuals is toward the truth, and when this happens the individual participates in shaping the future. In this these men were children of the Enlightenment. In this power of reason they remained Rationalists with a capital "R." There have never been philosophers who were more fully convinced that knowledge is salvation.

The knowledge that insured salvation was both theoretical and existential. As theoretical it was a rational understanding of the laws of historical development. Such were the theoretical systems developed by Marx, Nietzsche, and Freud which, properly apprehended and applied, are a means of salvation. As existential the knowledge is insight into one's own condition or the condition of one's society. This knowledge, objective and subjective, theoretical and existential, enables the individual to accept her situation and to share in the shaping of her future. This knowledge, always scientific, enables the individual to live with herself in her time and to live toward her future.

In this rationalism the individual is important, and in this affirmation the Enlightenment faith again reappears. But the individual is not the fundamental reality, and in this denial the Enlightenment faith is denied. "The individual is enabled," thus she is freed to do something, but she is not free to do anything. The individual is the determined bearer of her destiny; she is not, except as chosen by fate, the creative determiner of her own destination.

5. Out of the human conflict a fundamental harmony will emerge.

Once more the faith of the Enlightenment via Darwin appeared as a fundamental premise. The attitudes of the three men toward the inevitability and nature of the harmony were different. For Marx the social harmony, the complete disappearance of the conflict, was an absolute certainty. All of the laws of social history point toward the dawning of that day. For Nietzsche the unique harmony that constitutes the superman was the intensification of a creative tension. For Freud the individual harmony was inevitable if the person genuinely apprehended her past and participated, with this apprehension, in her present. As he lived into the twentieth century, however, Freud began to doubt the completeness of psychoanalytic cures in the case of all persons. In their faith in the emerging of harmony from conflict these men were the sons of the bourgeois Enlightenment. But Marx's optimism that the end of all conflict was around the next bend of social history contrasted with Freud's pessimism that there might be more bends in history than could yet be seen.

KARL MARX (1818–1883)

Until he was twenty-five Karl Marx lived in his country with his class and accepting his heritage. After he was twenty-five Marx lived in exile from his nation, class, and history. This dual fact was important in the development of his thought. His nation was Germany, but he became a man without a country. His class was the enlightened bourgeoisie, but he lost contact with that middle class. His history was that of the West with its religious and philosophical interpretation of human good, but he disdained any claims to moral theory through his break with traditional philosophy and religion. The years of acceptance were not ones of unquestioned conformity, nor the years of separation ones of absolute rejection. Still, it is true enough to say that at twenty-five, Marx made a break with his past. His major affirmations arose out of that life from which he exiled himself.

Marx's childhood was happy. His youth, excited by ideas, was happier still. During the formative period of his life he did not suffer hardship, but matured in congenial communities. Two men whom he always spoke of with respect were largely responsible for the happiness of his youth. Heinrich Marx, Karl's father, was an amiable, liberal, optimistic Jew who had embraced Christianity both from conviction, since it did not conflict with his Enlightenment rationalism, and from convenience, for it afforded privileges not granted to Jews. Ludwig von Westphalen, a minor government official, communicated to the young university student a love of literature, especially of Goethe, Dante, and Shakespeare. The friendship with both men sustained Karl and strengthened his belief in himself in the days of intellectual search before his own outlook was formulated.

When, at eighteen, Marx entered the University of Berlin, he was immediately confronted with the prominent Hegelian philosophy. In that philosophy, so comprehensive and consistent, he was introduced to the idea of historical laws that must be discovered by the rational mind. It was there that he recognized a pattern that permeated change, and he saw particular beings as manifestations of a Universal Spirit. Social institutions for Hegel could not be understood apart from discovering the laws of social history. These laws were the laws of "the dialectic," of omnipresent conflict being resolved through evolutionary progress. Freedom, then, could be a reality only for that person who discovered the historical laws of human life. This discovery led to the view that history moves toward a goal in which the Universal Spirit would be fully freed in social institutions. Shortly after he went to Berlin, Marx wrote to his father that he was wrestling with the new philosophy that was being preached to him, trying to prove it was false. He confessed failure to win his first bout with Hegelianism. He became a member of the "Younger Hegelians," a group dedicated to a liberal, social interpretation of Hegel's ideas. This led to his conception of what it means to be a philosopher and to his own vocation:

> The plain duty of the philosopher who carries the burden of civilization on his shoulders is therefore to promote such revolution by the special technical skills which he alone commands, that is by intellectual warfare.[22]

In 1841 Marx received the doctor of philosophy degree from the University of Jena. It would have been difficult to predict from his record what his future would be: his doctoral dissertation was on the philosophy of Heraclitus and Parmenides. Shortly thereafter, in 1843, he became editor of a journal, *Die Rheinische Zeitung*, and there began six years of conflict that led him into exile. However, it was through this continuing conflict that Marx's thought was forced into clearer focus.

Marx directed his first sympathies as an editor toward the peasants and the poor. He wrote articles analyzing the miserable condition of the peasants under the Prussian government and denouncing the harsh punishment meted out to the poor for petty thefts. From his first critical articles Marx had to maneuver adroitly to escape government censorship. When, on January 21, 1843, he advocated war against Russia as a way to promote liberty throughout Europe, his paper was suppressed. On June 19, 1843, Marx married Jenny von Westphalen, his childhood sweetheart, and together they went to Paris. To turn their backs upon Germany, whose atmosphere Marx found intolerable, for a foreign country was prophetic for the new family. The next few years were years of wandering, and for most of the remainder of their lives they lived in near poverty. But each new rejection, each new suffering, drove the two closer together.

In Paris Marx found in Ludwig Feuerbach (1804–1872) the view that social existence is the sum of material conditions. He found in Saint-Simon (1760–1825) the idea that class conflict is the propulsive force in history. From his meeting with émigré German workers he discerned a rising spirit of revolution. But it was from French and English economists that Marx learned his most important lesson, and it was this lesson that enabled him to win his wrestling bout with Hegelianism. For these "scientists" provided Marx with a method that rejected abstract philosophical reasoning for empirical data. He described his own view of his method in the preface to the second edition of *Capital* when he quoted with approval two Russian critics, one of whom pointed out that "the method of Marx is the deductive method of the whole English school."[23] The other writer commented at greater length:

> Marx only troubles himself about one thing; to show, by rigid scientific investigation, the necessity of successive determinate orders of social condi-

tions, and to establish, as impartially as possible, the facts that serve him for fundamental starting points. For this is quite enough, if he proves, at the same time, both the necessity of the present order of things, and the necessity of another order into which the first must inevitably pass over; and this all the same, whether men believe or do not believe it, whether they are conscious or unconscious of it. Marx treats the social movement as a process of natural history, governed by laws not only independent of human will, consciousness and intelligence, but rather, on the contrary, determining that will, consciousness and intelligence. . . . In a word, economic life offers us a phenomenon analogous to the history of evolution in other [*sic*] branches of biology. . . . The scientific value of such an inquiry lies in the disclosing of the special laws that regulate the origin, existence, development, and death [of] a given social organism and its replacement by another and higher one.[24]

In 1845 Marx criticized the Prussian king. When the Prussian government protested, he was exiled from Paris. In 1848 he was expelled from Brussels because he had written *The Communist Manifesto*. And in 1849, when as editor of *Die Neue Rheinische Zeitung*, Marx supported the democratic assembly against the autocratic government, he was tried by a jury for treason and acquitted, yet expelled from Cologne by the Prussian authorities. He went to London, where he remained until his death.

These, then, were the years of exile. Marx rejected his class, and from 1843 onward he increasingly lost contact with the bourgeoisie. From this exile he condemned the bourgeois (while recognizing their great achievements) and affirmed that through another class, the proletariat, history would move toward a classless society. He was exiled from his nation, and from his exile he condemned nationalism ("working men have no country"). Yet he affirmed that through developments which were to begin in Germany the world would enter an era of internationalism. Marx rejected his history, Judaism and Christianity, with its philosophical and moral tradition. Through the rejection of Judaism and Christianity he condemned religion but affirmed that irreligion would lead to the goal of prophetic religion, an era of justice. Through the rejection of philosophy he denied the possibility of philosophical truth since philosophies are the product of their time, and yet he proclaimed his own possession of the truth. Through his rejection of moral ideas he denied the validity of ethical judgments or slogans, and yet he advocated a new ideology which, replete with moral terms, would lead to a just society.

Karl Marx was scientist, prophet, and philosopher. He was a scientist who insisted upon factual data, making a careful analysis of the elements of social existence, commingling them into a comprehensive economic theory. The scientist in him denied the presence of value judgments in his thought. But he was also a prophet who had a sense of justice with a vision of a just world and who was possessed by a clairvoyant view of history with a conviction of human destiny. As philosopher he wove his scientific thought and prophetic feeling into a rational structure proclaimed as the true way for human life. While he was scientist and prophet and philosopher, he was also a person whose views were not fragmented but were focused into a multidimensional picture of human life.

THE VIEW OF HISTORY

History, to Marx, was the story not of this or that nation but of the human race, and the human race was ultimately one. This basic view did not mean that Marx was oblivious to the fact that civilizations, nations, and social groups have their own histories. It meant simply that he saw one universal will manifest through all histories whatever the particular accidents of their growth. He saw one universal goal as the culmination of all histories whatever their particular stages of attainment.

The phrase "universal will" was not understood in religious or teleological senses. The "universal will" was the "materialistic interpretation of history" or the "economic determinism." These catchphrases are easily misunderstood. Marx referred to his view as being "materialistic," but he did not mean that everything is reducible to physical materials. He was simply contrasting his own view with that of Hegelian idealism. Human history is not the working into time of a spiritual principle but the evolving in time of man's social existence.

> I was lead to the conclusion that legal relations, as well as forms of state, could neither be understood by themselves, nor explained by the so called general progress of the human mind, but that they are rooted in the material conditions of life which Hegel calls . . . civil society. The anatomy of civil society is to be sought in political economy.[25]

Marx reinforced this interpretation by contrasting his views with Hegel's:

> To Hegel the life process of the human brain, i.e., the process of thinking, which, under the name of "the Idea," he even transforms into an independent subject, is the demiurgos of the real world, and the real world is only the external, phenomenal form of "the Idea." With me, on the contrary, the ideal is nothing else than the material world reflected by the human mind, and translated into forms of thought.[26]

"Economic determinism" did not mean that all actions of individuals or nations were the direct result of simple economic motives, but that economic factors are the ultimate, most influential determinant of all significant human developments.

In 1859 Marx wrote a summary of his views of history.

> The general conclusion at which I arrived and which, once reached, became the guiding principle of my studies can be summarised as follows. In the social production of their existence, men inevitably enter into definite relations, which are independent of their will, namely relations of production appropriate to a given stage in the development of their material forces of production. The totality of these relations of production constitutes the economic structure of society, the real foundation, on which arises a legal and political superstructure and to which correspond definite forms of social consciousness. The mode of production of material life conditions the general process of social, political and intellectual life. It is not the consciousness of men that determines their existence, but their social existence that determines their consciousness. At a certain stage of development, the material productive forces of society come into conflict with the existing relations of production or—this merely expresses the same thing in legal terms—with the property relations within the framework of which they have operated hitherto. From forms of development of the productive forces these relations turn into their fetters. Then begins an era of social revolution. The changes in the economic foundation lead sooner or later to the transformation of the whole immense superstructure. In studying such transformations it is always necessary to distinguish between the material transformation of the economic conditions of production, which can be determined with the precision of natural science, and the legal, political, religious, artistic or philosophic—in short, ideological forms in which men become conscious of this conflict and fight it out. Just as one does not judge an individual by what he thinks about himself, so one cannot judge such a period of transformation by its consciousness, but, on the contrary, this consciousness must be explained from the contradictions of material life, from the conflict existing between the social forces of production and the relations of production. No social order is ever destroyed before all the productive forces for which it is sufficient have been developed, and new superior relations of production never replace older ones before the material conditions for their existence have matured within the framework of the old society. Mankind thus inevitably sets itself only such tasks as it is able to solve, since closer examination will always show that the problem itself arises only when the material conditions for its solution are already present or at least in the course of formation. In broad outline, the Asiatic, ancient, feudal and modern bourgeois modes of production may be designated as epochs marking progress in the economic development of society. The bourgeois mode of production is the last antagonistic form of the social process of production—antagonistic not in the sense of individual antagonism but of an antagonism that emanates from the individuals' social conditions of exis-

tence—but the productive forces developing within bourgeois society create also the material conditions for a solution of this antagonism. The prehistory of human society accordingly closes with this social formation.[27]

This is a clear picture of Marx's view of history and vision of the future with all the presuppositions that formed the basis for his thought. It also contains his theory of how history progresses through "productive forces," "the mode of production," "productive relations," and "social revolution."

The "productive forces" refer to the constituent parts of the "mode of production" or the material means of existence. These consist of man, nature, and technique or the work of man, the materials employed in the work, and the means used in the work. The "productive relations" are primarily the economic relations that exist among the members of any society and also the relations of any economic phenomena, for example, that of surplus value to the accumulation of capital. More importantly for the ideological struggle, the "productive relations" also refer to the consciousness of relations that exists in the minds of persons engaged in securing the economic means of life. The equating of "productive relationship" with "property relationship" is indicative that the primary relations in society are class relations. Every individual, no matter what his personal preferences might be, is in a class. He either possesses or does not possess property that is essential in the productive process. The ownership or non-ownership of property also means, in a capitalist society, that the individual has or does not have freedom. The idea of class, then, becomes the central idea in Marx's view of history: "The history of all hitherto existing society is the history of class struggles."[28] This struggle means "social revolution," that is, a change in the productive relationships that shall end in a just and classless society.

> If the proletariat . . . by means of a revolution makes . . . itself the ruling class, and, as such, sweeps away by force the old conditions of production, then it will, along with these conditions, have swept away the conditions for the existence of class antagonism, and of classes generally, and will thereby have abolished its own supremacy as a class.[29]

Marx was aware that he was not the first to observe the existence of classes but, in a letter written in 1852, he claimed to be the first to recognize the importance and role of classes in the historical process:

> What I did that was new was to prove: (1) that the *existence of classes* is only bound up with *particular, historic phases in the development of production*; (2) that the class struggle necessarily leads to the *dictatorship of the proletariat*; (3) that this dictatorship itself only constitutes the transition to the *abolition of all classes* and to a *classless society*.[30] (Original italics)

The phrase "dictatorship of the proletariat" was especially important in Marx's writing, but the meaning of the phrase was nowhere given careful definition. It was not clear whether Marx referred to (a) an actual political dictatorship, (b) a political organization by a democratic assembly, or (c) as only a "dictatorship" like that possessed by the bourgeois in a capitalist economy.

THE ELEMENTS OF ECONOMICS

Marx described succinctly the purpose of *Capital*:

> It is the ultimate aim of this work, to lay bare the economic law of motion of modern society. . . . The present society is no solid crystal, but an organism capable of change, and is constantly changing.[31]

To accomplish this purpose he made a study of the "economic cell-form" and this study led to a descriptive analysis of capitalism. The "economic cell-form" was the theory of value which had two aspects, a labor theory of value and the theory of surplus value. Marx defined the value of a commodity in simple terms:

> We see then that that which determines the magnitude of the value of any article is the amount of labor socially necessary, or the labor time socially necessary for its production.[32]

This theory of economic value was an abstraction. It assumed that labor is efficient (the "labor time socially necessary"); that the economic structure consisted of perfectly balanced competition; and, finally, that there were no differences of value in the skill of the workers. All that mattered to determine the value of a product was the quantity of labor required.

This was essentially David Ricardo's theory of value, and, when coupled with Ricardo's theory of wages (that wages necessarily remained at the subsistence level), Marx arrived at his theory of surplus value. The worker sells the only commodity which he possesses, his labor power. In return he receives only those wages sufficient for the minimum livelihood for himself and his dependents. But his labor power produced commodities which are then exchanged for more money than is required for his wages. This is surplus value. The appropriation of surplus value by the bourgeois is the exploitation of the proletariat.

One of the remarkable features of Marx's writings was the interweaving of empirical analysis with moral judgment. This was true of the "theory of exploitation." The theory developed from an analysis of capitalism in that exploitation was not a personal matter but an essential result of the economic system. Exploitation was, for Marx, an economic fact. At the same time, exploitation was to be morally condemned. It was to be condemned all the more because the entrepreneur, recognizing surplus value as his immediate goal, began consciously to exploit his workers.

Marx's theory of value, central in his economic theory, rested upon more than the classical economics of capitalism. There were philosophical and moral roots in Marx's economic views. The labor theory of value was founded upon the egalitarianism of Locke and the theory of exploitation through surplus value rested upon the imperative of Kant. In Locke's view all men had equal rights to the property which was the product of the mixing of labor with natural goods. A peculiar egalitarianism became the basis for the belief that labor power determined the value of products. In Kant's view the central dictum was that man was never to be treated as a means. This attitude developed into Marx's sense of outrage at the capitalist who consciously exploited the use value of the worker. If the ethical bases of the economic theory have not been clear, it is only because Marx professed he despised moral preaching and loved scientific analysis.

Surplus value, then, was proclaimed as the primary economic law of modern society. As such, it had an influence upon the changing social organism in three areas: the capitalists, the workers, and the entire economic system. For the bourgeois there was the accumulation and concentration of wealth leading to increased competition. For the proletariat, marginal employment led to increased misery and degradation. For the system as a whole there were inevitable internationalization and periodic crises leading to self-destruction.

The drive to accumulate economic wealth was not accounted for by a simple self-interest principle. It was, rather, the result of a drive for survival. Capitalism was seen as an organism constantly changing, and to exist any capitalist must find new products or new ways to make old products more cheaply. The capitalist was thus forced to accumulate the means for the expansion of power in order to survive. The drive toward concentration similarly went back to the survival principle. Concentration was the inevitable product of the evolutionary process.

But this surplus value arising out of the concentration necessarily led to more misery for the workers. Accumulation and concentration of power (including, of course, mechanization of industry) resulted in unemployment. The worker who has only his labor power to sell finds that there are no purchasers for his product. "Instead of rising with the progress of industry [the worker] sinks deeper and deeper below the conditions of existence of his own class."[33] Nor is this all. The worker is only "an appendage of the machine," so that every technical advance increases "the repulsiveness of his work" and decreases his wages.[34]

For the system as a whole there was the internationalization of life. It is one of the great achievements of capitalism that it has drawn "even the most barbarian nations into civilization. . . . It compels all nations, on pain of extinction, to adopt the bourgeois mode of production."[35] But with internationalization the frontiers of capitalism are gradually destroyed. Accumulation and concentration continue apace; competition becomes more furious and more destructive. In a feverish passage, expressive of the peak of Marx's analysis and judgment, the culmination of the capitalist process is summarized:

> As soon as this process of transformation has sufficiently decomposed the old society from top to bottom, as soon as the laborers are turned into proletarians, their means of labor into capital, as soon as the capitalist mode of production stands on its own feet, then the further socialization of labor and further transformation of the land and other means of production into socially exploited and, therefore, common means of production, as well as the further expropriation of private proprietors takes a new form. That which is now to be expropriated is no longer the laborer working for himself, but the capitalist exploiting many laborers. This expropriation is accomplished by the action of the immanent laws of capitalist production itself, by the centralization of capital. One capitalist always kills many. Hand in hand with this centralization, or this expropriation of many capitalists by few, develop, on an ever extending scale, the co-operative form of the labor-process, the conscious technical application of science, the methodical cultivation of the soil, the transformation of the instruments of labor into instruments of labor usable only in common, the economising of all means of production by their use as the means of production of combined, socialised labor, the entanglement of all peoples in the net of the world-market, and this, the international character of the capitalistic regime. Along with the constantly diminishing number of the magnates of capital, who usurp and monopolise all advantages of this process of transformation, grows the mass of misery, oppression, slavery, degradation, exploitation; but with this too grows the revolt of the working-class, a class always increasing in numbers, and disciplined, united, organised by the very mechanism of the process of capitalist production itself. The monopoly of capital becomes a fetter upon the mode of production, which has sprung up and flourished along with, and under it. Centralisation of the means of production and socialisation of labor at last reach a point where they become incompatible with their capitalist integument. This integument is burst asunder. The knell of capitalist private property sounds. The expropriators are expropriated.[36]

"The expropriators are expropriated." Thus, in a simple declaration, Marx expressed the conclusion of his economic study which was also his prophecy and his hope. He had begun with the belief that human beings are determined by primary, nonrational forces. He had discovered that these forces were the economics of society. He had started with the faith that the individual is a natural, evolving being and had interpreted human beings in terms of their social origins, their historical pattern, and the goals of their history. Pointing to the essence of historical life as conflict between social classes, he proclaimed that some individuals can participate in shaping the future through a genuine knowledge of historical causation. From this activity of the fate-selected elite and from the class conflict the inevitable harmony, the classless society, would emerge.

"The knell of capitalist private property sounds. The expropriators are expropriated." This was not only a conclusion that was the result of Marx's desire to know the truth, it was a call to arms that arose from his moral passion. Beginning with a concern for human justice he proclaimed that his discovery of truth meant the destruction of all moral concepts that had been important in the Western tradition. Moved by fundamental economic forces, history moves relentlessly, amorally into the future. Yet Marx could not remain exiled from Western history. The ultimate aim of his life and thought, the final goal of society, was the profound expression of his concern for human good. In Marx there returns the vision of ancient prophets, the utopia of philosophers. For when the expropriators are expropriated, then "we shall have an association in which the free development of each is the condition for the free development of all."[37]

FRIEDRICH NIETZSCHE (1844–1900)

Friedrich Nietzsche described himself and his vocation as one of the true philosophers, the "philosophers of the future." Scornful of "philosophical laborers, and scientific men generally," Nietzsche proclaimed the genuine philosophers as skeptics, critics, and spiritual experimenters who possess "the certainty of value standards, the deliberate employment of a unity of method, a shrewd courage, the ability to stand alone and give an account of themselves."[38] The true philosopher is the destroyer and the creator. He is a destroyer, the surgeon of his time who "knows how to handle a knife surely and subtly, even when the heart bleeds."[39] But he is also the surgeon who finds and removes the diseased organs of contemporary life that a new life might be created.

> More and more it seems to me that the philosopher, being *of necessity* a man of tomorrow and the day after tomorrow, has always found himself, and *had* to find himself, in contradiction to his today: his enemy was ever the ideal of today. . . .
>
> Facing a world of "modern ideas" that would banish everybody into a corner and "specialty," a philosopher—if today there could be philosophers—

would be compelled to find the greatness of man, the concept of "greatness," precisely in his range and multiplicity, in his wholeness in manifoldness. . . .

And the philosopher will betray something of his own ideal when he posits: "He shall be greatest who can be loneliest, the most concealed, the most deviant, the human being beyond good and evil, the master of his virtues, he that is overrich in will. Precisely this shall be called *greatness*: being capable of being as manifold as whole, as ample, as full."[40] (Original italics)

The philosopher, then, with a vision of the greatness of man, is the destroyer of the mediocre, the habitual, worn-out virtues. His essential task is to "create values" that "with a creative hand . . . reach for the future."[41]

The fact that the name "Nietzsche" arouses the emotions of his readers indicates that Nietzsche, like Darwin, Marx, and Freud, touched the vital nerves of Western life. Nietzsche saw that the true philosopher was one who stood at the center of the real battles of humankind, the battles for the spirit of human beings, and he believed that individuals must either say "yea" or "nay" to their own message. Because he evokes adoration and hatred it is difficult to understand his message. Everyone who desires to comprehend Nietzsche's views must become emotionally involved with his affirmations and denials. He wrote with feeling and he must be understood with feeling. This is not to deny the presence of reason in his writing. It is to assert that he was a thinker whose rational statements always end with an exclamation point or a question mark directed toward the reader.

Nietzsche did not try to be of much help to those who would attempt to grasp his meaning. He was a volatile, epigrammatic writer who rarely explained calmly the full details of his meaning. Some of his phrases are well known: "the will to power," "the transvaluation of values," the announcement that "God is dead," and that "I am the first immoralist." These are emotion-laden expressions that lead to easy misunderstanding. Nietzsche made no attempt to explain them carefully. He did, indeed, speak of the quiet ideas that rule humankind: "It is the stillest words which bring the storm. Thoughts that come with doves' footsteps guide the world."[42] But his own words were never still nor did they come on doves' footsteps but in the beak of an eagle.

If he can so easily be misunderstood, what is one to make of Nietzsche's statements about himself? How is this man to be dispassionately, objectively understood who, in his autobiography, writes chapters on "Why I Am So Wise," "Why I Am So Clever," "Why I Write Such Excellent Books," and "Why I Am a Fatality"? How is one to approach with the sympathetic intellect this person who claims of himself that "he breaks the history of mankind in two. Man lives either before or after him"?[43] It is difficult to know how to approach properly one who said of his *Thus Spake Zarathustra* that

This work is utterly unique. Let us leave the poets out of consideration: it may be that nothing has yet been produced out of such a superabundance of strength. . . . A Goethe or a Shakespeare would not have been able to breathe for a moment in this terrific atmosphere of passion and elevation; . . . compared with Zarathustra, Dante is no more than a believer, and not one who *creates* truth for the first time. . . . All the spirit and goodness of every great soul combined could not create one of Zarathustra's discourses.[44] (Original italics)

The existential quality of Nietzsche's writing also makes comprehension difficult because it was a social as well as personal existentialism. He wrote out of his contemporary social situation as a critic of his society, and his words cannot be understood when abstracted from that nineteenth-century European order in which nationalism, industrialism, capitalism, and science were fused in a middle-class civilization.

The details of Nietzsche's life, moreover, are not likely to be particularly helpful in understanding his thought. For is Nietzsche's attitude toward women explained by the fact that following the death of his father, he was raised in a household of women? Does Nietzsche's eleven years of insanity preceding his death indicate that within his philosophy there are the inevitable seeds of self-destruction? He has been interpreted in these ways, but the important point about the biography of any thinker is not to provide superficial similarities between the external details of the life and thought, but to give clues toward the spiritual meanings of the observable events. With Nietzsche, more than with most philosophers, the inner meaning of outward life is difficult to divine. He knew it to be so.

A man whose sense of shame has some profundity encounters his destinies and delicate decisions, too, on paths which few ever reach and of whose mere existence his closest intimates must not know: his mortal danger is concealed from their eyes, and so is his regained sureness of life. Such a concealed man . . . *wants* and sees to it that a mask of him roams in his place through the hearts and heads of his friends. . . . Every profound spirit needs a mask: even more, around every profound spirit a mask is growing continually, owing to the constantly false, namely *shallow*, interpretation of every word, every step, every sign of life he gives.[45] (Original italics)

How is this mask to be removed, that Nietzsche's ideas might be recognized? By reading and rereading his own words in the context of his life. This is to know that the ethical assumptions of his time were always at work within his life, fusing with his knowledge and spiritual restlessness, to condemn contemporary society and man.

Biographical details, if not too much is read into them, can be of some help in partly lifting the mask. If one has a knowledge of Luther and nineteenth-century Lutheranism it may be helpful to know that Nietzsche's father and both grandfathers were Prussian Lutheran ministers. When Friedrich was a year old his father died, and the family moved to the small town of Naumburg where the boy Nietzsche lived with his mother, grandmother, two maiden aunts, and a sister. Plato's *Symposium* was one of the first books that had a deep attraction for him. At the University of Bonn he was not happy with the perennial antics of student fraternities, nor with the popular religion. He became interested in Schopenhauer's *The World as Will and Idea* and in classical life. In his studies of Greek culture he discovered contrasting ways of life, the Dionysian and Apollonian. The former, with its ecstatic joy, its ceaseless seeking and yearning, its impassioned creativity and fulfillment, matched the needs of his own inner life.

At the age of twenty-five Nietzsche began ten years of teaching philology at the University of Basel and became friends with older colleagues Franz Overbeck and Jacob Burckhardt. Overbeck was a New Testament scholar and church historian who, through his scholarship, lived in the contrast between primitive and nineteenth-century Christianity. Burckhardt, like Nietzsche, looked at contemporary life through the history of man's spiritual life. Nietzsche became the intimate friend of Richard Wagner, the composer of *Tristan und Isolde*, and initially found in him the expression of creativity, of the passionate will, of the longing of love to overreach itself. This friendship of spiritual devotion and envy stimulated Nietzsche's own creative ambition. But when the ambitious Wagner, influenced by his wife, was disloyal to previous beliefs in composing *Parsifal,* with its otherworldly longing and resignation, Nietzsche broke the friendship. It was a break leading toward greater independence, and never again did Nietzsche have an older friend with any degree of spiritual dominion over him. In 1889 his mind became disordered, apparently as the result of syphilis, and until his death in 1900 he was nursed by his mother and his sister. Nietzsche's attitude toward women, including the women in his family, was always full of contradictions, but they, at least, were loyal to him. After his death the loyalty of his sister led to a worship that has, as much as any other single factor, been a mask hiding the real Nietzsche.

THE ETHIC OF NIETZSCHE

Nietzsche's view of reality and of ethics was, in essence, simple: All of life consists in the will to power. This is the reality. All of human life, when it is great, should consist in an endless self-overcoming. This is the ethic.

The will to power was announced by Zarathustra: "Wherever I found a living thing, there found I Will to Power."[46] At the first this was not to be understood in ethical terms; this was not a program that Nietzsche advocated. It was simply a fact of life. Any natural body, if it is living,

> will have to be an incarnate will to power, it will strive to grow, spread, seize, become predominant—not from any morality or immorality but because it is *living* and because life simply *is* will to power.[47] (Original italics)

In Zarathustra it was evident that this will to power was not to be understood as a struggle for survival.

> He certainly did not hit the truth who shot at it the formula: "Will to existence": that will doth not exist! . . . Only where there is life, is there also will; not, however, Will to Life but so teach I thee Will to Power![48]

This theme was repeated in the posthumous *Will to Power*:

> The only reality is this: *the will of every center of power to become stronger*, not self-preservation, but the desire to appropriate, to become master, to become more, to become stronger. . . .
> Life, which is our best known form of being, is altogether "will to the accumulation of strength" all the processes of life hinge on this: everything aims, not at preservation, but at accretion and accumulation. Life as an individual case (a hypothesis which may be applied to existence in general) strives after the maximum feeling of power; life is essentially a striving after more power; striving itself is only a straining after more power; the most fundamental and innermost thing of all is this will.[49] (Original italics)

When this will, this striving present in all life, manifested itself in an individual human being it generated a self-created individual. The will to power thus appeared as a "self-surpassing," a value to be reverenced.

"Self-surpassing" was the basic faith of Nietzsche. All his thought can be seen to revolve around his affirmation and advocacy of the will to power as a self-overcoming. The doctrine appeared first in Zarathustra's speech on "Self-Surpassing":

> And this secret spake Life herself unto me. "Behold," said she, "I am that *which must ever surpass itself.*"
> To be sure, ye call it will to procreation, or impulse towards a goal, towards the higher, remoter, more manifold: but all that is one and the same secret. . . .
> Whatever I create, and however much I love it, soon must I be adverse to it, and to my love: so willeth my will. . . .
> Verily, I say unto you: good and evil which would be everlasting—it doth not exist! Of its own accord must it ever surpass itself anew.

> With your values and formulae of good and evil, ye exercise power, ye valuing ones: and that is your secret love, and the sparkling, trembling, and overflowing of your souls.
>
> But a stronger power groweth out of your values, and a new surpassing: by it breaketh egg and egg-shell.
>
> And he who hath to be a creator in good and evil—verily, he hath first to be a destroyer, and break values in pieces. . . .
>
> And let everything break up which can break up by our truths! Many a house is still to be built![50] (Original italics)

For Nietzsche good and evil do not exist as absolutes. For where a good exists, it must be overcome; where an evil resides, it is to be surpassed. Yet there was a human absolute for Nietzsche. It was that will to power exists as a continuous act of self-overcoming. This is the individual's highest good, this is destiny; this is what Nietzsche loved in being human. Nietzsche required of the highest individuals that again and again, they are to surpass themselves, to overcome what they have become, and to go beyond where they have arrived.

> What is the greatest thing ye can experience? It is the hour of great contempt. The hour in which even your happiness becometh loathsome unto you, and so also your reason and virtue. . . .
>
> It is not your sin—it is your self-satisfaction that crieth unto heaven; your very sparingness in sin crieth unto heaven!
>
> Where is the lightning to lick you with its tongue? Where is the frenzy with which ye should be inoculated?
>
> Lo, I teach you the Superman: he is that lightning, he is that frenzy![51]

What Nietzsche recognized as essential for the superior individual he claimed for himself: "My *strongest* characteristic is self-overcoming" (original italics).[52]

But "self-overcoming" is a figure of speech. Its meaning hinged upon a particular view of overcoming and a specific conception of the self. What was Nietzsche's will to power that is a self-surpassing? First of all, it was not a political will but, as Nietzsche expressed it, an "*instinct for freedom*" (original italics),[53] or "the striving for excellence."[54] These were the essential characteristics. But what kind of freedom, what kind of excellence could identify Nietzsche's superior individual?

In Zarathustra Nietzsche described the will to power in ecstatic terms. That ecstasy must be participated in for any possible meaning to be communicated. But in *Beyond Good and Evil* he described with more objectivity the freedom and excellence of that superior individual which he advocated:

> First there is an independence, a spiritual self-sufficiency.
>
> Today the concept of greatness entails being noble, wanting to be by oneself, being able to be different, standing alone and having to live independently.[55]

This spiritual independence enables an individual not only to love his enemies but also to hate his friends. For friends are more dangerous than enemies, since by their very love they can dominate and destroy one's individuality.

Second, the superior individual reveres himself. Nietzsche asked the penetrating questions, "What is noble? what does the word 'noble' still mean to us today?" To these queries he found an answer stark in its simplicity: There is "some fundamental certainty that a noble soul has about itself, something that cannot be sought, nor found, nor perhaps lost. *The noble soul has reverence for itself.*"[56] Reverence for the self Nietzsche described in his words and his life as "egoism." His outbursts of self-praise may have been the attempt to prove to himself and to reveal that he possessed one essential characteristic of the superior man.

> Egoism belongs to the nature of a noble soul—I mean that unshakable faith that to a being such as "we are" other beings must be subordinate by nature and have to sacrifice themselves. The noble soul accepts this fact of its egoism without any question mark, also without any feeling that it might contain hardness, constraint, or caprice, rather as something that may be founded in the primordial law of things: . . . *It knows itself to be at a height.*[57] (Original italics)

In the distinguished individual there is great spiritual variety. Thus, the superior person is conceived in terms of spiritual conquest and self-conquest.

> The most spiritual men, as the *strongest*, find their happiness in what others would find their destruction: in the labyrinth, in hardness against themselves, in experiments. Their joy is self-conquest: asceticism becomes in them nature, need, and instinct. The difficult task is considered by them a privilege; playing with burdens which would crush others, a *recreation*. Knowledge a form of asceticism. They are the most venerable kind of man: that does not exclude their being the most cheerful and the kindliest.[58] (Original italics)

Such an individual is the natural authority of others,

> A man who says, "I like this, I take this for my own and want to protect it and defend it against anybody"; a man who is able to manage something, to carry out a resolution, to remain faithful to a thought, to hold a woman, to punish and prostrate one who presumed too much; a man who has his wrath and his sword and to whom the weak, the suffering, the hard pressed, and the animals, too, like to come and belong by nature.[59]

More than this, the distinguished individual is an authority over himself. He gives style to his own character, and lives according to the "four virtues: of courage, insight, sympathy, and solitude."[60] This characteristic of self-mastery combined with the will to power means that *the good man is for Nietzsche the passionate man who is the master of his passions*" (original italics).[61]

The distinguished individual is a person of power whose will seeks the fullness of life and seeks to overflow that life in order to create a new world, new values:

> The noble type of man experiences *itself* as determining values; it does not need approval; it judges, "what is harmful to me is harmful in itself"; it knows itself to be that which first accords honor to things; it is *value creating*. Everything it knows as part of itself it honors: such a morality is self-glorification.[62] (Original italics)

These bridges to the Superman, these "genuine philosophers" who live out of the inner vitality of life, are the heralds of the future announcing that man's future is man's will. As harbingers of a new dawn, they are the "commanders and legislators" and give new value to existence. Indeed, their "'knowing' is *creating*, their creating is a legislation, their will to truth is—*will to power*."[63] The new creating is neither a spasmodic nor a temporary act since "not the intensity but the duration of high feelings makes high men" (original italics).[64]

How are these characteristics created? When an individual possesses the potentialities of becoming distinguished, what are the means by which essential qualities are developed? The answer to this question, presented with many variations, was simple. The individual becomes superior through discipline and suffering, through exploitation and competition.

"Under peaceful conditions," said Nietzsche, the "warlike man sets upon himself."[65] By this aphorism he was not extolling the military aspects of war but praising the fact that warfare requires a certain hardness, discipline, and obedience. These must be exerted by the self toward the self since "Profound suffering makes noble; it separates."[66] For these reasons Nietzsche attacked those modern individuals with compassion who would do away with suffering. "The discipline of suffering, of *great* suffering—do you not know that only *this* discipline has created all enhancements of man so far?"[67]

The discipline that Nietzsche advocates was more than discipline of suffering. He recognized the need for obedience, an obedience that alone could give freedom and mold the great life. The obedience is that the self obeys its own nature and when its nature is that of greatness, then such obedience will, in time, develop the great individual. In Zarathustra obedience had been recognized as the law of all life with the corollary principle that it is more difficult to command freely than merely to obey the commandments of others. In *Beyond Good and Evil* obedience was seen as the key to freedom and creativity, as the means to the higher life:

What is essential "in heaven and on earth" seems to be, to say it once more, that there should be *obedience* over a long period of time and in a *single* direction: given that, something always develops, and has developed, for whose sake it is worth while to live on earth; for example, virtue, art, music, dance, reason, spirituality—something transfiguring, subtle, mad, and divine.[68] (Original italics)

The necessity of such self-mastery, such suffering, such obedience was the reason that Nietzsche valued asceticism. The discipline he advocated was a form of asceticism that does not destroy the passions but uses, controls, organizes, and sublimates them. Nietzsche was critical of traditional religion; he denounced the extreme form of asceticism that was a self-flagellation and denial of life rather than a joyful affirmation. Yet he recognized that "Asceticism and puritanism are almost indispensable means for educating and ennobling a race that wishes to become master over its origins among the rabble and that works its way up toward future rule."[69] And he saw the greatest asceticism as directed toward self-creation.

"Giving style" to one's character—a great and rare art! It is exercised by those who see all the strengths and weaknesses of their own nature and then comprehend them in an artistic plan until everything appears as art and reason. . . . It will be the strong and domineering natures who enjoy their finest gaiety in such compulsion, in such being bounded, and in such perfection under a law of one's own.[70]

Self-discipline was seen not as an asceticism that extirpates the passions but one that refines and redirects them.

Accepting the assumption of the age that "life is essentially conflict," Nietzsche saw in this truth not only a fact to be recognized but also a value to be approved. For it is through competition and exploitation that a higher life arises. When Nietzsche asked the question, "How and where has the plant 'man' flourished most strongly so far?" he received the answer: through enormous peril; through pressure and compulsion; through an unconditional will to power; through "hardness, forcefulness, slavery, danger in the alley and the heart, life in hiding, stoicism, the art of experiment and devilry of every kind, that everything evil, terrible, tyrannical in man, everything that is kin to beasts of prey and serpents."[71]

This view of what life at its best actually is, this interpretation of the distinguished individual and of how this person becomes distinguished, led Nietzsche to value solitude, a vital life and nature, great healthiness of body, strong sexuality, cruelty, war, and conflict. The new men are the "born, sworn, jealous friends of *solitude*"[72] who find in and through solitude the highest sense of self. They should remain faithful to the earth, which involves a loyalty to the body (in which "there is more sagacity . . . than in thy best wisdom")[73] and a great healthiness. Respect and adoration for the physical self would find its expression in sexual vitality. Cruelty, too, was valued, because "almost everything we call 'higher culture' is based on the spiritualization of *cruelty*."[74] Warfare was praised as a great good, though it is not always clear what Nietzsche meant by "war," for often he seems to use the word metaphorically rather than literally.

Nietzsche's total moral philosophy hinged upon his basic judgment that the individual must ever surpass himself. His vision of reality as will to power enabled Nietzsche to value self-surmounting. This was his "holy yea" to life. And this, too, determined his denials. For his passionate rejections were always those factors in existence that destroyed or restricted the self-surmounting of the free individual.

Nietzsche's rejections were based upon what he interpreted as another fact of human history. The will to power ever manifests itself in gradation of human ranks. "There is an order of rank between man and man, hence also between morality and morality."[75] As he surveyed the history of moral ideals Nietzsche reached the conclusion that there is a *"master-morality* and [a] *slave-morality."* In the former it is "the exalted, proud states of the soul [that] are experienced as conferring distinction and determining the order of rank," while in the slave-morality "those qualities are brought out and flooded with light which serve to ease existence for those who suffer."[76]

In his initial judgments Nietzsche viewed this distinction between two types of morality as historical fact. He also claimed as fact the judgment that aristocratic societies, being creative minorities, were responsible for the development of the best humanity. In his own words, he was a great despiser because he was a great adorer. But what, then, did Nietzsche detest, what did he reject? What was it that he wanted to say "Nay" to?

His first, his fundamental rejections were of contemporary society and contemporary human beings. Throughout he attacked the common individual and the social order of his day. Nietzsche saw everywhere in his Europe forces that were destroying human beings, their individuality, and their capacity to surpass themselves. With all the passion and fury that possessed him he lashed out at contemporary life:

> What is it precisely which I find intolerable? That which I alone cannot get rid of, which makes me choke and faint? Bad air! Bad air! That something misbegotten comes near me; that I must inhale the odour of the entrails of a misbegotten soul! . . . But from time to time do ye grant me . . . one glimpse, grant me but one glimpse only, of something perfect, fully realized, happy, mighty, triumphant, of something that still gives cause for fear! A glimpse of a man that justifies the existence of man, a glimpse of an in-

carnate human happiness that realises and redeems, for the sake of which one may hold fast to *the belief in man*! For the position is this: in the dwarfing and leveling of the European man lurks *our* greatest peril, for it is this outlook which fatigues—we see to-day nothing which wishes to be greater, we surmise that the process is always still backwards, still backwards towards something more attenuated, more inoffensive, more cunning, more comfortable, more mediocre, more indifferent, more Chinese, more Christian man, there is no doubt about it, grows always 'better'—the destiny of Europe lies in this—that in losing the fear of man, we have also lost the hope in man, yea, the will to be man. The sight of man now fatigues. . . . We are tired of *man*.[77] (Original italics)

So Nietzsche described "the European of today" as a "smaller, almost ridiculous type, a herd animal, something eager to please, sickly, and mediocre."[78]

What is it that Nietzsche detested in the society of his day? He despised the loss of will, the herd morality that was a morality of utilitarianism and pleasure, the conformity that led to mediocrity. He rejected the democratization of man and, worse, the democratization of woman that destroyed the proper role and relation of both sexes. He denounced the petty Christianization of life with its sense of sin, otherworldliness, and world-weariness. Human beings, proclaimed Nietzsche with utter horror, had ceased to desire to be or become anything. Skepticism, scientific objectivity, "art for art's sake": all of these were but manifestations of one dread disease, the paralysis of will. Nor was this surprising since the prevalent morality was the morality of the herd-animal. Society is dull in its mediocrity, in its insistence upon conformity: "'Be like them! Become mediocre!' is now the only morality that still makes sense, that still gets a hearing."[79]

The qualities that Nietzsche rejected in contemporary morality were those that destroyed the free individual. In particular, the popular bases for morality—pleasure and pain—he thought absurd and life-destroying.

Whether it is hedonism or pessimism, utilitarianism or eudaemonism—all these ways of thinking that measure the value of things in accordance with *pleasure* and *pain*, which are mere epiphenomena and wholly secondary, are ways of thinking that stay in the foreground.[80] (Original italics)

Democratization of life, absurdly considering that everyone was equal, destroyed the essential relations of things, that there are degrees of rank among people and differences of rank between men and women. The intensity with which Nietzsche wrote about women expressed his respect for woman at the same time that he rejected any thought of woman's equality:

> To go wrong on the fundamental problem of "man and woman," to deny the most abysmal antagonism between them and the necessity of an eternally hostile tension, to dream perhaps of equal rights, equal education, equal claims and obligations—that is a *typical* sign of shallowness.[81] (Original italics)

The distinction between men and women is revealed in a simple aphorism: "The happiness of man is, 'I will.' The happiness of women is, 'He will.'"[82] The granting of equality to women destroyed the feminine character. "Everything in woman is a riddle, and everything in woman hath one solution—it is called pregnancy."[83] This was particularly true when a woman accepted the advice of Zarathustra, to "let the beam of a star shine in your love! Let your hope say: 'May I bear the Superman!'"[84] The democratization of women weakened the desire for creating new human life, and it corrupted woman's unique spiritual capacities.

> What inspires respect for woman, and often enough even fear, is her *nature*, which is more "natural" than man's, the genuine, cunning suppleness of a beast of prey, the tiger's claw under the glove, the naivete of her egoism, her uneducability and inner wildness, the incomprehensibility, scope, and movement of her desires and virtues—
>
> What, in spite of all fear, elicits pity for this dangerous and beautiful cat "woman" is that she appears to suffer more, to be more vulnerable, more in need of love, and more condemned to disappointment than any other animal.[85]

Through the emancipation of women, the life of each woman was retrogressing, and the power of woman was weakened.

Finally, in his hatred of contemporary society Nietzsche lashed out at Christianity with its moods of sin, otherworldliness, and world-weariness. The church, he proclaimed, was perpetrating a "pious fraud." In its repeated emphasis upon sin, despising the body, and longing for another world, Christianity was destroying the most sacred quality of human life, that will to power that led to responsibility for and creation of the self. Nietzsche saw in the religion of his time nothing but the decay and destruction of the holiness of life.

As he rejected contemporary society, contemporary individuals, and Christianity, Nietzsche's great detestation caused him to reject religion as it had been in the past and human beings as they had hitherto existed. Religion he abhorred, especially Christianity and Judaism, because in preaching compassion and brotherly love and in proclaiming the providence of God, it had destroyed human worth and responsibility. He rejected human beings because, with all the past achievements of self-creating, he could find no individual who represented his ideal of what human life ought to be. No one had yet been able to become himself; no one had yet created a will that ever creates, that ever goes beyond what it has become.

These rejections clarify the ultimate rejection: "God is dead." The uttering of this faith, which many in the nineteenth century believed without understanding its consequences, caused Nietzsche to tremble. He related a story of a madman who passionately sought God and was mocked by all the disbelievers in the marketplace. Their laughing provokes him to frenzy.

> Where is God gone? . . . I mean to tell you! *We have killed him*—You and I! We are all his murderers! . . . God is dead! God remains dead! And we have killed him! How shall we console ourselves, the most murderous of all murderers? The holiest and the mightiest that the world has hitherto possessed, has bled to death under our knife—who will wipe the blood from us? . . . Shall we not ourselves have to become Gods, merely to seem worthy of it? There never was a greater event, and on account of it, all who are born after us belong to a higher history than any history hitherto![86] (Original italics)

Nietzsche shuddered at this proclamation because its meanings were many-sided and profound. He saw that the people of his time no longer genuinely believed in God, not even those who professed to believe. "What are these churches now, if they are not the tombs and monuments of God?"[87] But he saw further. All absolutes had been destroyed; there was no longer any objective reality to which the values of the world could be anchored. It was this dire prognosis that demanded that individuals must become gods; it was this that must lead to a Superman. For the Superman is one who, in the absence of permanent values, creates ever anew, through his powerful will, his own values.

In this great rejection Nietzsche thought that he was denying the reality of all absolutes. Yet there appeared, again and again, in his philosophy, moral absolutes. The death of God, which was the powerlessness of a God-reality to evoke the loyalties of individuals and to determine human values, meant that a new reality must appear, the image of Superman. There must be, asserted Nietzsche, a "transvaluation of values." But this demand did not mean a relativism of values. It meant that what individuals of the past and present have found to be values were false and must be overturned. The power of being human must be turned in a new direction, one of continual self-creating, self-responsibility, and self-domination. There were absolutes enough here, and they were those of late-nineteenth-century thought. These were the assumptions of his culture that Nietzsche accepted and wove into his own powerful philosophy. These were the viewpoints with which he began that were refocused in his unique vision.

Beginning with a moral passion that desired human goodness and greatness, Nietzsche saw humans as natural, evolving beings who could continually surpass themselves. But rejecting a facile evolutionism, he also saw all of life as essentially conflict in which the individual's existence was determined by primary nonrational forces. Still, he believed the strong individuals, those of independence and knowledge, could exert their will and create their own future. Thus, from the conflict within one's own life as from the conflict with others, there could emerge for the superior individual a harmony of achievement. But it was a harmony which must include its own tension, for there never could be a final harmony in which the free individual might cease to exert his will to power or to halt his transformation.

SIGMUND FREUD (1856–1939)

Sigmund Freud was scientist and philosopher, prophet and priest. He was scientist and philosopher in his yearning for the truth, in his patient observation of psychophysical data, in his construction of a psychological theory and philosophical worldview. He was prophet and priest in his judgment of disorder in human life, in his concern for healing disease, and in his proclamation of a new way of life. Freud thus combined in his way of thinking and feeling the rational approach of the Greeks, the existential concern of the Hebrews, and the objective naturalism of the scientists.

The life of Freud was lacking in those exciting events that mark the heroes of history. From his birth on May 6, 1856, his life appeared to have been relatively quiet and uneventful, though finally it was his inner life, and not his outward behavior, that constituted his biography. There was one period of six months in Freud's forty-first year that was remarkable in its intensity and significance. In those days are clues to the sources of his personality, the development of his psychological theory, his rejections of traditional religion and ethics, and his affirmation of a new means of salvation.

By 1897 Freud had established the basic foundations of psychoanalysis. As with most great discoverers he was not completely conscious of what he had discovered, but he sensed its significance and he found that his new insights increased the inner and outer difficulties of his life.

As a child Freud "was moved . . . by a sort of curiosity, which was, however, directed more towards human concerns than towards natural objects."[88] Influenced by Darwin's theories of evolution and by Goethe's essay on Nature he decided to become a medical student. At the University of Vienna he knew what it was to be excluded because he was a Jew, but this, he later reported, only served to lay foundations for "a certain degree of independence of judgment."[89] There Freud came under the influence of an excellent teacher and laboratory assistants, and after graduation, for a period of some fifteen years, he became friendly with and somewhat dependent upon a number of physicians and scientists. Three of these men were particularly important in

Freud's intellectual development: Jean Charcot (1825–1893), the famous neurologist in Paris, who interested Freud in mental diseases, particularly in hysteria; Josef Breuer (1842–1925), the Vienna physician, who developed cures for hysteria by hypnosis and to whom Freud said he was indebted for the theory of the unconscious; and Wilhelm Fliess (1858–1928), the Berlin physician and biologist, who, through a deep friendship of more than ten years, provided Freud with a sounding board for his earliest theories. There were, indeed, interesting elements in these friendships of Freud. Having attained, as he said, a "degree of independence of judgment," he yet needed during these years one intimate friend upon whom he was dependent. In every case (with the exception of Charcot, with whom Freud's relation was quite temporary), as his unique ideas and psychological independence developed together, there came a sharp break in personal relations. Consequently, for a number of years after these ruptures, and partly as the result of his great discoveries, Freud was isolated.

By May 31, 1897, when the six months of epochal events began, Freud had already developed certain basic elements of psychoanalytic theory. These elements were not clearly defined or related in his own mind, nor did he comprehend the full meaning or significance of his views, but the groundwork had been laid. In 1895 he had published, with Breuer, *Studien über Hysterie,* which emphasized the importance of emotions and of the unconscious; described neurotic symptoms as the result of inhibiting (or "damming-up") an emotion; and presented a therapy by inducing patients, through hypnosis, to remember significant events in their past, thus freeing them to redirect the blocked emotions. Thereafter, and largely through direct observation of his patients, Freud made the unexpected discovery that a sexual quality was always related to the neurosis. His belief in universal determinism, coupled with what he called his "fondness for the prehistoric in all human manifestations,"[90] led him to recognize that mental disorders had their roots in infantile experiences. This, in turn, enabled him to find the process of repression (at first called "defense"), whereby a person "forgets" significant but painful experiences.

By the beginning of 1896 *The Interpretation of Dreams* was, according to Freud, "finished in all essentials."[91] This book, one of the most influential that Freud wrote, presented as its essential thesis that "a dream is the (disguised) fulfillment of a (repressed) wish."[92] About the same time, noting that his patients began to talk aimlessly when asked to relate their experiences, Freud inaugurated the method of "free-association" by which the patient reported faithfully anything entering her consciousness. With these theories developing gradually in his mind, in 1896 Freud for the first time used the term "psychoanalysis." One particular view had appeared to him the keystone of his ideas. Patient after patient remembered that in her childhood she had been seduced. The father of the child was almost invariably involved in the report, so Freud became convinced that a father's seduction of his child caused a later neurosis. For four years this was a basic doctrine. Then in May 1897, Freud dreamed that he "was feeling overaffectionately" toward his daughter. He was honest enough to draw a painful conclusion from that dream. On May 31 he wrote to Fliess, "The dream of course shows the fulfillment of my wish to catch a *Pater* [father] as the originator of neurosis and thus [the dream] puts an end to my ever-recurring doubts."[93] With that dream Freud's theory began to fall apart, though he was not yet conscious of this fateful fact. In the same letter he announced that

> another presentiment tells me, as though I already knew—but I know nothing at all—that I shall very soon uncover the source of morality. Thus, the whole matter is still growing in my expectation and gives me the greatest pleasure.[94]

The mood quickly changed to one of "intellectual paralysis" for in less than two weeks he wrote:

> Incidentally, I have been through some kind of neurotic experience, curious states incomprehensible to [consciousness], twilight thoughts, veiled doubts, with barely a ray of light here or there. . . . I believe I am in a cocoon, and God knows what sort of beast will crawl out.[95]

He did not know what was happening. It was the beginning of his self-analysis that would lead Freud back into the recesses of his infancy, coupled with his objective scientific work. Both would have serious consequences and two months later, on August 14, he wrote in a brief letter to Fliess about both:

> Things are fermenting in me; I have finished nothing; am very satisfied with the psychology, tormented by grave doubts about my theory of the neuroses, too lazy to think, and have not succeeded here in diminishing the agitation in my head and feelings. . . .
> The chief patient I am preoccupied with is myself. . . . The analysis is more difficult than any other. It is, in fact, what paralyzes my psychic strength for describing and communicating what I have won so far. Still, I believe it must be done and is a necessary intermediate stage in my work.[96]

Freud's self-analysis did not make progress until he rejected his favored father-seduction theory of neuroses. That rejection was the result of scientific reasoning that led him to doubt his patients' abilities to distinguish between true memories and fantasies of childhood. Then, beginning on October 3, there was compressed into a few letters a report of his self-analysis which formed the turning point of his life and thought.

There is very little happening to me externally, but internally something very interesting. For the last four days my self-analysis, which I consider indispensable for the clarification of the whole problem, has continued in dreams and has presented me with the most valuable elucidations and clues. . . . To put it in writing is more difficult than anything else for me; it also would take me too far afield. I can only indicate that the old man plays no active part in my case, but that no doubt I drew an inference by analogy from myself onto him; that in my case the "prime originator" was an ugly, elderly, but clever woman, who told me a great deal about God Almighty and hell and who instilled in me a high opinion of my own capacities; that later (between two and two and a half years) my libido toward *matrem* [mother] was awakened, namely, on the occasion of a journey with her from Leipzig to Vienna, during which we must have spent the night together and there must have been an opportunity of seeing her *nudam* [naked] . . . that I greeted my one-year-younger brother (who died after a few months) with adverse wishes and genuine childhood jealousy; and that his death left the germ of [self-]reproach in me. I have also long known the companion of my misdeeds between the ages of one and two years; it is my nephew, a year older than myself. . . . The two of us seem occasionally to have behaved cruelly to my niece, who was a year younger. This nephew and this younger brother have determined, then, what is neurotic, but also what is intense, in all my friendships. . . .

I have not yet grasped anything at all of the scenes themselves which lie at the bottom of the story. If they come [to light] and I succeed in resolving my own hysteria, then I shall be grateful to the memory of the old woman who provided me at such an early age with the means for living and going on living.

In the same letter, dated the following day, October 4, he continued,

Today's dream has, under the strangest disguises, produced the following: she was my teacher in sexual matters and complained because I was clumsy and unable to do anything.

(Neurotic impotence always comes about in this way. The fear of not being able to do anything at all in school thus obtains its sexual substratum.) . . . Moreover, she washed me in reddish water in which she had previously washed herself. . . . And she made me steal zehners (ten-kreuzer coins) to give to her. . . . The dream could be summed up as "bad treatment." Just as the old woman got money from me for her bad treatment, so today I get money for the bad treatment of my patients.[97]

Freud later confirmed a portion of this interpretation by asking his mother whether she remembered the nurse. "Of course," she told him, "an elderly person, very clever, she was always carrying you off to some church; when you returned home you preached and told us all about God Almighty."[98]

Freud found that "being totally honest with oneself is a good exercise." From his exercise he arrived at his Oedipus theory. It was first mentioned in his letter to Fliess of October 15, 1897, when he reported that from the recent self-analysis,

A single idea of general value has dawned on me. I have found, in my own case too, [the phenomenon of] being in love with my mother and jealous of my father, and I now consider it a universal event in early childhood.[99]

He then attributed the power of Sophocles' *Oedipus Rex* to this universal experience; *Hamlet* was also interpreted with the new theory, in that Hamlet's early passion for his mother and hatred of his father explained both his sexual coldness and his moral conscience ("His conscience is his unconscious sense of guilt").[100] The self-analysis continued. Freud wrote Fliess on October 27,

I am gripped and pulled through ancient times in quick association of thoughts; my moods change like the landscapes seen by a traveler from a train; and as the great poet, using his privilege to ennoble (sublimate), puts it:
    Und manche liebe Schatten steigen auf;
    Gleich einer alten, halbverklungenen Sage,
    Kommt erste Lieb' und Freundschaft mit herauf.

    [And the shades of loved ones appear;
    with them, like an old, half-forgotten myth,
    First love and friendship.][101]

Through analysis he started to grasp the real power of resistance, that refusal to remember what has been repressed. He recognized and later reported (in a letter of November 14) the origins of repression ("it was a question of the abandonment of former sexual zones") and the diverse causes of specific types of neurosis.[102] He then stated that normal repression accounts for morality:

What, now, does normal repression furnish us with? Something which, free, can lead to anxiety; if physically bound, to rejection—that is to say, the affective basis for a multitude of intellectual processes of development, such as morality, shame, and the like. . . . From this we can see that, with successive thrusts in development, the child is overlaid with piety, shame, and such things.[103]

One important consequence of this interpretation was that Freud began "linking the neurotic process and the normal one."[104]

It was about this time, through interest in scientific reflection, that the self-analysis was interrupted. There is no external evidence that he engaged in systematic self-analysis again, although there are many reports of what he termed "a small bit of my self-analysis."[105]

On December 3, 1897, Freud returned to childhood memories. "At the age of three years I passed through the station when we moved from Freiberg to Leipzig, and the gas flames which I saw for the first time reminded me of spirits burning in hell."[106] This memory helped him to explain origins of religious and moral belief, for a week later he reported that

> The dim inner perception of one's own psychic apparatus stimulates thought illusions, which of course are projected onto the outside and, characteristically, into the future and the beyond. Immortality, retribution, the entire beyond are all reflections of our psychic internal [world].[107]

The self-analysis had momentous consequences for the life and the thought of Freud. For his personal life the experience was a turning point toward an apparent independence, even dominancy, of personality and self-assurance. For his psychological thought the analysis was the culmination of the formative years and the great discoveries, when different elements of the psychology were being welded together. For his ethical and religious thought the self-inquiry enabled Freud to give an account of human values.

Prior to the time of his self-analysis, Freud's life was marked by basic anxieties with great changes of moods, inner uncertainties, and an apparent dependence upon others. His phobia of travel by train, his experiences of dread of death, and his strange intimate friendships are symptoms that "there is ample evidence that for ten years or so roughly comprising the nineties, he suffered from a very considerable psychoneurosis."[108] The personality of Freud was not changed instantaneously, but, beginning with the rigorous, painful self-analysis, there gradually "emerged the serene and benign Freud, henceforth free to pursue his work in imperturbable composure."[109] During those years of change Freud knew great loneliness, but the isolation strengthened his independence of judgment. In 1902 he began a psychological discussion group that was the forerunner of the national and international psychoanalytical societies which provided Freud with a position of personal and intellectual dominance from about 1910 until his death.

The initial period of self-analysis provided Freud with his basic psychoanalytic theory, and by the turn of the century the essential elements of psychoanalysis had been formulated in his mind; although he continued to modify and develop his theories throughout his life, the basic pattern never changed. The time of self-analysis was also important for Freud's conception of human values. In his analysis there were references to dreams as wish-fulfillment, to erotic experiences, and to the importance of infancy. There was also preoccupation with moral and religious ideas.

The beginning of Freud's self-analysis also coincided with his expectation that he would discover the sources of morality. The analysis uncovers as his most important memories experiences with his nurse and mother that had overt religious and moral meanings, so that "many a pride and privilege are made aware of their humble origins."[110] The interruption of the analysis occurred about the time he found the source of human valuations in repression. The explanation that religious and moral ideas have their sources in infantile psychological experiences remained an essential part of Freud's views throughout his life. But such an explanation only obscures the actual Freudian ethic, which he never described in moral terms. The total psychoanalytic view was based upon the experience and advocacy of a therapy for individuals, and this therapy, coupled with the explanation of the psychological sources of morality, was the replacement of one ethical position for another. To understand the significance of the substitution of a Freudian therapeutic ethic for all other moralities, it is necessary to review briefly psychoanalytic theory and therapy.

PSYCHOANALYTIC THEORY

In his autobiography, written in 1925, Freud with characteristic succinctness described psychoanalytic theory:

> The theories of resistance and repression, of the unconscious, of the aetiological significance of sexual life and of the importance of infantile experiences—these form the principal constituents of the theoretical structure of psychoanalysis.[111]

The theoretical structure of psychoanalysis in its broad outlines is not difficult to understand, although the intricate details of the theory are exceedingly complex and, for mastery, require years of arduous study. That complexity of detail, however, should not obscure the magnificent simplicity of the total system.

1. The theory of the unconscious

The fact of unconscious mental life is the fundamental basis of psychoanalytic theory. Many theories of human nature had recognized "the unconscious," but, prior to Freud, no significant thinker had made it the key explanatory principle of human behavior. The central idea of the unconscious is that there are activities that have mental aspects (e.g., perceptions, conceptions, and desires) of which the individual is not aware. In Freudian theory the unconscious came to be divided into two types: the preconscious, which may be accessible to thought, and the unconscious, which is not available to any normal mental processes. The importance of the unconscious lies in the fact that elements of the unconscious continually erupt, in a disguised form, into the conscious life.

2. The aetiological significance of sexual life

In the attempt to find a primary nonrational cause for human psychological development, Freud discovered sex. Human beings have always experienced the power of sexuality and some persons have described in general terms the force of the sex drive, but Freud was the first to proclaim seriously that sex is the basic force creating specific human conditions. *Three Essays on the Theory of Sexuality* (1905), which, with *Interpretation of Dreams,* he regarded most highly, explained that

> What we describe as a person's "character" is built up to a considerable extent from the material of sexual excitations and is composed of instincts that have been fixed since childhood, of constructions achieved by means of sublimation, and of other constructions, employed for effectively holding in check perverse impulses which have been recognized as being unutilizable.[112]

In recognizing the significance of sexual experiences as a causative factor in human life, Freud repeatedly emphasized that he was widening the meaning of sex.

> That extension is of a twofold kind. In the first place sexuality is divorced from its too close connection with the genitals and is regarded as a more comprehensive bodily function, having pleasure as its goal and only secondarily coming to serve the ends of reproduction. In the second place the sexual impulses are regarded as including all those merely affectionate and friendly impulses to which usage applies the exceedingly ambiguous word "love."[113]

Freud used the term "libido" as "sexual longing" or "that force by which the sexual instinct is represented in the mind."[114]

This conception of libido and widening of the term "sex" was accompanied by Freud's repeated assertion that one of his most important discoveries was that of "infantile sexuality." Long before Freud it was apparent that infants are pleasure-seeking, that they have "affectionate and friendly impulses." What Freud did that was new was to insist upon the essential sexuality of many pleasure-gratifying acts. He recognized that

> sexuality has many manifestations besides the simple genital union of coitus. The instinct does not begin in this finished form. . . . On the contrary,

it has to pass through a rather complicated development before this stage of what Freud termed "genital primacy" is reached. It begins diffusely from the excitability of many "erotogenic zones" of the body. He maintained, for instance . . . that the infant is impelled to suck not only by hunger . . . but also by the desire for erotic gratification even when it is not hungry. This is continued later as thumb sucking, the sucking of other objects such as pencils, and in adult life as amorous kissing . . . . There is an unbroken line in this development, so Freud saw no reason for refusing it the same name "sexual" throughout.[115]

The suggestion was often made to Freud that psychoanalysis might find greater acceptance if he would use other than sexual terminology to define his central thesis, but he always refused. As he wrote to Jung in 1907,

Even if we were not to call the driving force in our broadened conception of sexuality "libido" it would still remain the libido and every time we follow it up we should get back to the very thing from which the new nomenclature was supposed to divert us. . . . What is demanded of us is after all that we deny the sexual instinct. So let us proclaim it.[116]

3. The importance of infantile experiences

Freud's probing mind, influenced by evolutionary biology, continually sought genetic explanations. "My fondness for the prehistoric in all human manifestations,"[117] he wrote in 1899, and this fondness led him to discover the significance of infantile experiences. When he had located infantile sexuality, the next logical step was to find its relation to the development of human character. This occurred through the repression into the unconscious of infantile sexual experiences. There are obviously many such experiences, but the most important Freud discovered in his self-analysis, when he detected in his own childhood an antipathy toward his father and a love of his mother. He then claimed that this was a universal experience of childhood. This love of the mother by the son, of the father by the daughter, according to the Oedipus theory, was not a "pregenital" pleasure seeking but an actual genital wish. In 1920 Freud claimed the recognition of this Oedipus complex "distinguishes the adherents of psychoanalysis from its opponents." He also maintained that

It represents the peak of infantile sexuality, which, through its after-effects, exercises a decisive influence on the sexuality of adults. Every new arrival on this planet is faced by the task of mastering the Oedipus complex; anyone who fails to do so falls a victim to neurosis.[118]

4. The theories of repression and resistance

A repression occurs when the self is unable to retain in consciousness a particular idea or image representative of an instinct. The repression may be of two types: (a) the repression may prevent any symbolization of an instinct to enter awareness; and (b) a conscious symbolization of an instinct may be dismissed from awareness. The essential cause of repression, then, is that the self "recognizes" that the desire to satisfy a given impulse would produce more pain than pleasure.

Strictly speaking, it is not an impulse that is repressed but the particular symbolization or manifestation of an impulse. The impulse remains what it always is, impulsive, and, though a particular realization of the impulse is prohibited, it continues to make its appearance in all sorts of disguised forms. The actor changes his costume but plays the same role, and it is precisely the reappearances, in diverse garbs, of repressed manifestations of impulses that are so important for the development of character.

"Resistance" is the force whereby the self fights against the reappearance of what has been repressed and, more particularly, against admission of the basic impulse that has been repressed. The description of these elements constituted what Freud referred to as the "dynamic theory." By 1900 these elements formed a part of his thinking, although they were not at that time finally defined. Later he made one important modification of his dynamic theory by adding a "death instinct" which paralleled the eros or libido instinct. With this addition there were two basic drives in all human life, the constructive "love" instinct and the destructive wish for death.

In addition to these four elements of the dynamic theory Freud later postulated two other systems: the Economic and the Topographical. The "Economic" described the constant psychological force in terms of two principles, "pleasure-pain" and "reality." Pleasure and pain determine the nature of wishing, that is, the basic force for psychical life. A wish, however, may be in opposition to reality, and in the recognition of this opposition Freud made use of the assumption that life is essentially conflict. "Reality—wish-fulfillment"; he wrote, "it is from this contrasting pair that our mental life springs."[119]

In the "Topographical system" Freud divided the mental life into the id, the ego, the superego. The id is "the reservoir of the instinctive impulses."[120] (The term id was taken from the Greek "idioplasma" which is a combination of *idios,* meaning "one's own, personal, distinct," and *plasma,* "form, something that has been molded.") There were obviously many instinctual needs that in their nonconscious force seek only to be satisfied, but the most important for the construction of the mental life are the urgent erotic impulses. The ego is "the most superficial portion of the id and one which is modified by the influence of the external world."[121] The ego is thus a mental organization constructed out of the conflict between the pleasure-pain and reality principles, and with responsibility for self-preservation it controls voluntary mental and physical activity. The superego "develops out of the id, dominates the ego and represents the inhibitions of instinct characteristic of man."[122] The superego consists of the internalization of moral demands derived from early experience, usually from identification with the parents.

In the creation of this psychological theory Freud was influenced throughout by the assumptions of late-nineteenth-century ethics. With these assumptions woven into his thought he arrived through the unexpected route of medicine and psychology at his "initial goal of philosophy." "For that," he said, "was what I wanted originally, when it was not yet clear to me to what end I was in the world."[123] In his theories he realized his presentiment that he would "uncover the source of morality."[124]

Freud began with assumptions regarding man as the product of the natural evolution of deterministic forces, including the primacy of conflict and the centrality of nonrational elements in life. He discovered the origins of individual morality in infantile experiences. This discovery, in his mind, destroyed the possibility of any objective ethical standards, for the kind of moral attitudes an individual develops depends upon his own particular resolution of the Oedipus relation. Acceptance of moral standards, therefore, is a matter of recognizing "truth" not in certain values but in the unique way of resolving conflicts in control of the libido.

Because the psychological development of the individual was not sufficient to account for social morality, Freud was led to apply his theory to social origins. Just as the prehistory of the individual accounts for individual morality, so the prehistory of the society accounts for social morality. Here, too, the Oedipus theme was central, so that "the problems of social psychology, too, should prove soluble on the basis of one single concrete point—man's relation to his father."[125] Freud described the original events in words which, he warned, lack precision because of the nature of the subject.

> All that we find [in Darwin's primal horde] is a violent and jealous father who keeps all the females for himself and drives away his sons as they grow up. . . . One day the brothers who had been driven out came together, killed and devoured their father and so made an end of the patriarchal horde. . . . The violent primal father had doubtless been the feared and envied model of each one of the company of brothers: and in the act of devouring him they accomplished their identification with him, and each one of them acquired a portion of his strength."[126]

Following this act there was the reaction of remorse that found expression in a sense of guilt, and with this reaction society and social taboos were created.

Society was now based on complicity in the common crime; religion was based on the sense of guilt and the remorse attaching to it; while morality was based partly on the exigencies of this society and partly on the penance demanded by the sense of guilt.[127]

Seen in this way, social, like individual, morality has no objective standards, but is equally the result of the attempt to resolve the fundamental Oedipal relationship, so that for Freud it was true to say on both counts, that "In the beginning was the Deed."[128]

Thus the assumptions of Freud and his psychological theories led inexorably to a rejection of ethics. There can be no objective moral standards since moral ideas and attitudes are all explained psychologically as the consequence of individual or social experiences which occurred in childhood and may have been repressed or misremembered. Individuals have been shaped by nonrational forces beyond their control, and often even beyond their knowledge. Yet in Freud's rejection of ethical objectivity there was an inner contradiction and a paradox. The inner contradiction was that Freud, as a psychoanalyst, made value judgments about human beings and society, attempted to cure human disorders, and advocated for all persons a normal unity of life. The paradox was that Freud approved his own morality, desired that more persons might embody lofty ethical ideals, and lived by traditional moral virtues. Both the contradiction and paradox must be examined in more detail to understand Freud's real ethic.

THE FREUDIAN ETHIC

Freud denied that morality possesses an objectivity, and yet his theory of human behavior involved value standards which he claimed were rooted in objective truth. This was possible because Freud was concerned, as a physician, with curing disease and not with promoting moral ideals. Day after day persons who were sick came to him. He early found that their diseases were not, in the main, physical, but disorders of the mind, the results of their experiences and often involving repressive, moralistic parents or society. He learned that the cure did not create paragons of virtue but individuals with a certain unity of character. Thus, he attacked the prevailing morality without recognizing that the attack was based upon an ethical standard, and he promoted a curative process without admitting that his image of normality involved an ethical judgment. This blindness was both the product of a desire for value-free objectivity and the result of his experience of moralistic ideas. "The publicity with which moral demands are made often makes an unpleasant impression on me," Freud wrote in 1915. "What I have seen of religious-ethical conversions has not been very inviting."[129]

Because of the central position of sexuality in his psychology Freud's main, and continuing, attacks upon social standards were directed toward the rigid social repression of sexual instincts. "Sexual morality as society, in its most extreme form the American one, defines it, seems to be very contemptible. I stand for an incomparably freer sexual life."[130] In 1908 he emphasized that the central cause of neuroses was civilization's restriction of sexual activities.

Unable to change immediately the demands of society, Freud was faced with the necessity of curing individuals whom a moralistic society helped to make neurotic. The methods of psychoanalytic cure, he stated, are not difficult to acquire but the process is exceedingly painful for the patient and requires great insight, tact, and patience from the analyst. Through the patient's free association a discovery is made of resistance and, beyond the resistance, that which is being repressed. As the patient moves deeper and deeper into her past, there comes the critical moment when there is a crucial transference of her emotional attitudes (previously directed toward a key person in early experiences) to the analyst. This is the final expression of resistance, of a refusal to see the true facts of her life, and the point of the cure is to enable the patient to gain insight into the real, original causes of her disorder. The at-first painful acceptance of her original condition leads to a new order in life. It is not to be supposed, however, that a person becomes more moral through her self-acceptance. "Why should analyzed people be altogether better than others?" asked Freud. "Analysis makes for unity, but not necessarily for goodness."[131] What was desired from the therapeutic process was that hysteria would be reduced to where it was manageable, enabling the individual to function properly in society.

The recognition that the cure did not necessarily make for "goodness" helped to prevent Freud from seeing that the unity is itself an ethical reality. Through the application of the psychoanalytic therapy there is realized the assumptions which he received from his time that through knowledge of the life forces the individual is enabled to participate in shaping her future so that out of the human conflict there emerges a fundamental harmony.

There was also the paradox in Freud's psychological and value thought in that proclaiming an ethical relativism, he yet approved of his own moral standards, expressed the wish that individuals might be more ethical, and, in his life and work, often embodied high ethical ideals. In his self-criticism Freud was aware of his own virtue. In 1915 he wrote:

> I consider myself to be a very moral person who can subscribe to the excellent maxim of Th. Vischer: "What is moral is self-evident." I believe that in a sense of justice and consideration for others, in disliking making others suffer or taking advantage of them, I can measure myself with the best

people I have known. I have never done anything mean or malicious and cannot trace any temptation to do so, so I am not in the least proud of it. . . .

When I ask myself why I have always behaved honorably, ready to spare others and to be kind wherever possible, and why I did not give up doing so when I observed that in that way one harms oneself and becomes an anvil because other people are brutal and untrustworthy, then, it is true, I have no answer. Sensible it certainly was not. In my youth I never felt any special ethical aspirations, nor have I any recognizable satisfaction in concluding that I am better than most other people. . . . If only more of this valuable constitution were to be observed in the others! I have the secret belief that if one possessed the means of studying the sublimations of instincts as thoroughly as the repressions of them one might come across quite natural psychological explanations. . . .[132]

There are a number of interesting points raised by this personal letter. (1) What can Freud have meant by the statement, which his biographer says was "a favorite quotation,"[133] that "Morality is self-evident"? This was inconsistent with his psychological explanations and ethical relativism. The dismissal of a very difficult philosophical problem with a quotation indicates that Freud was actually concerned only with the question of psychological origins and was never troubled by the issue of validity of moral standards. His ethical relativism was not carefully thought out but was a conclusion drawn hastily from psychological descriptions. (2) In his honest self-judgment there is also a fresh naivete. But in his conclusion that he was better than most other persons there is no indication that Freud had any comprehension of what was involved in an ethics of inner character and external behavior. (3) The prediction that moral goodness might be explained in the future by "quite natural psychological explanations" meant that, in 1915, Freud had not discovered the sources of *specific* types of moral goodness. The assumptions with which he began, as well as his earliest discoveries in psychoanalysis, provided him with "natural psychological explanations."

Freud was somewhat harsh in his judgment of human beings. "The unworthiness of human beings, even of analysts," he confessed, "has always made a deep impression on me, but why should analyzed people be altogether better than others?"[134] In writing to the clergyman-psychoanalyst Oskar Pfister, he said

I don't cudgel my brains much about good and evil, but I have not found much "good" in the average human being. Most of them are in my experience riff-raff, whether they loudly proclaim this or that ethical doctrine or none at all.[135]

Throughout his life Freud possessed a restless energy, a desire to achieve his goals. What were those goals? What were the motives that enabled Freud to work through years of isolation and of opposition? Ambition and, in particular, the desire for fame were important factors. But the man who, in the time of his greatest loneliness, felt strengthened against all daily cares and worries by the feeling that, if given the time, he would leave to humankind something which would justify his existence was surely motivated by more than personal ambition.

It is not possible to easily decipher an individual's secret motives. Those motives, as Freud has convinced us, may be hidden from the individual herself as well as from observers of her life. But trying to live imaginatively with Sigmund Freud makes it appear that, with all of his idiosyncrasies, two powerful forces were present in his life: a concern for the human individual and a desire to know the truth.

The concern for the individual was not that human beings should possess the virtues of saints, but that they should live as normal men and women. Confronted with disturbed, disordered persons, Freud longed that they might be cured so that a human order might enter their lives. He had, he admitted, a "love of form," and this referred to a form for human life as well as an appreciation of a psychological system.

On one occasion Freud recognized that human love might conflict with the desire for truth. He refused to make an absolute judgment that one was superior to the other.

> Whether the demand of absolute truthfulness may not sin . . . against the aims of love itself I should not like to answer with an absolute negative. Truth is only the absolute goal of science, but love is a goal of life quite independent of it and conflicts between the two great powers are very well conceivable. I do not see any necessity for regularly subordinating one to the other as a matter of principle.[136]

Freud possessed a longing for the "absolute goal of science." This was one of the most powerful forces working in him. Again and again he reported his desire to gain philosophical knowledge and to understand the entire functioning of the mental life. He exemplified the courage and determination required of intellectual explorers.

> I am by temperament nothing but a conquistador—an adventurer, if you want it translated—with all the curiosity, daring, and tenacity characteristic of a man of this sort. Such people are customarily esteemed only if they have been successful, have really discovered something.[137]

The concern for human individuals, the love of truth—these were two of the motives that enabled this modern conquistador to make his discoveries, and to be treasured for that work.

THE UNIQUE CONTRIBUTION OF
DARWIN, MARX, NIETZSCHE, AND FREUD

The channels flow into the river; the river rushes to the sea. The eddies and pockets of water swirl, and down in the delta, when the current rises, the banks sometimes break and the river floods. These four individuals have brought us to the end of our journey. They have left us facing an open sea. They have delivered us into the last Western century, and we are still riding along the currents they have created.

There is, it should be said at the outset, a contradictory element in linking these men together, for though they shared similarities, they were each uniquely alone in their quest and their vision.

(1) But they were all four men who felt themselves emerging from an old order and crossing over into a new. It was an old order of industrialism, capitalism, nationalism, and science, an order that would become increasingly mesmerized by technology. But these four men saw beyond these inherited and hypnotic boundaries, and spoke, each out of his own particular vision, of a new world that only they could see. While not all of them felt themselves to be prophets, each of them was. But they were prophets, reluctant or not, of a new kind.

For these men did not see seek to restore us to an earlier vision, to renew a lost insight, to reconnect to an old world. Rather, they brought a new vision that startled and alarmed those who were the first to receive it. In many ways they ruptured the past with their visions. They were not seeking to fuse their insights with those of the past, but to step beyond, and in doing so they often repudiated the culture that had nourished them.

(2) In the broad strokes they shared a similar past: they were the children of the European Enlightenment and of Romanticism. In each family there had been religious figures and something of that religious destiny was embedded in them—in their sense of being called, in being committed, in being prophets. Each had a felt need for salvation, but the old religious concepts remained closed to them, and they had to seek elsewhere for sustenance. Yet they shared one crucial thing in common: they each had a concern for human good and a determination to know the truth, and they believed that individuals could make choices and thereby free themselves from the restraints they found themselves in, and create for themselves a new destiny and a greater and more inclusive freedom. They were also, for the most part, each cut off from their own time. Some were exiles; all suffered for their ideas. All trembled in the face of the vision they explored, some with humility, some with triumphant expectation. They had few friends, and mostly strove on in silence and isolation. The life they sought was in the mind, and the exploration was by thought, a solitary activity by its very nature. Their courage was to be alone, and to know themselves as alone, and they were each singular in that courage.

And yet as similar as they are, they were also distinctly different. They worked at vastly different occupations, and each carved out for himself a particular landscape he sought to map and name. These were landscapes which rarely shared a common border, but did share some common themes.

(3) They each believed that the life of the individual and society was determined by basic nonrational forces. Their personal responses to these forces varied greatly, and cumulatively they undermined the earlier mechanistic vision. But as much as each of them hoped for a better world, of freer individuals living in healthier communities, there lay underneath this hope a darker sense that human beings may not be able to control the forces that flow through their lives. There was a respect for the power of the nonrational, and an uncertainty about an individual's or a community's ability to shape that power for its own ends.

(4) They also believed that while human beings are natural, evolving beings, conflict is the essential touchstone in life. Some of this conflict arose because humans had one aspiration and the nonrational forces seemed to have another. Some came because this dichotomy was also inherent in each individual. Humans are often divided against themselves. The Romantic vision was also based on conflict, but it was a vision where conflict was the source of life, not its end; where conflict could be lived through, fully experienced, expropriated, and harmonized into a new whole. Some of these four men continued to maintain that faith, but it was a faith placed deep into the future, nearly, if not entirely, out of reach for those who were alive today. Conflict for these four men then became a condition of being, rather than a stage of being. It took on a permanence, an indelible presence in the lives of individuals, communities, nations, and the planet itself. It was certainly possible that there would be no final harmonization, and that the conflict that was central in their thought was also paradigmatic.

(5) While each of these men rejected the morality of the past and sought his own "transvaluation of values," and while each has had a significant impact on the last Western century, still it is a current paradox that ethics in itself was not a central concern for any of them. For the most part they approached the subject only obliquely. Each personally felt the injustices of history, both personal and collective, and each sought through his vision to shape a new future for himself and for others. Yet this shaping was not primarily conceived of in ethical terms. This fact itself has become a foreshadowing of our present condition, for many of our ethical challenges have come from sources where that was not the intention.

(6) Finally, perhaps the most significant contribution these four men made, individually and collectively, was not in the world they were attempting to create, but in the vision of the world they left behind. This, too, was not their intention, for in many ways these four men were Romantics:

they sought to unite thinking and feeling, to shape the future, and to give meaning to lives and hope to individuals. As troubling as their visions were for themselves, they experienced them hopefully, and yet the legacy they left has so far proved otherwise.

Where they felt certain, we have been left with doubt. Where they felt confident, we have been left unsettled. Where they expressed their dreams, we have often had their nightmare. Collectively they shifted the ground of mystery and the sense of certainty. Their challenges to the inherited traditions were meant to be radical, permanent, and exclusive. They were looking not back, but forward. They were seeking not to connect, but to reach out. But they still innately believed that out of the present conflicts a new harmony could emerge, and yet the world they bequeathed to us is one in which no vision is secure or uncontested. That was not their purpose, but it has been their result. Nevertheless, we must admire these last men of Western history. After them the sources of the challenges to ethics have not been so much individuals, as communities of individuals: ethnic, feminist, cultural, sexual, ecological, and aboriginal. These four men stand on the last shore of Western ethical history. They are our last prophets. After them, the sea is open.

NOTES

1. T. R. Malthus, *Essay on the Principle of Population,* selected and introduced by Donald Winch (Cambridge: Cambridge University Press, 1992), pp. 23, 228.

2. David Ricardo, *Principles of Political Economy and Taxation* (London: E. P. Dutton [Everyman Edition], 1912), p. 52.

3. Ernest Barker, *National Character and the Factors in Its Formation* (New York: Harper and Brothers, 1927), p. 17.

4. Quoted in C. J. H. Hayes, *Essays on Nationalism* (New York: Macmillan, 1926), 1: 44–45.

5. H. W. Carr, *National and After* (New York: Macmillan, 1945), p. 8.

6. C. J. H. Hayes, "Nationalism," in *Encyclopedia of the Social Sciences* (New York: The Macmillan Co., 1937), 2: 246.

7. Sir William Cecil Dampier, *A History of Science and Its Relation with Philosophy and Religion,* 3d rev. ed. (Cambridge, Mass.: Harvard University Press, 1942), p. 219.

8. Ernst Jones, *The Life and Work of Sigmund Freud* (New York: Basic Books Inc., 1955), 1: 28.

9. Charles Singer, *A Short History of Science to the Nineteenth Century* (Oxford: Clarendon Press, 1941), p. 376.

10. Ibid.

11. Ruth Moore, *Charles Darwin* (New York: Alfred A. Knopf, 1955), pp. 52–53.

12. Ibid., p. 59.

13. Dampier, *A History of Science,* p. 295.

14. Moore, *Charles Darwin,* pp. 110–11.

15. Ibid., pp. 122–23.

16. Ibid., pp. 131–32.

17. Ibid., p. 137.

18. Quoted in Dampier, *A History of Science,* p. 296. "Bulldog" remark is on p. 298.

19. Quoted in Singer, *A Short History of Science,* pp. 379–80.

20. Ibid., p. 380.

21. Isiah Berlin, *Karl Marx: His Life and Environment* (New York: Oxford University Press, 1959), pp. 6–7.

22. Ibid., p. 64.

23. Karl Marx, *Capital: A Critique of Political Economy,* trans. from the third German edition by Samuel Moore and Edward Aveling (Chicago: Charles H. Kerr, 1919), 1: 21.

24. Ibid., pp. 22–24 passim.

25. Berlin, *Karl Marx,* p. 125.

26. Marx, *Capital,* p. 25.

27. Karl Marx, *A Contribution to the Critique of Political Economy,* introduction by Maurice Dobb (New York: International Publishers, 1970), pp. 20–22.

28. Karl Marx, *Communist Manifesto,* in *Capital: The Communist Manifesto and Other Writings,* ed. Max Eastman (New York: Modern Library, 1932), p. 321.

29. Ibid., p. 343.

30. Quoted in George H. Sabine, *A History of Political Theory,* 3d ed. (New York: Holt, Rinehart and Winston, 1961), p. 768.

31. Marx, *Capital,* p. 14.

32. Ibid., p. 46.

33. Marx, *Communist Manifesto,* p. 333.

34. Ibid., p. 328.

35. Ibid., p. 325.

36. Marx, *Capital*, pp. 836–37.

37. Marx, *Communist Manifesto*, p. 343.

38. Friedrich Nietzsche, *Beyond Good and Evil: Prelude to a Philosophy of the Future,* trans. Walter Kaufmann (New York: Random House, 1961; reprint Vintage Books, 1989), pp. 211, 210.

39. Ibid., p. 210.

40. Ibid., p. 212.

41. Ibid., p. 211.

42. Friedrich Nietzsche, *Thus Spake Zarathustra,* ed. Manuel Komroff (New York: Tudor Publishing Company, 1936; originally trans. Thomas Common [New York: The Modern Library, 1905]), p. 44.

43. Friedrich Nietzsche, "Why I am a Fatality," *Ecce Homo*, in *The Philosophy of Nietzsche* (New York: The Modern Library, 1927, 1954), p. 8.

44. Nietzsche, "Thus Spake Zarathustra," *Ecce Homo*, in *The Philosophy of Nietzsche* (New York: The Modern Library, 1927, 1954), p. 6.

45. Nietzsche, *Beyond Good and Evil*, p. 40.

46. Nietzsche, "Thus Spake Zarathustra," p. 34.

47. Nietzsche, *Beyond Good and Evil*, p. 259.

48. Nietzsche, "Zarathustra," p. 34.

49. Friedrich Nietzsche, *The Will to Power,* in *The Complete Works of Friedrich Nietzsche,* ed. Oscar Levy (London: George Allen and Unwin, Ltd., 1924), 15: 698.

50. Nietzsche, "Thus Spake Zarathustra," p. 34.

51. Ibid., prologue III.

52. Quoted in Walter A. Kaufmann, *Nietzsche: Philosopher, Psychologist, Anti-Christ* (Princeton, N.J.: Princeton University Press, 1950), p. 15.

53. Friedrich Nietzsche, "Genealogy of Morals," II, see 18, in Friedrich Nietzsche, *On the Genealogy of Morals,* trans. Walter Kaufmann (New York: Random House, 1989), p. 200.

54. Ibid., p. 167.

55. Nietzsche, *Beyond Good and Evil*, p. 212.

56. Ibid., p. 287.

57. Ibid., p. 265.

58. Kaufmann, *Nietzsche*, p. 324.

59. Nietzsche, *Beyond Good and Evil*, p. 293.

60. Ibid., p. 284.

61. Kaufmann, *Nietzsche*, p. 246.

62. Nietzsche, *Beyond Good and Evil*, p. 260.

63. Ibid., p. 211.

64. Ibid., p. 72.

65. Ibid., p. 76.

66. Ibid., p. 270.

67. Ibid., p. 225.

68. Ibid., p. 188.

69. Ibid., p. 61.

70. Nietzsche, *Gay Science*, p. 290, in Kaufmann, *Nietzsche*, p. 200.

71. Nietzsche, *Beyond Good and Evil*, p. 44.

72. Ibid.

73. Nietzsche, "Thus Spake Zarathustra," p. 4.

74. Nietzsche, *Beyond Good and Evil*, p. 229.

75. Ibid., p. 228.

76. Ibid., p. 260.

77. Friedrich Nietzsche, *The Genealogy of Morals,* trans. Horace B. Samuel (New York: Bom and Liveright, n.d.), p. 112.

78. Nietzsche, *Beyond Good and Evil*, p. 62.

79. Ibid., p. 262.

80. Ibid., p. 225.

81. Ibid., p. 238.

82. Nietzsche, "Thus Spake Zarathustra," p. 18.

83. Ibid.

84. Ibid.

85. Nietzsche, *Beyond Good and Evil*, p. 239.

86. Nietzsche, *The Joyful Wisdom,* in *The Complete Works of Friedrich Nietzsche,* ed. Oscar Levy (New York: The Macmillan Company, 1924), 10: 125.

87. Ibid., p. 125.

88. Sigmund Freud, *An Autobiographical Study,* trans. James Strachey (New York: W. W. Norton and Company, Inc., 1952 [1935]), p. 13.

89. Ibid., p. 15.

90. Ernst Jones, *The Life and Work of Sigmund Freud* (New York: Basic Books Inc., 1955), 1: 330. An alternate translation is in *Complete Letters* (see #93), Letter to Fliess, 30 Jan. 1899. "predilection for the prehistoric in all its human forms," p. 342.

91. Jones, *The Life and Work of Sigmund Freud*, 1: 351.

92. Freud, *An Autobiographical Study*, p. 85.

93. Letter to Fliess, 31 May 1897, in *The Complete Letters of Sigmund Freud to Wilhelm Fliess, 1887–1904,* trans. and ed. Jeffrey Moussaieff Masson (Cambridge, Mass.: The Belknap Press of Harvard University Press, 1985), p. 249.

94. Letter to Fliess, 31 May 1897, *The Complete Letters*, p. 249.

95. Letter to Fliess, 22 June 1897, *The Complete Letters*, p. 254.

96. Letter to Fliess, 14 Aug. 1897, *The Complete Letters*, p. 261.

97. Letter to Fliess, 3 Oct. 1897, *The Complete Letters*, pp. 268–69.

98. Letter to Fliess, 15 Oct. 1897, *The Complete Letters*, p. 271.

99. Ibid., p. 272.

100. Ibid., p. 273.

101. Letter to Fliess, 27 Oct. 1897, *The Complete Letters*, p. 274. (The poem, the Dedication from Goethe's *Faust*, is translated and footnoted in the text.)

102. Letter to Fliess, 14 Nov. 1897, *The Complete Letters*, p. 279.

103. Ibid., p. 280.

104. Ibid., p. 281.

105. Letter to Fliess, 3 Jan. 1899, *The Complete Letters*, p. 338.

106. Letter to Fliess, 3 Dec. 1897, *The Complete Letters*, p. 285.

107. Letter to Fliess, 12 Dec. 1897, *The Complete Letters*, p. 286.

108. Jones, *The Life and Work of Sigmund Freud*, 1: 304.

109. Ibid., 1: 320.

110. Letter to Fliess, 27 Oct. 1897, *The Complete Letters*, p. 274.

111. Freud, *An Autobiographical Study*, p. 74.

112. Sigmund Freud, *A Case of Hysteria, Three Essays on Sexuality and Other Works*, in *Complete Psychological Works,* ed. James Strachey (London: The Hogarth Press and the Institute of Psycho-analysis, 1953), 7: 238–39.

113. Freud, *An Autobiographical Study*, p. 70.

114. Jones, *The Life and Work of Sigmund Freud*, 2: 282.

115. Ibid., 2: 283–84.

116. Letter to Jung, 7 Apr. 1907, in Jones, *The Life and Work of Sigmund Freud*, 2: 436.

117. Jones, *The Life and Work of Sigmund Freud*, 1: 330. (see n. 92).

118. Freud, *A Case of Hysteria*, p. 226; footnote added, 1920.

119. Letter to Fliess, 19 Feb. 1899, *The Complete Letters*, p. 345.

120. Definitions in this paragraph from Sigmund Freud, "Psychoanalysis," in *Encyclopaedia Britannica* (Chicago: Encyclopaedia Britannica, Inc., 1968), 18: 721.

121. Ibid.

122. Ibid.

123. Letter to Fliess, 1 Jan. 1896, *The Complete Letters*, p. 159.

124. Letter to Fliess, 31 May 1897, *The Complete Letters*, p. 249.

125. Sigmund Freud, *Totem and Taboo*, in *Complete Psychological Works* ed. James Strachey, 7: 157.

126. Ibid., pp. 141–42.

127. Ibid., p. 146.

128. Ibid., p. 161. The quotation is from Goethe's *Faust*, part 1, section 3.

129. Letter to J. J. Putnam, 8 July 1915, in Jones, *The Life and Work of Sigmund Freud*, 2: 418.

130. Ibid.

131. Letter to J. J. Putnam, 17 June 1915, in Jones, *The Life and Work of Sigmund Freud*, 2: 182.

132. Letter to J. J. Putnam, 8 July 1915, in Jones, *The Life and Work of Sigmund Freud*, 2: 418.

133. Letter to J. J. Putnam, 7 June 1915, in Jones, *The Life and Work of Sigmund Freud*, 2: 416.

134. Letter to J. J. Putnam, 17 June 1915, in Jones, *The Life and Work of Sigmund Freud*, 2: 182.

135. Letter to J. J. Putnam, 9 Oct. 1918, in Jones, *The Life and Work of Sigmund Freud*, 2: 457.

136. Letter to Sandor Ferenczi, 10 Jan. 1910, in Jones, *The Life and Work of Sigmund Freud*, 2: 446.

137. Letter to Fliess, 1 Feb. 1900, *The Complete Letters*, p. 398.

CONCLUSION

RETROSPECT AND PROSPECT: A PERSONAL VIEW

> History may be servitude,
> History may be freedom. See, now they vanish,
> The faces and places, with the self which, as it could, loved them,
> To become renewed, transfigured, in another pattern.
>
> T. S. Eliot[1]

When I was a boy, until I left home for college I lived with my family on the banks of the James River. It was four miles to the other shore and so it was natural for a child to imagine, far out in the channel, the three small ships of the first immigrants sailing upstream. We picnicked at Jamestown Island, climbing about the ruins of the old church, playing that the Indians were coming through the swamp, remembering the first awful winter and malaria. We were heroes filled with hope; we were at home in our world. Better yet were the bicycle trips twenty miles from our house to Yorktown. There we saw the cannon balls still embedded in the houses; we heard in imagination the dejected British band playing, "The World Turned Upside Down"; we visited the lovely white Moore house where General Washington received the surrender of Lord Cornwallis. But best of all were the visits to Williamsburg even before the restoration. There was the ground where the House of Burgesses had been; the Raleigh Tavern where young Tom Jefferson danced with Belinda in the Apollo Room; the beautiful Bruton Parish Church with its enclosed pews where so many great early Americans had worshiped; and, somehow most moving of all for a child, that architectural gem, the Wren building. It was here that Jefferson studied ethics under Doctor Small, a professor of mathematics, which Jefferson described as "my good fortune, that probably fixed the destinies of my life."

I went to Stonewall Jackson School, and so he, too, became a hero for his courage and commitment. It was painful to recall that frightening evening when, at dusk, his own men mistook him for the enemy and killed him. (Strangely, that story became for a child a myth of life.) Lee, of course, was the greater hero and, as in many Southern homes, there on the sunporch was the picture of him astride Traveller sitting with such straight dignity it was impossible to see how he could ride without being jarred from the saddle. Even a boy could understand that night he was offered command of the Union forces, a night he spent pacing the floor, and even a boy could be proud when he decided to stay with his native Virginia, yet believe he made the wrong decision. We also often visited Fortress Monroe, listened to band concerts and played on the battlements, knowing that President Lincoln had come to that very spot during the war. (One did not then have to ask, "What war?") Living where and with whom I lived it was not surprising that Lincoln was as great a hero as Lee, and, indeed, when about ten the only fight I had with my best friend was because he insulted Lincoln. So when I visited Gettysburg, I was a confused boy and didn't know whether to hope that (this time) Lee would get key battle orders through on time or to hear and believe Lincoln talking about "a new nation, conceived in liberty, and dedicated to the proposition that all men are created equal."

On Sunday afternoons we would drive in the Model T through the beautiful Hampton Institute campus. On those rare, most wonderful times of all our bachelor uncle would stuff his pockets with hard peanut candy and take us on the rollicking streetcar the ten miles to the college where we would go to a concert. I cannot know all that we talked about on those trips, but at some early age Booker T. Washington became a hero and I was led to understand that if only I was as conscientious as he, I might make something of my life. (My admiration for him, of course, caused me real trouble in the sixties when many black friends scorned him.) It was my Southern grandmother who first came to admire Washington. She had been four when her home in Georgia was burned by stragglers from Sherman's army. Her clearest memory, next to the burning and the fear, was of the handsome Yankee captain who saved her life. (She fell in love with him, and of such childish loves perhaps later reconciliations are made.) A few years ago I visited Auburn, where she had later moved so her children could go to college. As we drove by a black church, my uncle said, "Once when Mama was teaching a Sunday School class there she asked, 'Who died for your sins?' Hands went up, and the first small child to answer said, 'Booker T. Washington.' 'Well,' she said, 'That's not who I had in mind, but he will do.'" It is no wonder he became a hero in our family.

Others, closer in time, were more remote, but to a young boy they also became heroes: Theodore Roosevelt and his "Square Deal," Woodrow Wilson and his dreams of a peaceful world, a world made safe for democracy. All of these persons were dead before I first heard about them. Yet to a child they were very much alive, and still are today. "The communication/Of the dead is tongued with fire beyond the language of the living."[2] For a young boy the fire of every one of these persons was the fire of liberty, and, since then, though I have come to recognize the human flaws in each, it is that flame that still burns most fiercely, most dangerously.

I have reported these myths of my life for various reasons. One is to make clear that what I understand ethics to be has been a part of my life as long as I can remember. Another is to make clear that any writing about the history of ethics is not a personal academic exercise but a personal, painful experience. For my life, like that of so many others in our nation and world (especially the West), is at stake now and dependent upon precisely how we preserve and expand our ethical tradition. Often I wish that I could be as simple and as clear as Augustine:

> "What do you want to know?"
> "God and the soul."
> "Nothing more?"
> "Nothing more."

But my life has often not been that simple or clear, and so I must ask myself, as I believe everyone must: "What do I want to know?" And for me the answer is: what it is to be fully human in a human society. For this is the theme of Western ethics: what it means to be and to become a human individual in a human community. And, of course, this answer leads inevitably to other concerns which, more often than not, appear to us as questions: education; equality; friendship; faith; freedom; politics; love; and what is the essential nature of the individual's relationship with the self, others, society, and the world.

For me the purpose of studying and writing about the history of Western ethics has always been to help myself and others create and understand my own ethic with greater clarity, for the ultimate goal is the passionately integrated life. And in the first place I believe this can be done only when I understand and share with others what has been given to us by our past. For each individual's ethics are formed in those special border crossings between the individual and her community. For the history of ethics is the history of the discovery of moral truth, and of the loss of moral truth, and it is through the recognition of this discovery and loss, that each individual can come to embody the truth in her own life. And I believe that the embodiment of that truth, or the failure to embody it—which has a close connection with beauty —is the most important fact about a person's life.

So, I believe that part of our tradition (which is both Greek and Hebraic) is that we study ethics in order to become good, that is, more fully human. Of course, it is not possible to arrive at a final, complete, and accurate truth in understanding one's own ethic or that of others. There is no perfect expression of an ethic. But what we can have is the habit of active thought about life. This comes from making connections, from creating insights, and then, though rational thought, whether alone or with others, from correcting, adapting to, and improving in clarity and depth those connections and insights. Yet, while looking back as we must, still we must live in our own time, for moral philosophy also arises from and is directed toward personal moral experience.

What, then, is the nature of our own time? George Steiner in his famous Charles Eliot Norton lecture at Harvard makes a striking assertion about the essential requirement for a responsible theory of culture in our time:

> A theory of culture, an analysis of our present circumstance, which does not have at [its] pivot a consideration of the modes of terror that brought on the death, through war, starvation, and deliberate massacre, of some seventy million human beings in Europe and Russia, between the start of the First World War and the end of the Second, seems to me irresponsible.[3]

These words might well have been written about moral philosophy except in that case the pivot is in the experience rather than the consideration of the modes of terror. And it is not just the experience of those modes of terror that is essential for the creation of an adequate ethic. It is the full integration of the experience into a life in order that, later, the experience emerges transmuted in a moral philosophy.

In our age then, who are these persons who have experienced, and who still experience, the modes of terror? They are the refugees, the displaced persons, the prisoners of war and of conscience. They are those who have been forced by the nation states to move from their homes, from all that is familiar and beloved in their lives. They are forced to move without possessions to an alien place. Their freedom and community are taken from them: they move as prisoners or, at best, as dependents, their communities destroyed. They are forced either to begin a new life or to die. For the twentieth century will be known as the century of the homeless.

These persons are the reality and the symbol of the twentieth century, as they are likely to be of the twenty-first, and there have been and are literally millions of them. For it is not only in German concentration camps or in Russian pogroms, but on every continent and in every country that the violated have existed and exist. For whenever we try to think of human life in our time, some of the most compelling images are those of the strangers we have seen who have been forced to leave their homes and can never return to the familiar land and life they have loved. Millions of these travelers are now silent, for they have accepted the burden of death. Millions are refugees whose numbers increase incrementally each year. Since no one can have an image of millions, consequently the image that most often disturbs the mind is that of individual persons, their plight and suffering. And yet when we multiply that individual by the millions, how, we wonder, can the moral ideals of the West thrive?

These homeless are not only the literal refugees and prisoners, those who would be recognized by the United Nations High Commissioner for Refugees or Amnesty International. In a more fundamental way, we see our own lives in theirs. For in an elemental sense, and in a way unprecedented for so brief a time in human history, repeated waves of new cultures have flooded in upon the old, forcing almost all persons to flee from the familiar and the beloved, to make radical adjustments, and to begin a new life in a spiritual sense or to die.

In this respect it is important to recognize what the displaced persons have contributed to the new cultures in which they have shaped their new lives. For their contributions to the renewal of European culture, whether on the Continent, in Britain, America, Israel, or the European Pacific, have been incalculable. In the natural and social sciences, in all the arts (where would contemporary painting, music, and literature be without them?), in history, in diplomacy and politics, in business and the professions: everywhere there has been creative development in Western culture, it has been the violated of our time, those who have experienced the violence and known the anomie, who have made many of the most significant contributions. But this has not happened in moral philosophy. Here the contribution of the displaced has been more ambiguous. Here the refugees have not contributed directly to a moral philosophy but rather to a moral life. For it is they who have manifested the indomitable spirit of individual struggle, who have embodied and enacted human freedom in ways unsurpassed by any previous persons in history. They have shown us what it means to be a person in a human community, to be a free person in a free world.

This is what the displaced persons have done. Indeed, the very depth of the ethical life of many refugees accounts in large part for their extraordinary contributions in all fields except ethics. Those contributions can be seen as the expression of the will to live, to be free, and to find meaning in the world. For it has been an enormously difficult task for the violated of our time to live as persons and to manifest the meaning of their lives in creative human work.

These images of those who have felt forced from their homes will not fade. This is another reason why I wanted to begin this final chapter with a personal history, for are we not all now, refugees from a familiar past, immigrants in an alien present? So the inescapable questions come before our moral lives: how can we who are spiritual refugees become transformed into spiritual pilgrims? How can the stranger carve out a home in this new world?

How, in short, can we create from our past and in our own difficult present, a living moral faith by which we all might live?

Moral philosophy arises from moral experience. In any period of history, therefore, an ethic adequate for the needs of persons living fully in their time can be created only by those who have lived deeply in that age, allowing the age to live in them. But how the transition is made from this crucial experience to the ethic, from an encased, enclosed life to one of freedom, makes all the difference, for the transition cannot take place immediately or suddenly, though in the act of making, of creating this project, we are, in fact, creating our own lives. For this act of self-creation there must be, first, remembrance and reflection. Then there must be engagement, the creation of new insights, and a freshness of faith which we have not known before. The study of ethics can, at least, help us in this exploration. It can help us make of our history a living tradition, whose final goal is to develop a creative, free moral agent.

REMEMBRANCE

It has never been an easy marriage, but it has endured; even more, it has been a constant source of renewal for everyone in the Western family. The marriage here is the original couple of Western ethics: the Greek and the Judeo-Christian traditions. These two parents have been the primogenitors in the creation of a shared Western ethical identity, a basic Western moral personality. For all ethical experience and thought since the establishment of the ethical identity in the West has been related to Greek and Hebraic experience, though it is far from certain that this will be the case in the future. But the origins of our family tree are clear, for it is the Greek philosophers and the Hebrew prophets who have together established our identity and set the essential tasks that have determined our growth and failure. Others have added and elaborated on this basic moral core, but it is these two who are our rightful ancestors. For both, the essential question was one of authority: What is the source of authority? For one, the answer was a conversational thinking, while for the other, it was manifested in a living relationship with a Holy Other.

For the Greeks it was the sense that there were truths external to human beings. This sense of truth brought with it the centrality of certain words: reason (as a means both of discovery and of directing action once the discovery has been made), dialogue, ideas, order, structure, goals, purpose (the conflict between means and ends), the individual, happiness, balance, and harmony. For the Greeks, justice was discoverable, interpretable, and enforceable. Friendship was essential to the full life, and thinking (as impersonal objectivity) was directed toward the world as empirical fact.

For the Hebrews it was the covenant: a determinative bond between a nonhistorical Holy Other and a historical people. This covenant also accented certain words like: promise, trust, responsibility, faithfulness, loyalty, duty and thus correspondingly their opposites: sin, and then the treatment of sin: forgiveness. For both there was the awareness of the essential conflict between justice and love, and in between the two, the centrality of suffering. Crucial to both was the sense of embodiment, of living one's ideals and of service to the community. For both, ethics was a matter of individual and social fulfillment.

The Roman Stoics and Augustine expanded the understanding of ethics to the whole world, and felt that ethics could provide a comprehensive ordering of life. Though their understanding of the source was vastly different, for both a reasonable valuing became the basis of all life. This living unity of thought and action, of history and eternity was carried over into the medieval age where the major figures there embraced a shared sense of meaning, an overarching order that gave each individual a sense of her own place and value. But while faith was the *sine qua non* for this segment of history, at the same time there was a growing seed in faith's soil: that of individuality. In the Renaissance this seed would break the surface, prosper and flower in the Enlightenment of the eighteenth century and from there into the political foundations of democracy itself, but also ontologically the individual became the focus of all values.

As the Renaissance and Reformation broadened into the scientific revolutions of the seventeenth century, the old unity was shattered. There were multiple possibilities for creating meaning, and values became a matter of personal choice rather than adherence to a community standard. From a plethora of often conflicting sources the individual was left free, or cut adrift, to create her own individual ethical stance. The search, the journey, the quest became the central underlying metaphor for this creative act. Equally implicit in this quest was a sense of optimism, a sense that this best of all possible worlds could yet be made even better; that goodness was natural; and that there were principles, natural human rights, which were universal and could transcend political boundaries. But the inherent worth of the individual was the cornerstone. Gradually, however, the world shifted from a religious foundation to a secular and political one, and it was the state that guaranteed the principle of the right of religious freedom, the right to worship as one chose.

The Romantics deepened and expanded these sensibilities, adding feeling as a value in itself, but it was really Darwin and Marx, Nietzsche, and Freud who opened and closed the last Western century. In the wake of their thought, the foundations themselves were questioned: natural goodness, optimism, the independence of the individual. In fact human beings and human values were lifted from the center of creation to a peripheral space, and the nonrational forces moved to the center of the way the individual creates values. Darkness replaced the dawn. Conflict became permanent and not merely a stage in the process of becoming. Individuals and communities were seen as divided against themselves. Doubt replaced certitude. Power replaced peace. The individual was still the focus of forces from within and without, but now she was besieged, and often an outcast, expelled and exiled from home.

What began, then, as confidence in authority with the Greeks and the Hebrews has changed to doubting authority. What began with a confidence in reason has changed to a fear of the irrational. What began as a sense of unity with the universe has changed to a sense of alienation from the natural and the spiritual worlds. As we look around our modern terrain we seem to be living in the ruins of ancient beliefs, caught up in irreconcilable conflicts with no moral exemplars and no clearly defined responsibilities. Thus we seem homeless ourselves. And yet, this is only a partial vision, for in fact, beyond the doubts of the present, what our ethical tradition has bequeathed us are some clear insights into some fundamental assumptions that support our Western ethical personality as well as some clear ethical convictions, which, as we look at both, have become permanent presuppositions in the Western moral character.

Consequently, we must begin our inspection by acknowledging that there is a developing Western ethic which we may easily miss if we pay too much attention to special individuals and their differences; or if we attempt to ignore the Jewish-Christian tradition which, whatever one may think of it, has been a constant influence upon the ethic, including the philosophers; or, finally, if we become too preoccupied with contemporary political and moral problems. For there is an ethical tradition of the West that contains essential and enduring moral insights and convictions. But in order to glimpse the lineaments of these insights and convictions, it is important to step back and view the history of Western ethics as a whole; by doing that, we can notice six major assumptions that have endured throughout.

(1) In the first place, the major concern of the Western ethic has always been the human person in a human community. It has always focused its attention on what it means to be a person, or what it means to be becoming a person; therefore, one of its central concerns has always been what personal relations are and should be, as well as what social institutions are and do, and what they should be and should do. The most important materials of ethics are, therefore, found within the living experiences of the self and of groups, and ethical reflection and creation begins with such intimate personal experience. It begins with a sense of place, both temporal and physical. It begins in our homes and our sense of what home is and where we feel and have felt at home. It begins on the James River of each of our own lives.

(2) With this focus upon the individual in community, there has always been an accompanying dual emphasis on individual rights, which historically is the ethic of goals, and on individual responsibilities, which historically is

the ethic of motive or duty. Concurrent with this double emphasis is the accompanying sense of the equality of value of all persons and the sense that institutions are made for human beings.

(3) A focus on these emphases has tended to produce ethics characterized by: (a) seeking, that is, by an intellectual curiosity and questioning; (b) a focused concern on practical application of values; and (c) a significant emphasis on discipline, that is, the use of reason to understand and to order behavior and emotions. Although it should be noted that as central as reason is in understanding what is happening to and in us, including what should happen, we neither receive nor live by the ethic of rationality.

(4) There is the shared view that ethical truth exists; that in opposition to all ethical skepticism, irrationalism, and subjectivism there is the conviction that there are fundamental and real differences between moral good and evil, right and wrong. And that whatever an individual or a community may postulate as the ethical truth is always objective, a truth that is discovered in human creation.

(5) However, this truth, *as known,* is always a relative or relational truth. Moral truth is related to the structure of personal existence. Since personal existence is not a static structure but is ever in process, and since it is always rooted in changing historical, social, cultural situations, the ethical truth will be related to the particular person in each particular culture. This means that during one's own life time each individual must work out, more or less satisfactorily, her own ethical existence. Each is led to the discovery of moral truths by acceptance of assumptions provided by the ethical community in which she lives, as modified by individual experience and expressed through individual reflection. But the experience and reflection change over time.

(6) This final emphasis upon the individual is the cornerstone of the Western ethic. Every person who lives experiences some ethical fulfillment, and has some aspirations and sense of responsibility. To comprehend what accounts for the fulfillment, to understand the basic origins of the aspirations and obligations would be to understand fundamental aspects of the moral truth. Thus, the ethical life of the self comes prior to and accompanies ethical thought and creation. We do not begin ethical reflection as we *may* begin mathematical reflection or scientific study, i.e., with little or no prior experience in the field, but able to proceed by carefully paced steps from the simplest to the complex. No matter at what age a self-conscious moral reflection begins, it begins not at the beginning but in the middle, in the midst of life with conflicting experiences, values, beliefs, and societies pressing upon us. This is the essential paradox of Western ethics: that the tongues of the dead are voiced "in the language of the living," that though "last year's words belong to last year's language/And next year's words await another voice,"[4] still the voice we are, the voice we are becoming, is also the renewed, trans-

figured voice that others have known. For we are simultaneously creators and caretakers. We are the intersection of numerous borders and vast crossings.

Given these assumptions, and recognizing that the history of Western ethics is not one continuous success story nor even a continuous story, we can now state some of the clear convictions that have been developed in our Western tradition:

1. Every individual has the right to life and to the means to life.

2. The direction of the ethical life is the self-realization of one's own full potential.

3. As ethical individuals we have a moral responsibility for our own actions.

4. Our political society exists to guarantee these rights and to ask us to account for our responsibilities.

5. As human beings, with kindness, dedication, courage, and love we can make these rights and responsibilities real for all persons.

As we interrogate our memory, certainly, these are some of our basic Western ethical convictions. Still, the nagging question is: are they sufficient? Are they adequate to help us face the world that is opening before us? For prior to the twentieth century every major moral philosopher in Western history dealt in his or her theory with social and personal ethical problems, and generalizing from moral experience, created a normative theory. But increasingly in the modern world the "ethical communities" have been dispersed or diffused and thus the moral philosopher has, in the chaos of the contemporary world, been left without the support of what is necessary as the starting point for a normative ethic. Now in the West, there is no adequate social base for the construction of an ethic. Today there is no compelling moral consensus. So, while every age has developed ethical principles appropriate to its own time, and while we, too, must develop new principles, still it is far from certain that we will be successful, for today the practical situation is unprecedented. For this is, for those of us in the West, the last Western century, and we must ask ourselves what it is that has made this century unique.

REFLECTION

What can we say has happened to Western life in the twentieth century? What are the essential characteristics of our time, and what are the effects that these characteristics have had on modern life?

First, the organizational revolution, which has silently transformed our society and our lives. It refers to the omnipresent fact that with our great organizational skill, we have developed organizations for everything, and that there is scarcely anything we can do without intricate organizations, from making love to getting an education to controlling a free-enterprise system. This institutionalizing of our lives has a profound effect upon us; all the more important, perhaps, because we usually take our institutions for granted. But their power over us, I believe, can hardly be overestimated.

Along with this is the sense that the institutions of Western culture have become dysfunctional, no longer adequately meeting essential human needs. No matter whether the institutions were thought of as socially patterned ways or socially organized structures there has developed a widespread dissatisfaction and even despair with them: "institutionalized racism," foreign policy and the military, education, health, politics, sex and the family, entertainment and the news media, housing programs, religion, transportation, law enforcement, welfare. It is impossible to look at any institutionalized way that human beings have organized their lives and not find serious criticism and considerable reason for criticism. Nor is it important at the moment to inquire whether the considerable reason is sufficient reason. The important point is that to a great extent human beings do not feel that the institutions "fit" their lives and needs, resulting in despair, malaise, and distraction.

Second, the technological-electronic revolutions. We live among machines, and in machines, and even for machines. And we live with the mass media so intimately that they live in us. We live in a time of unparalleled ability to transmit or transport information, goods, and persons throughout the world. And yet this immediacy, paradoxically, makes intimacy less likely, makes privacy more fragile, and creates vast pockets of stress and alienation.

Third, we have lived through social catastrophe and social success. The catastrophe of twentieth-century violence was unimaginable in the nineteenth, and even today, incomprehensible. What is the meaning of this: that millions of young adults have been killed, stalked like animals, destroyed without thought; that women, old men, and children in literally hundreds of cities of Europe, Asia, Africa, and Latin America have, in our lifetimes, been carelessly killed; that millions of persons have been and still are refugees, in strange places, without homes and without hope? What is the meaning of this violence, these random acts of genocide and terrorism, these outbursts of ethnic conflicts and the rise of crime in our daily lives and communities? And what is the meaning of this: that simultaneously with these events, the West and parts of Asia have created an ongoing prosperity, indeed, a life of opulence, of such wealth, luxury, and waste as the world has never seen before?

Fourth, we have witnessed exponential rises in population and vast shifts in residences. From the moon this movement must resemble a cancer—a vast march of cells across a living body. But this displacement of individuals, whether by choice, fear, or accident, has seen the burgeoning growth of the cities, the decline of the rural areas, and the spreading tentacles of the suburban streets. In 1900, for example, the population of the world was 1.6 billion; in 2000, it will be 6.1 billion. In 1900 there were sixteen cities with a population in excess of one million; in 2000 there will be nearly 150. This process can perhaps best be illustrated by noticing where our families live and how they live, for, paradoxically, crowding persons together in cities actually tends to separate them from each other; and, surprisingly, suburbanizing them has the same effect. The resulting pressures that have been placed upon families have been immense and have, as often as not, crushed them.

Fifth, individuals have continued to give their greatest love to the lowest common denominator. Nationalism has been the twentieth-century god, and the major violence of the century has been the direct consequence of the nation-state and of the individual's loyalty to it. The incipient transnationalism, whether it be the European Common Market, the rise of economic unions like NAFTA, or the expansion of the United Nations, is still not the dominant ethos. In addition, there is the proliferation in importance of the pluralistic societies contained within each nation. Group identities are formed along ethic, racial, ideological, sexual, and religious lines and these strong ties make border crossings, whether in marriage or friendships, whether political or economic, difficult and often dangerous. Accompanying these multiple sources of identity have been the various social revolutions that have taken place in the West, for more often than not these have come about because a group of people who have felt themselves marginalized have banded together and asserted their rights. This is true of the movements in labor unions, African Americans, the dispossessed, the immigrants, or the assertive rights on behalf of women or the sexual revolution.

Sixth has been the centralization of power. This refers to the fact that in times of crisis the control of life has been centered to the fullest possible extent allowed by the technology and the institutions. And following crises, the power centers strive to maintain their control.

Seventh, the thought of our time has exerted powerful influences in our lives. That thought is so varied, so vast but whether it is philosophical, theological, scientific, economic, or political, it seems to have had two prime characteristics: a tendency toward extremes and toward providing an esoteric salvation. It sometimes seems that persons in our time have not been able to believe anything unless they could believe it all the way, and believe that it provided the one sure way to salvation: the scientific method, pacifism, psychoanalysis, Marxism, fundamentalism, and fascism. Attitudes toward these have been extreme, and their devotees have often held them out as the one sure hope for humankind.

Finally, the most significant factor of the twentieth century has been the fact that there seem to be no new consensual moral norms being established. Indeed, there seems to be a weakening in the values of vocation, in a sense of the importance of personal integrity, and in the centrality of sexuality and personal relationships. There seems to be a retreat from the public arena to the private; fewer causes, no crusades. A diminution of will. And at the same time there is discernible a growing chasm between professed virtues and practices, leading to a greater confusion, conflict, and malaise. Accompanying all this is a pervasive absence of a personal and inclusive cause that gives life significance, an absence of the feeling that it might be possible to create a sustaining set of ideas, values, or beliefs that can help one understand and enjoy life. There is a fragmentation of will, a thwarting or wasting of talents, a stifling of creativity, and an eroding of sensitivity both in the moral and the aesthetic realms. But perhaps the greatest concern here is that life is increasingly thought of in terms of threats, problems, and the lack of meaning.

Now, if we put these together—the organizational and technological revolutions, the social catastrophes and successes, the shifts in population and allegiances, the centralization of power and the blind faith of modern thought—we can begin to sketch the effects of these characteristics upon our lives.

(1) There is a lack of community. A community of persons is a spiritual thing: it rests upon the worthiness of the goals of the persons in the community and depends upon mutual respect and mutual trust; therefore, it is marked by an openness of communication. But these characteristics are largely lacking in our society. A contemporary individual does not act as though he or she believes or perhaps even knows the doctrines of Plato and Jesus, so important in Western history, that the ultimate forces at work in human life operate by persuasion and not by force. Whenever problems arise the tendency seems to be for individuals to want to win, to impose their views upon others rather than to cooperate, compromise, and attempt to talk out their problems patiently together.

(2) With this lack of community has come an increasing erosion of the human personality. This is true because personality and community exist together. This depersonalization has happened so quickly and so quietly that we may not be aware of how it has happened to us. But it is marked by such qualities as a denial of our responsibility and a tendency to blame other persons and other situations for what we have become. There is also a brutalization of life or sandpapering of our sensitivity; an unwillingness to engage in sharp self-criticism; a lovelessness, both toward the self and toward others.

(3) There exists in us conflict and confusion. But the conflict of two hundred years ago did not lead to confusion because beneath the conflict there was an automatic, real harmony. The conflict of one hundred years ago, or fifty, did not lead to confusion because through the conflict we believed we were progressing, howsoever painfully, to a social utopia and psychological

salvation. But the present conflicts within ourselves and within our society have no such common beliefs in harmony or progress. This is particularly evident when we look, for example, at the status of women almost anywhere in the world.

(4) This lack of community, this loss of personality, this conflict and resultant confusion is all related to the absence of inclusive causes for which to live. This, indeed, is, I think, the most significant thing that has happened to us: we have lost that living sense of a meaning in life that is a harmonizing and a motivating force in our lives; we have lost that living sense of the sacredness of common things.

(5) There is a decreasing sense of self-direction, or a decreasing sense of the adventure and control of the self in all of its relations. This refers, obviously, to the self-adventure and self-control of personality, to the self's adventure and control of personal relations and of society. It means also that for most persons there are no felt personal relations with what is ultimate and inescapable; and for many who are so minded the relations are artificial, insignificant, and irrelevant to the daily concerns of life.

These, then, are the tremors that have shaken the Western world in the twentieth century, creating simultaneously a sense of disorientation and a series of distractions. We live with the imminent threat of eviction from our own tradition, if we are not in fact homeless already. These characteristics of our time and their effects have brought us a significant set of interlaced concerns that human beings have never had to face before. At the same time, there is a double-waved challenge coming to us from our own future.

ENGAGEMENT

We cannot escape our history. We cannot hide from the time in which we live, and we must not hide from what has happened and is happening to us. This means, obviously, that we cannot act as though we have not been deeply involved in the holocaust of the great wars, or partners in the great hatreds of our time; that we cannot escape technology or its influences; that we cannot return to a pre-twentieth-century kind of society or family or nature. The way out is not in retreat or in sleep.

But more than this: I am convinced that none of the popular panaceas of the twentieth century can adequately reconstruct human life in the twenty-first. The scientific method, public education, socialism, world government, psychoanalysis—these are pleasant panaceas to play with, but none of them is adequate to make us fully human.

Positively, we can begin by recognizing that we have reached the end of an age: call it what you will—the end of the modern world, the end of the

Protestant epoch, the end of the Christian era, the end of Western civilization, or the birth of the postmodern world. The name is not as important as the fact that we have arrived at an end, we have reached the edge. And beyond us are uncharted seas and unmapped lands. If we believe that beyond us there is a promised land, it is certainly one that we cannot see and, therefore, like any real adventurer, we must live by trust and hope and not by sight. For those living on the edge of time, the past can be of some help, indeed, of indispensable help, but we must be wary of living by our past. In that way is certain failure.

But we can also begin by recognizing that the history of ethics is complex, confusing. This is true partly because the history has had various origins, at different places and in different social and personal contexts, and dealt with different problems. Yet, often these sources have used the same words, which in themselves have imprecise and changing meanings. So, our own ethic is often confused and complex, inheritors as we are of these various sources. And now the situations in which we apply our values are equally complex, confusing, and changing.

But as we scan the history of ethics, we can notice that most discoveries of new ethical truths occur when an individual and/or a community resolves practical moral problems and when individuals creatively reach toward new principles and perspectives. Of course, the times of resolving practical moral problems and reaching toward new ethical truths are times of extraordinary conflict and usually, as viewed from within the time, intellectual ferment and frequently spiritual chaos. Such a time is certainly the twentieth century since the First World War. But we also notice that normally ethical groups do not conflict with each other, unless one tries to maintain itself as the only legitimate ethical perspective. Consequently, the major conflicts in Western ethics have occurred not between ethical communities but within the communities and a framework of common assumptions. Most of these ethical conflicts have, therefore, been resolved by more inclusive views or finer perceptions of individuals in later moral communities.

This brings us to the first challenge of the twenty-first century, the challenge to revise our own ethical beliefs. This challenge will come simultaneously in two waves, from within and from without. In the first place new surges of immigrants, new technologies, and new imaginative insights will continue to create *within* the Western tradition the kinds of tensions that we have observed before. At the same time the essential conflict between the values of Adam Smith and those of John Locke will continue to exert pressure on the surface of all of our lives. The challenge between free enterprise and democratic ideals appears now only in the shadows, but increasingly as the distribution of wealth continues to separate us, the question will be put more bluntly: how can we resolve the very real conflicts between the basic values of an amoral self-interested free-enterprise system which allows wealth to accumulate in the hands of a few, and the values of democratic institutions which are committed to principles of self-evident and inalienable rights equally shared by all? It is possible that this conflict cannot be turned into a dance of partners, and that one of these value systems will attempt to fully dominate the other. But the hope is that, with the collapse of communism having brought the question from the shadows, creative individuals can find new, unifying common commitments which can bond these two into a new creative marriage, for without this bond, the acrimony of the parents will most certainly continue to be manifested in the disrupted lives of their children.

But simultaneous with the attempt to resolve these internal tensions, there will be a more significant wave, and this is that for the first time Western ethics will have to confront not just challenges to particular beliefs or insights, but to the very presuppositions that underpin the entire set of Western beliefs. Because for the first time individuals, communities, and nations within the Western tradition will be confronting other traditions which have also been developing for millennia their own ethical insights, perspectives, principles, and traditions. At first we will probably confront these traditions over particular issues, unaware perhaps that underlying these issues is a rich history and a fully developed ethic which does not correspond to our own. We will, perhaps, be further handicapped because as we deal with these new traditions, we will not, at least at first, have at our disposal a history of the ethical tradition that we are confronting, and so there is likely to be greater misunderstanding and misapprehension, and we are likely, if we are not careful, to find ourselves in the position of trying to assert our own beliefs as the only legitimate beliefs. Reconciliation between whole systems is something that has never been attempted before, and we have no model to follow to guide and assist us.

In addition, from the insights of anthropology, we will be forced to recognize the inherent malleability of most beliefs, and of most systems of beliefs. Contrasting cultural conditions can produce a wide variety of value systems which are, at times, almost diametrically opposed. If this is true, then as we face new cultural beliefs, we must face them with humility rather than disdain, with a listening ear rather than a rigid mind. But even if we are open to listening and to receiving, it still may be difficult to tolerate what we hear, much less to embrace it. One thing is clear, however, and that is that for Western ethics, the twentieth century is the last Western century. This set of dual waves, from within and from without, will, like any storm, permanently alter the Western landscape. Standing on the beach facing this double tsunami, what can we hope for? What can we bring to this experience that will not only help us endure it, but assist us to make with it new lives lived in a greater harmony in a larger world and with greater satisfactions? Facing all these challenges, what can we do to become more fully human?

First, and overarching all, we must experience dignity in our own persons, we must have a firsthand acquaintance with human dignity. In the West, we have lived and fought on slogans: the dignity of man, the four freedoms, freedom and equality, justice and mercy, the importance of the individual. It is important that we experience these within ourselves, in our personal lives and relations. But more specifically, what does this mean?

(1) We must develop a sense of the significant, and a sensitivity to the significant. This means that we develop our ability to distinguish for ourselves, and not at the dictation of friends or authorities, between the first rate and the second rate, between the profound and the superficial, between the sincere and the hypocritical.

(2) It is essential that we recognize, understand and—in such manner as we are able—oppose the threats to human personality wherever those threats arise. This means, of course, an understanding of what is happening to human life in our world, an understanding that takes us beyond the front page of the newspaper or beyond a half an hour's world news. It means an intellectual restlessness, alertness; a hunger that is important enough and also a recognition and understanding of, and an opposition to, those demonic, destructive forces in human life and society and, most difficult of all, in the self. Accompanying this, there must be that sense of the sacred that, knowing no limits, can permeate all of life.

(3) There must be an active acceptance of others *as* others. This implies the recognition that others are selves whose experience of life is as important to them as ours is to us. It means, too, the understanding that we do not possess all the truth about life, that there are many possible solutions to our common problems, and that we can learn from diverse peoples. And the acceptance of others as others also suggests that when we war with them, we do not embark on a holy crusade but with a sense of a tragedy that has engulfed us all. And perhaps, most difficult of all, this relation to others makes it essential that we accept their rejection of us, accepting it not with an inner rejection of them, not with bitterness, nor with furious pride but with the awareness that this may be, if we allow it, a means toward the purification of ourselves and the achievement of our society. Rejection, like difference of opinion, is not a defeat but an opportunity.

But acceptance also implies sympathy, although today we have no accurate word for that eighteenth-century term "sympathy" which was, for David Hume and Adam Smith, an essential way of knowing the other. For Hume and Smith sympathy was defined as one person's experience of the other's experiencing. It is not my experience of your experience where I remain myself looking upon and responding to you; but rather, it occurs when I place myself in your situation and in an imaginative sense become you. I have *your* experience, yet without losing my "self." In a real sense and to some degree I have your pain, your joy, your perplexity, your insight. Such sympathy is, therefore, absolutely essential to my acceptance of the other. For if ever I am to know you as you, I must, in key respects, accept you as you are and are becoming, letting you be the person you essentially are. This acceptance of you is doubly necessary as a means to the knowledge of you. In such accepting there is also the participating in a community with you. And one of the fundamental problems in this regard is to find the right psychological distance from you and nearness to you, a distance that is always shifting.

For the knowledge of selves points to the fact that we discover the inner life, whether of others or the self, in much the same way we find the inner meanings of a work of art. If successful in achieving knowledge, we see a person in much the same ways as we see a painting; we listen to a person in much the same way as we listen to music; we observe a person in much the same way that we observe a play, an opera, a dance; we read a person as we read a book. In all these aesthetic approaches we see, listen, observe, read, and respond immediately with our feelings. Later we may ask questions and develop theories. These frequently seem to be, and sometimes are, exclusively about the work of art. But the most important questions have to do with whether we "understood" the work; and this is the question basically whether our feelings in responding to it were both justified and adequate.

(4) There is a need for self-criticism that goads one to correction and further achievement. And, in particular, there is a need for some fair estimate of one's self, that is, for a continuing Socratic inquiry regarding the self and its powers. Together with this, and harder to achieve, is that acceptance of failure when it occurs in such a manner that one becomes a stronger individual through the defeat.

(5) Closely related to this self-knowledge, acceptance, and discovery is a sense of history. There is as great a need for a sense of our past, of belonging to the history that has entered our lives, for making history personal. This is a return to tradition, but not a traditionalism. It is the accurate recognition that much that is vital in our time and in us has come from our past. The simplest way to clarify this point, perhaps, is to say that we do not need to look *at* our past but *with* our past. We do not need to look at Socrates and Thucydides, at Isaiah and Paul, Francis of Assisi and Aquinas, at Machiavelli and Jefferson; but what we need to do is to stand where they stood and to look with them. We need to look at them with the "sympathy" of David Hume and Adam Smith.

(6) This way of looking would lead, I believe, to an experimental spirit, to an acceptance of change which is one of the most powerful forces of our time. And this would occur not simply because we would recognize the changes of history but, more importantly, because we would experience the spirit in which many of the individuals of our past accepted change.

(7) With this comes the discovery of a cause. Here, once more, living

with others in our past can help us, for it will serve to remind us that most worthwhile causes are not handed to individuals so much as discovered or created by them. And that this discovery has usually occurred gradually, sometimes maturing slowly, through loyal living with other persons. Such loyal living has often helped individuals in the West to discover, in after-days, a pattern that at the time they did not recognize.

In the first seven points I have focused a good deal on the past, when what should be obvious is that it is important now, in this new age, to take these same insights and ways of living with others and to face the immigrants and the homeless who are coming to our shores or are already living with us. Beyond all this, however, there are two final qualities that are essential: I will relate them briefly; but I believe that, except for the overarching experience of dignity, they are most important of all, providing a motive force and a meaning for the remainder. These are the qualities of courage and love to perform and achieve with the self, and with others, all of these factors required of us.

This courage is of great significance, and it gradually becomes a daily requirement, in this new century, to live with a sense of significance and self-criticism, accepting others as others, opposing the threats to personality, and risking chance and change.

This love is of all kinds: *eros, philia, agape, charitas.* For life is, or can become, a unity only though the activating power of love of all kinds. This love is our first real and last home, a river that connects what is inland to the sea, that brings the waves of immigrants, of persons or ideas or beliefs, and bids them welcome. And this exploration by love, with love, will inevitably reveal to us the deeper and necessary connections between knowing another and being known, and lead us to see the connection between all these relationships and becoming a self. For if the knowledge of selves has to do with memory and reflection and engagement, then it has also to do, most simply, with truth and love. The ultimate norm and the basic drive to knowledge, as Plato so clearly affirmed, is erotic. It is also the love of the suffering servant and of the Christ on the cross. It is a love modulated by, transformed by, the truth of the ways things are. It is the longing to know. Memory is such a longing for truth. But the memory and the longing and even the truth have their origin, as both Plato and Aristotle knew, in wonder. All knowledge begins in this wonder, such a wonder the self knows when it enters the presence of others, when it is present with itself, when it is aware of being known. The art of knowing persons begins here, in this wonder, moving toward a greater and greater unfolding of love:

> heard, half-heard, in the stillness
> Between two waves of the sea.
> Quick now, here, now, always—

A condition of complete simplicity
(Costing not less than everything)
And all shall be well and
All manner of thing shall be well
When the tongues of flame are in-folded
Into the crowned knot of fire
And the fire and the rose are one.[5]

NOTES

1. T. S. Eliot, "Little Gidding," III: 13–16, in *Four Quartets* (New York: Harcourt, Brace & World, Inc., 1943), p. 36.

2. Ibid., I: 53–54, p. 32.

3. George Steiner, *In Bluebeard's Castle* (New Haven: Yale University Press, 1971), p. 30.

4. Eliot, "Little Gidding" I: 53, p. 32; II: 65–66, p. 35.

5. Ibid., V: 37–46, p. 39.

BIBLIOGRAPHY

Abelard, Peter. *Peter Abelard's Ethics.* Translated by D. E. Luscombe. Oxford: Clarendon Press, 1971.

Ady, Cecilia May. "Florence and North Italy." *Cambridge Medieval History.* Vol. 8. New York: Macmillan Company, 1924.

Anselm. *Proslogium; Monologium; An Appendix in Behalf of the Fool by Gaunilon; and Cur Deus Homo.* Translated by Sidney Norton Dean. Chicago: Open Court Publishing Co., 1930.

Antoninus, Marcus Aurelius. *The Meditations.* Translated by G. M. A. Grube. New York: The Bobbs-Merrill Company, Inc., 1963.

———. *The Meditations of Marcus Aurelius Antoninus.* Translated by A. S. L. Farquharson. New York: Oxford University Press, 1989.

Aristotle. *The Basic Works of Aristotle.* Edited by Richard McKeon and translated by W. D. Ross. New York: Random House, 1966.

Arnold, Matthew. "Dover Beach." In *The Norton Anthology of Poetry.* New York: W. W. Norton & Co., 1975.

Auden, W. H. "Squares and Oblongs." In *Poets at Work: Essays Based on the Modern Poetry Collection at the Lockwood Memorial Library, University of Buffalo.* Edited by Rudolf Arnheim et al. New York: Harcourt Brace and Co., 1948.

Augustine. *The Basic Writings of St. Augustine.* Edited by Whitney J. Oates. 2 vols. New York: Random House, 1948.

———. *The Confessions of St. Augustine.* Translated by John K. Ryan. Garden City, N.Y.: Doubleday, 1960.

Bainton, Roland. *Here I Stand: A Life of Martin Luther.* New York: Abingdon-Cokesbury Press, 1950.

———. *The Reformation of the Sixteenth Century.* Boston: The Beacon Press, 1952.

Barker, Ernest. *National Character and the Factors in Its Formation.* New York: Harper and Brothers, 1927.

Becker, Carl. *The Declaration of Independence.* New York: Alfred Knopf, [1922] 1942.

———. *The Eve of the Revolution.* New Haven: Yale University Press, 1918.

Berlin, Isaiah. *Karl Marx: His Life and Environment.* New York: Oxford University Press, 1959.

The Bible, King James Version.

The Bible, Revised Standard Version.

Birley, Anthony. *Marcus Aurelius.* Boston: Little, Brown and Company, 1966.

Blake, William. *The Marriage of Heaven and Hell.* Introduction and Commentary by Sir Geoffrey Keynes. London and New York: Oxford University Press, 1975.

Bolotin, David. *Plato's Dialogue on Friendship: An Interpretation of the* Lysis *with a New Translation.* Ithaca, N.Y.: Cornell University Press, 1979.

Bowers, Claude. *Jefferson in Power: The Death Struggle of the Federalists.* Boston: Houghton, Mifflin, 1936.

Brown, Peter. *Augustine of Hippo: A Biography.* Berkeley and Los Angeles: University of California Press, 1967.

Bunyan, John. *Grace Abounding to the Chief of Sinners.* Oxford: Clarendon Press, 1962.

———. *Pilgrim's Progress.* Edited by James Wharey. Oxford: Clarendon Press, 1928.

———. *The Pilgrim's Progress.* New York: New American Library, 1964.

Burgess, J. W. *Political Science and Comparative Constitutional Law, Sovereignty and Liberty.* Boston: Ginn, 1898.

Butler, James, and Karen Green, eds. *Lyrical Ballads and Other Poems: 1797–1800.* Ithaca, N.Y.: Cornell University Press, 1992.

Calhoun, Robert Lowery. *Lectures on the History of Christian Doctrine.* 2 vols. New Haven: Yale Divinity School, 1948.

Calvin, John. *Calvin: Theological Treatises.* Translated by Rev. J. K. S. Reid. Philadelphia: The Westminister Press, 1954.

———. *Institutes of the Christian Religion.* Translated by Henry Beveridge. Vol. 1. Grand Rapids, Mich.: Wm. B. Eerdmans Publishing Company, 1953.

Carr, H.W. *National and After.* New York: Macmillan, 1945.

Cassirer, Ernst. "Enlightenment." *Encyclopedia of the Social Sciences.* Edited by Edwin R. A. Seligman. Vol. 5. New York: Macmillan, 1931.

———. "Giovanni Pico della Mirandola, A Study of the History of Renaissance Ideas." *Journal of the History of Ideas.* Vol. 3. New York: College of the City of New York, 1942.

———. *Rousseau, Kant, Goethe.* Translated by James Gutman, Paul Oskar Kristeller, John Herman Randall, Jr. Princeton: Princeton University Press, [1945] 1970.

Chinard, Gilbert. *Thomas Jefferson: The Apostle of Americanism.* Boston: Little, Brown, 1939.

Clapham, John Harold. "Commerce and Industry in the Middle Ages." *The Cambridge Medieval History.* Vol. 6: *Victory of the Papacy.* New York: Macmillan Company, Cambridge University Press, 1929.

Cochrane, Charles Norris. *Christianity and Classical Culture.* Oxford: Clarendon Press, [1940] 1980.

Coleridge, S. T. *Biographia Literaria.* Edited by J. Shawcross. Vol. 2. London: Oxford University Press, 1907.

———. *Collected Letters of Samuel Taylor Coleridge.* 1801–1806. Edited by Earl Leslie Griggs. Vol 2. Oxford: The Clarendon Press, 1956.

———. *The Complete Poetical Works of Samuel Taylor Coleridge.* Edited by Ernest Hartley Coleridge. Vol. 1. Oxford: The Clarendon Press, 1957.

———. *The Table Talk and Omniana.* Edited by T. Ashe. London: George Bell and Sons, 1909.

Collingwood, R. G. *The Idea of Nature.* Oxford: Clarendon Press, 1945.

Constitution of the United States.

Coulton, C. G. *Two Saints: Saint Francis and Saint Bernard.* Cambridge, Mass.: Harvard University Press, 1955.

Dampier, Sir William Cecil. *A History of Science and Its Relation with Philosophy and Religion.* Third Revised Edition. Cambridge, Mass.: Harvard University Press, 1942.

Descartes, René. *Principles of Philosophy.* Translated by Valentine Roger and Reese Miller. Netherlands: Reidel Publishing Company, 1983.

De Selincourt, Ernest, ed. *The Journals of Dorothy Wordsworth.* Vol. 1. New York: The Macmillan Company, 1941.

———. *Dorothy Wordsworth.* London: Oxford University Press, 1933.

———. *Wordsworth The Prelude.* (Text of 1805) Oxford: Oxford University Press, 1970.

Dick, Oliver Lawson. *Aubrey's Brief Lives.* Ann Arbor: University of Michigan Press, 1957.

Dodds, E. R. "Augustine's *Confessions:* A Study of Spiritual Maladjustment." *Hibbert Journal* 26 (1927–28): 459–73.

Eliot, T. S. *Four Quartets.* New York: Harcourt, Brace & World, Inc., 1943.

Englebert, Omer. *Saint Francis of Assisi.* New York: Longmans, Green, and Company, 1950.

Fleming, Thomas. *The Man from Monticello: An Intimate Life of Thomas Jefferson.* New York: William Morrow, 1969.

Fosdick, Harry Emerson. *Great Voices of the Reformation.* New York: Random House, 1952.

Freeman, Kathleen. *Ancilla to the Pre-Socratic Philosophers.* Cambridge, Mass.: Harvard University Press, 1966.

Freud, Sigmund. *An Autobiographical Study.* Translated by James Strachey. New York: W. W. Norton and Company, Inc., [1935] 1952.

———. *Complete Psychological Works.* Edited by James Strachey. Vols. 7 and 8. London: The Hogarth Press and the Institute of Psycho-analysis, 1953.

———. "Psychoanalysis." *Encyclopaedia Britannica.* Vol. 18. Chicago: E. B. Inc., 1968.

Gabriel, Ralph H. "Thomas Jefferson and Twentieth-Century Rationalism." *Virginia Quarterly Review* 26, no. 3: 329–42.

Gibbon, Edward. *The Decline and Fall of the Roman Empire.* Edited by J. B. Bury. Vol. 1. New York: Fred De Fau and Company, 1906.

Gilson, Étienne. *Heloise and Abelard.* Ann Arbor: University of Michigan Press, 1960.

Goodwin, Robert. *Selected Writings of St. Thomas Aquinas.* Everyman's Library edition by Ernst Rhys. New York: Bobbs-Merrill Educational Publishing, 1954.

Haller, William. *The Rise of Puritanism.* Philadelphia: University of Pennsylvania Press, [1938] 1972.

———. *Tracts on Liberty in the Puritan Revolution 1638–1647.* Vol. 2. New York: Columbia University Press, 1933.

Haller, William, and Godfrey Davies. *The Leveller Tracts 1647–1653.* New York: Columbia University Press, [1944] 1964.

Hammarskjöld, Dag. *Markings.* London: Faber and Faber, Ltd., 1964.

Hartman, Herbert. *Hartley Coleridge.* London: Oxford University Press, 1931.

Havens, Raymond Dexter. *The Mind of a Poet.* Vol. 1. Baltimore: Johns Hopkins University Press, 1941.

Hawke, D. F. *Benjamin Rush: Revolutionary Gadfly.* Indianapolis: Bobbs-Merrill, 1971.

Hayes, C. J .H. "Nationalism." *Encyclopedia of the Social Sciences.* Vol 2. New York: The Macmillan Company, 1937.

———. *Essays on Nationalism.* Vol. 1. New York: Macmillan, 1926.

Hazlitt, William. "On the Living Poets." *Lectures on the English Poets.* Introduction by A. R. Waller. London: J. M. Dent and Sons Ltd., [1910] 1955.

Hobbes, Thomas. *The English Works of Thomas Hobbes of Malmesbury.* Vol. 4. Germany: Scientia Verlag Alen, 1966.

———. *Leviathan.* New York: E. P. Dutton Co., 1914.

———. *Leviathan.* New York: J. M. Dent & Sons, 1928.

———. *Leviathan.* Cambridge: Cambridge University Press, 1991.

Hunt, Gaillard. *The Debates in the Federal Convention of 1787.* Westport, Conn.: Greenwood Press, 1970.

Jaeger, Werner. *Paideia: The Ideals of Greek Culture.* Translated by Gilbert Highet. 3 vols. New York: Oxford University Press, 1939, 1943, 1944.

Jefferson, Thomas. *Papers of Thomas Jefferson.* Edited by Julian P. Boyd. 12 vols. Princeton, N.J.: Princeton University Press, 1950.

———. *Thomas Jefferson: Revolutionary Philosopher, A Selection of His Writings.* Edited by John S. Pancake. Woodbury, N.Y.: Barron's International Series, 1976.

———. *The Works of Thomas Jefferson.* Edited by Paul Leicester Ford. Vol. 9. New York: G.P. Putnam, 1905.

———. *The Writings of Thomas Jefferson.* Edited by Andrew A. Lipscomb and Albert Ellery Bergh. Memorial Edition. 20 vols. Washington: Thomas Jefferson Memorial Association, 1903.

Jones, Ernst. *The Life and Work of Sigmund Freud.* 2 vols. New York: Basic Books Inc., 1955.

Kant, Immanuel. *The Categorical Imperative, A Study of Kant's Moral Philosophy.* Translated by H. J. Paton. New York: Harper and Row, [1947] 1965.

———. *The Critique of Pure Reason.* Translated by Norman Kemp Smith. London: Macmillan, [1929] 1968.

———. *Groundwork of the Metaphysics of Morals.* First Section in *The Moral Law.* Translated by H. J. Paton. London: Hutchinson, [1948] 1976.

———. *Foundations of the Metaphysics of Morals.* Translated by Lewis White Beck. Indianapolis: Bobbs-Merrill, 1959.

Kaufmann, Walter A. *Nietzsche: Philosopher, Psychologist, Anti-Christ.* Princeton, N.J.: Princeton University Press, 1950.

Keats, John. *Autobiography of John Keats.* Edited by Earle Vonard Heller. London: Oxford University Press, 1933.

———. *The Letters of John Keats.* Edited by Hyder E. Rollins. Cambridge, Mass.: Harvard University Press, 1958.

Kirk, Kenneth E. *The Vision of God: The Christian Doctrine of the Summum Bonum.* New York: Longmans, Green, and Co., [1931] 1937.

Koch, Adrienne. *Jefferson and Madison: The Great Collaboration.* New York: Alfred A. Knopf, 1950.

Kuno, Fischer. "Life and Character of Baruch Spinoza." *Spinoza: Four Essays.* Edited by W. Knight. London: Williams and Norgate, 1882.

Leavis, F. R. *The Common Pursuit.* New York: George W. Steward Publisher, 1952.

Lindsay, A. D. *Kant.* London: Ernest Benn Limited, 1934 [The Folcroft Press Inc., 1970].

Locke, John. *Works of John Locke.* Edited by Thomas Tegg et al. 6 vols. London: 1823; reprinted by Scientia Verlag-Aalen, Germany, 1963.

Luther, Martin. *A Compend of Luther's Theology.* Edited by Hugh Thomas Kerr. Philadelphia: West Minister Press, 1943.

———. *Martin Luther: Selections From His Writings.* Edited by John Dillinger. New York: Anchor Books, 1961.

———. *Works of Martin Luther.* Philadelphia: Muhlenberg Press, 1930–43.

Machiavelli, Niccolo. *Florentine History.* Translated by W. K. Marriott. London: J. M. Dent & Company, 1909.

———. *The Prince and Other Works.* Translated by Alan Gilbert. Chicago: Packard and Company, 1941.

MacKiney, Loren Carey. *The Medieval World.* New York: Farrar & Rinehart, Inc., 1938.

Mackinnon, James. *Calvin and the Reformation.* New York: Longmans, Green, and Co., 1936.

Malthus, T. R. *Essay on the Principle of Population.* Selected and introduced by Donald Winch. Cambridge: Cambridge University Press, 1992.

Maritain, Jacques. *The Angelic Doctor.* New York: Dial Press, 1931.

Marx, Karl. *Capital: A Critique of Political Economy.* Vol 1. Translated from the third German edition by Samuel Moore and Edward Aveling. Chicago: Charles H. Kerr, 1919.

———. *Capital: The Communist Manifesto and Other Writings.* Edited by Max Eastman. New York: Modern Library, 1932.

———. *A Contribution to the Critique of Political Economy.* Introduction by Maurice Dobb. New York: International Publishers, 1970.

Masson, David, ed. *The Collected Writings of Thomas De Quincey.* Vol. 2. Edinburgh: Adam and Charles Black, [1889] 1964.

Masson, Jeffrey Moussaieff., ed. and trans. *The Complete Letters of Sigmund Freud to Wilhelm Fliess, 1887–1904.* Cambridge, Mass.: The Belknap Press of Harvard University Press, 1985.

Merriam, C. E., Jr. "The Political Theory of Thomas Jefferson." *Political Science Quarterly* 17, no. 4: 25–46.

Mill, John Stuart. *The Spirit of the Age.* Chicago: University of Chicago Press, 1942.

Milton, John. *The Works of John* Milton. Vol. 15. New York: Columbia University Press, 1933.

Moffatt, James. *A New Translation of the Bible.* New York: Harper & Brothers Publishers, 1935.

Moore, Ruth. *Charles Darwin.* New York: Alfred A. Knopf, 1955.

More, Thomas. *The English Works of Sir Thomas More.* Edited by W. E. Campbell. Vol. 1. New York: Lincoln MacVeagh, 1931.

Morgan, Edmund S. *Challenge of the American Revolution.* New York: W. W. Norton, 1976.

———. *The Meaning of Independence.* Charlottesville: University of Virginia Press, 1975.

Muckle, J. T. *The Story of Abelard's Adversities: A Translation with Notes of the "Historia Calamitatum."* Preface by Étienne Gilson. Toronto: Pontifical Institute of Medieval Studies, 1964.

Namier, L. B. *England in the Age of the American Revolution.* St. Martin's Street, London: Macmillan and Co., Limited, 1930.

Niebuhr, Richard. *Christ and Culture.* New York: Harper & Row Publishers, 1951.

Niebuhr, Richard, and Waldo Beach. *Christian Ethics.* New York: Ronald Press Company, 1955.

Nietzsche, Friedrich. *Beyond Good and Evil: Prelude to a Philosophy of the Future.* Translated by Walter Kaufmann. New York: Vintage Books, [Random House, Inc., 1966] 1989.

———. *The Complete Works of Friedrich Nietzsche.* Edited by Oscar Levy. Vols. 10 and 15. London: George Allen and Unwin, Ltd., 1924.

———. *The Genealogy of Morals.* Translated by Horace B. Samuel. New York: Boni and Liveright, n.d.

———. *The Philosophy of Nietzsche.* New York: The Modern Library, 1927, 1954.

———. *Thus Spake Zarathustra.* Edited by Manuel Komroff. New York: Tudor Publishing Company, [Originally translated by Thomas Common. New York: The Modern Library, 1905] 1936 .

Nock, Albert Jay. *Jefferson.* New York: Harcourt Brace, 1926.

Oliver, James H. *The Ruling Power: A Study of the Roman Empire in the Second Century after Christ through the Roman Oration of Aelius Aristides.* Philadelphia: The American Philosophical Society, 1953.

Owen, W. J. B., ed. *Wordsworth and Coleridge Lyrical Ballads 1798.* London: Oxford University Press, 1969.

Parrish, Stephen Maxfield, ed. *Coleridge's Dejection: The Earliest Manuscripts and the Earliest Printings.* Ithaca, N.Y.: Cornell University Press, 1988.

Pauck, Wilhelm. *The Heritage of the Reformation.* Boston: The Beacon Press, 1950.

Paulsen, Friedrich. *Immanuel Kant: His Life and Doctrine.* Translated by J. E. Creighton and Albert Lefevre. New York: Scribners, 1902.

Peterson, Merrill D., ed. *The Portable Thomas Jefferson.* New York: Viking, 1975.

Pico della Mirandola, Giovanni. *The Renaissance Philosophy of Man.* Edited by Ernst Cassirer. Illinois: University of Chicago Press, 1948.

Plato. *The Collected Dialogues of Plato.* Bollingen Series LXXI. Edited by Edith Hamilton and Huntington Cairns. New York: Pantheon Books, 1964.

———. *The Dialogues of Plato.* Translated by Benjamin Jowett. 2 vols. New York: Random House, 1937.

———. *Gorgias.* Translated with notes by Terence Irwin. Oxford: Clarendon Press, 1979.

———. *Gorgias.* Text and Commentary by E. R. Dodds. Oxford: Oxford University Press, 1959.

———. *Great Dialogues of Plato.* Translated by W. H. D. Rouse. New York: New American Library, 1956.

———. *The Republic of Plato.* Translated by Allan Bloom. New York: Basic Books, 1968.

———. *The Republic of Plato.* Translated by Francis M. Cornford. London: Oxford University Press, 1941.

Plotinus. *The Six Enneads.* Translated by Stephen Mackenna and B. S. Page. Chicago: Encyclopaedia Britannica, Inc., 1952.

Radice, Betty, trans. *The Letters of Abelard and Heloise.* Harmondsworth, Middlesex: Penguin, 1974.

Rae, John. *Life of Adam Smith.* New York: Augustus M. Kelly, [1895] 1965.

Rashdall, Hastings. *The Universities of Europe in the Middle Ages.* Vol. 1. Oxford: Clarendon Press, 1936.

Reynolds, Joshua. *Discourse XIII.* In *The Creative Imagination: Enlightenment to Romanticism* by James Engell. Cambridge, Mass.: Harvard University Press, 1981.

Ricardo, David. *Principles of Political Economy and Taxation.* London [Everyman Edition]: E. P. Dutton, 1912.

Robertson, D. B. *The Religious Foundations of Leveller Democracy.* New York: King's Crown Press, 1951.

Rogers, Arthur Kenyon. *The Socratic Problem.* New Haven: Yale University Press, 1933.

Rosi, Mario. *Modern Language Review* 44 (1949): 421–32.

Roth, Leon. *Spinoza.* London: Ernest Benn Ltd., 1929.

Sabatier, Paul. *Life of St. Francis of Assisi.* New York: Scribners, 1894.

Sabine, George H. *A History of Political Theory.* New York: Holt, Rinehart and Winston, 1961.

Schevill, Ferdinand. *History of Florence from the Founding of the City through the Renaissance.* New York: Harcourt, Brace and Company, 1936.

Schillp, Paul. *Kant's Pre-Critical Ethics.* Evanston, Ill.: Northwestern University, 1938.

Sharrock, Roger. "Spiritual Autobiography in Pilgrim's Progress." *Review of English Studies* 24 (1948).

Shenk, W. *The Concern for Social Justice in the Puritan Revolution.* London: Longmans, Green and Co., 1948.

Shorey, Paul. *What Plato Said.* Chicago: University of Chicago, 1933.

Short, William. *The Franciscans.* Wilmington, Delaware: Glazier, 1989.

Singer, Charles. *A Short History of Science to the Nineteenth Century.* Oxford: Clarendon Press, 1941.

Smith, Adam. *An Inquiry into the Nature and Causes of the Wealth of Nations.* Edited by R. H. Campbell and A. S. Skinner. 2 vols. Oxford: Clarendon, [1776] 1976.

———. "Lectures on Justice, Police, Revenue and Arms." *Moral and Political Philosophy.* Edited by Herbert W. Schneider. New York: Hafner, 1948.

Smith, Adam. *The Theory of Moral Sentiments*. Edited by D. D. Raphael and A. L. Macfie. Oxford: Clarendon Press, 1976.

Smith, John Alexander. *The Nicomachean Ethics of Aristotle*. Translated by D. P. Chase. Longon: J. M. Dent & Sons Ltd., 1911.

Spinoza, Baruch. *The Correspondence of Spinoza*. Edited by Wolf. New York: The Dial Press, 1927.

———. *Ethics*. Edited by James Guthman. New York: Hafner Publishing Co., 1949.

———. *Spinoza's Ethics and "De Intellectus Emendatione."* Translated by A. Boyle. New York: E. P. Dutton and Co., 1910.

———. *Writings on Political Philosophy*. Edited by A. G. A. Balz. New York: D. Appleton Century Company, 1937.

Steiner, George. *In Bluebeard's Castle*. New Haven: Yale University Press, 1971.

Taylor, A. E. *Plato, The Man and His Work*. New York: Methuen, 1926.

Taylor, F. S. *A Short History of Science and Scientific Thought*. New York: W. W. Norton and Co., 1949.

Taylor, H. O. *The Medieval Mind*. Vol. 1. Cambridge: Harvard University Press, 1949.

Thomas Aquinas. *Summa Theologiae*. Translated by Thomas Gilby. Vol. 18. New York: McGraw-Hill Book Company, 1964.

Thompson, James Westfall. *An Economic and Social History of the Middle Ages, 300–1300*. New York: Century Co., 1928.

———. *The Middle Ages*. 2 vols. New York: Alfred A. Knopf, 1931.

Thucydides. *The History of the Peloponnesian War*. Edited by Sir Richard Livingstone. New York: Oxford University Press, 1943.

———. *The Peloponnesian War*. Translated by Rex Warner. New York: Penguin Books, 1978.

Trevelyan, George. *Illustrated English Social History*. New York: Longmans, Green and Co., 1930.

———. *Illustrated English Social History*. Vol. 3. London: Longman's, Green, 1949–1952.

Troeltsch, Ernst. *The Social Teaching of the Christian Churches*. Translated by Olive Wyon. Vol. 1. New York: Macmillan Company, 1950.

Ward, A.W., ed. *The Cambridge Modern History*. New York: Macmillan Company, 1907.

Whitehead, Alfred North. *Science and the Modern World*. New York: Mentor Book, 1925.

Woodhouse, A. S. P. *Puritanism and Liberty*. Chicago: Chicago University Press, 1951.

Wordsworth, William. *The Complete Poetical Works of Williams Wordsworth*. Edited by Alice N. George. New York: Houghton Mifflin and Co., [1904] [1932] 1953.

———. *The Poetical Works of Wordsworth*. Edited by Thomas Hutchinson and revised by Ernest De Selincourt. London: Oxford University Press, 1959.

Wright, Benjamin Fletcher, ed. *The Federalist*. Cambridge, Mass.: The Belknap Press of Harvard University Press, 1961.

INDEX